W9-CEI-760

McGraw-Hill Ryerson Series in Canadian Politics
General Editor Paul W. Fox

POLITICS AND THE MEDIA IN CANADA
Arthur Siegel

CANADA IN QUESTION: Federalism in the Eighties, Third Edition
Donald V. Smiley

THE REVISED CANADIAN CONSTITUTION: Politics as Law
Ronald I. Cheffins and Patricia A. Johnson

SOUTHERN EXPOSURE: Canadian Perspectives on the U.S.
David Flaherty and William McKercher

FEDERAL CONDITION IN CANADA
Donald V. Smiley

THE JUDICIARY IN CANADA: The Third Branch of Government
Peter H. Russell

POLITICAL PARTIES AND IDEOLOGIES IN CANADA, Third Edition
William Christian and Colin Campbell

LOCAL GOVERNMENT IN CANADA, Third Edition
C. Richard Tindal and S. Nobes Tindal

Also Available
THE CANADIAN POLITICAL SYSTEM, Fourth Edition
Richard J. Van Loon and Michael S. Whittington

SEVENTH EDITION

POLITICS:
C A N A D A

PAUL W. FOX
Victoria College
University of Toronto

GRAHAM WHITE
Department of Political Science
University of Toronto

McGRAW-HILL RYERSON LIMITED
Toronto   Montreal   New York   Auckland   Bogotá
Caracas   Hamburg   Lisbon   London   Madrid   Mexico
Milan   New Delhi   Paris   San Juan   São Paulo
Singapore   Sydney   Tokyo

POLITICS: CANADA, seventh edition

© McGraw Hill Ryerson Limited, 1991, 1987, 1982, 1977, 1970, 1966, 1962.
ISBN: 0-07-551101-0

1 2 3 4 5 6 7 8 9 0 W 0 9 8 7 6 5 4 3 2 1

Printed and bound in Canada

Sponsoring Editor: Catherine O'Toole
Senior Supervising Editor: Rosalyn Steiner
Copy Editor: Pat Banning
Cover and text design: Carole Giguere
Technical Artist: Carole Giguere
Permissions Editor: Norma Christensen

Canadian Cataloguing in Publication Data
Main entry under title:

Politics : Canada
7th ed.
Includes bibliographical references.
ISBN 0-07-551101-0

1. Canada – Politics and government – 1963–1984.*
2. Canada – Politics and government – 1984–   .*
I. Fox, Paul W., date –   . II. White, Graham, date

JL11.P64 1991   320.971   C90-095598-8

CONTENTS

Preface   IX

Bibliographical Abbreviations   XI

1   CULTURE AND CONSTITUTION

4 Regionalism

5 French Canada

2 PROCESS

6 Public Opinion

7 Political Parties

PREFACE TO THE SEVENTH EDITION

Once again this new edition of *Politics: Canada* has a great deal of fresh material. About half of the contents consists of items that have not appeared in previous editions. All of these selections are drawn from very recent publications or are articles prepared especially for this edition of *Politics: Canada*.

Original material seems to be a growing feature in each successive edition. This time there are eleven articles that have been prepared particularly for the new edition. I am indebted greatly to the authors for their generosity and their labours and would like to thank them warmly for their contributions. My co-editor, Graham White, and our colleague, Nelson Wiseman, have each written two articles, while William Christian and Colin Campbell, John Eichmanis, Lawrence LeDuc, Evert Lindquist, Lorna Marsden, Paul Thomas, and Joseph Wearing have contributed one each.

I would like to express my gratitude also to the authors whose work has appeared in previous editions and who have been kind enough to revise their articles and bring them up to date for this edition. No one declined to take on the task and not one failed to meet the deadline, even when it was suddenly advanced. That is a double measure of co-operation, which only an editor can truly appreciate, but which should be acknowledged publicly. I am pleased to do so here, thanking Agar Adamson, Carl Baar, Brian Land, Evert Lindquist, John McMenemy, and Desmond Morton. Peter Russell should be thanked also for being willing to take on this job, though in the end he contributed two new articles with co-authors.

I should like to thank also those authors whose work has been reprinted here with their permission or by arrangement with their publisher. The contribution of each of these more than 40 individuals is significant and appreciated. None of them, by the way, should be held responsible for the title put on his or her material when it differs from the original. On occasion, I have taken the liberty of altering original titles in order to make them fit the pattern of the chapter in which they appear or to stimulate discussion among students by posing controversial assertions or questions. The desire to provide good argumentative matter is also the reason for juxtaposing contradictory articles wherever possible.

I should add that the freedom taken in designing titles has not been extended to distorting the contents of these articles. Although many selections have been edited rigorously, I have tried very hard to maintain the integrity of the authors' arguments and evidence.

The lengthy bibliographies that follow each chapter reflect the large amount of research and publication that continues to be done in the field of Canadian government and politics. Though the bibliographies are extensive, they are by no means exhaustive. In an effort to keep them to a reasonable length, the co-editor and I have deleted most items published before 1980, except for a few classics. For material published prior to 1980, a reader should consult the bibliographies in earlier editions of *Politics: Canada*. To save space, most bibliographical references have been entered only once, usually in the chapter where the subject matter seemed most appropriate. However, since some items deal with more than one subject, we have made liberal use of cross-references. For reasons of economy, also, the names of most publishers and periodicals have been abbreviated. Full information is provided in the list of Bibliographical Abbreviations that follows this preface. Rose Antonio deserves great thanks for typing the bibliographies so expertly.

Finally, I would like to thank my co-editor, Professor Graham White, for his invaluable assistance and hard work. He joins me in thanking Catherine O'Toole, sponsoring editor, McGraw-Hill Ryerson, for her support and encouragement. A special word of appreciation goes to Rosalyn Steiner, supervising editor, for her painstaking care in shepherding the book through publication.

Victoria College   Paul Fox
University of Toronto   July 18, 1990

BIBLIOGRAPHICAL ABBREVIATIONS

Publications

A.R.C.S.	*American Review of Canadian Studies*
C.B.R.	*Canadian Bar Review*
C.H.R.	*Canadian Historical Review*
C.J.E.	*Canadian Journal of Economics*
C.J.E.P.S.	*Canadian Journal of Economics and Political Science*
C.J.I.S.	*Canadian Journal of Information Science*
C.J.P.S.	*Canadian Journal of Political Science*
C.J.S.	*Canadian Journal of Sociology*
C.P.A.	*Canadian Public Administration*
C.P.P.	*Canadian Public Policy*
C.P.R.	*Canadian Parliamentary Review*
C.R.S.A.	*Canadian Review of Sociology and Anthropology*
C.T.J.	*Canadian Tax Journal*
D.L.R.	*Dalhousie Law Review*
I.J.	*International Journal*
J.C.S.	*Journal of Canadian Studies*
McG.L.J.	*McGill Law Journal*
M.J.P.S.	*Midwest Journal of Political Science*
O.	*Optimum*
O.H.L.J.	*Osgoode Hall Law Journal*
O.L.R.	*Ottawa Law Review*
P.O.	*Policy Options*
Q.L.J.	*Queen's Law Journal*
Q.Q.	*Queen's Quarterly*
S.P.E.	*Studies in Political Economy*
U.T.F.L.R.	*University of Toronto Faculty of Law Review*
U.T.L.J.	*University of Toronto Law Journal*

Publishing Companies, Associations, Councils, Institutes, Foundations.

Ampersand	Ampersand Communications Services Incorporated
B. and M.	Burns and MacEachern
C.B.C.	Canadian Broadcasting Corporation
C.E.L.A.	Canadian Environmental Law Association
C.I.I.A.	Canadian Institute of International Affairs
C.I.P.A.	Canadian Institute on Public Affairs
C.L.I.C.	Canadian Law Information Council
C.P.S.A.	Canadian Political Science Association

C.T.F.	Canadian Tax Foundation
C.M.H.C.	Central Mortgage and Housing Corporation
C.I.S.	Centre for International Studies
C.U.C.S.	Centre for Urban and Community Studies
C.-M.	Collier-Macmillan
C.P.A.	Community Planning Association
C.C.	Copp Clark
C.U.P.	Carleton University Press
D. and G.	Deneau and Greenberg
E.C.C.	Economic Council of Canada
F. and W.	Fitzhenry and Whiteside
H.R.W.	Holt Rinehart and Winston
H.M.	Houghton Mifflin
I.C.	Information Canada
I.R.P.P.	Institute for Research on Public Policy
I.I.R.	Institute of Intergovernmental Relations
I.P.A.C.	Institute for Public Administration of Canada
I.R.C.	Industrial Relations Centre
I.U.S.	Institute of Urban Studies
J.L.S.	James, Lewis and Samuel
K.P.	King's Printer
L. & O.	Lester and Orpen
L.&O.D	Lester & Orpen Dennys
M. & S.	McClelland and Stewart
McG.-Q.U.P.	McGill-Queen's University Press
McG.-H.	McGraw-Hill
McG.-H.R.	McGraw-Hill Ryerson
O.E.C.	Ontario Economic Council
O.I.S.E.	Ontario Institute for Studies in Education
O.U.P.	Oxford University Press
P.-H.	Prentice-Hall
P.U.L.	Les Presses de l'Université Laval
P.U.M.	Les Presses de l'Université de Montréal
P.U.Q.	Les Presses de l'Université du Québec
Q.P.	Queen's Printer
R.M.	Rand McNally
R.K.P.	Routledge, Kegan, Paul
S. and S.	Supply and Services
U.A.P.	University of Alberta Press
U.B.C.P.	University of British Columbia Press
U.O.P.	University of Ottawa Press
U.T.P.	University of Toronto Press
W.L.U.P.	Wilfrid Laurier University Press

POLITICS:
CANADA

CULTURE AND
CONSTITUTION

SOCIO-POLITICAL ISSUES

THE ESSENTIAL POLITICAL GOODS

Ronald Manzer

From the comparative perspective of Canadian history and the experience of other political communities, the people who live in Canada today enjoy very high standards of material prosperity, physical security, and human rights. Conventional measures of socio-political development—such as average income, rates of mortality and morbidity, incidence of political and criminal violence, equality of opportunity for education, and protection of civil liberties—indicate a relatively high and historically increasing level of well-being. Only a few other political communities can claim to provide for the basic needs of their citizens at a level comparable to that attained in Canada.

None the less, Canada's high average standard of living disguises serious and persistent maldistributions. For example, a hard core of 15 per cent, perhaps more, of the population endures material poverty in the midst of affluence. Racial and sexual inequalities deny sizable numbers of Canadians secure enjoyment of their dignity and self-respect. An upper-status group possessing position, expertise, and wealth is firmly in control of economic and political power, lessening the potential for an authentically democratic polity.

In addition to serious inadequacies in the present distribution of political

From *Public Policies and Political Development in Canada*, Toronto. Reprinted by permission of University of Toronto Press. © University of Toronto Press 1985. Ellipsis points indicate text omitted.

goods, Canadians face disquieting prospects for more severe shortfalls in the satisfaction of their basic needs. In one issue-area after another public policies seem to have reached an impasse. More than a decade of policy-making effort to cure weak economic growth, high unemployment, and persistent inflation has produced no convincing remedies for a stubborn "stagflation." Considerable scientific evidence and a popular awareness of the adverse impact of the industrial system on the natural environment have so far resulted only in weak and vacillating corrective regulation. A social order founded on bargaining among power élites verges on immobility when dominant organized socio-economic interests fail to agree, and veers toward injustice when agreement is obtained at the expense of weak, unorganized segments of society. The integrity of the Canadian political community is threatened by the internal strains of two linguistic–cultural communities and four or five economic regions and by the very mixed blessings of an American penetration that reinforces internal divisions and complicates their accommodation. Policies for cultural development and humanistic education that aim at the higher values of individual self-realization consistently are the last to be supported and the first to be eviscerated in disputes over collective priorities.

In the past, Canadians have benefitted from the richness of their physical resources and the general benignity of their external relationships, which have facilitated the growth of their well-being. On the whole, they also have been fortunate in the political choices they have made. A complex array of federal, provincial, and local public policies has been instrumental in achieving high levels of need satisfaction.

In the future, the challenge of remedying maldistributions of primary political goods and overcoming impasses in making essential public policies will continue to demand imaginative and sometimes difficult political choices. Making good choices will require a better core of policy knowledge, far-reaching institutional reform, and a new commitment to the principles of liberal democracy.

The challenge of public policy and political development in Canada is one involving policy knowledge and political institutions. Genuine puzzlement about the theoretical assumptions on which to base public policy inhibits the development of policies in such diverse issue-areas as economic stabilization, corrections, and public education. Grave doubts about the responsiveness and effectiveness of federal, provincial, and local political institutions cast a pall on our tentative attempts to create fresh formulations for old policy designs.

Underlying the questions of relevant policy knowledge and effective political institutions is a more basic question about the validity of contemporary political ideas and values. Ultimately, the challenge of public policy and political development in Canada is one of political principles and public purposes.

PUBLIC PURPOSE

The usual justification for government in general and for public policies in particular is the satisfaction of human needs. In their eventual outcomes, specific programs or particular actions to implement policies usually fall far short of their initial promise to serve human needs, and often they are deliberately perverted to satisfy the wants of a few rather than the needs of many. None the less, if we are to understand and evaluate the development of public policies we must have a concept of public purpose that can relate the satisfaction of human needs to the functions of good government.

The construction of a list of human needs is necessarily somewhat arbitrary, but for purposes of policy analysis the fivefold classification of basic needs suggested by Abraham Maslow is a useful schema. First, physiological needs are the requirements for physical survival and the relief of pain. People must have clean air to breathe and adequate food, drink, sleep, and shelter. Second, safety needs are needs for order, predictability, and dependability of the environment. People vary greatly in their capacities to cope with disorder or unpredictability in their personal lives and social relationships, but there are evident limits to go beyond which results in neurosis or psychosis. Third, people have basic needs for love, affection, and a sense of belongingness. The belongingness needs represent the deep, persistent desire of people to get together, to be together, and stay together. Fourth, people need esteem and respect from other people, and they need self-esteem and self-respect. "Satisfaction of the self-esteem need leads to feelings of self-confidence, worth, strength, capability, and adequacy, of being useful and necessary in the world. But thwarting of these needs produces feelings of inferiority, of weakness, and of helplessness." Fifth, self-development needs are the needs people have to actualize their full potential as human beings, not simply to survive in safety, with friends, respected, but to achieve to the fullest extent possible what they are capable of becoming.

According to Maslow, these five sets of needs are hierarchically ordered, with higher degrees of "gratification health" being achieved as higher levels of needs are satisfied. If all needs are unsatisfied, physiological needs will predominate. When physiological needs are satisfied, a concern for predictability and dependability of the environment grows. Then, as physiological and safety needs are satisfied, needs for belongingness, esteem, and self-development successively become predominant.

Maslow is ambiguous about the points at which individual priorities change from one set of needs to another. Basic needs will obviously persist, and subtle transformations express the increasing complexity of expanding desires. Sexual desire grows into love, and love requited demands mutual respect and freedom for self-development. Food and drink prepared with skill and taken with friends become a means of self-expression and affection. In spite of this ambiguity, the higher the level of needs satisfied, the healthier and closer to realizing their human potential people will be. A person who is safe, loved, and respected, for example, will be healthier and closer to full human development than a person who is safe but rejected and unloved.

Each set of basic human needs may be satisfied by planned or spontaneous individual private action, collective private action, or collective public action.

A person may act alone to obtain food and shelter, or small groups of people may combine their activities in voluntary co-operative effort to produce goods and services that cannot be produced by one person working alone. For many components of basic human needs, public policies that guide collective public action may be an effective approach to their satisfaction.

Each of the five sets of basic human need has a corresponding conception of political good. They are "good" because they represent conditions known to be agreeable, beneficial, commendable, right, or proper for the satisfaction of basic needs. They are "political" because they can only be realized through public collective action, and consequently they provide justification for compulsory collectivization.

Welfare as a political good implies, for example, that people should have adequate food and shelter and that they should have access to health services adequate to reduce the incidence of illness and to extend their average length of life to what is attainable with current technology. Welfare as a political good also implies a justification for formulating public policies wherever appropriate to achieve the basic conditions for human survival.

Security is a political good because people need, and governments can act to provide public order and social stability. Security in a political community means protection of people's lives and property; tolerable rates of change in economic, social, and political relationships; and some guarantee of protection from aggression originating outside the community. When security is provided as a political good, a person's entire needs for consistency and predictability are not thereby satisfied; but public security will provide a basic framework of regulated behaviour and will help to ensure dependable outcomes over a wide range of economic, social, and political relationships.

Fraternity expresses the political conditions for the existence within a large political community of primary autonomous groups in which people can get together, be together, and stay together. To the extent that fraternity is their purpose, public policies will aim to ensure that diversity of groups is accepted, that tolerance prevails, and that primary relationships involving families, friends, neighbourhoods, churches, and workplaces are protected and developed.

Equality is a political good because satisfaction of esteem needs depends on it. Who shall be treated alike for what purposes is a recurring question in politics and policy-making. Differences arise over which social and personal characteristics (such as age, sex, and ethnicity) are relevant in determining equality; over which particular personal, social, economic, and political activities should be considered; and over the best approach to resolving these differences in specific public policies. However, if people properly expect equality of treatment in carrying out certain activities but do not get it, they will feel deprived of esteem and respect and will usually lack self-esteem or self-respect. Their unsatisfied need becomes a justification for public policies that promote equality.

Liberty is a political good because people need a private sphere respected by others, especially the state, in which self-expressive activity may be pursued. As a political good, liberty also recognizes the existence of the right and power of each person to participate in collective decisions. No matter how well other needs may be met, self-development requires the double freedom of independence and participation.

From the standpoint of making and implementing public policies to satisfy basic needs, welfare is a political good for which governments can provide directly. Welfare represents basic needs that commonly are satisfied by improving conditions arising in the natural environment—for example, by larger supplies of food, better quality of shelter, or wider availability of health services. Assuming they are correctly designed, public policies that are intended to promote welfare will accomplish their purposes directly during the stage of implementation as general economic production is expanded, as hospitals are built and doctors are trained, or as food and shelter are supplied to the poor.

Security is a political good for which public policies also can provide directly as long as government action is backed by effective coercion. Security as a political good satisfies basic needs by reducing threats arising from the human environment—for example, by deterring criminal violence, containing political instability, or protecting national sovereignty. Again assuming they are correctly designed, public policies that are intended to increase security will accomplish their purpose directly during the stage of implementation as long as the state can exercise successfully its ultimate coercive power. Thus, for example, larger numbers and better organization of domestic policy and more vigorous enforcement of the law can deter criminal behaviour, and international diplomacy and military preparedness can protect the sovereignty of the community in the international system as long as sufficient coercive power exists to apprehend law-breakers and to resist potential external aggressors.

Fraternity, equality, and liberty are political goods for which public policies cannot provide directly. They represent basic needs that cannot be satisfied simply and directly by material changes in environmental conditions. Creating a sense of belongingness, feelings of mutual respect, or a sense of freedom involves changes in personal relationships and attitudes that cannot be achieved by coercion. Public policies aimed at attaining these political goods can try to protect and promote a natural and human environment in which people are able to love and respect one another and realize their full potential; but no policy can guarantee that love, respect, and self-development will actually result. That depends upon the responses of people who in these matters cannot be coerced.

The important differences in the implications of the five political goods for governmental action suggest the utility of simplifying an analysis of the patterns of public policy into a study of three categories of governmental functions. First, the function of creating economic progress includes a range of policies designed to achieve and maintain a high standard of material welfare. Maslow argued that physiological needs are prepotent, and hence it is scarcely surprising that much policy-making is devoted to their satisfaction. Second, the function of maintaining social order involves another range of public policies designed to achieve and maintain a high level of public order and social stability, primarily by regulating the way people behave toward one another. Although resorting to coercion is costly and necessarily limited in its actual development, social order can in principle be created and maintained by force. Third, the function of furthering individual development requires public policies designed to create or maintain the conditions for satisfying those aspects of basic needs for belongingness, esteem, and self-development that are obtainable through political action. Public policies directed at encouraging full human development are qualitatively different from those aiming at economic progress or social order. Coercion can produce facilitating conditions for individual development, but neither in principle nor in practice can it directly produce full human development.

The classification of basic needs in terms of political goods and governmental functions provides a useful framework for analysing the purposes and assessing the results of government and public policies, but it will not direct us to any obvious resolutions of political differences or put an end to partisan debate. Welfare, security, fraternity, equality, and liberty are comparative ideas; for a number of reasons disagreements can arise about how much of each should be provided in given circumstances. The question is always open as to how much of each good is necessary in order to satisfy basic physiological, safety, belongingness, esteem, and self-actualization needs. People accord different weight to the enjoyment of different goods, and they have different views of the future. In any political community people will be widely distributed in their levels of "gratification health," and these differences will be reflected in their politics and their expectations of governments. People also differ in the extent to which they see collective public action, as opposed to individual private or voluntary co-operative action, as the appropriate way to satisfy basic needs.

How much of each good is needed, which goods should have priority, what relative importance should be given to different functions of government, and what balance should be struck between private and public action to satisfy basic human needs are questions that have no easy, objective answers. They are questions on which people living in a political community will differ, often intensely, whether they simply follow their own self-interest or take seriously their moral responsibilities to others. As a result, in order to understand and evaluate public policies both concepts of public purpose and concepts of political ideology are needed. ● ● ●

WOMEN AND POLITICS—MANY PARTICIPATE BUT FEW ARE SELECTED

Janine Brodie

INTRODUCTION

[*Women and Politics in Canada*] documents the experience of 327 Canadian women who, as candidates for public office, ventured into the male-dominated world of politics. It is similar to other studies concerned with the political status of women in western democracies: it begins with a curious contradiction. Most of us do not condone dramatic inequities in the distribution of political power and social resources. In fact, a fundamental premise of our democratic value system is that no one social group is or should be systematically excluded from the exercise of political power. Yet we rarely question one of the most enduring and universal manifestations of political domination and subordination—the virtual exclusion of women from public office. Many years after their formal admission into the politics of liberal democracies, women remain outside the corridors of political power. The case of women is the most prevalent and obvious problem of political participation and representation in the policy-making structures of liberal democracies.

Popular political ideology provides that every citizen ought to have a chance to seek public office. In practice, however, only a very small proportion of the population actually does. While most citizens are legally entitled to seek elected office, subtle social and political practices effectively narrow the large field of potential political candidates to a select few. Among the social groups most consistently excluded from the ranks of political candidates (and consequently from public office) are the working class, minority ethnic and religious groups, and women. Statistically speaking, however, women are the most under-represented social group in the elected assemblies of western democracies. Women constitute more than one half of the population, but rarely more than a handful of its elected representatives are women. Few aspects of social life are more completely and universally male-dominated than politics. Indeed, if one observation best describes the political behaviour of women in liberal democracies today, it is that few seek and even fewer achieve public office.

One need only survey the composition of the national legislatures of the western world to appreciate the scope of this under-representation. Women appear to achieve their highest rates of election in countries that have electoral systems based on proportional representation as in Scandinavia. For example, in 1981, 25 per cent of Finnish, 23 per cent of Swedish and 8.5 per cent of Western German national legislators were women. In Britain, however, the

From *Women and Politics in Canada*, Toronto, McGraw-Hill Ryerson, 1985. By permission of the author.

TABLE 1   **Women as a % of 1983 Provincial Legislatures***

British Columbia	12.3	Quebec	6.6
Alberta	7.6	New Brunswick	6.9
Saskatchewan	7.8	Nova Scotia	1.9
Manitoba	12.3	Prince Edward Island	6.3
Ontario	4.8	Newfoundland	5.8

*Table number changed from original
Source: Sylvie Arend, *Prendre Nos Droits: Prendre Nos Places*

first large western nation to elect a woman as Prime Minister, only 3 per cent of the members of the House of Commons were women. In 1980, women constituted only 4.4 per cent of the American Congress and 2 per cent of the Senate. The proportions of women in office are even smaller in France, Australia and Japan.

Canada is not an exception to this general observation about the gender-based division of political power in western democracies. Most Canadian women were granted the right to vote and seek public office at about the same time as their British and American counterparts. Due to Canada's federal structure, however, women's suffrage has a rather complex history. In the provinces west of Ontario, women were granted the right to vote and contest office in provincial elections as early as 1917. The federal franchise was extended to women in 1921. (Some women were allowed to vote in the 1917 federal election as male surrogates.) The right to contest provincial office, however, was withheld from women until 1934 in New Brunswick and 1940 in Quebec. Many municipalities have property qualifications, so many women could not run for municipal office until as recently as 1970. (The qualifications discriminated against females, who are less often property owners than males.)

In the several decades since suffrage was achieved, women have been integrated only partially into the mainstream of Canadian politics. This pattern is shared by all western democracies. For some time, women lagged behind men in the performance of even the least demanding acts of democratic citizenship, such as voting. Since the early 1970s, however, the "gender gap" has closed at the level of mass or citizen politics. Women now read about politics, vote and attend political meetings as frequently as men do; only negligible gender differences remain. Women, in other words, have achieved parity with men at the level of citizen politics in Canada.

Elite politics remains virtually an exclusive male domain. National data indicating women's involvement in municipal politics are unavailable, but records from provincial and federal elections underline the pronounced gender biases in the composition of our elected assemblies. Canada's first female legislators, Louise McKenney and Roberta Macadams, were elected at the provincial level, in Alberta, in 1917. In 1983, however, only 6 per cent of a total of 1172 provincial legislators were women (see Table 1). Women presently constitute only 5 per cent of provincial cabinets.

TABLE 2   **Women Candidates and MPs in Canadian General Elections, 1921–1980***
(per cent women)

Year	Candidates	M.P.s
1921–1967	2.4[a]	0.8
1968	3.5	0.4
1972	6.4	1.8
1974	9.4	3.4
1979	13.8	3.6
1980	14.4	5.0
1984	14.5	9.6

[a] Average for elections between 1921 and 1967.
* Table number changed from original.
Sources: Report of the Royal Commission on the Status of Women; Reports of the Chief Electoral Officer of Canada (1972–1984).

At the federal level, a mere sixty-five women have become members of Parliament between 1921—when the first woman, Agnes Macphail, was elected to the House of Commons—and 1984. As Table 2 indicates, women constituted 2.4 per cent of all candidates for federal office and less than one per cent of those elected between 1921 and 1968. Since 1968 the percentage of women candidates and federal members has progressively increased. Yet, even at the peak of women's participation in federal elections, in 1984, less than 15 per cent of all candidates for federal office and 10 per cent of those elected were women. There are only six women in the federal Cabinet, the heart of political power and policy-making in Canada. These striking statistics point to a serious flaw in the fabric of representational democracy in Canada, and prompt one obvious question: why have women been so dramatically under-represented in our elected assemblies?

CITIZENS AND POLITICIANS

Most of the research concerning women's political participation concentrates on the behaviour of females in the general public, rather than on female politicians. This might be because there are only a small number of female political leaders to study. More important are the theoretical reasons for concentrating on the participation of women in citizen politics. Put simply, evidence of gender differences in rates of mass political participation often is taken as an explanation for the limited involvement of women in élite politics. Both macro-historical theories and micro theories of the sociology of political participation posit a causal link between mass political behaviour and élite recruitment.

The macro-historical perspective is concerned with the integration of newly enfranchised groups into the mainstream of democratic politics. It proposes that the equal integration of women into democratic decision-making structures (like the integration of all newly enfranchised groups) follows two distinct and necessarily consecutive stages. First, the voting participation of newly enfranchised groups must rise until it matches that of already established groups in the electorate. Only after the first stage has been accomplished can we expect to find representatives of these late entrants participating in élite politics in any significant numbers. The recruitment of women to public office depends on women voters. Women must vote in the same numbers as men— the already "established group" in the electorate.

Lester Milbrath's hierarchy of political involvement perhaps best suggests how the link between mass political behaviour and élite recruitment has been established in micro theories of political participation. Milbrath argues that the citizens of any democratic polity can be ranked on a ladder of political activities. The ladder has four distinct and ordered steps. At the bottom of this hierarchy are the "Apathetics," who neither care about politics nor vote. "Spectators" are placed a step above the "Apathetics" because they take some interest in politics and engage in the least demanding acts of democratic citizenship such as voting or putting campaign signs on their lawn. "Transitional Participants" comprise the next step up the ladder of political involvement. Transitional participants may attend political meetings, contact public officials or contribute financially to a party. At the top are the "Gladiators"—party members, strategists and fund-raisers. Candidates for public office and office-holders are at the apex. In liberal democracies, élite recruitment is viewed as the "most active" stage of political involvement.

Milbrath's model of political involvement makes a number of assumptions about the nature of political participation, but only two concern us here. The first is the assumption of unidimensionality. The wide range of political acts on the hierarchy are not seen as differing qualitatively; that is, they are not treated as essentially distinct forms of human behaviour. Instead, Milbrath suggests that such divergent political activities as voting and office-holding differ only in terms of the time and energy invested in each. The major distinction among Milbrath's four types of political actors is the amount of effort they put into politics.

The model also assumes that political participation is cumulative. By making this assumption, Milbrath establishes a link between mass political participation and office-holding. In the terms of his model, "cumulative" means that those at any one level on the ladder also perform the political acts that define the lower levels. "Transitional Participants" also engage in activities such as voting, which define the "Spectator" level. Transitional forms of political activity, in turn, are preconditions for gladitorial or élite politics. The transitional level, in other words, provides the "pool of eligibles" for public office. The existence of biases in liberal–democratic recruitment, therefore, simply reflects the under-participation of certain social groups at lower levels of the hierarchy of political involvement—especially the composition of the "pool" from which full-time politicians emerge.

Both the macro and micro explanations rely on similar evidence to explain the dearth of women in public office. Both focus on gender differences in rates of mass political behaviour and both assume that the election of women is dependent on the development of parity between the genders in mass political participation. Early voting studies reported that women were less likely to vote than men. This finding was taken as evidence that women had not yet achieved the first and necessary stage in the political integration of "late entrants" into the politics of liberal democracies. Similarly, early political participation studies indicated that women were less likely than men to move up the ladder of political involvement to the transitional level. From the micro perspective, too, gender biases in élite recruitment could be attributed to the seeming inability of women to enter the ranks of the eligibles for public office at rates similar to men. Both explanations for male dominance at the élite level, therefore, held only so long as gender differences were apparent in mass political participation.

Recent developments in patterns of mass politics undermine the notion that the election of women in significant proportions will necessarily follow if the "gender gap" is closed at the mass level. In Canada and elsewhere, women now appear to engage in mass or citizen politics as frequently as men do. This parity between the genders has not been reflected in our elected assemblies. The equal integration of women at the level of mass politics, in other words, does not appear to have dramatically expanded the opportunities for women to enter the ranks of political decision-makers.

The fundamental weakness in arguments that posit a causal relationship between gender differences at the mass level and the recruitment of women to public office appears to be the assumption of unidimensionality. If only from a common sense perspective, unidimensionality is difficult to accept. Citizen and élite politics are different spheres of political activity. Each makes quite different demands on the individual. Each is characterized by distinct social norms and political processes. Popular political ideology instructs all citizens, from a very early age, that engaging in citizen politics—voting, being informed, taking sides in partisan debates—is both a necessary and desirable pursuit for all members of a democratic polity. Moreover, such participation is a part-time and intermittent activity. Individuals may differ among themselves according to the interest, time and resources they can afford to invest in mass politics. But, with sufficient measures of these qualities, they can determine their own level of political involvement.

Interest and resources, however, clearly are not sufficient for advancement in élite politics. Running for and achieving public office shapes the individual's lifestyle and usually requires special skills and organizational ties. Moreover, the point of entry to élite politics is in no small way controlled by others. Electorates, local notables, party officials and public opinion, to name a few, all intervene to determine who will become political decision-makers in liberal democracies. Elite politics is not simply a more active stage of citizen participation; it is a distinct form of political activity.

The passage of individuals from citizen politics to elected office is the purview of political recruitment studies. Ideally, the studies are concerned with the social and political processes through which political positions are filled. Few studies, however, trace the pathways and experiences of women who cross the threshold from mass to élite politics. Most of us simply have rested comfortably with a few general explanations for why women *do not* become involved in élite politics.

WHY WOMEN ARE NOT POLITICIANS

At least until very recently, the mainstream recruitment literature has not regarded women as a special category of politicians. Rather, the recruitment literature has accepted uncritically a few broad explanations of why élite politics essentially is incompatible with the female experience. (One is the explanation based on mass participation.) The literature has emphasized a number of other factors that contribute to the dearth of female politicans. For some time, the absence of women in the elected assemblies of western democracies was attributed to physiological factors, although "hormone-based" explanations find little support today. The continued exclusion of women from the ranks of political decision-makers has also been attributed to a male conspiracy that subjugates women to a subordinate and dependent social status. Overall, however, the "socialization paradigm" and gender role constraints have become the most popular explanations for division of political power by gender.

The "socialization" explanation contends that women do not seek elected office because, in western democracies, women are socialized to be apolitical. Young girls are taught differently than young boys: females are encouraged— indirectly through example and directly through cultural prescriptions and sanctions—that politics is better left to the men. They are encouraged to *abstain* from the public world of politics (and business and the professions) so that they can better fulfill the responsibilities of homemaking and child-rearing, roles reserved for women alone. As a result of this socialization process, men and women learn to expect that only men should pursue a career in politics. The cultural exclusion of women in political leadership roles, then, becomes self-reinforcing. The nearly exclusive election of males to public office creates the expectation that only males should seek office. Cultural norms prescribe and sustain male dominance in politics. The gender-based division of political power is firmly entrenched, and is transmitted from generation to generation via the values and expectations of men and women.

The "gender-role explanation" is closely related to the "socialization paradigm," but it is different in that it concentrates on the *situations* imposed on women as they perform the traditional female gender roles that have been prescribed by dominant cultural norms. The "gender-role explanation" asserts that women do not abstain from political activism as much as they are *inhibited* from participating by the constraints of female gender roles, especially those of wife and mother.

All modern societies have more or less rigid sexual divisions of labour. The relegation of women to the "private sphere," to the tasks of mothering and homemaking, is said to undermine women's ability to enter full-time politics in a number of ways. First, since homemaking is not financially remunerated, it is assigned little prestige in industrialized societies where income is a major ranking variable in the social hierarchy. Second, homemaking isolates women from the public sphere, from business and politics. It provides them with ambiguous social skills and few of the social contacts that facilitate a political career. Finally, female gender roles are said to put women at a disadvantage in the political world because of the time-consuming nature of the roles themselves. Child-rearing, for example, often delays women's entry into politics until after their children have grown. Since full-time child-rearing generally is assumed by females alone, males often get a head start in a highly competitive and apprenticeship-oriented recruitment system. The "gender-role" or "situational" explanation, then, suggests that women may aspire to public office, but that they usually are delayed or fully inhibited from crossing the threshold from private to public life by gender-role demands and constraints.

Both the "socialization" and "gender-role" arguments suggest that men and women are provided with quite distinct social cues and tangible opportunities to compete for public office. Neither, however, is a sufficient explanation for the division of political power by gender. Socialization processes may transmit and reinforce the expectation of male dominance in politics, but they are not as rigid as is sometimes supposed. Some women do deviate from these norms by seeking and sometimes achieving public office. Also, gender roles do not prohibit all wives and all mothers from seeking and gaining elected office. Indeed, the few studies examining the backgrounds of female politicians demonstrate that many enter élite politics directly from these roles. Both arguments suggest that men and women do not share the same symbolic or structural environment when they try to move from mass to élite politics, but the arguments tell us little about those women who do contest political office. At best, they provide us with underlying perspectives to begin the study of women's recruitment to public office. ● ● ●

AN INDIAN PERSPECTIVE ON CANADIAN POLITICS
Marie Smallface Marule

Our strength as Indians derives from our tribal identity. The Canadian government, very deliberately and systematically, is seeking to undermine our tribal

From Little Bear, Leroy; Bolt, Menno; and Long, J.D., eds, *Pathways to Self-Determination: Canadian Indians and the Canadian State*, Toronto. Reprinted by permission of University of Toronto Press. © University of Toronto Press 1984. Some notes from the original have been omitted.

identity by imposing policies on Indians that emphasize individualism and materialism. This policy of "detribalization" subverts our consensual political system, our kinship system, our communal ownership system, and our collective economic system. This policy represents the biggest problem in our efforts to revitalize our Indian societies and governments.

In traditional Indian societies, whether band or clan, authority was a collective right that could be temporarily delegated to a leader, under restrictive conditions, to carry out essential activities. But the responsibility and authority always remained with the people. In situations where the collectivity temporarily delegated authority to a leader, that person had to have the respect of the entire tribe, not merely the support of a majority of voters. Obedience to the leader derived from the respect that the people had for him. The coercive imposition by the Canadian government of an elected form of government on Indians is in direct conflict with traditional forms of government. The elective model is based on individual ownership of land and the delegation of authority from above, and it has created serious problems in our Indian communities. This is particularly true among the prairie tribes, where there has always been a strong tradition of decision-making by consensus rather than by individuals in authority.

I have had an opportunity to observe how the consensus approach to decision-making works in practice. In the mid-1970s when I worked for the executive council of the National Indian Brotherhood, they used this approach because they recognized a flaw in the system of majority rule. They saw that majority rule forces decisions on the minority, thereby creating divisions. The few times that the executive council attempted to use the majority-rule system of decision-making, it resulted in the abstention of those who didn't agree with it. They would not directly oppose it, but they did not pay any attention to it either. Thus, it was possible to work together only on those things where they all agreed. On matters of disagreement, each was left to take his own approach.

It is not known to what degree the Canadian government has been successful in its efforts to eliminate traditional Indian attitudes and values. It is assumed by many that very little remains of traditional Indian ideology and philosophy because the traditional Indian lifestyle is no longer in evidence; that is, we don't live in tepees anymore. This assumption holds that traditional values and beliefs changed when our lifestyles changed. Implicit in this assumption, also, is the notion that Indian culture must remain static to remain Indian. But the history of our people is a history of successful adaptation to change while countering oppression and resisting imposition of undesired changes. A specific and important example of such resistance to imposed change can be observed in the Indians' refusal to submit to pressures by the Canadian government to adopt its system of individualized land allotment.

Why is the issue of Indian government taking centre stage at the present time? The answer is to be found in the policy goals of the Canadian government.

They want to revise the Indian Act to accelerate the detribalization of Indians. Their ultimate goal is the termination of Indian status and the complete assimilation of our people into Canadian society. The first major attempt by the Canadian government to advance this objective was made in 1969. The 1969 White Paper on Indian policy sought to terminate Indian status and rights within a five-year period. It was unsuccessful. Now the Canadian government sees an opportunity to use the Constitution to achieve the same end. Embodied in the Constitution as it now stands is the falsehood that international political and legal principle gives to the Canadian government the right to terminate our special status as Indians. But if they truly have this right, why do they bother to pacify us by throwing a few words on aboriginal rights into the Canadian Charter of Rights and Freedoms? Why do they dangle the mirage of Indian government in front of us at this time? I say it is to divert our attention from their policy goals, which are in contravention of international political and legal principles.

When a delegation of the Union of British Columbia Indian Chiefs went to the United Nations to address the Under-Secretary-General of Political Affairs, Decolonization, and Trusteeships, they said, "Look here! You are ignoring us. You have addressed the colonial situations in Africa and Asia, but you have ignored the Western Hemisphere. Why is it that you are allowing colonial situations to exist in the Western Hemisphere?" Significantly, after the UBCIC brought this issue to the attention of the UN, the Canadian government suddenly became willing to negotiate changes to the Canadian Charter of Rights and Freedoms, adding protection for treaty and aboriginal rights along with traditional rights and freedoms. But this provision is not acceptable to the UBCIC because the charter contains no acceptable definitions of aboriginal and treaty rights. Furthermore, the provision governing Indian rights will be subject to the constitutional amending formula. This formula requires agreement by the provincial governments before any changes can be effected on Indian treaty and aboriginal rights.

It is no secret that the interests of the provincial governments are in direct conflict with Indian interests. This conflict of interest derives from Indian land claims. Currently, large parts of Canada are under tenancy by indigenous peoples. For example, 80 per cent of the population of northern Saskatchewan is native Indian; in northern Manitoba, it is 90 per cent. Now and historically these territories belong to the indigenous people. Yet the consequence of the constitutional amending formula will be to leave Indians with whatever territories the provinces choose to surrender, which may be nothing. Some say that claiming these territories for Indians is a very idealistic and unrealistic position to take, a symbolic position. But that is not the position of the native people. The UBCIC rejected the proposed constitutional package, saying:

> As long as we have no involvement in amendments that affect Indian people, then what we are offered is nothing. It is not better than what it was before. We

are better off with S91(24) of the BNA Act and the interpretation that administration of the trust now reverts back to Britain upon the independence of Canada.

To create division among Indians in their stand on the Constitution, the Canadian government decided to bait the constitutional trap. It leaked information that it was about to pass "Indian-government" legislation that would empower Indian band councils to assume the authority currently exercised by the minister of Indian Affairs. By leaking news of this "significant concession," the Canadian government sought to induce some Indians to support the constitutional package. Even if this proposed "concession" turns out to be genuine, however, it offers Canadian Indians no more than what the United States gave to its Indians in the Indian Reorganization Act of 1934. This is an act to institutionalize legal authority over Indians. For American Indians this act brought with it European concepts of authority and the associated structures, systems, and institutions. The Canadian Indian-government legislation is rumoured to have an "opting-in" provision so that bands will not have to accept it if they do not want to. Ostensibly, bands will be allowed to opt into the Indian-government system when they are "ready." But there is an underlying threat that, if a band refuses to opt in when the government deems it should, its funds can be cut off.

The tactic of cutting off funds in order to coerce us to surrender our authority and responsibility is not new. The Canadian government used it during the last century by withholding rations in times of famine and disaster. Today social assistance is being manipulated in the same manner to subordinate and intimidate Indians. How can Indian people take political control of their communities when 80 per cent of them are dependent on the Canadian government for social assistance? We cannot declare political independence so long as we are dependent on Canadian government welfare. . . .

Indian communities that have worked to get rid of their dependence on the Canadian government have not found it easy, but some have done it. The Neskainlith Indian people of the Shuswap nation have said,

> We are going to do something about this dependency of ours. We are going to regain some degree of self-reliance. We are going to cut our dependency on money and on the Canadian government which controls every facet of our lives.

They are struggling to this end, and it is truly marvellous to see the progress they are making. They are showing that dependence is a matter of attitude.

There is a belief among some of our Indian people that by replacing the white bureaucrats in the Indian Affairs Department with brown people we will remedy all that is wrong with our situation. The experience of the United States Bureau of Indian Affairs (BIA) shows that this approach offers no solution to Indian problems. Sixty per cent of BIA employees are of native descent, and sixteen of the top twenty-five administrative positions are currently held by native people. Yet the BIA continues to function as an ineffective, oppressive agency because of its structure, its systems, and its processes. Currently some of our provincial organizations are acting on the assumption that by organizing themselves along the lines of the Indian Affairs Department they will be able to do more for their people than Indian Affairs now does. This too is a fallacy; furthermore, it is a fatal mistake for us to assume that solutions to our problems can be found in European-Western structures, systems, and processes.

Let us now turn to consider workable alternatives available to us. We talk about sovereignty and claim it for ourselves, but we have not yet begun to exploit the opportunities that are open to us to exercise it. British Columbia Indians have begun to take a leadership role in asserting their sovereignty. Why are British Columbia Indians more progressive than Alberta Indians in this regard? I have a personal theory about this: people living in poverty have less, individually, to lose and are more willing to risk what little they have to achieve their rights. In British Columbia, where there are smaller communities, a smaller land base, fewer resources, and less material wealth, Indians are willing to risk the consequences of confrontations with the Canadian government. In Alberta, where Indians have a larger land base, greater resources, and greater individual material wealth, they are acquiescing to the system that the Canadian government has imposed because they are afraid of losing what they have.

There exists in Alberta also a more entrenched Indian élite than one finds in British Columbia. This is because the benefits of economic development on Indian reserves tend to accrue to a privileged minority, and in Alberta there has been more economic development on Indian reserves. Emergence of an élite class in Alberta Indian communities has inhibited the development of traditional Indian government because élite interests are well served by the kind of political and economic system advocated by the Department of Indian Affairs. Such a system enables the élite group to conduct band affairs in such a way as to maintain and advance its [own] interests. This élite group of Indians does not want its people to regain authority over their own affairs because that would require leaders to be accountable to their people. In effect, the élite class of Indians is fronting for the Indian Affairs Branch by persuading the mass of band members to accept what the Canadian government is pushing. The élite are telling Indian people that if the proposed Indian-government legislation is passed by the Canadian government, Indians will have what they want—self-determination. What they are not saying is that the systems, the institutions, the structures associated with legislated Indian government will be the same as those under the Indian Affairs Department.

In Indian communities élitism is sometimes promoted by people who go to university and return home believing they have the right, the authority, and the wisdom to tell people what they should do or what is best for them. They assume that they should hold a superior economic and social position in the community. Elitism is a European ideology and philosophy. It is completely contrary to our traditional philosophy and ideology, and it is very dangerous to the survival of Indian communities.

Reassertion of the peoples' authority is a critical issue if Indian government is to have any real meaning. The Neskainlith Indians of the Shuswap nation, whom I mentioned earlier, are doing just that. These people are standing up and challenging their leaders, asking the fundamental question: "Who gave you your authority—the people, or the Canadian government?" They are struggling to re-establish and revitalize traditional processes of decision-making, which eliminate the danger of élitism. Without revitalization of the traditional system of leadership and of leadership selection, I foresee that Indian society will evolve into a two-class system of "haves" and "have-nots."

An alternative model of government available to Indians is one that places the locus of authority in the smallest political unit. The larger, more encompassing political units would play only a delegated, *co-ordinating* function. Under such a model we would resurrect family-clan groups and band communities. Each band would select its representatives to send to the tribal council. These representatives would get their direction from their band constituents. They would have specified responsibilities and limited authority. Thus, the tribal unit would function as it did traditionally, acting only in instances where the bands comprising the tribal unit had shared concerns, but ultimate authority would continue to rest within each band community.

The next step in building Indian government would be to resurrect and reactivate the tribal confederacies to act as encompassing units in matters of shared tribal concerns, such as commerce, trade, and political representation at a higher level. The confederacies, like the tribal units, would function in the traditional manner, that is, in the spirit of specified responsibilities with limited authority. With such constraints a political unit is less vulnerable to rule by bureaucracy because the authority to build a "top-down" bureaucracy is lacking. By vesting authority in the smallest political unit, the necessary administrative structures are kept as close as possible to the people. This increases the likelihood that they will be more sensitive and responsive to community needs than are the currently functioning oversized (Canadian and Indian) political-bureaucratic organizations to be found in Ottawa and the provincial capitals. An example of rebuilding Indian societies along the lines I have described can be observed in the Shuswap nation in British Columbia. The Shuswap nation comprises twenty-four bands united in a tribal confederation. The Shuswaps are related to other Salish groups, thus offering the potential to go on organizing into a confederation of Indian nations.

A model such as I am advocating would require a degree of communal sharing. Many people believe the concept of communal sharing is extinct in Indian communities, but I think it is very much alive. It merely hasn't been allowed to function. It hasn't had an opportunity to express itself in contemporary Indian society.

In all of this, I am detailing what I consider to be the best path to the development of an Indian political unit that can negotiate effectively with the government of Canada. We must have such a united political body because, if we try to negotiate on the basis of one Indian nation at a time, we are much less likely to succeed than if we do it as a united people. But in all of this we must be careful to honour an important traditional principle—that is, not to dictate to any Indian community how it should deal with its internal affairs. We as Indians hold many interests in common on which we can work together. We must work together on those commonalities but not involve ourselves in trying to force all our people into accepting the same solutions.

The model of government I have described offers potential advantages not only to Indians but to all Canadians. Canadians today are having serious problems with their political institutions. Consider, for example, the municipal governments' relationships to the provincial governments. These relationships are as paternalistic and bureaucratic as is the band council–Department of Indian Affairs relationship. They have similar problems of jurisdiction over resources, of indebtedness, dependence, and the alienation of people from central government. They also have the limitations that are inherent in a fragmented authority that is unable to deal effectively with the problems confronting it. Like band councils they are subject to a variety of unco-ordinated small political units (hospital boards, school boards, and so on) all beholden to a central government and lacking the authority for integrated planning that could give a meaningful sense of community to the people. Yet this municipal-government structure is now being offered to Indians as an alternative, a *better* alternative, to our existing situation.

Franz Fanon, in writing about the process of colonization and decolonization, identifies several sequential stages and impacts upon individuals and society. While his account may be overly dramatic, I have found parallels between the stages and impacts he describes and what our people are experiencing, particularly our experience in the last two generations. Indians are currently in the stage, identified by Fanon, where we believe that we are an inferior people. This sense of inferiority is evident in the way we are negotiating the terms of Indian government with the Canadian government. There is an underlying attitude that we have nothing of value in our communities, that the good things are to be found outside of our communities, that we must have federal officials tells us what to do.

A specific example of our sense of inferiority can be observed in the prevailing assumption among our people that we have to go to university for knowledge. Yet we have our elders to give us guidance. They have no university education, but they have a lifetime of understanding and wisdom to offer us. Until about ten years ago we had very few Indians in universities, but we survived and achieved. When I worked with the National Indian Brotherhood, only two members of the executive council had any university training. Yet they were all very knowledgeable about the white man's system—not only knowledgeable, but wise about it, knowing all its traps and pitfalls.

I observe a sense of inferiority, also, in our assumption that we need hospitals and doctors to have good health. Yet the evidence shows these have not contributed to our good health. They represent only an ineffective curative, not a preventative approach. Indians had far better health under the traditional system than we have today.

If we really want to help ourselves, we must revitalize our institutions. We must turn to our own traditional structures, systems, and processes. This does not mean that we have to return to the way we were two or three hundred years ago. Given our experience and knowledge about the failures of the European institutional structures, systems, and processes, why should we repeat their mistakes? Why, for example, should we adopt an educational system that not only fails to meet the needs of its students but also alienates them in the process? Yet we are currently on a course of introducing that type of educational system into our Indian communities. I believe we are uncritically adopting European–Western institutional approaches because of our sense of inferiority. We are doing it because we do not have confidence in our ability to build something that will be workable, more appropriate to our needs, and more effective. I am convinced that Indians can find in their traditional philosophies and ideologies better and more meaningful approaches than those offered by the Canadian government. We have something to offer that even other Canadians can look to as a better alternative to their existing institutions.

I know it is difficult to change institutions once they are established. This is where Indians are fortunate. We have not fully accepted the Canadian model of political, economic, and social administration and management as our own model on the reserves. We still have a chance to shape our institutions so they will conform to our traditional philosophies and ideologies and to adapt these to contemporary times so they will be as useful as they were previously to our community. But it is essential that Indians insist on traditional institutions, systems, and processes as the framework for any discussion of Indian government. Our traditional philosophies and ideologies are absolutely vital to our future. They must be clarified to give our people a real alternative.

My proposed approach to Indian government is not an easy route. Most things worthwhile are not easy to obtain. It will require much thought and planning. Without careful deliberation our "solutions" will only multiply our problems. In this process of thinking and planning, we must beware of the traitors in our midst—those of our people who have already accepted élitism, materialism, and individualism, who are trying to convince us that the Canadian way is the only way. Yes, it may be inevitable that our greatest enemies are within our own ranks.

THE POLITICAL ECONOMY TRADITION IN CANADA

Wallace Clement and Glen Williams

The pioneering of political economy approaches gave some of Canada's leading social scientists international recognition for their contributions to world scholarship during the period from the 1920s to the 1950s. After being all but abandoned during the next two decades, a *new* Canadian political economy can be dated from the popularization of nationalist issues identified in the 1968 report of a federal government task force on foreign ownership in Canadian industry, known commonly as "The Watkins Report," and the 1970 publication of Kari Levitt's *Silent Surrender: The Multinational Corporation in Canada*. The revived tradition was launched in earnest by the first Canadian Political Economy sessions in 1976 at the Learned Society meetings in Quebec City, organized by Daniel Drache. These sessions thereafter became a regular feature of the annual "Learneds."

Central to the first decade of the new Canadian political economy were three collections of articles: *Close the 49th Parallel Etc.: The Americanization of Canada*, edited by Ian Lumsden in 1970; *Capitalism and the National Question in Canada*, edited by Gary Teeple in 1972; and *The Canadian State: Political Economy and Political Power*, edited by Leo Panitch in 1977. Intellectual work proceeded rapidly enough for Wallace Clement and Daniel Drache to compile *A Practical Guide to Canadian Political Economy* in 1978, drawing together an eclectic set of readings from a variety of disciplines relevant to the revived political economy tradition. Of continuing importance was the 1979 creation of the learned journal *Studies in Political Economy: A Socialist Review* (twenty-six issues had appeared by the summer of 1988). Through the 1980s, the revival was not only under way, it was flourishing. The wealth of published research it produced was documented in 1985 by Daniel Drache and Wallace Clement's *The New Practical Guide to Canadian Political Economy*. This time the *Guide* required a host of contributors and twenty-five sub-fields to introduce the subject. This extensive output by a new generation drawing on an older tradition revealed that the new Canadian political economy had come of age.

But, as we look toward the 1990s, this tradition is at another crossroads. A generation of scholars has established the new Canadian political economy on a solid foundation, but it is now time for reflection and rejuvenation. ● ● ●

POLITICAL ECONOMY: ROOTS AND MEANING

Political economy has held different meanings over time, and, more important, political economy has been incorporated into both liberal and Marxist world

From *The New Canadian Political Economy*, Kingston, McGill-Queen's University Press, 1989. By permission.

views. "Classical" European political economy is associated with Adam Smith and David Ricardo, British economists who wrote as capitalism blossomed around the turn of the nineteenth century. Their focus was on the development of commodity markets and the relations of production made manifest by the labour theory of value. . . .

Smith founded the study of political economy in its modern sense as the application of scientific methods of analysis to human society. . . .

Especially interesting to Smith was the transition from farming to commerce. The social and economic inefficiencies of feudal agriculture were gradually broken down by the rise of the towns and the accompanying development of industrial capitalism through the unconscious operation of the "invisible hand" of the market. . . .

From this vision of an "invisible hand" that shapes socially beneficial ends from the chaos of individuals seeking to promote their own selfish purposes, Smith derived his theory of the minimal state. He believed that government intervention in the market, no matter how well intentioned, could serve in the end only to distort the social benefits that would flow from the free competition of industry and capital. The minimal state, Smith argued, would prevent the state from returning to the role it had taken on in previous economic eras as a line of defence for the rich against the poor.

Political economy became a popular label widely employed in nineteenth-century studies of liberal economics and society. There was considerable debate about its exact meaning, but most definitions were compatible in a general fashion with Smith's search for scientific insight into the mechanisms of socially organized production. . . .

Karl Marx, also writing in the nineteenth century, developed his political economy in critique of the dominant liberal or bourgeois political economy that had grown from the work of Smith and Ricardo. Their analysis of markets and profits within capitalism was the orthodoxy against which Marx raged. Smith and Ricardo were the theoreticians of capitalism against feudalism, whereas Marx's task was to expose the internal contradictions of capitalism in seeking the release of new relations of production. Nevertheless, at a macro level, Marx's analysis shared important similarities with Smithian political economy, including a stress on "scientific" social analysis, a stage theory of economic development, the centrality of labour in creating value, and a view of the state as alien and repressive. At the core of Marx's political economy was a notion most fully elaborated by Ricardo—the labour theory of value—but for Marx the commodity "labour" had a dual quality. Not only does labour produce more than its cost of reproduction (surplus value), and so provide the basis for capitalist exploitation and economic growth, but labour has consciousness, an ability to act politically to transform the conditions of its sale. Exploitation and struggle are the hallmarks of Marx's political economy. . . .

Marx's political economy has come to be known as "historical materialist." It is materialist in the sense that it focuses on the processes whereby material requirements are satisfied. It is historical in its concern for social processes that transform societies. A historical materialist approach seeks to understand the dynamic of change in the transformation of production and reproduction with particular attention given to the tensions, struggles, and contradictions within societies and between them. Political institutions were given an important place by Marx in the regulation of social conflict. As Bob Jessop has argued so persuasively, Marx's historical materialist analysis of the state and politics had its "discontinuities and disjunctions" but offered an open richness that has spurred a "wide range" of state theories. Derived from Marx, these state theories focus generally on the mechanisms through which government social and economic policies help to stabilize the dynamic process of capitalist accumulation.

To summarize, while political economy is based on a tradition that investigates the relationship between the economy and politics as they affect the social and cultural life of societies, within political economy there have been divergent tendencies. Broadly, the liberal political economy tradition has placed determinate weight on the political system and markets, while the Marxist tradition grants primacy to the economic system and classes. Such facile statements, however, underplay the complexity of positions within each tradition. Political economy at its strongest has focused on processes whereby social change is located in the historical interaction of the economic, political, cultural, and ideological moments of social life, with the dynamic rooted in socio-economic conflict. The best of political economy has avoided "economism," which attributes all explanations to the laws of motion of capitalism, instead impregnating materialism with "human agency," whereby the decisions and actions of people are integral to explaining the course of history. . . .

FROM CLASSICS TO CONTEMPORARIES: INNIS

Through their pioneering of the staples approach to understanding Canadian economic development, Harold Adams Innis (1894–1952) and W.A. Mackintosh (1895–1970) became the founders of the political economy tradition in Canada. Although they at first appeared to proceed from shared assumptions, their conclusions began to diverge markedly with the passage of time. Whereas Mackintosh's message could be absorbed (and eventually obscured) within orthodox neo-classical economics, Innis's analysis was so forcefully original that his commanding presence has been evident throughout the history of the tradition. Innis has stood sometimes as inspiration, sometimes as foil, for those who have worked to create the new Canadian political economy.

As testimony to his staying power, aspects of Innis's staples thesis are recounted in virtually all the chapters. Its essence is that Canada was developed to exploit a series of raw materials for more industrially advanced metropolitan nations. Canada's reliance on resource exports led to a failure to capture the benefits of the "linkages" associated with the inputs into production and processing of the raw materials, thereby locking it into a spiral of dependent relations. Apparent similarities between Innis's staples thesis and later Latin American dependency theories led the founders of the new Canadian political economy to proclaim Innis a forerunner of their own application of *dependencia* analysis to Canada. . . . it was a product more of wishful imagination than of careful analysis. Unlike dependency theory, the staples approach was not rooted in neo-Marxist models of socio-regional exploitation.

But Innis was much more than a staples theorist, contributing to a wide range of issues like regionalism, culture, and communications still central to the study of contemporary Canadian life. He also remained relevant because, like those in the new political economy, he worked outside the mainstream of neo-classical doctrine. Innis's critique of neo-classical political economy was, however, derived not from Marx but from his reading of Adam Smith and the radical heretic of US economics in the early twentieth century, Thorstein Veblen. Innis recorded that Veblen was "the first to attempt a general stocktaking of general tendencies in a dynamic society saddled with machine industry, just as Adam Smith was the first to present a general stocktaking before machine industry came in."

In a revealing tribute to Veblen, Innis recorded many features of Veblen's work that characterized his own method. In contrast to ahistorical and static neo-classical analysis, Veblen's approach was "dynamic," Innis wrote, since it focused on "the study of processes of growth and decay" of economic institutions. Also in contrast to neo-classical orthodoxy, Veblen's humanistic interdisciplinary perspective was grounded in the premise that economic man "is not simply a bundle of desires that are to be saturated by being placed in the path of the forces of the environment, but rather a coherent structure of propensities and habits which seeks realization and expression in an unfolding activity." Another important area of agreement between Innis and Veblen was their stress on the significance of understanding the relationship between machine technology and the character of human activity. This was to become an especially important theme in Innis's later work on culture and communications. Finally, Innis admired what he perceived to be Veblen's detached, unbiased, apolitical, scientific approach, "protecting him from absorption into the partialities of modern movements. His anxiety has always been to detect trends and escape their effects." Veblen, like Innis, was an "individualist . . . in revolt" against mass society.

FURTHER LINKS WITH THE PAST:
PENTLAND AND MACPHERSON

Innis provided the new Canadian political economy with a non-Marxist alternative to the neo-classical models that today still dominate the training of professional economists. Pentland and Macpherson, as we shall see, provided a

Marxist-influenced basis for the rejection of the dominant liberal models of social analysis.

H. Clare Pentland (1914–1978) has been an important, if somewhat underground, figure in both the rediscovery and the revitalization of Canadian political economy. Pentland's work asked central questions about the making of Canadian labour, in terms of both labour market and class formation, within an immigrant society undergoing industrialization and resource exploitation. Pentland became widely known through a few seminal journal articles, but close followers have always referred to his doctoral thesis, defended in 1961, and a major report prepared for the Task Force on Labour Relations in 1968. Not until 1981 was his thesis, *Labour and Capital in Canada 1650–1860*, finally published under the editorship of Paul Phillips. While Pentland's main work was produced in the 1960s and was not published until the 1980s, its major influence for the revival of Canadian political economy was in the 1970s. Significant critiques of Pentland's work have now begun to appear, testament to both the continuing importance of his contribution and also the more scrutinizing gaze of the new political economy's ever stronger foundation of empirical research. . . .

Crawford Brough Macpherson, better known as "C.B." (1911–1987), also continues to have a major impact on Canadian political economy. His justly famous *Democracy in Alberta: Social Credit and the Party System* was first published in 1953, and he went on to build a world-wide following as a political theorist, culminating in 1985 with *The Rise and Fall of Economic Justice*. Macpherson's greatest contribution to the new political economy has been through his extensive writings on theories of property, on democracy, and on the development of a theory of rights.

In their own ways, both Pentland and Macpherson fostered and influenced the growth of a strong neo-Marxist presence within Canadian political economy. However, Canadian neo-Marxism has owed its vigour also to a post-1960s resurgence, centred in western Europe, of left intellectual analysis. Not surprisingly, controversies marking the new Canadian political economy in the 1980s have centred on the respective contributions of Innis and Marx. Debate was sparked by a special issue of *Studies in Political Economy*, where David McNally, Leo Panitch, and Ray Schmidt critiqued "Innisian-inspired" dependency perspectives, especially the weakness of class analysis within the Canadian dependency school. This critique initiated energetic responses by Ian Parker, Daniel Drache, and Mel Watkins defending the relevance of Innis.

At issue has never been whether Innis was a Marxist—of course, he was not—but whether there was a common ground of mutual relevance between the class and dependency/Innisian perspectives within contemporary Canadian political economy. Clement has argued, using the case of mining, that Innis's massive empirical contribution can enrich class analysis. Such an undertaking is informed by Innis's insights, but the more powerful explanation is Marxist. For the most part, the tension between the two approaches has been creative for the new political economy. The challenge continues to be to produce fresh paradigms that build on the insights of traditional ones.

SCOPE AND METHOD IN
CANADIAN POLITICAL ECONOMY

Despite their work being complementary, we have seen that classical and contemporary, liberal and neo-Marxist, class and dependency political economists have proceeded largely from radically different premises. At the risk of overgeneralizing, we will now explore, through consideration of scope and method, how these distinct strands can be woven back together into the fabric of Canadian political economy.

The object of political economy research is typically macro-level description and/or explanation of material practices. The subject of this research knows no boundaries, as long as the analysis develops the subject's reciprocal linkages to related subjects and fields of inquiry. Consequently, political economy analysis is interdisciplinary, bridging such organized disciplines as history, economics, geography, philosophy, anthropology, literature, communications, psychology, political science, and sociology. At its best, political economy makes the connection between the economic, political, and cultural/ideological moments of social life in a holistic way. As well, researchers typically use a historical developmental approach in order to locate their subject in time, hence the focus on social change and transformation. Finally, research is frequently spatially sensitive: that is, the subject is defined territorially through a relational linkage with other domestic and international territories.

While founded in an era of nationalism, the new Canadian political economy has always been outward-looking: both concerned about the impact of international forces on Canada and open to incorporating international theoretical movements into its research. In the late 1960s, the dependency literature, drawn from the experience of Africa, Latin America, and the Caribbean, stimulated debate. As it matured, however, the new political economy has become more integrated within a wider international political economy centred in western Europe. Increasingly, it has become more truly comparative in its methodology, moving away from the classical political economists' universe, centred in Great Britain and the United States, toward developing comparisons with other smaller, late-industrializing countries in Scandinavia and Australasia.

Some have mistakenly attributed economic determinism to Canadian political economy, but it has focused primarily on human agency—choices and decisions made by political, economic, and social actors and their effects. These choices are defined both historically and territorially and are mediated through cultural and ideological factors on the one hand and forms of social organization and/or technology on the other. Where liberal political economists might emphasize culture and technology, neo-Marxists would stress ideology and social organization. The concept of agency is employed here to convey the sense that social outcomes are not predetermined. However, the "definition" and "mediation" of these choices indicate that social and material boundaries extensively structure decision-making. Canadian political economy's different theoretical perspectives often hotly debate the different weights they ascribe to "agency" and "structure" in determining outcomes.

Political economy's methodological insight is to study the effects of totalities from a materialist perspective. Social relations are located within the context of the economic, political, and ideological/cultural dimensions on the one hand and within the dimensions of time and space on the other. To understand the forces of change, political economy requires a broad base. In Innis's terms, this means that political economy is concerned with linkages, but these linkages are conceptual as well as material. Relations within political economy are not static forces. To the contrary, political economy seeks to discover tensions within society as it produces struggle and resistance. To know how societies are, and can be, transformed is the primary goal of political economy. Frequently this means challenging conventional wisdoms and ideological structures in the popular, academic, and political domains.

. . . Canadian political economy covers a great deal of ground. . . . it is an eclectic tradition in terms of subject, ideology, and specific approach. It does not lay exclusive claim to any special research techniques, nor does it promote a homogeneous "line." Political economy in Canada prides itself on its openness, its willingness to engage in disputes over theoretical paradigms, and its eagerness to incorporate new discoveries. Its vibrancy comes from the prolific research of its practitioners and the engagement of its followers. ● ● ●

FREE TRADE, MEECH LAKE,
AND THE FUTURE OF CANADA

Donald V. Smiley

● ● ● The free trade agreement with the United States which came into effect on 1 January 1989 is, of course, the second major federal issue of the past two years. There are three federal dimensions of this matter. First, the provinces were very much involved with Ottawa in the early stages of the formulation of the agreement and the scope of FTA as finally accepted by the Canadian and American governments was decisively shaped by the distribution of jurisdiction between Ottawa and the provinces. In the *State of the Federation* collection Douglas Brown, formerly an intergovernmental affairs officer with the New-

Adapted by the editor from a review article by the late Donald V. Smiley entitled "Meech Lake and Free Trade: Studies in Canadian Federalism," which appeared in *Canadian Public Administration*, 32, 3, Fall, 1989, published by the Institute of Public Administration of Canada. By permission.

foundland government and now associate director of the institute, gives a valuable account of the very intense involvement of the provinces with the federal government in the earlier phases of free trade and the decline of such involvement in the latter period of "brinkmanship" negotiations between the most senior officials of the two national governments. He suggests tentatively that " . . . in the final power play, protecting the Canadian position could not allow for the niceties of federal-provincial diplomacy" (p. 91). In a companion essay Shellagh Dunn analyses the strategies of each of the provinces in relation to the free trade issue.

Ottawa was able to dispense for the most part with provincial involvement in the latter phases of the FTA negotiations and thus to blunt the opposition of the governments of Ontario and Prince Edward Island to free trade. This proved possible because the federal government was able to convince Washington to agree to an arrangement which in its trade aspects, as distinct from those related to energy and investment, was almost entirely within federal jurisdiction, except for the provisions relating to wine. However, in the discussions about the definition of subsidies which are now beginning, it is unlikely that the Americans can be persuaded to keep certain provincial policies and practices out of the negotiations—for example, those related to procurement by the provincial governments and their public corporations. More immediately, it appears that the agreement curtails provincial powers in respect to investment and energy policies.

Secondly, it is at least possible that FTA will have the result of extending the scope of federal legislative power. While the issue is complex, existing law seems to have moved away from the provincializing thrust of the 1937 Labour Conventions decision of the Judicial Committee which determined that federal powers could not be extended solely because Canada had entered into some sort of international arrangement and of a very narrow definition of the trade and commerce power. It seems likely that in future judicial decisions related to Canadian–American economic relations the courts will take notice, explicitly or otherwise, of FTA and its political ratification by the Canadian voters in the general election of 1988.

Thirdly, the compliance requirements of the FTA may give rise to American pressures on Ottawa to take action against the provinces in respect to matters within the latters' jurisdiction. Section 103 provides that "the Parties to this Agreement shall ensure that all necessary measures are taken in order to give effect to its provisions, except as otherwise provided in this Agreement, by state, provincial and local governments." It has been pointed out that this is much stronger than the GATT provision in which each government is committed to take "such reasonable measures as may be available to it" to secure observance. In the extreme, might Americans go so far as to pressure Ottawa to use such heavy constitutional weapons against the provinces as disallowance, the exercise of the declaratory power, or refusing contributions to established shared-cost programs?

How, then, are Meech Lake and free trade related, if at all? There is an influential nationalist strain in English–Canadian political thought which as had its most articulate exponent in Donald Creighton. According to this general line of analysis, provincialism and continentalism are corollaries and thus both Meech Lake and the FTA proceed in the same direction by weakening the power of the national government.

Ideological explanation provides an alternative way of linking the Meech Lake and free trade issues. Left-right cleavages are only one of the several axes on which Canadians are divided in their politics. In fact, one could go even further and say that if anyone set out in a deliberate way to construct a political system which would effectively frustrate such cleavages, the result might not look very different from the one Canadians have evolved. There is of course the French–English dimension, and the federalism which divides Canadians along territorial lines is pervasive. The Charter of Rights and Freedoms has a thrust towards encouraging political mobilization and political allegiances around the axes of sex, ethnicity, race, religion, aboriginal rights, physical or mental disability and so on. Janine Brodie and Jane Jenson in their book-length analysis set out to explain the failure of the left in Canada to have the political system mobilized on class lines. In large part, the explanation is that the bourgeois parties have had a high degree of success in frustrating *definitions* of politics in terms of class. Although Brodie and Jenson do not make this point, it might be argued that mainstream federalist scholars in Canada, with their preoccupations in French–English and provincial cleavages, have contributed to such non-class definitions and there is little reference to class or ideology in the publications of the institute.

Yet political events upend political analysis, and it seems to me that the circumstances of the federal general election of 1988 make explanations of the Canadian system which ignore ideology unpersuasive. Thus:

—the free trade issue mobilized Canadian interest groups on an ideological basis more clearly than ever before. The business community and interests closely associated with it supported the FTA with almost no dissent. The anti-free trade forces did not encompass a class in any strict Marxian sense but rather corresponded in a broad way to what Duncan Cameron and Daniel Drache call the "public sector consensus" opposed to rolling back the size and power of the state and enhancing market forces as allocators of economic resources.

—ideological conflicts about free trade have at least the potential to create new kinds of relations between the francophone community of Quebec and other Canadians. Within that province there seems to be an elite consensus favouring the philosophy of the market economy in a less diluted form than this has been articulated by Prime Minister Mulroney and other leaders of the national PC party. The Parti Québécois has, it seems, cut itself off from its former social democratic moorings, and in a deft way Jacques Parizeau has associated separatism with free trade on the general argument that as Quebec becomes increasingly more integrated into the continental economy it will become decreasingly less vulnerable to English-Canadian threats that the attainment of sovereignty would bring about serious economic disruptions. Thus in Quebec, as in the United Kingdom and the United States, the market-economy philosophy is associated with nationalism. This monopolization of Quebec political space by the right both federally and provincially imposes difficulties for the relations between *québécois* and other Canadians, particularly those English-speaking Canadians on the left of the political spectrum. Among social democrats there has been a considerable sympathy for Quebec nationalism and autonomism. Yet some English–Canadian social democrats are embittered that this was not reciprocated with any considerable Quebec opposition to free trade in a general election where the anti-free trade forces become closely associated with the maintenance of social programs and in general with government interventionism. Thus, as in the past, Canadian and Quebec nationalisms are proceeding in contradictory directions.

—the response of the individual provinces to free trade has been influenced by ideology. I have already suggested how this has impinged on Quebec. Perhaps too ideology can in part explain the opposition of the government of Ontario to the FTA in the face of some evidence that in strictly economic terms that province might be expected to gain more than any other part of Canada by free trade. A similar explanation may be applied to the circumstance that of all the Atlantic provinces only Prince Edward Island opposed the agreement. On the other side, the two provinces most solicitous of autonomy, Quebec and Alberta, appear to have put aside this concern by supporting the FTA, although this results in some restriction over provincial discretion in respect to investment and energy. A commitment of the governmental and other elites of those provinces to the free-market philosophy would seem to have had some influence here.

The ideological polarization of the Canadian political system which was occasioned by the free trade debate was only partial and may prove to be temporary. But so long as there is a Quebec consensus more attuned to free-market thinking than that prevailing elsewhere in Canada it is likely that ideology will have some considerable impact on the evolution of the federal system.

Since the PCs came into national power in 1984 there has been less federal–provincial tension than in the Trudeau years. Detractors of the Mulroney government attribute this almost entirely to Ottawa's willingness to accede to the provinces in respect to Meech Lake, regional development, energy and investment policies and so on. While those factors are important, an adequate explanation for such relative harmony is more complex. The norms of the new set of powerful actors in intergovernmental affairs, including most importantly the prime minister himself, incline towards co-operation rather than conflict and no incumbent first minister is disposed to articulate his views in such a coherent way as did Trudeau, Blakeney, Levesque and Lougheed. The federal minister responsible for federal–provincial relations, Senator Lowell Murray, has been skilful in both articulating the government's policy and mollifying provincial sensibilities. The economic nationalism pressed by the Trudeau government after it returned to power in 1980 has given way to a view dominant in Ottawa and most of the provinces which sees national and provincial boundaries as irrelevant to trade, energy development and investment.

Perhaps, however, the norm of intergovernmental co-operation has its dangers for basic political values. This is the argument pungently and cogently made by Albert Breton in his Supplementary Statement to the Macdonald Report. In his elaboration of "competitive federalism" Breton suggests that the governmental order will better maximize the preferences of citizens if there are a large number of checks on particular actors in the state systems. Cooperative federalism on the other hand is unduly secretive and depresses the legitimacy of the political process by forestalling public participation in it, as well as shackling the federal government from tackling the problems it alone can solve by proscribing unilateral federal action.

We can reasonably expect some heightening of federal–provincial tension in respect to both fiscal federalism and constitutional reform. In his excellent monograph on *National Citizenship and Provincial Communities* Peter Leslie analyses the former. He suggests that "the line between economic policy and social policy is becoming increasingly tenuous" (p. 55). In this context, the goals of economic efficiency and equity, the latter including interprovincial fiscal equalization and the maintenance of equal country-wide standards in respect to particular social services, are likely to be more sharply juxtaposed than in the past. Perhaps Leslie takes more seriously than he should section 36 of the Constitution Act, 1982, which gives constitutional recognition to the obligation of Ottawa to ensure that the provinces have enough resources to provide "reasonably comparable levels of public services at reasonably comparable levels of taxation." Leslie gives up-to-date information to show how far we are from this goal as enunciated by the Rowell–Sirois Commission in 1940 and suggests that the "capping" of federal equalization payments as defined proportions of GNP in 1982 and 1987 as perhaps inconsistent with the requirements of section 36. But it is devoutly to be hoped that the courts will not become involved in deciding this kind of question.

It is very hazardous to predict what kinds of linkages will be made between the more particularized aspects of federal–provincial relations, fiscal and otherwise, and attempts to redefine the basic nature of the Canadian political community through constitutional reform. It is reasonably certain that constitutional change will be high on the public agenda for the foreseeable future. The Meech Lake Accord of course requires annual first ministers' conferences on the constitution. Even if the Accord does not come into effect, it seems that

Senate reform is permanently on the first ministers' agenda until unanimous federal–provincial agreement is secured for change under section 41. Apart from legislatures and governments, the constitution has become an important symbolic focus for a large number of Canadian groups and this by itself will cause constitutional reform to be prominent in public debate. . . .

BIBLIOGRAPHY

Canadian Politics—General

Armour, L. *The Idea of Canada and the Crisis of Community*. Ottawa: Steel Rail Publishing, 1981.

Axworthy, T., and Trudeau, P.E., (eds.). *Towards a Just Society: The Trudeau Years*. Toronto: Viking, 1990.

Banting, K., (ed.). *State and Society: Canada in Comparative Perspective*. Toronto: U.T.P., 1986.

Blair, R., and McLeod, J., (eds.). *The Canadian Political Tradition: Basic Readings*. Toronto: Methuen, 1987.

Brimelow, P. *The Patriot Game: National Dreams and Political Realities*. Toronto: Key Porter, 1986.

Brooks, S., (ed.). *Political Thought in Canada*. Toronto: Irwin, 1984.

Byers, R.B., (ed.). *Canadian Annual Review of Politics and Public Affairs 1986*. Toronto: U.T.P., 1990. (Annual.)

Cairns, A., and Williams, C., (eds.). *Constitutionalism, Citizenship and Society in Canada*. Toronto: U.T.P., 1985.

Cameron, S. *Ottawa Inside Out: Power, Prestige and Scandal in the Nation's Capital*. Toronto: Key Porter, 1989.

Campbell, C. *Canadian Political Facts: 1945–1976*. Toronto: Methuen, 1977.

Carty, K., and Ward, P., (eds.). *National Politics and Community in Canada*. Vancouver: U.B.C.P., 1986.

Cassidy, C., Clarke, P., and Petrozzi, W., (eds.) *Authority and Influence: Institutions, Issues and Concepts in Canadian Politics*. Oakville: Mosaic Press, 1985.

Clift, D. *The Secret Kingdom: Interpretation of the Canadian Character*. Toronto: M. & S., 1989.

Dawson, R.M., and Dawson, W.F., rev. by Ward, N. *Democratic Government in Canada*. Toronto: U.T.P., 1989.

Fletcher, F., and Wallace, D. *Canadian Politics Through Press Reports*. Toronto: O.U.P., 1985.

Forbes, H.D., (ed.). *Canadian Political Thought*. Toronto: O.U.P., 1985.

Forsey, E. *How Canadians Govern Themselves*. Ottawa: Secretary of State, 1988.

Gagnon, A.G., and Bickerton, J., (eds.). *Canadian Politics: An Introduction to the Discipline*. Peterborough, Broadview, 1990.

Gibbins, R. *Conflict and Unity: An Introduction to Canadian Political Life*. Toronto: Nelson, 2nd ed., 1990.

Gollner, A.B., and Salee, D., (eds.). *Canada Under Mulroney: An End of Term Report*. Montreal: Vehicule Press, 1988.

Guy, J.J. *People, Politics and Government: Political Science: A Canadian Perspective*. Don Mills, Ontario: C.-M., 2nd ed., 1990.

Jackson, R.J., and Jackson, D. *Politics in Canada*. Scarborough: P.-H., 2nd ed.,1990.

Kent, T. *Getting Ready for 1999: Ideas for Canada's Politics and Government*. Halifax: I.R.P.P., 1989.

Khan, R.A., MacKown, S.A., and McNiven, J.D. *An Introduction to Political Science*. Georgetown, Ontario: Irwin-Dorsey, 2nd ed., 1984.

Kierans, E., and Stewart, W. *Wrong End of the Rainbow*. Toronto: Harper & Collins, 1989.

Kornberg, A., and Clarke, D., (eds.). *Political Support in Canada: The Crisis Years*. Durham, North Carolina: Duke University Press, 1983.

Landes, R., (ed.). *Canadian Politics: A Comparative Reader.* Scarborough, Ontario: P.-H., 1985.

Landry, R.,(dir.). *Introduction à l'analyse des politiques.* Québec City: P.U.L.,1980.

Levy, G. "Is the Canadian Governing Process Going American?" *C.P.R..* 12, Autumn, 1989.

Mahler, G. *Contemporary Canadian Politics: An Annotated Bibliography, 1970-1987.* New York: Greenwood, 1988.

Mahler, G., and March, R., (eds.). *Canadian Politics 90/91, Annual Editions.* Guilford, Connecticut: Dushkin, 1990.

Mallory, J.R. *The Structure of Canadian Government.* Toronto: Gage, rev. ed., 1984.

Marchak, M.P. *Ideological Perspectives on Canada.* Toronto: McG.-H.R., 2nd ed., 1981.

McMenemy, J. *The Language of Canadian Politics: A Guide to Important Terms and Concepts.* Toronto: Wiley, 1980.

Merritt, A.S., and Brown, G.W. *Canadians and Their Government.* Markham, Ontario: Fitzhenry, 1985.

Morris, R. *Behind the Jester's Mask: Canadian Editorial Cartoons about Dominant and Minority Groups, 1960-1979.* Toronto: U.T.P., 1989.

Owram, D. *The Intellectual and the State in Canada 1900-1945.* Toronto: U.T.P., 1986.

Pammett, J., and Pepin, J.-L., (eds.). *Political Education in Canada.* Ottawa: I.R.P.P., 1988.

Pocklington, T.C. *Liberal Democracy in Canada and the United States.* Toronto: H.R.W., 1985.

Redekop, J.H., (ed.). *Approaches to Canadian Politics.* Toronto: P.-H., 2nd ed., 1982.

Scott, F. *A New Endeavour: Selected Political Essays, Letters and Addresses.* Ed. by Horn, M. Toronto: U.T.P., 1986.

Simpson, J. *Spoils of Power: The Politics of Patronage.* Toronto: Collins, 1988.

Stewart, G. *The Origins of Canadian Politics: A Comparative Approach.* Vancouver: U.B.C.P., 1986.

Van Loon, R.J., and Whittington, M.S. *The Canadian Political System: Environment and Structure and Process.* Toronto: MG.-H.R., 4th ed., 1987.

Verney, D.V. *Three Civilizations, Two Cultures, One State: Canada's Political Traditions.* Durham, North Carolina: Duke University Press, 1986.

Ward, N., (ed.). *Dawson's The Government of Canada.* Toronto: U.T.P., 6th ed., 1987.

White, W.L., Wagenberg, R.H., and Nelson, R.C. *Introduction to Canadian Politics and Government.* Toronto: H.R.W., 5th ed., 1990.

Whittington, M., and Williams, G., (eds.). *Canadian Politics in the 1990's.* Toronto: Nelson, 1990.

Canadian Political Science

Brooks, S., and Gagnon, A. *Between Vanguard and Clerisy: Social Scientists and Politics in Canada.* Montreal: M-Q.U.P., 1988.

Cairns, A.C. "Alternative Styles in the Study of Canadian Politics," *C.J.P.S.,* 7, 1, March 1974.

Cairns, A.C. "Political Science in Canada and the Americanization Issue," *C.J.P.S.* 8, 2, June, 1975. (Comment by D.P. Shugarman, *ibid.,* 9, 1, March, 1976.)

Courtney, J., Kawchuk, K., and Spafford. D. "Life in Print: Citation of Articles Published in Volumes 1-10 of the *C.J.P.S.,*" 20, 3, September, 1987.

English, J. "The Second Time Around: Political Scientists Writing History," *C.H.R.*, 67, 1, March 1986.

Kornberg, A., and Thorp, A. "The American Impact on Canadian Political Science and Sociology," in Preston, R., (ed)., *The Influence of the United States on Canadian Development*. Durham, North Carolina: Duke University Press, 1974.

Sproule-Jones, M. "The Enduring Colony? Political Institutions and Political Science in Canada." *Publius: The Journal of Federalism*, 14,1, Winter, 1984.

Young, R.A. "Political Scientists, Economists and the Canada-US Free Trade Agreement." *C.P.P.*, 15, March, 1989.

Foreign Policy

(See also "Canadian Nationalism" and "Canada and the U.S.A.")

Adams, P.A., and Solomon, L. *In the Name of Progress: The Underside of Foreign Aid*. Toronto: Energy Probe, 1985.

Brecher, I., (ed.). *Human Rights, Development and Foreign Policy: Canadian Perspectives*. Halifax: I.R.P.P., 1990.

Brownsey, K., (ed.). *Canada–Japan: Policy Issues for the Future*. Halifax: I.R.P.P., 1989.

Chenoweth, D. "Political Parties, Provinces and Canadian Foreign Policy: Trudeau and Beyond," *A.R.C.S.*, 15, 2, Summer, 1985.

DeWitt, D.B., and Kirton, J. *Canada as a Principal Power*. Toronto: Wiley, 1983.

Eayrs, J. *In Defence of Canada: Vol. 1. From the Great War to the Great Depression; Vol. II, Appeasement and Rearmament; Vol. III, Peace- making and Deterrence; Vol. IV, Growing Up Allied; Vol. V, Indo-China: Roots of Complicity*. Toronto: U.T.P., 1961, 1965, 1972, 1980, 1983, respectively.

Gillies, D. "Commerce over Conscience: Export Promotion in Canada's Aid Program." *I.J.*, 44, 1, Winter, 1988–89.

Griffith, F., (ed.). *The Politics of the Northwest Passage*. Montreal: M.-Q.U.P., 1987.

Hervouet, G. *Les politiques étrangères régionales du Canada: éléments et matériaux*. Québec: P.U.L., 1983.

Holmes, J., (ed.). *Canada and International Security Institutions*. Toronto: C.I.S., University of Toronto, 1986.

Holmes, J., and Kirton, J., (eds.). *Canada and the New Internationalism*. Toronto: C.I.I.A., 1988.

Honderich, J. *Arctic Imperative: Is Canada Losing the North?*. Toronto: U.T.P., 1987.

Ismael, T. *Canada and the Arab World*. Edmonton: U.A.P., 1985.

Jockel, J. *No Boundaries Upstairs*. [NORAD]. Vancouver: U.B.C.P., 1987.

Keating, T., (ed.). *The Provinces and Canadian Foreign Policy*. Toronto: C.I.I.A., 1986.

Lyon, P.V., and Tomlin, B.W. *Canada as an International Actor*. Toronto: Macmillan, 1979.

Matthews, R., and Pratt, C., (eds.). *Human Rights in Canadian Foreign Policy*. Montreal: M.-Q.U.P., 1988.

McFarlane, P. *Northern Shadows: Canadians and Central America*. Toronto: Between the Lines, 1989.

Middlemiss, D., and Sokolsky, J. *Canadian Defence: Decisions and Determinants*. Toronto: Harcourt Brace Jovanovich, 1989.

Nossal, K. *The Politics of Canadian Foreign Policy*. Toronto: P.-H., 2nd ed., 1989.

Painchaud, P., (ed.). *From MacKenzie King to Pierre Trudeau: Forty Years of Canadian Diplomacy, 1945–1985.* Quebec: P.U.L., 1989.
Regehr, E. *Arms Canada: The Deadly Business of Military Exports.* Toronto: Lorimer, 1987.
Robinson, B. *Diefenbaker's World: A Populist in Foreign Affairs.* Toronto: U.T.P., 1989.
Stairs, D. "The Political Culture of Canadian Foreign Policy." *C.J.P.S..* 15, 4, December, 1982.
Stairs, D., and Winham, G.R., (eds.). *Selected Problems in Formulating Foreign Economic Policy.* Toronto: U.T.P., 1985.
Taras, D., (ed.). *Parliament and Canadian Foreign Policy.* Toronto: C.I.I.A., 1985.
Taras, D., and Goldberg, D., (eds.). *The Domestic Battleground: Canada and the Arab-Israeli Conflict.* Montreal: M.-Q.U.P., 1989.
Tomlin, B. "The Stages of Prenegotiation: The Decision to Negotiate North American Free Trade." *I.J.*, 44, 2, Spring, 1989.
Tomlin, B., and Molot, M., (eds.) *Canada Among Nations 1988–89.* Toronto: Lorimer, 1989. (Annual)
Tucker, M.J. *Canadian Foreign Policy: Contemporary Issues and Themes.* Toronto: McG.-H.R., 1980.

Political Leadership

Dion, L. "The Concept of Political Leadership," *C.J.P.S.*, 1, 1 March, 1968.
Esberey, J.E. *Knight of the Holy Spirit: A Study of William Lyon MacKenzie King.* Toronto: U.T.P., 1980.
Fox, P.W. "Psychology, Politics and Hegetology." *C.J.P.S.*, 13, 4, December, 1980.
Pal, L., and Taras, D., (ed.). *Prime Ministers and Premiers: Political Leadership and Public Policy in Canada.* Scarborough, Ontario: P.-H., 1988.

SOCIAL ISSUES

Business and Society

(See also Chapter 12, "Business Government Relations")

Antoniou, A., and Rowley, R. "The Ownership Structure of the Largest Canadian Corporations, 1979." *C.J.S.*, 11, 3, Fall, 1986.
Atkinson, M.M., and Coleman, W.D. *The State, Business, and Industrial Change in Canada.* Toronto: U.T.P., 1989.
Brooks, S. "State as Entrepreneur: from CDC to CDIC." *C.P.A.*, 26, 1, Winter, 1983.
Coyne, D. "Corporate Over-concentration." *P.O.*, 7, 3, April, 1986.
Finkel, A. *Business and Social Reform in the Thirties.* Toronto: Lorimer, 1979.
Francis, D. *Controlling Interest: Who Owns Canada?* Toronto: Macmillan, 1986.
Gorecki, P., and Stanbury, W.T. *The Objectives of Canadian Competition Policy: 1888–1983.* Montreal: I.R.P.P., 1984.
Niosi, J. *The Renaissance of Canadian Business.* Toronto: Lorimer, 1981.
Rea, K.J., and Wiseman, N., (eds.). *Government and Enterprise in Canada.* Toronto: Methuen, 1985.
Stanbury, W.T. *Business Interests and the Reform of Canadian Competition Policy. 1971–1975.* Toronto: Methuen, 1977.
Stanbury, W.T. *Business-Government Relations in Canada.* Toronto: Methuen, 1986.

Canadian Nationalism

Bell, D., and Tepperman, L., *The Roots of Disunity: A Look at Canadian Political Culture*. Toronto: M. & S., 1979.

Canada. *Report of the Royal Commission on National Development in the Arts, Letters, and Sciences* [Massey Report]. Ottawa: Q.P., 1951.

Carty, R.K., and Ward, W.P., (eds.). *Entering the Eighties: Canada in Crisis*. Toronto: O.U.P., 1980.

Cook, R. *The Maple Leaf Forever: Essays in Nationalism and Politics in Canada*. Toronto: Macmillan, 1971.

Drache, D. "Whatever happened to Canadian nationalism?" *Canadian Dimension*, 18, October–November, 1984.

Feldman, E., and Nevitte, N. *The Future of North America: Canada, the United States and Quebec Nationalism*. Cambridge: Harvard University Press, 1979.

Forbes, D. *Nationalism, Ethnocentrism and Personality*. Chicago, University of Chicago Press, 1985.

Gibbins, R. "Models of Nationalism: A Case Study of Political Ideologies in the Canadian West." *C.J.P.S.*, 10, 2, June, 1977.

Grant, G. *Lament for a Nation: The Defeat of Canadian Nationalism*. Toronto: M. & S., 1965.

Hardin, H. *A Nation Unaware: The Canadian Economic Culture*. Vancouver: J.J. Douglas, 1974.

Harvey, T.G., and Harvey, S. *Political Culture in a Canadian Community*. Toronto: Copp Clark, 1973.

Hutcheson, J. *Dominance and Dependency: Liberalism and National Policies in the North Atlantic Triangle*. Toronto: M. & S., 1978.

Levitt, J. *A Vision Beyond Reach*. Ottawa: Deneau, 1982.

Litvak, I.A., and Maule, C.J. *The Canadian Multinationals*. Toronto: Butterworths, 1981.

Marchak, P. *In Whose Interests?: An Essay on Multinational Corporations in a Canadian Context*. Toronto: M. & S., 1979.

Mathie, W. "Political Community and the Canadian Experience: Reflections on Nationalism, Federalism, and Unity." *C.J.P.S.*, 12, 1 March, 1979.

Meisel, J. "Political Culture and the Politics of Culture." *C.J.P.S.*, 7, 4, December, 1974.

Migue, J.-L. *Nationalistic Policies in Canada: An Economic Approach*. Montreal: C.D. Howe Institute, 1979.

Niosi, J. *The Economy of Canada: A Study of Ownership and Control*. Montreal: Black Rose, 1978.

Resnick, P. *The Land of Cain: Class and Nationalism in English Canada, 1945–1975*. Vancouver: New Star Books, 1977.

Rotstein, A. *The Precarious Homestead: Essays on Economics, Technology and Nationalism*. Toronto: New Press, 1973.

Rotstein, A. "Is There An English-Canadian Nationalism?" *J.C.S.*, 13, 1, Summer, 1978.

Rugman, A.M. *Multinationalism in Canada: Theory, Performance, and Economic Impact*. Boston: Martinus Nijhoff, 1980.

Russell, P. (ed.). *Nationalism in Canada*. Toronto: McGraw-Hill, 1966.

Smiley, D.V. "Canada and the Quest for a National Policy," *C.J.P.S.*, 8, 1 March 1975.

Stevenson, G. "Foreign Direct Investment and the Provinces: A Study of Elite Attitudes," *C.J.P.S.*, 7, 4, December, 1974.

Symons, T.H.B. *To Know Ourselves: The Report of the Commission on Canadian*

Studies. Ottawa: Association of Universities and Colleges of Canada, Vols. I and II, 1975.

Teeple, G. (ed.). *Capitalism and the National Question in Canada*. Toronto: U.T.P., 1972.

Young, R.A. "National Identification in English Canada: Implications for Quebec Independence." *J.C.S.*, 12, 3, 1977.

Canada and the U.S.A.

Armstrong, W.C., Armstrong, L.S., and Wilcox, F.O., (eds.). *Canada and the United States: Dependence and Divergence*. Cambridge, Massachusetts: Balinger, 1982.

Beigie, C.E., and Hero, A.O., (eds.). *Natural Resources in U.S.-Canadian Relations*. Vol. I, Boulder, Colorado: Westview Press, 1980.

C.P.P. Special issue on "Canada-U.S. Trade and Policy Issues," 8, October, 1982.

Cameron, D. (ed.). *The Free Trade Deal*. Toronto: Lorimer, 1988.

Cameron, D. (ed.). *The Free Trade Papers*. Toronto: Lorimer, 1986.

Clark, S.D. "Canada and the American Value System," *The Developing Canadian Community*. Toronto: U.T.P., 2nd ed., 1968.

Clarkson, S. *Canada and the Reagan Challenge: Crisis and Adjustment 1981–85*. Toronto: Lorimer, 2nd ed., 1985.

Doran, C.F. *Economic Interdependence, Autonomy, and Canadian/American Relations*. Montreal: I.R.P.P., 1983.

Doran, C., and Sigler, J. *Canada and the United States: Enduring Friendship, Persistent Stress*. Englewood Cliffs, New Jersey: P.-H., 1985.

Drache, D., and Cameron, D., (eds.). *The Other Macdonald Report*. Toronto: Lorimer, 1985.

Flaherty, D.H., and McKercher, W.R., (eds.). *Southern Exposure: Canadian Perspectives on the United States*. Toronto: McG.-H.R., 1986.

Fox, W.T.R. *A Continent Apart: The United States and Canada in World Politics*. Toronto: U.T.P., 1985.

Gold, M., and Leyton-Brown, D., (eds.). *Trade-offs on Free Trade: The Canada U.S. Free Trade Agreement*. Toronto: Carswell, 1988.

Hillmer, N., and Schiller, N. *Partners Nevertheless: Canadian-American Relations in the Twentieth Century*. Toronto: Copp Clark, 1989.

Holmes, J.W. *Life with Uncle: The Canadian-American Relationship*. Toronto: U.T.P., 1981.

I.J.. Special issue on "The North American Political Economy," 42, 1, Winter, 1986–87.

Lamont, L., and Edmonds, D., (eds.). *Friends So Different: Essays On Canada and the United States in the 1980s*. Ottawa: O.U.P., 1989.

Laxer, J. *Leap of Faith: Free Trade and the Future of Canada*. Edmonton: Hurtig, 1986.

Lipset, S.M. "The United States and Canada," *Revolution and Counter- Revolution*. New York: Basic Books, 1968.

Lipset, S.M. "Historical Traditions and National Characteristics: A Comparative Analysis of Canada and the United States." *C.J.S.*, 2, 2, Summer, 1986.

Lipset, S.M. *Continental Divide: The Values and Institutions of the United States and Canada*. Montreal: Canadian-American Committee, 1990.

Mount, G.S., and Mahant, E.E. *An Introduction to Canadian-American Relations*. Toronto: Methuen, 1984.

Murray, J.L., (ed.). *Canadian Cultural Nationalism: The Fourth Lester B. Pearson Conference on the Canada-U.S. Relationship*. Toronto: Macmillan, 1978.
Redekop, J. "A Reinterpretation of Canadian-American Relations." *C.J.P.S.*, 9, 2, June, 1976.
Stairs, D., and Winham, G., (eds.). *The Politics of Canada's Economic Relationship with the United States*. Toronto: U.T.P., 1985.
Whalley, J., (ed.). *Canada/U.S. Free Trade*. Toronto: U.T.P., 1985.
White, R. *Fur Trade to Free Trade: Putting the Canada-U.S. Trade Agreement in Historical Perspective*. Toronto: Dundurn Press, 1988.
Willoughby, W.R. *The Joint Organizations of Canada and the United States*. Toronto: U.T.P., 1979.
Wonnacott, R.J. *Canada/United States Free Trade: Problems and Opportunities*. Toronto: O.E.C., 1985.
Woodside, K. "The Canada-United States Free Trade Agreement," review article with bibliography. *C.J.P.S.*, XXII, 1, March, 1989.

Elites and Power

Brym, R.J., (ed.). *The Structure of the Canadian Capitalist Class*. Toronto: Garamond Press, 1985.
Carroll, W.K. "The Individual, Class and Corporate Power in Canada." *C.J.S.,*. 9, 3, Summer, 1984.
Carroll, W.K. *Corporate Power and Canadian Capitalism*. Vancouver: U.B.C.P., 1986.
Carroll, W.K. "The Canadian Corporate Elite: Financiers or Finance Capitalists?" *S.P.E.*, 8, Summer, 1982.
Clement, W. *The Canadian Corporate Elite: An Analysis of Economic Power*. Toronto: M. & S., 1975.
Clement, W. *Continental Corporate Power: Economic Linkages Between Canada and the United States*. Toronto: M. & S., 1977.
Clement, W. *Class, Power and Property: Essays on Canadian Society*. Toronto: Methuen, 1983.
Forcese, D.P. *The Canadian Class Structure*. Toronto: McG.-H.R., 3rd ed., 1986.
Fournier, P. *The Quebec Establishment: The Ruling Class and the State*. Montreal: Black Rose, 2nd rev. ed., 1978.
Hunter, A.A. *Class Tells: On Social Inequality in Canada*. Toronto: Butterworths, 2nd ed., 1986.
Johnston, W., and Ornstein, M. "Class, Work and Politics." *C.R.S.A.*, 19, 2, May, 1982.
Johnston, W., and Ornstein, M. "Social Class and Political Ideology in Canada." *C.R.S.A.*, 22, 3, August, 1985.
Love, R. *Income Distribution and Inequality in Canada*. Ottawa: E.C.C., 1980.
Newman, P.C. *The Canadian Establishment*. Toronto: M.& S., Vol. 1, 1979; Vol. 2, 1981.
Newman, P.C., and Moncreiffe, I., *Debrett's Illustrated Guide to the Canadian Establishment, 1983*. Toronto: Methuen, 1983.
Niosi, J. *Canadian Capitalism: A Study of Power in the Canadian Business Establishment*. Toronto: Lorimer, 1981.
Olsen, D. *The State Elite*. Toronto: M. & S., 1980.
Ornstein, M. "The Political Ideology of the Canadian Capitalist Class." *C.R.S.A.*, 23, 2, May, 1986.

Ornstein, M. "The Social Organization of the Canadian Capitalist Class in Comparative Perspective." *C.R.S.A.*, 26, 1, February, 1989.

Osberg, L. *Economic Inequality in Canada*. Toronto: Butterworths, 1981.

Ossenberg, R. (ed.). *Power and Change in Canada*. Toronto: M.& S., 1979.

Panitch, L. "Dependency and Class in Canadian Political Economy." *S.P.E.*, . 6, Autumn, 1981.

Porter, J. *The Vertical Mosaic: An Analysis of Social Class and Power in Canada*. Toronto: U.T.P., 1965.

Presthus, R. *Elite Accommodation in Canadian Politics*. Toronto: Macmillan, 1973.

Presthus, R. *Elites in the Policy Process*. Toronto: Macmillan, 1974.

Prottis, J.I., and Chartrand, J-P. "Cultural Division of Labour." *C.R.S.A.*, 27, February 1990, 23–48.

Veltmeyer, Henry. *The Canadian Class Structure*. Toronto: Garamont Press, 2nd ed., 1990.

Williams, A.P. "Access and Accommodation in the Canadian Welfare State: The Political Significance of Contacts Between State, Labour and Business Leaders." *C.R.S.A.*, 26, 2, May 1989.

Williams, A. P. "Social Origins and Elite Politics in Canada: The Impact of Background Differences on Attitudes Towards the Welfare State." *C.J.S.*, 14, 1, Winter, 1989.

Ethnic Groups and Immigration

Anderson, A.B., and Frideres, J.S. *Ethnicity in Canada: Theoretical Perspectives*. Toronto: Butterworths, 1982.

Black, J.H., and Leithner, C. "Immigrants and Political Involvement: The Role of the Ethnic Media." *Canadian Ethnic Studies*, 20, 4, 1988.

Bolaria, B.S. *Oppressed Minorities in Canada*. Toronto: Butterworths, 1980.

Breton, R., Reitz, J.G., and Valentine, V. *Cultural Boundaries and the Cohesion of Canada*. Montreal: I.R.P.P., 1980.

Canada, Parliament, House of Commons, *Equality Now, Report of the Special Committee on Visible Minorities in Canadian Society*. Ottawa: S. and S., 1978.

Charon, M., (ed.). *Between Two Worlds: The Canadian Immigrant Experience*. Montreal: Quadrant, 1984.

Dahlie, J., and Fernando, T., (eds.). *Ethnicity, Power and Politics in Canada*. Toronto: Methuen, 1980.

Dreidger, L. *The Ethnic Factor: Identity in Diversity*. Toronto: M.H.-R, 1989.

Elliott, J. *Two Nations, Many Cultures: Ethnic Groups in Canada*. Scarborough, Ontario:, P.-H., 1983.

Ferguson, E. *Immigrants in Canada*. Toronto: University of Toronto Guidance Centre, 2nd rev. ed., 1977.

Goldstein, J.E., and Bienvenue, R.M., (eds.). *Ethnicity and Ethnic Relations in Canada*. Toronto: Butterworths, 2nd ed., 1985.

Hawkins, F. *Canada and Immigration: Public Policy and Public Concern*. Montreal: I.P.A.C., 2nd ed., 1989.

Hawkins, F. *Critical Years in Immigration: Canada and Australia Compared*. Montreal: McG.-Q.U.P., 1989.

Herberg, E., (ed.). *Ethnic Groups in Canada: Adaptations and Transitions*. Toronto: Nelson, 1989.

J.C.S. Special issue on "Multiculturalism," 17, 1, Spring, 1982.

Kallen, E. *Ethnicity and Human Rights in Canada*. Toronto: Gage, 1982.

Li, P.S., and Singh, B. *Racial Minorities in Multi-cultural Canada*. Toronto: Garamond, 1983.

Malarek, V. *Haven's Gate: Canada's Immigration Fiasco*. Toronto: Macmillan, 1987.

Menezes, J. (ed.). *Decade of Adjustment: Legal Perspectives on Contemporary Social Issues*. Toronto: Butterworths, 1980.

Nevitte, N., and Kornberg, A., (eds.). *Minorities and the Canadian State*. Oakville, Ontario: Mosaic Press, 1985.

Pletsch, A., (ed.). *Ethnicity in Canada*. Marburg, University of Marburg, 1985.

Ramcharan, S. *Non-White Immigrants in Canada*. Toronto: Butterworths, 1980.

Sunahara, A.G. *The Politics of Racism: The Uprooting of Japanese Canadians During the Second World War*. Toronto: Lorimer, 1981.

Takata, T. *Nikkei Legacy: The Story of Japanese Canadians from Settlement to Today*. Toronto: N.C. Press, 1983.

Ujimoto, V., and Naidoo, J. *Asian Canadians: Aspects of Social Change*. Ottawa: Canadian Asian Studies, 1984.

Ujimoto, K.V., and Hirabayashi, G., (eds.). *Visible Minorities and Multiculturalism: Asians in Canada*. Toronto: Butterworths, 1980.

Westfall, William, *et al.*, (eds.). *Religion/Culture: Comparative Canadian Studies*. (Canadian Issues, Volume 7). Ottawa Association for Canadian Studies, 1985.

Whitaker, R. *Double Standard: The Secret History of Canadian* Immigration. Toronto: L. & O.D., 1987.

Labour, Poverty, Housing, Welfare

Banting, K.G., *The Welfare State and Canadian Federalism*. Montreal: McG.-Q.U.P., 2nd ed. 1987.

Barber, C., and McCallum, J. *Unemployment and Inflation: The Canadian Experience*. Toronto: Lorimer, 1980.

Bernier, I., and Lajoie, O., (eds.). *Family Law and Social Welfare Legislation in Canada*. Toronto: U.T.P., 1985.

Block, W.E., and Olson, E.O., (eds.). *Rent Control, Myths and Realties: International Evidence of the Effects of Rent Control in Six Countries*. Vancouver: Fraser Institute, rev. ed., 1981.

Block, W.E. *Focus: On Discrimination, Affirmative Action and Equal Opportunity*. Vancouver: Fraser Institute, 1985.

Djao, A.W. *Inequality and Social Policy: The Sociology of Welfare*. Toronto: Wiley, 1983.

Esland, G., and Salaman, G., (eds.). *The Politics of Work and Occupations*. Toronto: U.T.P., 1981.

Freeman, Bill. *1005: Political LIfe in a Union Local*. Toronto: Lorimer, 1982.

Grayson, J. Paul, "Plant Closures and Political Despair," *C.R.S.A.*, 23, 3, August, 1986.

Guest, D. *The Emergence of Social Security in Canada*. Vancouver: U.B.C.P., rev. ed., 1985.

Ismael, J.S., (ed.). *Canadian Social Welfare Policy: Federal and Provincial Dimensions*. Toronto: I.P.A.C., 1985.

Markson, E.W., and Botra, G.R. *Public Policies for An Aging Population*. Toronto: Heath, 1980.

McClain, J., and Doyle, C. *Women and Housing*. Toronto: Lorimer, 1983.

Montgomery, R., and Marshall, D.R., (eds.). *Housing Policy for the 1980's*. Toronto: Lexington Books, 1980.

Morton, D. *Labour in Canada*. Toronto: Grolier, 1982.

Moscovitch, A. *The Welfare State in Canada: A Selected Bibliography, 1840 to 1978.* Waterloo, Ontario: W.L.U.P., 1983.

Moscovitch, A., and Drover, G., (eds.). *Inequality: Essays on the Political Economy of Social Welfare.* Toronto: U.T.P., 1981.

Moscovitch, A. "The Welfare State Since 1975." *J.C.S.*, 21, 2, Summer, 1986.

Nightingale, D.V. *Workplace Democracy: An Inquiry into Employee Participation in Canadian Work Organizations.* Toronto: U.T.P., 1982.

Palmer, B., (ed.). *The Character of Class Struggle: Essays in Canadian Working Class History, 1850–1985.* Toronto: M. & S., 1986.

Palmer, B. *Working-Class Experience: The Rise and Reconstitution of Canadian Labour, 1800–1980.* Toronto: Butterworths, 1983.

Pentland, H.C. *Labour and Capital in Canada.* Toronto: Lorimer, 1981.

Phillips, P., and Phillips, E. *Women and Work: Inequality in the Labour Market.* Toronto: Lorimer, 1983.

Riddell, C., (ed.). *Canadian Labour Relations.* Toronto: U.T.P., 1985.

Rose, A. *Canadian Housing Policies, 1935–1980.* Toronto: Butterworths, 1980.

Ross, D.P. *The Working Poor; Wage Earners and the Failure of Income Security Policies.* Toronto: Lorimer, 1981.

Ross, D.P. *Canadian Fact Book on Poverty, 1983.* Ottawa: C.C.S.D., 1983.

Stone, L.O., and Fletcher, S. *A Profile of Canada's Older Population.* Montreal: I.R.P.P., 1980.

Walters, V. "Occupational Health and Safety Legislation in Ontario: An Analysis of Its Origins and Content." *C.R.S.A.*, 20, 4, November, 1983.

Yelaja, S.A., (ed.). *Canadian Social Policy.* Waterloo, Ontario: W.L.U.P., 2nd ed., 1987.

Native Peoples

Adams, H. *Prisons of Grass: Canada from the Native Point of View.* Toronto: New Press, 1975.

Asch, M. *Home and Native Land: Aboriginal Rights and the Canadian Constitution.* Toronto: Nelson, 1988.

Bartlett, R.H. *The Indian Act of Canada.* Saskatoon, Saskatchewan: U. of S., Native Law, 1980.

Barsh, R.L., and Henderson, J.Y. "Aboriginal Rights, Treaty Rights and Human Rights: Indian Tribes and 'Constitutional Renewal.' *J.C.S.*, 17, Summer, 1982.

Boisvert, D.A. *Forms of Aboriginal Self-Government.* Kingston: Queen's University, I.I.R., 1985.

Boldt, M., and Long, J.A., (eds.). *The Quest for Justice: Aboriginal Peoples and Aboriginal Rights.* Toronto: U.T.P., 1985.

Boldt, M., and Long, J.A. "Tribal Traditions and European-Western Political Ideologies: The Dilemma of Canada's Native Indians." *C.J.P.S.*, 17, 3, September, 1984. (See also Flanagan, T., "Comment," *ibid.*. 18, 2, June, 1985.)

Breton, R., and Grant, G., (eds.). *The Dynamics of Government Programs for Urban Indians in the Prairie Provinces.* Montreal: I.R.P.P., 1984.

Canada, Mackenzie Valley Pipeline Inquiry. *Northern Frontier, Northern Homeland: The Report of the Mackenzie Valley Pipeline Inquiry.* [Berger Report]. Ottawa: S. and S., 1977, 2 volumes.

Cassidy, F. "Aboriginal Governments in Canada: Emerging Field of Study." *C.J.P.S.*, 23, 1, March, 1990.

Cassidy, F., and Bish, R.L. *Indian Government: Its Meaning in Practice.* Halifax: I.R.P.P., 1989.

Cassidy, F., and Dale, N. *After Native Claims? The Implications of Comprehensive Claims Settlements for Natural Resources in British Columbia.* Lantzville and Halifax: Olichan and I.R.P.P., 1988.

Colvin, E. *Legal Process and the Resolution of Indian Claims.* Saskatoon, Saskatchewan: U. of S., Native Law, 1981.

Cowie, I. *Future Issues of Jurisdiction and Co-operation between Aboriginal and Non-aboriginal Governments.* Kingston: I.I.R., Queen's University, 1987.

Cumming, P.A. *Native Rights in Canada.* Toronto: Edmond Montgomery, 3rd ed., 1985.

Driben, P., and Trudeau, R.S. *When Freedom is Lost: The Dark Side of the Relationship Between Government and the Fort Hope Band.* Toronto: U.T.P., 1983.

Franks, C.E.S. "Aboriginal Self-Government in Canada." *Q.Q.*, 94, 3, Autumn, 1987.

Frideres, J.S. *Native People in Canada: Contemporary Conflicts.* Scarborough, Ontario: P.-H., 2nd ed., 1983.

Gibbins, R., and Ponting, J.R. "An Assessment of Self-Government in Canada." In Cairns, A. and Williams, C., Research Coordinators, *The Politics of Gender, Ethnicity and Language in Canada.* Toronto: U.T.P., 1986.

Gifford, M.N *et al. Indians and the Law.* Vancouver: B.C., Continuing Legal Education, 1982.

Hawkes, D. (ed.). *Aboriginal Peoples and Government Responsibility: Exploring Federal and Provincial Roles.* Ottawa: C.U.P., 1989.

Hawkes, D. *Aboriginal Self-Government: What Does it Mean?* Kingston: Queen's University, I.I.R., 1985.

Hawkes, D., and Peters, E. *Implementing Aboriginal Self-Government: Problems and Prospects.* Kingston: I.I.R., 1986.

Hawkes, D., and Peters, E. *Issues in Entrenching Aboriginal Self- government.* Kingston: Queen's University, I.I.R., 1987.

Hawkes, D. *Negotiating Aboriginal Self-Government: Developments Surrounding the 1985 First Ministers' Conference.* Kingston: Queen's University, I.I.R., 1985.

Hawley, D.L. *The Indian Act Annotated: Indian Law in Canada.* Toronto: Carswell, 1984.

Hodgins, B., and Benidickson, J. *The Temagami Experience: Recreation, Resources, and Aboriginal Rights in the Northern Ontario Wilderness.* Toronto: U.T.P., 1989.

House of Commons. Report of the Special Committee on Indian Self-Government, *Indian Self-Government in Canada,* [Penner report]. Ottawa: S. and S., 1983.

Inuit Committee on National Issues. *Completing Canada: Inuit Approaches to Self-government.* Kingston: Queen's University, I.I.R., 1987.

Johnston, P. *Native Children and the Child Welfare System.* Toronto: Lorimer, 1983.

Krotz, L. *Urban Indians: The Strangers in Canada's Cities.* Edmonton: Hurtig, 1980.

Little Bear, L., Boldt, M., and Long, J.A., (eds.). *Pathways to Self- Determination: Canadian Indians and the Canadian State.* Toronto: U.T.P., 1984.

Long, A., and Bolt, M., (eds.). *Governments in Conflict? Provinces and Indian Nations in Canada.* Toronto: U.T.P., 1988.

Morse, B.W. *Aboriginal Self-Government in Australia and Canada.* Kingston: Queen's University, I.I.R., 1985.

Morse, B.W., (ed.). *Aboriginal Peoples and the Law: Indian, Métis and Unit Rights in Canada.* Ottawa: C.U.P., 1985.

Peters, E. *Aboriginal Self-government Arrangements in Canada.* Kingston: Queen's University, I.I.R., 1987.

Ponting, J.R. "Public Opinion on Aboriginal Peoples' Issues in Canada." *Canadian Social Trends.* Winter, 1988.

Ponting, J.R., and Gibbins, R. *Out of Irrelevance: A Socio-Political Introduction to Indian Affairs in Canada*. Toronto: Butterworths, 1980.

Richardson, B. (ed.). *Drumbeat: Anger and Renewal in Indian Country*. Toronto: Summerhill Press, 1989.

Robinson, E., and Quinney, H.B. *The Infested Blanket: The Canadian Constitution Genocide of Indian Nations*. Winnipeg: Queenston, 1985.

Schwartz, B. *First Principles: Constitutional Reform with Respect to the Aboriginal Peoples of Canada. 1982–84*. Kingston: Queen's University, I.I.R., 1985.

Schwartz, B. *First Principles, Second Thoughts: Aboriginal Peoples, Constitutional Reform and Canadian Statecraft*. Halifax: I.R.P.P., 1988.

Sealey, D.B., and Lussier, A.S. *The Métis: Canada's Forgotten People*. Winnipeg: Métis Federation Press, 1975.

Weaver, S.M. *Making Canadian Indian Policy: The Hidden Agenda, 1968–1970*. Toronto: U.T.P., 1980.

Zlotkin, Norman. *Unfinished Business: Aboriginal Peoples and the 1983 Constitutional Conference*. Kingston: Queen's University, I.I.R., 1983.

Political Economy Tradition

(See also Bibliography, Chapter 3.)

Banting, K., (ed.). *The State and Economic Interests*. Toronto: U.T.P., 1985.

Clement, W. *The Challenge of Class Analysis*. Ottawa: C.U.P., 1988.

Clement, W., and Williams, G., (eds.). *The New Canadian Political Economy*. Montreal: M-Q.U.P., 1989.

Drache, D., and Clement, W., (eds.). *The New Practical Guide to Canadian Political Economy*. Toronto: Lorimer, 1985.

Jenson, J. "'Different' but not 'Exceptional': Canada's Permeable Fordism." *C.R.S.A.*, 26, 1, February, 1989.

Laxer, G. "Foreign Ownership and Myths about Canadian Development." *C.R.S.A.*, 22, 3 August, 1985.

Laxer, G. "The Schizophrenic Character of Canadian Political Economy." *C.R.S.A.*, 26, 1, February, 1989.

Marchak, P. "Canadian Political Economy." *C.R.S.A.*, 22, 5, December, 1985.

Moscovitch, A., and Albert, J., (eds.). *The "Benevolent" State: The Growth of Welfare in Canada*. Toronto: Garamond, 1987.

O'Connor, J. "Welfare Expenditure and Policy Orientation in Canada in Comparative Perspective." *C.R.S.A.*, 26, 1, February, 1989.

Panitch, L., (ed.). *The Canadian State: Political Economy and Political Power*. Toronto: U.T.P., 1977.

Resnick, P. *Parliament vs People: An Essay on Democracy and Canadian Political Culture*. Vancouver: New Star, 1984.

Williams, G. *Not for Export: Toward a Political Economy of Canada's Arrested Industrialization*. Toronto: M. & S., 1983.

Wolfe, D. "The Canadian State in Comparative Perspective." *C.R.S.A.*, 26, 1, February, 1989.

Women

Adamson, N., Briskin, L., and McPhail, M. *Feminist Organizing for Change: The Contemporary Women's Movement in Canada*. Toronto: O.U.P., 1988.

Armstrong, P., and Armstrong, H. *The Double Ghetto: Women and Their Work in Canada*. Toronto: M. & S., rev. ed., 1984.

Bashevkin, S.B. *Toeing the Lines: Women and Party Politics in English Canada*. Toronto: U.T.P., 1985.

Bashevkin, S.B. "Women's Participation in the Ontario Political Parties, 1971–1981." *J.C.S.*, 17, 2, Summer, 1982.

Bashevkin, S.B. "Free Trade and Canadian Feminism: The Case of the National Action Committee on the Status of Women." *C.P.P.*, 15, December 1989.

Brodie, J. *Women and Politics in Canada*. Toronto: McG.-H.R., 1985.

Burt, S. "Women's Groups and Government: The Charter of Rights and the Ad Hoc Lobby." *Atlantis*, 14, 1988, 74–81.

Burt, S. "Canadian Women's Groups in the 1980s: Organizational Development and Policy Influence." *C.P.P.*, 16, March 1990.

Burt, S., Code, L., and Dorney, L., (eds.). *Changing Patterns: Women in Canada*. Toronto: M. & S., 1988.

Cairns, A., and Williams, C., (eds.). *The Politics of Gender, Ethnicity and Language in Canada*. Toronto: U.T.P., 1985.

Canada, Report of the Royal Commission on the Status of Women. Ottawa: Information Canada, 1970.

Cleverdon, C.L. *The Women's Suffrage Movement in Canada*. Toronto: U.T.P., 1974. (First published in 1950.)

Connelly, M.P. *Last Hired, First Fired: Women and the Canadian Work Force*. Toronto: Women's Press, 1979.

Doerr, A. "Women's Rights in Canada: Social and Economic Realities." *Atlantis*, 9, 2, Spring, 1984.

Doerr, A., and Carrier, M. *Women and the Constitution*. Ottawa: Canadian Advisory Council on the Status of Women, 1981.

Evans, P.M. *Perspective on Work, Women and Welfare: A Dual Labour Market Analysis*. Toronto: U. of T., Social Work, 1983.

Findlay, S., and Randall, M., (eds.). "Feminist Perspectives on the Canadian State." Special issue of *Resources for Feminist Research*, 1989.

Fine Balances: Equal Status for Women in Canada in the 1990s.. Ottawa: Canadian Advisory Council on the Status of Women, 1987.

Kay, B. *et al.* "Gender and Political Activity in Canada, 1965–1984." *C.J.P.S.*, 20, 4, December, 1987.

Kealey, L., and Sangster, J. *Beyond the Vote: Canadian Women and Politics*. Toronto: U.T.P., 1989.

Kome, P. *The Taking of 28: Women Challenge the Constitution*. Toronto: Women's Press, 1983.

Kome, P. *Women of Influence: Canadian Women and Politics*. Toronto: Doubleday, 1985.

Kopinak, K. "Women in Canadian Municipal Politics: Two Steps Forward, One Step Back." *C.R.S.A.*, 22, 3 August, 1985.

Lamoureaux, D., and Michaud, J. "Les parlementaires candiens et le suffrage féminin: un aperçu des débats." *C.J.P.S.*, 21, 2, June, 1988.

Maroney, H.J., and Luxton, M., (eds.). *Feminism and Political Economy*. Toronto: Methuen, 1988.

Miles, A., and Finn, G., (eds.). *Feminism in Canada*. Montreal: Black Rose Books, 1982.

Morgan, N. *The Equality Game: Women in the Federal Public Service (1908–1987)*. Ottawa: Canadian Advisory Council on the Status of Women, 1988.

Penney, J. *Hard Earned Wages: Women Fighting for Better Work*. Toronto: Women's Press, 1983.

Sangster, J. *Dreams of Equality: Women on the Canadian Left, 1920–1950.* Toronto: M.& S., 1989.
Tancred-Sheriff, P., (ed.). *Feminist Research: Prospect and Retrospect.* Montreal: McG.-Q.U.P., 1988.
The State Bibliography. An annotated Bibliography on Women and the State in Canada. RFR/DRF, 252 Bloor St. W., Toronto: 1989.
Vickers, J., and **Brodie**, J. "Canada," in Hills, J., Lovenduski, J., (eds.), *The Politics of the Second Electorate.* London: R.K.P., 1981.
Winn, C. "Affirmative Action for Women: More than a Case of Simple Justice." *C.P.A.*, 28, 1, Spring, 1985.

THE CONSTITUTION

THE NATURE OF CONSTITUTIONS
AND CONSTITUTIONALISM

Ronald I. Cheffins and Patricia A. Johnson

In recent years, the Canadian Constitution has been the subject of considerable debate, scrutiny and important change. It is not correct to say, however, as members of the media often have, that Canada has a new constitution. That this statement is incorrect in every respect will be illustrated throughout this work.

THE 1982 REVISIONS

In 1982 the United Kingdom Parliament made important changes in the Canadian Constitution, but the changes fell far short of a complete revision of the Constitution which might have resulted in a totally new format. The essence of that legislation, namely, the Constitution Act, 1982 provided for a domestic amending process, a Charter of Rights, an additional subsection with respect to the existing division of powers, a provision that there be a conference on the rights of the aboriginal peoples of Canada, and provisions with respect to equalization and regional disparities. The Act, however, did not in any substan-

From *The Revised Canadian Constitution: Politics as Law*, Toronto, McGraw-Hill Ryerson, 1986. By permission.

tial way change the content of the many British statutes relating to Canada which have been enacted since 1867.

As an example of this limited change, the British North America Act, 1867, which formed the basis of Canada's constitutional structure, was altered only in relatively minor ways: its name was changed, and subsection 91(1), the subsection of the Act dealing with amendment, was repealed, as was subsection 92(1) dealing with provincial constitutions. It should be noted, however, that section 20 which was also repealed, and subsection 92(1), were incorporated into the Constitution Act, 1982 and thus no substantial change has been made in the content of these sections. Therefore, the only real change in what was formerly known as the British North America Act, 1867 was the repeal of subsection 91(1) which, as will be explained later, dealt with those classes of subjects still reserved for the United Kingdom Parliament.

Similarly, if one looks through the whole series of British statutes and orders in council relating to Canada, one finds that in almost every respect the only change made is in name. In most instances the change is from "British North America Act" to "Constitution Act." For example, the British North America Act, 1915 is now referred to as the Constitution Act, 1915. Presumably the reason for the change in name is to remove the word "British" from the statutes so as to eradicate as much as possible any underlining of Canada's historical relationship and ties with Great Britain.

The Schedule to the Constitution Act, 1982 should be referred to for an overview of these changes. This schedule includes the British statutes and orders in council relevant to Canada in Column I, and in Column II indicates the sections of those thirty legal documents that have been amended or repealed. Column III indicates the new names of the documents. The only statute other than the British North America Act, 1867 which has been amended in any substantial respect is the Statute of Westminster. Section 4 and subsection 7(1) of the latter still contemplated British statutory authority with respect to Canada.

The other major change effected in 1982, in addition to the adoption of a domestic amending process and a Charter of Rights, was the passage by the British parliament of the Canada Act. This Act is important in that it provides that henceforth "[N]o Act of the Parliament of the United Kingdom passed after the *Constitution Act, 1982* comes into force shall extend to Canada as part of its law." This statute is, in effect, a "signing-off" and merely provides that no British statutes passed after the Constitution Act, 1982 shall have force or effect in Canada. It is interesting and important to note, however, that the Constitution Act, 1982 and the majority of the proceeding thirty statutes and orders in council listed in the Schedule remain statutes or orders in council of either the United Kingdom Parliament or the Privy Council of the United Kingdom, respectively.

The use of the word "patriation" has created a great deal of confusion in that many Canadians probably assume that our basic constitutional documents are now similar in legal status to the Constitution of the United States. In the United States, the Constitution was the result of a constitutional convention and is not the product of any legislative enactment. This is not true in Canada where the majority of our entrenched constitutional documents, ranging from the Constitution Act, 1867 down to the Constitution Act, 1982, are and presumably will always remain statutes of the United Kingdom Parliament. What has changed, however, is that these statutes, though British in their legal origin, can no longer be amended by the United Kingdom Parliament. As a result of the amending formula contained in the Constitution Act, 1982, these British statutes can now be amended only by a Canadian process as outlined in the Act. Thus our situation is more similar to that of Australia than to that of the United States in that our basic constitutional law is composed of British statutes amendable by a wholly domestic Canadian process. Later in this work the domestic process will be described and critically analyzed. Similarly, there will be a detailed examination of most of the important British statutes described in the opening words of this book, with an analysis of their significance and impact on Canada's political and legal functioning.

However, before looking in detail at the provisions of the Canadian Constitution, we will turn to an examination of the functions of a Constitution generally, and an analysis of how these functions are fulfilled by our constitutional structure.

THE NATURE AND FUNCTIONS OF A CONSTITUTION

A Constitution must first provide for the creation of the basic organs and institutions of public authority. Second, it must define the powers possessed by each of the public institutions and in some respects define the relationships between these various institutions. Third, a Constitution must provide for the processes by which law is created, and at the same time provide for the limitations on the power exercised by the officials of public institutions. Thus a Constitution assigns legal responsibility, defines the limits of authority, and establishes the processes which must be followed before this authority can be exercised. Furthermore, a constitutional document must provide for a method of change, both of political leadership and of the basic constitutional framework, the latter by way of amendment to the Constitution.

In Canada it is necessary to look at a whole series of statutes and other legal documents to ascertain how, at least to some extent, power is allocated in the Canadian system. However, as will be demonstrated later, many of the rules with respect to the functioning of authority in a constitutional system are not defined in authoritative legal documents but rather are the result of consensus among the actors in a political and constitutional system. It must always be remembered that the legal rules of the Constitution are inextricably linked with the informal functioning of the political process. It is impossible to detach the legal rules of the constitutional game from the political process which gives the entire polity vitality and life. It must also be remembered that quite often the legal rules are very misleading when examined without reference to the historical and political context of the country. Thus throughout this work there will be a repeated effort to illustrate constitutional rules in the light of the political setting in which they exist.

A further important concept of constitutionalism is that which is usually referred to as the rule of law. This concept is that legitimate actors in the political system have only such authority as is vested in them by law, and that any attempt to move beyond the peripheries of this authority is illegal, or to use the constitutional term, *ultra vires*. This particular notion is especially underlined in Canada by the fact that ours is a federal system, which means that the basic state authority is divided between the central government on the one hand and the provincial governments on the other. The allocation of power is provided for in relevant sections of the Constitution Act, 1867, but these terms are often vague and imprecise and accordingly lead to considerable conflict between the levels of government. There is a tendency for each level of government to attempt to expand its authority and to push into the areas assigned to the other level of government. It is in this context that we see the development of the idea of the judiciary as a referee, adjudicating questions as to the appropriate demarcation of authority between the central government and its provincial counterparts.

Particularly, however, since the passage of the Charter of Rights, a new limitation has been imposed on the authority of governmental institutions. Once again it is the responsibility of the judiciary to determine when governments or their agents overstep the boundaries of legitimate authority. A good deal of power is thus put in the hands of the judiciary in defining the proper limits of governmental power. Inevitably, this involves the courts in drawing lines beyond which various government agencies and other political actors cannot go. This was illustrated in the case of *Roncarelli v. Duplessis*, in which Premier Duplessis of Quebec had instructed the Quebec Liquor Commissioner to cancel the liquor licence of Mr. Frank Roncarelli, who operated a restaurant in the city of Montreal. The Supreme Court of Canada held that Mr. Duplessis, even though premier of the province and attorney general of Quebec, had no legal authority to give instructions to any public servant with respect to whether Mr. Roncarelli should or should not possess a liquor licence. The court said that the sheer fact of holding the offices of premier and attorney general does not give an official any authority above and beyond that vested by law in those offices. Accordingly, Mr. Duplessis was ordered by the Supreme Court of Canada to pay to Mr. Roncarelli over $50 000 in damages for his unlawful actions.

This case serves admirably to illustrate how the Constitution imposes limits on office holders with respect to functions they are not authorized by law to perform. Until recently, however, most of the decisions, as outlined earlier, tended to centre on the appropriate jurisdictions of federal and provincial governments. In future not only will the courts continue to play this major role, but they will also be increasingly called upon to determine whether a government has overstepped the barriers created by the Charter of Rights which was enacted as part of the Constitution Act, 1982. In this respect we see a substantial push in the direction of the American system and, accordingly, a heightened role for the judiciary. Whether our judiciary will become as active as the American judiciary is, of course, impossible to predict. Most of our judges have been trained in a tradition which accords considerable deference to legislative dominance. But even with a judiciary conditioned to legislative dominance there is no doubt that judges will still inevitably be pushed to apply the Charter quite frequently to strike down either the activity of governmental authorities or the actual provisions of statutes. This, of course, is the most important impact arising from the legal actions of 1982, namely, the drafting of the Charter of Rights and the resultant increased role for the judiciary in our constitutional system.

As mentioned above, until 1982 the chief area in which the courts have had to function as referee has been in the determination of the jurisdictional lines between the authority vested in the federal parliament and the authority vested in the provincial legislatures, a necessary feature of a federal state. Federalism is a system which in its purest sense vests power in at least two levels of government by virtue of the country's basic constitutional law. This means that certain areas of authority are assigned to the central government while other areas are given to the regional governments, and that neither government can interfere with the jurisdiction of the other. K.C. Wheare developed the theoretical concept that in a pure federal system the different levels of government have independent power, each free from dominance and control by the other level of government.

There is little doubt that Canada meets, in a practical sense, the test devised by Wheare in that certain features of the Constitution which allow for a high degree of federal intervention in the provincial sphere have now fallen into disuse. In particular, the power of the lieutenant governor, an appointee of the central government, to refuse to give assent to a bill or to reserve it for the attention of the central government is no longer employed. Similarly, the power of the central government to disallow provincial legislation has not been utilized since 1942. In addition, the authority of the central parliament to pass remedial legislation in the area of education, as provided for by section 93 of the Constitution Act, 1867, has never been used although the possibility of its utilization arose at one point in the context of the Manitoba School Crisis of 1896. Thus Canada probably represents one of the purest examples of a truly functioning federal system.

The Constitution Act, 1867, is the starting point for determining the jurisdictional limits of the federal parliament and the provincial legislatures. A number of sections deal with this division of powers including sections 91, 92, 93, 94, 95, 101, 117 and 132. Although this material will not be dealt with in any detail at this point, it should be noted that sections 91 and 92 of the 1867 statute constitute the most important legal provisions for assigning legislative authority. Of these two sections, however, only a few subsections have provided the basis for most of the power of the respective legislatures and consequently have formed the basis of most of the political and legal debate about jurisdictional lines. The struggles have been particularly intense in economic matters, centring around control of commercial activity and regulation of the economy. In recent years, cases dealing with natural resources have been highly significant and have cast the courts in a central role in determining who has control over the ownership and regulation of natural resources. In one case, so bitter were the feelings of the Saskatchewan government after the decision in the case of *Canadian Industrial Gas and Oil Ltd.* v. *Government of Saskatchewan* that section 92 of the Constitution Act, 1867 was amended in 1982 to deal with some of the results of that case, particularly the power of the province to impose indirect taxes on certain aspects of natural resource production. Thus, a federal system produces a host of legal and fiscal questions which are of vital concern to governments and private citizens as well as constitutional lawyers.

This discussion leads to a central theme of [*The Revised Canadian Constitution: Politics as Law*]: that talk of a new constitution is very misleading because, except for the just mentioned addition to section 92 on natural resources, the remainder of the provisions with respect to the division of powers in the 1867 statute remains unaltered. We thus have the same division of powers, at least in pure legal theory, that we had in 1867. Naturally the courts have played a major role in determining through judicial decisions the exact meanings of the words of sections 91 and 92 of the Constitution Act, 1867, but the compromise of 1982 did not change the language of the original statute.

Another important area not reformed by the Constitution Act, 1982 is that of the basic institutions of Canadian government at both the federal and provincial levels. In fact, the result of that Act is the freezing of the existing institutional structure of Canada. We now see that the Supreme Court of Canada, by and large, can no longer be changed by the Parliament of Canada alone. We also see that the monarchy has been entrenched. This, in our view, has the effect of entrenching the cabinet system of government because that system is so tightly linked with the office of the Queen and her representatives. This point will be dealt with in considerable detail later in this work. Similarly, aspects of the legislative system have now been entrenched and cannot be changed without the use of a fairly rigid amending formula. One of the tragedies of the compromise of 1982 is that the functioning of the parliamentary system—and its increasing tendency to fall under executive dominance—has not been reviewed and revised. These facts reinforce our objection to the suggestion that Canada has a "new" Constitution. It is our view that we have failed to draft a new Constitution with respect to the area in which it is most needed, namely, the functioning and interrelationship between executive government in Canada and the legislative process.

Furthermore, in the process of constitutional review which led to the passage of the Constitution Act, 1982, no serious examination of the legislative process was carried out. The electoral system as practised in this country should have been reviewed in considerable depth in order to deal with the problems created by one party having dominance in one province, while another party has dominance in a totally different region of the country. The Pepin–Robarts Committee set up by the federal government asked very serious questions about electoral reform. These questions were not addressed by the government of Canada when it placed before the House of Commons its unilateral proposals for revision to the Canadian Constitution. We are left with an unfortunate situation as a result of the Constitution Act, 1982: certain aspects of the electoral system are subject to change only as a result of the utilization of the cumbersome amendment formula provided for in that Act. This is further evidence that Canada does not have a new Constitution but merely an addition to the existing model. The fundamental operation of the basic institutions of Canadian government at both the federal and provincial levels has been left intact, often, in our view, to the detriment of the functioning of the Canadian polity.

THE POLITICAL IMPETUS LEADING TO THE PASSAGE OF THE CONSTITUTION ACT, 1982

We will examine later in some detail the history of events leading up to the passage of the Constitution Act, 1982 but it would be remiss in this chapter not to touch upon and introduce briefly the political impetus which led to its enactment. The finding of a domestic amending formula had been a concern of Canadian politicians since 1927 and, in fact, six attempts to achieve patriation were made prior to the events of 1982. These attempts seemed to lack a sense of urgency until the very serious drives of 1964 and 1971 brought the federal government and the provincial governments close to agreements on a domestic amending formula. In both 1964 and 1971 patriation failed because Quebec objected to the proposed formulas. On both occasions Quebec took the view that it wanted other concessions in terms of a widening of provincial jurisdiction over various matters, particularly in cultural and economic fields, before it would agree to an amending formula. In those instances the federal government was not prepared to go ahead without the agreement of the government of Quebec. We see here at least some recognition of the "compact theory" that basic federal–provincial relations are not to be altered without the agreement of the federal and provincial governments.

After the failure of 1971 a period of time elapsed before the dramatic events of 1981 and 1982 occurred. The election of the Parti Quebecois separatist government in 1976, and its referendum on the question of sovereignty-association of Quebec with the rest of Canada in 1980, opened the way for Prime Minister Pierre Trudeau to take unilateral action on the Constitution. The then leader of the Liberal party in Quebec, Claude Ryan, had argued against any form of Quebec separation with a plea that he would fight for the renegotiation of the Canadian constitutional structure. He, in fact, issued what came to be known as the "Beige Paper" outlining dramatic revisions to the Canadian constitutional system. It was particularly noteworthy that the essential theses of this paper were the widening of Quebec's economic and political jurisdiction, and the greater participation of provincial representatives in the context of federal institutions. This potential promise of a constitutional new deal for Quebec was very helpful to those who opposed the sovereignty-association proposal in the Quebec government's referendum question.

Using the opening presented by the defeat of the Levesque government's referendum, Trudeau unilaterally introduced into the federal House of Commons a resolution involving "patriation" of the Constitution and passage of a charter of rights. His argument was that the Quebec referendum had been defeated on the promise of constitutional change and that, therefore, he was taking this opportunity to put forward changes for ultimate enactment by the British parliament. Most of the provinces were both shocked and outraged by this dramatic departure from the previous constitutional practice and began a series of steps, leading ultimately to a major decision of the Supreme Court of Canada, opposing the unilateral action of the prime minister. Claude Ryan, who had led the fight against the Quebec separatists' referendum, was incensed by the actions of the federal government and vociferously expressed his opposition to the federal proposals. Trudeau, recognizing the opportunity to place his stamp on Canadian history and at the same time divert attention from Canada's rapidly deteriorating economic situation, decided to push ahead at all costs. After a number of political and legal skirmishes, nine of the provinces and the federal government ultimately agreed on a compromise package to forward to the parliament of Great Britain for its enactment as the Constitution Act, 1982.

The major concession by the federal government was the acceptance of the provincial proposals with respect to an amendment formula. The federal proposal in this area, which had been based on the Victoria solution of 1971, was entirely jettisoned. The question of native rights was put off, to be dealt with at a conference to be held within one year. Then, as previously mentioned, an amendment was made to section 92 of the British North America Act, giving the provinces greater control over natural resources and their taxation. Trudeau was able to keep the Charter of Rights and Freedoms within the resolution to be forwarded to London. The provinces, however, did obtain the concession that either the federal or provincial legislatures could enact a statute which would operate without some portions of the Charter of Rights being applicable to it.

Certainly one strong factor in the push by Trudeau for the Charter of Rights and Freedoms was the question of language rights. It had been one of his long-time commitments to dramatically increase French-Canadian participation in all levels of federal government activity. Similarly, he was concerned about guaranteeing French language and educational rights at the provincial level in the English-speaking provinces. This objective is achieved in a very clear way in the context of the Constitution Act, 1982. Thus bilingualism is now, by and large, solidly entrenched in the Canadian federal governmental context.

One of the chief motivating factors—both political and legal—in including the rest of the Charter of Rights and Freedoms was the American experience. In the United States the courts had used the Bill of Rights as an important tool in diminishing states' rights. It obviously occurred to the central planners that the Charter of Rights would impact much more substantially on provincial jurisdiction than on federal jurisdiction. Thus it was anticipated that the courts would begin to make important decisions that were previously in the hands of the provincial legislatures.

The prime minister's advisors were also not unaware of the fact that in the United States constitutional law courses centre on the interpretation of the Bill of Rights, rather than on the division of powers between federal and regional legislatures. Thus it was envisaged that true to our usual practice of imitating the United States, Canadian law teachers would more and more teach the Canadian Constitution from an American perspective of focussing on entrenched rights rather than from the traditional Canadian approach of focussing on the division of power and the evolution of Canada's political and conventional heritage.

There are others who argue that when Trudeau briefly resigned as leader after the defeat of the Liberal government at the polls in 1979, he was concerned that writers of his political obituary concentrated almost exclusively on his proclamation of the War Measures Act and the resultant infringement on civil liberties. It has been argued that he wanted to rewrite his place in history so as to be identified with the Charter of Rights rather than with the repression of the War Measures Act.

Another line of argument is that Trudeau is a rationalist, which means that he has a Cartesian or Utopian view of what the world should be, and considers that a constitution and legislation should mould the human condition to meet this idealistic model. Trudeau supporters would argue that the Charter of Rights is part of the legal technique for modelling humanity along the lines of an ultimate rationalist view for the betterment of mankind. It is somewhat difficult to accept this line of argument in view of Trudeau's conduct at the time of the proclamation of the War Measures Act and his general treatment of persons who did not share a viewpoint similar to his own. It is, in our view, much more likely that while with respect to language rights he was genuinely motivated towards extending French language rights throughout Canada, with respect to other aspects of the Charter the realist argument that a charter is a homogenizing influence was probably the most important reason for his inclusion of them. This is consistent with Trudeau's ongoing hostility towards provincial rights, seeing them as an obstruction to the achievement of his goal of a Canada in which the central government is overwhelmingly dominant.

THE RELATIONSHIP BETWEEN LAW AND POLITICS

In 1969 one of the authors of [*The Revised Canadian Constitution: Politics as Law*] wrote

> [l]aw, in my view, is that part of the overall process of political decision-making which has achieved somewhat more technical, more obvious and more clearly defined ground rules than other aspects of politics. It is still, however, an integral subdivision of the overall political process. The student of politics, law and legal philosophy is concerned, among other things, with the question of allocation of all types of resources, and with questions of the relationships between individual citizens and between the citizen and the state, as well as the relationships between states. The study of the legal and political process in any nation is a study of how decisions are made, who makes them, what the decisions are, how they influence subsequent events, and how alternative decisions might have led to different results.

The authors see no reason to alter their views with respect to the relationship between law and politics. In fact, the Charter of Rights, and its inevitable interpretation and application by the judiciary, is bound to place the courts much more in the forefront of the political process. In addition to having to determine legality based on the dividing lines of the federal system, they will now have to add another perspective of consideration, namely, whether the legislation also violates the Charter of Rights. True, commentators can argue that this is purely a legal process to be determined by legal reasoning. The difficulty, however, is that the Charter of Rights is couched in very general terms, including such phrases as "freedom of expression," which leave the judiciary considerable latitude in defining the restraints to be placed on a legislature with respect to the limitation of freedom of expression.

It is impossible to predict how far we will move down the American road; one can only pause and reflect on the Supreme Court decision in *Roe* v. *Wade*. In that case state laws prohibiting abortion during the first three months of pregnancy were struck down as unconstitutional, as being in violation of the Fourteenth Amendment of the United States Constitution. The Fourteenth Amendment provides that it is unconstitutional for a state to "deny to any person within its jurisdiction the equal protection of the laws." Who could have possibly envisaged that these very general words would involve the court in the forefront of policy making with respect to the legality of abortion?

This point has been raised simply to illustrate how the rather general rules of entrenched rights can lead the courts into very unusual directions. It is, of course, fairly well known that in the United States the courts have ended up virtually administering the rules relating to busing in order to provide for racial integration in the public schools, and have laid down rules with respect to the functioning of penal institutions. They have even ordered electoral redistribution of state upper houses on the ground that they violate the equal protection clause of the Constitution. This is not to imply that the Canadian courts will automatically follow the American route, because the inherent tradition of parliamentary supremacy will, for some time, remain embedded in our legal consciousness. However, as stated earlier, it seems inevitable that the courts will be drawn into an ever increasing number of political disputes because of the passage of the Charter of Rights.

As a result we can expect the Canadian public will become more sensitized to the judiciary being a participant in the political process. Even when acting as a referee in determining legislative boundaries between the central and provincial governments, the Supreme Court is finding it more difficult to avoid being identified with political issues. The Charter of Rights has, and will, further politicize the judiciary in the conception of the public. It will also involve directing more matters to the judiciary for final determination and away from the elected representatives. Many may approve of this direction, especially lawyers and law professors to whom will now accrue the potential heritage of the United States with its excessively lawyer-dominated society. Certainly this may have been one of the objectives of Prime Minister Trudeau and his advisors when drafting the Charter of Rights. They have through that medium been able to take issues out of the political arena and transpose them into legal forms.

The result of these manoeuvres has been to turn many political matters into legal issues. Thus we see a transposition in the direction of turning political solutions into legal ones; we have moved clearly and inexorably in the American direction of politics as law.

JUDGING THE JUDGES:
THE SUPREME COURT'S FIRST ONE HUNDRED
CHARTER DECISIONS

F.L. Morton, Peter H. Russell, Michael J. Withey

INTRODUCTION

On April 16, 1982, Canada formally amended its written constitution by adding the Charter of Rights and Freedoms. The Charter explicitly authorized judicial

An abridged version of a paper presented at the annual meeting of the Canadian Political Science Association held in Victoria, B.C., May 27–29, 1990. Professor Morton is a member of the Department of Political Science, The University of Calgary; Professor Russell is a member of the Department of Political Science, University of Toronto; Mr. Withey is a graduate student in political science at The University of Calgary. By permission.

review and the power of all courts to declare offending statutes void. At the time this constitutional transplant of American-style judicial review into the Canadian hybrid of British-style parliamentary democracy posed important questions of both theoretical and practical interest. Canada had already modified the Westminster model of parliamentary supremacy with an overlay of federalism *cum* judicial review. Within their respective jurisdictions, however, the "exhaustion theory" held that both levels of government were supreme. The Charter appeared to challenge this supremacy, and perhaps the structure of federalism itself. Suffice it to say that in the intervening eight years, the Charter, or, more precisely, the Charter through the courts, has had a broad, varied, and significant impact on the practice of politics in Canada. In November, 1989, the Supreme Court of Canada handed down its one hundredth Charter of Rights decision. This paper presents a statistical overview of these first one hundred Charter cases. It identifies trends with respect both to the Charter's impact on the Court and the impact of the Court's decisions on the Charter.

. . . By identifying patterns not discernible through the study of leading Charter cases, quantitative analysis can generate empirically supported generalizations—that is, new understanding—of how the Charter is affecting the Supreme Court and how the Court is shaping the Charter.

This is not to deny the limitations of quantitative analysis of judicial decision-making. It is not a substitute for jurisprudential analysis. For supreme courts—indeed, for all appellate courts in common law countries—the reasons given to justify a decision are often more important in the long run than a decision's basic outcome or "bottom line." In this respect judicial decision-making differs significantly from executive or legislative decision making. A single decision on a right or freedom—because of the far-reaching implications of its supporting reasons—can outweigh in importance dozens of other decisions on the same right or freedom which go in the opposite direction. Statistical analyses treat all cases equally, when in fact they are clearly not all of equal significance. Similarly, statistical classifications of cases in terms of their bottom line outcomes—for example "upholding" or "denying" a Charter claim—do not capture important jurisprudential subtleties. A decision which upholds a Charter claim might do so through opinions which actually narrow the meaning of the Charter right involved. . . .

THE CHARTER'S IMPACT ON THE COURT'S CASE LOAD

The Charter has clearly changed the composition of the Supreme Court's case load. Table 1 shows that since the Court's first Charter decision in May, 1984 the volume of Charter cases steadily increased. By 1987 it constituted nearly one-quarter of the Court's annual output of decided cases, and has remained at that level since. This means that in a short span of eight years roughly 25 percent of the Court's time and other resources are now being spent on Charter

TABLE 1   **Charter Decisions by all Supreme Court Decisions, 1981–1989**

Year	All SCC decisions	SCC Charter decisions	Percent of total
1981	111	0	0%
1982	117	0	0%
1983	87	0	0%
1984	63	4	6%
1985	83	11	13%
1986	81	11	14%
1987	95	23	24%
1988	104	25	24%
1989	126	29*	23%
	867**	104*	12%

unit of analysis: case

* Only Table 1 uses all Charter decisions through the end of 1989—104 cases. The other tables are based on the first 100 decisions.

** Data provided by Sylvie Roussel, Noel Décary, Aubrey and Associates, *Supreme Court News*. (Hull, Quebec)

cases. Significantly, the corresponding percentage for the U.S. Supreme Court is almost identical. During the same time period the American Court decided 169 Bill of Rights decisions out of a total of 732 written decisions, or 23 percent. This institutional parallel was unthinkable prior to the Charter, and supports Lipset's recent hypothesis that the Charter is "Americanizing" the practice of politics in Canada.

This surge of Charter litigation contrasts sharply with the development of the 1960 Canadian Bill of Rights. From 1960 to 1982 the Supreme Court decided only 34 Bill of Rights cases, an average of slightly over one per year. The high success of Charter claims in the Court's first two years of decision-making, as shown in Table 2, seems to have stimulated use of the Charter. The Supreme Court sent a message to the legal profession and lower court judges that it was prepared to take the constitutionally entrenched rights of the Charter much more seriously than the Bill of Rights. Under the latter, the Supreme Court did not hand down a ruling that supported a rights claim until its 1969 *Drybones* decision, and even this turned out to be the exception, not the rule.

The total of 63 cases decided in 1984 represented the Court's lowest annual output since it took over as Canada's highest court in 1949. It was not until 1988 that the Court returned to the 100 plus level which has been its norm since 1949. . . .

The advent of the Charter has not meant an abatement of constitutional cases involving federalism. Indeed, the Supreme Court and lower courts still prefer, where possible, to settle a constitutional case on federalism grounds rather than on the Charter. During the period of the Court's first one hundred Charter cases, it also decided 31 federalism cases. This means that the Court's constitutional mandate is in this respect actually wider than that of the United States Supreme Court, which has virtually abandoned any active role as an umpire of federalism.

TABLE 2   **Outcome of Supreme Court's First 100 Charter Decisions**

Year	Charter claimant Loses	Charter claimant Wins	Inconclusive	Totals
1984	1	3 (75%)	0	4
1985	3	7 (64%)	1	11
1986	8	3 (27%)	0	11
1987	16	6 (26%)	1	23
1988	17	8 (32%)	0	25
1989 (–Nov.)	16	8 (31%)	2	26
Totals	61	35 (35%)	4	100

With Charter litigation added to constitutional litigation based on the division of powers, the Supreme Court has become much more concerned with constitutional issues than was the case in the past. It would be a mistake, however, to regard the Canadian Supreme Court, even with its new Charter responsibilities, as simply a "constitutional court." Constitutional cases continue to account for only one-quarter to one-third of the cases it decides. This figure is only slightly lower than the comparable figure for the American Supreme Court for the same time period—44 percent.

On the other hand, the Charter has contributed to the further decline of private law and a corresponding increase in public law cases. As Monahan correctly pointed out, the decline in private law cases decided by the Court dates back to 1974, when appeals as of right in private law cases were abolished. Prior to 1974, private law cases constituted approximately one-half of the cases decided by the Supreme Court each year. Since 1974, private law cases have steadily declined to the point where they account for less than a quarter since the adoption of the Charter. . . . To conclude, while the Charter has not made the Supreme Court into an exclusively "constitutional court," it has contributed to the Court's transformation into a decidedly "public law" court.

OUTCOME OF CASES

In the 34 Bill of Rights cases decided by the Supreme Court of Canada between 1960 and 1982, the rights claimant won only five times—a "success rate" of only 15 percent. Table 2 shows how markedly different the Supreme Court has treated rights claims under the Charter. Thirty-five of the first one hundred Charter cases were won by the litigant. Once again there is a strong parallel with American experience. During the same time frame, the non-government litigant won 61 of the 169 Bill of Rights decisions handed down by the American Supreme Court, a "success rate" of exactly 36 percent!

During its first two years of Charter decisions (1984 and 1985), the Court awarded victories to a stunning 67 percent (10 of 15) of the Charter claimants who came before it. The success rate of Charter litigants fell off steeply after this initial burst of judicial enthusiasm, averaging 27 percent to 32 percent over the last four years. During these six years, there has been a turnover of six justices, and the Mulroney government has filled all six vacancies. This has tempted some commentators to attribute the sharp drop in Charter success rates to the change in the Court's personnel. David Beatty, for example, has described the six Mulroney appointees as "conservative judges . . . [who] are very deferential to the legislature [and] don't want to hold a law unconstitutional."

This analysis is only superficially persuasive. . . . there is no consistent empirical support for Beatty's thesis that Prime Minister Mulroney has used his appointment power to shape an ideologically "conservative" or self-restrained Supreme Court.

A more probable explanation for the drop in the success rate of Charter claims after 1985 is a philosophical shift among some of the same justices who began the Court's Charter interpretation in 1984. In retrospect, these first two years can be seen as a sort of Charter "honeymoon." Not only were many of these first 15 cases strongly activist, but all save two were unanimous. The written judgments in these decisions manifested a very sanguine—some might say, naively optimistic—view of the Court's new role under the Charter. The Court seemed intent on minimizing any tension between its new mode of American-style judicial activism and its traditional, constitutional functions. The judges seemed to be trying to convince their public—and perhaps themselves—that they were simply carrying out the legal implications of the Charter. The Court wanted to have its cake and eat it too, and, for a brief moment, it did. Like all honeymoons, this one came to an end. As the Court ventured deeper into "Charterland," it was no coincidence that the success rate for Charter cases began to fall precipitously while at the same time the number of dissenting opinions soared. The number of unanimously decided Charter decisions dropped from over 85 percent in 1984–85 to the 60 percent range since then. The falling success rate and growing division on the Court both reflect the same hard reality—the inescapably contentious character of modern judicial review.

The seeds of this change were already present in the Court's 1984 and 1985 Charter decisions. As Monahan observed, these early Charter decisions were characterized by two very different and conflicting tendencies. On the one hand, the Court repeatedly invoked the rhetoric of judicial activism (especially Lord Sankey's "living tree" metaphor) and repeatedly ruled in favour of Charter litigants. At the same time, the Court drew a sharp distinction between law and politics, characterizing its new role under the Charter as purely legal. Monahan argued that this somewhat schizophrenic behaviour was symptomatic of an underlying "crisis" on the Court over its new role under the Charter and "the relationship between law and politics."

This tension was also evident in the Court's use—or misuse—of the "living tree doctrine" to justify its new Charter activism. While the "living tree" doctrine originated in Lord Sankey's now famous dicta in the *Persons Case*, it developed primarily in the context of the law of Canadian federalism. In this context, it came to be widely used—primarily by English-Canadian jurists favouring a more centralist constitutional order—to encourage judges to accommodate new policy initiatives of Canadian governments through a "flexible" interpretation of the BNA Act, especially the enumerated grants of power in sections 91 and 92 of that Act. Its practical effect is a form of judicial self-restraint that defers to majoritarian or democratic influences in Canadian government. By contrast, when the focus of the "living tree" doctrine is shifted from the law of federalism to the law of civil liberties, the roles of courts and legislatures are reversed. Rather than expanding legislative powers, the "living tree" doctrine expands limitations on legislative power. Rather than accommodating legislative problem-solving, judges are encouraged to give a "large and liberal" interpretation to Charter provisions in order to correct legislative errors. The continued use of the same legal metaphor of the "living tree" obscures the radical revaluation that has occurred. While the original version of the "living tree" entails judicial self-restraint, the new version promotes judicial activism.

While Monahan's characterization of the problem as a "crisis" may be overstated, there was clearly a tension between the Court's legalistic pretense and its activist behaviour. In 1986, this tension came to a head for at least some of the justices, who adopted a more cautious or self-restrained approach to their Charter work. This shift was particularly evident in the three cases decided early in 1986 rejecting language rights claims and in the cases rejecting claims of organized labour decided later in 1986 and early 1987.

The growing sense of caution and judicial self-restraint can also be seen in the Court's handling of section 1 "reasonable limitations" claims by the Crown. Section one involves what is widely recognized as a highly discretionary "balancing test" between the policy interests of the government and the interest of the litigant in having his Charter rights upheld. From 1984 through 1987, the Court rejected all but one of the 11 section 1 defences that were presented by the Crown. By contrast, in 1988 and 1989, it accepted 8 of 14. These data simply confirm what was already an open secret: that the Court has become badly divided on how to handle the section 1 issue.

To conclude, the simultaneous drop in the success rate and increase in dissenting opinions after 1985 cannot be explained as an effect of "conservative" Mulroney appointments to the Court. Rather, it represents the working out of the tension between the activist behaviour and legalistic pretense in the Court's earlier decisions. There are real tensions between judicial review of constitutional rights and parliamentary democracy, and it was inevitable that these would surface and produce disagreement among the justices. The same disagreements have fueled constitutional debate in the U.S. for the past 20 years, and the advent of the Charter has brought "an American debate . . . to Canada." It has not—at least not yet—brought the corollary American practice of "court packing" into Canadian politics. The most that can be said at this point about the Mulroney Supreme Court appointments is that they have been chosen according to traditional, non-ideological criteria, and they have neither impeded or hastened any prior trends in the Court's approach to Charter interpretation.

Even at the current, lower levels of success, the Charter has served as a catalyst for a new era of judicial activism unparallelled in Canadian history, and on a par with contemporary American practice. . . .

A final caveat is in order about the tendency of Beatty and others to use "liberal" and "conservative" as synonyms for "judicial activism" and "judicial self-restraint" when discussing the Charter of Rights. This usage is as misleading as it is common. It reflects a simplistic attitude of "the more rights, the better," an attitude that fails to grasp either the complexity or ambiguity of "rights." The wrong-headedness of this common practice can be illustrated by comparing judges with legislators. It is simply perverse to describe a politician who supports state intervention to regulate or redistribute private power as a "liberal," and simultaneously to describe a judge who strikes down such laws as a "liberal." Similarly, it is hardly clear why a politician who votes against interventionist, statist projects should be described as a conservative, while a self-restrained judge who votes to uphold the same laws is described as a conservative. Judicial activism and judicial self-restraint denote the willingness or reluctance of judges to use the power of judicial review to revise or obstruct the decisions of legislatures and the executive. They may be used with equal facility for either conservative or liberal ends. There is thus nothing to be gained and much to be lost by conflating the two sets of terms. . . .

TREATMENT OF COURTS OF APPEAL

With the exception of one reference by the federal government, all of the Supreme Court's first one hundred Charter decisions have come on appeal from intermediary courts of appeal. This permits a comparison of the Supreme Court's decisions with those of the lower appeal courts in the same sets of cases. As indicated by Table 3, 68 percent—or about two of every three—of the Charter decisions appealed from the lower courts have been upheld by the Supreme Court. This figure contrasts sharply with the comparable American figure. In its 169 Bill of Rights decisions during this same time period, the American Supreme Court overturned 111 lower court decisions. This contrast suggests that the American Court makes more strategic use of its discretion to choose which appeals to hear; that is, it selects cases that it initially intuits as "mistakes" that should be given a hard second look. The American Court's more critical screening process may be explained by the much higher demand for its services—over 5000 appeal requests annually. By comparison, the Canadian Supreme Court selects its 100–125 cases a year from only 400 appeal petitions. It can thus afford to be more generous with its discretion to grant leave to appeal.

The 68 percent "uphold" figure for Charter decisions is marginally higher than the global average for all Supreme Court decisions during this same time

TABLE 3 **The Supreme Court's Treatment of Courts of Appeals' Charter Decisions**

Courts of Appeal	Number of Charter Decisions		Total	% Upheld
	Upheld	Reversal		
British Columbia*	17	2	19	89%
Alberta	9	4	13	69%
Saskatchewan	5	2	7	71%
Manitoba	4	2	6	67%
Ontario	25	6	31	81%
Quebec	7	11	19**	37%
New Brunswick	1	1	2	50%
Nova Scotia	1	2	3	33%
PEI	1	1	2	50%
Newfoundland	1	1	2	50%
Federal Court	3	2	5	60%
	74	34	109***	68%

* Includes one decision made when sitting as Yukon Court of Appeals.
** Includes one case that upholds in part, reverses in part.
*** Totals more than 100 because it includes ten additional S.C.C. Charter decisions which were not counted in this study because they raised the identical issues as cases that were already counted. Because they originated in different courts of appeal, however, they are included in Table 3.

Total is 109, rather than 110, because one decision came as a reference directly from the federal government, with no lower court decision to review.

period. Between 1982 and 1989, the Supreme Court heard 559 appeals and dismissed 59 percent of them. This means that for courts of appeal in general, the Charter is not posing any new or special problems in their relationship with the Supreme Court.

However, as Table 3 also shows, the reversal rates have varied quite widely for the different courts of appeal. The most remarkable difference is the very high reversal rate (63 percent) in appeals from Quebec. Only Nova Scotia has a reversal rate even close to Quebec's, but that is for only three cases. Charter ideology alone cannot account for the relative frequency with which the Supreme Court has reversed Quebec's Court of Appeal. The courts of appeal whose Charter decisions have been most frequently upheld by the Supreme Court—British Columbia, Ontario and Saskatchewan—differ widely in their Charter profiles. British Columbia's Court of Appeal has been fairly self-restrained, Saskatchewan's fairly activist, and Ontario's in the middle. The Charter activism or self-restraint of an appeal court is thus not an accurate predictor of how its decision will be reviewed by the Supreme Court.

Table 4 [omitted here] presents a closer look at those 35 Supreme Court Charter decisions that reversed lower court of appeal decisions. The number of reversals in favour of the Charter litigant (22) were twice as numerous as those favouring the Crown (11). Thus, when the Court did reverse lower court decisions, it was much more likely to do so in favour of the individual. This also means that for this set of one hundred cases, the Supreme Court supported the Charter claimant more frequently (35 percent) than the appeal courts collectively (25 percent). ● ● ●

TREATMENT OF DIFFERENT CHARTER RIGHTS

Table 5 shows which Charter rights and freedoms have formed the basis of the Supreme Court's first 100 decisions and how they were decided. The unit of analysis is Charter cases. We have classified each of the one hundred cases according to the right or freedom on which the case primarily turned and the outcome in terms of whether the litigant achieved the practical objective of his or her litigation. In civil cases, a "win" denotes the Charter claimant received the remedy requested—the nullification of a statute or regulation, a declaratory judgment, an injunction, and so forth. Likewise in criminal cases, a "win" denotes the Court awarding the Charter litigant/accused the remedy he requested—the exclusion of evidence, the nullification of a statute, a reinstatement of a verdict of "not guilty," an order for a new trial, and so forth. In cases where the Charter claimant receives some but not all of the remedies requested, the result of the case is coded as "inconclusive."

Table 5 clearly shows the extent to which legal rights cases have dominated the Court's Charter agenda—74 of its first one hundred decisions. This trend has been evident from early on. Most commentators agree that it favours both the Court and the Charter, as judicial expertise and authority are highest in this area. Also, legal rights cases arise predominantly in the making and enforcement of criminal law—a purely federal jurisdiction—and thus tend not to become embroiled in the politics of federalism or language. This is not to minimize the importance or extent of the changes effected by the Court in this area. As Manfredi has shown, criminal process issues contain important substantive dimensions. The Court has used the Charter to develop a new constitutional code of conduct for Canadian police officers in dealing with suspects and accused persons, and in the process has pushed the Canadian criminal process away from the "crime control" toward the "due process" side of the ledger.

Ironically, while this policy area represents the Court's most extensive *de facto* efforts at law reform, it has thus far escaped public notice. American experience shows that this type of judicial policy-making can become an issue of partisan political conflict. Beginning with Richard Nixon's 1968 presidential campaign, the Republican Party has criticized "liberal" judges for being "soft on criminals" and successfully exploited the "law and order" issue, particularly as it relates to the appointment of federal judges. It will be of both theoretical and practical interest to see if a Canadian political party will try to make a political issue out of the Supreme Court's Charter-inspired reform of the criminal law process.

Fundamental Freedoms are a distant second, accounting for sixteen cases. The distinctively Canadian sections of the Charter—mobility rights and lan-

TABLE 5 **Different Categories of Charter Cases by Result**

	Charter claimant			
	Wins	Loses	Inconclusive	Totals
Fundamental Freedoms	5	11	0	16
Democratic Rights	0	0	0	0
Mobility Rights	1	2	0	3
Legal Rights*	27	42	5	74
Equality Rights	1	4	0	5
Language and Education Rights**	4	3	0	7
Aboriginal Rights***	0	0	0	0
Totals	38	62	5	105

Note: The following five cases are counted in two categories, thus making the total number of cases 105.

Morgentaler v. *The Queen*: counted as Legal Rights and Fundamental Freedoms
Black and Co. v. *Law Society of Alberta*: counted as Fundamental Freedoms and Mobility Rights
Irwin Toy v. *A.-G. Quebec*: counted as Fundamental Freedoms and Legal Rights
Reference re Bill 30 (Ontario): counted as Fundamental Freedom and Equality Right
Borowski v. *The Queen*: counted as Legal Rights and Equality Rights

* Including s.23(2).
** Includes sections 16–23 of Charter, sections 93 and 133 of BNA Act, s.23 of Manitoba Act and s.16 of Saskatchewan Act.
*** Includes s.25 of Charter and s.35 of Constitution Act, 1982.

guage rights—have generated only three and seven cases, respectively. On the other hand, they have been relatively more successful than the other sections. The two unsuccessful mobility rights cases dealt with the extradition of criminals and the rights of non-citizens—issues peripheral to the nation-building objectives of the primary author of section 3, Pierre Trudeau. By contrast, the one successful section 3 case struck down Alberta's restrictions on non-resident lawyers and law firms—precisely the type of interprovincial barrier targeted by Trudeau. Within months of the decision, almost every major law firm in Alberta had announced mergers or associations with large Toronto-based firms.

Nor do the small number of language rights cases accurately reflect their considerable political impact. The Court's 1984 decision in the *Quebec Protestant School Boards Case* forced the Quebec government to realize that they had lost control of education and culture, and gave them the incentive to enter into new negotiations with Ottawa, negotiations that led eventually to the 1987 Meech Lake Accord. The Supreme Court's 1988 decisions dealing with language rights in Saskatchewan, Alberta and Quebec, and the political responses that they provoked, have in turn contributed heavily to the demise of Meech Lake. In both instances the Supreme Court affirmed the existence of minority language rights, and in both instances the governments affected enacted new legislation that negated the judicial ruling. Critics of Meech Lake seized upon Quebec's use of the section 33 override as an indicator of what to expect under the "distinct society" clause.

Section 15, the multi-pronged equality rights section, did not come into force until 1985. While it has flooded the lower courts with litigation, it has not yet had much of an impact at the Supreme Court level. However, now that the Court has begun in *Andrews* to lay the foundations of equality rights jurisprudence, a larger proportion of cases coming before the Court will likely deal with equality rights.

NULLIFICATION OF STATUTES

Section 32 of the Charter declares that its enumerated prohibitions apply to "all matters within the authority" of Parliament and the legislatures of each of the provinces. Cases such as *Dolphin Delivery* and *Daigle* show that occasionally it is difficult to say where "state action"—and thus the reach of the Charter—ends and "private action" begins. As a basic rule, however, Charter litigation can be directed at three forms of government actions: primary legislation or statutes; secondary legislation or administrative rules and regulations; and the conduct of government officials. Table 6 presents a breakdown of the Court's first one hundred Charter decisions according to the "object" of the challenge.

Executive conduct has been under review in just over 50 percent of the Court's Charter cases. This is significantly lower than the proportion for Charter cases generally. Earlier studies by both Morton and Monahan found that two out of every three Charter cases are challenges to "conduct"—usually the actions of the police in the enforcement of criminal law. The Supreme Court, it would appear, has been more willing to grant leave to appeal when statutes are challenged than when conduct is challenged.

This has implications for the new role of the Court under the Charter. If the Supreme Court followed the trend of the lower courts and heard primarily "conduct cases," it would reduce the potential for direct clashes between the Court and legislatures over the substantive policy choices implicit in most Charter challenges to statutes. It would also weaken the "anti-democratic" critique of judicial review. The Court's decision to hear a roughly equal number of statute and conduct cases has thrust it into a more competitive relationship with Parliament and provincial legislatures, and made the "legitimacy issue"

TABLE 6   **Object of Charter Challenge by Result of Case**

| | Charter claimant | | |
	Wins	Loses	Inconclusive	Total
Statute	18	29	2	49
Conduct	18	32	1	51
Regulation	2	1	0	3
Totals	38	62	3	103*

*Total greater than one hundred because some Charter cases involve challenges to both statute and conduct, or both statute and regulation, etc.

TABLE 7   **Nullification of Federal and Provincial Statutes**

	Upheld	Nullified	Total
Federal	16	8	24
Provincial	15	11	26
Totals	31	19	50

more explicit and thus more difficult to ignore. This may have been a contributing factor to the end of the Court's initial "Charter honeymoon" described above. The legitimacy issue becomes even sharper when we focus on the judicial nullification of statutes, the subject of Table 7.

Table 7 shows that in the seven years since its adoption, the Supreme Court has used the Charter to strike down a total of 19 statutes, in whole or in part. Remarkably, this figure is almost identical with the number of statutes declared invalid by the U.S. Supreme Court for Bill of Rights violations during the same time period—20.

The 19 Charter nullifications also contrast sharply with the Court's deferential, British-style exercise of judicial review under the 1960 Bill of Rights. Under the latter, the Court struck down only one statute—an obscure and unimportant section of the Indian Act—in 22 years. The magnitude of this change can be appreciated by comparing this figure to the number of statutes declared *ultra vires* on sections 91–92 federalism grounds during the same time frame—only 10 in 31 cases. The Charter has clearly replaced federalism as the primary basis for the Court's exercise of judicial review.

More provincial legislation (11 statutes) has been declared invalid under the Charter than federal (8 statutes). This is consistent with Morton *et al.'s* earlier study of all appeal court nullifications under the Charter, which found that the quantitative impact of the Charter on federal and provincial statutes was roughly equal, but that there were some interesting qualitative differences. The invalidated provincial statutes tended to be of a substantive character and more recently enacted. The same trend is present in the federal and provincial statutes declared invalid by the Supreme Court, which are presented in Table 8 [omitted here].

Seven of the eight nullifications of federal statutes were procedural in character, and half were based on the legal rights provisions of the Charter. By contrast, nine of the eleven nullifications of provincial statutes were substantive in character, and seven of them were based directly or indirectly on French-English minority language and education issues—a perennial source of conflict in Canadian politics.

Table 8 [omitted here] shows that five of the eight invalidated federal statutes involved criminal law. Parliament's exclusive power over criminal law makes federal legislation in Canada a prime target for Charter challenges. This contrasts with the United States, where the states have the primary responsibility for making criminal law. As a result, the American Supreme Court's application of the Bill of Rights, via the Fourteenth Amendment, applies primarily to the states. As noted above, most of the federal legislation overturned by the Court on Charter grounds have involved procedural issues and have not involved major policy concerns.

The major exceptions—and they are major—were the *Singh* and *Morgentaler* decisions. The latter is the most famous—or infamous—Charter decision to date. *Morgentaler* overturned the abortion provisions of the Criminal Code and forced the Mulroney government to deal with the politically charged abortion issue. The government struggled for more than two years to frame a new abortion policy. In June 1990, after several failed attempts, Parliament in a free vote adopted Bill C-43, a compromise measure that leaves abortion in the Criminal Code but allows therapeutic abortions when a pregnancy threatens the life or health of the mother. Bill C-43 abolishes the old requirement of committee approvals, and now leaves the determination of the threat to health to a woman and her doctor. In this respect, it closely follows Chief Justice Dickson's judgment in the *Morgentaler* decision. The legal vacuum created by the government's inaction led to a variety of different provincial responses to the funding and access issues, and also a series of abortion injunction cases. The most dramatic, *Daigle* v. *Tremblay*, went all the way to the Supreme Court for an unprecedented emergency hearing during the summer recess of 1989.

The *Singh* decision is less well known but hardly less dramatic in its effects. *Singh* struck down the procedures for hearing applications for refugee status under the Immigration Act. It forced the government to provide a mandatory oral hearing for refugee applicants. This decision has had the unintended consequences of creating a backlog of 124 000 refugee claimants; an amnesty for 15 000 claimants already in Canada; $179 million dollars in additional costs; and a new refugee law that some critics say is more unfair than the original one. The new refugee law took effect January 1, 1989. Eighteen months later, the government announced that the "new" Immigration and Refugee Board would quadruple its capacity to keep up with applications. This would allow the Board to hire an additional 280 public servants (to add to the present 496) at an additional cost of $20 million. This increase brings the annual budget of the new Board to $80 million.

Only five provinces have lost legislation to Charter challenges: Quebec, British Columbia, Alberta, Saskatchewan and Manitoba. Of the five, Quebec has clearly been most affected. Not only has it had the highest number of nullifications (five), but the statutes affected represented recent policy initiatives that were important to the Quebec government—all but one in the fields of language and education. By contrast, none of the other provincial legislation which has been overturned represented recent policy commitments considered important by the provincial governments. For Quebec, the Court's decisions striking down various sections of Bill 101 have been serious policy setbacks. . . .

In one sense, Quebec presents the clearest example of the counter-majoritarian character of judicial review, where the Court uses the Charter to protect the rights of a local minority against the local majority. From a different perspective, however, the same decisions, particularly in conjunction with the language rights cases from Manitoba and Saskatchewan, show how the Charter, through the Supreme Court, can serve as a vehicle for majoritarian democracy rather than limitation on it. These results parallel similar developments in the United States, where seven times more state laws (970 in total—850 since 1870) have been declared unconstitutional than federal laws (135). Leading American commentators argue that rather than being a restraint on Congress and the president, the American Supreme Court has more often been "an active participant in the ruling national coalitions that dominate American politics," especially when it comes to curbing state or local policies that are offensive to the ruling national coalition. The Supreme Court's lead in attacking racial segregation in the South is only the most well-known example of the use of judicial review to restrain what is perceived as "aberrant" behaviour of regional majorities. Both the U.S. and Canadian experiences support Shapiro's broader comparative thesis that the primary function of judicial review is not legal but political—namely, to "aid the central authorities in breaking into the cake of local custom and bringing [central] government influence down into the villages."

The greater impact of the Charter on provincial law-making also supports earlier predictions about the potential of the Charter to act as a force for policy uniformity throughout Canada. Whether this will serve a "nation-building" function, as its proponents hoped, or be a politically divisive influence remains to be seen. The prolonged and bitter debate over the "distinct society" clause in the Meech Lake Accord reflects the Charter's disproportionate impact on Quebec, and suggests a growing cleavage between Francophone Quebec and the rest of Canada concerning the value of the Charter. Quebec nationalists hoped that the "distinct society" clause would mitigate the impact of the Charter on Quebec's attempts to protect and promote the use of the French language. For the same reason, many English Canadians—especially those within Quebec—were equally strongly opposed to the "distinct society" clause.

JUDICIAL DISCRETION: REASONABLE LIMITATIONS AND THE EXCLUSION OF EVIDENCE

Frequently in Charter cases, after the Court has found that a right has been violated, it goes on to a second stage of analysis to consider whether the law abridging the right is a "reasonable limitation' under section 1 or whether, if it is a criminal case, the evidence should be excluded under section 24(2). Both these types of second stage determinations are crucial to the practical outcome of Charter cases. They are also both highly discretionary, and thus reliable indicators of judicial self-restraint or activism. Tables 9 and 10 [omitted here] present data on the outcome of these second stage determinations in

Supreme Court decision making. The most significant feature of both tables is the contrast in outcomes between the early years and more recent years, evidence which further supports the thesis that after an initial burst of activism, the Court has moved toward a practice of greater self-restraint.

Section 1 states that the rights and freedoms enumerated in the Charter are "subject to such reasonable limitations prescribed by law as can be demonstrably justified in a free and democratic society." Rather than treat this as a self-evident, declaratory truth (i.e., no right is absolute), the Court has made section 1 an integral step in Charter interpretation. If the Court finds that the statute in question restricts a Charter right, the judges then proceed to determine if this limitation is "reasonable" and "demonstrably justifiable." . . .

The close division in outcomes and the division within the Court on section 1 and section 24(2) arguments reflect the rather discretionary and subjective nature of applying these sections of the Charter. Deciding whether legislation is "reasonable" or whether the admission of unconstitutionally obtained evidence "would bring the administration of justice into disrepute" are not likely to become precise arts. The divisions which have developed within the Court over the Court's proper role under the Charter can be understood as both cause and effect of its changing and divided record on section 1 and section 24(2) issues.

DIVISIONS WITHIN THE COURT

Table 11 shows how the Supreme Court's initial consensus on the Charter has broken down. Since the opening activist "honeymoon," the Court has become increasingly divided in its approach to the Charter. Table 11 presents the percentage of unanimous Supreme Court Charter decisions in Charter and non-Charter cases. Note first how the former has fallen steadily. Since 1986 there have been dissents in two out of every five Charter decisions. Meanwhile, the percentage of unanimous decisions in non-Charter cases has remained relatively steady in the 80 percent range, which is the same as pre-Charter practice. This means that the growing dissensus on the Court is limited to Charter cases. A 60 percent unanimity rate is still high by American standards, where it is unusual for more than 20 percent of the Supreme Court's decisions to be unanimous. However, prior to the 1930s—that is, before the Bill of Rights became an active part of its workload—the American Court also enjoyed unanimity in over 80 percent of its decisions. With the advent of "modern judicial review," its preoccupation with rights and emphasis on judicial discretion, this consensus quickly evaporated. Since these conditions now apply in Canada, the declining consensus on the Canadian Court associated with the advent of the Charter may only be the beginning of a longer trend toward still greater dissent.

"Dissent is usually not a game played in solitude; the great majority of all Supreme Court dissents are concurred in by two, three or four justices." So

TABLE 11   **Unanimity in Charter and Non-Charter Cases**

Year	Charter Decisions	Unanimous Judgments	
		Charter	**Non-Charter**
1984	4	100%	88%
1985	11	82%	83%
1986	11	55%	89%
1987	23	61%	85%
1988	25	64%	85%
1989	26	61%	77%
Totals	100	65%	

wrote C. Herman Prichett about the American Supreme Court. While it is true to a lesser degree of the Canadian Supreme Court, the study of dissenting voting patterns suggests that they are not random but reflect a shared judicial philosophy. Table 12 presents one way of analyzing dissenting votes in the Supreme Court of Canada's first one hundred Charter decisions.

The patterns of inter-agreement among the nine justices who participated in a substantial number of the Court's first one hundred Charter cases are displayed in Table 12. The top line records the number of cases in which a justice dissented. The numbers below indicate the number of times the other justices also dissented in the same cases. Solo dissents are shown in brackets. The table is arranged so that each judge is placed closest to those with whom he or she joined in dissent most often and furthest from those with whom they dissented least often. A difficulty in interpreting levels of inter-agreement within the Canadian Supreme Court arises from fact that the full Court rarely participates in decisions. Indeed, nine justices participated in only eight of these first one hundred Charter cases. Thus, to some extent, levels of inter-agreement may be affected by the frequency with which justices participate in the same cases. Nonetheless, even with this caveat, a fairly clear pattern emerges from Table 12. There has been a tendency for three justices—Wilson, Lamer, and Dickson—to cluster together at one end of the Court, while Justice

TABLE 12   **Pattern of Division: Voting Blocs Inter-Agreement in Dissents**

1984–1989 Terms	No	Wilson	Lamer	Dickson	Estey	Beetz	LeDain	Laforest	L'Heureux-Dubé	McIntyre
No. of Dissents		**13**	**9**	**6**	**3**	**3**	**1**	**3**	**3**	**11**
Wilson		(5)	4	3	1			1	1	
Lamer		4	(2)	3		1		1		
Dickson		3	3	( )		1		1		
Estey		1			(1)					1
Beetz			1	1		( )				1
LeDain							( )			1
Laforest		1	1					(1)		1
L'Heureux-Dubé		1	1						( )	2
McIntyre				1	1	1	1	1	2	(5)

McIntyre has been relatively isolated at the other end of the Court. McIntyre received some support from L'Heureux-Dubé after she joined the Court in 1987. Note that McIntyre has never been joined in dissent by Wilson, Lamer, or Dickson.

IDEOLOGICAL DIVISION OF THE INDIVIDUAL JUSTICES

While Table 12 indicates how the Court has divided over Charter interpretation, it does not provide any information as to the direction of the division. Tables 13 and 14 leave no doubt about the ideological nature of the cleavage within the Court. Wilson and Lamer are at the most activist end of the court, while McIntyre and L'Heureux-Dubé have been the justices most inclined to favour judicial self-restraint. Table 13 [omitted here] shows the vote orientation of the justices in all of their Charter decisions—unanimous as well as split decisions. Wilson has supported the Charter litigant in over half the cases she has participated in—a startling 53 percent. At the other extreme are L'Heureuex-Dubé (15 percent) and McIntyre (23 percent), both less than half the rate of Wilson. Lamer, at 47 percent, is closest to Wilson, followed by Estey (47 percent). The rest of the justices fall into a wide middle ground ranging from 30 percent (LaForest) to 39 percent (Beetz). The Court average is 35 percent.

Table 14 [omitted here] indicates the same pattern with regard to dissents in split decisions. All of Wilson's and Lamer's dissents have come in decisions in which the Charter claimant has lost, whereas all but one of McIntyre's and L'Heureux-Dubé's dissents have been in cases in which the majority has favoured the Charter claimant.

It is interesting to observe the position of the then Chief Justice Dickson. Certainly, his voting record in Tables 12 and 13 shows that he has leaned toward the more activist end of the Court and has been more inclined than any other justice to join Wilson and Lamer. On the other hand, he has not isolated himself at that end of the Court and has been able to play the role of an activist-leaning leader on the Court. Evidence for this can be found in the fact that his overall voting record of favouring the Charter claimant in 37 percent of his decisions is almost the same as the overall Court average. Also, he has never dissented by himself.

Tables 15 through 17 throw further light on the ideological differences within the Court. Table 15 records the tendency of the justices' dissenting and concurring opinions to give a broader or narrower interpretation of the Charter. This table includes concurring opinions which are often written to mark out a significant departure from the interpretation advanced in the main opinion on either the majority or dissenting side. Hence it is likely to give a fuller picture of the orientation of a justice's Charter jurisprudence. Table 15 shows an even sharper cleavage than the voting tables. Whereas not one of the concurring and dissenting opinions of L'Heureux-Dubé and McIntyre supported a broader

TABLE 15 **Direction of Charter Interpretation in Dissenting and Concurring Opinions**

	Broader	**Narrower**	**Same**
Wilson	28	2	1
Lamer	11	1	4
Dickson	12	1	3
Estey	2	4	1
Beetz	1	4	5
LeDain	2	4	2
LaForest	5	5	2
L'Heureux-Dubé	0	3	0
McIntyre	0	16	6

interpretation of the Charter section in question, all but three of those in which Wilson, Lamer, and Dickson have participated argue for a wider interpretation.

Tables 16 and 17 [omitted here] are a further index of judicial activism and judicial self-restraint. They focus on how the justices have responded to second-stage Charter decisions based on the section 1 "reasonable limitations" defence and section 24(2) motions to exclude unconstitutionally obtained evidence. The willingness of a justice to accept a section 1 defence of a statute that he or she has already found to limit a Charter right is an important indicator of self-restraint. Table 16 shows that L'Heureux-Dubé and LaForest were the justices most deferential to the legislature in applying section 1. Justice McIntyre, it would seem, was more inclined to exercise his self-restraint at the first stage of Charter cases by giving a narrow interpretation of Charter rights, thereby avoiding the need to even consider section 1 arguments in 14 cases.

The striking feature of Table 17 on the exclusion of evidence is not a polarization at opposite ends of the Court but the distinctive record of L'Heureux-Dubé and McIntyre. While most of the Court has been slightly more inclined to exclude evidence once a Charter violation has been established, these two justices have favoured admitting it by a ratio of more than 2:1. This pattern further supports the classification of L'Heureux-Dubé and McIntyre as exponents of judicial self-restraint, in this case driven perhaps by a "crime control" view of criminal justice.

The data presented in Tables 11 to 17 make it clear that there is growing disagreement on the Supreme Court over how the Charter should be interpreted. The number of unanimous decisions has decreased every year, while the number of dissenting opinions has risen steadily. Nor is this division random. The data show a clear pattern of voting blocs. The Court has divided into two wings and a centre. The activist wing is led by Justice Wilson and includes Justice Lamer and usually the Chief Justice. This bloc has provided the most consistent support for Charter litigants, given broader interpretations to Charter rights, and frequently dissented together—usually when the majority votes against the Charter claimant. They are also less likely to accept "section 1 defences" and more likely to exclude evidence under section 24(2).

The other wing exemplifies the philosophy of judicial self-restraint and has been led by Justice McIntyre. While McIntyre lacked reliable allies, he managed to attract all members of the Court to join him in dissent at least once, except for the three members of the activist wing. Since her appointment in 1987, Justice L'Heureux-Dubé has frequently voted with Justice McIntyre. Justice LaForest is an occasional member of this bloc. All of them have been much less likely to support Charter claims, tend to give narrower interpretations of the Charter, are more receptive toward "section 1 defences" and more reluctant to dismiss illegally obtained evidence. The "leader" labels apply to Wilson and McIntyre because they are on the opposite ends of the activist-restraint spectrum in every table but one. They also "lead" the Court in the number of dissents and the number of solo dissents, yet have never dissented together.

In sum, Wilson and McIntyre have developed very different theories of proper judicial review under the Charter, theories that consistently lead them to very different results. Lamer and Dickson seem to share Wilson's activist perspective, but are less consistent in following it. L'Heureux-Dubé and, to a lesser extent, LaForest are sympathetic to McIntyre's vision of judicial self-restraint. The other justices have hewn to a more pragmatic, middle ground. These differences make it clear that in "border line" cases—and thus far, no cases have involved clear-cut violations of well-established rights—it is the judge, not the Charter, that determines the outcome of the case.

This conclusion should come as no surprise to those familiar with the American Supreme Court. Particularly since 1937, it too has fragmented into different voting blocs with even wider discrepancies between the voting records of the judges. On the Burger Court (1968–1986), for example, support for civil liberties claims ranged from a high of 90.6 percent for Justice Douglas to a low of 19.6 percent for Justice Rehnquist.

Canadian and American experiences diverge at this point, however. In the U.S., the perception of federal judges as essentially political actors has given rise to an increasingly partisan competition over judicial appointments. The "Bork Affair" was only the most recent and most visible incident in this struggle. Such nakedly partisan attempts to shape the outcome of the Supreme Court's decisions by strategic judicial appointments sits poorly with traditional concepts of judicial independence and impartiality. In practice, however, it is consistent with interest group behaviour in contemporary Western democracies. As V.O. Key has written: "Where power rests, there influence will be brought to bear." Courts that act politically will come to be treated politically.

In Canada, however, there has thus far been no evidence that the federal government has let ideological criteria influence its Supreme Court appointments. Nor has there been much popular interest in following the American practice of subjecting the views of Supreme Court justices to public examination before they are appointed. Unlike Americans, it would appear that Canadians prefer to remain in a state of ideological innocence about their judges.

This traditional, legalistic view of judges may be the legacy of the dominant English influence in Canadian law prior to 1982. Further evidence of differences within the Court on Charter issues may well transform this condition in the future.

A recent exception to this is the apparently successful effort by Canadian feminist organizations to have the Canadian Judicial Centre sponsor special education seminars for judges on sexual equality and "systematic discrimination." From a political science/judicial process perspective, this is analogous to the efforts of American feminists to prevent judges like Robert Bork from being appointed, except that this "lobbying" occurs after the appointment and is directed at the appointee rather than the appointers. The common denominator of both tactics is the perception that judges can and do use their discretion in interpreting constitutional rights to alter public policy. Since there is no opportunity to exert influence prior to the appointment, such as the hearings of the Senate Judiciary Committee in the U.S., Canadian interest groups are forced to seek access after the appointment. This novel spectacle of "special education" seminars for judges provides just such a forum. Not surprisingly, anti-feminist groups have protested this "privileged audience" with the judges. Since presumably other Canadian interest groups would also welcome the opportunity to present their points of view to Canadian judges, it will be interesting to see whether this practice is expanded or eliminated.

At a minimum, the growing perception of "different judges, different rights" is likely to produce demands that the Supreme Court cease its current practice of sitting in panels of seven or fewer justices—something they did in approximately 75 percent of their first one hundred Charter decisions. In these cases, the outcome of a Charter challenge may be largely determined by the selection of justices for the panel that hears the case, rather than the merits of the case. The prospects of a Charter claimant are much better before a five-judge panel which includes Chief Justice Dickson and Justices Lamer and Wilson rather than one which includes Justices McIntyre, L'Heureux-Dubé, and LaForest. Awareness of this fact will generate increasing pressure to organize the Court's work so that all nine justices participate in Charter cases.

CONCLUSIONS

The Charter has ushered in a new era for the Supreme Court of Canada. Nineteen eighty-two marks a turning point for the Court equal in importance to the abolition of appeals to the J.C.P.C. in 1949. In only eight years, the Charter has come to constitute roughly one-quarter of the Supreme Court's annual workload. The Court has made a clean break with the British-style judicial self-restraint that characterized its interpretation of the 1960 Canadian Bill of Rights. The Court has upheld Charter claimants in 35 percent of its first one hundred decisions, and declared 19 statutes void for Charter infractions.

The comparable figures for the Bill of Rights were 15 percent and one statute. In all three of these important respects—composition of docket, success rate and nullification of statutes—there is no longer any appreciable difference between the Supreme Court's Charter work and the American Supreme Court's work under the Bill of Rights.

Like its American counterpart, the Supreme Court now routinely finds itself in the thick of the political process. Seventy-five percent of the Court's Charter work has dealt with legal rights and criminal justice. While most of these decisions have not touched on issues of great public interest, the exceptions are important: abortion and language rights in particular. The impact of the Charter on the provinces has been qualitatively greater than its effect on federal law-making.

Our study confirms a growing dissensus within the Court over Charter interpretation since 1986, and argues that this accounts for the decline of successful Charter challenges after 1985. We document the division on the Court between activists (Wilson and Lamer) and non-activists (McIntyre and L'Heureux-Dubé), and suggest that such division was more or less inevitable, given the inescapably contentious character of modern judicial review. Comparative data from American experience suggests that such division is to be expected and is even likely to increase.

For the country too, the Charter, which was promoted as an instrument of national unity, is ironically becoming a source of disunity so far as Quebec's relationship to the rest of Canada is concerned. The Supreme Court's application of the Charter, while by no means the sole explanation of this tendency, has been a contributing factor. Among the provinces, Quebec's legislature experienced the most serious reversals in the Supreme Court's first one hundred Charter cases. Likewise, the Quebec Court of Appeal has been reversed more often than any other provincial court of appeal. With respect to the Charter, Quebec may already be well on its way to becoming a distinct society.

SHORTCOMINGS AND DANGERS IN THE CHARTER

Roy Romanow

After the constitutional resolution was proclaimed in 1982 various symposia and conferences were held to discuss the impact of the new Charter of Rights on the life of Canadians. From the very beginning we all recognized that the Charter represented a dramatic shift in our political system from one based

From *Canadian Parliamentary Review*, Vol. 9, No. 1, Spring, 1986. By permission.

on political accommodation of conflicts to, in effect, a system of judicial intervention. We commented on the effect of the Charter in transferring responsibility for societal conflict from the political to the judicial process.

What we did not fully anticipate was exactly how widespread the phenomenon of transfer of authority was going to be. In the constitutional negotiations in 1980 we realized judges would henceforth be dealing with major political issues such as abortion, pornography, Sunday closing and capital punishment. What we did not foresee was the extent to which the basic rules for society, heretofore resolved by the political process—basic rules pertaining to social, economic and political issues—would be affected by the Charter. A challenge to Sunday closing by-laws as being unconstitutional was to be expected, but that the administration of the *Combines Investigation Act* or the right of trade unions to negotiate dues checkoffs or closed shops would also be challenged was less expected. Yet both of those cases have already been dealt with by the courts. It therefore seems that the Charter will be important not only in "traditional" human rights cases but it will have an essential political role in accommodating competing economic and social interests among groups, regions, the provinces and the federal government in ways which will have a profound implication for Parliament, and for Canada as a whole.

We must also not overlook some potential problems in the way the Charter will affect Canadian life. Many citizens are expecting genuine reform, through the Charter, when it comes to deserving Canadians, such as handicapped people. In classic civil rights cases, such as discrimination on the basis of race and religion, the Charter, once it has worked its way through the courts, will be a valuable weapon against discrimination and therefore improve our society. But in matters which do not lend themselves so readily to a traditional civil liberties approach, there is a danger that the aspirations raised by the Charter will not be fulfilled.

The Charter contains very general language. Its protection can be sought by the privileged and the powerful as well as by the disadvantaged. It will be argued, for example, that the Charter protects the right of corporations to operate without interference of consumer protection laws; that it prohibits political activities by trade unions, perhaps even that it is incompatible with progressive taxation. Adjudication of these kinds of Charter issues will now take place before the courts, and will go up the chain of judicial appeals. The cost of the proceedings will be more easily borne by the corporations and privileged people than by ordinary Canadians, the handicapped, the welfare recipients or the native people.

So the Charter can be an instrument for social progress but it can be something more than that unless we are vigilant as a society and as parliamentarians to make sure that we look beyond the pure black and white of the Charter and ask what kind of society we really want in Canada. We must insure that the kind of a system which has allowed us to develop as a humane, caring society in Canada continues. We have to be vigilant in the shift from the legislatures over to the court rooms.

Let me outline why the scope of the Charter was largely unforeseen. First of all, the Charter of Rights itself is an act of compromise. Section 1, the so-called derogation clause, is an act of compromise which does permit the political process to prevail in certain circumstances. Section 33, the "notwithstanding clause," is also compromise and there are other examples. Perhaps we thought that, because the Charter was a product of compromise, it would be not as far-reaching in its consequences as some might have hoped for and perhaps others had feared.

A second reason is the history, in Canada, of the interpretation of bills of rights. As we know, the Diefenbaker *Bill of Rights*, although it applied only to the federal law, permitted the courts to strike down discriminatory legislation. There was a short period where the court was very activist, but after the 1974 *Lavalle* decision the court adopted the position that it would not get into the policy determinations of what was good for our society, policy determinations as set out by Parliament and the legislatures. As a result, the Diefenbaker *Bill of Rights* was not given very much life by the courts in Canada. To some extent, some felt that would be the case with the Charter of Rights as well, even though the Charter is an amendment to the Constitution and not just an ordinary statute.

The expectations raised by the introduction of the Charter of Rights, however, have unleashed a new and fundamental attitudinal change toward the political process in Canada.

Former Prime Minister Trudeau described the Charter as both a shield and a sword on behalf of the average Canadian. The unleashing of this force has brought what some have described as a kind of "Americanized" search for rights, which makes the Canadian Charter of Rights and Freedoms different from the old Diefenbaker *Bill of Rights*. We have seen in many cases an importation of American jurisprudence. Not in the *acceptance* of that jurisprudence by the courts but in the *advocacy* of civil rights cases by counsel before the courts.

There is, of course, a distinct difference between American and Canadian society. Let me just give you one example. In the United States where they have had a *Bill of Rights* in the Constitution for some two hundred years, the ethos of the rugged individualist is much more imbedded than in Canada. The right to medical treatment in the United States has been frequently raised. In private hospitals in the United States a person who cannot pay for emergency treatment may be turned away. Those who argue for a right to medical treatment in the United States sometimes attempt to demonstrate that the protections in the American *Bill of Rights* to life and liberty should guarantee the access to medical treatment. They seek a remedy through legal action. In Canada, we have responded to the concern about medicare in a political fashion. There is no specific right to medical treatment found in any legal document including the Charter of Rights or the Diefenbaker *Bill of Rights*. There has been a political response to the need for medical treatment which reflects a belief that the community at large benefits if it pursues that particular objective.

My biggest concern about the Charter is that, in the search for individual rights unleashed by it, we forget to ask what are the demands of justice. I agree with the great English jurisprudential scholar John Finiss who said the conclusory force of aspirations to rights also has the potential to confuse the rational process of determining what justice requires. The question which must be addressed before the Charter can be effectively applied is "what are the demands of justice," as understood and applied to the Canadian ethic and the Canadian body politic.

There are many areas where this is an important and complicated question to answer. The question of trade unions is one. The trade union movement and legislation pertaining to the trade union movement are susceptible to challenges as a result of the Charter of Rights and Freedoms. We have several cases before the Supreme Court of Canada right now. Trade unions and their causes—the causes of wages, standard of living, poverty, technology, job security—are, in varying degrees, the issues of all Canadians. Trade union interests embrace not only individual rights but also collective rights. In the determination of the validity of laws permitting closed shops, membership dues and checkoffs, we have to guard against the total dismantlement of the trade union movement as a positive social force in our community as a whole because of alleged violations of individual freedom of choice.

We may have debates about this issue, but I would argue that other aspects of our society are in the same kind of a situation. If you look at some of the recent Supreme Court decisions, such as *Southam* v. *Hunter*, where the issues were the right of the public to make sure that the freedom of the press was maintained by breaking down monopolies and due process, the corporate interest won. In the *Big M Drug Mart* case, where the issue was Sunday closing, the corporate interest won. The cruise missile case was again a public interest versus a government interest. Who won? Although these cases were concerned with complex legal issues (and I am doing a disservice for dealing with them so summarily), the danger here, in my opinion, is that in the context of the Charter of Rights and the interpretation of it by the courts of our country, we may see a dismantling of the values and the principles, collective and individual, which are the foundation of our society.

This may be a pessimistic view of the Charter, and perhaps too critical of the courts who, after all, are well qualified to decide many of these issues. But in other ways courts are not as well qualified as parliamentarians to ask "What are individual rights all about, and what are the demands of justice?"

The Charter must be a vehicle for justice. In order to ensure that, I would argue we must look for ways and means to support, financially and otherwise, those individuals and organizations which have as their mandate the advancement and the protection of the disadvantaged in our society. Bluntly speaking, this means money. The Charter will be used by the large corporations and the large school boards just as easily as by individuals, in fact more easily. We need to, I think, as an institution fund organizations through mechanisms like LEAF, the Legal Education Action Fund.

Secondly, we must accept the fact that the Charter, while an important tool for the advancement of individual human rights, is limited. It talks about protection and advancement of equality "before and under the law" but it is not in itself a mechanism for solving social and political problems facing this country. There is an important political role for Parliament and the legislatures to play. This role may be anticipatory. It may mean introducing legislation in advance of a court decision thus complying with the provisions of the Charter in a way which thwarts possible negative judicial intervention. It is still the role of politicians to accommodate the interests of the disadvantaged and the needy and to articulate the interest of the collectivity.

And finally, what parliamentarians and others interested in the law have to do is to rethink the manner in which the courts have traditionally fulfilled their functions. As you know, the courts are responsible to no one, except other judges. They are not elected. Now more than ever their judgements have to be clear, logical, and reasonable in order for us to understand what they mean. Perhaps we should look to a new method of appointing judges. If they are going to be so important in deciding these kinds of political issues then maybe it is time that our parliamentary institutions, in full daylight, if I may put it that way, examine carefully exactly who is going to be deciding these very important economic and social trade-offs.

I want to make one last point as a "provincialist" if I might. Heretofore, in constitutional matters, our courts have been basically dealing with division of powers issues. Does a piece of provincial legislation fall within the scope of the constitutional powers assigned to that province? It has been a great system because it has allowed flexibility. It has permitted people, if I may use my own province of Saskatchewan as an example, to experiment and to do things under our constitutional mandate which have become part of what it means to be Canadian. I use medicare, again, as an example. We did that under our provincial constitutional powers.

I could cite other examples of the flexible federalism which has permitted diversity within a united nation. I think we want to preserve this kind of body politic. I think we want to make sure that there is not too much uniformity as the result of the Court's interpretation of the Charter, and the natural levelling tendency in the interpretation of the Charter. We want to make sure that flexible federalism, which has been the genius of Canadian political life, is maintained. That too will require a very active legislature and Parliament.

QUEBEC'S USE OF THE NOTWITHSTANDING CLAUSE WAS RIGHT

Reg Whitaker

If there were any lingering doubts about the profound impact of the Charter of Rights on Canadian politics, they have been forcefully removed by the crisis precipitated by the Supreme Court's decision on the constitutionality of Quebec's language law (the so-called "Law 101"). Within a week of the decision, the largest and most militant nationalist demonstrations in more than a decade swept Montreal, the Quebec government felt compelled to override both the federal Charter and its own human rights code in amending the language law, three Quebec cabinet ministers resigned in protest, and the Meech Lake constitutional accord was thrown into grave doubt. A handful of judges armed with the Charter have certainly shown that they can turn Canada upside down in a hurry.

Expressions of regret, or even outrage, at Quebec's use of the notwithstanding clause to override the Charter of Rights, seem to have been nearly universal throughout English Canada. There is something very suspicious about this sudden English Canadian rejection of the principle of the notwithstanding clause, Section 33 of the Charter. Not only is it in strange contrast to the insistence on the inclusion of this clause by the provincial premiers in 1981, but it is also in strange contrast to the near-universal silence which greeted the use of s.33 by the Saskatchewan government of Grant Devine a few years ago, in a bill legislating striking provincial employees back to work. Could it be that English Canada has a double standard for interpreting its constitutional principles? Could it be that this principle (that individual or minority rights should not be overridden) appears in all its majestic clarity only when it is the rights of the anglophone minority in Quebec which are in question? Certainly the example of Manitoba Premier Gary Filmon seems to lend credibility to this interpretation: the man who brought the legislature of Manitoba to a halt in order to deny franco-Manitobans rights directed by a Supreme Court decision suddenly discovers the inalienable nature of minority rights! If the spectacle were not so profoundly sad, it would be hilarious.

Under these circumstances, it is worth pondering just what state the country would now be in if the override clause had not been available to the Quebec government.

The sign provisions of 101 are strongly supported by the majority in Quebec. This is partly for reasons intrinsic to the purposes of the language law. If French is to be secured within the boundaries of Quebec, it is important to maintain an urban landscape of signs and symbols that reinforces the predominance of

From *Policy Options*, Vol. 10, No. 4, May, 1989, published by The Institute for Research on Public Policy. By permission.

French, and clearly indicates to immigrants the linguistic character of the province.

Nowhere else in Canada or North America is there a secure base for the French language; only Quebec has the capacity to legislate the external reassurances that it is truly home to francophones. This may be symbolism, but it is deeply important symbolism that the majority will not allow to be snatched away—especially by a federal court sitting in Ottawa.

In fact, the Court itself recognized that the maintenance of a *"visage linguistique"* (the Court used the French phrase even in its English text) is a valid purpose of public policy, which could even justify the legislation of the "marked predominance" of French over English in commercial advertising.

It is also symbolic in another, related sense. The Supreme Court's ability (in the absence of the override power) to threaten the integrity of the sign provisions of 101 raises the spectre of the "thin-end-of-the-wedge." If the courts could gut the sign provisions of 101 under Charter guarantees of freedom of expression, what might prevent further challenges to the more important parts of the law, especially the language-of-work sections?

Assurance that the francophone majority can earn a living in their own language is absolutely vital to the intent of 101; without it, the law would be merely empty rhetoric. Is it really necessary to reiterate the past history of injustice, whereby the francophone majority were subordinated in the workplace to the language of the minority who happened to control the levers of economic power? Such a situation was intolerable, but no more intolerable than a judicial attack on the legislative instrument which has helped the majority to emancipate itself from this subordination.

An insecure legislative guarantee of the French language is clearly intolerable to a linguistic majority in Quebec which is also a tiny minority in an anglophone North America.

The security provided by 101 has underwritten Quebec's continued adherence to Canadian federalism—as some honest anglophones in Quebec have admitted, although more often in private than in public. The corollary of this proposition is obvious: if the notwithstanding clause did not exist to protect 101 or its successors, independence would once again become a viable option.

On grounds of political prudence, both the existence of s.33 and its use by the Bourassa government seem amply justified. But the anti-Quebec clamour which has broken out in English Canada explicitly eschews reasoning based on political prudence. Instead, the issue has been debated as a question of *rights*.

More precisely, the question has been couched as a conflict between "collective rights," claimed by Quebec and rejected by English Canada, and "individual rights," claimed by English Canada and rejected by Quebec.

Premier Robert Bourassa explicitly noted that in coming up with an amended version of 101, he was compelled to make a "difficult adjudication" between individual and collective rights. His three anglophone ministers who resigned cited their adherence to individual over collective rights. Politicians outside

Quebec have echoed this argument in condemning Bourassa's decision—including some politicians who were pretty reluctant to accept the idea of an entrenched Charter of Rights when it was advanced by the Trudeau Liberal government in 1980–81.

Yet even taken at face value, this philosophical debate misses the first test of political relevance: it does not deal with the facts. In the distinction between individual and collective rights regarding language there is less than meets the eye. To hear English Canadian politicians talk, one would think that the primacy of individual rights had been (to quote one resigning Quebec minister) "imbibed with their mother's milk." Are memories so short that we must be reminded that the Charter of Rights is less than seven years old? Or that so-called collective rights are much older and more deeply entrenched in our constitutional and political practices?

In the BNA Act of 1867 there is no reference to individual rights, as such. There are clear references to collective rights in regard to language and religious education. The language provisions (s.133) state that laws, parliamentary debates and court proceedings may be in either English or French at the federal level—and in Quebec.

The latter was the only province of which bilingualism was demanded and it is clear from the context that the object of s.133 was to protect the collective rights of the anglophone minority. For the same reasons, Quebec alone was saddled with an appointed upper chamber of its legislature (abolished only in the 1960s), the purpose of which was to protect the anglophone Protestants of Quebec from the francophone Catholic majority.

Similarly s.93, dealing with minority education, is premised upon the collective rights concept: separate schools are guaranteed for the "Queen's Protestant and Roman Catholic subjects," where they form minorities. This provision, recently upheld by the Supreme Court in the Ontario separate schools reference case against a challenge based on the Charter, is as forceful a statement of collective rights as can be imagined. Again, in the context of the 1867 act, it is clear that the main object was to protect the Protestant minority in Quebec.

In short, the concept of collective rights is an original element of the Canadian constitution, one which is arguably better entrenched than the more recent concern with individual rights. It is ironic that collective rights were largely designed to serve the anglophone Protestant minority of Quebec, the very minority which is now claiming the primacy of individual rights against the threat of the collective rights of the francophone majority.

Of course, much has changed in the nature of Canadian society and politics since 1867 to alter the contextual meaning of rights in the late twentieth century. On the one hand, the adoption of the Charter of Rights is both a cause and effect of a growing rights-consciousness among the Canadian people.

This assertiveness has found expression both in individual rights and in the growth of what may be called "group rights." The latter lie somewhere between collective and individual rights, in that they express group conditions of disability and unequal treatment (women, visible ethnic minorities, disabled people, etc.), without recognizing any collective body as exercising the rights. The "distinct society" clause of the Meech Lake Accord, on the other hand, seems to reaffirm the older collective rights notion, in that the Quebec government is designated as bearing the right, and obligation, to advance the distinct character of Quebec society.

A second, and crucial, contextual factor is the rise of the new Quebec nationalism and the renegotiation of the fundamental bargain which has underlain the relations between English and French Canada. Parts of this bargain are evident in the revised constitution of 1982, the Official Languages Act, Quebec's language law, and the "distinct society" clause. Since this bargain is threatening to unravel over the bilingual signs issue, it is important to understand just what is involved, and what is not.

Like many important political accommodations striking a delicate balance between conflicting social forces, it is the essence of this bargain that it is tacit, and not articulated in the clear and unequivocal language of constitutional principles. In societies divided along lines of linguistic and cultural community, universalist principles may only deepen divisions. Skillful compromises which do not speak their name are usually wiser, although difficult to sustain.

The language sections of the Charter of Rights were designed by former Prime Minister Pierre Trudeau in the name of individual rights. The Parti Québécois launched 101 in the name of collective rights. Irreconcilable principles? In practice, not at all. Individual language rights actually presuppose collective rights: two language groups, English and French, are recognized as having an historically privileged priority, one not accorded to other linguistic groups. The Liberal view was not as far away from the PQ position as the rhetoric indicated. And indeed, in practice the Liberal position was much more flexible than might have been anticipated.

As for the PQ position, its apparent hard-line defence of collective rights was by no means as illiberal as many have assumed. Even the philosophical defence of 101 upon its first introduction in the National Assembly by Dr. Camille Laurin—always considered the most culturally nationalist of PQ ministers— was rather liberal in inspiration.

French, argued Dr. Laurin, was at a distinct disadvantage in North America and it was the obligation of the government of Quebec to intervene so as to right that disadvantage and thereby guarantee equality of opportunity for francophones.

In keeping with this liberal perspective, the traditional rights of the anglophone minority were protected by 101. Indeed, every aspect of English language use touching upon freedom of expression as traditionally understood (but not commercial signs) was protected: anglophones are free to express themselves in their own English language media and institutions of education, as well as to receive health and social services in their own language. So concerned was the PQ to maintain a liberal face to their legislation that they withdrew a clause in the original draft of 101 that would have exempted the law from the Quebec Charter of Human Rights—to the ultimate chagrin of the Quebec government, when this was used against 101 in the Supreme Court decision.

However tempered with liberalism, the legislative intent of 101 is at bottom concerned with sovereignty—but not sovereignty in the sense of sovereignty-association or independence. Rather, language is a sovereignty issue in Quebec in that it revolves around the sovereign right of the Quebec community, through those political institutions under its control, to legislate the priority of the French language within the boundaries of the community.

The historical irony is that the PQ's very success in framing and implementing a clear, effective and relatively liberal language law—arguably its major achievement in two terms in office—was also the single act which did most to undermine the PQ's own option for sovereignty-association. If Quebec could exercise sovereignty in legislating language within the framework of the Canadian federation, perhaps it did not require sovereignty in the full political sense. Here indeed was the very basis for a tacit accommodation between the Liberal federalists and the PQ *indépendentistes*. The protection of the essentials of 101 could underwrite Quebec's continued membership in the federation.

Despite the apparent antagonism between the Lévesque and Trudeau governments, the writing of the language provisions of the Charter of Rights in 1980–81 constitutes a compromise between the spirit of national bilingualism as an individual right and the collective right of Quebec to make the French language secure within its jurisdiction.

S.23 of the Charter on minority language educational rights was drawn up in such a way as to prevent any possible challenge to one of the key provisions of 101: the requirement that immigrants to Quebec have their children educated in French. Along with the language of work, this is perhaps the most crucial part of 101, given the demographic threat to a francophone majority in Montreal posed by the previous tendency of immigrants to opt for English language schooling.

In effect, the Trudeau government secured this section from a Charter challenge. Moreover, s.15 on equality rights did *not* include "language" as one of the explicit grounds upon which individuals could claim they were suffering from discrimination. Although this may not be enough to prevent a challenge to the language-of-work sections of 101, it would make such a challenge more difficult to sustain.

Interestingly enough, the silence of the federal Charter equality sections regarding language stands in contrast to Quebec's Human Rights Charter, which boldly states that, "Every person has a right to full and equal recognition and exercise of his human rights and freedoms, without distinction . . . based on [among other categories] language."

It should be noted as well that the Quebec code refers to all aspects of life within Quebec, while the federal Charter is limited to relations between citizens and the state. In other words, the federal definition of language rights is more circumscribed and, in this sense at least, less liberal than the Quebec definition. It is no accident that the federal Charter drafters showed such caution.

These little-heralded compromises suggest a deeper compromise. There was no desire to undermine 101 once it was recongized that to do so would be subversive of the federalist position in Quebec. In the end, the collective rights position and the individual rights position dovetailed together.

The Mulroney position on language rights after 1984 does not seem to differ in any significant way from his predecessor; if anything, as prime minister, Brian Mulroney has been more forthcoming with praise for the Quebec language law than Trudeau could ever allow himself to be in public. One may thus speak with some confidence of bipartisan continuity in Ottawa (much to the chagrin of certain Tory backbenchers).

Of course, neither side could publicly admit what in practice had happened. Trudeau was unwilling to admit that to win his struggle to keep Quebec in Canada, he had had to give way on the principal ground of individual rights. The PQ would not admit that sovereignty had been rendered less attractive by their own achievement in securing the place of the French language. It would be wrong to suggest any explicit understanding, as such. Historic compromises may sometimes be easier if neither party draws up a list of demands for negotiations, but each allows the force of circumstance to rule.

Such compromises are also inherently unstable, as conditions change. The PQ, especially once it was out of office, was increasingly disposed to welcome the weakening of 101 by judicial review, so as to encourage a revival of separatist sentiment. To this same end, the PQ has contributed in its own way to the heightening of linguistic tensions between the majority and minority language communities in Montreal.

For its part, the federal position has an Achilles heel in regard to the position of the francophone minorities outside Quebec. It is the essence of this tacit accommodation that no facile equation can be made between majorities and minorities in Quebec and the rest of Canada.

The francophones of Quebec are a majority only in that province, but a weak and threatened minority in the larger picture. Extraordinary measures are required to protect the French language within the sole jurisdiction where French is the majority tongue. Francophone minorities outside Quebec are doubly vulnerable and deserve some constitutional protection and an attitude of liberality on the part of the anglophone majority which is in no way threatened in the security of its language.

The case of the anglophones of Quebec is not analogous to the francophone minorities outside Quebec: Quebec anglophones constitute a minority tied to an overwhelming linguistic and cultural majority outside the province, which, moreover, enjoys an institutional network of support within Quebec (English education from primary school to university; English language TV and radio stations and newspapers, etc.), which is unparalleled among linguistic minorities in Canada.

How curious that it is the English Canadian politicians—contrary to cultural stereotypes—who are insisting on Cartesian rigour in equating majorities and minorities across Canada, while it is Quebec politicians who are pleading for the recognition of special circumstances. Quebec is right. Cartesian logic may be satisfying to rationalist philosophers but when applied to the untidy world of politics its effect can be mischievous.

The Supreme Court has, in one blunt action, threatened a delicate and complex balance between individual and collective rights. To be sure, the justices tried to soften the blow by admitting that the intent of 101 to maintain a certain *visage linguistique* was valid public policy. Unfortunately, they then muddied the waters by suggesting that while French could be granted even "marked predominance," the blanket denial of the use of English on signs did constitute an infringement on freedom of expression (defined for this purpose as including commercial advertising).

The Quebec legislature was then directed to wrestle with the unenviable task of determining what would constitute an acceptable level of "marked predominance." Would a ratio of 2- or 3-to-1 be acceptable, while a ratio of 10- or 20-to-1 would be unacceptable?

If so, why? The Court was no help at all in this. The National Assembly might have been forgiven for invoking the notwithstanding clause out of sheer irritation, if nothing else. In any event, since the language law is, as I have already suggested, essentially a sovereignty issue to the Quebec community, any interference by a federal court would be unacceptable, so the exact degree of judicial meddling is, in a sense, irrelevant.

Whether or not the Court's reasoning can be considered good jurisprudence I will leave to others more qualified to determine. But this question begs another, more important question: is good jurisprudence necessarily political prudence? In this case the answer is clear, and unsettling. The Court might be "right" legally and at the same time very wrong politically.

Should Canadians regret the use of the notwithstanding clause? No. We should rather see its use in this case as a demonstration of the wisdom of maintaining such a clause in the Charter. It may be the only way to temper the political havoc which could otherwise be wrought by the rationalist application of individual rights without regard to circumstance—especially in a society divided by language and culture.

Any attempt to remove the notwithstanding clause from the constitution, as has been rashly suggested by some English Canadian politicians, would under present circumstances be an act of folly. It would quite justifiably be seen by Quebec as an attempt to remove its capacity to defend its vital interests. However symbolically satisfying the distinct society clause of Meech Lake might be to the Quebec government, the notwithstanding clause offers a surer, tested guarantee of the integrity of the Quebec community.

NO, IT WAS WRONG

P.K. Kuruvilla

Since announcing his decision to invoke the notwithstanding clause of the Canadian Charter of Rights and Freedoms to ban all but French outdoor commercial signs in Quebec, Premier Robert Bourassa has presented at least five major arguments to justify his action.

First, francophones in Quebec constitute a frail and small minority in North America and his government, therefore, has a responsibility to protect their language, culture and identity by taking extraordinary measures when necessary. Second, francophones in Quebec simply want to feel at home in their own province, be masters in their own house, and to run their own affairs. Third, Quebec is sovereign within its own jurisdiction and its obligation to bilingualism at present need not go beyond the requirements of the Constitution Act of 1867 and the 1982 Constitution, which are restricted to the legislature, courts and educational institutions. Fourth, Quebec has no lessons to learn from any other provinces on the protection of minorities. And fifth, the rest of Canada must accept that Quebec is a very distinct society in which the collective rights of francophones have predominance over individual rights contained in the Charter of Rights and Freedoms, or Quebec might once again seriously consider the option of separation.

It seems unrealistic to expect the federal Tories, who have been lately politically in bed with Premier Bourassa, or the opposition parties who have been falling over each other in supporting the Meech Lake Accord, hoping vainly to win votes in Quebec, to stand up now and put their boots to Mr. Bourassa for his betrayal of the anglophones in his province. Nevertheless, if they would pull up their socks and take a closer look at his arguments, it should be clear to them that they are lamentably light on logic and fairness.

For instance, take his first argument: the highest court in the land, while conceding the importance of safeguarding the predominant status of the French language and culture in Quebec, had cautioned him in no uncertain terms that he could promote the preponderance of French, but not at the expense of the freedom of expression of the anglophones and other non-francophones in his province. Similarly, even if he is sincere, is it realistic to

From *Policy Options*, Vol. 10, No. 4, May, 1989, published by The Institute for Research on Public Policy. By permission.

hope that by systematically suppressing some of the basic linguistic and cultural rights of the anglophone minority in Quebec, he can put an end to the inevitable and perennial pull of the Canadian and U.S. mass culture and remain solidly French in North America?

So also, even if English signs are a true impediment in the path of French language and culture, how could a "compromise" which bans them from outside improve the situation? As several critics have correctly asked, since people presumably spend at least as much time inside stores as outside them, how can they be stopped from viewing both linguistic faces? As a newspaper editorial succinctly pointed out, perhaps the real purpose of the ban against exterior English signs may be simply to send a clear and unmistakable message to the anglophone minority in Quebec—a message which tells them, "You don't belong here . . . your language pollutes the atmosphere and even to see it on a sign is an insult; pack up and go."

Furthermore, the alleged frailty of the French language and culture in North America cannot be by any stretch of imagination a totally new phenomenon. Having ostensibly survived all historical hostile forces and even prospered for over a century, does Quebec now have to go out of its way to extinguish minority language rights and to help fan the flames of francophone nationalism?

In the same way, if it had to be done, why did Quebec's own Charter of Rights take the trouble of promising freedom of expression to all Quebeckers in the first place? Why did the Liberal party in Quebec bother to include bilingualism as a major plank in its platform until recently? Above all, why did Mr. Bourassa himself make his election pledge in 1985 to make French predominant on signs but not to forbid other languages?

Concerning Mr. Bourassa's second argument, one can easily understand why francophones want to feel at home in their province and be masters in their own house. However, here again, as the Supreme Court painstakingly pointed out in its judgement, "the exclusivity for the French language" which they want to establish in order to attain this goal does not accurately reflect the reality of their present-day society. Notwithstanding what Quebec's ultra nationalists like Mr. Bourassa may fondly wish, that reality cannot and must not exclude the legitimate interests of anglophones and other minority groups in their midst.

Concerning Mr. Bourassa's third argument, which is based on Quebec's obligation under bilingualism, it must not be overlooked that during the past two decades, the federal government has been committed to bilingualism in a big way and billions of dollars have been spent to provide it across the country and to bridge the linguistic and cultural gap between anglophones and the francophones. Many enlightened Canadians outside Quebec have also been feeling a certain sense of pride about the various measures their national government has taken to repair past injustices towards French Canadians and the linguistic neighbourliness they themselves have been nurturing.

More recently, most other provinces have also been steadily inching their way along the road to bilingualism, by bestowing more educational and other rights on their francophone minorities in a political and practical, if not strictly constitutional, manner. It is true that Quebec has not been begging for bilingualism. Nevertheless, it is unfortunate that at a time when the rest of Canada has been assiduously attempting to make more accommodation and steadily stretching its hand of goodwill and better neighbourliness, Quebec under both the Parti Québécois and the Liberals has been stubbornly spurning it and systematically sowing the seeds of discord between its francophone and anglophone communities.

Regarding the argument that Quebec has no lessons to receive from other provinces and it has the best-treated minority, one is in fact at a loss to fathom which other provinces recently have so wantonly and vengefully legislated the use of language to deprive their minorities of their traditionally enjoyed freedom of expression, including "commercial expression" as Quebec has done. One may also add that it is very unlikely that the minority rights Mr. Bourassa is boasting about would have existed merely because of the good nature and generosity of the government of Quebec. On the contrary, these rights may have been grudgingly tolerated until now simply because they were constitutionally stipulated at the inception of the federation. Fortunately for the minorities, the BNA Act did not contain a notwithstanding clause which a Quebec government could have blissfully exploited whenever it wished, as Mr. Bourassa is now able to do.

Finally, on closer scrutiny, the argument based on the paramountcy of collective rights and the possibility of separation does not seem to hold much water. First, the Supreme Court has already categorically rejected the notion that the collective rights of francophones must have priority over individual rights in the Charter. One might also ask: suppose the anglophone majority in the country is also inclined to adopt an insensitive and undemocratic attitude towards francophones in Quebec and elsewhere, what would be the ramifications for francophones?

Furthermore, the paramountcy of the collective rights of francophones and the possibility of Quebec's separation from the rest of Canada are precisely two of the principal planks in the Parti Québécois platform as well. It is difficult to comprehend the rationale and propriety of a supposedly non-separatist party callously raising the spectre of separatism as soon as its own cultural agenda begins to clash with that of the rest of the country.

It is obvious that our political system is predicated on the lofty presumption that its constituent parts, while pursuing their legitimate self-interest, would show respect for the needs of the country as a whole and make necessary compromises however difficult they might be, in order to strengthen the sinews of its nationhood.

However, the government of Quebec at the present time seems to be almost exclusively concerned about its own future and not the future of Canada as a whole. Needless to say, if it continues to be parochially preoccupied with province-building only and no nation-building at all, sooner or later, Canada as we know it today will have to cease to exist, with Quebec no more an integral part of it.

BIBLIOGRAPHY

Constitution

(See also Bibliographies in Chapters 5 and 12.)

Asch, M. *Home and Native Land: Aboriginal Rights and the Canadian Constitution.* Toronto: Nelson, 1988.

Cairns, A.C. *Constitution, Government and Society in Canada: Selected Essays.* Toronto: M. & S., 1988.

Canadian Government Publishing Centre, *Constitution of Canada, Office Consolidation, 1867–1982.* Ottawa: S. and S., 1984.

Cheffins, R. I., and Johnson, P.A. *The Revised Canadian Constitution: Politics as Law.* Toronto: McG.-H.R., 1986.

Conklin, W. *Images of a Constitution.* Toronto: U.T.P., 1989.

Forsey, E.A. *Freedom and Order: Collected Essays.* Toronto: M.& S., 1974.

Heard, A. "Recognizing the Variety among Constitutional Conventions." *C.J.P.S.*, 22, 1, March, 1989.

Hogg, Peter. *Constitutional Law of Canada.* Toronto: Carswell, 2nd ed., 1985.

Hogg, P.W. *Canada Act Annotated.* Toronto: Carswell, 1982.

La Forest, G.V. *Disallowance and Reservation of Provincial Legislation.* Ottawa: Department of Justice, 1955.

Laskin, B. *Canadian Constitutional Law: Cases, Text, and Notes on Distribution of Legislative Power.* Toronto: Carswell, 4th ed., 1975.

Lederman, W.R. *Continuing Canadian Constitutional Dilemmas: Essays on the Constitutional History, Public Law, and Federal Systems of Canada.* Toronto: Butterworths, 1981.

Lysyk, K. "Constitutional Reform and the Introductory Clause of Section 91: Residual and Emergency Law-Making Authority." *C.B.R.*, 57, 1979.

McWhinney, E. *Constitution-making: Principles, Process, Practice.* Toronto: U.T.P., 1981.

Meekison, J.P., Romanow, R.J., and Moull, W.D. *Origins and Meaning of Section 92A: The Constitutional Amendment on Resources.* Montreal: I.R.P.P., 1985.

Milne, D. *The New Canadian Constitution.* Toronto: Lorimer, rev. ed., 1989.

Monahan, P. *Politics and the Constitution: The Charter, Federalism and the Supreme Court of Canada.* Toronto: Methuen, 1987.

Russell, P.H., (ed.). *Leading Constitutional Decisions*, Carleton Library No. 23, Toronto: M. & S., rev. ed., 1973.

Sharman, C. "The Strange Case of a Provincial Constitution: The British Columbia Constitution Act." *C.J.P.S.*, XVII, 1, March 1984.

Strayer, B.L. *The Canadian Constitution and the Courts.* Toronto: Butterworths, 2nd ed., 1983.

Verney, D.V. "Parliamentary Supremacy versus Judicial Review: Is Compromise Possible." *Journal of Commonwealth and Comparative Politics*, 27, 2, July, 1987.

Vipond, R.C. "Constitutional Politics and the Legacy of the Provincial Rights Movement in Canada." *C.J.P.S.*, 18, 2, June, 1985.

Whyte, J.D., and Lederman, W.R., (eds.). *Canadian Constitutional Law: Cases, Notes, and Materials on the Distribution and Limitation of Legislative Powers Under the Constitution of Canada.* Toronto: Butterworths, 2nd ed., 1977.

Yalden, R. "Liberalism and Canadian Constitutional Law: Tensions in an Evolving Vision of Liberty." *U.T.F.L.R.*, 47, 2, Fall, 1988.

Bilingualism and Biculturalism

(See also Bibliography in Chapter 12, "Bilingualism and Biculturalism.")

Allaire, U., and Miller, R.E. *Canadian Business Response to the Legislation on Francization in the Workplace.* Toronto: C.D. Howe Institute, 1980.

Association of Canadian Studies. *Demolinguistic Trends and the Evolution of Canadian Institutions.* Montreal: 1989.

Beaujot, R.P. "A Demographic View on Canadian Language Policy." *C.P.P.*, V, 1, Winter, 1979.

Beaupre, R.M. *Construing Bilingual Legislation in Canada.* Toronto: Butterworths, 1980.

Breton, A., and Breton, R. *Why Disunity? An Analysis of Linguistic and Regional Cleavages in Canada.* Montreal: I.R.P.P., 1980.

Canada, Commissioner of Official Languages. *Annual Report, 1989.* Ottawa: S. and S., 1989. (Annually from 1971.)

Canada, Commissioner of Official Languages. *Language and Society.* Ottawa: 1987. (Quarterly, commencing 1987).

Canada. *A Preliminary Report of the Royal Commission on Bilingualism and Biculturalism.* Ottawa: Q.P., 1965.

Canada. *Report of the Royal Commission on Bilingualism and Biculturalism.* Ottawa: Q.P. Book 1, *General Introduction and the Official Languages*, 1967; Book II, *Education*, 1968; Book III, *The Work World*, 2 vols., 1969; Book IV, *The Cultural Contributions of the Other Ethnic Groups*, 1970; Books V, VI, *Federal Capital and Voluntary Associations*, 1970.

Cartwright, D.C. *Official Language Populations in Canada: Patterns and Contacts.* Montreal: I.R.P.P., 1980.

Doern, R. *The Battle over Bilingualism: The Manitoba Language Question, 1983–85.* Winnipeg: Cambridge, 1985.

Gibson, F.W., (ed.). *Cabinet Formation and Bicultural Relations: Seven Case Studies.* Studies of the Royal Commission on Bilingualism and Biculturalism, No. 6. Ottawa: Q.P., 1970.

Gill, R.M. "Language Policy in Saskatchewan, Alberta and British Columbia and the Future of French in the West." *A.R.C.S.*, 15, 1, Spring, 1985.

Lachapelle, R., and Henripin, J. *The Demolinguistic Situation in Canada.* Montreal: I.R.P.P., 1982.

La Federation des Francophones hors Québec. *The Heirs of Lord Durham: Manifesto of a Vanishing People.* Toronto: Burns and MacEachern, 1978.

Laponce, J. *Languages and Their Territories.* Toronto: U.T.P., 1987.

Russell, P. *The Supreme Court of Canada as a Bilingual and Bicultural Institution,* Documents of the Royal Commission on Bilingualism and Biculturalism, No. 1. Ottawa: Queen's Printer, 1969.

Wardhangh, R. *Language and Nationhood: The Canadian Experience.* Vancouver: New Star, 1983.

Amending the Constitution

(See also other sections in this Bibliography and Chapter 3 for Meech Lake.)

Chandler, M. "Constitutional Change and Public Policy: The Impact of the Resource Amendment (Section 92A)." *C.J.P.S.*, 19, 1, March, 1986.

Kilgour, D.M. "A Formal Analysis of the Amending Formula of Canada's Constitution

Act, 1982." *C.J.P.S.*, 16, 4, December, 1983. (See also comments by Levesque and Moore, *ibid.*, 17, 1, March, 1984, and comment by Mintz and reply by Kilgour, *ibid.*, 18, 2, June, 1985.)

LaSelva, S.V. "Federalism and Unanimity: The Supreme Court and Constitutional Amendment." *C.J.P.S.*, 16, 4, December, 1983.

Meekison, J.P., Romanow, R.J., and Moull, W.D. *Origin and Meaning of Section 92A: The Constitutional Amendment on Resources.* Montreal: I.R.P.P, 1985.

Russell, P., *et al. The Court and the Constitution: The Supreme Court Reference on Constitutional Amendment.* Kingston: Queen's University, I.I.R., 1982.

Smith, J. "Origins of the Canadian Amendment Dilemma." *D.L.R.*, 61, 1981/1982.

The Charter and Civil Rights

(See also other sections in this Bibliography.)

Anisman, P., and Linden, A.,, (eds.). *The Media, The Courts and the Charter.* Toronto: Carswell, 1986.

Bayefsky, A.F. "Parliamentary Sovereignty and Human Rights in Canada." *Political Studies.* 21, 2, June, 1983.

Bayefsky, A., and Eberts, M., (eds.). *Equality Rights and the Canadian Charter of Rights and Freedoms.* Toronto: Carswell, 1985.

Beatty, D. *Putting the Charter to Work.* Montreal: McG.-Q.U.P., 1987.

Becton, C., and MacKay, A.W. *The Courts and the Charter.* Toronto: U.T.P., 1985.

Belobaba, E.P., and Gertner, E., (eds.). "The New Constitution and the Charter of Rights: Fundamental Issues and Strategies." *Supreme Court Law Review*, 1982.

Berger, T. *Fragile Freedoms: Human Rights and Dissent in Canada.* Toronto: Clarke Irwin, 1981.

Bilodeau, R., (ed.). *Human Rights and Affirmative Action.* Montreal: Canadian Human Rights Foundation, 1985.

Borovoy, A. *When Freedoms Collide: The Case for Our Civil Liberties.* Toronto: L. & O. D., 1988.

Boyer, J.P. *Equality For All, Report of the Parliamentary Committee on Equality Rights.* Ottawa: S. and S., 1984.

Boyle, C. *et al. Charterwatch: Reflections on Equality.* Toronto: Carswell, 1987.

Colvin, E. "Section Seven of the Canadian Charter of Rights and Freedoms." *C.B.R.*, 68, September 1989.

Côté, A., and Lemonde, L. *Discrimination et Commission des droits de la personne.* Montréal, Saint-Martin, 1988.

Dworaczek, M. *The Canadian Bill of Rights and the Charter of Rights and Freedoms: A Bibliography.* Monticello, New York: Vance, 1987.

Elkins, D. "Facing Our Destiny: Rights and Canadian Distinctiveness." *C.J.P.S.*, 22, 4, December, 1989.

Flanagan, T., Knopff, R., and Archer, K. "Selection Bias in Human Rights Tribunals: An Exploratory Study." *C.P.A.*, 31, 4, Winter, 1988.

Fogarty, K. *Equality Rights and the Limitations in the Charter.* Toronto: Carswell, 1987.

Gibson, D. "Reasonable Limits Under the Canadian Charter of Rights and Freedoms." *Manitoba Law Journal*, 15, 1, 1985.

Green, L. "Are Language Rights Fundamental?" *O.H.L.J.*, 25, 1987.

Greene, I. *The Charter of Rights.* Toronto: Lorimer, 1989.

Hiebert, J. "Fair Elections and Freedom of Expression under the Charter." *J.C.S.*, 24, 4, Winter, 1989–90.

Hiebert, J. "The Evolution of the Limitation Clause." *O.H.L.J.*, 28, 1, Spring, 1990.

Hutchinson, A.C., and **Petter, A.** "Private Rights/Public Wrongs: The Liberal Lie of the Charter." *U.T.L.J.*, 38, 3, Summer, 1988.

Kallen, E. *Label Me Human: Minority Rights of Stigmatized Canadians*. Toronto: U.T.P., 1989.

Kaplan, W. *State and Salvation: The Jehovah's Witnesses and Their Fight for Civil Rights*. Toronto: U.T.P., 1989.

Knopff, R. "What do Constitutional Equality Rights Protect Canadians Against?" *C.J.P.S.*, 20, 2, June, 1987.

LaSelva, S. "Mandatory Retirement: Intergenerational Justice and the Canadian Charter of Rights and Freedoms." *C.J.P.S.*, 20, 1, March, 1987. "Comment" by Drummond, R., and "Reply" by LaSelva, S., *ibid.*, 21, 3, September, 1988.

Lederman, W.R. "The Power of the Judges and the New Canadian Charter of Rights and Freedoms," Charter Edition. *U.B.C., Law Review*, Vol. 1, 1982.

Lysyk, K. "Enforcement of Rights and Freedoms Guaranteed by the Charter" 43. *Advocate* 165, 1985.

Macdonald, R.A. "Postscript and Prelude—the Jurisprudence of the Charter: Eight Theses." *Supreme Court Law Review*, 4, 1982.

MacKay, A.W. "Freedom of Expression: Is it All Just Talk?" *C.B.R.* 68, December, 1989.

Magnet, J.E. "The Charter's Official Languages Provisions: The Implications of Entrenched Bilingualism." *Supreme Court Law Review*, 163, 4, 1982.

Mandel, M. *The Charter of Rights and the Legalization of Politics in Canada*, Toronto: Wall and Thompson, 1988.

Manning, M. *Rights, Freedoms and the Courts: A Practical Analysis of the Constitution Act, 1982*. Toronto: Edmond-Montgomery, 1983.

McDonald, D.C. *Legal Rights in the Canadian Charter of Rights and Freedoms: A Manual of Issues and Sources*. Toronto: Carswell, 1982.

McKercher, W.R., (ed.). *The U.S. Bill of Rights and the Canadian Charter of Rights and Freedoms*. Toronto: O.E.C., 1983.

Mitchnick, M.G. *Union Security and the Charter*. Toronto: Butterworths, 1987.

Morton, F.L. "The Political Impact of the Canadian Charter of Rights and Freedoms." *C.J.P.S.*, 20, 1, March, 1987.

Ratushny, E., and **Beaudoin, G.-A.**, (eds.). *The Canadian Charter of Rights and Freedoms*. Toronto: Carswell, 2nd ed., 1988.

Roher, E. "Limiting the Charter." *P.O.*, 8, 8, October, 1987.

Russell, P.H. "The Effect of a Charter of Rights on the Policy-making Role of Canadian Courts." *C.P.A.*, 25, 1, Spring, 1982.

Russell, P. "The Political Purposes of the Canadian Charter of Rights and Freedoms." *C.B.R.*, 61, 1983.

Russell, P.H. "The First Three Years in Charterland." *C.P.A.*, 28, 3, Fall, 1985.

Sniderman, P., *et al.* "Political Culture and the Problem of Double Standards: Mass and Elite Attitudes Toward Language Rights in the Canadian Charter of Rights and Freedoms." *C.J.P.S.*, 22, 2, June, 1989.

Tarnopolsky, W.S., and **Beaudoin, G.A.** (eds.). *The Canadian Charter of Rights and Freedoms: Commentary*. Toronto: Carswell, 1982.

Tenofsky, E. "The War Measures and Emergencies Acts: Implications for Canadian Civil Rights and Liberties." *A.R.C.S.*, 19, Autumn, 1989.

Wakeling, T.W., and **Chipeur, G.D.** "An Analysis of Section 15 of the Charter After the First Two Years or How Section 15 Has Survived the Terrible Twos." *Alberta Law Review*, 25, 3, 1987.

Background to the New Constitution

Axworthy, T. "Colliding Visions: The Debate Over the Canadian Charter of Rights and Freedoms, 1980–81." *Journal of Commonwealth and Comparative Politics*, 24, 3, November, 1986.

Banting, K., and Simeon, R., (eds.). *And No One Cheered: Federalism, Democracy and the Constitution Act.* Toronto: Methuen, 1983.

Beck, S., and Bernier, I. *Canada and The New Constitution: The Unfinished Agenda.* Montreal: I.R.P.P., 1983.

Cairns, A.C. *The Canadian Constitutional Experiment: Constitution, Community and Identity.* Killam Lectures, Dalhousie University, Halifax, N.S., 1983.

Cairns, A.C. "The Politics of Constitutional Renewal in Canada," in K. Banting and R. Simeon (eds.), *Redesigning the State: The Politics of Constitutional Change in Industrial Nations.* Toronto: U.T.P., 1985.

Davenport, P., and Leach, R.H., (eds.). *Reshaping Confederation: The 1982 Reform of the Canadian Constitution.* Durham, North Carolina: Duke University Press, 1984.

McWhinney, E. *Canada and the Constitution 1979–82: Patriation and The Charter of Rights.* Toronto: U.T.P., 1982.

Morin, C. *Lendemains piégés: du référendum à la nuit des long couteaux.* Montréal: Boréal, 1989.

Romanow, R., Whyte, J., and Leeson, H. *Canada Notwithstanding: The Making of the Constitution 1976–1982.* Toronto: Methuen, 1984.

Russell, P., *et al.The Court and The Constitution.* Kingston: Queen's University, 1982.

Schwartz, B. *First Principles: Constitutional Reform with Respect to the Aboriginal Peoples of Canada, 1982–1984.* Kingston: Queen's University, I.I.R., 1985.

Segal, H., and Nurgitz, N. *No Small Measure: The Progressive Conservatives and the Constitution.* Ottawa: Deneau, 1983.

Sheppard, R., and Valpy, M. *The National Deal: The Fight for a Canadian Constitution.* Toronto: Macmillan, 1984.

Judicial Review

Bale, G. "Law, Politics, and the Manitoba School Question: The Supreme Court and the Privy Council." *C.B.R.*, 63, 3, September 1985.

Cairns, A.C. "The Judicial Committee and Its Critics." *C.J.P.S.*, 4, 3, September, 1971.

Griffiths, C.T., Klein, J.F., and Verdun-Jones, S.M. *Criminal Justice in Canada.* Toronto: Butterworths, 1980.

Hogg, P.W. "Is the Supreme Court of Canada Biased in Constitutional Cases?" *C.B.R.*, LVII, 4, December, 1979.

Hogg, P.W. "Comments on Legislation and Judicial Decision." *C.B.R.*, 60, 1982.

Law Reform Commission. *Judicial Review and the Federal Court.* Ottawa: S. and S., 1980.

Manfredi, C. "Adjudication, Policy-making and the Supreme Court of Canada: Lessons from the Experience of the United States." *C.J.P.S.*, 2, June, 1989.

Monahan, P. *Politics and the Constitution: Federalism and the Supreme Court of Canada.* Toronto: Carswell/Methuen, 1987.

Russell, P.H. "The Anti-Inflation Case: The Anatomy of a Constitutional Decision." *C.P.A.*, 20, 4, Winter, 1977.

Russell, P.H. "History and Development of the Court in National Society: The Canadian Supreme Court." *Canada-United States Law Journal*, 3, Summer, 1980.

Scott, F. "Section 94 of the British North America Act," in *Essays on the Constitution*. Toronto: U.T.P., 1977.

Smith, J. "The Origins of Judicial Review in Canada." *C.J.P.S.*, 16, 1, March, 1983.

Whyte, J.D. "Legality and Legitimacy: The Problem of Judicial Review of Legislation." *Q.L.J.*, 12, 1, 1987.

Wilson, B. "Decision-Making in the Supreme Court." *U.T.L.J.*, 36, 3, Summer, 1986.

FEDERALISM

BACKGROUND TO MEECH LAKE

Graham Fraser

OTTAWA

The Meech Lake Accord is the latest attempt to address a fundamental question in Canadian life.

The nub of the question is this: is Canada a partnership between two peoples or a federation of 10 equal provinces?

For 30 years, Canada has wrestled with different versions of this question and its ramifications.

Biculturalism or multiculturalism? Dualism or pan-Canadian federalism? . . .

The key question throughout the debate has been very simple: does Quebec get more power or not?

For 22 years, from 1960 until the patriation of the constitution in 1982, the nature of the bargaining was straightforward. Successive Quebec governments made the following offer to Ottawa: Give us more powers, and we will let you bring the British North America Act to Canada.

Throughout that period, different ideas were put forward for a redistribution of power, and different constitutional proposals failed: the so-called Fulton–Favreau Formula in 1965 and the Victoria Charter in 1971 among them.

Ironically, when the constitution was patriated and amended with a Charter of Rights and Freedoms in 1982, the Quebec National Assembly ended up not

From *The Globe and Mail*, Toronto, March 24, 1990. By permission.

with more powers but with fewer. For the Charter settled with one stroke a question that had been at the heart of political debate for 15 years—who could go to English school—by imposing criteria.

Although he had supported Mr. Trudeau's action, Brian Mulroney set out in 1984 to make it possible for Quebec to sign the new Constitution.

In 1985, the Quebec Liberal Party adopted a constitutional policy that set out the terms for the negotiations.

These focused on three themes: the recognition of Quebec as a distinct society, guarantees of its cultural security and the return of power to influence the evolution of Canada's constitutional future.

Those three themes translated into Robert Bourassa's five points:

- the recognition of Quebec as a distinct society;
- the recognition of Quebec's role in jointly selecting immigrants;
- a role for Quebec in choosing Supreme Court judges;
- the limitation of federal spending power;
- a veto for Quebec in future constitutional changes.

Mr. Bourassa campaigned on these points in the 1985 election campaign, and when he became Premier, they were his conditions for agreeing to sign the 1982 Constitution.

In the summer of 1986, the premiers agreed to address the question of Quebec's conditions as a priority, and on April 30, 1987, Mr. Mulroney and the 10 premiers met at Meech Lake to see if it would be worthwhile to hold a First Ministers' Conference.

From that day-long meeting, an agreement emerged. In a nutshell, Quebec's conditions were met by making them available to all provinces. Special status was avoided by increasing the role for all provinces in certain federal institutions.

On the question of Quebec as a distinct society, the First Ministers agreed to the following formula: The constitution would be interpreted in a way consistent with:

First, the recognition that the existence of what they called "French-speaking Canada, centred in but not limited to Quebec, and English-speaking Canada, concentrated outside Quebec but also present in Quebec" is a fundamental characteristic of Canada;

Second, "the recognition that Quebec constitutes within Canada a distinct society."

Then, the Parliament of Canada and the provincial legislatures were to be committed to "preserving" the fundamental characteristic of Canada, while the government of Quebec would have the role "to preserve and promote the distinct identity of Quebec."

Quebec's desire for a role in immigration was met by offering other provinces such an arrangement if they wished to negotiate it. Provinces were given the right to propose a list of candidates for the Supreme Court and the Senate from which the federal government would choose. On the issue of spending power, the provinces were given the right to compensation if they chose to opt out of shared-cost programs in areas of exclusive jurisdiction, provided they developed their own programs compatible with national objectives. Finally, to meet Quebec's desire for a veto, unanimity was required for amendments to federal institutions.

In addition, a number of agenda items, including fisheries, senate reform and the economy, were added to the annual meetings of First Ministers.

A month later, on June 3, this initial agreement was translated into a constitutional amendment.

Some changes were negotiated to deal with concerns that were raised during the month of May.

The recognition of the existence of French Canada and English Canada was changed to the recognition of the existence of French-speaking Canadians and English-speaking Canadians. A clause was inserted to ensure that nothing in the accord would affect the clauses in the 1982 Constitution that dealt with multiculturalism or aboriginal peoples.

This clause provoked considerable concern that women's rights included in the 1982 constitution would be undermined.

Other elements that provoked controversy were the distinct society clause, the unanimity provisions for federal institutions and the restrictions on spending powers.

Some critics argued that the fact that the Quebec government could "preserve and promote" Quebec's distinct identity while the federal government and the provinces only had the role of "promoting" the fundamental characteristics of Canada was a formula that would result in a French-only Quebec and nine English-only provinces.

Others argued that the unanimity clause and the clauses concerning a provincial role in nominations to the Senate and the Supreme Court were both discriminatory against the Northern territories.

And some felt that the opting-out provisions for shared-cost programs would make it impossible for Ottawa to introduce new federal social programs, such as a national child care program.

The federal government and eight of the 10 provinces ratified the Meech Lake accord.

However, three provincial governments changed, electing premiers who challenged the accord: New Brunswick's Frank McKenna, Manitoba's Gary Filmon and Newfoundland's Clyde Wells.

Mr. McKenna has proposed to end the deadlock by passing the accord, with a companion resolution that is designed to meet a number of the criticisms.

Among other things, the federal government would be given a role to "preserve and promote" the fundamental characteristics of Canada, sexual equality rights would be added to the clauses on aboriginals and multiculturalism, and the territories would be given a role in naming senators and Supreme Court judges.

But in meeting the criticisms, the proposals may have simply fudged the central dilemma of Canadian dualism that lies at the heart of the debate.

In her book The Question of Separatism 10 years ago, author Jane Jacobs made the point succinctly:

"The issue of how to combine duality of French and English Canada with federation of 10 provinces remains insoluble because it is inherently insoluble," she wrote.

THE MEECH LAKE ACCORD

1. The *Constitution Act, 1867* is amended by adding thereto, immediately after section 1 thereof, the following section:

"2.(1) The Constitution of Canada shall be interpreted in a manner consistent with

(a) the recognition that the existence of French-speaking Canadians, centred in Quebec but also present elsewhere in Canada, and English-speaking Canadians, concentrated outside Quebec but also present in Quebec, constitutes a fundamental characteristic of Canada; and
(b) the recognition that Quebec constitutes within Canada a distinct society

(2) The role of the Parliament of Canada and the provincial legislatures to preserve the fundamental characteristic of Canada referred to in paragraph (1)(a) is affirmed.

(3) The role of the legislature and Government of Quebec to preserve and promote the distinct identity of Quebec referred to in paragraph (1)(b) is affirmed.

(4) Nothing in this section derogates from the powers, rights or privileges of Parliament or the Government of Canada, including any powers, rights or privileges relating to language."

2. The said Act is further amended by adding thereto, immediately after section 24 thereof, the following section:

"25.(1) Where a vacancy occurs in the Senate, the government of that province to which the vacancy relates may, in relation to that vacancy, submit to the Queen's Privy Council of Canada the names of persons who may be summoned to the Senate.

(2) Until an amendment to the Constitution of Canada is made in relation to the Senate pursuant to section 41 of the *Constitution Act, 1982*, the person

summoned to fill a vacancy in the Senate shall be chosen from among persons whose names have been submitted under subsection (1) by the government of the province to which the vacancy relates and must be acceptable to the Queen's Privy Council for Canada."

3. The said Act is further amended by adding thereto, immediately after section 95 thereof, the following heading and sections:

"Agreements on Immigration Aliens

95A. The Government of Canada shall, at the request of the government of any province, negotiate with the government of that province for the purpose of concluding an agreement relating to immigration or the temporary admission of aliens into that province that is appropriate to the needs and circumstances of the province.

95B.(1) Any agreement concluded between Canada and a province in relation to immigration or the temporary admission of aliens into that province has the force of law from the time it is declared to do so in accordance with subsection 95C(1) and shall from that time have effect notwithstanding class 25 of section 91 or section 95.

(2) An agreement that has the force of law under subsection (1) shall have effect only so long and so far as it is not repugnant to any provision of an Act of the Parliament of Canada that sets national standards and objectives relating to immigration or aliens, including any provision that establishes general classes of immigrants or relates to levels of immigration for Canada or that prescribes classes of individuals who are inadmissible into Canada.

(3) The *Canadian Charter of Rights and Freedoms* applies in respect of any agreement that has the force of law under subsection (1) and in respect of anything done by the Parliament or Government of Canada, or the legislature or government of a province, pursuant to any such agreement.

95C.(1) A declaration that an agreement referred to in subsection 95B(1) has the force of law may be made by proclamation issued by the Governor General under the Great Seal of Canada only where so authorized by resolutions of the Senate and House of Commons and of the legislative assembly of the province that is a party to the agreement.

(2) An amendment to an agreement referred to in subsection 95B(1) may be made by proclamation issued by the Governor General under the Great Seal of Canada only where so authorized

(a) by resolutions of the Senate and House of Commons and of the legislative assembly of the province that is a party to the agreement; or
(b) in such other manner as is set out in the agreement.

95D. Sections 46 to 48 of the *Constitution Act, 1982* apply, with such modifications as the circumstances require, in respect of any declaration made pursuant to subsection 95C(1), any amendment to an agreement made pursuant to subsection 95C(2) or any amendment made pursuant to section 95E.

95E. An amendment to sections 95A to 95D or this section may be made in accordance with the procedure set out in subsection 38(1) of the Constitution Act, 1982, but only if the amendment is authorized by resolutions of the legislative assemblies of all the provinces that are, at the time of the amendment, parties to an agreement that has the force of law under subsection 95B(1)."

4. The said Act is further amended by adding thereto, immediately preceding section 96 thereof, the following heading:

"General"

5. The said Act is further amended by adding thereto, immediately preceding section 101 thereof, the following heading and sections:

"Courts Established by the Parliament of Canada"

6. The said Act is further amended by adding thereto, immediately after section 101 thereof, the following heading and sections:

"Supreme Court of Canada"

101A.(1) The court existing under the name of the Supreme Court of Canada is hereby continued as the general court of appeal for Canada, and as an additional court for the better administration of the laws of Canada, and shall continue to be a superior court of record.

(2) The Supreme Court of Canada shall consist of a chief justice to be called the Chief Justice of Canada and eight other judges, who shall be appointed by the Governor General in Council by letters patent under the Great Seal.

101B.(1) Any person may be appointed a judge of the Supreme Court of Canada who, after having been admitted to the bar of any province or territory, has, for a total of at least ten years, been a judge of any court in Canada or a member of the bar of any province or territory.

(2) At least three judges of the Supreme Court of Canada shall be appointed from among persons who, after having been admitted to the bar of Quebec, have, for a total of at least ten years, been judges of any court of Quebec or of any court established by the Parliament of Canada, or members of the bar of Quebec.

101C.(1) Where a vacancy occurs in the Supreme Court of Canada, the government of each province may, in relation to that vacancy, submit to the Minister of Justice of Canada the names of any of the persons who have been admitted to the bar of that province and are qualified under section 101B for appointment to that court.

(2) Where an appointment is made to the Supreme Court of Canada, the Governor General in Council shall, except where the Chief Justice is appointed from among members of the Court, appoint a person whose name has been submitted under subsection (1) and who is acceptable to the Queen's Privy Council for Canada.

(3) Where an appointment is made in accordance with subsection (2) of any

of the three judges necessary to meet the requirement set out in subsection 101B(2), the Governor General in Council shall appoint a person whose name has been submitted by the government of a province other than Quebec.

(4) Where an appointment is made in accordance with subsection (2), otherwise than as required under subsection (3), the Governor General in Council shall appoint a person whose name has been submitted by the government of a province other than Quebec.

101D. Sections 99 and 100 apply in respect of the judges of the Supreme Court of Canada.

101E.(1) Sections 101A to 101D shall not be construed as abrogating or derogating from the powers of the Parliament of Canada to make laws under Section 101 except to the extent that such laws are inconsistent with those sections.

(2) For greater certainty, section 101A shall not be construed as abrogating or derogating from the powers of the Parliament of Canada to make laws relating to the reference of questions of law or fact, or any other matters, to the Supreme Court of Canada."

7. The said Act is further amended by adding thereto, immediately after section 106 thereof, the following section:

"106A.(1) The Government of Canada shall provide reasonable compensation to the government of a province that chooses not to participate in a national shared-cost program that is established by the Government of Canada after the coming into force of this section in an area of exclusive provincial jurisdiction, if the province carries on a program or initiative that is compatible with the national objectives.

(2) Nothing in this section extends the legislative powers of the Parliament of Canada or of the legislatures of the provinces."

8. The said Act is further amended by adding thereto the following heading and sections:

"XII—CONFERENCES ON THE ECONOMY AND OTHER MATTERS

148A. A conference composed of the Prime Minister of Canada and the first ministers of the provinces shall be convened by the Prime Minister of Canada at least once each year to discuss the state of the Canadian economy and such other matters as may be appropriate.

XII—REFERENCES

149. A reference to this Act shall be deemed to include a reference to any amendments thereto."

Constitution Act, 1982

9. Sections 40 to 42 of the Constitution Act, 1982 are repealed and the following substituted therefore:

"40. Where an amendment is made under subsection 38(1) that transfers legislative powers from provincial legislatures to Parliament, Canada shall provide reasonable compensation to any province to which the amendment does not apply.

41. An amendment to the Constitution of Canada in relation to the following matters may be made by proclamation issued by the Governor General under the Great Seal of Canada only where authorized by resolutions of the Senate and House of Commons and of the legislative assembly of each province:

(a) the office of the Queen, the Governor General and the Lieutenant Governor of a province;
(b) the powers of the Senate and the method of selecting Senators;
(c) the number of members by which a province is entitled to be represented in the Senate and the residence qualifications of Senators;
(d) the right of a province to a number of members in the House of Commons not less than the number of Senators by which the province was entitled to be represented on April 17, 1982;
(e) the principle of proportionate representation of the provinces in the House of Commons prescribed by the Constitution of Canada;
(f) subject to section 43, the use of the English or the French language;
(g) the Supreme Court of Canada;
(h) the extension of existing provinces into the territories;
(i) notwithstanding any other law or practice, the establishment of new provinces; and
(j) an amendment to this Part".

10. Section 44 of the said Act is repealed and the following substituted therefor:

"44. Subject to section 41, Parliament may exclusively make laws amending the Constitution of Canada in relation to the executive government of Canada or the Senate and House of Commons."

11. Subsection 46(1) of the said Act is repealed and the following substituted therefor: "46.(1) The procedures for amendment under sections 38, 41 and 43 may be initiated either by the Senate or the House of Commons or by the legislative assembly of a province."

12. Subsection 47(1) of the said Act is repealed and the following substituted therefor:

"47.(1) An amendment to the Constitution of Canada made by proclamation under section 38, 41 or 43 may be made without a resolution of the Senate authorizing the issue of the proclamation if, within one hundred and eighty days after the adoption by the House of Commons of a resolution authorizing its issue, the Senate has not adopted such a resolution and if, at any time after the expiration of that period, the House of Commons again adopts the resolution."

13. Part VI of the said Act is repealed and the following substituted therefor:

"PART VI

CONSTITUTION CONFERENCES

50.(1) A constitutional conference composed of the Prime Minister of Canada and the first ministers of the provinces shall be convened by the Prime Minister of Canada at least once each year, commencing in 1988.
(2) The conferences convened under subsection (1) shall have included on their agenda the following matters:

> (a) Senate reform, including the role and functions of the Senate, its powers, the method of selecting Senators and representation in the Senate;
> (b) roles and responsibilities in relation to fisheries; and
> (c) such other matters as are agreed upon."

14. Subsection 52(2) of the said Act is amended by striking out the word "and" at the end of paragraph (b) thereof, by adding the word "and" at the end of paragraph (c) thereof and by adding thereto the following paragraph:
"(d) any other amendment to the Constitution of Canada."
15. Section 61 of the said Act is repealed and the following substituted therefor:
"61. A reference to the *Constitution Act 1982*, or a reference to the *Constitution Acts 1867 to 1982*, shall be deemed to include a reference to any amendments thereto."

General

16. Nothing in section 2 of the *Constitution Act, 1867* affects section 25 or 27 or the *Canadian Charter of Rights and Freedoms*, section 35 of the *Constitution Act, 1982* or class 24 of section 91 of the *Constitution Act, 1867.*

CITATION

17. This amendment may be cited as the *Constitution Amendment, 1987.*

OBJECTIONS TO THE MEECH LAKE ACCORD

Clyde K. Wells

● ● ● In 1986 Gil Rémillard, the Quebec Minister of Intergovernmental Affairs, put forward five proposals that he said were essential to address Quebec's concerns. Those proposals were as follows:

Abridgement by the editor of a speech given by the Premier of Newfoundland and Labrador on February 14, 1990. By permission.

1. Explicit recognition of Quebec as a distinct society (in a revised preamble to the Constitution);
2. The recognition of a right to veto;
3. A limitation on the federal spending power;
4. Quebec's participation in appointing judges to the Supreme Court of Canada;
5. A guarantee of increased powers in matters of immigration.

These proposals are certainly a reasonable basis for negotiation and there is no doubt that the Meech Lake Accord was responsive to them. But, we will have gained nothing if, by accepting the five proposals as minimum acceptable demands, we make the people of one province happy and in the process create a great resentment and dissatisfaction in the people of most if not all of the remaining provinces. . . .

This is why changes in the Constitution cannot deal with the concerns and demands of a single province, however meritorious, in isolation. Although the changes may focus on the concerns of one province they must address those concerns in a manner that takes into account the impact on other provinces and all Canadians, and in a manner that respects the fundamental constitutional precepts which, I believe, most Canadians would agree to be as follows:

Firstly, there is more to being a Canadian than being a resident of a particular province or territory. We have a sense of national citizenship and community that transcends our provincial identities. Being a Canadian must mean that a citizen can go to any province and still be a full Canadian. Canada has a national identity that is more than the sum of its parts, an identity which must be provided for and reinforced by the Constitution. Canada must never be allowed to degenerate into an association of provinces and territories, known to the world as the "Canadian Economic Community."

Secondly, every citizen of the country is equal to every other citizen, something which is now firmly entrenched in the Canadian Charter of Rights and Freedoms. It is also reflected in the principle of one-citizen one-vote, which underlies our system of representation based on populations, in one of the Houses of Parliament. This is the first of the two basic equalities of every federal nation.

A third fundamental precept of the Canadian federation is that every province is equal, in its status and rights as a province even though there may be great disparity in population or economic power. This is the second of the two basic equalities of a federal nation and was, of course, explicitly acknowledged in the preamble to the Meech Lake Accord itself. That principle of provincial equality must be reflected in the other House of Parliament [the Senate] to ensure the national decisions are balanced to take into account the interest of the majority of the provinces, as well as the interest of the majority of the people.

Fourthly, Canada is today, as it will be in the future, the beneficiary of contributions of people from a variety of cultural and ethnic backgrounds. But, the nation was founded on the basis of an understanding between the French- and the English-speaking peoples of the colonies in North America, then administered by Britain to build a bilingual nation, something which has now evolved into a collective commitment to build a bilingual nation from coast to coast. This constitutional precept must also be appropriately reflected in Parliament and the functioning of our national institutions.

Finally, the nation and the provinces are collectively committed to promoting equal opportunities for the well-being of all Canadians; furthering economic development to reduce disparity in opportunities, and providing essential public services of reasonable quality to all Canadians. This commitment to redistribution and sharing among Canadians is essential to strengthening the national community and our sense of national identity and responding to the Canadian sense of fairness and justice. Canadians considered it so important that we spelled it out in section 36(1) of the Constitution Act, 1982.

If these are in fact the five precepts that, for the vast majority of people of Canada, reflect the nation that they want Canada to be, then they lead to two inevitable consequences.

First, the Constitution must be written, and from time to time amended, to reflect these precepts in a constantly changing world. And second, our national political institutions must be established and function in a manner that will ensure the fair and full implementation of these precepts.

Instead of addressing the legitimate concerns of Quebec in a manner that respected the fundamental precepts of the nation and took in account the impact on other provinces, the prime minister proposed the Meech Lake Accord, which I suggest is seriously inconsistent with the fundamental constitutional precepts of this nation. He appears to have persuaded the premiers of the day to accept it, and still argues that it should be supported, on the basis of his contention that in 1982 the federal government and the other nine provinces somehow ganged-up on Quebec and imposed constitutional changes that "excluded" Quebec, an action which he claims would not have been taken against Ontario.

Nothing could be further from the truth. Quebec had a government at that time that was dedicated to seeking the separation of Quebec from Canada and would not have agreed to anything that promoted Canadian federalism. The federal government at the time was led by a strong French Canadian, Pierre Trudeau, and included several strong French-Canadian ministers, all of whom, I believe, had the best interests of both Canada and Quebec at heart. In the end, all but two federal members of parliament from Quebec supported the 1982 reforms, and a substantial number of Liberal Party members of the Quebec National Assembly did likewise. . . .

. . . The people of Canada are not rejecting Quebec.

They are rejecting the dismantling of federalism in Canada. They are rejecting a Canada with a class "A" province, a class "B" province and eight class "C" provinces. . . .

I believe the Meech Lake Accord can be rewritten to "reflect faithfully Quebec's five original proposals, while remaining faithful to federalism." An examination of provisions of the Accord in the context of the five proposals will demonstrate the basis for that belief.

EXPLICIT RECOGNITION OF QUEBEC AS A DISTINCT SOCIETY

The Meech Lake Accord as it is, is unacceptable because it goes beyond the explicit recognition of Quebec as a distinct society in the preamble, that was originally contemplated by Quebec. In addition, it also gives the Quebec legislature and government the special role that no other province has "*to preserve and promote the distinct identity of Quebec referred to in paragraph (1) (b) [which requires that the constitution be interpreted in a manner consistent with the recognition of Quebec as a distinct society]*." The role of a legislature is to legislate, or pass laws. Clearly, therefore, the Meech Lake Accord creates a special legislative status for one province. No federation is likely to survive for very long if one of its supposedly equal provinces has a legislative jurisdiction in excess of that of the other provinces.

Most constitutional scholars also agree that the total effect of Section 2 of the Meech Lake Accord will permit the Quebec legislature to discharge its affirmed special role in a manner that could override the Charter of Rights and Freedoms (with the exception of sections 25, 27 and 35).

We are also concerned that the special constitutional role accorded to the legislature and government of Quebec would be used to enact laws further restricting Quebec's recently passed Bill 178. Such actions then trigger resentment and negative reactions in other provinces. Those actions and reactions would serve only to increase prejudice and drive an ever bigger wedge between French and English Canadians, and mutual resentment would inevitably build to the point where its divisive force could no longer be contained. With the rigid amending formula the Accord would impose, there would be no way to reverse the situation. Canada would inevitably evolve into two linguistic enclaves and national disintegration and discord would likely follow. . . .

All these potential difficulties could be avoided and Quebec's original proposal could be faithfully met by an explicit recognition of Quebec as a distinct society in the preamble. A revised Accord could easily provide for that and be faithful to federalism.

THE RECOGNITION OF A RIGHT TO VETO

The Meech Lake Accord accommodates Quebec's request for a constitutional veto by extending the veto to all provinces. This will effectively halt all significant future constitutional change. The current amending formula is already quite rigid; the Meech Lake Accord, by requiring unanimity in several more areas, would place Canada in a permanent constitutional strait jacket.

While an amending formula requiring unanimity may appear to be consistent with the fundamental precept of the equality of the provinces, in fact it is inconsistent since it effectively destroys all hope of Senate reform and will prevent Newfoundland and Labrador and the other smaller provinces from ever becoming full participating provinces of Canada. It would also prevent the Northwest Territories or the Yukon becoming provinces unless they could obtain the approval of all the provincial legislatures.

I believe, however, there is a means of addressing Quebec's proposal for constitutional veto in a manner that would be faithful to federalism. In every federation there are two essential equalities, each of which must be given a voice in the affairs of the federation. The first is the equality of each citizen, which is given a voice in the legislative chamber (in Canada, the House of Commons) elected on the basis of representation by population. The second is the equality of each constituent part (state or province) in its status and right as a constituent part, which is given a voice in a second legislative chamber (in Canada, it should be the Senate) in which there is a equal representation from each constituent part.

Canada, however, has or is perceived to have a third equality, namely, the equality of each of the two founding linguistic cultures. Being the principal homeland of the French language and culture in Canada, together with having the civil law system, has always been the basis on which Quebec has claimed an entitlement to a constitutional veto. Our constitutional challenge has always been to find the means of accommodating this third equality. Special legislative status or a general constitutional veto for Quebec is not an appropriate way to provide a voice for this third equality because, of course, it would destroy the second equality, namely, the equality of the provinces. Rather, it must be done at the national level and on a basis that is directly related to and commensurate with the need to accommodate that third equality.

It is on this basis that Newfoundland had proposed that all constitutional amendments affecting language, culture and the proportion of civil law judges on the Supreme Court of Canada should be subject to separate linguistic votes in the Senate which would have the effect of requiring the separate approval of the majority of senators from Quebec for any such amendment. In that way Quebec, through its senators acting at the national level, would have an effective veto over constitutional amendments affecting language, culture and the proportion of civil law judges on the Supreme Court of Canada, without giving to the Quebec legislature or government a status that no other provincial legislature or government had. Such an alternative would enable us to faithfully respond to Quebec's request and at the same time be faithful to federalism.

A LIMITATION ON THE SPENDING POWER

The concern of most Canadians about the limitation on the federal spending power for national programs in areas of exclusive provincial jurisdiction is that it would unduly limit the federal government's capacity to initiate and implement national programs designed to promote national standards of social and economic well-being for the people of Canada. Quebec (and other provinces sharing its view, including Newfoundland) does have a legitimate concern that unilateral federal action in the exercise of its spending power could encroach on areas of exclusive provincial jurisdiction, and we therefore support the basic limitation on the federal spending power set out in the Meech Lake Accord.

We feel, however, it is necessary to add a new subsection to the Meech Lake Accord provisions, to provide that the opting-out with compensation provisions would not apply "to any national program expressly declared by Parliament to be a response to the commitment set out in section 36 (1) of the Constitution Act, 1982." This ensures that the federal government will be able to implement national or regional programs, with minimum national standards and full provincial participation, designed to meet the fundamental precept set out in section 36 (1) without the deterring effect of one or more provinces claiming entitlement to compensation. Indeed, it should provide an incentive to the federal government to develop such programs. . . .

QUEBEC'S PARTICIPATION IN APPOINTING JUDGES TO THE SUPREME COURT OF CANADA

Quebec has a civil law system, and all of the remaining nine provinces have, in common, the common law system. In such circumstances it is not all inappropriate that one-third of the judges of the Supreme Court of Canada should have a civil law background, and effectively be appointed from members of the Bar of Quebec.

The Meech Lake proposal, however, would result in the Government of Quebec effectively appointing three of the judges, and the governments of the other provinces could only collectively provide lists from which the federal government would be forced to choose the remaining six judges. That is unacceptable.

Newfoundland believes that it is not faithful to federalism for all Supreme Court appointments to be made only from a list of names submitted by provincial governments, something which effectively cedes the power to appoint judges to Canada's highest court to certain of the provinces. In addition, among other things, the Meech Lake provisions create no mechanism to break any deadlock that would inevitably occur when the federal government disagreed with the provincial nominations; they leave unspecified a fair means of distributing nominations among the Atlantic provinces; finally, they prohibit the appointment of judges from the Northwest Territories and Yukon.

It is noteworthy that even the judges of the provincial supreme courts are appointed by the federal government with no right in any of the provinces to submit lists. In such circumstances, it is even more difficult to justify restricting the Government of Canada to choosing common law judges to be appointed to the Supreme Court of Canada from a list collectively submitted by the common law provinces, and effectively giving Quebec the right to appoint the civil law judges by submitting a very restricted list.

Quebec and the other provinces can, however, be given appropriate roles in the appointment of Supreme Court of Canada judges by requiring that all civil law judges appointed by the federal government to the Supreme Court of Canada be subject to the approval of the senators from Quebec, and all common law judges appointed to the Supreme Court of Canada be subject to the approval of the senators from the common law provinces. . . .

A GUARANTEE OF INCREASED POWERS IN MATTERS OF IMMIGRATION

With respect to the immigration provisions, Newfoundland understands the Quebec government's concerns to ensure sufficient reinforcement of the francophone community through immigration. In this connection, a special administrative agreement with the federal government has been in force since 1978 (the "Cullen–Couture Agreement") to give Quebec a special role with respect to its participation in the selection of immigrants, pursuant to the concurrent federal–provincial powers over immigration set out in section 95 of the Constitution Act of 1867. That agreement and agreed amendments could be enhanced by constitutional provision.

Newfoundland is also prepared to explore additional acceptable ways to address Quebec's special interest in the selection of immigrants. Once again, however, the Meech Lake provisions go far beyond this and leave Parliament with the power only to set "national standards and objectives" including establishing "general classes of immigrants," prescribing classes that are inadmissible, and settling the total number for any year. On the other hand, all provinces can henceforth conclude separate immigration agreements with the federal government which will then be constitutionally entrenched and thereafter only able to be amended by either the general amending process or "such other manner as is set out in the agreement."

In my view, the immigration provisions in the Meech Lake Accord unacceptably weaken the critical federal power over immigration and the essential federal role in providing new Canadians with a sense of attachment to Canada as opposed to the particular province to which they initially immigrate. As well, I do not understand how the Constitution can "guarantee" that any province will get a fixed proportion of the total number of immigrants and, more specifically, that the province of Quebec has the right to exceed its fixed proportion by 5% for demographic reasons. . . .

CONCLUSION

. . . Renewed negotiations and a lively public debate over the Meech Lake Accord should not be viewed in a negative light. Rather, it provides constructive opportunity for all Canadians to examine the significant challenges to the Canadian society and economy that lie ahead and the respective federal and provincial roles in meeting those challenges. This will allow the Canadian people to discuss alternatives to the Meech Lake Accord that will accommodate Quebec's special concerns but, at the same time, be faithful to the fundamental precepts of federalism and strengthen our sense of national community and national identity, rather than lead to national disintegration and discord.

It is urgent now to move beyond the Meech Lake Accord and to put in place a constitutional structure that the whole nation, including Quebec, can embrace.

Constitutions and constitutional change are not just affairs of governments and of first ministers. The Constitution belongs to the people of Canada—the ultimate source of sovereignty in the nation. In light of the importance of constitutional change, I suggest that perhaps the worst flaw in the Accord was the closed process which resulted in eleven first ministers telling the 26 million people of Canada how they will be governed in the future, instead of the 26 million people of Canada telling the eleven first ministers how they will govern. . . .

IN DEFENCE OF THE ACCORD

Robert L. Stanfield

● ● ● In 1982, the Parliament at Westminster, exercising its ancient colonial powers at the request of the Parliament of Canada and the legislatures of our English-speaking provinces, imposed constitutional changes on Quebec. No doubt these were legally binding on Quebec as well as the other provinces, but the government and legislature of Quebec rejected them and Quebec withdrew from the constitutional life of Canada. . . .

The Meech Lake Accord, if ratified by all provincial legislatures, will restore common sense to politics in Canada. In 1982 we abandoned, temporarily I hope, one of the fundamental challenges inherent in the creation of Canada in 1867: the challenge of English- and French-speaking Canadians living together in mutual respect for mutual benefit. . . .

Furthermore, French-speaking Quebecers feel increasingly insecure about

An abridgement by the editor of an address given by the Honourable Robert L. Stanfield to the Dalhousie Law School on October 19, 1989. By permission.

their language. The drastic fall in the birthrate among Quebecois and the dominance of English in communications systems and in entertainment in largely English-speaking North America seem to the French-speaking to threaten the future use of French in Quebec.

Consequently since the late 1960's we have seen governmental efforts in Quebec to strengthen the current and future roles of French in Quebec. They have believed that French requires more than equality to survive there. These efforts have created resentment among English-speaking Canadians, who see French-speaking Quebecers as a majority in Quebec abusing their power, rather than as a small minority in English-speaking North America trying to preserve their language and culture, which is how Quebecers see themselves. . . .

Quebecers knew that the power to protect and enhance the French in Canada was largely within provincial, not federal, jurisdiction. Quebecers knew that even if it wanted to do so the federal government could not effectively protect or enhance the French language, and they did not forget that the great majority of voters in Canada are English-speaking, often with little or no desire to protect and enhance French. Consequently when Quebecers began to worry about the future of French in Quebec they looked to their own government, not to the government of Canada, for leadership and action. During the 1970's successive governments of Quebec made French more than equal in Quebec. This infuriated English-speaking Canadians, who had in fact long ago made English more than equal in other provinces, but nevertheless wanted Ottawa to stop Quebec from doing what they themselves had done. . . .

The Levesque government when elected in 1976 passed Bill 101, designed to make French the working language in Quebec, and generally the predominant language in Quebec. This was probably the most popular thing the P.Q. did, as far as Quebec's French-speaking majority was concerned. Indeed, some suggest that Bill 101 caused the separatists to lose the referendum on separatism in 1980 because Bill 101 showed that Quebecers did not need to separate in order to protect French. . . .

I believed and I still believe that the exercise of 1982 endangers Canada as a country. We gave the separatists a stick to beat us with. They could always claim, correctly, that Quebecers were thereafter compelled to live under a Constitution they had rejected by a bi-partisan resolution of their legislature, the National Assembly. Ottawa had not only missed an opportunity for constitutional renewal following the favorable vote in the referendum. Ottawa had betrayed the French-speaking Quebecers who had voted for constitutional renewal.

Fortunately Premier Bourassa replaced René Levesque and personally sought constitutional renewal. Shortly after his election in 1985 he prepared a list of five points on which Quebec sought satisfactory agreement. He was the first premier of Quebec who would say precisely what Quebec needed for constitutional settlement, and he produced the shortest list of demands ever to come out of official Quebec. In 1986 the premier of the other provinces agreed with Ottawa that trying to reach agreement with Quebec should be the first priority of constitutional discussion. Two years of preliminary discussions led to Meech Lake in 1987.

Mirabile dictu, an accord was reached which would become effective when the Parliament of Canada and all the provincial Legislatures approved the Accord. I was amazed by Bourassa's moderation. Instead of the traditional demands for increased powers under Section 92 of the British North America Act he agreed that Quebec be described as a distinct society in an interpretation clause of the Constitution. Instead of disputing the existence of the federal spending power in areas of provincial jurisdiction, as Quebec had always done, he accepted the more accommodating position that in national shared cost programs a province be entitled to opt out and receive reasonable compensation if its program was compatible with national objectives. He agreed that if Ottawa chooses judges and senators from lists prepared by provincial premiers, this would meet Quebec's requirements. He agreed that matters such as the creation of new provinces and changes to the Senate be added to the list of items already requiring unanimous provincial consent in the Constitution of 1982. . . .

I do not argue the Meech Lake Accord is perfect. But any defects it may have are small indeed compared to the unholy mess it was intended to clear up. Politics is the art of the possible. It is a matter of choices. English-speaking Canada cannot have everything it wants if it wants to bring Quebec back in. . . .

Some critics have expressed concern about the distinct society-duality section in the Accord. There are two separate concerns: one, that the clause would give additional powers to Quebec and, secondly, that the clause would enable Parliament and the provincial Legislatures to override the Charter.

The all-party joint committee, after hearing constitutional experts and many others including Pierre Trudeau, decided that the clause, which is only an interpretive clause, could not give a province legislative power in any area clearly within federal jurisdiction, and that the clause would be of minor significance in determining future distribution of powers between Ottawa and the provinces. . . .

As to possible effects on the Charter of Rights, the only way Meech Lake could possibly affect a charter right would be by way of Section 1 of the Charter itself. A government could argue that the objectives of the distinct society-duality clause must be considered when a court is deciding whether legislation is demonstrably justified in a free and democratic society. If it is so justified the legislation could limit a right under Section 1 of the Charter. I believe it would be very difficult—perhaps not impossible, but very difficult—to persuade our courts that a clear violation of a charter right is justified in a free and democratic society in order to preserve linguistic duality or to promote a distinct society. A government that wishes to reduce charter rights is much more likely to use the notwithstanding clause.

Also I ask why worriers about charter rights have not expressed concern about Section 25 of the Charter. "The Charter shall be interpreted in a manner consistent with the preservation and enhancement of the multicultural heritage of Canada."

This clause, also, would have to be given weight in determining whether legislation affecting a charter right was justified in a free and democratic society. This and the Meech Lake distinct society-duality clause are both interpretation clauses. Indeed, most provinces would be far more likely to try to justify infringement of a right by claiming it is enhancing multiculturalism than by claiming its preserving linguistic duality. . . .

I cannot see the slightest excuse for having a multicultural clause in the Charter and excluding the distinct society-duality clause from our Constitution.

Concerns have been strongly expressed that Meech Lake may weaken the equality rights of women. I wish to emphasize that under the Charter and Meech Lake the equality rights of women appear to be ironclad. Women can point not only to the equality provisions of Section 15 of the Charter, but also to Section 28, which reads: "Notwithstanding anything in this Charter, the rights and freedoms referred to in it are guaranteed equally to male and female persons."

The rights in Section 28 cannot be infringed by resort to the notwithstanding clause of the Charter, which can be used only respecting rights provided by Sections 1, and 7 to 15 of the Charter. Section 28 also prohibits resort to any other clause of the Charter as a justification for limiting women's equality rights. This means that these rights cannot be weakened by legislation justified in a free and democratic society. Since Section 1 is the only vehicle by which Meech Lake could possibly affect the Charter it means that Meech Lake could not possibly affect the equality rights of women.

The Accord has been attacked for allegedly weakening the power of the federal government to establish national shared-cost programs with national standards in fields of exclusive provincial jurisdiction. . . . Meech Lake does not permit a province to get its share of federal money if it wished to stay out unless its own program is compatible with national objectives, i.e., the objectives of the national plan. Thus Meech Lake strengthens Ottawa's ability to negotiate shared-cost programs with national objectives. . . .

. . . Bourassa in 1985 made proposals to Ottawa and the other provinces, which, with modification and two years of consideration, were passed by the Government and the Parliament of Canada with the support of all the national party leaders, and endorsed by the premiers of all the provinces. Three premiers who have taken office since the Accord are now raising objections. If Canadians throw away this second opportunity for reconciliation we will deserve our fate. . . .

Since the 1982 Constitution is already legally binding on Quebec and since the Meech Lake Accord would make relatively few legal changes, the importance of Meech Lake goes beyond the changes it proposes. For the Quebec government and non-separatist Quebecers it represents the formal acceptance by the rest of Canada that a francophone presence and space exists in Canada, is an essential part of the Canadian fabric, and contributes to defining the Canadian identity. For the federal government and for the provincial governments which support Meech Lake it represents, not a weaker Ottawa, but a new vision of the federal-provincial relationship and hopefully the end of the debate about the place of Quebec in Confederation.

[ ]

FIRST MINISTERS' COMMUNIQUÉ AND THE LEGAL OPINION

[Editor's note: The prime minister and provincial premiers met from June 3 to June 9, 1990, to resolve their differences on the proposed constitutional amendment known as the Meech Lake Accord. At the conclusion of their week-long deliberations in the National Conference Centre in Ottawa, they issued a communiqué and a legal opinion on the meaning of the clause in the Accord that gave Quebec status as a "distinct society." In a final public session all of the first ministers signed the communiqué, although Premier Wells of Newfoundland reserved the right to submit the Accord to a vote in his legislature or in a provincial referendum. The ministers did not sign the legal opinion which was issued under the signature of six constitutional lawyers and attached to the communique as an appendix.]

THE COMMUNIQUE

Whereas on April 30, 1987, the Prime Minister of Canada and the premiers reached agreement in principle on means to bring about the full and active participation of Quebec in Canada's constitutional evolution;

And whereas on June 3, 1987, all first ministers signed the 1987 Constitutional Accord and committed themselves to introducing as soon as possible the Constitution Amendment, 1987, in Parliament and the provincial legislative assemblies;

And whereas the Constitution Amendment, 1987, has been authorized by Parliament and the legislative assemblies of Quebec, Saskatchewan, Alberta, Prince Edward Island, Nova Scotia, Ontario and British Columbia:

1. THE MEECH LAKE ACCORD

The premiers of New Brunswick, Manitoba and Newfoundland undertake to submit the Constitution Amendment, 1987, for appropriate legislative or public consideration and to use every possible effort to achieve decision prior to June 23, 1990.

2. SENATE REFORM

After proclamation, the federal government and the provinces will constitute a commission with equal representation for each province and an appropriate number of territorial and federal representatives to conduct hearings and to report to Parliament and the legislative assemblies of the provinces and territories, prior to the first ministers conference on the Senate to be held by the end of 1990 in British Columbia, on specific proposals for Senate reform that will give effect to the following objectives:

• The Senate should be elected.
• The Senate should provide for more equitable representation of the less populous provinces and territories.
• The Senate should have effective power to ensure the interests of residents of the less populous provinces and territories figure more prominently in national decision-making, reflect Canadian duality and strengthen the government of Canada's capacity to govern on behalf of all citizens, while preserving the principle of the responsibility of the government to the House of Commons.

Following proclamation of the Meech Lake accord, the Prime Minister and all premiers agree to seek adoption of an amendment on comprehensive Senate reform consistent with these objectives by July 1, 1995.

The Prime Minister undertakes to report semi-annually to the House of Commons on progress achieved towards comprehensive Senate reform.

The Prime Minister and all premiers reaffirming the commitment made in the Edmonton Declaration and the provisions to be entrenched under the Constitution Amendment, 1987, undertook that Senate reform will be the key constitutional priority until comprehensive reform is achieved.

If, by July 1, 1995, comprehensive Senate reform has not been achieved according to the objectives set out above under Section 41 of the Constitution Act, 1982, as amended by the Constitution Amendment, 1987, the number of senators by which a province is entitled to be represented in the Senate will be amended so that, of the total of 104 senators, the representation of Ontario will be 18 senators, the representation of Nova Scotia, New Brunswick, British Columbia, Alberta, Saskatchewan, Manitoba, and Newfoundland will be 8 senators each, and the representation of all other provinces and the territories will remain unchanged.

In the case of any province whose representation declined, no new appointments would be made until that province's representation had by attrition declined below its new maximum.

In the event of such a redistribution of Senate seats, Newfoundland would be entitled to another member of Parliament in the House of Commons under Section 51A of the Constitution Act, 1867.

3. FUTURE CONSTITUTIONAL AMENDMENTS

(1) Charter—Sex Equality Rights:
- Add Section 28 of the Canadian Charter of Rights and Freedoms to Section 16 of the Constitution Amendment, 1987.

(2) Role of the Territories:
- In appointments to the Senate and the Supreme Court of Canada.
- In discussions on items on the agenda of annual constitutional and economic conferences where, in the view of the Prime Minister, matters to be discussed directly affect them.

(3) Language issues:
- Add to the agenda of constitutional conferences matters that are of interest to English-speaking and French-speaking linguistic minorities.
- Require resolutions of the House of Commons, the Senate and the legislative assembly of New Brunswick to amend that province's Act Recognizing the Equality of the Two Official Linguistic Communities in New Brunswick (Bill 88).

(4) Aboriginal constitutional issues:
First ministers' constitutional conferences to be held once every three years, the first to be held within one year of proclamation; representatives of aboriginal peoples and the territorial governments to be invited by the Prime Minister to participate in the discussion of matters of interest to the aboriginal peoples of Canada.

The Prime Minister of Canada will lay or cause to be laid before the Senate and House of Commons, and the premiers will lay or cause to be laid before their legislative assemblies, a resolution, in the form appended hereto, and will seek to authorize a proclamation to be issued by the Governor-General under the Great Seal of Canada to amend the Constitution of Canada as soon as possible after proclamation of the Constitution Amendment, 1987.

4. AGENDA FOR FUTURE CONSTITUTIONAL DISCUSSIONS

(1) Creation of new provinces in the Territories:
The Prime Minister and all premiers agreed future constitutional conferences should address available options for provincehood, including the possibility that, at the request of the Yukon and Northwest Territories to become provinces, only a resolution of the House of Commons and Senate be required.

(2) Constitutional recognitions:
The Prime Minister and premiers took note of repeated attempts by first

ministers over the past 20 years to draft a statement of constitutional recognitions. All such attempts were unsuccessful.

The Prime Minister and premiers reviewed drafts submitted by the federal government and Manitoba, Saskatchewan, Ontario and British Columbia, and agreed to refer immediately the drafts to an all-party special committee of the House of Commons. Public hearings would begin across Canada on July 16, 1990, and a report on the substance and placement of the clause—in a manner consistent with the Constitution of Canada—would be prepared for consideration by first ministers at their conference in 1990.

(3) Constitutional reviews:

The Prime Minister and all premiers agreed jointly to review, at the constitutional conference required by Section 49 of the Constitution Act, 1982, the entire process of amending the Constitution, including the three-year time limit under Section 39 (2) of that Act and the question of mandatory public hearings prior to adopting any measure related to a constitutional amendment, including revocation of a constitutional resolution.

Pursuant to Section 50 of the Constitution Act, 1982, as proposed in the Constitution Amendment, 1987, the Prime Minister and the premiers also committed to a continuing review of the operation of the Constitution of Canada, including the Canadian Charter of Rights and Freedoms, with a view to making any appropriate constitutional amendments.

5. SECTION 2, CONSTITUTIONAL AMENDMENT, 1987

The Prime Minister and the premiers took note of public discussion of the distinct society clause since its inclusion of the Meech Lake accord. A number of Canada's most distinguished constitutional authorities met to exchange views on the legal impact of the clause. The Prime Minister and premiers reviewed their advice and other material.

The Prime Minister, in his capacity as chairman of the conference, received from the above-noted constitutional authorities a legal opinion, which is appended to the final conference communique.

6. NEW BRUNSWICK AMENDMENT

- Add a clause that within New Brunswick, the English linguistic community and the French linguistic community have equality of status and equal rights and privileges.
- Affirm an additional role of the legislature and government of New Brunswick: To preserve and promote the equality of status and equal rights and privileges of the province's two official linguistic communities.

The Prime Minister of Canada will lay or cause to be laid before the Senate and House of Commons, and the premier of New Brunswick will lay or cause to be laid before the legislative assembly of New Brunswick, a resolution, in the form appended hereto, and will seek to authorize a proclamation to be issued by the Governor-General under the Great Seal of Canada to amend the Constitution of Canada as soon as possible after proclamation of the Constitution Amendment, 1987.

THE LETTER

Dear Prime Minister:

In response to certain concerns which have been expressed in relation to Section 1 of the proposed Constitution Amendment, 1987 (Meech Lake accord), it is our pleasure to confirm our opinion on the following.

In our opinion, the Canadian Charter of Rights and Freedoms will be interpreted in a manner consistent with the duality/distinct society clause of the proposed Constitution Amendment, 1987 (Meech Lake accord), but the rights and freedoms guaranteed thereunder are not infringed or denied by the application of the clause and continue to be guaranteed subject only to such reasonable limits prescribed by law as can be demonstrably justified in a free and democratic society, and the duality/distinct society clause may be considered, in particular, in the application of Section 1 of the Charter.

The Constitution of Canada, including sections 91 and 92 of the Constitution Act, 1867, will be interpreted in a manner consistent with the duality/distinct society clause. While nothing in that clause creates new legislative authority for Parliament or any of the provincial legislatures, or derogates from any of their legislative authority, it may be considered in determining whether a particular law fits within the legislative authority of Parliament or any of the legislatures.

Gerald-A. Beaudoin, OC, QC, professor of law,
University of Ottawa.
B. Jamie Cameron, associate professor,
Osgoode Hall Law School, York University.
E. Robert A. Edwards, QC, assistant deputy attorney general,
government of British Columbia.
Peter W. Hogg, QC, professor,
Osgoode Hall Law School, York University.
Katherine Swinton, professor,
Faculty of Law, University of Toronto.
Roger Tasse, OC, QC, barrister and solicitor.

POSTSCRIPT

[*Editor's note: Following the conference, New Brunswick was the only one of the three abstaining provinces in which the Accord was passed in its legislature. In Manitoba a Cree member of the Assembly, Elijah Harper, refused to accede to the unanimous consent, which was necessary for the Accord to be introduced into the Assembly, while in Newfoundland Premier · Wells, having decided to submit the Accord to a free vote of the Assembly, delayed putting the amendment to a vote when he was angered by Ottawa's alleged manipulation. With two provinces having failed to approve the amendment within the three-year period that was inaugurated when it was first passed by a legislature (which happened to be Quebec), the Accord expired on June 23, 1990.*]

CO-OPERATIVE, EXECUTIVE, AND INTRASTATE FEDERALISM

Garth Stevenson

CO-OPERATIVE FEDERALISM

The administrative approach to managing and resolving intergovernmental conflicts did not really begin to develop before the turn of the century, and it reached its fullest development in the period roughly from 1945 until 1970. During the two decades following the Second World War, it was the predominant method of dealing with federal-provincial conflict, largely supplanting both the party-political and the judicial approaches. This was the heyday of "co-operative federalism," a phrase borrowed from the United States, which both celebrated, and purported to describe, the way in which the federal system operated at that time. By the late 1960s, however, administrative or "co-operative" federalism was already being transformed into executive federalism, which will be considered subsequently.

Administrative or co-operative federalism, its proponents like to argue, was based on the virtues of compromise, flexibility, and pragmatism. It was also based on the assumption that all disputes and problems could be resolved through the application of these virtues, and that some mutually acceptable position could always be discovered. Certainly the administrative approach to the resolution of conflict contrasted with the judicial approach in that it did

From *Unfulfilled Union: Canadian Federalism and National Unity*, 3rd edition, Toronto. © 1989. Gage Publishing Limited. Used by permission of publisher and author.

tend to promote such compromises and was thus more effective in resolving certain kinds of dispute, such as those over fiscal matters. The administrative approach also appealed to governments which, for one reason or another, preferred not to seek a clear definition of jurisdictional boundaries, or which did not believe it was possible to find one.

While it had certain advantages over the judicial approach, the administrative approach tended to replace the party-political approach to conflict resolution for somewhat different reasons. As bureaucracies became larger, more powerful, more functionally specialized, and more removed from partisan influence and pressure, they assumed increasingly autonomous roles in seeking accommodation with their counterparts at the other level of government. As specialists of various kinds came to predominate in certain sectors of the public service, they tended to discover that they held interests, goals, and assumptions in common with similar specialists at the other level of government, and that these took precedence over considerations of intergovernmental competition, party rivalry, or even constitutional propriety. Thus administrative methods of problem-solving were preferred. Politicians acquiesced in this, partly by necessity (since they could no longer control all the detailed activities of their departments), partly because it lacked the risks of the judicial approach, and partly because they were themselves acquiring bureaucratic perspectives. It is significant that the administrative character of federalism became most pronounced under the St. Laurent government, at a time when the governing federal party had become almost a part of the bureaucratic machinery.

The growth of administrative or co-operative federalism was very closely associated with the growth of conditional grants and shared-cost programs. . . . Inseparable from both was the proliferation of federal-provincial committees, councils, meetings, and other forms of contact at various levels of officialdom, which served as the mechanisms by which problems were resolved in an administrative manner.

These bodies have been catalogued and described by a number of writers. Gerard Veilleux discovered in the 1960s that about four-fifths of them were concerned with the areas of general government (including finance), statistics, health and welfare, natural resources, and agriculture. This list suggests the areas in which administrative approaches to the resolution of intergovernmental conflict were generally successful and popular. Finance is the area least amenable to solutions achieved through the judicial process; health and welfare . . . and shared-cost programs were most important; agriculture is a shared jurisdiction under the BNA Act. The inclusion of resources appears anomalous from our present perspective, but at the time Veilleux wrote they would have been mainly renewable resources, which are closely associated with agriculture.

Donald Smiley has suggested some of the circumstances under which co-operative federalism is most likely to be successful. The officials who do the negotiating should have real authority to speak on behalf of their governments;

they should have a common frame of reference, such as might result from shared professional training and expertise; they should be more committed to the success of the program than to other types of goals; they should be willing to compromise, and also to share confidential information with one another. Finally, there should not be too much public interest or involvement in the matters at issue.

Viewed in a somewhat different way, co-operative or administrative federalism seems to be a fairly effective remedy for the types of conflict that arise from the organizational imperatives of different levels of government. It can prevent or resolve such conflicts, at least to some degree, through the countervailing impact of professional or programmatic goals that cut across, instead of reinforcing, the jurisdictional rivalries between the two levels. Co-operative federalism cannot, however, deal very successfully with the conflicts that originate outside the governmental and bureaucratic milieu and that result from more fundamental antagonisms between the interests of different classes or class fractions. Whether producers or consumers benefit from resource developments, whether industries are established in the East or in the West, whether jobs go to anglophones or francophones—these are not the types of question to which co-operative federalism provides answers. This is one reason for its obsolescence.

EXECUTIVE FEDERALISM

In recent years the term "executive federalism," first coined by Donald Smiley, has come to be used more frequently than "co-operative federalism." Although the fact may not always be explicitly stated or even recognized, the change in terminology corresponds to a real change in the nature of intergovernmental relations, and one that began to take place a few years before the terminology was changed to correspond with it. Although one cannot state any precise date at which it occurred, the change was in fact fundamental. Co-operative federalism was characterized by the fragmentation of authority within each level of government, the absence of linkages between different issues and functional domains, the forging of specific intergovernmental links by different groups of specialized officials, and the lack of publicity or public awareness of what was happening.

Executive federalism, on the other hand, is characterized by the concentration and centralization of authority at the top of each participating government, the control and supervision of intergovernmental relations by politicians and officials with a wide range of functional interests, and the highly formalized and well-publicized proceedings of federal-provincial conference diplomacy. While co-operative federalism tended to subordinate the power, status, and prestige of individual governments to programmatic objectives, executive federalism does exactly the opposite.

Despite its recent rise to prominence, the origins of executive federalism and its most characteristic institutional manifestation, the first ministers' conference, can be traced back fairly far in Canadian history. Contacts between the Prime Minister and individual premiers were fairly frequent in the early period when partisan political considerations exercised a decisive influence on federal-provincial relations. Laurier summoned all of the premiers to a conference in 1906 to discuss the proposed changes in statutory subsidies to the provinces. There was a one-day conference in 1910 to discuss company law reform and a longer one in 1918, mainly to discuss problems of post-war reconstruction. In 1927 Mackenzie King organized a major conference to commemorate the sixtieth anniversary of Confederation, at which an extensive agenda was discussed. There were four more conferences during the Depression, mainly to discuss problems of relief and federal-provincial-municipal finance, an abortive conference to discuss the Rowell–Sirois Report in 1940, and a conference on postwar reconstruction and fiscal arrangements in 1945. As it turned out, the postwar pattern of federal-provincial finance required a first ministers' conference to discuss the arrangements at least every five years, and two additional conferences were also held in 1950 to consider the amendment of the constitution, a topic that had also been discussed in 1927 and 1935.

Federal-provincial first ministers' conferences were thus by no means unknown, but they took place at fairly infrequent intervals and could hardly be considered the predominant mechanism of interaction between the two levels of government, at least when considering the more mundane topics that dominated the federal-provincial agenda. Only for major changes in fiscal arrangements or for the consideration of amendments to the BNA Act were they considered essential. For the most part federal-provincial relations in the postwar period remained fragmented, specialized, unco-ordinated, and dominated by officials. Gerard Veilleux estimated in his book that only one-tenth of federal-provincial meetings and conferences involved elected politicians as participants. By contrast, a study done for the government of Alberta in 1975 found that by that time politicians participated in almost one out of every four meetings. It is also significant that at least one first ministers' conference took place almost every year from 1963 onward. The federal government in fact proposed in its "Victoria Charter" that the obligatory requirement of an annual conference be written into the constitution, corresponding to the requirement that there be an annual session of Parliament.

The most important reason for the shift from co-operative to executive federalism was that federal-provincial conflicts were becoming too serious, too profound, and too sensitive to be safely entrusted to the diplomatic and managerial skills of subordinate officials. In particular the evident dissatisfaction of Quebec during the Quiet Revolution could not be accommodated by traditional means. Federal-provincial relations had to be politicized and conducted at the highest level, as in the case of the Pearson-Lesage negotiations over the Canada and Quebec pension plans. At the same time or subsequently a number of other serious conflicts emerged which involved provinces other than Quebec: conflicts over tax-sharing and the financing of health, education, and welfare, over economic relations with the United States, over regional development and the competitive scramble for investment, and over the division of benefits from mineral resources. All of these matters were clearly "political" rather than "administrative" in the sense that large numbers of people outside the bureaucracy were aware of their significance and deeply interested in their outcomes. In fact the complex of problems, and particularly the situation in Quebec, provided grounds for apprehension that the survival of the federal state itself might be called into question.

This exacerbation of conflict led to a renewed emphasis on intergovernmental competition and to a tendency to give the institutional interests of governments priority over functional or programmatic objectives. A distrust of co-operative federalism followed, accompanied by a belief that the fragmentation of authority and the lack of co-ordination that it entailed were luxuries that no self-respecting, government could afford. Quebec nationalists had always argued, correctly from their point of view, that the proliferation of specialized and fragmented intergovernmental relationships, such as those that arose from shared-cost programs, was a potential menace to the integrity of their provincial state and its ability or willingness to defend its own interests. This belief had caused Maurice Duplessis to refuse some conditional grants and had caused a later generation of Quebec nationalists to denounce the co-operative federalism of the 1960s as a fraud and a delusion. Similar reasoning became increasingly apparent on the part of other provincial governments, and even of the federal government itself. This led to the development of new mechanisms for the conduct of intergovernmental relations.

These sentiments arising out of intergovernmental competition reinforced certain incentives toward centralization and concentration of power within each of the eleven governments that had arisen simultaneously from other causes. There was a widespread conviction in the 1960s that administrative structures and procedures could and should be reformed to make them more "rational." The centralized setting of priorities and the control of expenditure, through a process that related decisions on expenditure to more fundamental decisions on objectives, were viewed as fundamental to successful administration and policy-making. The desire to control expenditure was particularly strong on the part of Canadian provincial governments, which saw themselves after 1966 as faced with mounting expenditures on legitimization coupled with the diminishing likelihood that the "tax room" made available to them by the federal government would increase proportionately.

All of these pressures to centralize and concentrate authority were manifested in organizational changes at both the federal and provincial levels. Intergovernmental competition certainly played a part in promoting these changes, although they occurred so rapidly that it is not easy to determine which level of government initiated the trend and which level responded. At the federal level the establishment of the Treasury Board as a separate department and the proliferation of cabinet committees and support staff took place under Prime Minister Pearson. It was followed under Prime Minister Trudeau by a dramatic expansion of the Prime Minister's Office and the Privy Council Office, and by the creation in 1974 of a separate Federal-Provincial Relations Office reporting directly to the Prime Minister. From 1977 to 1980 there was also a Minister of State for Federal-Provincial Relations.

At the provincial level there has also been a tendency to expand and improve the machinery for co-ordinating intergovernmental relations. Until the 1960s such machinery was practically non-existent. In 1961 Quebec established a Ministry of Federal-Provincial Affairs, and in 1967 the name of the ministry was changed to Intergovernmental Affairs. Until 1976 this portfolio was always held by the Premier, but in that year Claude Morin, who had been the deputy minister under Lesage and Johnson, became a full-time Minister of Intergovernmental Affairs. From the outset the ministry was responsible for Quebec's international activities as well as its relations with other Canadian provinces, but in 1984 these functions were separated and placed under different ministers. After the change of government in 1985, both portfolios were held by Gil Remillard.

Quebec's example in establishing a department to conduct its intergovernmental relations was followed by Alberta in 1972, Newfoundland in 1975, Ontario in 1978, and both British Columbia and Saskatchewan in 1979. The Saskatchewan department lasted only four years before it was abolished, but the others have continued. In Newfoundland, and since 1985 in Ontario, the intergovernmental affairs portfolio has been held by the Premier. The Alberta and Ontario departments follow the original Quebec model most closely in that they combine responsibility for international and federal-provincial activities. Ontario's was also responsible for the province's relations with its municipalities until 1981, when a separate department was organized for that purpose.

Opinions differ on the question of whether the proliferation of intergovernmental affairs departments and other central agencies has made federal-provincial relations better or worse. Their detractors argue that they have contributed to the erosion of co-operative federalism by reducing the autonomy of the functional departments such as agriculture, health, and welfare, and that they have a vested interest in intergovernmental competition and conflict. Their defenders respond that the intergovernmental affairs departments are at most a symptom, and certainly not a cause, of the transition from co-operative to executive federalism, and that the nation-wide network of intergovernmental affairs specialists is itself, like the functional networks that it partly replaced, a contributor to national unity.

Whatever the truth of these assertions, it seems indisputable that the success of executive federalism in resolving problems has not been impressive. When the sessions are televised, participants tend to read speeches to the cameras rather than negotiating seriously, but when negotiations take place in secret the governments cannot be held accountable for the results. Consensus is rarely achieved among governments representing different regions, political parties and jurisdictional interests. When it is not achieved the public demands a scapegoat, and each government argues that some other government is at fault. Even the Pepin-Robarts Task Force, in a report otherwise distinguished by an excessive sympathy for the provincial governments, expressed awareness of the dangers:

> The spectacle of Canadian governments wrangling constantly among themselves has done nothing to reduce cynicism about public affairs and it has presented Canadians with the image of a country deeply divided against itself.

Media coverage of the conferences, portraying the federal government as merely one of "eleven senior governments," has undermined its legitimacy and has dangerously elevated the status of the premiers, who increasingly tend to argue that they collectively represent the national interest. Although Richard Simeon's observations of executive federalism in the 1960s led him to conclude that there was an unwritten rule against provinces "ganging up" on the federal government, this has not been evident recently. Yet when most or all of the provinces attend the conference armed with a common set of demands agreed upon in advance, there can be little hope of serious negotiation.

Another problem with executive federalism is its tendency to erode the power and influence of the legislature at both levels. Legislatures are weakened when they must legislate within the parameters of executive agreements arrived at in secret without their participation. Opposition parties, especially at the federal level, are placed in the position of being forced either to acquiesce in the agreements arrived at or to criticize the members of their own party who have participated in making them. Accountability also suffers when each government involved in an agreement can deny responsibility by claiming that undesirable features of the agreement were insisted upon by one of the other governments involved. At the same time executive federalism is arguably a consequence, as much as a cause, of the domination of legislatures by cabinets, or more precisely, of a parliamentary form of government. Certainly in the United States, with its separation of powers, nothing of the sort would be possible. Neither the President nor state governors could assume that an executive agreement would be acceptable to Congress or the state legislatures.

As discussed below, Canada's federal institutions, particularly Parliament, have recently borne the brunt of much criticism to the effect that they do not adequately reflect the diversity of regional interests and that conflicting interests are, therefore, almost inevitably expressed as conflicts between the two levels of government. While there is some truth to this impression, it really explains only half the problem. The other half is the impact of parliamentary institutions and party discipline at the provincial level, where majorities and governments are subjected to even fewer checks and balances than they are at the federal level. Unlike an American state, a Canadian province does not have separation of powers, nor a rigid constitution, nor an upper house. The government's majority in the legislature is often overwhelming, and the legislature is typically in session for only a few months of the year. Natural resource revenues, external borrowing, and profit-making ventures such as provincial liquor boards weaken the legislature's control over the public purse. The checks and balances which the BNA Act provided by establishing the office of lieutenant-governor are now widely viewed as illegitimate, and are practically never used. Electoral campaigns focus on the premier's leadership, particularly his role in federal-provincial relations, so that members of the legislature are elected on the party label as docile members of a "team" and are not expected to have independent thoughts on important issues. Far more than at the federal level, and more than in any other liberal democracy, power is concentrated in the hands of a few persons or even one person. The illusion that what the premier wants is what the province wants is easily perpetuated. This in turn makes Canada appear like a collection of ten private fiefdoms, in which the provincial boundary is the most significant basis of political interest or allegiance. The diversity of interests within each province, and the many interests and associations that unite individuals and groups across provincial boundaries, are given little expression.

INTRASTATE FEDERALISM

Although federalism was defined in the first chapter of this book in a way that emphasized the co-existence of two distinct levels of government, some recent writing on the subject, particularly in Canada, has emphasized another aspect of federalism, namely the representation of the provinces or sub-national states and their interests within the institutions of the central government. The terms interstate and intrastate federalism have been devised to distinguish between these two aspects, with interstate federalism referring to the relations between two distinct levels of government and intrastate federalism referring to the representation of the component parts within the central institutions. While both the academic study of and popular impressions of Canadian federalism have traditionally emphasized the interstate aspect, recent years have seen an increasing emphasis on intrastate federalism.

Students of intrastate federalism argue that the central institutions of the Canadian state, and particularly the House of Commons and the Senate, fail to provide adequate representation of the diversity of provincial and regional interests. As a result, those interests must seek representation through the provincial governments and the accommodation of interests can only take place through intergovernmental bargaining or, if that fails, through intergovernmental conflict. This line of argument, while increasingly popular, is rather ambiguous in its motives and conclusions. As Donald Smiley and Ronald Watts point out in a useful book on the subject, proponents of institutional reform along the lines of intrastate federalism may be seeking either to strengthen or to weaken the federal level of government, and the two motives are not always clearly distinguished. Intrastate federalism might strengthen the federal level by increasing its legitimacy and by persuading regionally concentrated interests to seek their objectives through it rather than through the provincial governments. On the other hand, it might weaken the federal level by making it increasingly difficult to devise coherent and effective policies, by promoting political instability, and by encouraging the provincial governments to meddle in national politics. While many intrastate federalists are no doubt sincerely devoted to the first objective, the fact that the governments of Alberta and British Columbia have been among the most enthusiastic proponents of the concept gives considerable grounds for apprehension.

Elements of intrastate federalism are, of course, to be found in the status quo, and there is some evidence that they were more effective in the early years of Canadian federalism than they are today. The Fathers of Confederation seem to have taken the Senate seriously as a means of representing regional diversities, if one is to judge by the amount of time devoted to discussing that institution at the conferences that preceded Confederation. Party discipline in the House of Commons was less rigid in the nineteenth century than it is now; members often broke ranks with their party on regionally sensitive issues like the Riel affair, the Pacific railway, or Catholic education in New Brunswick. The federal civil service, being recruited through political patronage, could be influenced by the regional concerns of ministers and members of Parliament. Most importantly, the cabinet consisted of persons closely tied to provincial party organizations, and often with political experience at the provincial level, who ensured that their own province received its fair share of patronage and public expenditure. To some extent the cabinet is still an agency of intrastate federalism even today, as suggested by the rigid convention requiring at least one minister from each province. Its effectiveness in this regard has been eroded, however, by the technocratic background of many ministers, the extent to which ministers are influenced by the non-political bureaucracy, and the increasingly complex organization and processes of the cabinet itself.

Since few seem to wish a return to the type of cabinet and civil service that existed under Macdonald and Mackenzie, recent proposals to strengthen intrastate federalism have concentrated on the House of Commons and the Senate. The two major complaints about the Commons have been in relation to the rigid party discipline and the electoral system. Party discipline means that members, particularly on the government side of the house, must defer to the collective decision of their party rather than speaking out publicly for regional interests. Since the collective decision will naturally reflect mainly the interests of the provinces with the largest number of representatives, the interests of small provinces, or of provinces where the party in question has little support, will receive inadequate representation.

The electoral system, as Alan Cairns argued in a classic article in 1968, worsens the problem by magnifying regional variations in the support of the different parties, and creating the possibility that the caucus of the governing party will seriously underrepresent certain provinces. Thus the Progressive Conservative caucus elected in 1979 contained only two members from Quebec and the Liberal caucus elected in 1980 contained only two members from the West, both of whom were from Winnipeg. The absence of representatives from petroleum producing provinces seemed to many westerners a credible explanation for the subsequent introduction of the National Energy Program by the Liberal government.

Party discipline is a complex phenomenon that goes to the heart of responsible government, and criticism of it leads logically to the rejection of the parliamentary system itself, something which relatively few Canadians seem willing to contemplate. The electoral system is a more tempting target of criticism. The Task Force on Canadian Unity, which reported at a time when Quebec had only two representatives in the government caucus, recommended that about sixty additional members of the House of Commons should be elected by proportional representation. A few months later the Quebec Liberal Party's "beige paper" suggested more cautiously that the idea of proportional representation should be considered. The federal New Democratic Party supported a proposal similar to that of the task force. However, the election in 1984 of a government with substantial support from every province caused interest in the idea to subside, at least temporarily.

SENATE REFORM

The principal target of intrastate federalists has always been the Senate. This is so, in part, because the institution itself is unpopular, but also because it was ostensibly designed to represent regional diversities, and because the second chambers of other federal countries, particularly the United States, appear to do so more effectively. Proponents of Senate reform, who seem to be heavily concentrated in western Canada, have a more specific motive; they believe that a revitalized Senate would counteract what they consider to be the excessive influence of Ontario and Quebec in the House of Commons.

There are almost infinite possible variations of a hypothetical reformed Senate, and the subject cannot be pursued in detail here. Generally speaking, proposals can be placed in one of two categories: a Senate that would be wholly or partially appointed by the provincial governments or legislatures, and one that would be elected by the people of each province. Germany, India, and the United States before 1913 provide possible prototypes of the first version, while Australia and the present-day United States are the prototypes of the second, Switzerland combines elements of both.

When intrastate federalism first became fashionable in the 1970s, the first version appeared to have more support, presumably because it was less of a break with Canadian tradition and with the elitist strands in our political culture. (It might be noted in passing that the interprovincial conference of 1887 called for provincial appointment of half the senators, so the idea is far from new.) In 1978 the Trudeau government introduced Bill C-60, which would have provided for half the senators to be elected by the House of Commons and half by the provincial legislatures. A second chamber modelled after the German Bundestag, with all its members appointed as delegates from the provincial governments, was proposed by the government of British Columbia, the Task Force on Canadian Unity, and the Quebec Liberal Party's "beige paper." The government of Alberta belatedly climbed on the bandwagon in 1982, but changed its mind three years later. All these proponents of the German model were probably more interested in weakening rather than strengthening federal institutions, a fact which undermined their credibility. Critics pointed out that the Bundestag only works in Germany because the main role of the states is to implement and administer federal legislation. In Canada the combination of federal legislation with provincial administration exists only in the field of criminal law.

In 1984 a joint parliamentary committee on Senate reform, after considering the various alternatives, recommended a Senate that would be directly elected by the people. Subsequently a committee of the Alberta legislature reached the same conclusion and the government of Alberta, possibly because polls showed that most Albertans favoured an elected Senate, soon abandoned its flirtation with the German model. Instead it began to promote what it called a "triple E" Senate, meaning elected, equal, and effective. By "equal" it meant that each province should have the same number of senators regardless of population, a view that is an article of faith in most of western Canada. As anyone who has lived there can attest, almost any real or imagined misfortune suffered by the West is attributed to the fact that Ontario and Quebec together have a majority of the seats in the House of Commons.

In any event, the "triple E" proposal deserves very critical examination. Australian experience, including a constitutional crisis in 1975 that led the governor general to dismiss the elected government, suggests that an elected second chamber works badly in a system of responsible government, unless the same party has a majority in both houses. Australian experience also suggests that a "triple E" Senate would not seriously reduce the discontent of Canada's peripheries. Tasmania, Queensland, and Western Australia complain about the domination of New South Wales and Victoria just as much as western and Atlantic Canada complain about the domination of Ontario and Quebec. Equal representation for Ontario and Prince Edward Island, despite the hallowed example of the United States, would be difficult to justify in a liberal democracy. The authors of the U.S. constitution were not liberal democrats in the modern sense (Thomas Jefferson was, but he did not attend the convention), and the disproportion in size between the larger and smaller states at that time was far less than the disproportion between the larger and smaller provinces in present-day Canada. An additional reason for rejecting the "triple E" proposal is that it would reduce francophones to a minority of about 10 percent in an important federal institution.

When Australia was drafting its federal constitution, the view was expressed that responsible parliamentary government on the British model was inappropriate in a federal country. The question raised by that comment is a real one and should be considered rationally, not through appeals to imperial history, ethnic solidarity, or anti-Americanism. Nonetheless, the worst possible solution would be to Americanize our institutions in Ottawa while retaining the present authoritarian and centralized institutions in the provincial capitals. If there is a problem, it must be dealt with at both levels simultaneously.

[Editor's note: for Senate Reform, see also Chapter 11, *infra*.]

THE POLITICAL FUTURE OF THE NORTHWEST TERRITORIES: A TEST FOR CANADIAN FEDERALISM

Graham White

When southern Canadians think about political developments in the north, they often focus on the prospects for provincial status for the Yukon and the Northwest Territories. The unspoken premise is that although the north, compared to the south, may be politically immature, underpopulated, and lacking a stable economic base, politics there will still follow the pattern set by the provinces. This assumption may be valid for the Yukon, but for the NWT it is dubious.

The essence of federalism lies in the ability of regional political units to control important aspects of their own politics and policies while the central government sets national policies and controls certain aspects of governing. From this perspective political developments in the Northwest Territories will constitute an important test of Canadian federalism. The issue of how and when provincial status is attained is only one aspect of this test. More significant, perhaps, will be the ability of the federation to adapt to unconventional structures and processes of government in the NWT, and to tolerate substantial regional deviations from provincial norms that the people of the Northwest Territories demand from their government.

This paper examines the course of recent political developments in the Northwest Territories and considers possible future directions of politics there. The emphasis is on large-scale constitutional issues such as possible division of the territories, land claims, and Native self-government within the context of a social structure which differs markedly from that of southern Canada.

An original article prepared for this edition by the author. By permission.

SOCIETY AND ECONOMY IN THE NORTHWEST TERRITORIES

The Meech Lake Accord acknowledged the reality that Quebec represents a "distinct society" within Canada. In terms of language, culture, geography, and economics, however, the NWT stands out as the most distinctive society in Canada.

The 53 000 residents inhabit a land mass of 1.3 million square miles; in other words, a population which would fit into Toronto's Skydome is spread across an area larger than India. Yellowknife, the capital, has a population of 14 000; four other centres number about 2500 people; the balance of the population lives in some 60 isolated communities, most of which have fewer than 1000 residents. Except in the southwest corner of the territories there are virtually no roads, travel is by air or by sea. By the standards to which most Canadians are accustomed, the climate is harsh.

The Northwest Territories is rich in natural resources, particularly oil and natural gas, though exploitation of these resources has been restricted for geographic, economic, and political reasons. Manufacturing (other than arts and crafts) and agriculture are all but non-existent; beyond natural resources, the mainstays of the economy are tourism, services, hunting, trapping and fishing, and government. Given the weakness of the wage economy and the limits on the ability and willingness of the private sector to cope with small numbers and long distances, it is hardly surprising that government is critically important in the lives of territorial residents; in 1987–88 the average per capita spending by the government of the Northwest Territories was $16,379, compared to the national average of $4,600.

The most significant feature of society in the NWT is that aboriginal people make up a majority (roughly 58 percent) of the population. This fact alone distinguishes it in crucial ways from the Yukon, whose Native population is only 25 percent of the total. Approximately 35 percent of the NWT's population are Inuit, constituting the overwhelming majority in the eastern Arctic, the area north and east of the tree line. Another 23 percent are Dene or Métis. The Dene are the Indians of the western Arctic, who are concentrated in the Mackenzie Valley. The Métis (who constitute about 7 percent of the population) are of mixed Dene-white origins; although they differ in some significant ways, for example, in legal status, from the Dene, for most practical social and political purposes, the Dene-Métis may be considered a single group. The balance of the territorial population, some 42 percent, are non-Native, mainly whites of European ancestry.

The split between Native and non-Native means far more than simply competing interests within a single political system. The gulf between Native and non-Native culture, for example, is far wider than that between English and French Canada. One primal division is identified by Gurston Dacks, a leading analyst of territorial politics: "whereas the aboriginal population feel a spiritual attachment and a sense of responsibility as stewards of the land, the non-aboriginal population sees the land primarily as a source of economic opportunity, and mining and oil and gas development as more profitable than wildlife harvesting."

Other crucial differences relate to concepts of political authority and to methods of reaching political decisions. The basis of politics in Western democracies is the individual. Decision making is premised on majoritarian principles, that is, the view favoured by the majority of individuals (usually ascertained by voting) carries the day. Politics among the Inuit and Dene–Métis of the Northwest Territories are conducted along very different lines. Here the good of the collectivity takes precedence over the good of the individual (although, unlike in Western liberal thought, the capacity of the collectivity to coerce the individual into accepting a group decision is limited). Moreover, decisions are reached by "consensus," by exhaustive discussion, until all points of view have been heard and a course of action acceptable to all emerges. The wisdom and experience of elders is much valued; leaders, whose responsibility to consult extensively with their communities is taken very seriously, tend to have far less power and authority vested in them than is typical in non-Native politics.

CONSTITUTIONAL DEVELOPMENTS

Constitutionally, the Northwest Territories has experienced in two or three decades many of the developments that took two centuries to unfold in the rest of Canada. Until the 1960s the Northwest Territories was governed by a committee of civil servants in Ottawa. Although the first elections to the territorial council (now the Legislative Assembly) were held in 1951, it was not until 1975 that all positions on the council became elective and the last civil servant removed. Until the early 1980s the federally appointed commissioner chaired meetings of the territorial cabinet and only in 1986 did he cease running government departments.

During this same period Ottawa began transferring to the territorial government responsibility for policy areas that elsewhere in Canada fall within provincial jurisdiction such as health, transportation, and municipal government. However, in important ways, the Northwest Territories remains a colony of the federal government. It does not, like the provinces, enjoy a constitutionally enshrined existence; Ottawa could, by a simple act of Parliament, legislate the Northwest Territories out of existence or change it in other fundamental ways. All territorial laws are subject to veto by the minister of Indian Affairs and Northern Development. These formal powers are of decreasing significance; like the federal disallowance power over provincial legislation, the longer they remain disused, the less likely that they will ever be deployed. Of greater practical import is the federal government's retention of important powers in such fields as energy and natural resources and the heavy dependence of the territorial government on federal finances: more than 80 percent of the government of the Northwest Territories' budget comes from Ottawa in grants and transfer payments (far higher than any province).

Ottawa, in effect, has permitted the Northwest Territories to become, for most purposes, a self-governing colony. Without question, the trend to further devolution of authority from the federal to the territorial government will continue. Just as clearly, however, Ottawa is unwilling to grant the Northwest Territories provincial status until fundamental uncertainties over Native land claims, over moves toward Native self-government, and over possible division of the territories are resolved.

Many leaders of the powerful Native organizations such as the Dene Nation, the Métis Association of the Northwest Territories, and the Inuit Tapirisat do not regard the Government of the Northwest Territories (GNWT) as a legitimate representative institution, but as a foreign institution, imposed by a colonial power. Until 1979 the Dene refused to take part in territorial elections because they did not accept the legitimacy of the GNWT. Since 1979 Native members have held the majority of seats in the legislative assembly, but the acceptance of the GNWT by Natives remains problematic. As a committee of the assembly put it:

> the government of the Northwest Territories was set up and evolved without the full understanding and consent of the indigenous people. Now that they do understand, full consent is denied. Loyalty and commitment, hence the very stability of a jurisdiction, rely upon consent. A government must pay for imposition with continual dissatisfaction, tension, and significant dissent.

Although Natives have assumed positions of power in the GNWT, this has by no means solidified support for it among the Native population. Indeed, a crucially important, often bitter, battle continues to rage between the territorial government and the Native groups as to who really acts as the legitimate political embodiment of the Natives in the Northwest Territories.

DIVISION

The possibility of dividing the Northwest Territories along east-west lines has been on the political agenda since the 1960s. In response to vigorous public campaigns, the federal government agreed to hold a plebiscite on division. In the 1982 plebiscite, 56 percent supported the notion of division, while 44 percent were opposed. Significantly, whereas 80 percent of eastern Arctic voters favoured division, only 39 percent did in the west. Ottawa's approval of any division scheme is contingent upon, among other things, agreement on a mutually satisfactory boundary. It was clear from the outset that any boundary generally would follow the tree line (which is not so much a precise line as a zone), but both east and west laid claim to parts of the Beaufort Sea and of the so-called "barren lands" of the central Arctic. Protracted negotiations between representatives of the Inuit and the Dene-Métis resolved all but a few crucial disputes over the potential boundary, but this was enough to bring the process to a halt. With impetus towards division lost, the Native groups shifted their prime attention to the land claims process.

Arguments over division relate both to practicalities and to ideals. The duplication of costly administrative structures in two numerically small jurisdictions is a frequently raised objection, particularly given the dependence on Ottawa for financing. So too is the difficulty involved in recruiting and training two professional public services. Conversely, however, the often debilitating tension between east and west, which characterizes current politics in the Northwest Territories, would be eliminated by division. Moreover, the governments of two territories could more readily tailor their policies to the needs of their own populations, which would be much less disparate—geographically, culturally, and economically—than at present.

The fundamental thrust for division, however, reflects nationalism and a desire to give political form to regional and cultural identity. The Inuit feel remote and isolated from Yellowknife, which is 2500 km (and two time zones) from communities in the eastern Arctic—roughly the distance from Thunder Bay to Vancouver. They believe that their interests are not adequately considered by politicians and bureaucrats in the west, where conditions are very different. One of their highest political priorities, protecting and fostering their language and culture, would be far better served, they believe, were they firmly in control of their own government. As one eastern MLA put it, "For our people, it is a way of life, it is a way of thinking, it is a vision, it is our hope. Nunavut for us is self-government, self-determination, a greater measure of control over our lives."

With final resolution of the land claims apparently in sight, the prospect of division has once again come to the fore in the Northwest Territories. Inuit leaders are eager to see the creation of a *Nunavut* (our land, in Inuktitut) territory and are actively pressing the issue. At the urging of Inuit MLAs, in the fall of 1989 the legislative assembly reaffirmed its support for the creation of Nunavut by a 22–0 vote. Although establishment of *Denedeh* is still sought by some in the Dene-Métis community, others are hesitant; in a western Arctic territory Natives would find themselves in a minority. Many Dene-Métis leaders hope to achieve their political goals through self-government rather than through division. In the east the Inuit constitute over 80 percent of the population and division would for most practical purposes bring with it self-government there.

FORM OF GOVERNMENT

The form of government and the conduct of politics in the Northwest Territories are unlike those of any province. The most significant differences are the absence of political parties and the influence of Native political approaches. The form and principles of the Northwest Territories government are based on the British parliamentary model, but certain elements of "responsible government" in the Westminister sense either are absent or are present in unconventional ways.

The procedures of the 24-member legislative assembly are premised on British-style rules and incorporate such familiar features as an impartial Speaker, a question period, nonconfidence motions, and prohibitions against noncabinet members bringing forward financial measures. As is the case elsewhere in Canada, the cabinet derives its authority from its ability to retain the confidence of the House.

Other features of the assembly strike southern Canadians as decidedly unusual. Ministers, including the first minister (called the government leader), are elected by all 24 MLAs. Many important issues are discussed and resolved by the "caucus" of 24 meeting in private. Proposed government bills and even the government's spending estimates are sent to legislative committees for review prior to being made public, and cabinet is very responsive to MLAs' suggestions and criticisms about them. Without parties, candidates seek election—and re-election—as independents; on the plus side this means that members are neither beholden to party leaders nor cowed by party discipline; while on the negative side, voters have no opportunity to pass judgment on the government's record.

Although ordinary MLAs exert far more influence over the government than private members in any other Canadian legislature, the eight-member cabinet is clearly the prime locus of political power in the government of the Northwest Territories. Cabinet generally acts as a cohesive unit, though the norm of cabinet solidarity is not so well-developed as elsewhere in Canada. Since the government leader does not select his cabinet (though he does assign them responsibilities, and is empowered by the assembly to discipline them), his power over them is substantially less than that exercised by other Canadian first ministers. Moreover, the government leader appears to lack the power to dissolve the assembly in favour of new elections that first ministers in fully responsible systems enjoy (subject of course to approval by the representative of the crown).

The system is described as "consensus government." Yet if certain elements of Native political culture are evident in the assembly, relations between the executive and the legislature are primarily based on the British model, in which a powerful cabinet dominates policy making, often to the exclusion of the private members. Still, although consensus government as it operates in the NWT is a far cry from the true Native consensual decision making, it is also very different from the accepted Canadian model.

The contrast with the Yukon is instructive. Government and politics there are much more conventional by Canadian standards. They are dominated by the political parties of the Canadian mainstream. The absence of parties in the Northwest Territories does not reflect underdevelopment compared with the Yukon or the south so much as it represents a conscious rejection, by almost all Natives and by many non-Natives, of the very notion of a party system, with its artificial divisions, its destructive competition, and its corollary of rigid party discipline. Residents of the Northwest Territories believe that their political needs are unique and not at all suitable to party domination—especially parties rooted in the political divisions of the south. (In federal politics candidates run as standard-bearers for the three principal political parties; many territorial politicians are known to have affiliations to the southern parties, but they count for little in Northwest Territories politics.)

LAND CLAIMS AND SELF-GOVERNMENT

In most of Canada the term "public government" would seem redundant, since government is by definition public. In the Northwest Territories, however, it is very much an open question whether the principal form of government will be the traditional public form (that is, applicable to all) or will be essentially aboriginal self-government. Technically, self-government and land claims are separate issues, but the reality is that the two are inextricably bound together.

Native land claims are not unique to the Northwest Territories; in recent years they have become a common feature of the Canadian political landscape. In essence they represent demands by Native peoples for recognition that vast tracts of land were never ceded to the British or Canadian governments, or that treaties signed between Natives and governments were never intended to transfer complete ownership and control of Native lands to government. (Native cultures have no concept of private ownership of land, a notion deeply ingrained in European societies; instead, Natives look upon themselves as the collective stewards of the land.)

Land claims, generally, have three components: monetary compensation for lands that have already been or will be developed for the benefit of non-Natives; full ownership and control (including all mineral and development rights) over certain lands; and significant influence over such matters as wildlife management and resource development in other areas. Typically, the areas under complete Native control are relatively small compared to the areas of partial control.

The land claims in the Northwest Territories rank among the largest, most far-reaching in Canada. In 1984 the smallest of the three claims was settled. The Inuvialuit (the Inuit of the Mackenzie Delta) received 5000 square miles of land outright, $152 million (over 14 years) and are involved in the management of the balance of the Delta region. An agreement-in-principle was reached in 1988 with the Dene-Métis, but it came close to foundering over disagreements on specific provisions. In April, 1990 negotiations on a final settlement were completed between the Dene-Métis and the federal government, subject to approval by the individual Native communities. The settlement provided for a cash payment of $540 million (over 20 years), direct control over 70 000 square miles of land with effectively the balance of the Western Arctic subject to Native agreement on important resource development issues. Finally, an agreement-in-principle between the Inuit and Ottawa was signed in early 1990; expectations are that finalization of the details will not be difficult. The scope of the Inuit settlement is effectively that of the projected Nunavut territory, including 136 000 square miles of land to be completely controlled by the Inuit. In addition, the package includes $612 million in cash over 20 years.

Settlement of land claims constitutes a significant development in several respects. Symbolically, it is important for Native peoples to gain formal recognition by the federal government of their unique status and their special relationship with the land. Culturally, the capacity to protect and promote the hunting and trapping, so central to the Native way of life, is highly significant. Economically, the money (virtually all of which goes to Native organizations rather than to individuals) will provide capital for the Natives of the Northwest Territories to finance their own businesses and economic development opportunities. Politically, settlement of the claims clears the way for Native self-government.

Although public opinion surveys indicate that a majority of Canadians support the notion of aboriginal self-government, probably few have a clear idea of what it would entail. In part this reflects the fact that even among Native groups substantial disagreement exists as to how it might work in practice.

Native groups in the Northwest Territories have yet to work out in detail their ideas of how self-government would operate, but it is clear that they envision a fundamental reordering of governmental structures and responsibilities. Quite simply, they wish to provide, in an authoritative fashion, most of the public services currently provided by the territorial and federal governments, including education, social services, justice, and economic development. Moreover, they reject the notion of having powers delegated to them by other governments, in the manner of municipalities; they want autonomy from other levels of government. They hope to achieve independent status more akin to that of the provinces vis-à-vis the federal government.

Given the large Native population in the Northwest Territories and the extent of the land claims settlements, such visions of Native self-government are clearly incompatible with the continued existence of the territorial government in anything like its present form (regardless of whether division occurs). The territorial government would continue as the public government for non-Natives, but granting Native self-government in its more extreme form would necessarily strip the GNWT of its principal powers over most of its citizens. Accordingly, in a way unimaginable in provinces where self-government agreements have been or are being worked out, the prospect exists in the Northwest Territories for irreconcilable conflict between public government and aboriginal self-government. Of course, considerable leeway exists for a significant measure of Native self-government of a less radical form that would not pose a threat to the continued existence of the territorial government. How insistent the Native groups will be is very much an open question, as are the responses of the federal and territorial governments.

Through the 1980s negotiations between the Native groups and the federal government focused on the land claims rather than on self-government. Moreover, since self-government discussions are typically complex and difficult, the federal government cannot deal with a large number of negotiating processes at once; for a variety of reasons federal efforts have concentrated on reaching self-government agreements with Natives in British Columbia and Alberta. In short, as of mid-1990 the process of negotiating native self-government in the Northwest Territories had yet to begin in earnest. Thus, the manifold questions arising from the Natives' quest for self-government will not be resolved for some time.

In a way unimaginable elsewhere in Canada, the future of the government and the legislative assembly of the Northwest Territories is highly uncertain, pending the outcome of the movements toward division and toward Native self-government. Whether there will be one political unit or two and whether they will attain provincehood, remain territories, or achieve some intermediate status, fundamental issues relating to the form of government, the style of decision making, and the nature of Native–non-Native political relationships remain to be resolved. Clearly, future political developments in the Northwest Territories will carry it in directions unfamiliar to most Canadians. As such, the Northwest Territories will represent an intriguing test of the adaptability of Canadian federalism.

BIBLIOGRAPHY

Federalism and Federal Problems

(See also Bibliographies in Chapters 1, 2, 4, and 5.)

Armstrong, C. *The Politics of Federalism: Ontario's Relations with the Federal Government 1867–1942*. Toronto: U.T.P., 1981.

Bakvis, H. *Federalism and the Organization of Political Life: Canada in Comparative Perspective*. Kingston: Queen's University, I.I.R., 1981.

Bakvis, H., and Chandler, W. (eds.). *Federalism and the Role of the State*. Toronto: U.T.P., 1987.

Banting, K. *The Welfare State and Canadian Federalism*. 2nd ed., Montreal: McG-Q.U.P., 2nd ed., 1987.

Beckton, C.F., and MacKay, A.W., (eds.). *Recurring Issues in Canadian Federalism*. Toronto: U.T.P., 1985.

Bernard, A. *Politics in Canada and Quebec*. Adapted by J. Driefelds. Toronto: Methuen, 1981.

Black, E.R. *Divided Loyalties: Canadian Concepts of Federalism*. Montreal: McG-Q.U.P., 1975.

Bothwell, R., Drummond, I., and English, J. *Canada Since 1945: Power, Politics and Provincialism*. Toronto: U.T.P., 2nd ed., 1989.

Breton, A., and Scott, A. *The Design of Federations*. Montreal: I.R.P.P., 1980.

Brown-John, L., (ed.). *Centralizing and Decentralizing Trends in Federal States*. Lanham, Maryland: University Press of America, 1988.

Cairns, A.C. "The Governments and Societies of Canadian Federalism." *C.J.P.S.*, 10, 4, December, 1977.

Cairns, A.C. "The Other Crisis of Canadian Federalism." *C.P.A.*, 22, 2, Summer, 1979.

Carty, R.K., and Ward, W.P., (eds.). *Entering the Eighties: Canada in Crisis*. Toronto: O.U.P., 1980.

Courchene, T.J. *Economic Management and the Division of Powers*. Toronto: U.T.P., 1985.

Courchene, T.J. *et al.*, (eds.). *Federalism and the Canadian Economic Union*. Toronto: U.T.P., 1983.

Chandler, W., and Zollner, C.W., (eds.). *Challenges to Federalism: Policy-Making in Canada and the Federal Republic of Germany*. Kingston: Queen's University, I.I.R., 1989.

Elton, D., Engelmann, F., and McCormick, P. *Alternatives: Towards the Development of an Effective Federal System for Canada*, Amended Report. Calgary: Canada West Foundation, 1981.

Federal-Provincial Programs and Activities: A Descriptive Inventory, 1986–1987. Ottawa: Federal-Provincial Relations Office, 1987.

Hodgins, B. *et al.*, (eds.). *Federalism in Canada and Australia*. Peterborough, Ontario: Broadview Press, 1989.

Hodgins, B.W., Wright, D., and Heick, W.H. *Federalism in Canada and Australia: The Early Years*. Waterloo, W.L.U.P., 1978.

Hueglin, T.O. *Federalism and Fragmentation: A Comparative View of Political Accommodation in Canada*. Kingston: Queen's University, I.I.R., 1984.

James, P., and Michelin, R. "The Canadian National Energy Program and its Aftermath: Perspectives on an Era of Confrontation." *A.R.C.S.*, 19, Spring, 1989.

Krasnick, M., Norrie, K., and Simeon, R., (eds.). *Case Studies in the Division of Powers*. Toronto: U.T.P., 1985.

Krasnick, M., Norrie, K., and Simeon, R., (eds.). *Division of Powers and Public Policy*. Toronto: U.T.P., 1985.

Krasnick, M., Norrie, K., and Simeon, R., (eds.). *Intergovernmental Relations*. Toronto: U.T.P., 1985.

Leslie, P. *Federal State, National Economy*. Toronto: U.T.P., 1987.

Leslie, P. *Federal Leadership in Social and Economic Policy*. Kingston: Queen's University, I.I.R., 1988.

Leslie, P. *National Citizenships and Provincial Communities: A Review of Canadian Fiscal Federalism and Ethnonationalism in a Federal State: The Case of Canada*. Kingston: Queen's University, I.I.R., 1988.

Lower, A. "The Prime Minister and the Premiers." *Q.Q.*, 87, 4, Winter, 1980.

Mahler, G. *New Dimensions of Canadian Federalism: Canada in a Comparative Perspective*. Cranbury: Fairleigh Dickinson University Press, 1987.

Meekison, J.P. (ed.). *Canadian Federalism: Myth or Reality?* Toronto: Methuen, 3rd ed., 1977.

Milne, D. *Tug of War: Ottawa and the Provinces Under Trudeau and Mulroney*. Toronto: Lorimer, 1986.

Monahan, P.J. "At Doctrine's Twilight: The Structure of Canadian Federalism." *U. of T. L.J.*, 34, 1984.

Murray, C. *Managing Diversity: Federal-Provincial Collaboration and the Committee on Extension of Services to Northern and Remote Communities*. Kingston: Queen's University, I.I.R., 1984.

Norrie, K., Simeon, R., and Krasnick, M. *Federalism and Economic Union in Canada*. Toronto: U.T.P., 1985.

Olling, R., and Westmacott, M., (eds.) *Perspectives on Canadian Federalism*. Toronto: P.-H., 1988.

Petter, A. "Federalism and the Myth of the Federal Spending Power." *C.B.R.*, 68, September 1989.

Reid, J. "Federal-Provincial Conferences: Their Implications for Legislators and Political Parties." *C.P.R.*, 4, 3, Autumn, 1981.

Rémillard, G. *Le fédéralisme canadien*. Montréal: Québec/Amérique, 1980.

Rémillard, G. *Le fédéralisme canadien*. Tome 2, *Le rapatriement de la Constitution*. Montréal: Québec/Amérique, 1985.

Robertson, G. "The Global Challenge and Canadian Federalism." *C.P.A.*, 32, 1, Spring, 1989.

Savoie, D.J. *The Canada-New Brunswick General Development Agreement*. Montreal: McG.-Q.U.P., 1981.

Savoie, D.J. "Competitive Federalism: The Case of Direct Delivery of Federal Programmes." *J.C.S.*, 21, 1, Spring, 1986.

Schultz, R. *Delegation and Cable Distribution Systems: A Negative Assessment*. Kingston: Queen's University, I.I.R., 1981.

Schultz, R., and Alexandroff, A. *Economic Regulation and the Federal System*. Toronto: U.T.P., 1985.

Scott, A. *Divided Jurisdiction Over Natural Resources*. Kingston: Queen's University, I.I.R., 1980.

Scott, F. R., *Essays on the Constitution: Aspects of Canadian Law and Politics*. Toronto: U.T.P., 1977.

Shugarman, D., and Whitaker, R., (eds.). *Federalism and Political Community: Essays in Honour of Donald Smiley*. Peterborough: Broadview Press, 1990.

Simeon, R. *Natural Resource Revenues and Canadian Federalism: A Survey of the Issues*. Kingston: Queen's University, I.I.R., 1980.

Simeon, R. "Intergovernmental Relations and the Challenges to Canadian Federalism." *C.P.A.*, 23, 1, Spring, 1980.

Simeon, R. *The Political Economy of Canadian Federalism: 1940 to 1984.* Toronto: U.T.P. 1985.

Simeon, R. "Considerations on Centralization and Decentralization." *C.P.A.*, 29, 3, Fall, 1986.

Simeon, R., (ed.). *Must Canada Fail?* Montreal: McG-Q.U.P., 1977.

Smiley, D. V. "Territorialism and Canadian Political Institutions." *C.P.P.*, III, 4, Autumn, 1977.

Smiley, D. V. "The Challenge of Canadian Ambivalence." *Q.Q.*, 88, 1, Spring, 1981.

Smiley, D. V. *The Federal Condition in Canada.* Toronto: McG-H.R., 1987.

Smiley, D. V. and Watts, R. L., *Intrastate Federalism in Canada.* Toronto: U.T.P., 1985.

Smith, J. "Canadian Confederation and the Influence of American Federalism." *C.J.P.S.*, 21, 3, September, 1988.

Smith, P. "The Ideological Origins of Canadian Confederation." *C.J.P.S.*, 20, 1, March, 1987.

Stevenson, G. *Unfulfilled Union: Canadian Federalism and National Unity.* Toronto: Gage, 3rd ed., 1988.

Stevenson, G. (ed.). *Federalism in Canada: Selected Essays.* Toronto: M.& S., 1989.

Swan, J. "The Canadian Constitution, Federalism, and the Conflict of Laws." *C.B.R.*, 63, 2, June, 1985.

Thorburn, H. G. *Planning and the Economy: Building Federal- Provincial Consensus.* Toronto: Lorimer, 1984.

Thur, L.M., (ed.). *Energy Policy and Federalism.* Toronto: I.P.A.C., 1981.

Veilleux, G. "Intergovernmental Canada: Government by Conference: A Fiscal and Economic Perspective." *C.P.A.*, 23, 1, Spring, 1980. (See also comments by Dupre, J.S., *ibid.*)

Verney, D. "The 'Reconciliation' of Parliamentary Supremacy and Federalism in Canada." *Journal of Commonwealth and Comparative Politics*, 21, 1, March, 1983.

Vipond, R. "1787 and 1867: The Federal Principle and Canadian Confederation Reconsidered." *C.J.P.S.*, 22, 1, March, 1989.

Waller, H., Sabetti, F., and Elazar, D. *Canadian Federalism: From Crisis to Constitution.* Lanham, Maryland: University Press of America, 1988.

Watts, R., and Brown, D., (eds.). *Canada: The State of the Federation, 1989.* Kingston: Queen's University, I.I.R., 1990. (Annual; previous editors include Leslie, P., Dunn, S., Pollard, B.).

Whitaker, R. *Federalism and Democratic Theory.* Kingston: Queen's University, I.I.R., 1983.

Wiltshire, K. "Working with Intergovernmental Agreements — The Canadian and Australian Experience." *C.P.A.*, 23, 3, Fall, 1980.

Wiltshire, K. *Planning and Federalism: Australian and Canadian Experience.* St. Lucia, Queensland: University of Queensland Press, 1986.

Woodrow, R.B., *et al. Conflict over Communications Policy: A Study of Federal-Provincial Relations and Public Policy.* Montreal: C.D. Howe Institute, 1980.

Finances

Auld, D.A.L., and Miller, C. *Principles of Public Finance: A Canadian Text.* Toronto: Methuen, 2nd ed., 1982.

Bird, R.M., (ed.). *Fiscal Dimensions of Canadian Federalism.* Toronto: C.T.F., 1980.

Bird, R.M. *Federal Finance: An International Perspective.* Toronto: C.T.F., 1985.

Brown, M. *Established Program Financing: Evolution or Regression in Canadian Fiscal Federalism*. Canberra: Australian National University, 1984.

Canada, Parliamentary Task Force on Federal-Provincial Fiscal Arrangements, [Breau Committee]. *Fiscal Federalism in Canada*. Ottawa: S. and S., 1981.

C.P.P., special issue on "Financing Confederation," 8, 3, Summer, 1982.

C.T.F. *The National Finances: An Analysis of the Revenues and Expenditures of the Government of Canada, 1989–90*. Toronto: C.T.F., 1990. (Annual.)

C.T.F. *Provincial and Municipal Finances, 1989*. Toronto: C.T.F., 1990. (Biennial.)

Carmichael, E.A. *Tackling the Federal Deficit*. Montreal: C.D. Howe Institute, 1984.

Carter, F. "How to Tame the Spending Power." *P.O.*, 7, 8, October, 1986.

Carter, G.E. "Established Programs Financing: A Critical Review of the Record." *C.T.J.*, 36, 5, Sept-Oct, 1988.

Courchene, T.J. *et al. Ottawa and the Provinces: The Distribution of Money and Power*. Toronto: O.E.C., 1985, 2 Vols.

Courchene, T.J. *Equalization Payments: Past, Present and Future*. Toronto: O.E.C., 1984.

Delamaide, D. *Debt Shock*. Toronto: L. & O. D., 1984.

Kabir, M., and Hackett, D.W. "Is Atlantic Canada Becoming More Dependent on Federal Transfers?" *C.P.P.*, 15, March, 1989, (See also Dickson, V., Murrell, D., "Comment" *C.P.P.*, 15, March, 1990.)

Krasnick, M., Norrie, K., and Simeon, R., (eds.). *Fiscal Federalism*. Toronto: U.T.P., 1985.

LaForest, G.V. *The Allocation of Taxing Powers Under the Canadian Constitution*. Toronto: C.T.F., 2nd ed., 1981.

Moore, M. "Some Proposals for Adapting Federal-Provincial Financial Agreements to Current Conditions." *C.P.A.*, 24, 2, Summer, 1981.

Perry, J.H. *Background of Current Fiscal Problems*. Toronto: C.T.F., 1982.

Phidd, R.W., and Doern, G.B., (eds.). *The Politics and Management of Canadian Economic Policy*. Toronto: Macmillan, 1978.

Watson, W. "Simpler Equalization." *P.O.* 7, 8, October, 1986.

Meech Lake Proposed Amendments

Baines, B. "Gender and the Meech Lake Committee." *Q.Q.*, 94, 4, Winter, 1987.

Barker, P. "The Accord and Medicare." *P.O.*, 9, 9 November, 1988.

Behiels, M. (ed.). *The Meech Lake Primer: Conflicting Views of the 1987 Constitutional Accord*. Ottawa: U.O.P., 1989.

Canadian Public Policy. Special Issue on the Meech Lake Accord, 14, September, 1988.

Canadians for a Unifying Constitution, with Friends of Meech Lake, *Meech Lake: Setting the Record Straight*. Ottawa: Ampersand, 1990.

Cook, R. "Alice in Meechland or the Concept of Quebec as 'A Distinct Society.'" *Q.Q.*, 94, 4, Winter, 1987.

Dean, J. "Living with Unanimity." *P.O.*, 9, 9, November, 1988.

Gibbins, R. (ed.). *Meech Lake and Canada: Perspectives from the West*. Edmonton: Academic Printing and Publishing, 1988.

Hogg, P. *Meech Lake Constitutional Accord Annotated*. Toronto: Carswell, 1988.

Isaak, P., Roper, P., and Stebelsky, S. "Why the Deal [Meech Lake Accord] Should be Blocked." *P.O.*, 10, 9, November 1989.

Johnston, D., (ed.). *Pierre Trudeau Speaks Out on Meech Lake*. Toronto: General Paperbacks, revised, 1990.

Manitoba Task Force on Meech Lake. *Report on the 1987 Constitutional Accord.* Winnipeg: 1989.

Mintz, E. "How the Deal [Meech Lake Accord] Can Be Saved." *P.O.*, 10, 9, November, 1989.

New Brunswick Legislative Assembly, Select Committee on the 1987 Constitutional Accord. *Final Report.* Fredericton: 1989.

Robertson, G. *A House Divided: Meech Lake, Senate Reform and the Canadian Union.* Halifax: I.R.P.P., 1989.

Special Joint Committee of the Senate and the House of Commons on The 1987 Constitutional Accord. *Report,* 1987.

Swinton, K., and Rogerson, C. *Competing Constitutional Visions: The Meech Lake Accord.* Toronto: Carswell, 1988.

Thomas, C.. (ed.). *Navigating Meech Lake: The 1987 Constitutional Accord.* Kingston: Queen's University, I.I.R., 1988.

Vipond, R.C. "Whatever Became of the Compact Theory? Meech Lake and the New Politics of Constitutional Amendment in Canada." *Q.Q.*, 96, 4, Winter, 1989.

REGIONALISM

THE DIFFERENT DIMENSIONS
OF REGIONALISM IN CANADA

Peter McCormick

To assert the importance of regionalism in Canadian politics is neither original nor interesting; it has all the shock value of observing that forests contain trees or lakes are wet. Normally the discussion proceeds immediately to examine specific examples of regionalism (Quebec or the West or the Maritimes), or to look at the question of what should be done about it (national identity-building or Senate reform or whatever). The purpose of this article is to proceed in the other direction, to ask what sort of a thing regionalism in general or Canadian regionalism in particular might be, if only to make sure that we are not stretching a single word rather further than it is useful to ask it to stretch.

It is immediately clear that politically relevant regionalism is several sorts of things rather than just one generic type. Quebec is a region and the West is a region and the Maritimes is a region; but when we talk about Quebec we focus on language and politics, when we talk about the Maritimes we stress historical links and interaction, and when we talk about the West we bring up questions of resource producing regions as distinguished from resource consuming regions, and so on for the North, the Prairies, the Atlantic, and all the other regions that appear in the literature from time to time. Each example suggests

From *Journal of Canadian Studies/Revue d'études Canadiennes*, Vol. 24, No. 2, Summer, 1989. By permission.

a "regionalism" of quite different implications and effects, often difficult to translate or to compare. Quebeckers often see English Canada as a monolith (much to the chagrin and disgust of Western Canadians) because there is a single language bloc accompanied from time to time by the appearance of a united front against Quebec. Western Canadians earn the reputation of anti-French rednecks by speaking disparagingly of a unified central Canada using its economic and political power to keep the West in check, because from their point of view language differences are less significant than the imperatives of economic interests. Neither is insincere about their protestations and assumptions, but each is using the notion of regionalism in a different sense.

As an initial effort at brush-clearing, I will identify the major dimensions of politically relevant regionalism. The core of regionalism is a persisting, territorially-linked diversity that has actual or potential political implications, and the extent to which the different dimensions are or are not present or strong generates different *varieties* of regionalism. . . .

DISTRIBUTIONAL REGIONALISM

The first dimension of regionalism is the most straightforward: some provinces are different because their population is distinctly different in terms of basic demographic factors such as religion or ethnicity or the like. Clearly it makes a difference to the politics of a province if significant numbers of its inhabitants speak English or French or both or neither, or if the strongest church is Catholic or Presbyterian or Methodist or Unitarian, or if large blocs of people hail from the Ukraine or Glasgow or Ulster or Vietnam, and these differences may reverberate long after all the original settlers have become senior citizens.

We might call this dimension of regionalism "distributional," and acknowledge that the differences to which it refers can be gratuitous, almost accidental. . . .

This brand of regionalism is conceptually simplistic, but it can nonetheless be of profound political importance. Canada's fundamental territorial cleavage, that between French and English, is the classic but not the only example. It is a matter of historical accident that Canada's French Canadians wound up in Quebec rather than in some other geographical location, because there is nothing about the rivers, rocks and fields of that province that predisposes one to express political ideas in the language of Molière. It is similarly a matter of historical accident that they remained clustered in Quebec rather than spreading more evenly across the country. . . .

The comment about francophones might be replicated in more moderate terms for the variety of ethnic groups that have become part of the Canadian mosaic in successive waves of immigration. The distribution of these groups across the Canadian provinces is far from even. A broad census category such as "other European" shows minimal numbers in the Atlantic region, massive concentration in the Prairie provinces, and scattered clusters in the major urban centres of central Canada; breaking the broad category into more specific elements shows Italians concentrated in Toronto, Ukrainians in northern Alberta, and so on. Canadians of Asian origin are statistically much more significant in British Columbia and southern Alberta than in most other parts of the country. . . .

The impact of religion on Canadian politics has been parallel, although of declining importance in an increasingly secular society. The initial confrontation between primarily Protestant anglophones and overwhelmingly Catholic francophones was complicated by waves of immigrants from Eastern Europe and other parts of the world. In some parts of the country, but not in others, the balance within Catholic ranks between French and Irish was upset by the newcomers who were neither, and then again only in some parts of the country the Protestant/Catholic balance was further confused by the arrival of significant numbers of Orthodox believers. Similarly, Protestant ranks are far from monolithic, and (for example) the uneven receptivity of fundamentalism has helped to create areas such as "Bible Belt" southern and central Alberta and the Okanagan where MPs are pilloried by their constituents for mild right-to-life statements that are thought commonplace, even wishy-washy, in central Canadian cities. The politics of ethnicity and the politics of religion have been closely intertwined, crisscrossing each other to create regional concentrations that make the differences relevant to political regionalism.

Stretching the point slightly, because they are less gratuitous and sometimes more structural in nature, the category of distributional regionalism might be extended to include other demographic factors as well. Age, education, length of residence, and rural/urban location are all factors that impact directly on politics, and all show considerable diversity from one province to another. The politics of a province with a significant number of recent arrivals, whether from other provinces or other countries (such as British Columbia, or Alberta in the 1970s) is different from that of a province where most families measure their residence in the region in generations (such as Nova Scotia or Prince Edward Island); a province with an aging population will be politically different from one with a high proportion of young adults; and so on. Such regional concentrations are far from surprising in a country as large and geographically diverse as Canada, although the counterexample of Australia suggests that such variations are not unavoidable but just that they have not been avoided in Canada.

These distributional differences impact upon politics in several ways. First, they may contribute directly to a political culture and a set of political values that are specific to the region and distinct from those of other regions. It used to be commonplace to suggest that some regions of Canada were more tolerant of political corruption, more concerned about whether candidates for office could deliver the goods than the details of their personal lives, than other regions; it used to be said that some religious affiliations were more accepting than others of church guidance in political affairs; it used to be suggested that immigrant groups tended to retain a gratitude and a political loyalty to the government and party in power that permitted them to enter and assisted them in settling; and so on.

Second, even in the absence of differences in political culture, distributional regionalism can contribute to differences in specific policies or programs that are demanded or opposed. The interest of francophones in bilingual policies, of Eastern European immigrant groups in multiculturalism or in pressuring the Soviet bloc on human rights, of recent Asian immigrants in changes to immigration policy are obvious examples. Similarly, the relative political salience of such issues as higher old age pensions, property tax reductions for senior citizens, and universal day-care is clearly linked to the relative proportions of senior citizens and young parents in any given region.

Third, local concentrations of ethnic or racial or religious minorities not only have their own political agenda and style, but often provoke a response from the other groups with whom they are in contact. Nativism is typically the response of a status-threatened resident population to the arrival of newcomers who are distinctive in physical attribute or life-style or both, externalizing in a scapegoat pervasive and unavoidable anxieties. The 1919 Winnipeg General Strike was the occasion for identifying foreigners generally with Bolshevik radicals, leading to some legally very dubious deportations; as late as the 1940s British Columbia denied the right to vote to Canadian citizens of Japanese descent; and the Ku Klux Klan made a brief but politically significant appearance in Saskatchewan, peddling anti-immigrant and anti-Catholic rather than anti-Negro slogans. . . .

Fourth, whether or not a specific demographic minority gets involved in politics, and the kind of politics in which it becomes involved, are also connected to the way in which it is distributed among the constituent units of the federation. Alan Cairns has spelled out the logic: a territorially concentrated minority is the natural clientele of regionalist movements, but a territorially dispersed minority is the natural clientele of the central government. The *francophones hors du Quebec*, as a national minority that is also a regional minority in every province, are naturally drawn to the federal government and receive a more sympathetic hearing there than they would in any provincial capital, and the same tends to be the case for the native peoples' organizations. The connection between minority status and political regionalism is not automatic, but must be catalyzed by the distributional "accident" of territorial concentration.

. . . The large Asian presence in British Columbia must be included in any explanation of why that province, rather than Nova Scotia, excluded Japanese Canadians from the provincial franchise, just as the distribution of francophones within Canada helps to explain why the *Gens de l'Air* dispute involves the air corridors over Quebec rather than Saskatchewan. This is *obvious*, but it is still important. Every demographic group is a group of electors, and therefore a potential source of support to a government that appeals to its interests or behaves in the way it approves and expects. Governments respond to or anticipate the demands of their electorates, and electorates of different demographic characteristics lead those governments in different directions. This is not a very subtle form of regionalism, but it is regionalism nonetheless.

ECONOMIC/OCCUPATIONAL REGIONALISM

The second dimension of regionalism we might call "economic/occupational," differing in that it is not gratuitous but directly generated by Canada's geographic diversity. It may be banal to observe that one is more likely to find dock-workers in British Columbia than Saskatchewan, more likely to find farmers in Saskatchewan than Nova Scotia, more likely to find fishermen in Newfoundland than Alberta, more likely to find miners in British Columbia than Prince Edward Island, and so on; but the banal observations have significant political consequences.

The first consequence is differences in political culture and behaviour, and in the context of political activity. Given that personal experiences in the workplace are an important part of political socialization, it is only to be expected that the different occupational patterns generated by the different resource and economic bases of the various provinces will themselves contribute to differences in political styles and expectations. For example, not only is British Columbia the most unionized province in Canada, making unionized labour a more significant factor in politics there than elsewhere in Canada, but in important sectors such as mining and forestry union/management relations have been characterized by confrontation, militancy and protracted ill-tempered strikes. The interior of the province is dotted with forestry and mining towns that present the worker/management duality in terms of unavoidable starkness, unsoftened by the distractions of physical separation or the presence of other economic groups. This has helped to give British Columbia politics a radical tinge and a polarization between labour and business that is unusual in Canada. The loose, business-oriented umbrella of Social Credit is only the most recent successor to the formal Liberal/Conservative coalition after World War II in the grand cause of keeping the socialists out of power.

The unusual socio-economic conditions of Prairie farmers, the paradoxical elements of which are so nicely caught by C.B. Macpherson's classic phrase "independent commodity producer," created the populist political and organizational style that emerged in the aftermath of World War I. Although the roots of this style were deeper in the Prairies than elsewhere, the Progressive movement had a massive and enduring impact on Canadian politics, directly in the 1920s and then through its two successors, the Social Credit movement and the Co-operative Commonwealth Federation, the latter the forerunner of the present New Democratic Party. The populist style was characterized by an emphasis on grass roots democracy, suspicion of outsiders and of the "Fifty Big Shots" of the financial system, a faith in the common man, a dislike of parliament and party that led to the creation of informal coalition governments and the renunciation of official opposition status, and a distrust of formal leaders so profound that on at least two occasions (Alberta 1919, Manitoba 1923) leaderless parties won a majority of the seats in a provincial legislature. As its farmer class foundation dwindles and rural regions diminish in population and political importance, the impact of this regionally based phenomenon is fading, although there are still occasional echoes, as when the Western Canada Concept's recent leadership race permitted the party membership from a dozen locations to vote directly on the new leader of the party through satellite age telecommunications. The Progressives might well have approved of such an innovative marriage of direct democracy and technology.

But the second set of consequences of economic/occupational regionalism—that is, the differences in political interests that exist as a result—is just as significant and even more enduring. It is not just that Vancouver dockworkers undergo a different political socialization from that of Ontario factory workers, or that both again are different from Newfoundland fishermen, but that a policy or a state of affairs that favours one may harm another. The economic interests of the various groups trade off in what can be perilously close to a zero-sum game. Indeed, as Hugh Thorburn suggests, "the structure of federalism in itself is an incentive to view political issues in zero sum terms." It is of course oversimplification to consider Canada as divided into a politically dominant resource-consuming centre composed of Ontario and Quebec, and a politically marginal resource-producing hinterland composed of the rest of the country (oversimplification if only because it assimilates the resource-producing northern regions of the central provinces to their metropolitan cores), but this nonetheless catches a duality that has been recurrently pivotal in Canadian politics. It was clearly evident, for example, during the Western Canadian resource boom of the 1970s and hovers in the background of the debate over free trade with the United States.

The successful economic sectors of any region constitute a regional elite that contributes campaign funds and leadership to supportive political groups, while their employees are voters who oppose measures that threaten their prosperity and job security. The impact is by no means limited to provincial politics. In a country as diverse as Canada, national economic policies impact quite differently upon different parts of the country, and the political reactions both exhibit and reinforce regionalism. All provincial governments act to promote the economic opportunities of their region and urge the federal government to do likewise, while existing occupational groups pressure governments at both levels to act in ways that are favourable to them. This seems appropriate enough, because, as Thorburn points out, "when the British North American provinces were united in 1867, the object of the enterprise was economic development." Where geographic diversity implies a different resource base for economic activity, a political regionalism based directly upon economic and occupational considerations will quite probably result.

There is a pervasive tendency, at least one that I often perceive, to assume that a regionalism with cultural dimensions is more real or genuine or important than one which is fundamentally economic, although one need only state it in such bald terms to sense its absurdity. When one person whose grandparents moved West from Ontario in 1900 has a row over freight rates with another person whose grandparents did not, both using the same language, idioms, and ideological assumptions throughout, this is still regionalism. Indeed, one could just as easily reverse the tendency and argue that it is regional differences grounded in economics that are real, while those that grow from purely cultural factors are less important. After all, many wars have been fought over language and history and religion, but an equally depressing number have been fought over raw materials and markets and access to trade routes. If some mysterious cataclysm were to obliterate the population of Quebec (plague? an errant US cruise missile? a Canadian Chernobyl?) and the territory were to be incrementally restocked by new immigrants, then it is unlikely in the extreme that the language of education for St. Leonard or the issue of the *Gens de L'Air* would again emerge as a focus for politics. But if a similar disaster were to depopulate Saskatchewan or Alberta, and immigrants were to filter back into that territory, then within a generation they would be complaining about freight rates and tariff policies and saying "Damn the CPR." However, the argument over the "true" form of regionalism is an empty one, flowing from the erroneous assumption that if we are using one word we must be referring to only one thing; in fact, Canadian regionalism comes in many forms, each of which is real and important.

PERCEPTUAL REGIONALISM

The third dimension of regionalism concerns the extent to which a region is subjectively perceived as such by its inhabitants; we might call this "perceptual" dimension. For an observer to impose regional divisions from "above" and outside can mean very little, and Harold Clarke *et al.* write ironically of an Atlantic region that is more clearly perceived from the West than by its inhabitants. Mildred Schwartz falls into precisely this trap when she creates her five regional "containers" that Simeon criticizes. It is quite a different thing to let the regions create themselves from the self-perceptions of their inhabitants, to discover those geographical units that are perceived by the people within them to constitute real entities, to find the regional containers whose self-definition creates an "us" that is to be distinguished and defended from "them." It is this type of regionalism that creates a real potential for political mobilization.

On the basis of the results of the 1974 election survey, Jon Pammett wrote an intriguing article on regional self-perceptions. The question that provided Pammett's data asked a random sample of Canadians whether they felt that regionalism was an important dimension of Canadian politics, and then asked those giving an affirmative response what region they felt they lived in. The results are as provocative as they are difficult to categorize. A majority of Canadians thought in regional terms and could name a region with which they identified, although a significant number (varying from 20% in Saskatchewan to 40% in New Brunswick) did not. Regional identification was more pronounced among the young, which suggests that it is a waxing rather than a waning force. . . .

However, although a majority thought in regional terms, they did so in a variety of ways. They fragmented between those who identified specific provinces, those who thought in terms of vaguely multi-provincial groupings such as "West" or "Prairies" or "Central" or "Maritime" or "Atlantic," those who indicated regions smaller than provinces, and those who thought of regions in non-geographic terms (including "French Canada" and similar designations). What looks perfectly clear from outside (such as the traditional division of Canada into the four Senatorial regions of Atlantic/Maritime, Quebec, Ontario, and West) becomes far less clear when individuals spontaneously identify their own region. Apart from the obvious problem of one-sided polarities (that is, there is a self-designated west but no corresponding east, and a self-conscious French Canada but no parallel English Canada), there are some fascinatingly intricate patterns, as New Brunswickers seem to opt out of a region called the Maritimes and Manitobans do not identify with the Prairies. Even within a single province regional perceptions point in several different directions: how does an inhabitant of Alberta who saw himself as part of the Prairies identify with a neighbour who spoke of the West, and how would either or both make common cause with one who saw himself simply as an Albertan?

Regional self-identification is the raw material of regional agitation, but clearly there is opportunity here for a variety of strategies. Region is a strong evocative symbol, but its pull is neither straightforward nor unidirectional. Regionalism is multifaceted, in that any of a variety of regional identifications might evoke a positive response among some portions of a given population. It follows that the imposition of one definition of a region upon the assumptions of that population and the external actors who must deal with it represents a victory for a specific set of interests that are advantaged by that definition, and a defeat for those interests that would be better served by an alternative definition. In general terms, "Translation of disputes into the terms of a particular discourse strengthens the position of those whose interests and values are represented in that discourse." Whether a political demand or complaint is couched in terms of region (sub-provincial, provincial, or super-provincial), or class, or ethnicity, or religion can alter the forum in which a solution is sought, the definition of allies and enemies, the focus on a specific office or individual, whether the complaint is narrowed (made more specific) or expanded (lumped together with "other things like it"), and so on.

To put the point in less abstract terms, imagine an orchard, the north half of which has thirty apple trees and twenty cherry trees, and the south half of which has twenty cherry trees and thirty peach trees. It is simply a matter of how one draws the line whether you have a small apple orchard and a small peach orchard, or a good-sized cherry orchard, and it can be more than a trivial question if the description will affect government subsidies or spraying schedules or irrigation allowances. When one substitutes occupational groups or ethnic groups for trees, the political relevance of persuading a group of people how to draw the line around themselves is clear. E.E. Schattschneider spoke of politics as a process by which certain interests were "organized in" and others were "organized out," and the same is no less true of the politics of regionalism. One particular version enjoys very real advantages in this regard, and will be considered as the fourth dimension of Canadian regionalism.

This is *not*, however, to say that the only regionalism that matters is self-aware perceptual regionalism that has been politically triggered, as Simeon suggests. His own example of the poor New Brunswick logger is a case in point. To the extent that large numbers of loggers live in New Brunswick and constitute a significant proportion of the population of that province, then this will have an impact on the style and content of the actions of their political representations (both federal and provincial), whether or not the loggers identified themselves in terms of that particular region as opposed to (say) being loggers, or poor, or francophone, or Catholic, or whatever. The addition of regional self-identification transforms rather than creates the regionalism. Since regional self-identification is so pervasive in Canada, the point is perhaps more theoretical than practical, but it is still worth making.

POLITICAL REGIONALISM

The fourth dimension of regionalism we might simply refer to as the political dimension, growing out what E.R. Black and A.C. Cairns refer to as "province-building." ...

The Black/Cairns thesis is that the outcome, sometimes intentional and sometimes gratuitous by-product, of provincial government action is an awareness of the region defined by those provincial boundaries, and that provincial governments are the beneficiaries of that feeling because they are the natural focus of such province-regionalism. The resulting loyalty is itself a resource of some value in the federal-provincial interplay that is such an important part of recent Canadian politics, so playing to the regional peanut gallery becomes both an end in itself (politics is about serving the people) and a means to an end (building support for re-election, gathering strength for a wrangle with the "feds"). ...

In the more than forty years since World War II, and especially in the quarter century since Quebec's so-called "quiet revolution" provincial governments have worked hard and successfully to re-establish in the eyes of the voting public a credibility and relevance that had been sand-bagged by the Great Depression and overshadowed by the national war effort. They were assisted by the historic accident that gave the provincial governments most of the juicy politically advantageous jurisdictions of the age of "positive government" (health, education, welfare). The federal government could buy itself a role through the device of conditional grants, but the constitution guaranteed that the provincial government would be an active participant with considerable leverage over the outcome.

The primary component in province-building was simply to provide the provincial voting public with the services they wanted, and to do so with a degree of responsiveness that would turn that public into a loyal clientele. The process has generated a double benefit, a double set of supporters for further expansion. The first set is obvious, the beneficiaries of existing or pending programs and policies. For social services as much as for junior colleges, for publicly-funded symphony orchestras and lottery-funded little leagues, the expanding services of provincial government has created clients, and what is at stake is less whether they demand increased funding (as such groups invariably do) than who they demand such funding from.

The second set of supporters is the provincial public service created in the process, whose numbers have not so much grown as exploded. In any intergovernmental disputes over jurisdiction, this group is necessarily a staunch supporter of the provincial government, whether it is a question of consolidating existing practices or further expanding provincial activities. Although they might have their doubts about some specific incumbent regimes, they are committed *a priori* to the provincial government as such, and to a strong and aggressive role for that government. Discussions of recent Quebec politics invariably mention the new government-employed francophone middle class as a political force of recent origins and great influence, and parallel observations can be made of the other provinces. The process is by no means finished even in a time of fiscal restraint. The adoption of equal pay policies, for example, will inevitably generate a clientele in the form of those persons (presumably mostly lower-paid women) who will benefit from the policies, the degree of their enthusiasm and loyalty being directly proportional to the perceived success of the policy. They will also create the need for a body of public servants to gather and process information on pay scales, to issue regulations for applying the policy, to provide information about powers and procedures, to receive and process complaints, to make decisions about those complaints, and to report on their own actions to the cabinet, legislature, and general public. . . .

But an equally important component in the province-building strategy has been the creation of a regional identification to reinforce the support earned by the effective provision of wanted services. If regionalism did not already exist, provincial governments would find it useful to invent it. The process is straightforward in a province like Quebec, where regional particularism is so pronounced that it would be impossible for any government to ignore it, whatever its motives or intentions, and in such surroundings it is easy to see government as being pushed by regionalism as well as contributing to it. In other provinces, where demographic factors are less unambiguous, the positive efforts of the provincial government are both more difficult and more visible, and their success is sometimes rather more in doubt. . . .

It is indicative of the pervasiveness of the province-building strategy that every province now has a provincial flag, although this visible symbol of regionalism enjoys varying degrees of recognition and enthusiasm from one province to another. . . .

The provincialist endeavour has enjoyed a considerable degree of success. Public opinion surveys in the 1970s showed that in every province save Ontario the public found the provincial government to be closer, more responsive, more trustworthy and more efficient than the federal government. The primary beneficiary of this shift in public opinion has typically been the provincial premier, and something of a ratchet effect seems to apply to the achievements of these enterprising individuals. Their status as regional spokesmen in the 1970s was parlayed into an entrenched role in the process of constitutional amendment with the passage of the Constitution Act, and under the Meech Lake Accord that would be further expanded to an entrenched right to annual First Ministers' meetings with an agenda at least partially determined by the provincial premiers. To cap the whole thing off, each and every provincial premier is to gain an absolute veto over constitutional amendments affecting the institutions of the national government. Things have come a long way from the 1880s, when the provincial premiers held a conference and Sir John A. Macdonald yawned and declined to attend.

The fly in the ointment is the fact that the regionalist card can be played with equal effectiveness by separatist movements, turning against the provincial government precisely those groups and sentiments that it effectively pre-empted from the national government. Especially in those provinces in which the regional sentiments are as much created by the government as spontaneous, there is a real element of irony. The example of the Alberta provincial election of 1982, when the Lougheed government over-reacted to a transient separatist threat that was easily obliterated, indicates that the provincial governments are perfectly aware what is at stake. Some aspects of Canadian regionalism may be contrived in their origins, but they can be spontaneous in their effects and implications.

CONCLUSION

The product of all four of the major components is the full flower of Canadian regionalism, a complicated amalgam of ethnic and linguistic differences with territorial dimensions, of local economic interests, of groups defining themselves in a variety of ways and mobilizing to achieve a variety of goals, and of provincial governments trying to build a stable power base by opportunism or design on a combination of calculated self-interest and emotional self-definition. At times, the serried ranks of regionalism seem rather like the elaborate mercenary armies of Renaissance Italy, dazzling to the eye but with a marked reluctance to face the showdown of battle, a thing of smoke and mirrors. Sometimes there is a large element of bluff that can safely be called. . . . But not all the rhetoric is bluff, and not all the threats are empty. Canadian regionalism is a mixture of show and of substance, of the spontaneous and the consciously created, frequently manipulated for political advantage but nonetheless pervasive and powerful. Just because a product is sometimes oversold does not mean that there is nothing to sell.

It is important to note the dimension that isn't; that is, the fact that I have left out that standard staple of regional analysis, "regional political culture," so ably discussed by (for example) Simeon and Elkins. The omission is deliberate, because I wish to suggest that the presence of such regional variations in political culture is neither the motor nor the essence of politically relevant regionalism. Schwartz, for example, divides Canada into five regions to examine the nature and extent of inter-regional differences in political life ("as it is" and "as it is seen") and considers the prospects for their persistence, but when she talks of the political consequences of the differences she assumes that they must be filtered through, or take the form of, regional differences in political culture (such as awareness, legitimacy, or efficacy) or the party system (national party ties or party structure). I disagree that such differences are the core of political regionalism, or even that they need to be present, and suggest the possibility of a significant and persisting impact of regionalism even in the absence of regional differences in political culture. For example, it has been argued that, as contrasted to fifty years ago when a rural and traditional and Catholic francophone Quebec confronted an urban and progressive and secular-cum-Protestant English North America, the differences in values, outlook, expectations, lifestyle, and political culture between Quebeckers and other Canadians has never been smaller, language alone remaining as a differentiator. No one would conclude from this that Quebec regionalism must be a dying force. Quite the contrary, the emotional salience of language has simply expanded to carry the psychological weight previously distributed across several differentiating factors. Political culture is an important component of the modern study of politics, but it is not all there is. ● ● ●

. . . Each specific manifestation of regionalism is a combination, in varying proportions, of each of the four dimensions, with that mixture subject to change over time as issues and economics rise and fall. For each province (or for each region defined in other terms) the combination is different. Some rest on a firmer and more constant foundation than others, some are grounded in emotion and others in more careful economic assessment, some are short-lived reaction to specific grievances or transient preoccupations while others grow from enduring cleavages, some are created by governments while others create governments in their own image.

For political purposes, perhaps the major difference to be noted is between those regionalisms that are basically cultural in origin and government-driving, such as Quebec, and those that are economic in origin and often government-driven, such as those of the West. It is not that one type is more real or more legitimate than the other, still less that one type is necessarily stronger and politically more effective, just that they build on a different base, follow a different dynamic, feed on different motives and challenges. Nor can it ever be forgotten that if regionalism of whatever form is active and visible, it is because some specific groups or interests benefit from that visibility, from that definition of the politically relevant. At the core of any analysis of any regionalism must be the question, "Who benefits?"

Regionalism in Canada is not a single story, but rather several different stories running along tracks that have tended in recent years to be parallel. How long this state of affairs will continue, how long the prevailing definitions will maintain their viability, how long provincial governments will be able to continue validating the process by rendering material and emotional services that a national government and community cannot, and whether they will always be able to command the genie they have conjured up—these are different questions to which neither the remote nor the recent past can give definitive answers.

REGIONAL ECONOMIC DISPARITIES— CAUSES AND REMEDIES

Royal Commission on the Economic Union and Development Prospects for Canada

REGIONAL DISPARITIES

What do we know about regional economic disparities in Canada? For a start, per capita earned or market income (excluding transfer payments) varies significantly among provinces. In 1981, for example, as Table 1 shows, New-foundland's per capita market income was only 53.8 per cent of the national average, while Alberta's was 114.1 per cent. In that year, only three provinces, Alberta, Ontario and British Columbia, were above the national average, although Saskatchewan was close, at 98.7 per cent. Manitoba and Quebec form the next group, at slightly over 90 per cent, followed by Nova Scotia at about 70 per cent, while the other three Atlantic provinces stood below two-thirds of the mean income. This general pattern has changed little over the 60

From the *Report of the Royal Commission on the Economic Union and Development Prospects for Canada* [Macdonald Commission], Ottawa, Supply and Services, 1985, Vol. II. Reproduced with permission of the Minister of Supply and Services Canada.

TABLE 1 Alternative Measures of Regional Income Disparities, 1971 and 1981*

Index	Year	Nfld.	P.E.I.	N.S.	N.B.	Que.	Ont.	Man.	Sask.	Alta.	B.C.	Vuw^a(%)
						(Canada = 100)						
Market income per capita^b	1971	55.1	53.6	69.3	66.5	88.5	119.6	93.2	79.1	98.3	109.6	0.285
	1981	53.8	57.5	69.6	63.2	90.7	110.5	92.7	98.7	114.1	110.3	0.274
Personal income per capita^c	1971	63.7	63.4	77.5	72.2	88.7	117.0	94.0	80.3	99.0	109.0	0.232
	1981	65.1	67.4	76.8	70.4	93.6	107.4	93.1	99.7	110.3	108.7	0.211
Personal disposable income per capita^d	1971	68.1	68.0	79.8	75.0	89.6	114.8	95.5	85.5	99.6	108.6	0.203
	1981	67.3	71.6	78.7	72.3	90.8	108.3	97.9	104.4	109.0	109.4	0.195
Personal disposable income per household^e	1971	90.1	76.2	84.9	84.4	94.1	111.1	91.6	82.8	97.6	99.4	0.136
	1981	87.6	79.2	83.0	79.7	91.5	107.0	95.5	103.4	109.4	101.5	0.130
Real personal disposble income per household^e	1971	89.9	N.A.	82.7	89.3	96.2	106.3	96.4	88.3	97.2	89.8	0.102^f
	1981	81.5	N.A.	82.5	83.7	94.9	103.2	101.1	111.4	109.3	90.9	0.125^f

a. Unweighted Coefficient of Variation.
b. Defined as wages and supplementary income, net unincorporated business income, net farm incomes, and interest, dividend and miscellaneous investment income, all calculated on a per capita basis for the region as a percentage of that for Canada.
c. Personal income is market income plus transfers to individuals.
d. Personal disposable income is personal income less personal income taxes and contributions to social security.
e. Regional price indexes calculated from inter-city partial consumer price index (Winnipeg = 100, May 1971) and city consumer price indexes.
f. The values for this measure exclude P.E.I. and hence cannot be compared to those for the other income measures.

*Table number changed from original.

Source: Based on data from Statistics Canada, *Cansim* (Matrices 555-562; 7002-7031) and *Census of Canada* (1971, 1981) as presented in Robert L. Mansell and Lawrence Copithorne, "Canadian Regional Economic Disparities: A Survey," in *Disparities and Interregional Adjustment, Vol. 64*, prepared for the Royal Commission on the Economic Union and Development Prospects for Canada (Toronto: University of Toronto Press, 1985).

years for which data are available, although individual rankings of provinces have occasionally altered.

Earned income is generally the initial measure of economic disparity, since it most accurately reflects the relative strength and productivity of the various economies. Other measures represent more fully the relative economic well-being of individuals. If we add transfers to individuals to their earned income, we can form a better picture of total personal income. By this standard, the poorest province is now at 65.1 per cent of the national average, and the richest is at 110 per cent; these figures still represent a difference of slightly more than three to two. If we add the effect of the progressive income tax by assessing after-tax income rather than gross income, discrepancies narrow further. Calculating income per household rather than per person has an additional dramatic effect. On these terms, Newfoundland's disposable income per household rises to 87.6 per cent of the national average, and Prince Edward Island and New Brunswick become the poorest provinces, with per capita incomes 79 per cent of the national average. The shortfalls in per capita income have now become less than half of what they were on the basis of earned per capita income. Adjusting for prices, in order to capture real purchasing power, produces another slight reduction in variations among provinces.

Why do earned incomes per person differ so markedly among regions? Two explanations tend to be offered, the first, perhaps, a little more frequently than the second: differentials in wage rates and differentials in employment rates. In other words, if Canadians actually employed in the poorer regions were to earn, on average, what their counterparts in wealthier areas earn, about one-half of the observed income disparity would disappear. The remainder would reflect the smaller proportion of people actually working. Thus the question becomes: Why do earnings and employment rates vary by region?

The most obvious answer to varying wages is that occupational and industrial structures vary. Fishermen do not make as much as corporate vice-presidents. If there are relatively more fishermen in Nova Scotia and relatively more executives in Ontario, earnings per capita will reflect the different occupational mix. Regional disparities in this circumstance, however, would reflect the usual spread of earnings across occupations or persons that characterizes all industrial societies.

Relatively little of the observed disparity appears to be grounded in occupational differences, however. Earnings for any given job, rather than differences in the types of job available, account for most of the income gap. The explanation for differential earnings lies in worker productivity. A number of factors might explain difference in output per employee. The "quality" and the amount of capital employed appear to account for some part of the gap: poorer regions have lower capital-to-labour ratios. Lower-income regions also have relatively fewer workers in the prime age groups and a work-force characterized by fewer years of education. Slower adoption of new technology, poorer management, fewer and smaller urban centres, and greater distance from important markets explain the remainder of the productivity gap.

To note these associations, however, is not to explain them. In fact, it is extremely difficult to sort out cause and effect. Education of the work-force appears to be lower in poorer regions because individuals with training are generally in a better position to migrate in search of better employment opportunities elsewhere. Lower capital expenditures per worker could simply reflect a poorer investment climate. The decision to adopt new technology as it becomes available depends primarily on the economic circumstances: the speed of adoption tends to reflect the buoyancy of the regional economy. Good managers tend to be promoted to head offices, irrespective of where they start out.

The other half of differentials in per capita earnings reflects lower employment rates in poorer regions. Typically, there are fewer people of working age in the poorer provinces; members of that age group, especially women, are less likely to seek work, and those in the labour force are more likely to experience unemployment. As with earnings, however, these patterns do not explain differences in employment rates. Lower participation reflects, but does not explain, a depressed economy.

REMEDIES

On the basis of this analysis, three theoretical approaches to the problems of regional economic development may be distinguished. The first approach stresses interregional adjustment within the national economy. It focuses on the question: What adjustments must occur to equalize the rewards of similarly situated workers in different provinces, given the present underlying forces in the economy? The primary issue is removal of impediments to movement of labour and capital to the areas of their most productive use, that is, interregional adjustment. Theoretically, such adjustment would reward both labour and capital. It would not, however, equalize per capita incomes in each province. If skill levels, management quality, available technology and endowment of natural resources differ, then, even with perfect adjustment, average incomes will differ. Moreover, adjustment occurs largely through mobility of capital and labour: accordingly, this approach offers no guarantee of any particular level of economic activity in any province.

The second approach is compensatory. It emphasizes measures, not to facilitate adjustment, but rather to compensate individuals in a given region for the situation in which the market leaves them. Equalization transfers, considered above, are the Canadian archetype of this solution.

The third approach is developmental. Its policies are intended to stimulate economic development by addressing the underlying factors that cause relative underdevelopment. The market imperfections and the characteristics that each region brings to the national economy become the subject of government policy. Some of these characteristics—distance from markets or natural resources, for example—are relatively fixed, though transportation policies can alleviate the disadvantages of distance. Other aspects of economic structure, however, are more amenable, in principle, to policy efforts, and these are the object of regional development policy more strictly defined.

Canadians have experience with all three approaches: people have moved; incomes have declined; transfer payments have been made, and economic development programs established. In spite of all this, there has been remarkably little change in the level of measured disparities, although the differences do vary somewhat over economic cycles, widening in hard times, converging in good ones.

1. INTERREGIONAL MARKET ADJUSTMENT

... Canadians have relied primarily on the individual decisions of private economic actors to facilitate adjustment through mobility of factors in response to changing economic incentives. Adjustment of this type has been quite effective in the past. For example, as the terms of trade shifted in favour of Western resource producers in the 1970s, not only labour but also capital and financial institutions responded. The subsequent shift away from resources has brought a corresponding flow of these factors to Ontario. The process of adjustment through the migration of labour and capital has been facilitated by a wide range of policies, including Employment Canada's efforts to match workers and opportunities, and grants or tax deductions against moving expenses to assist relocation. More generally, federal support for post-secondary education, health care and other public services help to overcome the barriers to mobility inherent in variations of provincial policy in these areas. Language policies also help to reduce some of the cultural barriers to personal mobility. We have already seen that equalization payments contribute to efficient reallocations of labour and capital.

2. COMPENSATORY POLICIES

The second policy option is compensatory. Equalization payments provide the obvious example. Provinces qualify for these payments by virtue of an unacceptably low taxation base. Payments flow, by design, to some provinces and not to others. They are intended to offset natural economic disadvantages, not to change the underlying forces of the economy. Another example is the regional differentiation of Unemployment Insurance (UI) terms and benefits. The variability within the UI system acknowledges that unemployment is more likely to occur in some parts of Canada than in others and to last longer when it does occur. More generous terms and benefits make up for these differences. It is, in general, these policies that produce the reduction of disparities in personal income treated earlier. The transfers applied can render market adjustments less necessary: they allow recipient regions to maintain consumption levels; they prevent real per capita incomes from falling; and they obviate the necessity for individuals to migrate who might otherwise have to do so. Hence the population base can remain intact, reducing downward pressure on wages. While these results may seem entirely positive in terms of individuals or families, from the market point of view, compensatory policies can hinder adjustment. Where there is a high level of transfers, wages and unemployment remain too high.

3. DEVELOPMENTAL POLICIES

The third policy option, while still explicitly regional in focus, is developmental in intent. It has been defined as follows:

> Economic development . . . refers to the structural transformation of an economy such that, over time, it becomes increasingly capable of sustaining its capacity for further expansion out of its own, internal resources. Since the prerequisites for such sustained expansion include an increasingly differentiated and integrated economic structure, combined with incentives for its key actors to accumulate capital, to innovate, and to be efficient, the goal of development policy is to ensure that such prerequisites are created.

Developmental policies are not designed to adapt to, or to compensate for, economic circumstances; rather they address the means of changing those circumstances or of supporting specific regions in their attempts to alter their own capacities in order to overcome their disadvantages.

These developmental approaches often emphasize a broader range of historical, political and even cultural factors than do market-based theories. Some, in particular, see a pattern of cumulative forces, in which the dynamics of the market lead to even greater concentration of productive forces at the centre. Availability of large markets, of economies of scale, of sophisticated specialized services, of a highly skilled labour pool, and like circumstances all attract capital and labour from peripheral regions. Consequently, these regions lose many of their most dynamic citizens and are able to offer fewer advantages to new investors. Cumulative growth at the centre, in this view, can thus lead to cumulative decline elsewhere. Regional policies seek to counter these forces.

Canada has employed some form of regional development policy throughout its history. Much of development policy aimed at sectors has had a strong regional basis where sectors have been concentrated in one or a few regions. In the oil and gas, auto, fisheries, and timber sectors, for example, a substantial portion of activity has been concentrated in a few regions. At the turn of this century, the federal government imposed export duties on unprocessed logs to increase the extent of processing in central Canada and British Columbia. During the Great Depression, relief measures were targeted regionally; the Prairie Farm Rehabilitation Act is a well-known example. Moreover, national development policies, such as those to enable or promote the movement of goods and services across the country have proved beneficial to the regions. The building and extending of our great national railways and highways fall into this category. Indeed, these implicitly regional policies have undoubtedly been more vital to regional development, broadly defined, than have the explicitly regional development programs of the Department of Regional Economic Expansion (DREE) and other comparable agencies.

Explicit regional efforts, however, had little part in federal economic policy immediately after the Second World War. Instead, emphasis was placed on promoting aggregate economic growth and stability, and on creating the outlines of the modern welfare state. The federal government expected that poorer regions, to the extent that they entered the calculations at all, would benefit from the general economic prosperity: "Regional development was seen as natural adjunct of national development." By contrast, from the close of the Second World War, Britain used regional policy as a pillar of its post-war full-employment policy. ● ● ●

EVALUATION

... In 1977, the Economic Council of Canada published a comprehensive study of regional economic development in which it attempted to evaluate the effectiveness of DREE grants. It compared unemployment, income and migration rates in the recipient regions before and after the inception of the grant program. It concluded that "job opportunities in the Atlantic region have improved over the last few years, although nothing much seems to have changed elsewhere." Nevertheless, it is impossible to establish that DREE policies necessarily had anything to do with this outcome.

To meet this uncertainty, the Economic Council undertook its own study of the success of grants in influencing firms' location in the Atlantic provinces. It found that 25 per cent of DREE-supported establishments were definitely influenced by the grant program, and that another 34 per cent were possibly so influenced. Little evidence was found that the subsidies "crowded out" other economic activity in the region, and so the net gain remained at 25 per cent to 59 per cent. As a final step, the Council compared the increment to national output from DREE-created jobs with the cost of providing those jobs. Even with conservative estimates of the grant's effectiveness in determining plant location, the program appeared to be successful. The additional contribution to national output from workers who would otherwise have been unemployed more than covered the cost of the funds used.

The Economic Council's overall evaluation of the industrial subsidy program was cautiously optimistic:

> Our own assessment of previous evidence, together with our analysis of data on the births and deaths of establishments in one region only (the Atlantic), has led

us to the view that the subsidy program is far less successful than published estimates of job creation would imply. To that extent, the critics are right. But the subsidies, nevertheless, seem successful enough to be a paying proposition. The value of the jobs created appears to outweigh the inefficiency involved in locating production inappropriately.

The Council was unable to come to any definite conclusion on the other components of regional development policy, such as the infrastructure grants.

Other writers have been more critical of the DREE programs. One, for instance, concluded that:

> In the current situation, the publicly-recognized RDIA goal is employment in certain depressed regions . . . DREE fails to achieve the greatest number of new jobs, and incurs a higher cost per new job created, by continuing with the subsidies which are inconsistent with their goals.

The specific complaint, based on rigorous statistical analyses of the program and its effects, was its bias towards capital-intensive production techniques. Another analyst was even more sweeping in the criticisms put forward:

> In view of all the uncertainties inherent in the subsidization of firms—the absence of solid evidence that investment in the designated regions is really increased, the even greater doubt about employment, the effects on distribution of income among persons, the possibility of inequity in the government's dealings with firms, the probable reduction in national income in Canada as a whole, and the lack of any real assurance that modernization and progress are fostered in the designated regions—I wonder if it might not be best for the federal government to restrict its subsidy program to the support of poor people . . . and to such transfers to provinces as are agreed upon in federal-provincial negotiations, and to keep its distance from firms' decisions about the location of investment.

A research paper prepared for this Commission summarized the available evidence on regional development initiatives:

> Despite widely varying policy thrusts and economic circumstances, there has been little improvement in the relative position of most of the poorer provinces as measured by income net of transfers . . . It seems reasonable to conclude that there has been no discernible progress with regard to regional development. This finding alone would appear to be a serious indictment of the many policy efforts, and very large public sector outlays that, it was argued, could achieve that goal.

Nevertheless, as Commissioners have noted, it may be that the policies have prevented regional imbalances from getting worse. Nor has it been shown conclusively that if Canada had devoted greater resources to regional development, more progress would have been made.

ATLANTIC CANADA: HOPE SPRINGS ETERNAL IN A TROUBLED CLIMATE

Agar Adamson

Those Canadians who do not reside in Atlantic Canada view the region rather like an eccentric relative, one who is fun to visit because his or her lifestyle is so quaint, but not a person with whom you wish to live—because you could not stand their eccentric behaviour. The inhabitants of these four provinces resolutely reject these scurrilous attacks, and rightly so. The traditional view of politics in Atlantic Canada is one which emphasizes parties, elections, patronage, regional disparity, and a dependency on government for various forms of economic assistance.

POLITICAL CULTURE

In Atlantic Canada politics is the very staff of life and the region's national sport. Especially in the three Maritime provinces, politics is followed literally from the cradle to the grave. Furthermore, nowhere else in Canada, with the possible exception of the two Territories, are people so dependent on government for employment and social welfare assistance.

Given the history of the region, including the apathy toward Maritime union, one might expect to find significant political and policy differences among these four provinces. However, the reverse is true. There is a regional political culture that is the basis for this similarity. Historically, many residents have been tied to a subsistence economy of renewable staples because both federal and provincial governments have consistently been unable to alleviate the region's poverty. Changes in technology, the sea, and more developed economies to the south and to the west have served as channels, as well as safety valves, for dissatisfaction. There has been little, if any, infusion of new blood from immigration into the region since the early years of this century. The prevailing political orientation of these four provinces has fundamentally revolved around the three elements of cynicism, traditionalism, and regionalism.

There is some argument as to whether or not Newfoundland and Labrador's political culture should be grouped with that of the three Maritime provinces. Every Newfoundland government since Confederation in 1949, particularly those formed by the Progressive Conservatives, has made it clear that Newfoundland should not be considered as one of the Maritime provinces. However, since his election in 1989 Liberal Premier Clyde Wells has shown a stronger interest than have any of his predecessors in regional co-operation.

Revision in May 1990 of an original article prepared for this book by the author, who is a Professor of Political Science at Acadia University, Wolfville, Nova Scotia. By permission.

Wells has attended several of the regularly scheduled meetings of the three Maritime premiers. Still, many differences remain between Newfoundland and the other three provinces, particularly in the area of policy development and federal–provincial relations. Since the political demise of former Premier J.R. Smallwood, there have been very few occasions when the region has presented a united front at federal–provincial first ministers' conferences. Nevertheless, the gradual demise of the outports has eroded many of the distinctive aspects of Newfoundland political culture, while integration into the Canadian political community has simultaneously reinforced the pervasive traditionalism and cynicism of Newfoundlanders. It would appear that Newfoundland's political culture, contrary to the Hartzian model, is converging with that of the three Maritime provinces.

Newfoundland has had one of the lowest political participation rates in Canada, while the Maritimes have had the highest. Here, too, one can see change: voter turnout in the Maritimes is decreasing somewhat, although still the highest in Canada, while the percentage of those who vote is increasing in Newfoundland.

There will always be a debate over both the precise composition and the extent of homogeneity of the Atlantic political culture. Political culture, after all, is an abstract concept based upon observable political phenomena.

MODERNIZATION

All four provinces are undergoing a process of "modernization." Although rural society remains important, the growth of urban centres, economic development, the influx of ideas from outside the region through the national media, and the return of people to the region have led to changes in political and social attitudes. While society is still essentially conservative, possibly the most conservative in Canada, modernization is taking place. How far this process will continue is debatable, for tradition, cynicism, and changes in the economy may impede any process of modernization.

Until recently the electorate in all four provinces accepted the old adage that "you do not bite the hand that feeds you," and thus would not vote against the party in power in Ottawa. This attitude has now changed, and the performance of the federal government has become an important issue in provincial elections, just as it has in other parts of Canada. It is not pure coincidence that in 1990 three of the four provinces are governed by the Liberal party.

The growth of New Democratic party support in the Halifax area is another sign of modernization. The NDP has articulated society's concern over such issues as child care and "equal pay for work of equal value." Groups wishing to protect the environment, even when it means loss of jobs, are becoming stronger and more numerous throughout the region. The Conservatives may have been successful in Nova Scotia in the 1988 provincial election because of their promise to clean up the Halifax harbour, which is one of Canada's largest cesspools.

Former New Brunswick Premier Richard Hatfield singlehandedly modernized his own party by opening it up to francophones. As well, he continued the progressive programs initiated by his Liberal predecessor, Louis Robichaud, in the Equal Opportunities Program of educational and local government reform. It is perhaps unfortunate that Hatfield may well be remembered by history for the eccentricities of his behaviour and his dramatic defeat in 1987 (58 to 0) rather than for his outstanding efforts to modernize his party and his province.

One of the side effects of a Hatfield modernization program, which made New Brunswick officially Canada's only bilingual province, plus the promotion of the French language in the public service, has been the rise of the Confederation of Regions Party (COR). COR's arrival in New Brunswick is a reaction to modernization. How successful this political movement will be is an open question. However, it may damage the Conservative efforts to rebuild under their new leader, Barbara Baird-Filliter, as both parties draw support from the same segments of society.

ECONOMIC DEVELOPMENT

The economic development of all four provinces is another form of modernization. The offshore developments of the 1980s in both Newfoundland and Nova Scotia led to changes; St. John's and Halifax, in particular, have become the growth poles for the region. It may be premature to say that modernization will drastically alter the accent on traditionalism found within Atlantic Canada's political culture, but these changes will have a positive impact.

Economic development lies at the heart of politics and public policy in Atlantic Canada. These four provinces consistently have the highest unemployment rates in Canada. Furthermore, they have been economically damaged by changes in technology: steam replaced sail, oil and natural gas replaced coal, and now science has improved the way fish are counted, leading to problems in the fishery. It is true that the region has not been as dependent upon a single-crop economy as have the Prairie provinces and, consequently, except for the fishery, has not suffered economic catastrophes in the way the Prairies have from time to time. Instead, poverty in the Atlantic region is oppressive and continuous, rather than episodic and spectacular.

Each provincial government, no matter its political ideology, has for years endeavoured to end this cycle of poverty by providing jobs through programs of economic development. Furthermore, the electorate constantly demands more jobs from its politicians at both the provincial and federal levels. Thus, we have witnessed provincial governments seducing industries to move into the region. Industrialists are well aware of this situation and will play one province off against the other: in 1986, for example, Litton Systems bargained with each of the Maritime provinces to see which one would give it the best incentives package (Nova Scotia won). Firms refuse to locate in the region without substantial governmental subsidies of one form or another.

The problem of distance to markets continues to plague the region. The high cost of shipping (freight rates within Canada) is equally as important in the East as it is in the West. The cost of electricity is also an issue in Prince Edward Island and Nova Scotia. Both of these provinces must use steam to generate electricity, which is costly to the consumer.

It is unfortunate that governments' attempts to promote industrialization and jobs are more noted for their failures (Bricklin automobiles, Sydney steel, heavy water, oil refineries, shipyards, cucumbers, and Clairtone) than for their successes (Michelin, McCain's, Volvo, and Cavendish Farms). The politicians' view is that any industry, no matter its social or environmental impact, is worth the investment because of the employment it creates. The only exception is Prince Edward Island, which refused to give Litton Industries all the financial assurances it demanded, and has also refused to purchase electricity generated by nuclear fission in New Brunswick.

The region has not been blessed with an abundance of natural resources. In the past the major resource industries have been the fishery, pulp and paper, lumber, base metals, coal and, in the case of Labrador and New Brunswick, water power. The discovery of hydrocarbons off the coasts of Newfoundland and Nova Scotia led both of those provinces to believe fervently that prosperity was just around the corner. The Buchanan government in Nova Scotia produced a succession of budgetary deficits in the expectation that offshore oil would provide sufficient funds to pay off its debts. However, the fall in world oil prices has delayed prosperity's arrival indefinitely. Without large-scale government grants the economic feasibility of these projects will continue to be questionable as long as the world price of oil remains below $20 (U.S.) a barrel. Nova Scotia does expect production to begin in 1991 on two small fields, but Hibernia, in spite of the federal Conservatives' promises of 1988, seems to be drifting away. Despite these setbacks, economic developments, particularly offshore, have assisted the modernization process within the region.

The four provincial governments have asserted themselves as legitimate actors in their sphere of constitutional jurisdiction, as is witnessed by New Brunswick's and Newfoundland's stand on the Meech Lake Constitutional Accord. Their policy outputs run the gamut from economic development to social welfare, most notably economic development, but one must not overlook the fact that each province has developed a network of social welfare policies. Of course, in the field of social welfare, including education, there is still much to be done. Each province has its own social problems, but general throughout the region are rural poverty and appalling housing. Another is the question of job training through the educational system. Because of the region's lack of an adequate tax base, the social welfare net is not what the politicians, particularly the Red Tories, would like it to be. The region remains dependent upon assistance from Ottawa. Indeed, federal money of one form or another (equalization grants, Established Programs Financing, other federal grants, military bases, decentralization of government departments, public works, unemployment insurance, etc.) accounts for more than half of the economy of the region. Thus, Atlantic Canada is greatly affected by federal policy. The deficit reduction policies of the Mulroney government found in the budgets of 1989 and 1990 have drastically impinged on the region.

The most recent examples of federal development policy are the Atlantic Canada Opportunities Agency (ACOA), established by legislation in 1987, and the 1990 Federal Fiscal Adjustment Package (FFAP). Since 1961 numerous agencies and ministeries have come and gone before ACOA was established. ACOA may be the most promising of any of these agencies. Instead of promoting mega projects and inducing industry from outside to locate in the region, ACOA is geared to assist the local entrepreneur and to work with businesses of all sizes located within the Atlantic provinces, plus those wishing to locate in the region.

ACOA, as originally conceived, was to be as nonpartisan and nonpolitical as possible. Unfortunately, evidence illustrates that ACOA has become nothing more than a continuation of previously existing patronage agencies. A major proportion of its five-year budget was distributed prior to the November, 1988 federal election, and following the election the newly appointed Board of Directors comprised almost entirely Conservative party supporters. If ACOA is to be successful and respected by the citizenry, it will have to return to the original concept and be nonpartisan. Furthermore, it will have to cease being an object of the minister of Finance's desire to reduce the deficit by extending the budget allocations for another two years, as was done in the 1989 federal budget. ACOA, if handled properly, has the potential to be the most significant federal regional disparity program announced in Atlantic Canada since the publication of the *Gordon Royal Commission Report* in 1957.

The fisheries package of 1990 is a slightly different proposition. Unlike ACOA, which evolved from a lengthy public policy process, FFAP is the response to an emergency. Assisted by earlier government policy, the number of fish plants increased from five hundred in 1977 to nine hundred in 1988. In these 11 years, approximately nine thousand new fishermen, using more sophisticated harvesting techniques, entered the fishery. At the same time federal government scientists found new and more accurate methods to count the fish. What all this has meant is that the fishery can no longer support the over one hundred thousand Atlantic Canadians who look to it for their livelihood. This has led to a federal aid package of $584 million to assist those who have lost their jobs and to help the many one-industry communities like Grand Bank and Gaultois, Newfoundland to diversify. The problem is, diversifying to what? Atlantic Canada, like the Prairies, is experiencing the demise of the small towns, and once again the ancient cry of "going down the road" is heard throughout the region.

What FFAP is designed to do is to persuade people to leave the fishery because the earlier governmental policy of expansion was an error. Although it may be "short-term pain for long-term gain," the question is what happens to the region's major natural resource industry in the meantime, and for how long? The fishery is not only a regulated industry, it is also a victim of the constitutional division of powers. The provinces have jurisdiction only when the fish are landed for processing.

Thus FFAP, unlike ACOA, is a result of a crisis brought about by changes in technology and inappropriate governmental policy. The collapse of the fishery means greater emphasis must be placed on economic development at a time when governments are curtailing expenditures in order to cut their deficits. For Atlantic Canadians, and especially those in the fishery, this means there is a long road ahead.

Another issue hanging over Atlantic Canada like the sword of Damocles is the Free Trade Agreement with the United States. As the results of the 1988 federal election illustrate, when 20 Liberals and only 12 PCs were elected, the agreement is not popular in the region, even though only PEI Premier Joe Ghiz opposed it. The legitimate fear in Atlantic Canada is that the discussions surrounding the definition of a government subsidy, which must be decided before 1999, will go in the Americans' favour. If this should happen, many of the existing Canadian government economic development programs will be curtailed because they will contravene the Free Trade Agreement. Such a turn of events would damage the region's economy.

CLIENTISM

It is, perhaps, debatable whether a state of "clientism" still exists in the region. It is true that governments in the region are reluctant to be openly hostile toward Ottawa and that voting records in the region have, until recently, illustrated a form of clientism. Yet it is doubtful if a specific form of political clientism exists today; there is, perhaps, a general spirit of this political phenomenon present in the region, particularly with respect to federal–provincial fiscal relations.

As the four provinces have only 32 seats in the House of Commons, they have little opportunity to influence the outcome of federal elections. Furthermore, Atlantic Canadians, like those in other rural sections of the country, are suffering from the increased urbanization of the political process. As most elections are now won or lost in the major urban centres, where most of the seats are, government policies are increasingly directed to the urban voters' interests at the expense of their rural compatriots. Recent government policies such as cutbacks in Via Rail, closure of post offices, and deregulation of the airline industry have not inconvenienced the residents of Toronto or Vancouver as much as those of Sydney and Cornerbrook.

Atlantic Canada may be overrepresented in the Senate (having 30 of 104 seats, or over 31 percent); however, the Senate seldom if ever acts as a body that defends regional concerns. Thus, the major protectors of the region's interests are the provincial governments and the region's representatives in the federal cabinet.

Fortunately, Atlantic Canada is usually blessed with strong and vigorous cabinet representation. The most recent example of this was Allan J. MacEachen, who used his position in the Trudeau cabinet to keep the region, and particularly his native Cape Breton, afloat with government grants of one form or other. The role of federal cabinet representatives cannot be overstated in this region. These members of Parliament are like the squire of feudal days who looked after his faithful tenants and handed out favours to them at harvest time.

The question of province-building and its impact on relations with Ottawa also arises. In the Atlantic region province-building has been of two types: the first is the aggressive and confrontational style of a Brian Peckford or a Clyde Wells; the second is the quiet diplomacy of a Buchanan or a Hatfield, or the mixed bag of a Joe Ghiz. Which is more successful depends upon the observer's point of view, though one would have to admit that Wells has not yet won many battles.

In regard to the bureaucracy, which directs public policy development, both New Brunswick and Newfoundland have been the most successful and, indeed, the most aggressive in bureaucratic reform. They have by far the most progressive public services in the Atlantic region.

The Maritimes have developed two interesting regional bureaucracies: the Maritime Provinces Higher Education Commission and the Council of Maritime Premiers. Both of these bodies co-ordinate regional policies in regard to transportation, education (including post-secondary), energy, and government services.

Atlantic Canadians can be easily distinguished from their compatriots by their relative lack of either political efficacy or political trust. There are curious contradictions in the Atlantic provinces' political culture. Although they distrust politics and politicians and feel incapable of effecting political change, Atlantic Canadians continue to invest high amounts of physical, intellectual, and emotional energy in politics. The traditional orientations of Atlantic Canadians have served to maintain a traditional party system. Perhaps the most obvious manifestation of this phenomenon is the stability and intensity of party attachments which, in many parts of Atlantic Canada, are a matter of heredity. For example, a respondent to a questionnaire sent to delegates answered the question "When did you become a member of the Progressive Conservative party?" with the answer "At conception."

Third parties have, in general, found the Atlantic provinces to be a virtual "wasteland." Only in a few pockets, such as industrial Cape Breton, have third parties had any success.

In New Brunswick both the Parti Acadien and Social Credit have withered and died on the vine, while the Confederation of Regions party remains an unknown, though threatening, entity. In Prince Edward Island, at least until the 1986 election, the New Democratic party candidates in some constituencies received fewer votes than there were spoiled ballots. In Newfoundland third parties, with the exception of the fights within the Liberal party in the final stages of Joey Smallwood's political life, have also been unsuccessful. Twice, the NDP have won federal by-elections only to lose the seat in a subsequent general election. In 1989 the NDP lost its toehold in the Newfoundland House of Assembly, and its popular vote fell dramatically. Only in Nova Scotia have third parties had any success. The NDP and its predecessor, the CCF, have been successful in industrial Cape Breton; indeed, the CCF formed the official Opposition immediately following the Second World War, when the Conservatives had no seats in the House of Assembly.

Atlantic Canadians, unlike their countrymen in western Canada, have never taken the opportunity to produce a regionally based party in order to present a unified voice in the House of Commons. They have always maintained that it was far more advantageous for them to work through the two major political parties rather than through any third party force. Whether or not this has been an advantageous line of action is debatable. However, it does illustrate the region's political traditionalism.

Politics in Atlantic Canada is changing, the old image of political strongmen walking across a small stage is no longer the complete picture of the political process in the region. Modernization and economic development have placed more stress on what governments do, or fail to do, than was the case a generation ago.

WESTERN GRIEVANCES—A LONG HISTORY

David Elton

Although political commentators often talk of the Canadian West as a meaningful political entity, . . . the individual provinces are more significant as social, economic, and political entities than this often-used regional designation would suggest. . . . Simultaneously, however, national identities have also been developed. ● ● ●

A REGIONAL IDENTITY

At the same time western Canadians were developing . . . strong provincial and national identities . . . a common regional identity was being forged. This

From R.D. Olling and M.W. Westmacott (eds.), *Perspectives on Canadian Federalism*, Scarborough, Prentice-Hall, 1988. By permission.

sense of regional identity is not based upon a positive reaction to government actions or symbols such as flags and logos, rather it is based upon recurring problems westerners have experienced in seeking to find practical political and economic solutions for dealing with property and natural resource development, the cost of supplies, and the sale of their products.

From early settlement days up to the present, westerners have run up against politically constructed barriers which limit their growth and development with regards to resource utilization, consumption, and the marketing of their products. . . .

PROPERTY AND NATURAL RESOURCES

When British Columbia entered Confederation in 1871, the province was given the same powers as those extended the four original provinces of Ontario, Quebec, Nova Scotia and New Brunswick; yet the three prairie provinces were denied control over crown lands on the grounds that the national government needed to retain control over crown lands to ensure the orderly flow of immigration into the region. This unequal constitutional treatment of Manitoba, Saskatchewan, and Alberta created considerable friction between the three provincial governments and Ottawa from the outset. . . .

During most of the first three decades of this century, and particularly during the decade following the First World War, demand for control over property and natural resources was the controversial centrepiece of federal-provincial relations between the three prairie provinces and Ottawa. While the federal government's decision in 1930 to transfer control over property and natural resources to Alberta, Saskatchewan and Manitoba placed them on an equal footing with British Columbia and the other provinces, Ottawa's unwillingness to treat the three provinces equally was one of the key factors in the development of a legacy of distrust and animosity which has never dissipated.

The contemporary equivalent of the struggle for constitutional control over property is the ongoing controversy over the production and sale of oil and gas. Beginning with the federal government's decision to set a ceiling on oil and gas prices in 1973, and culminating with the 1980 National Energy Policy, federal regulation of this industry has become a vivid symbol of Ottawa's colonial mentality towards western Canada.

TARIFF POLICIES

A second national policy which discriminates against residents of all four western provinces is the national government's tariff policy, set up to protect the domestic market for Canadian manufacturers from American and European competition. Most of these manufacturers are located in Ontario and Quebec. In effect, western Canadians are coerced into buying manufactured goods ranging from tools and clothing to household necessities at above their international market price, while at the same time selling their products, be they agricultural products such as wheat or hogs, forestry products, oil, gas, potash, coal, etc., in an open international market place. Given that most western Canadians live within a short distance of the American border and either visit the United States personally or communicate with neighbours who have recently returned from the U.S., they are constantly reminded of the practical costs of Canadian tariff policy.

Even though Canadian tariffs have been reduced considerably during the past two decades and manufacturing activity in western Canada has increased, western Canadians continue to pay more to maintain Canada's tariffs than they benefit. Canadian tariffs cost western Canada nearly 372 million dollars in 1983 alone, while at the same time benefiting central Canadians by over 474 million dollars. Given tariff reductions over the past several decades and the modest increases in manufacturing throughout western Canada during this same time period, it is understandable why Canadian tariff policy has been particularly aggravating to westerners.

TRANSPORTATION POLICY

National transportation policy constitutes a third set of national policies which western Canadians have found to be blatantly discriminatory. Since time when the federal government utilized western lands to pay for the building of the Canadian Pacific Railway in the late 1800s and permitted the railways to charge discriminatory freight rates, national transportation policy has been particularly aggravating for Alberta, Saskatchewan, and Manitoba. British Columbia, on the other hand, has never been concerned about transportation rates because the province is not landlocked and is favoured by competition between water transportation and rail to obtain optimal cost-benefits.

. . . The basic complaint centres around freight rate structures and programs which impose high rates on goods shipped into the three western land-locked provinces and encourages the shipment of non-processed goods out of the region.

THE NATIONAL INTEREST

Whether it be economists analysing voluntary export quotas on Japanese autos or federal revenue expenditure patterns, or the 1986 Auditor General's report focusing on grants handled by the Department of Regional and Industrial expansion, examples of regionally discriminatory practices by the national government abound. After having examined these and other federal government practices in a 1987 report prepared for the Canada West Foundation entitled "The Western Economy and Canadian Unity," McCormick and Elton conclude that the concept of "national interest" utilized by the national government often excludes the concerns and aspirations of western Canadians. They note: "The term 'the national interest' often takes on ominous overtones for western Canadians. When they hear it invoked, it is much like getting a phone call and being asked if you are sitting down: they know that bad news is on the way."

WESTERN ALIENATION

As a result of a broad range of policies such as those cited above, a longstanding and widespread disaffection with the national government has become embedded in the very heart of western Canada's political culture. This shared attitude, often referred to as western alienation, exists among a broad cross-section of western residents and has persisted regardless of the party in power or the number of western MPs on the government side of the House. Survey research over the 1979–85 period undertaken for the Canada West Foundation indicates that four of every five western Canadians believe the Canadian political system favours Ontario and Quebec. These sentiments have lead approximately one in 20 western Canadians to advocate separation or union with the United States. But approximately four out of five westerners continue to identify strongly with the Canadian political system while simultaneously expressing discontent over real and apparent discriminatory tendencies. . . .

REGIONAL COOPERATION

Although residents of the prairie provinces developed a strong regional identity in the early decades of this century, it has only been in the last two decades that a significant amount of formal cooperation between western provincial governments has taken place. The establishment of the Prairie Economic Council in 1965 by the provinces of Manitoba, Saskatchewan, and Alberta, followed by the creation of the Western Premiers Conference in 1973, which included British Columbia, are the most significant examples of formal interprovincial relations.

The Prairie Economic Council was created to provide a forum for the discussion of broad social and economic issues common to the region and where needed to permit cooperation on joint ventures. During the 1965–73 period, the Council met on 12 separate occasions and more than 200 items appeared on their agenda. These included water resource issues, tourism, freight rates, resource production, environmental regulation, power generation, educational programs, and highway construction. These discussions led to the initiation of a number of significant regional programs, such as the rationalization of university training programs for veterinary medicine, optometry, and occupational therapy, and the creation of a Prairie Provinces Water Board to administer an agreement allocating fresh water supplies throughout the prairie region.

The creation of the Western Premiers Conference and the inclusion of British

Columbia in the regional forum was occasioned by the January 1973 federal government Throne Speech, which proposed a Western Economic Opportunities Conference (WEOC). This initiative was taken by the newly elected minority Liberal Government, whose western representation had been reduced from 28 MPs in 1968 to 7 in 1972. Ottawa proposed WEOC to discuss western economic grievances and hopefully establish an agenda for future economic development and diversification.

. . . While the conference was clearly a historical event (it is the only regional federal-provincial conference that has been held to date), the meeting fell far short of attaining the expectations of either the federal or provincial governments. Rather than setting the stage for what the federal Throne Speech referred to as "concrete programs for stimulating and broadening the economic and industrial base of Western Canada," the meeting ended with few concrete accomplishments. . . . The creation of the Western Premiers Conference, although a byproduct, was in retrospect the most noteworthy accomplishment of WEOC.

Since 1973 the western premiers have met annually to discuss the coordination of regional policies and positions on federal-provincial relations. . . . Yet the most important function performed by the Western Premiers Conference has been that of providing a mechanism and forum for coordinating the western provinces' interactions with the federal government. For example, in 1976 the western premiers "expressed their concern over the increasing tendency of the government of Canada to legislate in subject areas which historically and constitutionally had been considered to be within the provincial sphere." This concern resulted in the production of three reports during the 1977–79 period which delineated dozens of policies, programs, and actions where the western provinces felt the federal government was intruding in areas of provincial jurisdiction.

FEDERAL–PROVINCIAL CONFLICTS

While there were a number of disagreements between individual western provinces and the federal government during the 1945–70 period (e.g., Alberta's stringent opposition to Medicare in 1968, British Columbia's confrontation with Ottawa over the Columbia River Treaty, etc.), there were three important factors in the late 1960s and early 1970s which led to increased confrontation between the western provinces and the federal government.

First, the late 1960s and early 1970s was a period of economic malaise in western Canada. All four western provinces had sought rapid economic development through an open-door investment policy, unrestricted resource development, and limited environmental controls. Yet each of the provinces was in a mild recession with job creation relatively stagnant, incomes falling somewhat, and generally a weak demand for the west's resource production.

The second factor which generated change in federal–provincial relations was that the 1969–72 period was one of rapid political change. In 1969, the NDP in Manitoba not only chose a new leader during the election campaign, but succeeded in defeating the governing Conservative party. In 1971 the Liberal government in Saskatchewan was defeated by the NDP led by Allan Blakeney, and the 36-year reign of the Social Credit party in Alberta came to an end when Albertans elected a Progressive Conservative party headed by Peter Lougheed. In 1972 the winds of political change made a clean sweep of the west when the 20-year reign of W.A.C. Bennett in British Columbia came to an end with the election of a New Democratic Party government headed by Dave Barrett.

In addition to these fundamental changes in provincial politics, the Liberal Party's fortunes in western Canada were dealt a severe blow in the 1972 federal election when their representation was reduced from 26 to 7 Members of Parliament. With four new premiers with new mandates to improve the economic performance of their provinces and a shift in partisan representation from the west in Ottawa, the stage was set for considerable change in federal–provincial relations.

The third factor influencing federal–provincial relations during the early 1970s was the turmoil over constitutional change generated by demands emanating from Quebec for greater provincial autonomy. The western provinces clearly had not actively sought increased provincial autonomy during the 1960s, but rather had focused on increasing federal government contributions to shared-cost programs. However, the growing sophistication of the western provincial bureaucracies, accompanied by a need for greater control over economic development, and the subsequent conflict over resource management and revenues of the 1973–76 period all played a role in convincing western leaders to seek both the protection and expansion of provincial constitutional powers. . . .

THE OIL AND GAS WARS

The war over oil and gas revenues struck at the very heart of western provinces–Ottawa relations. . . .

Formally the bone of contention between the western provinces (primarily Alberta) and Ottawa was the question of provincial jurisdictional rights over natural resources versus the federal government's regulation of interprovincial and international trade.

. . . The real issue was over which government would have the political power to regulate the oil and gas industry and thereby obtain the largest share of the billions of dollars of resource revenues which were to be generated from the sale of these resources.

During the 12-year period commencing with the September 1973 federal government announcement of a freeze on the domestic price of oil (followed ten days later with the announcement of an export tax on crude oil destined for the U.S.) and ending with the 1985 signing of the Western Accord, the battle for oil and gas revenues included a bewildering array of issues and activities. On a nearly continuous basis during the 1973–76 period and again from 1978–82, one or more of the following was taking place: (1) conferences between first ministers and/or energy ministers and their officials; (2) debates over whether and under what circumstances negotiations should be bilateral (i.e., between Alberta and Ottawa only) or multilateral (i.e., involving all ten provinces); (3) passage of a wide variety of provincial and/or federal legislation seeking to control the production, sale, and pricing of oil and gas; (4) temporary pricing agreements between the provinces and the federal government (e.g., 60–180 day pricing agreements) accompanied by premature assumptions that the battle was over; (5) constitutional court challenges; (6) disruptions in oil supplies; (7) the nearly spontaneous development of huge separatist rallies in Calgary and Edmonton.

From an Alberta perspective, the battle with Ottawa over control and regulation of oil and gas was a life and death struggle. The following excerpts from a speech by Peter Lougheed to the Canadian Club of Calgary at the outset of confrontations is an excellent example of the frustration and disenchantment over the federal government's decision to set domestic prices and impose an export tax on oil:

> This [the imposition of an oil export tax] appears to be the most discriminatory action taken by a federal government against a particular province in the entire history of Confederation. The natural resources of the provinces are owned by the provinces under the terms of Confederation. The action taken by Ottawa strikes at the very roots of Confederation. And why just an export tax on oil? Why not on lumber from British Columbia, potash from Saskatchewan, nickel from Manitoba, pulp and paper, asbestos, and gold from Ontario and Quebec? Why Alberta oil? . . . We are going to be forced to take certain actions we do not want to take and would not otherwise take. . . . We have to try to protect the Alberta public interest—not from the public interest of Canada as a whole—but from central and eastern Canadian domination of the West.

As a result of a mixture of bilateral (Alberta-Ottawa) and multilateral negotiations (all ten provinces and Ottawa), and notwithstanding the inordinately high profile given such things as inflammatory bumper stickers declaring "Let the eastern bastards freeze in the dark," a series of temporary pricing agreements were reached during the 1973–76 period through compromises on the part of both the producing provinces and the federal government. These compromises resulted in the producing provinces retaining control over much of the revenues generated from increased oil and gas prices and provided both Alberta and Saskatchewan with revenue surpluses worth hundreds of millions of dollars. These monies were used to establish savings trust funds which were used to facilitate economic development and diversification, and provide a financial cushion to make up for the loss of revenues that would take place when the resource base was depleted.

The federal government, on the other hand, not only clearly maintained its control over interprovincial and international trade, but also obtained adequate revenues to provide central and eastern Canadian consumers with oil and gas at well below the international market price. . . .

With the second dramatic increase in international oil prices in 1979 the uneasy truce between the western provinces and Ottawa was shattered. The battle over oil revenues played an important role in such significant political events as the defeat of Joe Clark's nine month old minority government, the creation of a National Energy Policy, and the establishment of a vibrant separatist movement centred in Alberta. It also generated other important events regarding federal-provincial relations that heretofore had not taken place. For example, the Alberta premier held meetings with federal members of Parliament from his province in an effort to influence Joe Clark's government in 1979. The first joint Alberta-British Columbia cabinet meeting was held in the summer of 1980 to show western solidarity on the resource issue. In addition, Alberta's premier held a number of bilateral meetings not only with other western premiers, but also with premiers in Atlantic Canada.

At the annual Premiers Conference held in Winnipeg in August of 1980, Lougheed succeeded in obtaining the support of nine of the ten provinces regarding Alberta's claim that the federal government should not interfere with provincial regulation of the production and sale of natural resources. The lone dissenting province was Ontario. . . .

It should be noted that the producing provinces on numerous occasions over the 1974–80 period had stated that they were willing to provide oil to other Canadians at below an artificially high international price in return for a reasonable rate of return for the production of a depleting resource. Thus the Ontario argument that consumers should set the price for the products they consume and also obtain the funds generated from their production was tantamount to the Ontario government flipping a coin and saying to western Canadians, "heads we win, tails you lose."

Notwithstanding widespread support among other provinces for Alberta's position the federal government brought down its National Energy Policy in October 1980. Alberta's response was immediate and calculated. First, Lougheed went on province-wide television and announced that unless Ottawa and Alberta could reach a settlement on oil pricing, Alberta would "turn down the taps" beginning five months hence (April 1, 1981) and further reduce oil production by the same amount on June 1 and September 1. To foreclose the possibility of the federal government using its emergency powers Lougheed was careful to assure Canadians that, while Alberta would not produce and sell this depleting resource at the fire sale prices specified in the National Energy Policy, Alberta would restore production immediately should a shortage of oil develop. This left the federal government in the position of being unable to stop the reduction of production and having to purchase the shortfall of oil on the international market. . . .

The second action was to launch a carefully structured case challenging the constitutionality of the federal government's export tax on natural gas. The Alberta case was based upon gas production from a specific well located on crown land and owned by the Alberta government. The Alberta argument was that the federal government's export tax was illegal because one government cannot tax another. Although it took some time for the courts to render their decision, Alberta won the case before the Supreme Court on a six to three decision.

The third action taken by Alberta was that of an extensive public relations campaign to inform Canadians of the discriminatory nature of the NEP. The campaign consisted primarily of an extensive speaking tour and media awareness briefings by the premier, his energy minister and officials, and a number of prominent oil industry executives and public-spirited Albertans. . . .

Shortly after Alberta's first round of oil production cutbacks in April 1981, a series of unpublicized bilateral meetings began between key officials of Alberta and the federal government in an effort to arrive at an acceptable compromise on oil pricing. Because no deal had been struck by June 1, oil production was reduced by another 60 000 barrels per day, requiring the federal government to increase subsidies to central Canadian refineries which now had to buy more oil on the international market. By September 1, the day the third reduction in oil production was to take place, Alberta and Ottawa announced that an accommodation had been reached and a five year oil pricing agreement had been negotiated. . . .

It wasn't until four years later, following the defeat of the Liberals and the election of Brian Mulroney's Conservative government, which obtained most of western Canada's seats, that the NEP would be dismantled and replaced by an agreement between Alberta, Saskatchewan, British Columbia, and the federal government. The agreement, called the Western Accord, replaced federal pricing regulations with international market discipline. Ironically, within months of the Western Accord international oil prices tumbled to approximately one-third their 1986 price, and western producers and western provincial governments found themselves facing massive cutbacks in energy exploration and layoffs within the industry of a magnitude never before experienced. Thus by the summer of 1986 the federal government found itself facing demands from both Saskatchewan and Alberta for federal loan guarantees and investments in oil sands projects and refineries.

At the same time that the decade-long war over oil and gas production and pricing was taking place, primarily between Ottawa and Alberta, Saskatchewan was doing battle with Ottawa through the Courts over provincial taxation powers regarding natural resources. At issue was the constitutionality of Saskatchewan's mineral income tax and royalty surcharges passed by the Saskatchewan legislature in 1973, and the province's ability to pro-ration potash production. The Supreme Court ruling on the taxation issue, handed down in November 1977, ruled in favour of the plaintiff, Canadian Industrial Gas and

Oil Ltd. (CIGOL), on the grounds that provincial legislatures did not have the authority to fix the price of goods to be exported from the province because this involved interprovincial or international trade and commerce, which were the exclusive responsibility of the federal government. This decision effectively put at risk $580 million in taxes which had already been collected by Saskatchewan from 1973 through 1977 and already spent by the Saskatchewan government on, among other things, the purchase of potash mines. Premier Blakeney announced that in spite of the Court decision his government would not return the funds to the oil companies and appealed for help from the federal government to find a means of obtaining a settlement with the industry. Following closely on the heels of the oil taxation case, the Supreme Court ruled in 1978 that the province's legislation dealing with the pro-rationing of potash production among the various potash mines in Saskatchewan (many of them now owned by the provincial government) was also unconstitutional because almost all of Saskatchewan's potash was exported and the province's pro-rationing scheme interfered with international trade. Because the federal government had intervened in this case on behalf of the plaintiff and challenged the provincial legislation, the Saskatchewan premier directly attacked the federal government for attempting to wrest control of natural resources from the provinces through influencing these Supreme Court decisions. The premier then went on to vow that, rather than change Saskatchewan's approach to the management of their resources, he would seek constitutional changes to reinforce provincial control over natural resources and permit the kinds of actions which the Supreme Court had found unconstitutional.

THE STRUGGLE OVER CONSTITUTIONAL CHANGE

● ● ● By the time constitutional matters were again revived in late 1976, following the Parti Québécois victory in Quebec, western Canadians and their governments, particularly in Saskatchewan, Alberta, and British Columbia were anxious to place a number of important items on the constitutional reform agenda. For Saskatchewan and Alberta control over natural resources was of greatest importance. For British Columbia it was the need for fundamental change to national institutions.

In the fall of 1978 British Columbia released a series of nine position papers dealing with the need for constitutional change. The list included acceptance of British Columbia as a distinctive region of Canada, reform of the Senate, reform of the Supreme Court, improved instruments for federal-provincial relations, a Bill of Rights for Canada, language rights, the distribution of legislative powers, and an amending formula for the constitution. From a B.C. perspective, Senate reform was the most important of the nine items. This recommendation was based upon B.C. Premier Bill Bennett's belief that "the federal government, in formulating national policy, does not understand and, therefore, does not take account of important regional needs and aspirations, including those of British Columbia." Bennett felt that the solution to federal inattention to regional matters was to be found, not in decentralizing power, but in providing for a greater provincial voice in national institutions. . . .

With some variations on specifics, British Columbia's proposal for the establishment of what became known as the "House of the Provinces model" was advocated by a number of organizations during the 1978–80 period, such as the Canada West Foundation, the Ontario Advisory Committee on Constitutional Reform, the national Conservative party, and the federal government's Task Force on Canadian unity.

Initially none of the other three western provinces showed any interest in promoting the B.C. proposal for Senate reform. . . . When the final agreement was reached in late 1981, two key western issues were included in Canada's new constitution. First, Alberta's version of the amending formula was entrenched in the constitution. This formula recognized the equality of the provinces, denying any one province an absolute veto by requiring the assent of two-thirds of the provinces containing 50 percent of the country's population for key constitutional reforms.

The second major western issue included in the Constitution Act, 1982 was Saskatchewan's desire to have provincial powers over natural resources increased. The constitutional problems that Saskatchewan experienced in the mid-1970s over taxation and regulation of resource production were effectively resolved in Section 92a of the Constitution. This provides for provincial indirect taxation of resources and the ability to regulate resource production even though it may impact interprovincial or international trade. The only limitation now placed upon provincial control of natural resources is that provincial taxation and regulation practices must apply equally across the country.

MEECH LAKE

Following the enactment of the Canada Act in 1982 constitutional debate was shelved in western Canada as it was throughout the country. Once again economic issues dominated federal-provincial relations. . . .

While these economic matters dominated centre stage in federal-provincial relations during the 1982–86 period, a number of highly publicized events pertaining to federal–provincial relations took place which influenced the western provinces' attitude towards further constitutional reforms. In each of these events the centripetal and centrifugal forces working upon western Canadians and their governments are evident and played a part in shaping provincial government behaviour regarding the federal government.

The first event was the creation in 1983 of a special legislative committee of the Alberta legislature to examine ways and means to reform Canada's Senate. Although the Alberta government had not paid much attention to the B.C. proposals on institutional reform in 1978–80, the position changed in response to considerable public pressure exerted by those advocating Senate reform based upon a Triple E formula (elected, equal representation from each province, and effective powers). In 1985 the committee reported back to the Alberta legislature and recommended the creation of a Triple E Senate as a necessary element of effective regional representation within the national government. . . .

Little interest was paid to this initiative outside Alberta as even the British Columbia government, which had championed Senate reform only four years earlier, refrained from placing the issue on their agenda. Similarly, in Saskatchewan and Manitoba no extensive debate over Senate reform took place within government circles. . . .

The second event affecting the attitudes of the western provinces to constitutional reform was a decision by the federal government to award a military fighter aircraft maintenance contract to Quebec rather than Manitoba. The decision to award the F-18 military fighter aircraft maintenance contract to Canadair of Montreal rather than Bristol Aerospace of Winnipeg, even though the latter submitted a better bid, was seen as blatant discrimination and a devastating blow to the Manitoba economy. This action gave concrete and immediate evidence to the argument made by those advocating Senate reform that the federal government discriminates against the west in favour of Quebec. It therefore forced Manitobans, who by and large are supportive of federal spending due to their status as a beneficiary of equalization payments and other federal fiscal programs, to seek some means to ensure that similar discriminatory acts would not take place in the future. Equally important, it created considerable animosity between the government of Manitoba and the federal government.

The third event was an attack on the federal government's procurement practices by parliament's Auditor General, western print media, and the government of British Columbia. The following statement by B.C. Premier Bill Van der Zalm at the 1986 annual First Ministers Conference held in Vancouver is a good example of the content and rationale for these criticisms.

> In addition to its tariff and deficit policies the federal government has consistently reaped more income from British Columbia than it returns in the form of expenditures, investment, and employment. Examples of British Columbia not getting its "fair share" are not hard to find. Your government, Prime Minister, spends billions of dollars annually—approximately $12 billion in fact over the past five years—through its procurement process. In 1985–86, of those billions of dollars, British Columbia companies and manufacturers received only 5.3 percent of the major contracts though we represent 11.4 percent of the people in Canada.

. . . Premier Vander Zalm's frustration with federal procurement policies is shared by all western provinces and serves to reinforce a strong sense of inequity which does little to endear the federal government to western premiers, particularly when the west is in a recession and experiencing much higher levels of unemployment than central Canada. This issue provided yet another concrete and contemporary example of what Senate reform advocates were complaining about.

The fourth event which helped shape the mindset of western premiers was the refusal of the federal government to provide financial aid to further develop Alberta and Saskatchewan's oil industry. Alberta's Premier Don Getty expressed his frustration at the lack of federal government appreciation for the situation in the oil industry by noting that in 1986 over 25 000 people had lost their jobs in the oil industry, that investment had been cut by over four billion dollars, and that Canada's future security of oil supply was threatened. . . .

The fifth event was the announcement of a billion dollar federal deficiency payment to farmers in 1986 to help them cope with a dramatic fall in international grain prices. Saskatchewan Premier Grant Devine was one of the primary advocates of this federal grant-in-aid and, politically speaking, the greatest beneficiary of the program: it played no small part in the reelection of his government in 1986. For Saskatchewan farmers, for Grant Devine, and to a lesser extent for Alberta and Manitoba grain farmers, who also benefited from the program, it was concrete evidence of the benefits of Confederation and a good reason to support the federal government.

An analysis of the five events discussed above indicates the extent to which there are stresses and strains on federal–provincial relations in the west, accompanied by periodic benefits. Three of the five events leading up to the Meech Lake meeting (i.e., the F-18 contract, federal procurement practices, and oil industry aid) generated considerable animosity between western provinces and the federal government. The growth of support for the creation of a Triple E Senate was spurred on by the fact that these three events provided ample evidence of federal government discrimination and inattention regarding the Canadian west.

Concurrent with the high profile examples of federal government discrimination and inattention, the farm deficiency payment provided evidence of federal largesse towards the west. Thus, at the same time westerners were becoming more convinced that the Canadian federal system didn't work for them, they were provided with concrete evidence that it does work, at least sometimes. It is the continued existence of these sometimes discriminatory, sometimes beneficial federal programs and policies that generates the often seemingly schizophrenic behaviour of western Canadians who are alienated from their national government and yet seek to obtain greater participation in national decision-making.

There are literally dozens of joint federal-provincial programs between each of the western provinces and Ottawa which have been initiated by one province or by the federal government and function without raising public or political consternation. Unlike some members of the public, western provincial leaders are well aware of the scope of these ongoing federal-provincial programs, yet they frequently choose to openly challenge the federal system. This behaviour indicates that there are considerable improvements still needed before Canada's federal system is capable of meeting the needs of its citizens regardless of their place of residence.

Given the foregoing, it is not hard to understand why Alberta Premier Don Getty went to Meech Lake in April 1987 with the ultimatum that while he was as interested as anyone in finding a way to have the Quebec provincial government sign the constitution, he would not agree to any constitutional changes that did not include some movement towards meaningful Senate reform. Similarly, it is not hard to understand why Manitoba Premier Howard Pawley indirectly threatened to scrap the Meech Lake Accord by insisting upon the continuation of strong federal government constitutional powers regarding spending powers in areas of provincial jurisdiction. Both positions are indicative of western aspirations to play a meaningful role in national decision-making and underline the strong commitment of westerners to Canada—not Canada as it has existed, but a Canada with a reformed federal system that guarantees balance, equity, and fairness for all Canadians.

BIBLIOGRAPHY

Regionalism

(See also Bibliographies in Chapters 3 and 5.)

Alexander, D. "New Notions of Happiness: Nationalism, Regionalism and Atlantic Canada." *J.C.S.*, 15, 2, Summer, 1980.

Alexander, D. *Atlantic Canada and Confederation: Essays in Canadian Political Economy.* Toronto: U.T.P., 1983.

Aucoin, P. *Regional Responsiveness and the National Administrative State.* Toronto: U.T.P., 1985.

Aucoin, P., and Bakvis, H. "Organizational Differentiation and Integration: The Case of Regional Economic Development Policy in Canada." *C.P.A.*, 27, 3, Fall, 1984.

Bercuson, D.J., (ed.). *Canada and the Burden of Unity.* Toronto: Macmillan, 1977.

Bercuson, D.J., and Buckner, P.A., (eds.). *Eastern and Western Perspectives.* Papers from the Joint Atlantic Canada/Western Canadian Studies Conference, Toronto: U.T.P., 1982.

Bickerton, J. "Underdevelopment and Social Movements in Atlantic Canada: A Critique." *S.P.E.*, 9, Fall, 1982.

Bickerton, J., and Gagnon, A. "Regional Policy in Historical Perspective: The Federal Role in Regional Economic Development." *A.R.C.S.*, 14, 1, Spring, 1984.

Breton, A., and Breton, R. *Why Disunity? An Analysis of Linguistic and Regional Cleavages in Canada.* Montreal: I.R.P.P., 1980.

Brym, R.J., (ed.) *Regionalism in Canada.* Toronto: Irwin, 1986.

Brym, R.J., and Sacouman, R.J., (eds.). *Underdevelopment and Social Movements in Atlantic Canada.* Toronto: New Hogtown Press, 1979.

Cameron, D. (ed.). *Regionalism and Supranationalism.* Montreal: I.R.P.P., 1981.

Cameron, D. "Regional Economic Disparities: The Challenge to Federalism and Public Policy." *C.P.P.*, 7, 1981.

C.P.P. Special issue on "Western Economic Transition," 11, July, 1985.

Careless, A. *Initiative and Response: The Adaptation of Canadian Federalism to Regional Economic Development.* Montreal: McG.-Q.U.P., 1977.

Cannon, J.B. "Explaining Regional Development in Atlantic Canada: A Review Essay." *J.C.S.*, 19, 3, Fall, 1984.

Courchene, T. "A Market Perspective on Regional Disparities." *C.P.P.*, 7, 1981.

Economic Council of Canada. *Living Together: A Study of Regional Disparities.* Ottawa: S. and S., 1977.

Gibbins, R. *Regionalism: Territorial Politics in Canada and the United States: A Comparative Analysis.* Toronto: Butterworths, 1981.

Gibbins, R. *Conflict and Unity: An Introduction to Canadian Political Life.* Toronto: Methuen, 1985.

Gidengil, E. "Centres and Peripheries: The Political Culture of Dependency." *C.R.S.A.* 27, February, 1990, 23–48.

Governments of New Brunswick, Nova Scotia, P.E.I. *Royal Commission Report on Maritime Union*, [Deutsch Report]. Fredericton: 1970.

Krasnick, M., Norrie, K., and Simeon, R., (eds.). *Disparities and Interregional Adjustment.* Toronto: U.T.P., 1985.

Lithwick, N.H. "Is Federalism Good for Regionalism?" *J.C.S.*, 15, 2, Summer, 1980.

Lotz, J. *Understanding Canada: Regional and Community Development in a New Nation.* Toronto: NC Press, 1977.

Manzer, R. *Canada—A Socio-Political Report.* Toronto: McG.-H.R., 1974.

Marchal, P. "The Two Dimension of Canadian Regionalism." *J.C.S.*, 15, 2, Summer, 1980.

Matthews, R. "The Significance and Explanation of Regional Divisions in Canada: Towards a Canadian Sociology." *J.C.S.*, 15, 2, Summer, 1980.

Matthews, R. *The Creation of Regional Dependency*. Toronto: U.T.P., 1983.

McCormick, P., Manning, E.C., and Gibson, G. *Regional Representation: The Canadian Partnership*. Calgary: Canada West Foundation, 1981.

Melvin, R. "Regional Inequalities in Canada: Underlying Causes and Policy Implications." *C.P.P.*, 13, 3, September, 1987.

Phillips, P. *Regional Disparities*. Toronto: Lorimer, 2nd ed., 1982.

Rasporich, A.W., (ed.). *The Making of the Modern West: Western Canada Since 1954*. Calgary: University of Calgary Press, 1984.

Rawlyk, G.A., (ed.). *The Atlantic Provinces and the Problems of Confederation*. St. John's: Breakwater, 1979.

Romanow, R., Ryan, C., and Stanfield, R. *Ottawa and the Provinces: Regional Perspectives*. Toronto: O.E.C., 1984.

Rutan, G. "Western Canada: The Winds of Alienation." *A.R.C.S.*, 12, 1, Spring, 1982.

Savoie, D.J., and Raynaud, A. *Essais sur le développement régional*. Montréal: P.U.M., 1986.

Savoie, D.J. *Regional Economic Development: Canada's Search for Solutions*. Toronto: U.T.P., 1985.

Senate, Canada. *Report of the Standing Senate Committee on National Finance, Government Policy and Regional Development*. Ottawa: S., and S., 1982.

Simeon, R. "Regionalism and Canadian Political Institutions." *Q.Q.*, 82, 4, Winter, 1975.

Simeon, R., and Elkins, D. "Regional Political Cultures in Canada." *C.J.P.S.*, 7, 3, September, 1974.

Sitwell, O.F.G., and Seifried, N.M.R. *The Regional Structure of the Canadian Ecomony*. Toronto: Methuen, 1984.

Thorburn, H.G. "Politics of Economic Development in Canada." *Q.Q.*, 90, Spring, 1983.

Webb, T. "DRIEing out DREE." [regional development policy], *P.O.*, 7, 4, May, 1986.

Westfall, W., (ed.). *Perspectives on Regions and Regionalism in Canada*. (Canadian Issues, Volume 5). Ottawa: Association for Canadian Studies, 1983.

Whalley, J. *Regional Aspects of Confederation*. Toronto: U.T.P., 1985.

Provinces and Territories

(See also Bibliography in Chapter 7.)

Abele, F., and Dickerson, M.O. "The 1982 Plebiscite on Division of the Northwest Territories: Regional Government and Federal Policy." *C.P.P.*, 11, 1, March, 1985.

Bell, G., and Pascoe, A. *The Ontario Government: Structure and Functions*. Toronto: Wall & Thompson, 1988.

Bienvenue, R.M. "Language Politics and Social Divisions in Manitoba." *A.R.C.S.*, 19, Summer, 1989.

Bercuson, D.M. "Regionalism and Unlimited Identity in Western Canada." *J.C.S.*, 15, 2, Summer, 1980.

Bishop, O.B., *et al.* (eds.) *Bibliography of Ontario History, 1867–1976: Cultural, Economic, Political, Social*. 2 vols, Toronto: U.T.P., 1980.

Burill, MacKay, I. (ed.). *People, Resources, and Power: Critical Perspectives on*

Underdevelopment and Primary Industries in Atlantic Canada. Fredericton: Acadiensis Press, 1987.

Caldarola, C., (ed.). *Society and Politics in Alberta.* Toronto: Methuen, 1979.

Chandler, M.A., and Chandler, W.M. *Public Policy and Provincial Politics.* Toronto: McG.-H.R., 1979.

Chorney, H., and Hansen, P. "Neo-Conservatism, Social Democracy, and Province-Building: The Manitoba Experience." *C.R.S.A.,* 22, 1, February, 1985.

Coates, K., and Powell, J. *The Modern North: People, Politics and the Struggle Against Colonialism.* Toronto: Lorimer, 1989.

Conway, J. *The West: The History of a Region in Confederation.* Toronto: Lorimer, 1983.

Dacks, G. *A Choice of Futures: The Politics of Canada's North.* Toronto: Methuen, 1981.

Elkins, D.J., and Simeon, R. *Small Worlds: Parties and Provinces in Canadian Political Life.* Toronto: Methuen, 1980.

Elliott, J.L. "Emerging Ethnic Nationalism in the Canadian Northwest Territories." *Canadian Review of Studies in Nationalism,* XI, 2, Fall, 1984.

Friesen, G. *The Canadian Prairies: A History.* Toronto: U.T.P., 1984.

Gagnon, A. Développement régional: Etat et groupes populaires. Hull: Asticuou, 1985.

Gibbins, R. *Prairie Politics and Society: Regionalism in Decline.* Toronto: Butterworths, 1980.

Gibbins, R. "Models of Nationalism: A Case Study of Political Ideologies in the Canadian West." *C.J.P.S.,* 10, 2, June, 1977.

Gill, R. "Federal, Provincial and Local Language Legislation in Manitoba and the Franco-Manitobans." *A.R.C.S.,* 12, 1, Spring, 1982.

Gill, R. "Federal and Provincial Language Policy in Ontario and the Future of the Franco-Ontarians." *A.R.C.S.,* 13, 1, Spring, 1983.

House, J.D. "Premier Peckford, Petroleum Policy and Popular Politics in Newfoundland and Labrador." *J.C.S.,* 17, 2, Summer, 1982.

Jamieson, B., (ed.). *Governing Nova Scotia: Policies, Priorities and the 1984–1985 Budget.* Halifax: School of Public Administration, Dalhousie University, 1984.

Jamieson, B. "Budgeting in the Atlantic Provinces in the 1980s." *C.T.J.,* 35, 2, March-April, 1987.

Kilgour, D. *Uneasy Patriots: Western Canadians in Confederation.* Edmonton: Lone Pine Publishers, 1988.

Leadbeater, D., (ed.) *The Political Economy of Alberta.* Toronto: Lorimer, 1981.

Leadbeater, D., (ed.) *Essays on the Political Economy of Alberta.* Toronto: New Hogtown Press, 1984.

Magnusson, W., *et al. The New Reality: The Politics of Restraint in British Columbia.* Vancouver: New Star Press, 1984.

Michael, J.M. *From Sissons to Meyer: The Administrative Development of the Yukon Government, 1948–1979.* Whitehorse: Government of Yukon, 1988.

National and Regional Interests in the North. Ottawa: Canadian Arctic Resources Committee, 1984.

Page, R. *Northern Development: The Canadian Dilemma.* Toronto: M.& S., 1986. (Natives)

Palmer, H., and Palmer, T. "The Alberta Experience." *J.C.S.,* 17, 3, Fall, 1982.

Richards, J., and Pratt, L. *Prairie Capitalism: Power and Influence in the New West.* Toronto: M. & S., 1979.

Robertson, G. *Northern Provinces: A Mistaken Goal.* Montreal: I.R.P.P., 1988.

Rowat, D., (ed.). *Provincial Policy-Making: Comparative Essays.* Ottawa: C.U.P., 1981.

Rowat, D. *Issues in Provincial Politics.* Ottawa: Carleton Univeristy, Department of Political Science, 1988.
Stevenson, I.G., and Pratt, L., (eds.). *Western Separatism: Myths, Realties and Dangers.* Edmonton: Hurtig, 1981.
Winter, J.R., (ed.). *The Atlantic Provinces in Canada: Where Do We Go From Here?* Halifax: Atlantic Provinces in Canada Conference, 1981.

Municipalities

(See also Bibliography in Chapter 7.)

Antoft, K., (ed.). *A Guide to Local Government in Nova Scotia.* Halifax: Dalhousie University, 2nd ed., 1985.
Artibise, A.F.J., and Linteau, P.A. *The Evolution of Urban Canada: An Analysis of Approaches and Interpretations.* Winnipeg: University of Winnipeg, 1984.
Baccigalupo, A. *Les administrations municipales québécoises: des origines à nos jours*, Tome I. *Les municipalités.* Montréal: Agence d'Arc, 1984.
Bird, R.M., and Slack, N.E. *Urban Public Finance in Canada.* Toronto: Butterworths, 1982.
Bolduc, R. "Incidence du rôle accru de l'Etat sur la démocratie locale." *C.P.A.*, 23, 1, Printemps, 1980.
Bourassa, G., and Léveillé, J. *Le système politique de Montréal.* Montréal: les cahiers de l'Acfas, 1986.
Brownstone, M., and Plunkett, T.J. *Metropolitan Winnipeg: Politics and Reform of Local Government.* Berkeley: University of California Press, 1983.
Cameron, K., (ed.). *Municipal Government in the Intergovernmental Maze.* Seminar Publication, Toronto: I.P.A.C., 1980.
Cullingworth, J.B. *Urban and Regional Planning in Canada.* New Brunswick, New Jersey: Transaction Books, 1987.
Dickerson, M.O., Drabek, S., and Woods, J.T., (eds.). *Problems of Change in Urban Government.* Waterloo, W.L.U.P., 1980.
Federation of Canadian Municipalites. Report of the Resource Task Force on Constitutional Reform. *Municipal Government in a New Canadian Federal System.* Ottawa: 1980.
Feldman, L.D., (ed.). *Politics and Government of Urban Canada: Selected Readings.* Toronto: Methuen, 4th ed., 1981.
Filion, P. "Core Redevelopment, Neighbourhood Revitalization and Municipal Government Motivation: Twenty Years of Urban Renewal in Quebec City." *C.J.P.S.*, 20, 1, March, 1987.
Frisken, F., (ed.) *Conflict or Cooperation? The Toronto-Centred Region in the 1980s.* Toronto: York University Urban Studies Program, March, 1982.
Frisken, F. "Canadian Cities and the American Example: A Prologue to Urban Policy Analysis." *C.P.A.*, 29, 3, Fall, 1986.
Goldberg, M.A., and Mercer, J. *The Myth of the North American City.* Vancouver: U.B.C.P., 1986.
Graham, K.A., *et al. Local and Regional Government in the Northwest Territories.* Kingston: Institute of Local Government, Queen's University, 1980.
Hamel, P., Léonard, J.F., and Mayer, R. *Les mobilisations populaires urbaines.* Montréal: Nouvelle optique, 1982.
Higgins, D. *Local and Urban Politics in Canada.* Toronto: Gage, 1986.
Higgins, D. "Municipal Politics and Government: Development.of the Field in Canadian Political Science." *C.P.A.*, 22, 3, Fall, 1979.

Hodge, G., and Gadeer, M.A. *Towns and Villages in Canada: the Importance of Being Unimportant.* Toronto: Butterworths, 1983.

Kay, B.J. "Urban Decision-Making and the Legislative Environment: Toronto Council Re-examined." *C.J.P.S.*, 15, 3 September, 1982.

Kennedy, L.W. *The Urban Kaleidoscope: Canadian Perspectives.* Toronto: McG.-H.R., 1983.

Kitchen, H.M. *The Role for Local Governments in Economic Development.* Toronto: O.E.C., 1986.

Kitchen, H.M. *Local Government Finance in Canada.* Toronto: C.T.F., 1984.

Laurentian University Review. Special issue on "City Government in Northern Ontario." 17, 2, February, 1985.

Magnusson, W. "Metropolitan Reform in the Capitalist City." *C.J.P.S.*, 14, 3, September, 1981.

Magnusson, W. "The Local State in Canada: Theoretical Perspectives." *C.P.A.*, 28, 4, Winter, 1985.

Morin, R. *Réanimation urbaine et pouvoir local: les stratégies des municipalitiés de Montréal, Sherbrooke, et Grenoble en quartiers anciens.* Montréal: P.U.Q., 1987.

Newfoundland. *Report of the Royal Commission on Municipal Government in Prince Edward Island.* Halifax: Maritime Municipal, 1984.

Nova Scotia. *Report of Royal Commission on Education, Public Services and Provincial-Municipal Relations*, [Graham Report], 4 vols, Halifax: Queen's Printer, 1974.

Paterson, T.W. *Lower Mainland.* Langley, B.C.: Sunfine, 1984.

Perks, W.T., and Robertson, I.M., (eds.). *Urban and Regional Planning in a Federal State: The Canadian Experience.* Toronto: McG.-H.R., 1979.

Plunkett, T.J., and Betts, G.M. *The Management of Canadian Urban Government.* Kingston: Institute of Local Government, Queen's University, 1978.

Rayside, D.M. "Small Town Fragmentation and the Politics of Community." *J.C.S.*, 24, 1, Spring, 1989.

Robarts, Hon. J.P. *Report of the Royal Commission on Metropolitan Toronto*, 2 vols. Toronto: Queen's Printer, 1977.

Robinson, I.M. *Canadian Urban Growth Trends.* Vancouver: U.B.C.P., 1981.

Rowat, D.C. *The Government of Federal Capitals.* Toronto: U.T.P., 1973.

Rowat, D.C. "A Note on the Uniqueness of the Study of Local Government." *C.P.A.*, 26, 3, Fall, 1983.

Rowat, D.C., (ed.). *Recent Urban Politics in Ottawa-Carleton.* Ottawa: Carleton University, 1985.

Sancton, A. "The Impact of Language Differences in Metropolitan Reform in Montreal." *C.P.A.*, 22, 2, Summer, 1979.

Sancton, A. *Governing the Island of Montreal: Language Differences and Metropolitan Politics.* Berkeley: University of California Press, 1985.

Stetler, G.A., and Artibise, A.F.J. *The Canadian City.* Toronto: C.U.P., rev. ed., 1984.

Tindal, C.R. *You and Your Local Government.* Toronto: Ontario Municipal Management Development Board, 1982.

Tindal, C.R., and Tindal, S.N. *Local Government in Canada.* Toronto: McG-H. R., 3rd ed., 1990.

Weller, G.R. "Local Government in the Canadian Provincial North." *C.P.A.*, 24, 1, Spring, 1981.

FRENCH CANADA

NATIONALISM IN QUEBEC:
AN INCOMPLETE SECULAR REVOLUTION

François-Pierre Gingras and Neil Nevitte

Nationalism is the most significant thread running through Quebec politics during the last 150 years. Historically, the particular character of Quebec nationalism, however, has been a function of the nature of Quebec society itself; changes in Quebec society have produced transformations in the style, substance, and form of Quebec nationalism. Today, most observers view the "Quiet Revolution" of the early 1960s as the single most important turning point in Quebec's recent history. For many it marked Quebec's coming of age, the moment when Quebec moved into the modern era. Traditional social, political, and cultural institutions, which in the past had been the pillars of a traditional order, came under attack. Not surprisingly then, for many, contemporary Quebec nationalism of the sort advanced by the Parti Québécois is directly related to the transformations implied by the Quiet Revolution.

This chapter has two goals. The first is to illustrate the continuity of Quebec's nationalism by tracing, in very broad terms, the socio-historical backdrop of contemporary Quebec nationalism. . . . The second goal is more theoretical. It will be argued that the changes encompassed by the Quiet Revolution are not

Francois-Pierre Gingras and Neil Nevitte, "Nationalism in Quebec: The Transition of Ideology and Political Support," in *Political Support in Canada: The Crisis Years*. Allan Kornberg and Harold Clarke, editors. Pages 293–322. Copyright © 1984 Duke University Press.

as complete as many have suggested and that the tension between the forces of tradition and the forces of modernity constitutes a key focus for understanding contemporary Quebec politics. Specifically, it will be shown that the push for secularization in Quebec, secularization being the cutting edge of the Quiet Revolution, has not run its course, and as a result religious values remain important in Quebec society. Moreover, the coexistence of traditional religious values and modern secular values in contemporary Quebec carries important consequences for political support and the expression of contemporary nationalism. . . .

Historically, the Roman Catholic Church exercised the most profound influence on traditional Quebec and consequently on the definition of traditional Quebec nationalism. The church's total penetration of society and its unparalleled organizational capacity made it a critical actor in the politics of the province and as such it was uniquely qualified to articulate national aspirations. These aspirations, summarized in the phrase *la survivance*, presumed that institutions such as the parish, the confessional schools, and the family would remain as the chief pillars of French-Canadian society. Substantively, traditional nationalism called for the safeguarding of religious and cultural rights and institutions, the rejection of liberalism, the protection of a traditional rural lifestyle, freedom from government intervention, and provincial autonomy. Not surprisingly, increased levels of industrialization and urbanization represented a challenge to these ideals, and progressively traditional Quebec nationalism took on the appearance of the collective reactions of a minority which perceived itself to be under seige.

THE ORIGINS OF CONTEMPORARY QUEBEC INDEPENDENTISM

. . . The Rassemblement pour l'Indépendance Nationale, created in 1960, was the first distinct organizational vehicle for modern Quebec nationalism. At the outset it advocated a form of nationalism which favored no specific socioeconomic group or political doctrine. Although the RIN advanced a number of national claims which had been part and parcel of the traditional independentist movements, such as French unilingualism and territorial claims to Labrador, the importance of the RIN was that it represented a significant departure from the essence of traditional nationalism. The RIN's nationalism was not a defensive ideology reacting to unsatisfied demands, but a moderately aggressive nationalism which could not be satisfied by concessions from, or "outputs" of, the federal system. . . .

The RIN was formed only a few months after Jean Lesage's Liberals had defeated the Union Nationale, whose leader and founder, Maurice Duplessis, had died. Since the reforms of the Lesage regime are widely regarded as having set in motion the changes identified with the Quiet Revolution, it is necessary to outline the nature of the Quiet Revolution in order to appreciate the context and direction of the RIN's program.

In general terms the Quiet Revolution represented a fundamental, qualitative change in the orientation of Quebec society. This involved an impetus toward greater participation by Québécois in a modern industrial economy, and a reorientation of values particularly with respect to the reaffirmation of the authenticity of Quebec culture. These two basic themes, the socioeconomic development of Quebec and the Québécois, and the value of orientations leading to cultural affirmation, were viewed as complementary. Attitudes toward Quebec culture changed: *survivance*, which expressed the culturally defensive posture of old Quebec, was replaced by *rattrapage*, reflecting a new confidence coupled with the realization that precious time had been lost in the social and economic development of Quebec. In all dimensions, political and economic, cultural and social, the Quiet Revolution was, according to conventional historiography, a transition from an old to a new order.

Over the years, independence became perceived by its advocates more as an instrument than as a goal per se. Independence represented the key to social and economic planning which was to be guided *by* the Québécois, *for* the Québécois. As Pierre Bourgault, the leader of the RIN, commented, "So far, we have never known where we were heading for, because others were deciding. We now want to decide ourselves, and be responsible for our successes as well as for our failures." The RIN postulated that the Québécois should invent a new, unique socioeconomic system that would take into account their cultural uniqueness as well as the North American context. . . .

The Parti Québécois emerged as the principal vehicle for contemporary Quebec nationalism in the wake of the RIN's annual convention in 1968. A severe crisis in the RIN featuring a split between the revolutionary neo-Marxist faction and Pierre Bourgault's middle-of-the-road faction culminated in a resolution to terminate the existence of the party. Actually, a considerable portion of the party's membership had already joined the newly created PQ, probably because the PQ was perceived to have better electoral prospects than the RIN. The PQ itself was an outgrowth of the Mouvement Souveraineté Association formed in 1967 by René Lévesque, a high-profile and well-respected former cabinet minister in the Lesage government of 1960–66. ● ● ●

The core of the independentist construction has been a belief in a uniquely Québécois collective personality manifested by a deeply-rooted attachment to "this only corner of the world where we may be fully ourselves." This has implied the maintenance of French as the normal language of use despite tremendous North American pressures in the direction of assimilation. More generally, not only do Québécois have the right to safeguard their collective personality (the right of all nations to live), but also they have a moral obligation not to betray the heritage preserved and developed through generations at the cost of uninterrupted efforts and sacrifices. Thus, independentists believe Québécois have two alternatives: on the one hand, there is the "comfortable" solution of losing the collective self through assimilation; on the other, there is the difficult solution which involves struggling for a status congruous with the size, personality, and perceived aspirations of the Québécois nation.

According to independentists, the achievement of the second solution is dependent upon the ability of the Quebec government to autonomously determine and implement its own policies in the fields of citizenship, immigration and manpower, communications, social security and health, justice, the economy, international relations, the internal constitution, and territorial integrity. They do not regard the Canadian political system as sufficiently flexible to allow for such a measure of autonomy. As a result, rupture is regarded as inevitable if Québécois decide to fully assert their collective self. . . .

In 1968, the MSA merged with other groups to form the Parti Québécois. The new party emphasized the instrumental nature of independence rather than the possibility of an association with English Canada. During its first few years of existence, the new party's strategy was to recruit members on the basis of their sympathy for the idea of sovereignty (or sovereignty-association) and the respectability brought by Lévesque to the movement; to develop a sophisticated social democratic program; and to try to persuade the electorate to "buy" the program (social democracy and independence). The program itself was largely inherited from the MSA and the RIN and was based on three key themes; planning, efficiency, and decentralization. It had clear technocratic biases, vesting in the government a major role in the definition and organization of the community. . . .

The pragmatic drift of the PQ was accelerated after the 1973 election—a contest which saw the party increase its popular vote total to 30 per cent but capture only six assembly seats. The party largely abandoned its earlier "educational mission," to display instead an image of being *the* alternative to the status quo. PQ strategists understood that in searching for popular support a new party had to stress three elements, namely, the identification of personal and collective interests reflected in the emphasis placed on the need for control over one's personal/collective destiny, including good government in the short run; the symbolic manifestations of these aspirations, such as slogans like "Quebec to the Québécois" and "for a real government," designed to confirm the loyalties of the supporters and to recruit new sympathizers; and the deep-rooted cultural values of the population, that is, nationalism, the French language, and social economic development.

The agenda that PQ strategists tried to set involved issues such as the need for a "real" government, freedom from the political scandals of the Liberal administration, reformed party financing, and so forth. Also, the party made an effort to recruit new members (and in the 1976 campaign, to gather votes) on semi-ideological and nonideological terms, while trying to "ideologically educate" the members after they had joined (instead of before). The rationale for the strategy was the view that the objective of independence might be accepted and shared only as the result of individual analyses and ideological maturation.

In the 1976 election the strategy was successful; it brought the party 41 per cent of the vote and enough seats to form a majority government. In this election the PQ did not ask the Québécois to vote for the elaborate program, but instead to cast a ballot for "good government." According to the logic of the party's leadership, good government implied an eventual constitutional rupture (with anticipated economic association) as only limited improvements might be made within the existing constitutional structure. And the Québécois, through a referendum, would tell the government when to go that far in the development of their collective self.

In 1976, the PQ promised to hold a referendum on sovereignty-association during its first term of office. After considerable procrastination May 20, 1980, was chosen and the Québécois were asked to give the government a mandate to *negotiate* sovereignty-association. All observers agree that the actual "soft" wording of the question was designed to draw more supporters than would have been attracted by a "straight" question calling the Québécois to express their support for sovereignty-association . . . or even independence. Some claimed that it was "an effort to deflect the discussion away from the theme of basic change in the Canadian political community and toward the interpreta-tion that what was being proposed was a series of changes to the regime." The strategy was successful to the extent that, according to data collected by Maurice Pinard and Richard Hamilton, more than 40 per cent of those who voted "oui" wanted to set in motion negotiations on a renewed federalism rather than to support sovereignty-association.

However, the presence of a substantial number of "neo-federalists" among "oui" voters was insufficient as 60 per cent of all voters cast a "non." A majority of Québécois were unwilling, or unready, to go even as far as giving a mandate to negotiate sovereignty-association. In fact, as will be argued later, this result suggests that a majority of Québécois have not yet accepted all of the new value orientations developed during the Quiet Revolution, including the polarized nationalist values conveyed in the independentist movement.

Prior to the Quiet Revolution, value orientations were largely religious-based as the Roman Catholic Church played a central role in Quebec's social and political life. But since that time, other new and more important forces were presumed to be at work in the province. According to some theorists, the institutional and structural changes in Quebec during the 1960s were merely symptoms of, and secondary to, the essence of the Quiet Revolution. For example, Guy Rocher has argued that it "was characterized by changes of mentality, attitudes and values among French Canadians in Quebec much more than by a change in the institutions and in the social structures as such." Similarly, Kenneth McRoberts and Dale Posgate have maintained that traditional beliefs and assumptions were "to a large extent abandoned," while Fernand Dumont has referred to the Quiet Revolution as a profound transmuta-tion of yesterday's arguments—arguments articulated by the leading upholders of the old order, the Roman Catholic Church. The Quiet Revolution, therefore, to the extent that it constituted a reaction against the past, represented a fundamental challenge to the heretofore untested hegemony of the Roman

Catholic Church as the definitive director of the social order. Secular spokesmen articulated a new vision of Quebec, a vision which was aclerical if not
anticlerical. Moreover, the elites engineering Quebec's transformation from the
old to the new order were not reluctant to implicate the Church as the agent
responsible for the social, economic, political, and cultural retardation of the
Québécois. Some observers hold, then, that the creation of a new order
requires not only the participation of the Québécois in the modern sectors of
the economy but also, analogously, participation in *new and modern values*.
So it is assumed that the atrophy of the institutions of the Roman Catholic
Church, particularly the educational and social service institutions, has been
paralleled by atrophy in the pertinence of Roman Catholic values traditionally
understood.

The argument of the Quiet Revolution theorists is powerful. By all accounts,
at least until 1960, Quebec culture *was* a traditional and essentially religious
culture. Thus Québécois nationalism, until 1960, may be interpreted as a
religious nationalism. If the dissociation of the religious component of Quebec
culture, under such motors as secular post-secondary education, reached
fruition in the Quiet Revolution, then a fundamental reorientation of Quebec
society, a genuine "cultural revolution," has indeed taken place.

First, there can be little disagreement with Michel Brunet's view that the
question of complete redistribution of power between church and state has
been settled. Clearly, the institutional power of the Church has declined and
the once organic relationship between church and state has been ruptured by
the introduction of hospital insurance and medicare, the creation of the Ministries of Cultural Affairs and of Education, and the establishment of an integrated
network of state agencies providing basic as well as specialized health and
social services. Second, at the grassroots level, Quiet Revolution theorists point
to falling attendance rates at Mass as further evidence of the decline of the
Church. Also, the number of priests ordained in the Roman Catholic Church
fell 58 per cent between 1960 and 1969. And interest in the parish, particularly
among the youth, has declined. Third, the Church has become disconnected
from significant interest groups in Quebec. With the death of Maurice Duplessis,
the Roman Catholic Church lost an important and sympathetic ally. By 1960,
the Church had lost its influence even with the Catholic Trade Unions in
Quebec. Most professional and student organizations and public interest committees created in the 1960s did not bother to appoint chaplains.

The evidence supporting the Quiet Revolution view of Quebec's social
change since 1960 is impressive. But, from the theoretical perspective adopted
here, it cannot yet be considered conclusive. . . . In our view, the institutional
evidence does not easily fit the Quiet Revolution framework. The victory
of Quebec's provincial Liberal party in 1960, said to represent grassroots
endorsement of a program of social change, actually involved only a net loss
of slightly more than 2 per cent of the eligible electorate by the Union Nationale,
compared to its vote total in the 1956 election. The so-called consolidation of
modernization values in the 1962 election also added only 3 per cent of

eligible voters to the Liberal party's votes total. Insofar as the Union Nationale represented traditionalism in the 1960s, it cannot be said that the values associated with the old order were "swept aside overnight."

Nor can it even be said Quebec society has embraced religious neutrality: as late as 1975, a study prepared for the Reorganization Committee of the School Council of the Island of Montreal reported that "more than 80 per cent of Catholics want religious instruction in school" and, "most parents, especially Catholics, think these classes should be compulsory." Attempts to deconfessionalize the school system have met with staunch opposition from an overwhelming majority of Protestants and Roman Catholics alike. . . .

The second reservation specifically relates to the role that Quiet Revolution theorists conventionally assign to the Church in Quebec. Viewing the disengagement of the Roman Catholic Church from the Quebec polity as synonymous with the secular, progressive thrust of the Quiet Revolution implies that the Church (at least in Quebec) is once and for all against change, and that the most significant dimension of religious influence in Quebec is institutionally expressed. Perhaps the capacity of the Church to respond to change has been underestimated to the extent that its homogeneity as a conservative organization has been overestimated. To be sure, there are conservative forces within the Church hierarchy, but there are also liberal, even radical elements which have exercised important influence. . . .

Our third reservation about the Quiet Revolution framework concerns the assumed relationship between changes in institutions and changes in societal values. Specifically, while Quiet Revolution theorists argue that it is values, not institutions, that are at the core of social change, the only evidence that is presented in support of the case is institutional and we have already questioned the integrity of these types of data. . . .

. . . The fact of the matter is that the Quiet Revolution was élite-induced social change. Thus, the institutional reforms of the 1960s may be a more accurate reflection of the interests of areligious élites rather than the values of the bulk of the Quebec population. Indeed, some interpreters of the Quiet Revolution agree on this point.

In sum, in our view the conventional interpretation of the Quiet Revolution as an explanation of contemporary Quebec politics appears to contain serious weaknesses. The flaws are not fatal but they may be misleading. The above reservations, collectively, are sufficiently significant to cast doubt on the straightforward view that the Quiet Revolution represented a sudden and wholehearted change for most Québécois. To summarize our critique, the conventional view of the Quiet Revolution can only be sustained by ignoring the evident capacity of traditional institutions, such as the Roman Catholic Church, to respond to change; by focusing only on a selectively narrow range of institutional evidence; and by assuming that elite-led institutional changes corresponded to changes in the attitudes of the Quebec population as a whole. . . .

. . . The critical issue in the analysis of secularization in Quebec, then, concerns the extent to which religious values continue to impinge on society.

Two aspects are of particular interest: first, to what extent do religious values play an important role in the definition of the Québécois collective identity? and second, to what extent do religious values structure the political domain? Attention must be directed not only to the privately held beliefs of the Québécois (personal religiosity) but also to the public aspects of religious beliefs (hereinafter designated cultural religiosity)....

... [In a mail questionnaire survey of the Quebec general public conducted in November 1976] only 29 per cent of the Québécois sampled thought that religion was not important to French-Canadian culture, while nearly half of the respondents (47 per cent) regarded religion as important or very important to French-Canadian culture. On that basis, it is difficult to make the argument that Quebec in 1976 had a truly secular culture....

... Our data suggest that the conventional interpretation of the Quiet Revolution does apply, but only to a relatively restricted segment of the Québécois— those under thirty-five years of age. For the other Québécois, religion continues to play an important role in the definition of French-Canadian culture. In our view, the fact that most Québécois do *not* carry a secular view of French-Canadian culture is crucial because it argues against the indiscriminate use of the conventional interpretation of the Quiet Revolution, and it gives further support to the idea that the process of secularization is far from complete. ● ● ●

To summarize, the above analysis suggests that significant political consequences flow from the incomplete secularization of Quebec society. First, a secular orientation to Quebec national culture is linked to an exclusivist orientation to the Quebec nation whereas a religious conception of the national culture encourages a dual set of loyalties; adherents are attracted simultaneously to the Quebec nation and to the Canadian state. These two conceptions, in turn, produce two varieties of nationalist ideologies which exist side by side. On the one hand, the secular nationalists are attracted to an independentist solution; on the other hand, the traditional nationalists, who also seek to promote and defend Quebec's national interest, tend to believe that Quebec's aspirations can be achieved within a Canadian federal state....

CONCLUSION

... The argument advanced here is that conventional interpretations of the Quiet Revolution can be misleading. There is no question that the Quiet Revolution did unleash secular forces in Quebec, enormously significant forces which, for example, were probably responsible for the victory of the PQ in 1976. What is problematic, however, according to our evidence, is that an uncritical acceptance of the Quiet Revolution paradigm tends to overdramatize the scope and nature of Quebec's socio-political change with the result that the continued significance of the tension between modernity and tradition has been diminished. Certainly, a fundamental realignment in Quebec politics has taken place, but the evidence clearly shows that the process of transformation from a traditional religious to a secular society is far from complete. Indeed, the coexistence of religious and secular orientations represents a very significant cleavage in Quebec—one which makes the outcomes of political events such as the referendum uncertain. Therefore, to presume that the values associated with the Quiet Revolution changed "overnight" or that they have percolated through all of Quebec society at the mass level produces an oversimplified image of contemporary Quebec politics.

To suggest that the transformation of Quebec politics is incomplete encourages the inference that the movement to a secular society in Quebec will be completed. Although the analysis of attitudes of Québécois does not use longitudinal data, it could be argued that, since the Quiet Revolution involved seemingly irreversible reforms in areas such as education, the attitudes of the Quiet Revolution cohort will eventually be extended to the whole population. This is a tempting and perhaps powerful argument. At the same time, this argument too may be something of an oversimplification, one which ignores other factors. A survey of patterns of political support in advanced industrialized societies, societies, which in fact left clericalism behind a long time ago, clearly shows that religious values are remarkably resilient and that the "religious factor" remains a powerful though often indirect force informing political preferences. The implication is that, even with the advancing Quiet Revolution cohort, future support for independentist goals such as sovereignty-association is far from a foregone conclusion in Quebec. Not only is it difficult to predict what patterns of political support will emerge from a maturing Quiet Revolution cohort—conventional wisdom holds that such cohorts tend to become progressively less "revolutionary"—but it is also plain that many Québécois continue to subscribe to traditional values. The unfortunate consequence of conventional Quiet Revolution interpretations is that attention is deflected away from this evidently significant traditional element in Quebec. The result, in our view, is that debate about the importance of such factors as religion has been prematurely foreclosed, or at least pre-empted.

QUEBEC POLITICS IN THE EIGHTIES AND NINETIES
Nelson Wiseman

QUESTIONING GINGRAS AND NEVITTE

Gingras's and Nevitte's article is stimulating for it goes against the grain of conventional wisdom. How sustainable and helpful is it in interpreting Que-

An original article prepared for this edition in March 1990 by the author, who is a member of the Department of Political Science, University of Toronto. By permission.

bec's recent past or future bent? Their notion that the Quiet Revolution created a thoroughly secular society can be tested by placing Quebec in comparative perspective. No revolution has been thoroughly secular. Witness the American (whose coins proclaim "In God We Trust") or the Russian (whose leadership after seven decades of imposed atheism now acknowledges "spiritual values"). The struggle between modernity and tradition exists in every state, in every revolution. Gingras and Nevitte assault the Quiet Revolution paradigm, an abstract concept, by reference to snapshots of public opinion in the 1970s. Their case that "a truly secular society" does not exist in Quebec may be made for every society. Religion, like art, politics, and cuisine, is a universal feature of the human experience—individually and collectively. Social scientists are concerned with degree, relativity, and spectrums but might use models, paradigms, and polar opposites to illuminate the former rather than to insist on the absolute existence of the latter.

Compared to pre-1960s Quebec and to other societies, Quebec has become a relatively secular society both in its institutions and popular values. Lingering traces and symbols of tradition might be evident in attitude surveys and in institutions—such as the large cross in the chamber of Quebec's National Assembly—but behavioural evidence is more compelling than opinion surveys or symbolic relics. To test Gingras's and Nevitte's report that "more than 80 percent of Catholics *want* religious instruction in school," we might examine the actual *behaviour* of Quebec's Catholics. It has been remarkably inconsistent recently, in regard to Catholic religious instruction, perhaps more so than in other Catholic societies. In 1989, for example, the Quebec government resorted to monetary incentives to stimulate the production of children and its Ministère de la Santé et des Services sociaux observed that "Quebec is currently experiencing one of the lowest birth rates in the world, a marriage rate among the lowest, a divorce rate, and a proportion of consensual unions that are higher than average for industrialized countries."

The conclusion might be, therefore, that although Quebec is not a totally secularized society, it is more secularized than most. Gingras's and Nevitte's 1976 survey findings suggest as much. Religion mattered little "only to a relatively restricted segment of Québécois—those under 35 years of age." That group, now in the 1990s, includes all those under 50 years of age, a large majority of Québécois. In retracing Quebec's politics in the 1980s and projecting them through the 1990s, the religious variable has not been totally exorcised, but it is, arguably, less relevant than it has ever been in Quebec's history.

QUEBEC IN THE EIGHTIES

Québécois were summoned to the polls seven times in the 1980s for three federal elections, three provincial elections, and a unique referendum. In none of the provincial elections did the winning party (the Parti Québécois in 1981, the Liberals in 1985 and 1989) run on a platform of political sovereignty for

Quebec, so they had no mandate to pursue it. In all three federal elections the winning party (the Liberals in 1980, the Conservatives in 1984 and 1988) won massive support in Quebec and secured the backing of the federal opposition parties for their constitutional policies affecting Quebec. The highest turnout of voters (86 percent) came in the 1980 referendum. It denied the PQ government (by a ratio of 60 percent to 40 percent) a modest mandate to negotiate what it termed "sovereignty-association," with a federal government led at the time by French Canadians who would presumably negotiate on behalf of English Canada.

To the extent that elections represent a link between public choice and public policy, therefore, Québécois repeatedly opted for federalist alternatives and parties through the 1980s. Nevertheless, as the 1990s begin to unfold, the question of Quebec's status in confederation is as problematic as ever. It has been a seminal issue since the 1960s. This sometimes flaming, sometimes simmering, perpetual "crisis" was initially stirred by the Quiet Revolution of the 1960s, fanned by the *indépendantist*-minded PQ in the 1970s, and compounded by the Quebec government's exclusion from a major revision of Canada's constitutional order in the 1980s.

Although the "crisis" is ongoing, the material conditions and psychological factors feeding it have been changing rather than stable. During the Quiet Revolution the provincial government modernized itself as well as Quebec's economy and society. The objectives included heightening the status of francophones by marshalling the power of the Quebec state at a time when francophones as a group were disadvantaged and underprivileged in their own province. By the 1980s the government succeeded in the strategy of being "maîtres chez nous." The incomes and occupational status of francophones increased so substantially that they no longer qualified as an "exploited" ethnic class. Ten of the 50 largest Canadian financial institutions were francophone.

Rattrapage had been attained and *dépassage* was the next step. A dynamic and confident business class came to the fore in the 1980s. Its energy overshadowed that of the once burgeoning public sector which had been unleashed by the Quiet Revolution. The vanguard role of the Quebec government, which referred to itself as the "principal motor" of the Quebec economy in the 1960s and as a "corporate state" in the second half of the 1970s, gave way to a new breed of corporate, private entrepreneurs. Nowhere was this better expressed than in the career paths of the best and the brightest: whereas 90 percent of the 1970 graduates of Quebec's leading business school—École des hautes études commerciales—took positions in the public sector, only 5 percent of the 1985 graduating class did so. Between the 1960s and the 1980s the public sector fell into disrepute, and the government went from regulating to empowering Quebec's business class.

The linguistic fears and aspirations of Quebec's francophones were allayed and echoed by Bill 101 which was passed in 1977 as "The Charter of the French Language." In the 1980s the language of the workplace of commerce became, irreversibly, French. The children of allophone immigrants (non-English, non-French) were compelled to enter the French language education system (even as some francophone parents were complaining of the resulting imbalance of French Canadians and non-French Canadians in many Montreal classrooms), professionals and others seeking provincial licences had to demonstrate a working knowledge of French, and French became the sole permissible language of communications between municipalities and the provincial government. L'Office de la langue française monitored and ensured that *francisation* took place in the private sector. With minor exceptions affecting the minority language education rights of English-Canadian citizens (guaranteed by Section 23 of the Constitution Act, 1982) and the right to use English in Quebec's legislature and courts (guaranteed by Section 133 of the BNA Act, 1867), the Quebec government was unrestrained in its linguistic promotion of French. Simultaneously, it presided over a strategic transfer of power from an aging, declining, and dispirited English-Canadian community to an emerging, vibrant, and self-assured francophone commercial elite.

Demographic trends drove the Quebec government's preoccupation with language. For over a century francophones and Québécois have made up a progressively decreasing percentage of Canada's population. At the beginning of the 1980s 27 percent of Canadians were Quebecers, but they are projected to shrink to about 20 percent by the end of the 1990s. Quebec governments—Liberal and PQ—have felt a special obligation to preserve and promote Quebec's distinctive linguistic character and to attain cultural sovereignty. From their perspective the long-term survival and development of North American francophones are at stake. Nevertheless, francophone mass opinion has diverged from elite opinion on this issue and has been more generous to anglophones. Surveys between the late 1970s through the mid 1980s, such as that in Gagnon and Montcalm, *Quebec: Beyond the Quiet Revolution*, pp. 186–87, revealed that even among PQ supporters a substantial majority of francophones favoured extending anglophone rights in education, communications, and services which their government was strenuously denying. At the same time 80 percent of anglophones felt it was "legitimate for the government of Quebec to protect the French language."

These mutually supportive attitudes contributed to a social peace in Quebec during most of the 1980s. Some anglophones and their institutions like the Sun Life Assurance Company, feeling threatened by the new Quebec, had departed in the late 1970s. Most anglophones, however, remained and accommodated themselves. Many became bilingual. The PQ modified Bill 101 so that the anglophone community was explicitly recognized, and internal communications in English were permitted in anglophone parapublic institutions delivering health, education, and welfare services. Robert Bourassa's Liberals went further in 1986, entitling anglophones to health and social services in English.

The social peace was temporarily breached, however, in 1988 over the language of commercial signs. Although the Quebec Liberals had promised in their successful 1985 election campaign to permit English signs, they left the matter to the courts for initial and tardy resolution. Despite the defeat of the PQ, francophone nationalism on the language question did not abate. One demonstration of 20 000 in 1986 featured leading intellectuals who demanded that Bill 101 not be tampered with further. Bourassa began to waffle, his caucus was deeply divided, and the Montreal Chamber of Commerce came down in favour of the law as it was. Bill 101's provisions for unilingual commercial signs were eventually struck down by the Supreme Court in 1988 as a violation of "freedom of expression" guaranteed by the Charter of Rights and Freedoms.

Bourassa responded by resorting to the legislative override, or the "notwithstanding" clause, provided in Section 33 of the Charter (ironically, part of the constitution imposed on Quebec in 1982). The resulting Bill 178 permitted some English signs inside stores but continued to prohibit them outdoors. This angered many English Canadians inside and outside Quebec, although the issue was merely, although powerfully, a symbolic one because the presence of English signs is not a threat to the ability of francophones to work and live in French nor is their absence anything more than a slight inconvenience to anglophones. In a paradoxical upshot the Quebec government endorsed the legal efforts of the Saskatchewan and Alberta governments to limit the expansion of francophone rights in those provinces. The Quebec government feared constitutional precedents which Quebec's anglophones might pursue on their own account.

What were the sources of such behaviour? In the early 1980s the two major protagonists in the struggle over the French-Canadian question were both Québécois: Pierre Trudeau and René Lévesque. Prime Minister Trudeau opposed special constitutional status for Quebec and strengthened French by constitutionalizing bilingual federal government services. He championed linguistic duality and equality throughout Canada, providing opportunities and assistance for francophones outside Quebec and for anglophones inside. But the provision of French services in Vancouver or St. John's was a cruel joke to Quebec nationalists, who noted that the general population continued to grow faster than the francophone population and, notwithstanding federal language policies, French was not increasing as a language spoken regularly in homes outside Quebec.

Trudeau's agenda prevailed for he outmanoeuvred Premier Lévesque. His Liberals captured an unprecedented 74 of Quebec's 75 seats in 1980. Then, soon after the PQ's referendum loss, Trudeau and his caucus—which was 53 percent Québécois—pushed unilaterally for constitutional change. This threw Lévesque into a tactical, defensive alliance with seven English-Canadian premiers who formed a "Gang of Eight." In developing a united front, Lévesque waived Quebec's historic claim to a veto over future constitutional adjustments. When Lévesque was deserted by the other premiers a few months later, his appeal to the courts that Quebec's historic veto had been violated was ruled on too late, in December 1982. The Constitution Act had already been proclaimed in April under the signatures of the Queen and three Québécois MPs (Trudeau as prime minister, Jean Chrétien as minister of justice, and André Oulette as registrar-general).

When Brian Mulroney, another Quebecer, came to power in 1984, he embraced Trudeau's bilingual vision but strove to accomplish what had eluded his predecessor: a constitutional revision in which all governments, including Quebec, were willing partners. He promised to attain Quebec's approval with "honour and enthusiasm." The election of Bourassa's Liberals in Quebec made the task easier. Although Bourassa denounced the 1981–82 constitutional process as a "humiliation" for Quebec, he was a federalist and, as a sign of good faith, lifted the PQ's blanket application of the "notwithstanding" clause to all new legislation. His five conditions for endorsing the 1982 constitution were considered moderate and served as the basis of the Meech Lake Accord of 1987. They included constitutional recognition of Quebec as a distinct society, limiting federal spending in areas of provincial jurisdiction, a provincial role in nominating Supreme Court judges, entrenching Quebec's existing role in immigration policy, and giving Quebec a veto in future constitutional change. In the negotiating process Bourassa compromised on resurrecting a Quebec veto.

These efforts of Mulroney and Bourassa came to naught, however, and the Accord unravelled as three new premiers, who had not been parties to the Meech deliberations, appeared in New Brunswick, Manitoba, and Newfoundland. Public opinion, moreover, was unenthusiastic about Meech. As the deadline for ratification approached, *The Globe and Mail* reported on February 12, 1990, that 70 percent of Canadians surveyed knew not very much or nothing at all about the Accord. Given what they did know, a majority in English Canada opposed it, and only a plurality of Quebecers (outnumbered collectively by opponents, the "don't knows" and the "not sures") supported it.

THE PQ IN THE 1980S

In the 1970s and 1980s Quebec had the third highest turnout rate (after P.E.I. and Saskatchewan) in provincial elections and the third lowest (ahead of Alberta and Newfoundland) in federal elections. On average about 80 percent of Quebecers voted in provincial elections, but only about 74 percent voted in federal elections. Whereas Ontarians were more oriented to federal rather than provincial politics in terms of voter turnout (76 percent versus 64 percent) and interest, Quebecers' opposite tendency suggested perhaps greater allegiance to and identification with their provincial government. An exception to this turnout pattern was in 1984–85, when more Quebecers voted in the federal election that returned Mulroney's Conservatives than voted in the provincial election that replaced the PQ with the Liberals. (In 1988–89 there was an equal turnout of 75 percent in both the federal and provincial elections.) In part, therefore, the PQ's demise in the 1980s was the product of some of its traditional supporters boycotting provincial elections after a period of more intense participation.

Why and how did the PQ stumble and lose power? During its first term (1976–81) it was an activist, social democratic, and nationalist force. It promised and was perceived to have delivered good government. It won over and initially pacified the labour movement (although it did not bond with it formally as had the New Democratic party in English Canada) by legislating the country's toughest anti-strike breaking law, suspending fines that had been levied on strikers, nationalizing some industries (for example, asbestos and automobile insurance), and by introducing the most progressive income tax regime in Canada. As Lévesque's *My Quebec* (1979) put it, the PQ wanted to reduce income disparities, ensure equality of opportunity, and increase francophone participation in enterprise. No sovereignty, however, he repeatedly assured Québécois, without a referendum.

Against this backdrop the PQ was re-elected in 1981 with an increased popular vote. The Liberals also gained votes, while the Union Nationale, the primary political expression of pre-secular Quebec, disappeared as a force. Ignoring the national question, the PQ was re-elected despite its association with the *souverainiste* project rather than because of it. The victory was, in part, also one of personality, since Lévesque towered over his Liberal rival, Claude Ryan, in public opinion. By distancing himself from any effort to secure sovereignty during a new mandate, Lévesque disappointed some PQ veterans who wanted it high on the agenda. When challenged on the issue after the election, Lévesque threatened to quit. In fear of losing him, the PQ hurriedly organized an internal party referendum, a "Renérendum," which overwhelmingly endorsed his position by 95 percent.

In its second term the PQ retreated from its social democratic posture. It consciously veered from left to right. The minimum wage, the highest in the country, was frozen and the francophone business elite, nurtured and pampered by the PQ, became critical of the state's activism. Social programs were cut back, and there was less disposition to create new state enterprises and more inclination to wholly or partially privatize some such as la Société des alcools du Québec and Hydro-Québec. The PQ also alienated its union supporters, especially those in the public sector, by severe measures such as imposed collective agreements that reduced salaries and restricted the right to strike.

While the PQ continued to be divided on the national question, Lévesque announced in 1984 that Quebec would no longer boycott federal–provincial meetings and that sovereignty would not be an issue in the next election. Several ministers, including Jacques Parizeau, left the cabinet, and when Lévesque resigned in 1985, Pierre-Marc Johnson, the son of a former Union Nationale premier, easily captured the PQ's leadership. Running on a platform stressing "national affirmation" rather than sovereignty, antagonizing much of their traditional constituency, Johnson and the PQ went down to a quick defeat. Johnson's resignation then led to Parizeau's ascension and to a more militant nationalist PQ position in 1988.

The 1989 re-election of the Liberals was no surprise. Parizeau had not attained Lévesque's popularity, and it was uncertain whether anyone else would ever lead the PQ back to power. Bourassa, meanwhile, had matured as an astute and canny politician. His handling of the sign language issue permitted his Liberals to move toward the nationalist pole, covering more of the spectrum, yet not appearing as extreme as the PQ, with its now unabashedly separatist agenda. In the process Bourassa lost some traditional anglophone support in west Montreal, where the single-issue Equality Party elected a small contingent of four MNAs. Most francophones and allophones, however, remained in the Liberal camp. Bourassa, who had first come to power in 1970, was in a secure and commanding position in the early 1990s. He had, at least temporarily, outflanked his more nationalist opponents and overwhelmed his anglophone critics. The decision to escalate or reduce tensions vis-à-vis English Canada was very much his to make in the aftermath of Meech Lake's demise.

FUTURE LIKE THE PAST?

The future is more difficult to foretell than the past is to retell. Although the PQ's program for sovereignty-association was rejected in the 1980s, the drive for sovereignty may be, paradoxically, recharged in the 1990s under the banner of the traditionally federalist Quebec Liberals. English Canada's rejection of Meech Lake, the gratuitously wounding, anti-French resolutions of dozens of Ontario municipalities, and the small but growing sentiment for sovereignty among Quebec's heretofore universally federalist economic elite are potential fuel for feeding a separatist fire. If Quebec opts for independence, there are massive hurdles to overcome before a divorce is achieved: from monetary, trade, and debt issues to the physical separation of the four Atlantic provinces from the five more westerly provinces. Without mutually beneficial arrangements both English Canada and Quebec would suffer.

In light of its cultural distinctiveness, and especially its assertiveness since the Quiet Revolution, Quebec's place in confederation will continue in the 1990s to be at the heart of the Canadian national question. What makes Canada's break-up less rather than more likely, however, is the sheer weight of history. Persistently recurring tensions over language and Quebec's status are certain and to be expected. Canadians and Québécois have demonstrated in the past, however, that they can live with them and co-exist peacefully and sympathetically. These very strains and accommodations help define what Canada is and what it is to be Québécois. There is no ultimate solution to the Quebec conundrum, although impossibly competing visions promising one will continue to arise in both English and French Canada. There is little point in being surprised by or lamenting the near constant state of crisis. The challenge in the 1990s, as it was between the 1960s and 1980s, is to continue to manage the tensions for mutual advantage, collective gain, and national development—Canadian and Québécois.

[   ]

FRENCH AND ENGLISH MINORITIES ARE DECLINING

Luc Albert

Census data indicate that there have been several distinct trends in the linguistic make-up of Canada since 1971. Both the proportion of the population in provinces other than Quebec with English mother tongue and that with French mother tongue in Quebec have risen. [Mother tongue is the language first learned and still understood.] As well, bilingualism has become more common, as a growing percentage of Canadians report they are able to conduct a conversation in both official languages.

ENGLISH INCREASING OUTSIDE QUEBEC

In the last decade and a half, the proportion of Canadians living outside Quebec with English mother tongue has increased. In 1986, 80.0% of people living in provinces other than Quebec reported English as their mother tongue; this was up from 78.4% in 1971 and 79.4% in 1981. During the same period, the proportion of this population with French mother tongue fell from 6.0% in 1971 to 5.0% in 1986.

Other than Quebec, New Brunswick has by far the largest share of its population with French mother tongue. In 1986, 33.5% of residents of this province had French as their mother tongue, down slightly from 34.0% in 1971.

The proportion of people with French mother tongue was much lower in the remaining provinces. The figure was around 5% in Ontario, Manitoba, and Prince Edward Island; 4% in Nova Scotia; 2% in Saskatchewan, Alberta, and British Columbia; and just 0.5% in Newfoundland. As well, the percentage of the population with French mother tongue fell in these provinces between 1971 and 1986.

The proportion of Canadians outside Quebec whose mother tongue was neither English nor French has also declined. In 1986, 14.9% of this population had a mother tongue other than an official language, down from 15.6% in 1971.

There is considerable provincial variation in the percentage of people with

From *Canadian Social Trends*, Statistics Canada, Spring, 1989. Reproduced with permission of the Minister of Supply and Services Canada, 1990.

Proportion of Quebec Residents with English Mother Tongue and Home Language, 1951–1986

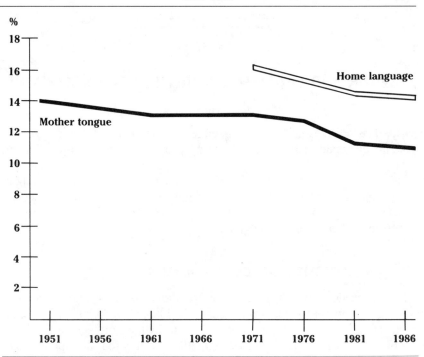

Source: Statistics Canada, Census of Canada.

a mother tongue other than English or French. In 1986, 22% of Manitoba residents, along with between 15% and 17% of those in Ontario, British Columbia, Saskatchewan, and Alberta, had a mother tongue other than English or French. In comparison, only 2% of people in Nova Scotia and around 1% of those in the other Atlantic provinces had a mother tongue other than one of the official languages.

FRANCOPHONE POPULATION INCREASING IN QUEBEC

The proportion of Quebec residents with French as their mother tongue has increased steadily in the last decade and a half. In 1986, French was the mother tongue of 82.8% of the people living in this province, up from 80.7% in 1971 and 82.4% in 1981.

There has also been a slight increase in the proportion of Quebec residents reporting a mother tongue other than English or French, from 6.2% in 1971 to 6.8% in 1986.

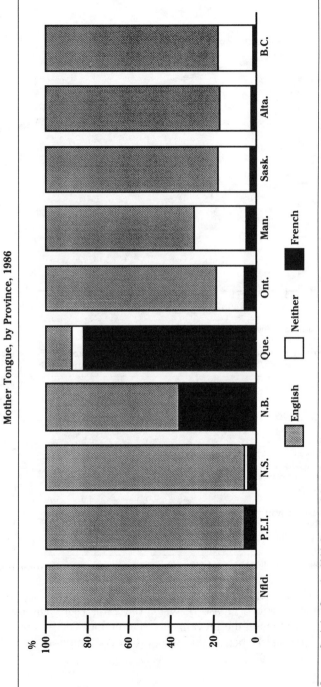

Mother Tongue, by Province, 1986

Source: Statistics Canada, 1986 Census of Canada.

Proportion of Canadians with French Mother Tongue and Home Language, 1951–1986

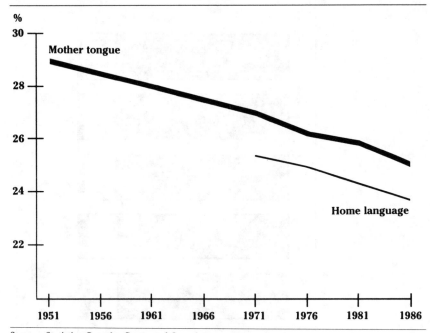

Source: Statistics Canada, Census of Canada.

Proportion of people in provinces outside Quebec with French mother tongue and home language, 1971 and 1986

	French mother tongue		French home language	
	1971	1986	1971	1986
		%		
Newfoundland	0.7	0.5	0.4	0.4
Prince Edward Island	6.6	4.7	3.9	2.8
Nova Scotia	5.0	4.1	3.5	2.9
New Brunswick	34.0	33.5	31.4	31.3
Ontario	6.3	5.3	4.6	3.8
Manitoba	6.1	4.9	4.0	2.8
Saskatchewan	3.4	2.3	1.7	0.9
Alberta	2.9	2.4	1.4	1.1
British Columbia	1.7	1.6	0.5	0.6
Total	**6.0**	**5.0**	**4.3**	**3.6**

Source: Statistics Canada, Census of Canada.

The actual number of people in Quebec with English mother tongue also continued to decrease between 1981 and 1986, although the decline was smaller than in the previous five-year period. The number of anglophones in Quebec fell 4% between 1981 and 1986, compared with a 12% decline between 1976 and 1981.

Much of the decline in Quebec's anglophone population is attributable to the fact that the number of these people leaving Quebec for elsewhere in Canada far exceeds the number entering the province from other regions. Between 1981 and 1986, 41,000 more anglophones left Quebec for other parts of Canada than came to Quebec from other provinces. This was down significantly from a net loss of 106,000 during the 1976–1981 period.

ENGLISH INCREASING, FRENCH DECLINING ACROSS CANADA

When figures from Quebec and the other provinces are combined, the results show that the proportion of all Canadians with English mother tongue has risen, while the percentage whose mother tongue is French has fallen. Between 1971 and 1986, the percentage of people with English mother tongue rose from 60.2% to 62.1%, while the proportion with French mother tongue declined from 26.9% to 25.1%.

Several factors have contributed to the overall decline in the proportion of Canadians whose mother tongue is French. These factors include low fertility in immigrants who speak French, as well as the linguistic assimilation of French-speaking minorities outside Quebec, and the tendency of people with mother tongues other than English or French to adopt the English language.

On the other hand, there has been little overall change in the proportion of Canadians with a mother tongue other than French or English. In the 1971–1986 period, the share of people with another mother tongue remained stable at around 13%.

However, there were changes in the proportion of people with different mother tongues. There was strong growth in the number of people reporting languages associated with the birthplaces of recent immigrants, notably Spanish, and Asiatic languages such as Chinese, Vietnamese, Persian (Farsi), and Tamil. On the other hand, the proportion of people with mother tongues such as German and Ukrainian has fallen.

MORE CANADIANS BILINGUAL

In 1986, more than four million Canadians reported they could conduct a conversation in both English and French. That year 16.2% of the population was bilingual, up from 13.4% in 1971 and 15.3% in 1981.

Quebec has the highest proportion of population which is bilingual. In fact, slightly over half of all Canada's bilingual population in 1986 lived in this province. That year, 34.5% of Quebec residents reported they could conduct a conversation in either official language.

The most bilingual group within Quebec was anglophone. In 1986, more than half (54%) of these people were bilingual, as were almost half (47%) of Quebec residents whose mother tongue was neither English nor French. At the same time, about a third (30%) of Quebec francophones were bilingual.

Proportion of people who are bilingual, by province, 1981 and 1986

Legend: □ 1981 ■ 1986

Provinces (left to right): Nfld., P.E.I., N.S., N.B., Que., Ont., Man., Sask., Alta., B.C.

Y-axis: % 0, 5, 10, 15, 20, 25, 30, 35

Source: Statistics Canada, Census of Canada.

In contrast, fewer than 6% of people residing outside Quebec with English or a language other than English or French, as their mother tongue reported they were bilingual in 1986. However, the vast majority of people outside Quebec with French mother tongue were bilingual. In 1986, almost four of every five (79%) of them were able to conduct a conversation in both official languages.

Outside Quebec, the most bilingual province was New Brunswick, where 29.1% of the population reported themselves as able to conduct a conversation in both official languages. In the remaining provinces, the proportion of the population which was bilingual ranged from around 12% in Ontario to less than 3% in Newfoundland.

Between 1981 and 1986, bilingualism increased in all provinces except Alberta, where the proportion reporting they were able to converse in both official languages was unchanged.

YOUTH MORE BILINGUAL

Young Canadians are generally more likely than other people to be bilingual. In 1986, 20.5% of the population aged 15–24 could conduct a conversation in either English or French; this compared with 19.9% of those aged 25–44, 16.8% of those aged 45–64, and 12.4% of people aged 65 and over. This suggests that French immersion programs in Canadian schools have contributed to the growth of bilingualism.

BIBLIOGRAPHY

French Canada

(See also the Bibliographies in other Chapters, especially in Chapters 4, 7, 8, and 12.)

Albert, A. "Conditions économiques et élections: le cas de l'élection provinciale de 1976 au Québec." *C.J.P.S.*, 13, 2, June 1980.

Albert, A. "La participation politique: les contributions monétaires aux partis politiques québécois." *C.J.P.S.*, 14, 2, June, 1981.

A.R.C.S. Special issue on "Quebec Today," 13, 2, Summer, 1983.

Angell, H. "Duverger, Epstein and the Problem of the Mass Party: The Case of the Parti Québécois." *C.J.P.S.*. 20, 2, June, 1987.

Arnopoulos, S.M., and Clift, D. *The English Fact in Quebec.* Montreal: McG.-Q.U.P., 1984.

Averyt, W.F. "Quebec's Economic Development Policies, 1960–1987: Between Etatisme and Privatisation." *A.R.C.S.*, 19, Summer, 1989.

Baccigalupo, A. *Les administrations municpales québécoises des origines à nos jours*, T.I. Montréal: Editions Arc, 1984.

Balthazar, L. *Bilan du nationalisme au Québec.* Montréal: l'Hexagone, 1986.

Bashevkin, S. "Social Change and Political Partisanship: The Development of Women's Attitudes in Quebec, 1965–1979." *Comparative Political Studies*, July, 1983.

Baugh, D.J. "Lessons from the Sign Law." *P.O.* 11, 2, March 1990.

Beaudry, M., Cloutier, E., and Latouche, D. *Atlas électoral du Québec 1970–1973–1976.* Quebec: 1979.

Behiels, M. *Quebec Since 1945: Selected Readings.* Toronto: Copp Clark, 1987.

Behiels, M. *Prelude to Quebec's Quiet Revolution: Liberalism versus New Nationalism, 1945–1960.* Montreal: McG.-Q.U.P., 1985.

Belanger, Y., and Fournier, P. *L'entreprise québécoise: développement historique et dynamique contemporaine.* Montréal: Hurtubise HMH, 1987.

Bellavance, M., Patry, M., and Parenteau, R. *L'Analyse des politiques gouvernementales.* Québec: P.U.L., 1983.

Bergeron, G. *A nous autres: Aide-mémoire politique par le temps qui court.* Montréal: Québec-Amèrique, 1986.

Bergeron, G., and Pelletier, R. *L'Etat du Québec en devenir.* Montréal: Boréal Express, 1980.

Bernard, A., and Descôteaux, B. *Québec: élections 1981.* Montréal: Edition Hurtubise HMH, 1981.

Bernard, A. *La politique au Canada et au Québec.* Montréal: P.U.Q., 2eme ed., 1977. (English version: Methuen, 1981.)

Bernard, L. *Réflexions sur l'art de se gouverner: essai d'un practicien.* Montrèal: Enap – Québec-Amérique, 1987.

Bernier, G., and Boily, R. *Le Québec en chiffres de 1850 à nos jours.* Montréal: ACFAS, 1986.

Bernier, R. *Le marketing gouvernemental au Québec: 1929–1985.* Montréal: Gaëtan Morin, 1988.

Bissonnette, L. *La passion du présent.* Montréal: Boréal, 1987.

Blais, A., and Crête, J. "Can a Party Punish its Faithful Supporters? The Parti Québécois and Public Sector Employees." *C.P.A.*. 32, 4, Winter, 1989.

Boismenu, G. *Le duplessisme: politique économique et rapports de force, 1944–1960*. Montréal: P.U.M., 1981.

Boismenu, G., *et al. Espace régional et nation*. Montréal: Boréal Express, 1983.

Boisvert, M.A. *Les implications économiques de la souveraineté association*. Montréal: P.U.M., 1980.

Bonhomme, J-P., *et al. Le Syndrome Postréférendaire*. Montreal: Stanke, 1989.

Borgeat, L., *et al. L'administration québécoise: organisation et fonctionnement*. Québec: P.U.Q., 1982.

Borins, S.F. *Language of the Skies: The Bilingual Air Traffic Control Conflict in Canada*. Montreal: McG.-Q.U.P., 1983.

Bourassa, G., and Leveilleé, J. *Le système politique de Montréal*. Montréal: A.C.F.A.S., 1986.

Bourgault, J. "Les hauts fonctionnaires québécois: Paramètres synergiques de puissance et de servitude." *C.J.P.S.*, 16, 2, June, 1983.

Bourhis, R.Y., (ed.). *Conflict and Language Planning in Quebec*. Clevedon, Avon: Multilingual Matters Ltd., 1984.

Bourque, G., and Destaler, G. *Socialisme et indépendance*. Montréal: Boréal Express, 1980.

Brière, M., and Grandmaison, J. *Un nouveau contrat social*. Ottawa: Les Editions Leméac, 1980.

Cabatoff, K., and Lezzoni, M. *Bibliographie sur l'administration publique québécoise*. Montréal: Université Concordia, 1985.

Caldwell, G. "Discovering and Developing English-Canadian Nationalism in Quebec." *Canadian Review of Studies in Nationalism*, 11, 2, Fall, 1984.

Clarke, H.D. "The Parti Québécois and Sources of Partisan Realignment in Contemporary Quebec." *Journal of Politics*, 45, 1, 1983.

Clift, D. *Quebec Nationalism in Crisis*. Montréal: McG.-Q.U.P., 1982.

Clift, D. *Le Pays Insoupçonné: Essai*. Montréal: Libre expression, 1987.

Cloutier, E., and Latouche, D., (dirs.). *Le système politique québécois*. Montréal: Hurtubise HMH, 1979.

Coleman, Q. *The Independence Movement in Quebec 1945–1980*. Toronto: U.T.P., 1985.

Coleman, W.D. "From Bill 22 to Bill 101: The Politics of Language Under the Parti Québécois." *C.J.P.S.*, 14, 3, September, 1981.

Collectif Clio. *L'Histoire de femmes au Québec depuis quatre siècles*. Montréal: Editions Quinze, 1982.

Comeau, R., (dir.) *Jean Lesage et l'éveil d'une nation: les débuts de la révolution tranquille*. Sillery: P.U.Q., 1989.

Constitutional Committee of the Quebec Liberal Party. *A New Canadian Federation*, [The beige paper]. Montreal: 1980.

Cook, R. *Canada, Quebec and the Uses of Nationalism*. Toronto: M.& S., 1986.

Cook, R., (ed.). *French-Canadian Nationalism*. Toronto: Macmillan, 1969.

Cook, R. *Canada and the French-Canadian Question*. Toronto: Macmillan, 1966.

Crean, S., and Rioux, M. *Two Nations: An Essay on the Culture and Politics of Canada and Quebec in a World of American Preeminence*. Toronto: Lorimer, 1983.

Crête, J., (ed.). *Comportement electoral au Québec*. Chicoutimi: Gaëtan Morin, 1984.

Crête, J., and Favre, P., (dirs.). *Générations et politique*. Qué; P.U.L., 1989.

Cuneo, C.J., and Curtis, J.E. "Quebec Separatism: An Analysis of Determinants with Social-Class Levels." *C.R.S.A.*, 11, 1 February, 1974.

Descent, L.D., *et al. Classes sociales et mouvements sociaux au Québec et au Canada*. [Bibliography] Montréal: Saint-Martin, 1989.

Dion, L. *Québec: 1945–2000, Tome I. A la recherche du Québec.* Québec: P.U.L., 1987.

Dion, L. *Le Québec et le Canada: les voies de l'avenir.* Montréal: Les Editions Québécor, 1980.

Directeur général des élections du Québec. *Référendum: Reçueil de la legislation.* Québec: Editeur officiel du Québec, 1980.

Dumont, F. *Le sort de la culture.* Montréal: L'Hexagone, 1987.

Dupont, P. *How Lévesque Won: The Story of the PQ's 1976 Election Victory.* Toronto: Lorimer, 1977.

Feldman, E.J., (ed.). *The Quebec Referendum: What Happened and What Next? A Dialogue the Day After with Claude Forget and Daniel Latouche,* May 21, 1980. Cambridge University, Consortium for Research on North America, 1980.

Fitzmaurice, J. *Quebec and Canada: Past, Present and Future.* New York: St. Martin's, 1985.

Forster, V.W. *Let Quebec Go!* Milden, Saskatchewan: Forster, 1984.

Fournier, P. *The Quebec Establishment: The Ruling Class and the State.* Montreal: Black Rose, 1976.

Fraser, G. *René Lévesque and the Parti Québécois in Power.* Toronto: Macmillan, 1984.

Gagnon, A., (ed.). *Quebec: State and Society.* Toronto: Methuen, 1984.

Gagnon, A., and Montcalm, M. *Quebec: Beyond the Quiet Revolution.* Scarborough: Nelson, 1989.

Gingras, F.-P., and Nevitte, N. "La Révolution en plan et le paradigme en cause." *C.J.P.S.,* 16, 4, December, 1983.

Girard, M., and Proulx, M. "Le système judiciare québécois: problematique et indicateurs d'efficacité." *C.P.A..* 30, 2, Summer, 1987.

Gow, J., *et al. Introduction à l'administration publique: une approche politique.* Chicoutimi: Gaëtan Morin, 1987.

Gow, J.I. *Histoire de l'administration publique Québécoise, 1867–1970.* Montréal: P.U.M., 1986.

Guindon, H. *Tradition, Modernity, and Nationhood: Essays on Quebec Society.* Edited by Hamilton, R., McMullan, J., Toronto: U.T.P., 1988.

Haggart, R., and Golden, A. *Rumours of War,* with new introduction by R. Stanfield. Toronto: Lorimer, 2nd ed., 1979.

Hamilton, R., and Pinard, M. "The Independence Issue and the Polarization of the Electorate: The 1973 Quebec Election." *C.J.P.S.,* 10, 2, June, 1977.

Hamilton, R., and Pinard, M. "The Parti Québécois Comes to Power: An Analysis of the 1976 Quebec Election." *C.J.P.S.,* 11, 4, December, 1978.

Handler, R. *Nationalism and the Politics of Culture in Quebec.* Madison, Wisconsin: University of Wisconsin Press, 1988.

Harvey, F. "La question régionale au Québec." *J.C.S.,* 15, 2, Summer, 1980.

Heintzman, R. "The Political Culture of Quebec, 1840–1960." *C.J.P.S.,* 16, 1, March, 1983.

Hero, Jr., A.O., and Daneau, M., (eds.). *Problems and Opportunities in U.S.–Quebec Relations.* Boulder and London: Westview Press, 1984.

I.I.R. *The Question: Debate on the Referendum Question, Quebec National Assembly, March 4–20, 1980.* Kingston: Queen's University, 1980.

I.I.R. *The Response to Quebec: The Other Provinces and the Constitutional Debate.* Kingston: Queen's University, 1980.

Johnson, D. *Egalité ou indépendance.* Montréal: Les éditions renaissance, 1965.

J.C.S. Special issue on "The State in Ontario and Quebec," 18, 1, Spring, 1983.

Kaplan, D.H. " 'Maîtres Chez Nous': The Evolution of French-Canadian Spatial Identity." *A.R.C.S.,* 19, 4, Winter, 1989.

L'Allier, J.-P. *Les années qui viennent.* Montréal: Boréal, 1987.

Lafleur, G.-A. *PQ-PLQ, élection 1981: étude de strategies électorales.* Québec: Université Laval, Laboratoire d'études politiques et administratives, 1985.

Laforest, G. "Fichte's *Reden* as a model: Léon Dion's Addresses to the Quebec Nation." *C.J.P.S.*, 22, 1, March, 1989.

Lapalme, G. *Pour une Politique: Le programme de la révolution tranquille.* Montréal: V.L.B., 1988.

Latouche, D. *Canada and Quebec, Past and Future: An Essay.* Toronto: U.T.P., 1985.

Lebel, J.-C. "Les sociétés d'Etat au Québec: un outil indispensable." *C.P.A.*, 27, 2, Summer, 1984.

Legel, M. *Le PQ: ce n'était qu'un début.* Montréal: Québec- Amérique, 1986.

Lemieux, V. *Personnel et partis politiques au Québec.* Montréal: Boréal Express, 1982.

Lemieux, V., and Ledoux, G. "Le contrôle de l'information gouvernementale: le cas du Québec." *C.P.A.*, 26, 3, Fall, 1983.

Lévesque, R. *My Quebec.* Toronto: Methuen, 1979. (French version, *La Passion du Québec.* 1978.)

Lévesque, R. *Memoirs.* Toronto: M. & S., 1986.

Lévesque, R. *Option Québec,* avec un essai de Bernard A. Montréal: Editions de l'Homme, 1988.

MacDonald, L.I. *From Bourassa to Bourassa.* Montreal: Harvest House, 1984.

Malone, M. *Une place pour le Québec au Canada.* Halifax: I.R.P.P., 1988.

Massicotte, L. "Le Parlement du Québec en transition." *C.P.A.*, 28, 4, Winter, 1985.

Massicotte, L. "Cohesion et dissidence a l'Assemblée nationale du Québec depuis 1867." *C.J.P.S.*, 22, 3, September, 1989.

Massicotte, L., and Bernard, A. *Le scrutin au Québec: Un miroir déformant.* Québec: Hurtubise, 1986.

McRoberts, K., and Posgate, D. *Quebec: Social Change and Political Crisis.* Toronto: M. & S., 3rd ed., 1988.

Milner, H. *Politics in the New Quebec.* Toronto: M. & S., 1978.

Milner, H. *The Long Road to Reform: Restructuring Public Education in Quebec.* Montreal: McG.-Q.U.P., 1986.

Monière, D. *Essai sur la conjoncture politique au Québec: pour la suite de l'histoire.* Montréal: Québec-Amérique, 1982.

Monière, D. *Le discours électoral: les politiciens sont-ils fiables?* Montréal: Québec/ Amérique, 1988.

Monière, D. *Les enjeux du référendum.* Montréal: Québec-Amérique, 1979.

Monière, D. *The Development of Ideologies in Quebec.* Toronto: U.T.P., 1981.

Morin, C. *Quebec versus Ottawa: The Struggle for Self-Government, 1960–72.* Toronto: U.T.P., 1976.

Morin, C. *L'art de l'impossible: la diplomatie québécoise depuis 1960.* Montréal: Boréal, 1987.

Morin, C. *Lendemains Piègés.* Montreal: Boreal Express, 1988. [The referendum and the constitutional negotiations]

Murray, V., and Murray, D. *De Bourassa à Lévesque.* Montréal: Editions Quinze, 1978.

Niosi, J. *La bourgeoisie canadienne: La formation et le développement d'une classe dominante.* Montréal: Editions Boréal Express, 1980.

Octobre 1979: Dix Ans Après. Montréal: P.U.M., 1980.

Pelletier, G. *Years of Impatience, 1950–1960.* Toronto: Methuen, 1984.

Pelletier, R. *Partis politiques et société québécoise, 1960- 1970.* Québec: P.U.L., 1984.

Pelletier, R., and Crête, J. "Realignements électoraux et transformations du personnel politique." *C.J.P.S.* 21, 1, March, 1988.

Pilette, D. *L'Urbanisme au Québec: organisation, legislation et perspectives politiques.* Montréal: Agence d'Arc, 1986.

Pinard, M. *The Rise of a Third Party.* [Social Credit in Quebec] McG.-Q.U.P., enlarged ed., 1975.

Pinard, M., and Hamilton, R. "Le référendum québécois." *P.O.*, 2, 4, September-October, 1981.

Piotte, J.-M. *La communauté perdue.* Montréal: VLB éditeur, 1987.

Le Processus électoral au Québec. Montréal: Editions Hurtubise HMH, 1980.

Proulx, M., and Girard, M. *Pour comprendre l'appareil judiciare québécois.* Québec: P.U.Q., 1985.

Québec, Assemblée nationale. *Répertoire des parlementaires québécois, 1867–1978.* 1980.

Québec, Conseil executif. *La nouvelle entente Québec-Canada: Propositions du gouvernement du Québec pour une entente d'égal à égal: la souvenaineté-association.* Québec: Editeur officiel, 1979,.(English version: *Quebec-Canada, A New Deal,* 1979.)

Québec. *Information et Liberté, Rapport de la Commission d'étude sur l'accès du citoyen à l'information gouvernementale et sur la protection des renseignements personnels.* Gouvernement du Québec, 1981.

Québec, Ministère des Affaires culturelles. *Bibliographie du Québec, 1821–1967.* Québec: Editeur officiel, 1978.

Quebec. *Report of the Royal Commission of Inquiry on Constitutional Problems.* [Tremblay Report] Quebec: 1956, 4 vols.

Quinn, H.F. *The Union Nationale: Quebec Nationalism from Duplessis to Lévesque.* Toronto: U.T.P., 1979.

Raboy, M., and Chodos, R. *Old Passions, New Visions: Social Movements and Political Activism in Quebec.* Toronto: Between The Lines, 1986.

Resnick, P. *Letters to a Québécois Friend,* with a Reply by Latouche, D. Toronto: McG.-Q.U.P., 1989.

Saint-Piere, J., Bédard, M.-A., and Caissie, F. *Répertoire des parlementaires québécois: mise à jour 1978–1987.* Québec, Assemblée nationale, 1987.

Saywell, J. *The Rise of the Parti Québécois, 1967–1976.* Toronto: U.T.P., 1977.

Shaw, W., and Albert, L. *Partition, The Price of Quebec's Independence.* Montreal: Thornhill Publishing, 1980.

Soldatos, P., (dir.). *Nationalisme et intégration dans le contexte canadien.* Montréal: Centre d'Etudes et de Documentation européenes, Université de Montréal, 1980.

Soulet, M. *Le silence des intellectuels: radioscopie de l'intellectuel québécois.* Montréal: Editions Saint-Martin, 1987.

Stein, M. *The Dynamics of Right-Wing Protest: Social Credit in Quebec.* Toronto: U.T.P., 1973.

Thomson, D. *Jean Lesage and the Quiet Revolution.* Toronto: Macmillan, 1984.

Thompson, D. *Vive le Québec libre.* Toronto: Deneau, 1988.

Trudeau, P.E. *Federalism and the French Canadians.* Toronto: Macmillan, 1968.

Vadeboncoeur, P. *To be or not to be, that is the question!* Montreal: l'Hexagone, 1980.

Vallières, P. *Les héritiers de Papineau: Itinéraire d'un nègre blanc'* (1960–1985). Montréal: Québec/Amérique, 1986.

Wood, J.R. "Secession: A Comparative Analytical Framework." *C.J.P.S.*, 14, 1, March, 1981.

PROCESS

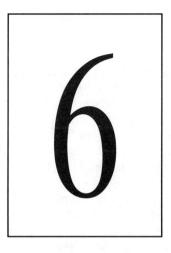

PUBLIC OPINION

THE PERILS OF POLLING—
AS EXEMPLIFIED IN THE '88 ELECTION

Alan Frizzell

It was fun being a pollster when you were the only one in town. After all, if anyone wished to disprove any of your findings, they would have to undertake another poll themselves, a costly undertaking in the cause of accuracy. True, when an election came around there was the awful risk of "getting it wrong," but that was a minor factor when compared to the rewards. And rewards there were, especially when the media discovered polling, and pollsters became commentators and experts rather than simply practitioners in the field of elementary statistics. But dark clouds began to gather over the Canadian pollsters in the 1970s. The business was becoming seriously congested, competition became fierce, the struggle for a media outlet intense. The danger was that as more and more public polls became available results would vary and lead to questions about, and criticisms of, methodology and interpretation. The image of the expert with the irrefutable data at his fingertips would be shattered. And that is what happened in the election of 1988.

For many Canadians the published polls in the election were at best an irritant, and at worst a corrupting influence on the democratic process. Calls to hot-line shows were overwhelmingly anti-poll and some candidates and

From A. Frizzell, J.H. Pammett, and A. Westell, *The Canadian General Election of 1988*, Ottawa, Carleton University Press, 1989. By permission.

journalists called for a ban on their publication during campaigns. The critics claimed that there were far too many polls and that those that were reported were inaccurate, biased and encouraged horse-race media coverage instead of a discussion of the issues in the election. The fact that the polls closest to election day accurately forecast the election outcome may have taken some of the sting out of these complaints, but it remains true that pollsters could do much better, and that if they are to avoid restrictive legislation designed to limit their activities they must develop some collective standards that will make their data more comparable and substantial.

Perhaps the pollsters could not have emerged unscathed from the election, even with perfect methodology. There has never been an election in Canada where the polls have come under such scrutiny or such criticism, and in a contest where political divisions were profound, polls which purported to show that one side or another was winning were bound to be found objectionable to some. Nevertheless, polling is a fact of life in Canadian politics. No political party plans campaign strategy without them, no government is prepared to risk major policy initiatives without gauging public opinion, and for major news organizations they are an indispensable reporting tool, both between and during elections.

It is only through media reporting of polls that the public is aware of polling numbers, and the evidence from the election indicates that the public was not served well by what was placed before them. This was partly due to the fact that pollsters have developed a disturbing tendency to do what they have always criticised journalists for doing; making sweeping political judgements and predictions which the limited polling data do not warrant. The dangers of this became apparent in the topsy-turvy world of Canadian politics after the 1984 election.

1984 AND BEYOND

The period between the 1984 and 1988 elections saw unprecedented volatility in the polls, and for the first time in Canadian politics each of the major parties found themselves at the top of the voting intentions stakes at some point and in third place on other occasions (Table 1).

The Tories ranged from a high of 60 percent support to a low of 22 percent while the Liberals had a low of 21 percent and a high of 45 percent. Given these astonishing swings, one would assume that pollsters would weigh their comments carefully. This, however, was not to be. Either because of the sin of hubris or a tendency to "Journalism Envy," pollsters were prepared to read into their numbers conclusions that would haunt them.

The fact that pollsters have come to see themselves as political commentators and gurus is worrying, especially since their prognostications are so often wrong. Newspaper columnists likewise may find that their prescriptions are

TABLE 1   **Party Voting Intentions—Gallup—1984–1988**
(Percentages for Major Parties)

	PC	LIB	NDP	Other
Oct. 84	60%	21%	17%	2%
Nov. 84	55	23	20	2
Dec. 84	54	24	20	2
Jan. 85	53	25	21	1
Feb. 85	53	25	21	1
Mar. 85	56	26	17	1
Apr. 85	54	24	21	1
May 85	45	31	22	2
June 85	44	33	21	2
July 85	40	33	26	1
Aug. 85	46	32	20	2
Sept. 85	48	29	22	1
Oct. 85	43	35	22	—
Nov. 85	40	36	24	—
Dec. 85	37	38	24	1
Jan. 86	41	36	23	—
Feb. 86	36	41	23	—
Mar. 86	41	34	25	1
Apr. 86	37	40	21	2
May 86	37	41	21	1
June 86	32	40	27	1
July 86	36	41	21	2
Aug. 86	33	41	24	2
Sept. 86	35	36	28	1
Oct. 86	31	38	29	2
Nov. 86	31	39	29	1
Dec. 86	30	45	25	—
Jan. 87	28	41	30	1
Feb. 87	22	44	32	2
Mar. 87	24	41	34	1
Apr. 87	24	42	32	2
May 87	26	42	30	2
June 87	24	39	35	2
July 87	23	35	41	1
Aug. 87	25	36	37	2
Sept. 87	25	36	37	2
Oct. 87	23	38	38	1
Nov. 87	25	40	33	2
Dec. 87	29	35	34	2
Jan. 88	30	36	31	3
Feb. 88	27	40	31	2
Mar. 88	28	37	31	4
Apr. 88	31	38	30	1
May 88	28	39	31	2
June 88	31	39	29	1
July 88	35	37	27	1
Aug. 88	34	35	30	1
Sept. 88	40	26	31	3

inaccurate, but pollsters are supposed to work from empirical data and their conclusions might reasonably be given more weight by the public at large.

In a recent book by the Liberal pollster Martin Goldfarb a series of comments typifies this self-importance. He writes: "Like a seer or oracle, the pollster plays a role that is viewed with a combination of respect, fear, intrigue and controversy." Moreover, Goldfarb argues that the pollster is no technician; he is a sage! "It is the interpretation of results—not the collection of data—that sets the good pollster apart from the ordinary one". Goldfarb is not forthcoming on what special qualities the pollster has that makes such insights possible. But even this accolade to the pollster is insufficient, for he goes on to say that the pollster is not merely "primus inter pares," but simply "primus." "He is the court confidante and knows more about the inner machinations of his court than anybody else—maybe even more than the leader."

Arrogance of this sort from pollsters is bound to cause trouble and that is what happened during the electoral off-season. For example, during the period when the NDP fortunes rose in the polls, Southam News pollster Angus Reid was quoted as saying that this was not temporary and that the party had become a genuine contender for power. This was despite the fact that much of the NDP strength was based on Quebec support which most analysts considered to be "vote parking"—voters registering their support in a convenient location until a real decision has to be made. The Tory pollster, Allan Gregg, in an end-of-the-year (1986) poll for *Maclean's* magazine, ordained that the Tories had six months to turn things around or face electoral defeat. Neither claim made any sense given the level of volatility in the political marketplace, and they were based on suppositions that had nothing to do with the available polling data.

There was, in addition, confusion among polls between the elections. There is regular polling by Angus Reid for Southam News, Environics Research for *The Globe and Mail*, and Gallup for the *Toronto Star* and other papers. Thus results are compared and differences highlighted. This was especially true for the two most regular polls, Reid and Gallup. There were two periods when differences were particularly evident and these differences led to concern on the part of the media sponsors.

The first was the period May to August 1987 when NDP support rose sharply, and the second was when there was a revival of Tory support between September 1987 and April 1988. In a confidential memo to Nick Hills, the General Manager of Southam News, and Allan Christie of the *Toronto Star*, Angus Reid explained that the earlier differences were "because the Gallup organization was somewhat later than us in detecting the trend in the direction of the New Democrats. Not surprisingly, there were considerable differences between us and Gallup during this period, with an average variance of 15.3 percent per month." By average variance Reid meant the total of differences in levels of support for each party in polls published at the same time. Reid made no attempt to explain why Gallup would take longer to detect a trend.

When the polls differed again later in the year, Reid argued that Gallup was once more late in detecting a trend, this time away from the Liberals. The issue came to a head when, in March 1988, each organization produced results that were considerably different. In an attempt to allay fears, Reid introduced a

TABLE 2   **Angus Reid's Two Month Lag Analysis**
(Percentages for Major Parties)

	Reid				Gallup		
	PC	**LIB**	**NDP**		**PC**	**LIB**	**NDP**
September 87	23	38	36				
October 87	28	35	35				
November 87	30	37	32	November 87	25	40	33
December 87	—	—	—	December 87	29	35	34
January 88	31	34	34	January 88	30	36	31
February 88	32	33	33	February 88	27	40	31
March 88	34	30	34	March 88	28	37	31
				April 88	31	38	30

table into his memo to show that Gallup was roughly two months behind his firm in their estimates of voting intentions (Table 2).

With considerable courage Reid predicted what the next Gallup would show when published in May, based on his assumption of the two month lag. His prediction was somewhat off the mark (Table 3).

TABLE 3

	Reid's Gallup Estimate	Actual May Gallup
PC	33	28
LIB	33	39
NDP	33	31

If Reid had difficulty explaining the inconsistencies, the public must have been even more baffled, and it was certainly true that many journalists were becoming highly sceptical of the numbers that were being published even before the campaign began. This scepticism would carry over to the election period itself.

THE CAMPAIGN POLLS

The revival of Tory fortunes in 1988 had been so staggering, and the problems of the Liberal party and its beleaguered leader so great, that for many the election appeared to be over before it started. The polls in the first two weeks of the campaign showed Tory support ranging from 42 to 46 percent. But despite this initial agreement, differences would emerge and the number of polls tended to highlight these (Table 4).

The last election was the most polled in Canadian history, with a total of 24 reported national polls, an increase from the 12 conducted in 1984.

Though the polls showed general trends in party support throughout the campaign, on any given day differing poll results might be published and this gave rise to the notion that there were far too many polls during the election. However, Canada has fewer polls than most Western countries during elections. In the British election of 1987 there were 73 national polls almost on a

TABLE 4   **Election Polls**
(Voting Intentions)

	Sample Size	PC	LIB	NDP	Other	Undecided
PUBLICATION DATE						
Oct. 3 Gallup	1,061	43	33	22	2	22
Oct. 5 Reid	1,512	45	26	27	2	25
Oct. 10 Gallup	1,017	41	32	46	1	13
Oct. 11 Environics	1,515	42	25	29	4	10
Oct. 14 CTV	1,100	46	27	26	1	18
Oct. 16 CBC	2,467	42	25	29	4	10
Oct. 17 Gallup	1,027	39	29	28	4	10
Oct. 21 CTV	1,100	43	25	30	2	10
Oct. 24 Gallup	1,034	40	28	29	3	19
Oct. 29 Reid	1,502	35	28	35	2	23
Oct. 29 CTV	1,100	35	39	23	3	19
Oct. 31 Gallup	1,034	38	32	27	3	11
Nov. 1 Environics	1,538	31	37	26	6	13
Nov. 2 Goldfarb	1,000	34	40	24	2	28
Nov. 4 CTV	1,101	40	37	20	3	16
Nov. 7 Gallup	1,041	31	43	22	4	10
Nov. 9 Environics	1,275	35	37	24	4	9
Nov. 10 Reid	1,501	39	35	24	2	22
Nov. 10 CBC	2,200	38	38	21	3	8
Nov. 11 CTV	1,100	39	39	20	2	15
Nov. 14 Gallup	1,026	35	35	26	4	8
Nov. 19 Reid	1,512	41	33	23	3	11
Nov. 19 Gallup	4,067	40	35	22	3	12
Nov. 19 CTV	2,720	43	32	20	5	15
Election Results		43	32	20	5	

daily basis during the primary and national campaigns, running into a total of hundreds.

The one election poll that seemed to be wildly out of line with the rest was the Gallup poll published on Nov. 7. While all the polls after the leaders' debates showed a remarkable Liberal resurgence, and in some cases a Liberal lead, the Gallup figures gave the Liberals an advantage of 12 percentage points. Most analysts consider that this was a "rogue poll," though they are at a loss to explain why this should be so. Lorne Bozinoff, vice-president of Gallup Canada Inc., argued that the poll was accurate and that after the debates the Liberals hit "a brief emotional high" before sliding back. No other poll found any evidence of this. Gallup later argued that the poll results may have been due to random error, the elusive 20th poll, and added that it was impossible for pollsters to know if they had encountered a "rogue poll." In fact there are many ways in which pollsters can gauge this, the most obvious being that in random sampling, demographic results such as sex and age breakdowns can be checked against census data to estimate the reliability of other results. Another problem with the same poll surfaced in the way the results were presented. Gallup disclosed results for the Atlantic region, Quebec, Ontario, the Prairies and B.C. Given that only 1041 respondents were interviewed, this means that the error margins for the regional results were huge.

Gallup was not the only polling group remiss in this regard. *The Globe and Mail* polling team published provincial results from a national sample of 1,275 eligible voters on Nov. 10. They estimated their Saskatchewan error margin at 13.5 percent. In an overall sample of this size a representative number of voters in that province would be 51, so that even by interviewing slightly more respondents than required, the numbers for a provincial breakdown were ludicrous.

Other problems with polling results were evident, notably in the number of undecided voters. This happened not only between organizations, but also within organizations throughout the campaign. Gallup ranged from 19 percent to 8 percent undecided, while Reid varied from 23 percent to 11 percent. In fact these differences are more apparent than real. Normally the rate of those who say they are undecided for whom to vote is anywhere from 8 to 12 percent. But another 4 to 8 percent of respondents refuse to answer a voting-intentions question, and there are also those who say they will not vote. Some polling companies report only the first of these figures while others lump all the categories together. When polling is irregular these differing practices are not much of a problem, but when polls are frequent, confusion results. Moreover, some polling firms ask respondents who are unsure about their voting choice if they are leaning to one particular party or another. The leaning respondents may or may not be included in the voting-intention numbers.

Another problem arises when one considers the nature of the vote question and its placement in the questionnaire. In the most recent Manitoba provincial election, one poll reported an undecided rate of 42 percent, largely due to the fact that the vote question was the first question asked. Most pollsters try to lead the respondent into the topic of the survey gently. Questions dealing with the respondent's interest in politics—such as, whether the respondent has been following the campaign or not—are ways of introducing the topic before directly asking about voting intentions. Angus Reid argues that this approach provides a context for the vote question. He asks about issues and perceptions of the party leaders before asking about voting intentions. Some would argue that the answers to the first questions will influence the responses to the vote question, thus causing what pollsters call "inter-item contamination."

The effect of differing techniques is to ensure that there will be differences between the polls during and between elections and when these differences emerge it should not be surprising.

During the election campaign some pollsters used their data to estimate the number of seats each party would win. This is not really difficult to do in theory; regional polling results are translated into seats on the basis of what has happened in the past. However, the regional sample sizes of most polls are so small as to make this technique risky at best, and in this election there was enough evidence of intra-regional variance to indicate that such predictions were little more than informed guesses.

It is not only in Canada that pollsters are trying to do too much with their numbers. In both the recent elections in the U.S. and the U.K. pollsters have behaved irresponsibly. In the former case there were many pre-primary polls which got the results all wrong—not surprising when one considers that actual primary turnout can be very low. What was worse was that there were polls produced in some States that had caucus elections where only a minuscule percentage of the population would actually vote, and in some cases these were presented as predictions of the likely outcome. In the 1987 British election the BBC was embarrassed by an election night prediction that the election was close and that there was a possibility of a hung parliament. This was based on a mixture of polling done the day before the election, election day polling and over-sampling in marginal constituencies. The election, of course, resulted in a landslide for Prime Minister Thatcher.

The irony of all this is that the pollsters could do a much better job without having to resort to dubious methodology or spurious prediction. All they need do is to ask more pertinent questions on issues and attitudes.

POLLS AND THE MEDIA

It is a sad fact that most of the media polling done in the election was concerned only with who was winning and losing. There was little examination of the issues, except for opinion questions on free trade, no explanation of why people were changing their minds or why they were voting the way they were. As usual, the exception to the rule was the CBC. The television news polls for the CBC delved into issues in detail and had a sample size that permitted regional analysis. For those reasons the CBC could use its polls to enhance other election coverage, but for most other news organizations the polling figures were so limited that this was not possible. For the media, polls are potentially an important reporting tool. They can direct election coverage and put into context the exaggerated claims of politicians. There are, however, other reasons for media polling. Since any news organization's poll is widely reported, the poll becomes advertising, and most major media organizations feel that they should have their own poll as a question of status. Of the major groups only the Sun chain of newspapers and the Global television network did not commission election polling.

All media reported polling results and the similarity in the number of stories in the press about polls is striking. Though there were slightly fewer stories in those papers which did not commission polls (*Halifax Chronicle Herald* and the *Winnipeg Free Press*), the differences were small (Table 5).

There figures do not indicate that there was an overemphasis on polls, since there was only an average of around 5 percent of stories where polls were the main topic. This would leave plenty of space for the coverage of issues. But the newspapers did leave themselves open to the criticism that when they did report on the polls they did not do so very responsibly. The Canadian Daily Newspaper Publishers' Association has outlined certain basic information that

TABLE 5   **Poll Stories as a Percentage of Election Items**

	Poll as main topic	Poll mentioned in story
Vancouver Sun	5.1	9.7
Winnipeg Free Press	4.7	10.9
Globe and Mail	5.2	14.4
Toronto Star	5.4	11.7
Montreal Gazette	4.7	16.3
La Presse	7.8	11.1
Halifax Chronicle Herald	4.8	7.9

should be included when polls are reported. Such factors as sample size, sponsorship, refusal rates and sample selection should all be included in the coverage. In fact there was no newspaper article in the last election that complied with all the guidelines. The stories that came closest were those in *The Globe and Mail*; these usually included a separate explanation of the methodology employed. It is difficult to understand why most newspapers don't include such information when polls have become so controversial.

The problem is even greater when polls are mentioned as secondary aspects in a story. Data which may well have been qualified when originally published are often commented on as gospel. While 73 percent of all poll stories were reported as straight news items, this was not the case for those stories where polls were the secondary topic. Forty percent of these were columns, editorials or news backgrounders. Indeed, a quarter of all news backgrounders mentioned polls at some point, indicating that poll information was used to make sense of the election campaign. Unfortunately, since almost all poll results were concerned with the horse race aspect of the election, this suggests that many news background items had a similar focus.

One other notable feature of the newspaper coverage was that poll stories tended to have a higher "attention score," meaning they were more prominently displayed, than non-poll items. This was true not only where polls were the main topic of the stories, but also when they were the secondary topic.

Broadcasters were much more concerned with polls than were newspapers. Global did not sponsor a poll yet it carried a higher percentage of poll items than the CBC which did (Table 6). As with newspapers, there was little mention of methodological limits. The CBC did introduce some qualifications, but the other broadcasters did not.

An innovation in poll reporting in Canada was introduced by the CBC. They developed a chart of all the polls giving each party a range of support as

TABLE 6   **Poll Stories as a Percentage of Coverage**

	Poll as main topic	Poll mentioned in story
CBC	8.9	19.9
CTV	14.9	21.0
Global	11.4	21.2

expressed by the polls. This poll-of-polls technique is much used in other countries. The only problem with the CBC model was that the range of support for each party was colour coded and as the campaign progressed the chart took on the appearance of a Salvador Dali painting. The CBC conducted only two polls, but they were comprehensive. CTV on the other hand used their resources to conduct much less elaborate rolling polls, the main component of which was the horse race.

While there is distress in some quarters that the media conduct so much polling during elections, this will have little effect on the amount of poll coverage in the future. The media get good value for their money from pollsters, who see their work for newspapers or television as good advertising for profitable market research or government contracts. Status is gained by the media outlet and despite the complaints about horse race coverage this is a legitimate aspect of election coverage. It is also true that the two major organizations that did not sponsor polls did consider doing so, but decided against it for reasons of cost rather than from journalistic considerations. The question is not how much polling will be done, but whether or not the media will improve the quality of what they do.

CRITICISMS

The furor over the Gallup poll giving the Liberals a commanding lead over the Tories gave rise to the issue of accuracy of the polls. Inconsistencies among published polls are bound to fuel notions that they are not really accurate predictors. In fact pollsters have long argued that polls should not be seen as predictors but as snapshots of opinion at a given time. Moreover, there is the problem of turnout. When asked if they will vote in an election, most respondents say they will, when in fact more than a quarter of the population will not vote. The latter problem can be partly solved by various techniques that predict turnout. However, the polls have been fairly accurate in predicting actual outcomes.

The three polls published two days before the election were close to the final outcome and, in the case of the CTV poll, bang on. Pollsters have learned that with the electorate so volatile, interviewing as close to election day as possible is necessary. Many polls increase their sample size for their last campaign poll. In the 1988 election Gallup interviewed over 4,000 respondents for its final election poll.

Politicians and business groups know how valuable polls can be. They spend considerable amounts of money on polling. But politicians are also very critical of published polls for other reasons. Bill Neville, a former journalist and now a Conservative strategist, has argued that the problem with polls is that their accuracy is almost irrelevant. Once they are out there they change the way people look at an election. There is widespread belief that polls influence the way people vote, yet neither of two theories that are supposed to explain

TABLE 7   **Differences Between Gallup Results and Voting Outcomes 1945-1988**

	Lib	PC	NDP	Other
1945	−2	+2	+1	−1
1949	−2	+1	+2	−1
1953	+1	0	0	−1
1957	+7	−5	−1	−1
1958	0	+2	−2	0
1962	+1	+1	−2	0
1963	−1	−1	+1	+1
1965	+4	−3	0	−1
1968	+2	−2	+1	−1
1972	0	−2	+3	−1
1974	0	0	0	0
1979	−2.5	+1.5	+1	0
1980	+4	−5	+3	−1
1984	0	0	0	0
1988	−3	+3	+2	−2

how they do this, the bandwagon and the underdog effects, applies consistently in Canadian elections. In the 1988 election campaign neither of these was consistently present.

In a poll dealing with how Canadians react to polls, *The Globe and Mail* discovered that only 13 percent of respondents admitted to being influenced in some way by them. However 64 percent thought that others were influenced by them. The survey results indicated that other influences, such as TV commercials, were much more important in influencing voting choice.

In fact it could be argued that the polls should have been more influential in this election. Indeed, if a voter wanted to vote against free trade, than a knowledge of party standings would have helped to decide whether to support the Liberals or the NDP. In fact the voting returns themselves indicate that if there was strategic voting on this issue, then there was not very much of it.

If polls do not determine voting choice in any significant way, they do influence politics, and this may explain the negative opinions of some politicians. Polls do tend to limit just how much politicians can control the agenda of an election. If an issue shows up in the polls as important to the public, journalists will question politicians about it, no matter how much those politicians would like to avoid it. Polls also influence the morale of party workers, though not always in an obvious way. Politicians have admitted that poor polling results can spur the campaign workers to greater efforts. But the dangers of despondency or complacency because of poll results are real enough.

Another effect of poor poll results between elections, or at the start of a campaign, is that potential candidates may decide to sit the election out. This may explain the difficulty the Liberals encountered in getting hold of star candidates at the beginning of the 1988 campaign. In this case one might consider polls as helpful; candidates who will run only if they are sure of election may not be the best servants of their parties or of the country.

Politicians may well see polls as a nuisance, but this does not mean they do not use them for their own purposes. They do not wish to see the polls banned—just their publication restricted. In 1980 former Tory minister Sinclair Stevens wanted to ban the publication of polls during an election and, more recently, *The Globe and Mail* columnist, Jeffrey Simpson, argued for a partial ban on the publication of election polls. The politician's argument is easily countered. What a politician wants is information for himself, but for nobody else.

Another argument is more difficult to deal with because it states that the democratic process is not well served by the publication of polls that tend to deflect interest away from the issues. The problem with this argument is that in Canadian politics there is evidence that voters are not overwhelmingly interested in, or informed about, the issues. The media tend to concentrate on factors other than the issues, and politicians often try to avoid speaking to the issues. A ban on the publication of poll results would be unlikely to change this situation. Though there are 10 countries in the non-communist bloc where there are some restrictions on the publication of election polls, notably France and South Africa, recent attempts to do this in the U.S. and Britain have been unsuccessful.

CONCLUSIONS

There have been attempts by pollsters in the past to impose some self-discipline on their industry, but these have come to nothing. Some marketing associations do have stated standards, but these do not address all of the complaints about political polls. It might be in the pollsters' best interest if they set in motion some form of self-regulation before it is imposed upon them. In particular there is a need for some form of agreement on minimum methodological standards or even a common methodological base. A standard way of computing the undecided vote should be determined, as well as the form and placement of the voting intentions question.

Pollsters in some countries insist that media sponsors print methodological outlines and that might well be proposed in Canada. In addition, a reasonable request might be that if the media are to ensure that polling contributes to the quality of election coverage, then they should demand much more comprehensive polling that will deal with the major issues of the campaign.

Though the polls were criticized, and in some cases rightly so, they did contribute to the election process in 1988. In a period of considerable volatility they pointed out major shifts of opinion during the campaign. They did give evidence that free trade was the major issue, and that opinions on that issue were more or less evenly divided. The evidence from the polls and from academic research is that voters are less committed to enduring party loyalties, that they make voting decisions late in campaigns, and that they base their decisions on short-term factors. All this suggests that in future elections polling will be even more useful in understanding what is going on in an election, if the pollsters can put their house in order.

THE DANGER IS PRIVATE POLLING

Paul Fox

Public opinion polls should not be banned. The real danger lies in the private polling conducted by affluent interests such as governments, political parties, candidates, or corporations that do not reveal the results to the public. Since knowledge is often power, the interests then have an advantage that the public does not have access to, even though the public may be paying for the polls through their taxes or other means.

Published polls should not be banned; they add to our knowledge. People learn something from polls that often provide useful and interesting information. The public finds them appealing because the polls give specifics, and the average citizen, submerged in a sea of piffle and waffle, longs for some facts to cling to.

This is a culture entranced by facts, whether relating to political preferences, the national debt, other people's incomes, sports scores, or the frequency of sexual relations. The media love polls for the same reason. They give a hard edge to the news that enables the media to make a good story out of them, dramatizing with the assurance of numbers the rise or fall of governments, the fate of leaders and politicians, and the public's opinion on gut-wrenching issues like abortion, the death penalty, and separatism in Quebec.

It doesn't much matter whether the facts quoted are true or false, whether the polling techniques are sound or shaky, or whether the purpose of the poll is benign or manipulative: polls are still popular and usually unquestioned.

They should be questioned, however. Even if they do not have much effect in influencing people how to vote, as experts like political scientist Richard Johnson at the University of British Columbia hold, they do have weaknesses.

They can be grossly misinterpreted, and even the best of them can be wrong in predicting outcomes like election results. In his accompanying article in this chapter, Alan Frizzell notes how the Gallup poll erred in proclaiming the Liberal party's ascendancy after the television debate during the 1988 federal campaign, in which Liberal leader John Turner shone, and this was only one of many monumental errors. In 1984 the polls all missed predicting John Turner's win in Quadra and the extent of Prime Minister Mulroney's breakthrough in Quebec. Errors are not confined to Canada. In the Australian election of 1980 almost every pollster predicted a victory for Labour, when in fact the Liberal National party won by a handsome majority.

Another problem is that the public is misled on occasion by deliberate misrepresentation or connivance. A special interest group wants a certain result and hires a pollster to get it, or makes use of an honest pollster's findings

A revision in 1990 of an article by the author which was published in the *Canadian Parliamentary Review*, Vol. 8, No. 4, Winter, 1985, based on the author's address to a joint conference of the Canadian Public Relations Society and the Couchiching Institute on Public Affairs held at the University of Toronto on Feb. 1–2, 1985. By permission.

in a way he or she didn't intend. A group may even conduct its own highly unscientific and self-serving survey to prove what it wants or, as a TV station did in 1988, suppress polling results that didn't confirm its desires.

Some of the techniques of polling are open to question also. To take one illustration, it is common practice for pollsters to allocate the undecided respondents in the same proportion as the decided. In very many polls a large percentage of respondents answer questions by saying that they "don't know," or are "undecided," or they "won't say." It is not unusual for 20, 30 or even 40 percent of a sample to make such a reply. Yet Gallup and most other pollsters round up the total in published figures to 100 percent, as though every one had given a specific positive reply. They may mention that a certain proportion was undecided, but when they give the figures of how the vote breaks down, say in a pre-election federal contest, they give figures for the Conservatives, Liberals, New Democrats, and others that total 100 percent. The way in which they reach that figure is to allocate the undecided in the same proportion as those who have made their choice known. This procedure is highly questionable, since undecided voters by definition are apt to be much less stable in their preferences than the declared.

The danger in this practice was demonstrated in the Carleton University School of Journalism's poll of delegates to the Conservative Convention in Winnipeg in 1983, which led to Joe Clark calling a leadership convention. The Carleton poll misallocated the undecideds and forecast that Clark would get 76.7 percent of the votes, when in fact he received about ten percentage points less.

The greatest danger in polling, however, comes from private polls whose results are not released to the public. Well-healed entities like governments, political parties, corporations, and special interest groups spend millions of dollars on private polling and use the secret results for their own advantage.

The Conservative government in Ottawa, for instance, commissioned a private poll to determine whether the general public endorsed the extensive and expensive plans for child day care which its supporters were pushing, and when the results were less than enthusiastic, the government quietly soft-pedalled its promises.

In the 1988 federal election, which was festooned with more public polls than ever before, the major political parties also engaged in a plethora of private polling. At the height of the campaign the Conservatives, Liberals, and New Democrats conducted private polls every night. This gave them an instant reading on voters' reactions to issues and candidates, and told them what policies to stress at that particular moment. There was an additional benefit in that the substantial sums spent on these private polls did not have to be reported as expenses under the Elections Act.

The argument that we should ban public opinion polls during an election misses the mark. What we should be talking about is what to do with the growing, new, secret private polls that give a boost to those who can afford to employ them.

The issue becomes particularly acute when candidates use polls to shape their presentation to the public. In the United States presidential election in 1984 Gary Hart was manufactured by his private pollster, who told him how to dress, how to speak, how to shape his own personality, and what policies to put before the voters. The temptation to be Mr. Nice Guy, who is in favour of everything and avoids all the controversial issues like abortion and capital punishment, is overwhelming. If a candidate gives back to the public only what a poll says the majority wants, there is little room for constructive leadership.

Manipulative polling is perverse. Private polling is dangerous. But manufacturing candidates by polling is the worst of the lot.

[   ]

GOVERNMENT-RELATIONS FIRMS ARE NOW PART OF THE SYSTEM

James Rusk

OTTAWA

It has taken two decades to mature, but the government-relations industry has established itself as an important and necessary participant in the Canadian public policy process.

Although trade associations, public interest groups and companies still deal directly with politicians and civil servants, they are more likely to turn to specialized companies to assist them in their efforts to make government go the way they would like.

Even though the advent of such firms—with the associated odor of money-buying influence—has been greeted with abhorrence in some quarters, the growth of the industry was as economically logical as an increase in diaper sales after a baby boom and, even critics agree, government relations is here to stay.

Indeed, if the industry needs a seal of approval from someone who started out on the other side of the fence, it gets it even from Gerry Caplan, a Toronto writer and commentator who was executive secretary of the federal New Democratic Party in the early 1980s.

After leaving the NDP post, Mr. Caplan was for more than a year associated with Public Affairs International, one of the three majors of Canada's government-relations industry.

From *The Globe and Mail*, June 5, 1989. By permission.

Although he went into the business with skepticism and left a critic, "I've come to believe that it is kosher. It is a plausible proposition that government has gotten so complex that a company, big or small, or an interest group cannot wheel their way through the intricacies without some advice."

Although the recent history of the industry tends to be personalized—which one-time politico or public servant joined which firm and landed what client— to see it solely in personal terms is to miss the basic point. No matter who the players were, the government-relations industry would have emerged in the 1970s and boomed in the 1980s.

Until well into the 1960s, the Canadian government was, by today's standards, relatively small and unintrusive. A coterie of career public servants, most of whom spent their lives mastering the minutiae of one area of public policy, worked out the details of policies under the direction of ministers who were likely to spend many years in the one portfolio.

If a company had a problem, it made a discreet call to its link with the party in power, usually a fund raiser or a lawyer who was wired into the party power structure. Otherwise, Ottawa and business left each other pretty much alone.

Then came the 1970s, with an explosion of government budgets, departments and regulatory activity and with the concurrent restructuring of the bureaucracy and decision-making process under the direction of clerk of the Privy Council Michael Pitfield.

Under Mr. Pitfield, process triumphed. Papers wended their way through a maze-like flow chart; deputy ministers and senior bureaucrats were shunted from department to department with scant regard for expertise; and business found that it could no longer know the players or the rules without a program.

The first-stage government-relations companies, such as Executive Consultants Ltd., were in the guidebook business. Bewildered business people came to town and paid a consultant to walk them through the government phone book. (Executive Consultants, still one of the main firms, was founded in the early 1970s by William Lee and William Neville, two former ministerial aides.)

But developments other than growing intrusiveness and internal complexity were also at work reshaping the political and policy processes.

Changes to electoral finance laws that limited business contributions and opened up party books to public view curtailed the role and power of bagmen.

Access to information laws, the emergence of single-interest groups, the television of the House of Commons question period, the end of the once-cosy relationship between journalists and politicians and the adoption of U.S.-style campaigning techniques fueled by opinion polls and driven by television, combined to open the system to new influences and new actors.

Business quickly found it was not easy to operate in this strange, often hostile environment and was forced to look for ways of strengthening relations with government.

But the trade and industry associations could achieve only limited goals as interlocutors for companies, which found they had increasingly specific requirements in their dealings with government.

While some larger companies beefed up their government-relations operations, many turned to government-relations specialists, even if only to supplement their own efforts.

If the business community needed any convincing that it had to get its act together, the 1980 National Energy Program and the 1981 federal budget, with its sweeping changes to the tax system—both of which were prepared in the bureaucracy with no effective input from the business community—convinced it.

The industry also got a shot in the arm when the Progressive Conservative Party won the 1984 election. Business, which had spent a generation dealing with one party in power in Ottawa, apart from the nine-month interregnum of the government of Joe Clark, scrambled to set up ties to the Tories.

Established government-relations companies moved quickly to bring on board political operatives with good Tory connections; new firms flaunting their ties to the party and the prime minister hung out their shingles.

Government Consultants International, founded by three men who were tight with Brian Mulroney—one-time Newfoundland premier Frank Moores, former Nova Scotia cabinet minister Gerald Doucet and Quebec City lawyer Gary Ouellet—muscled its way to the top rung with Public Affairs International and Executive Consultants.

The industry now seems to be maturing. The major companies in the business have institutionalized themselves by building links to the Liberal Party and the Conservatives (even Mr. Caplan concedes that the NDP does not figure in the government-relations game) and to the bureaucracy by recruiting senior public servants.

With institutionalization, the majors can survive a change in government; what they are up against are natural limits to their growth. The number of clients they can take is limited by confidentiality: too many clients reduce the amount of personal attention each one can get.

One growth strategy is to try to broaden the services a company provides. Public Affairs International, whose parent company, Public Affairs Resource Group Ltd. of Toronto, was recently purchased by WPP Group PLC of Britain, tries to sell clients a package of government-affairs services.

As well as advice, it can provide polling data from its subsidiary, Decima Ltd., and public relations strategy from its links with Hill and Knowlton, Inc. of New York.

Executive Consultants, which also provides clients with communications advice and opinion polling, has also developed international links. Last fall, Burson-Marsteller of New York bought a 49 per cent stake in the firm.

The institutionalization of the large firms has opened up opportunities for smaller companies that can provide intensive personal service to a small clientele.

While the smallness of these companies—most are one-person operations

run by a skilled political operative—might seem to be limiting, informal associations or "boutiques" have developed among groupings of firms that allow
them to take on larger projects or share their overhead.

But no matter the size of the firm, what it still has to sell is smarts. Sometimes,
that means tracking carefully the mundane details of government operations.
"There is no magic in this business; there is a hell of a lot of hard work and
it is often rather pedestrian work," said Government Consultants president
Ramsay Withers.

Sometimes, it means explaining the basics of business to civil servants
with little understanding of an industry. It almost always means explaining
government and its needs to clients, and consultants are often used to send
messages back to the business community.

Most important, however, companies hire consultants for their strategic
thinking. Even after two decades of growth and development, the one constant
in the industry is that the people who can provide what clients look for are
former political operatives—politicians or political aides—or civil servants.

[_____]

PRESSURE GROUPS AT WORK

A. Paul Pross

DEFINING PRESSURE GROUPS

Pressure groups are *organizations whose members act together to influence
public policy in order to promote their common interest.*

The chief characteristic of the pressure group is the fact that it tries to
persuade governments to pursue the policies it advocates. Persuasion takes
many forms, nearly all of them intended to exert political pressure on government. Most groups hope that the force of logical and well-prepared argument
will be sufficient to convince reluctant ministers and skeptical bureaucrats that
their proposals should be adopted. Failing that, many groups will look to an
aroused public to persuade government of the error of its ways, as pensioners
did when the 1985 budget proposed reducing their incomes. They may imitate
the response of the unions to the Trudeau government's wage and price
controls and withdraw from advisory boards and other joint activities, actions
that can not only embarrass government but deny it access to information.
They may threaten economic sanctions. When Indian organizations threatened
to boycott Expo '86 as a means of forcing the British Columbia government

From *Group Politics and Public Policy*, Toronto, Oxford University Press, 1986. By permission of
the publisher.

to discuss Haida land claims, the tactic was considered by some to be more effective than the demonstrations that had marked the first part of the campaign. In theory, the choice of tactics of persuasion is as extensive as the relationship between government and the society it serves.

Persuasion depends on organization. Modern governments are not easily convinced. Persistence; extensive knowledge of substantive issues and policy processes; and the financial resources necessary to communicate with the public as well as with government are all essential ingredients in a lobbying campaign. Common objectives must be identified, strategies worked out, modes of procedure adopted, responsibilities assigned, and consistent positions formulated if a group is to persuade government to take specific action and if it is to watch over the development and implementation of supporting policies. Above all, pressure-group activity must have continuity if it is to have lasting effect. These activities require organization, and it is the quality of organization that distinguishes the pressure group from the mob on the one hand and the movement on the other. The mob is an ephemeral thing, a product of chance. It may win clearly stated and immediately realizable goals. It cannot provide for the future because it cannot provide for its own continued existence. It lacks organizational capacity. In contrast, movements do exist over time, but they represent generalized progressions of public opinion. Organized groups participate in the progression, but the movement as a whole consists of too many distinct elements to be described as a coherent unit such as a pressure group. For this reason nationalist movements, for example, are not treated by most writers as pressure group activities, though we recognize that pressure groups take part in them. Organization—the association of individuals within a formal structure—is, then, the second defining characteristic of pressure groups.

Organizational capacity facilitates a third characteristic: the articulation and aggregation of common interests. Formal structures and constitutional procedures enable group members to identify the demands they wish to make on government and to explore the conflicts that arise when the objectives of some members clash with those of others. Debate, though it may entail disaffection and secession, brings these demands together and eventually achieves agreement and support.

Other groups besides pressure groups possess formal organization, the ability to articulate and aggregate common interests, and a willingness to act in the political system. Political parties are notable examples. The fourth characteristic of pressure groups—the desire to influence those who hold power rather than to exercise the responsibility of government—distinguishes them from these other organizations. Pressure groups focus on the special interests of a few and avoid trying to engage the support of the mass public, a restricted role that permits them to complement rather then to rival political parties in the process of political communication. The power they do exert is delegated to them by government and is narrowly defined. By delegating to professional associations the power to regulate their members, for example, the state acknowledges 'the political need to afford a measure of autonomy to those whose activities have been brought with the scope of the law', and admits that the state lacks the administrative capacity to 'fine tune' the relations between a professional group and the public. Even so, the state can always change the powers delegated or even withdraw them. . . .

PRESSURE GROUP TACTICS

Discourse, coercion, and corruption are the means groups use to obtain their goals. How they use these methods depends on their concerns, the resources they have at hand, and the environment surrounding the policy process.

Most pressure group persuasion is carried out through political debate. Briefs are presented to royal commissions, hearings of tribunals, and individual officials. Legal argument is used to weigh the validity of government policy. Placards shout distress, anger, hope, despair. Theatre, film, pantomime, music, and every conceivable kind of tactile art express opinions about government and are aimed, however indirectly, at government. Books are written; advertisements concocted; speeches rouse multitudes—or leave them indifferent—all in the name of rational discourse.

Threats and promises are implicit in much political debate. Few demonstrators thrusting placards at politicians or shouting into microphones are simply expressing their right to petition. They are also threatening to use the political process to work—and vote—against the party in power unless it accommodates their demands. Even more ominous are the messages contained in the murmur of voices around a boardroom table, the unemotional recitation of a brief or press statement, as the holders of economic power indicate whether or not they will challenge public policy by withholding investment, cutting back production, or eliminating services. The fury that leads protesting fishermen to burn government patrol boats may be less devastating. More commonly a hint of publicity acts as a powerful solvent for reducing the intransigence of groups and officials who prefer the status quo.

When driven, every interest will use whatever tools it can muster to protect its own. Even illegal means many not be excluded. It is increasingly common in Canada for extremists to explode their frustration at public policy. On another level, it is hard to say whether bribery and other forms of corruption are common. . . .

Even so, there are enough cases on record of the bribery and corruption of public officials for us to assume that on occasion lobbyists do buy policy decisions. . . .

These are the tools group representatives use to sway the policy decisions of politicians and civil servants. How they go about using them depends, as we have said, on the objectives of each group, and the political messages they give rise to; on the resources the group has to influence policy, and on the conditions that prevail at each gateway to the process. For some groups with extensive resources, sure that their views carry weight in policy circles, the polished tactics of traditional lobbying are ideal. They can afford to give 'the best power parties in Ottawa' where 'Cabinet ministers and deputy ministers mingle with captains of industry.' They can afford professional preparation of briefs and other documentation demanded by our increasingly bureaucratized policy process, as well as the costs of litigation or appearances before regulatory bodies. If necessary they can pay for campaigns of mass persuasion. For other groups access to the policy process, even at the local level, is hard to obtain because they do not understand the bureaucratic ways of policy-makers, because the trappings of democracy are beyond their means, or because their plight is too banal to stir a flicker of interest among crusading journalists. . . .

THE COMPLEXITY OF GOVERNMENT-GROUP RELATIONS

[Government] departments foster constant contact with their 'clientele'— sounding public opinion and obtaining new ideas. Usually this is done by identifying and building on relations with organized groups or specific interests concerned with the work of the agency. If interest groups do not exist, departments encourage their formation.

With this reciprocal relationship comes a growth in the complexity and number of ties that bind the various players in the [policy] community [the government agencies, the pressure groups, corporations, institutions, and individuals with a vested interest or an explicit concern in the policy field].

Thirty years ago lobbying and government were much less complicated. David Kirk, an official of the Canadian Federation of Agriculture, recalls that it was possible to 'work with just one minister and department. Policy recommendations would come up through the department; the minister would decide what he wanted to do; then he would take his proposals to Cabinet.' Action would be authorized with a minimum of fuss. Interdepartmental committees would not waver forever over the pros and cons of alternative options. If the minister were obstructive there would be little mystery about the reasons why, and it would be fairly clear whether ministerial lobbying would overcome the problem. Today lobbyists know that persuading key officials, or even ministers, will not suffice, since these apparently powerful personages will seldom act without receiving clear signals from other interested parties that they too support the proposed changes in policy. This does not mean that politicians avoid involvement in the selection of policy options; but it does reflect the fact that 'Cabinet ministers are in general enormously overextended and do not have adequate time to devote to any single special interest, unless it happens to be central to the management of the portfolio.' They are forced to rely on their officials. In most cases, the only alternative opinions available to the minister come from affected interest groups. . . .

LOBBYING THE CABINET

Most established groups prefer not to take action-oriented messages to the Cabinet and the central agencies. To do so would be to admit that they failed to reach agreement within the policy community and, in effect, are breaking ranks with the other members of the community. Invoking the superior authority of the political executive disturbs the balance of power within the policy community; and even if it achieves its purpose, it does so at the cost of goodwill and smooth working relations with their immediate associates. There are two even more important reasons why many groups do not appeal to the centre. First, they want to avoid Cabinet interference. Cabinet—particularly the inner Cabinet—occupies the overview position in the government: it is responsible for overriding the self-regarding tendencies of departments and their allies; for finding ways of co-ordinating the policies and programs of individual agencies, and ensuring that issues that have been organized out of politics are pushed back in. These responsibilities are often pushed aside by cabinet workloads and the natural tendency of ministers to defend their own departments by not encroaching on others', but since major reforms were made to the central policy structures during the Trudeau years, officials in the Privy Council Office, the Treasury Board, the Prime Minister's Office, and Finance have frequently assumed the task of representing Cabinet's co-ordinative and monitoring roles. Their many interventions during the 1970s earned them the dislike and bitter opposition of line agencies and their allies, who became determined to contain issues within the policy community and to reduce the central agencies' influence. This determination is given a further edge by the second reason for avoiding the involvement of the political executive; groups have discovered the fact that an appeal to the centre may force them to engage in public debate. The agenda of Cabinet and its committees is so constrained that only a few issues inherently and obviously of national importance find their way automatically to Cabinet consideration. The majority have to fight for a place on the agenda, usually by attracting the kind of media attention that persuades cabinet ministers that the public is concerned and wants policy decisions. This kind of publicity attracts the interest of opponents as well as the support of friends.

Nevertheless circumstances often force issues into Cabinet's purview—as in 1985 when the failure of two regional banks precipitated a major review of bank regulation and inspection. On such occasions groups must contend with the mysteries of central decision-making. It is then that the maintenance of offices in the federal and provincial capitals pays off. Since access to Cabinet is virtually impossible to obtain, groups must focus their attention on the officials of the central policy structures and aides of influential ministers— groups whose staff are familiar with the workings of the central agencies and who know their officials have a considerable advantage. Familiarity with the policy review process gives them a sense of when to inject supporting information and whether, when, and where to apply pressure, as well as the ability to monitor discussions at the centre and to use personal connections to communicate group concerns to officials. Some may be able to brief key ministers. Groups without staff members able to achieve this level of access— and they are probably the great majority, even among members of the various sub-governments—must secure the services of the many legal and consulting firms who specialize in this type of lobbying. Described as 'door openers for the lobbying trade,' firms like Executive Consultants Limited will, for a sizeable monthly retainer, advise clients on whom to see and what to say. Groups that are not affluent enough to pay for professional lobbying must depend on the pressure tactics we described earlier: communicating with MPs; asking friends and members with influence to intercede on their behalf with cabinet members and party officials; writing to cabinet members, and generally trying to create the impression that the public at large supports their cause.

Influential members of policy communities are chary of taking action-oriented messages to the centre, but they treat the delivery of legitimating messages as a mark of recognition—a telling point in the game of positional politics. Groups with particular influence—either because they represent a broad cross-section of the community or because they can command extensive economic resources—frequently have access to cabinets and from time to time make formal presentations to them. Thus for many years it was a tradition that the Canadian Federation of Agriculture, the Canadian Labour Congress, and business groups such as the Canadian Manufacturers' Association annually presented to the federal Cabinet briefs on the current state of government policy in fields concerning them and urged the executive to further measures that each group favoured. Some of the positions put forward in these briefs were 'ritual demands'—demands that the leadership and the politicians knew could not be met and followed up—that were presented as tokens of the group's long-term commitment to certain goals. Others, however, signalled to the executive the group's current policy agenda. These 'serious demands' were related to the group's mandate, its privileges and prerogatives, and other matters affecting the organizational integrity of the group, as well as to major current issues. Over the last decade, as the proliferation of pressure groups has made it more and more difficult for the federal government to appear to favour even very broadly based specific groups, the tradition of the cabinet briefing has been discouraged and major groups have had to be content with influencing those they hope will influence the Cabinet, namely the members of caucus. Thus in 1980 a representative of the Canadian Federation of Agriculture reported that 'in recent years' his organization had made presentations to the several federal caucuses, rather than to Cabinet. In the provinces, where such meetings still continue and may be more numerous, group briefs may be concerned with immediate issues and problems. In December 1974, for example, when the East Coast fishing industry was experiencing one of its recurrent crises, the Atlantic Chambers of Commerce highlighted the fishery's problems in their brief to the Nova Scotia Cabinet.

Groups reluctant to take specific concerns to cabinet level make an exception in the case of 'their' minister. The minister responsible for the community's lead agency is generally expected to be sympathetic to the community's concerns and to speak for them in Cabinet. Self-interest accounts for this. The community's successes tend to cast the minister in a favourable light; its failures nearly always find political expression, and unless handled adroitly, can undermine a promising ministerial career. . . .

LOBBYING THE BUREAUCRACY

In the 1970s Canadians became aware of how influential the bureaucracy had become. The widespread realization that in agency-group relations the agency tends to dominate fostered a small mythology of bureaucratic behaviour. An article in the September 1980 issue of *Canadian Business* describes some of the perceptions many interest group representatives developed of the lead agencies in their policy field, and indicates some of the strategies deployed to deal with them. Entitled 'Getting Your Way With a Bureaucrat,' its subtitle suggests a power relationship in which the official calls the shots: 'Show respect. Be patient. Take him seriously. Sounds easy, but a lot of businessmen don't know how to get to first base.' According to author Larry Smith, a consulting economist with experience as a federal civil servant,

> The need for business to be able to defend its interests before the civil service has never been greater. But many business representatives not only fail to advance their causes, but actually antagonize the very persons they wish to influence. The ineptness that many lobbyists bring to their relationships with the civil service arises from a single source—their failure to understand the bureaucracy's aims and the way it works. The bureaucracy is not, as too many business people tend to regard it, some inscrutable mandarinate out to thwart the legitimate ends of the free enterprise system. It is a collection of, for the most part, reasonably principled and reasonably intelligent civil servants who can be swayed by reasonable discourse.

To get their way, lobbyists were urged to adopt a set of procedures that reflected a shrewd understanding of how human foibles and motivations mingle with and leaven the operations of bureaucracy. The bureaucratic machine lives on information. It demands raw data from those it serves and sophisticated analyses from those who want to influence it. It is also complex and slow moving. Decisions are seldom made at a single point; they are generally the product of internal consultation and often reflect the public service's mandate to defend the public interest. These rationalistic aspects of bureaucracy intimidate many, who come to resent and fear the quest for information; they see the need for formal analysis and the complexity and slow pace of decision-making as an encumbrance. For the experienced lobbyist, however, the mingling of these classic attributes of bureaucracy with the normal, everyday need of human beings to advance and take satisfaction in their work offers an opportunity to exercise influence. Smith's message is that civil servants are human, 'reasonably competent and conscientious.' They are even 'susceptible to the most basic bargaining techniques.' The artfully prepared brief has greater impact if it is presented 'by someone the civil servant knows and may already have cooperated with. That circumstance alone guarantees a reading, which is the first, most critical step in advancing your case.' The request for information may be an opportunity to establish a contact and to do a favour. Respect for the civil servant's expertise and concern for the public interest builds trust that may be important in future bargaining sessions. Finally, the very complexity of the public service can be put to good use. Smith argues that 'when you are dealing with a complex organization, it is futile to try to impose simplicity where none exists. But handled knowledgeably, the very complexity of the bureaucracy can work to your advantage.' People who complain that 'I cannot find the right person to talk to; everyone refers me to someone else,' are turning an opportunity into a problem:

> . . . it is a mistake to take the absence of a single channel of responsibility as a vice; it is an outright virtue. If you are lobbying for a cause down a single pathway, a turn-down becomes a rejection without recourse or appeal. In the more tightly structured private sector, one imbecile often has the power to bring an entire line of activity to a complete halt. But in the civil service, where responsibility is diffused, any particular refusal need be only a roadblock around which it is possible to manoeuvre. The likelihood of ultimate success grows in direct proportion to the number of avenues of pursuit.

Aware that a single, knowledgeable official can guide him or her through 'the dark labyrinths of the mandarinate,' the effective lobbyist obtains referrals from one civil servant to another.

> The real challenge is to get each of them involved in your problem. Some civil servants, mistakenly believing that if the lobbyist states his problem precisely enough they can refer him to the right person, actually try to do so. Therefore, never state your area of concern precisely; use the most general, ambiguous terms possible without being incoherent. That forces the civil servant to generate a number of alternative referrals in the hope that one of them meets your needs. You, of course, want all of them.

But the canny lobbyist does not simply generate lists of names:

> . . . in your initial conversations with any civil servant, find out exactly what he does. Then try to find something about your problem that fits his bailiwick. Consider, for example, a company seeking support to make an investment in new plant. Each of the following aspects of the question involves *different* civil servants: job creation in general; job creation for a specific region; job creation for a minority; export stimulation; import substitution; improvement in the competitiveness of the market; enhancement of research and development; environmental improvement; and national unity. And that is a short list, any aspect of which may make the critical difference for obtaining a favourable

hearing. Broader lobbying causes, of course, involve an even wider range of possibilities.

Like much sophisticated advice, these suggestions over-simplify the world of policy formation and present too optimistic an account of the benefits to be derived from Machiavellian manipulation. Nevertheless they give us a glimpse of how lobbyists work with the public service and a sense of the rules they often apply. . . .

CONFRONTATION OR COOPERATION?

The sanctions against confrontation present many groups with a fundamental question: should we try to embarrass policy-makers and expand our public support by public criticism in the media, or is it better to work quietly behind the scenes and forsake a public image? To address this question many groups formulate a . . . guide to action: avoid confrontation, but remember that sometimes it is necessary to embarrass politicians and officials. On those occasions it is important to avoid the strident exposure that alienates them permanently and may antagonize the public as well. In the words of one activist:

> Avoid confrontation, but don't ignore its potential. Better to be seen as a lion than as a pussy cat! Confrontation—like the theatre that it strongly resembles— can generate emotions; rousing passions, touching people at their deepest levels, stimulating a catharsis. If the media are present they magnify and transmit the images to thousands of people. But confrontation is a two-edged sword: it can ruin an organization's credibility as well as enhancing it. Use it at specific times, to achieve specific goals (media coverage, mobilization of interest to reach politicians who have ceased to listen). Plan confrontation so that it is effective in achieving these goals, and keep it under control.

It is equally important to avoid boxing in policy-makers. They must have an 'out,' a compromise that will allow them to save face and permit them to maintain an equable relationship with the group in the future.

Simply cataloguing the rules lobbyists follow informally as they try to influence the lead agency in the policy community underlines the significant role of the bureaucracy in policy formation, and the extent to which its characteristics colour the policy community. . . .

SOLIDIFYING THE GROUP'S POSITION

Status, recognition, and position are essential to being consulted. Securing a recognized position in the sub-government is a first priority for any group intending to exert continuing influence on policy. For many this involves continual struggle and competition. The National Farmers' Union, after many years on the policy scene, still does not enjoy a privileged position in the agricultural policy community. Other groups, however, gain recognition form their work, or else their status was earned so long ago that it is no longer questioned. The Canadian Bankers' Association and the Canadian Tax Foundation, for example, are confirmed members of the policy community that regularly discusses fiscal policy with the Department of Finance. The Business Council on National Issues and the Canadian Federation of Independent Business, on the other hand, have only recently been created and have had to earn a consultative position in the community concerned with the economy. The CFIB mounted a flamboyant, belligerent publicity campaign that asserted the right of small business to be heard. The BCNI was equally flamboyant, but deliberately conveyed the impression that an organization speaking for the wealthiest corporations in the country would automatically have a seat in the councils of the mighty.

Once they have survived the first round in the game of positional politics, groups tend to become less vocal, less inclined to invoke public opinion on issues of the day. Problems of legitimacy give way to problems of communication. Instead of clamouring to be consulted, they are hounded for advice. When governments and their agencies decide that specific groups speak for a significant part of the population and that their views are legitimate, they turn to them frequently, inviting them to sit on advisory committees and consulting them on issues far afield from the immediate concerns of the groups themselves. Responding to these overtures takes considerable effort. Membership opinion may have to be elicited, or specialized knowledge tapped. More frequently the organization may have to dedicate the time of its research staff to the question at hand, diverting it from tasks more important to the group and its members. Even participation on advisory boards can siphon off valuable executive time.

Despite these problems groups hesitate to turn down invitations to advise and participate. Participation helps maintain the organization's position as an integral part of the policy community; taps it into the information flow; guarantees consultation on issues of real concern to the group; and provides opportunities for group representatives to form personal links with civil servants, leaders of other groups, and sometimes senior politicians. The cost of participation is, in short, the price the group pays for acceptance as a full-fledged member of the policy community.

Monitoring is an important aspect of any established group's relationship with its policy community, and particularly with the key agencies. Being a part of the information flow and establishing friendly ties with the representatives of other groups help the group keep abreast of opinion in influential circles, enabling it to anticipate proposals for policy change, and thus to react and adapt to them. Informal ties, and even a prominent place in the community, do not in themselves guarantee adequate monitoring of trends in public opinion and government thinking, however. It is often necessary to introduce more systematic monitoring devices, such as clipping and analysing the general and specialized press; scrutinizing government policy, proposed legislation, and policy reviews in related fields; following academic discussions that have a bearing on the policy field; and even commissioning research into emergent issues. Often groups will themselves organize seminars, workshops, and conferences whose major function is to engage in forecasting activities—summing up the results of current monitoring activities and extrapolating from them.

Position confers the privilege of consultation and of access to strategic information, both of which facilitate the process of bringing influence to bear. These privileges reconcile group members of the sub-government to the norms preferred by bureaucratic members. Indeed, these norms are not necessarily distasteful to groups that have worked their way to the sub-government. While competition and conflict are the hallmark of group efforts to secure the support of public opinion and also play a part in campaigns to influence the political and administrative executive, a search for consensus is an even more important part of the life of the sub-governments. Community members use consensus to keep issues from spilling over into the public arena. But consensus, as much as the predilections of officials, imposes norms and sanctions on group behaviour—particularly norms and sanctions of discretion and confidentiality.

The preoccupation with keeping issues out of politics also has much to do with the tendency to co-operate—the second feature of sub-government relations that concerns most of its members. For as long as organized groups have existed to influence government, they have allied themselves with other groups. There are several reasons for this. First, they promote stable relations between groups. As Kwavnick puts it: 'To leave a group outside the circle of accepted groups is to invite its leaders to adopt unorthodox tactics, to make exaggerated demands and, generally, to be a disruptive and uncertain element.' Second, alliances strengthen group credibility. Third, they broaden the base of support and increase the resources available to specific groups. Fourth, they also reflect the communal nature of policy-making. Most members of the sub-government are aware that they will have to live with one another in the future. Tomorrow they may in fact search out as allies the groups they are tempted to revile today. There is therefore an incentive not only for reaching compromises, and for exercising restraint and civility, but for acting in concert.

THE MEDIA STILL NEED IMPROVEMENT

Keith Davey

. . . [I want to compare] the media of today with the media of 20 years ago at the time of the Senate (Davey) Committee on Mass Media]. . . .

Extracted from a speech in the Senate of Canada by the Honourable Keith Davey, *Senate Debates*, May 9, 1990, pp. 1589–1595. By permission.

First let me provide you with my own ballpark analysis about how the media has fared in the last 20 years. The short answer, honourable senators, is extremely well. There were 112 dailies in 1970; in 1989 there were 109 dailies. Daily circulation is up 20 per cent to 5.3 million readers. Ad revenue for newspapers is off slightly, but newspaper advertising still commands 25 per cent of all available advertising revenue. The magazine industry doubled its circulation in the last 20 years. There are four times as many radio stations as there were then, collecting six times as much revenue, annually approximately $750 million. Constant television viewing was approximately 24 hours per week per viewer 20 years ago, and that is approximately what it is today, but there are almost twice as many television stations now as there were then.

Another important set of figures is the overall advertising revenue that was available 20 years ago as opposed to today. The all-media advertising revenue picture is startling. In 1970, at the time of the committee, it was $1 billion. In 1981 it was $4 billion, and in 1988 it was $7.5 billion. That is a breathtaking analysis by any standard. Media growth and profitability have outstripped Canadian industries generally and Canada itself. Marshall McLuhan was correct: The medium is the message, and the media must be held responsible.

Our first and primary concern, honourable senators, was the concentration of media ownership, especially the concentration of print ownership. Here the situation, I am sorry to say, in the last 20 years has gone from bad to worse, even without cross-ownership; that is, multimixed media ownership by various media conglomerates and so on which I have not had time to discuss. The situation was bad enough in 1970. Twenty years later it is that much worse. In 1970 there were 112 dailies, of which 60 per cent were group owned. In 1980 there were 120 dailies, 75 per cent of which were group owned. In 1989 there were 109 dailies, 80 per cent of which were group owned. I believe that leaves us with exactly 23 independent newspapers. Thomson controls 25 per cent and 32 newspapers; Southam owns 33 per cent and 17 newspapers. The situation is worse still in French Canada. Fifty per cent of the dailies were group owned in 1970, and now 90 per cent are group owned.

Honourable senators, gone is the *Telegram*, gone is the *Montreal Star*, gone is the *Winnipeg Tribune*, and gone is the *Ottawa Journal*. It is true they have been replaced by a series of *Sun* newspapers, which is owned and controlled by Maclean Hunter, the biggest media conglomerate in the country. Yes, *The Globe and Mail* is a significant newspaper, but all of those other Thomson dailies still take more out of their community than they put back in. Meanwhile, the *Toronto Star* has something of a love affair. David Jolley at the *Toronto Star* must blush and blanch when he meets with his friend, John Fisher of Southam. . . .

Since 1985 Torstar has owned 23 per cent of the voting stake in Southam, while Southam, in turn, has owned 23 per cent of the non-voting stake in Torstar. The Southam family, meanwhile, owns 22.6 per cent of Southam's stock. A standstill agreement preventing the *Star* from mounting a takeover expires next month. . . . The market value of all Southam Inc. stock, including its 16 dailies, is about $1.5 billion. . . .

The controversy over further concentration of media goes on unabated. A story in this morning's business section of *The Globe and Mail* was headlined by John Partridge as follows: "Southam buys giant stake in B.C.'s regional publishing industry."

> The Toronto-based media company announced yesterday that, in a complex series of transactions, it is trading an undisclosed amount of cash and a stake it owns in a Vancouver community newspaper publisher for 63 per cent of a new company that will own a total of 24 such papers and 14 weekly "specialty" publications in the B.C. lower mainland area.
> The deal will add to Southam's heavy presence in the region: it already owns Vancouver's two dailies, *The Vancouver Sun* and *The Province*.
> The new company is to be called Lower Mainland Publishing Ltd.

Honourable senators, the question we have to ask ourselves is: Does all of this print media concentration really matter? Should we bother about it? I think categorically the answer is "yes." I have never believed in a media conspiracy. I have never believed that there is a group of owners who get together and have breakfast to decide whatever it is they want to make the Canadian people believe on that particular day. I think that the conspiracy of media ownership is not realistic. But the fact is that the owners, the people who own and control the mass media, particularly the newspapers, are all the same kind of people doing the same kind of thing with the same kind of private enterprise rationale. . . . In our report we dealt with this question of concentration by quoting the distinguished American jurist, Justice Hugo Black. He stated:

> . . . the widest possible dissemination of information from diverse and antagonistic sources is essential to the welfare of the public. A free press is a condition of a free society.

Again, we said in our report that the prudent state must recognize that at some point enough becomes enough. If the trend towards ownership concentration is allowed to continue unabated, sooner or later it must reach the point where it collides with the public interest.

One-half of all Canadians read daily newspapers. That is the good news. The bad news is that more and more Canadians are spending less time reading those newspapers. Happily, the drop-off is marginal and unfragmented. Here is how some things have changed over 20 years; There is more ad revenue per capita; there are more tabloids, more morning newspapers, more and better television guides, more high technology, more "user friendly," more colour, more Sunday papers, higher weekend circulation, more international news viewed through Canadian eyes throughout the world, continuing myopic coverage of the rest of Canada in Quebec, more magazine-like newspapers and more products like newspapers and magazines. . . .

The fact is, however, that we really do not know what is happening in our society if we do not read newspapers. I frequently speak to student audiences—particularly grade 13 students and those in first year university—usually about the media. I like to point out to them that everything that Peter Mansbridge says on "The Journal" on a given night could appear on one-quarter of the front page of *The Ottawa Citizen*. This is just a fact. Fewer and fewer young people are taking the time to read. I think that is a sad reality. It is something about which we should be extremely concerned.

Whether we like it not, honourable senators—and I guess I do—print still orders society's agenda. True, it is television which defines how we respond to those items on the agenda, but it is still print which lines them up. . . .

On a sour note, there are fewer and fewer journalists of consequence in "small-town" Ontario. Small, honourable senators, is not better. Great journalists head for the big cities. Good on them, and good on you if you live in one of those big cities.

I also want to observe that press councils, which our committee helped to inspire, are working. They are not fast enough; they are not tough enough; and they are without enough public attention. What are we to think about the recent regrettable trend of allowing print advertising to pass for journalism? That is happening more and more, and it is a very distressing situation.

In 1970 we proposed a press ownership review board to deal with the problem. The Liberal government of the day did absolutely nothing. No government has done anything about it since. However, it is never too late in my opinion. Perhaps it is in the national interest. Perhaps it is time to unbundle, and there are some precedents.

In the report of the Special Senate Committee on Mass Media it says:

> . . . that this country should no longer tolerate a situation where the public interest in so vital a field of information is dependent on the greed or goodwill of an extremely privileged group of businessmen.

I will close my reference to newspapers with a reference to each of the three Toronto dailies. I wonder why the *Toronto Star* does not require a federal voice out of Quebec instead of just Robert MacKenzie, whose separatist bias is very clear. The *Toronto Star* should have more balance. . . .

Why must the *Toronto Sun* publish, as it does most days, literally dozens of nearly-naked women, hustling sleazy advertising? I counted 29 such advertisements last Monday. . . .

Finally, I should like to say a few words about *The Globe and Mail*. . . . I find *The Globe and Mail*'s love affair with the CBC quite distasteful. Should the cash star of the CBC be paying for public opinion polling or programming, and why should *The Globe and Mail* be in bed with the public broadcaster? Such mega media mergers I find very troubling, and so does my friend, Martin Goldfarb, who recently set up an inauguration of "Goldfarb's Lecture," an annual address of a public opinion polling at York University. In his first lecture he dealt with these. He said:

There are some events in Canada that I think need greater public and academic scrutiny. The fact that the two major television networks and two major newspapers have come together to poll the public on a regular basis—and that is *The Globe and Mail* and the CBC, and *The Toronto Star* and CTV—on a series of subject matter needs to be scrutinized in a careful way. Is this information simply to inform the public or is this information being used to engineer consent or to encourage the bias that these media themselves may have? The results of these polls are often reported as mega news with mega headlines. These polls are news events in themselves. The public should take very careful scrutiny of the impact of this new development with how polls are used in the media and how media themselves have joined together to create mega news events through the polling process.

Our second concern was about the quality of all those media voices. The questions we asked ourselves were: What is a good newspaper? What is a good television station? What is a good radio station? The response was essentially a very subjective determination. How successful is that newspaper or broadcasting outlet in preparing its audience for social change? Change then and now need not be feared if it is understood, which is not to suggest any built-in bias for or against anybody's notion of progress. It is rather to assist people to accept and to understand change. Indeed, there have been many examples of the media preparing us all for social change. ● ● ●

Honourable senators, I should like to talk about cultural survival. . . . It seems to me that we have more than enough American media entering this country on a daily basis, and continuing Canadian newspaper ownership must remain a priority.

Our committee produced the legislation, which culminated in Bill C-58, which, immodestly I believe, kept the Canadian magazine industry in business. . . . The Canadian magazine industry is in trouble, as it has been so often in the past. I have a quotation from the Canadian Magazine Publishers Association, April 3, 1990. Catherine Keachie, the Executive Director, writes:

> The magazine industry enjoys pre-tax profits of less than 5 per cent; and, according to Stats Canada, roughly 60 per cent of our magazines operate with no profits at all. The three main federal support measures that have contributed to a positive climate—Section 19 of the Income Tax Act, the traditional exemption from federal sales tax, and cheap postal rates—have been eroded with such alarming speed within the last two years that only Section 19 of the Income Tax Act appears to be safe, and the magazine industry is aware that Section 19 is not being enforced with any great vigilance.

● ● ● Honourable senators, I would like to say something about the television of 20 years ago. I would like to read two quotations from the report, which will give you the flavour of what television was like 20 years ago, and then we can look at what it is today. The report reads:

> Television is the most believed and most important medium for international

news, and for Canadian news of national importance. Television commercials are believed by Canadians to be more influential than advertisements in other media. Radio is the most immediate medium, the medium to which Canadians would turn first in an emergency, but it is also a soothing, relaxing background. Television is the medium for the whole family. And television is the most sensational of the media.

● ● ●   I am here this afternoon to assert that television gives Canadians their daily bath of American morality.

I know we must give people what they want, which is all too frequently lowest common denominator programming, and I know all about the dishes, the spoons, the satellites and the reality of international programming availability. The question, however, is: Why are we allowing this magnificent medium to Americanize us all? . . .

Here are some facts which most of you should know: The average Canadian spends 24 hours a week watching television. Canadian children—yours and my grandchildren—by age 12 have spent 12,000 hours watching television. That is more time than they spend in school. Only 28 per cent of what is available on Canadian TV is Canadian. Ninety-eight per cent of all Canadian television drama is American. What really goes on? For openers, our kids, who I think matter most, in fact, know more about American history than they do about Canadian history. The sad thing is that all of this is happening because some of us were fair and allowed it to happen. The American program became the name of the game.

I do not think it is ever too late to fight back. It is time for tough leadership from the CRTC and from the Government of Canada. Clearly a massive infusion of money to all levels of broadcasting must become a reality. Incidentally, I think all of this should have a far greater priority than the impending, inevitable HDTV, high-definition television.

This means that private broadcasters must offer more than good wishes. It means that the bloated cable industry will have to start paying something back to Canada. . . . Just to give you some idea, 42.4 per cent of Canada was wired by 1970 when gross cable revenue was $51.7 million. Eighteen years later, cable revenue in Canada has grown almost 20-fold to $1 billion, and 90 per cent of this country makes us the most wired country on earth. ● ● ●

Finally, honourable senators, the media we need or the media we deserve? Twenty years later, regrettably, it is still the media we deserve. Then, as now, we do not have the media we need; we still have the media we deserve. That, of course, is because an overwhelming majority of Canadians do not know, for example, who owns the newspapers they read. . . .

Perhaps by this time the media should have been able to deal with this public indifference. Perhaps by now the media should have instilled new insight and new vision into more Canadians. That has not happened, but I would submit, honourable senators, that it is something to think about. Thank you.

BIBLIOGRAPHY

Public Opinion and Polling

Hoy, Claire, *Margin of Error: Pollsters and the Manipulation of Canadian Politics.* Toronto: Key Porter Books, 1989.

Johnston, R. *Public Opinion and Public Policy in Canada.* Toronto: U.T.P., 1985.

LeDuc, L. "The Measurement of Public Opinion." In H.R. Penniman, (ed.). *Canada at the Polls: The General Election of 1974.* Washington, American Enterprise Institute, 1975.

Lemieux, V. *Les sondages et la democratie.* Québec: Institut québecois de recherche sur la culture, 1988.

Pinard, M. "A House Divided." [A review of poll results re: Sovereignty Association, 1962–80], *Report on Confederation*, 3, 6, May, 1980.

Wheeler, M. *Lies, Damn Lies, and Statistics: The Manipulation of Public Opinion in America.* New York: Liveright, 1974.

Pressure Groups and Lobbying

(See also Bibliography in Chapter 1, Social Issues.)

Boase, J. "Regulation and the Paramedical Professions: An Interest Group Study." *C.P.A.*, 25, 3, Fall, 1982.

Bon, D.L. *Lobbying: A Right? A Necessity? A Danger.* Ottawa: The Conference Board of Canada, 1981.

Calvert, J. *Government Limited.* Ottawa: Canadian Centre for Policy Alternatives, 1984.

Canada, Department of Consumer and Corporate Affairs. *Lobbying and The Registration of Paid Lobbyists: A Discussion Paper.* Ottawa: 1985.

Coleman, W.D. "Analysing the Associative Action of Business: Policy Advocacy and Policy Participation." *C.P.A.*, 28, 3, Fall, 1985.

Coleman, W.D., and Grant, W.P. "Regional Differentiation of Business Associations: A Comparison of Canada and the United Kingdom." *C.J.P.S.*, 18, 2, March, 1985.

Coleman, W.D., and Jacek, H.J. "The Roles and Activities of Business Interest Associations in Canada." *C.J.P.S.*, 16, 2, June, 1983.

Doran, C., and Sokolsky, J. *Canada and Congress: Lobbying in Washington.* Halifax: Centre for Foreign Policy Studies, Dalhousie University, 1985.

Faulkner, J.H. "Pressuring the Executive." *C.P.A.*, 25, 2, Summer, 1982.

Forbes, J.D. *Institutions and Influencing Groups in Canadian Farm and Food Policy.* Toronto: I.P.A.C., 1985.

Fulton, M.J., and Stanbury, W.T. "Comparative Lobbying Strategies in Influencing Health Care Policy." *C.P.A.*, 28, 2, Summer, 1985.

Gillies, J. *Where Business Fails.* Montreal: I.R.P.P., 1981.

Gillies, J., and Pigott, J. "Participation in the Legislative Process." *C.P.A.*, 25, 2, Summer, 1982.

Goldstein, J. "Public Interest Groups and Public Policy: The Case of the Consumers' Association of Canada." *C.J.P.S.*, 12, 1, March, 1979.

Hartnagel, T.F., Creechan, J.J., and Silverman, R.A. "Public Opinion and the Legalization of Abortion." *C.R.S.A.*, 22, 3, August, 1985.

Islam, H., and Ahmed, S.A. "Business Influence on Government: A Comparison of Public and Private Sector Perceptions." *C.P.A.*, 27, 1, Spring, 1984.

Laycock, D. "Representative Economic Democracy and the Problem of Policy Infuence: The Case of Canadian Co-operatives." *C.J.P.S.*, 22, 4, December, 1989.
Malvern, P. *Persuaders: Lobbying, Influence Peddling and Political Corruption in Canada*. Toronto: Methuen, 1985.
McBride, S. "Public Policy as a Determinant of Interest Group Behaviour: The Canadian Labour Congress' Corporatist Initiative, 1976–1978." *C.J.P.S.*, 16, 3, September, 1983.
Munton, D., (ed.). *Groups and Governments in Canadian Foreign Policy*. Proceedings of a Conference, Ottawa, Canada, 9–11 June 1982, C.I.I.A., 1985.
Paltiel, K.Z. "The Changing Environment and Role of Special Interest Groups." *C.P.A.*, 25, 2, Summer, 1982.
Presthus, R. *Elite Accommodation in Canadian Politics*. Toronto: Macmillan, 1973.
Presthus, R. *Elites in the Policy Process*. Toronto: Macmillan, 1974.
Pross, A.P. "Parliamentary Influence and the Diffusion of Power." *C.J.P.S.*, 18, 2, June, 1985.
Pross, A. P. *Group Politics and Public Policy*. Toronto O.U.P., 1986.
Riddell-Dixon, E. *The Domestic Mosaic: Domestic Groups and Canadian Foreign Policy*. Toronto: C.I.I.A., 1985.
Sarpkaya, S. *Lobbying in Canada—Ways and Means*. Toronto: CCH Canadian, 1988.
Saumier, A. "Business Lobbying." *C.P.A.*, 26, 1, Spring, 1983.
Sawatsky, J. *The Insiders: Power, Money and Secrets in Ottawa*. Toronto: M.& S., 1987.
Skogstad, G. "Interest Groups, Representation and Conflict Management in the Standing Committees of the House of Commons." *C.J.P.S.*, 18, 4, December, 1985.
Thompson, F., and Stanbury, W.T. *The Political Economy of Interest Groups in the Legislative Process in Canada*. Toronto: Butterworths, 1979.
Thorburn, H. *Interest Groups in the Canadian Federal System*. Toronto: U.T.P., 1985.
Vallance, I. "Interest Groups and the Process of Legislative Reform: Bill C–15—A Case Study." *Q.L.J.*, 13, 1, Spring, 1988.
Weaver, Sally, M. "The Joint Cabinet/National Indian Brotherhood Committee: A Unique Experiment in Pressure Group Relations." *C.P.A.*, 25, 2, Summer, 1982.

Participation

(See also Bibliographies, Chapters 1, 7, 8.)

Kroeker, H.V., (ed.) *Sovereign People or Sovereign Governments*. Montreal: I.R.P.P., 1981.
Nossal, K. "Rhetoric and Reality." *P.O.*, 7, 1, January, 1986. [Foreign policy and consultation papers.]
Resnick, P. *Parliament vs. People. An Essay on Democracy and Canadian Political Culture*. Vancouver: New Star, 1984.
Salter, L., and Slaco, D. *Public Inquiries in Canada*. Ottawa: Science Council of Canada, 1981.
Salutin, R. *Marginal Notes: Challenges to the Mainstream*. Toronto: L. & O. D., 1984.
Smith, L. G. "Mechanisms for Public Participation at a Normative Planning Level in Canada." *C.P.P.*, 8, 4, Autumn, 1982.
Yudelman, D. "The Practice of Consensus." *P.O.*, 6, 8, October, 1985. [Public input into the Macdonald Commission.]

The Media

Audley, P. *Voices of Our Own: A Study of Canada's Communication Industries.* Toronto: Lorimer, 1981.

Bain, G. "Dateline Ottawa:" *Saturday Night*, July, 1985.

Black, E. R. *Politics and the News: The Political Functions of the Mass Media.* Toronto: Butterworths, 1982.

Canada. *Royal Commission on Newspapers*, [Kent Commission]. Ottawa: S. and S., 1981.

Canada, Senate. *Report of the Special Senate Committee on Mass Media.* [Davey Report], 3 vols. Ottawa: Queen's Printer, 1970.

Canadian Study of Parliament Group. *Seminar on Press and Parliament: Adversaries or Accomplices?* Ottawa: Queen's Printer, April, 1980.

Caron, A.H., Mayrand, C., and Payne, D.E. "L'Imagerie politique à la télévision: les derniers jours de la campagne référendaire." *C.J.P.S.*, 16, 3, September, 1983.

Cocking, C. *Following the Leaders: A Media Watcher's Diary of Campaign '79.* Toronto: Doubleday, 1980.

Comber, M.A., and Mayne, R.S. *The Newsmongers: How the Media Distort The Political News.* Toronto: M.& S., 1986.

Desbarats, P. *Guide to Canadian News Media.* Toronto: Harcourt Brace Jovanovich, 1990.

Eaman, A. *The Media Society: Basic Issues and Controversies.* Toronto: Butterworths, 1988.

Ericson, R., Baranek, P., and Chan, J. *Negotiating Control: A Study of News Sources.* Toronto: U.T.P., 1989.

Fletcher, F.J. "Mass Media and Parliamentary Elections in Canada." *Legislative Studies Quarterly*, 12, 3, August, 1987.

Fotheringham, A. *Birds of a Feather: The Press and the Politicians.* Toronto: Key Porter Books, 1989.

Gossage, P. *Close to the Charisma.* Toronto: M.& S., 1986.

Hackett, R. "Coups, Earthquakes and Hostages? Foreign News on Canadian Television." *C.J.P.S.*, 22, 4, December, 1989.

LeDuc, L., and Price, R. "Great Debates: The Televised Leadership Debates of 1979." *C.J.P.S.*, 18, 1, March, 1985.

Lyman, P. *Canadian Culture and the New Technology.* Toronto: Lorimer, 1981.

McCormack, T. "The Political Culture and the Press of Canada." *C.J.P.S.*, 16, 3, September, 1983.

Ontario Press Council. *17th Annual Report, 1989.* Toronto: 1990. (Annual from 1972.)

Peers, F.W. *The Politics of Canadian Broadcasting, 1920–1951.* Toronto: U.T.P., 1969; *The Public Eye: Television and the Politics of Canadian Broadcasting, 1952–1968.* Toronto: U.T.P., 1978.

Reader's Digest Foundation and Erindale College. *Politics and the Media.* Montreal: Reader's Digest Foundation, 1981.

Salter, L. *Dimensions of the Message: Communication Studies in Canada.* Toronto: Butterworths, 1981.

Siegel, A. *Politics and the Media in Canada.* Toronto: McG-H.R., 1983.

Singer, D.B. *Communications in Canadian Society.* Toronto: Addison-Wesley, 1983.

Soderlund, W. *et al.* "Regional and Linguistic Agenda-Setting in Canada: A Study of Newspaper Coverage Issues Affecting Political Integration in 1976." *C.J.P.S.*, 13, 2, June, 1980.

Soderlund, W. "A Comparison of Press Coverage in Canada and the United States of the 1982 and 1984 Salvadoran Elections." *C.J.P.S.*, 23, 1, March, 1990.

Soderlund, W. *et al. Media and Elections in Canada*. Toronto: H.R.W., 1984.
Stewart, W., (ed.). *Canadian Newspapers: The Inside Story*. Edmonton: Hurtig, 1980.
Taras, D. "Television and Public Policy: The CBC's Coverage of the Meech Lake Accord." *C.P.P.* 15, 3, September, 1989.
Tataryn, L. *The Pundits*. Ottawa: Deneau, 1986.
Trueman, P. *Smoke and Mirrors: The Inside Story of Television News in Canada*. Toronto: M. & S., 1980.
Wagenberg, R. *et al.* "Campaigns, Images and Polls: Mass Media Coverage of the 1984 Canadian Election." *C.J.P.S.*, 21, 1, March, 1988.
Weimann, G., and Winn, C. *Hate on Trial: The Zundel Affair, the Media and Public Opinion in Canada*. Oakville, Ontario: Mosaic Press, 1986.

POLITICAL PARTIES

CAIRNS REVISITED—THE ELECTORAL AND PARTY SYSTEM IN CANADA

Nelson Wiseman

In 1968 Alan Cairns published a seminal article entitled "The Electoral System and the Party System in Canada, 1921–1965" (*Canadian Journal of Political Science*, I, 1, March, 1968) that illuminated and explored the impact of the Canadian electoral system on the party system. Cairns argued that the former conditioned the latter on a course that promoted regionalism or sectionalism in Canadian politics. The party system, paradoxically, was stimulating the very cleavages that brokerage parties like the Liberals and Conservatives were normally credited with healing. The sustaining power of Cairns's analysis was reflected in the fact that his article continued to be anthologized for two decades after its publication and, as one commentator remarked, Cairns "taught us that Canada's single-member plurality system manufactures regional differences more efficiently than it does parliamentary majorities."

Corollaries of this theorem were that the electoral system benefits disproportionately the winning party (historically, usually the Liberals) and regionally based minor parties (the Progressives, Social Credit, and the Créditistes). Conversely, minor parties with diffused support (the Reconstruction Party in 1935 and the CCF–NDP since then) are penalized. The electoral system also under-

An original article prepared for this edition in April 1990 by the author, who is a member of the Department of Political Science, University of Toronto. By permission.

represents the political diversity within regions. Quebec and Ontario, for example, looked more Liberal and Conservative, respectively, than they actually were in terms of votes between the 1920s and 1960s. Elections were thus transformed, so that looking at the results on a colour-coded map made an election appear more like a contest among regions than among parties.

The data providing the foundation for this analysis were indisputable and, unlike surveys, had no margin of error: *Reports of the Chief Electoral Officer*. Cairns offered five tables that covered 14 elections between 1921 (when a genuine multi-party system first appeared) and 1965 (when a third successive minority government in three elections over three years was in office and when the Créditistes were riding high in Quebec). Since then there have been seven more general elections and only two minority governments in over twenty years. Small sectional parties, moreover, have not elected an MP in a general election since 1979. This paper updates Cairns's data and reflects upon his analysis in the light of additional evidence.

Table 1 was offered by Cairns as evidence that the electoral system fails to produce, consistently and simultaneously, both a majority government and a numerically effective opposition. This, he claimed, was the rationale offered in defence of the single-member plurality system. Six of fourteen elections through 1965 did not produce majorities and, after defining an effective opposition as between one-third and one-half of all MPs, Cairns found the electoral system wanting 10 times out of 14 (for a 71 percent failure rate). Since 1968 these criteria produced failure in three cases of seven, and the cumulative total now stands at thirteen failures in twenty-one (or 62 percent of) cases. J.A.A. Lovink [in *C.J.P.S., III*, 4] has persuasively criticized Cairn's definition of a numerically effective opposition as too stringent, and pointed out that if the standard is lowered to one-quarter of MPs, the electoral system is efficient in most cases. Since 1921 it has succeeded in these terms in twelve cases of twenty-one (57 percent).

One may question the utility of any numerical criteria (beyond zero) in defining an effective opposition. Is the opposition in the Thirty-Fourth Parliament elected in 1988 more or less effective with 43 percent of the MPs than it was in the Thirty-Third Parliament with 25 percent of the MPs? The smaller opposition in the Thirty-Third thwarted the government's Free Trade Agreement; the larger opposition in the Thirty-Fourth saw it enacted. Canada's high level of party discipline combined with a party's parliamentary prerogatives provide the opposition with substantial resources to obstruct and/or influence a government no matter how small or few the opposition parties and their contingents. Social democratic MPs, for example, are fond of citing how only two Labour MPs in the 1920s "forced" the Liberals to introduce old-age pension legislation. "Most of Canada's social legislation was enacted by Liberal and, to a lesser extent, Conservative governments, but the party that first articulated the need and convinced Canadians that reform could be achieved was the CCF–NDP." This is not a party that sees itself nor is seen by others as "ineffective," yet it has never held more than 15 percent of Parliament's seats. If the numerical

TABLE 1 **Percentages of Votes and Seats for Government Party, 1921–1988**

	% Votes	% Seats		% Votes	% Seats
1921	41	49 (L)	1962	37	44 (C)
1925*	40	40 (L)	1963	42	49 (L)
1926	46	52 (L)	1965	40	49 (L)
1930	49	56 (C)	1968	45	59 (L)
1935	45	71 (L)	1972	38	41 (L)
1940	52	74 (L)	1974	43	53 (L)
1945	41	51 (L)	1979**	36	48 (C)
1949	50	74 (L)	1980	44	52 (L)
1953	49	65 (L)	1984	50	75 (C)
1957**	39	42 (C)	1988	43	57 (C)
1958	54	79 (C)			

* In 1925 the Conservatives received both a higher percentage of votes (47 percent) and seats (47 percent) than the Liberals. The Liberals, however, met Parliament and with Progressive support held office for several months.

** In 1957 and 1979 the Liberals received a higher percentage of votes (41 percent and 40 percent) than the winning Conservatives.

Sources: Alan C. Cairns, "The Electoral System and the Party System in Canada," *Canadian Journal of Political Science*, I, 1, March, 1968, pp. 55–80 and *Reports of the Chief Electoral Officer* for 1968 through 1988.

criteria defining effective opposition is eliminated altogether, the system has succeeded, rather than failed, in thirteen cases of twenty-one (62 percent).

We might go further and ask: are majority governments better or more successful than minority ones? Perceptions of an electoral system's "success" might change over time. If "success" is determined by either academic or public opinion, then opinion has shifted in both spheres. Cairns wrote soon after Canada had experienced four minority parliaments elected in five elections over an eight-year span. In the 1965 election the prime minister "emphasized, above all, the theme of majority government," and he described minority government as "bad for the democratic process in this country." For the Liberals it was *the* issue of the election. The public thought it "important" too: 60 percent said so in 1965 and between 69 percent and 72 percent in 1968 when Cairns wrote. The public's dislike and suspicion of minority government, however, was modified through the experience of minority government both in Ottawa and some of the provinces (Ontario and Manitoba). A more positive public predisposition to minority government emerged. In 1973 a Gallup Poll found that a majority of Canadians thought minority government is "good for the nation" and 64 percent preferred its continuation to another election. Parliamentarians also "had positive overall assessments of the minority experience" in Ontario and a study revealed "that all the normal functions attributed to the legislature were performed better in a minority situation." Minority governments became perceived as having enacted progressive social legislation, a fact noted by academics. "In Canada, minority government is held to be better because it is more socially conscious."

From this perspective the electoral system is less efficient when it produces majorities and more efficient when it produces minorities. Table 1, therefore, might be used to measure, but not to judge, the performance of the electoral

TABLE 2 **Bias of Electoral System in Translating Votes into Seats: Rank Order of Parties in Terms of Percentages of Vote**

Year	1		2		3		4		5	
1921	Libs.	1.21	Cons.	0.70	Progs.	1.20				
1925	Cons.	1.017	Libs.	1.015	Progs.	1.09				
1926	Libs.	1.13	Cons.	0.82	Progs.	1.55				
1930	Cons.	1.15	Libs.	0.82	Progs.	1.53				
1935	Libs.	1.57	Cons.	0.55	CCF	0.33	Recon.	0.05	Socred	1.68
1940	Libs.	1.43	Cons.	0.53	CCF	0.39	Socred	1.52		
1945	Libs.	1.24	Cons.	1.00	CCF	0.73	Socred	1.29		
1949	Libs.	1.49	Cons.	0.53	CCF	0.37	Socred	1.03		
1953	Libs.	1.32	Cons.	0.62	CCF	0.77	Socred	1.06		
1957	Libs.	0.97	Cons.	1.087	CCF	0.88	Socred	1.091		
1958	Cons.	1.46	Libs.	0.55	CCF	0.32	Socred	0		
1962	Cons.	1.17	Libs.	1.01	NDP	0.53	Socred	0.97		
1963	Libs.	1.17	Cons.	1.09	NDP	0.49	Socred	0.76		
1965	Libs.	1.23	Cons.	1.13	NDP	0.44	Cred.	0.72	Socred	0.51
1968	Libs.	1.30	Cons.	0.88	NDP	0.46	Cred.	1.06		
1972	Libs.	1.09	Cons.	1.16	NDP	0.65	Socred	0.71		
1974	Libs.	1.24	Cons.	1.03	NDP	0.40	Socred	0.83		
1979	Libs.	1.01	Cons.	1.34	NDP	0.51	Socred	0.43		
1980	Libs.	1.18	Cons.	1.11	NDP	0.57				
1984	Cons.	1.50	Libs.	0.51	NDP	0.56				
1988	Cons.	1.33	Libs.	0.88	NDP	0.75				

Independents and very small parties have been excluded from the table.

The measurement of discrimination employed in this tables defines the relationship between the percentage of votes and the percentage of seats. The figure is devised by dividing the former into the latter. Thus 1—(38 percent seats/38 percent votes), for example—represents a neutral effect for the electoral system. Any figure above 1—(40 percent seats/20 percent votes) = 2.0, for example—indicates discrimination for the party. A figure below 1—(20 percent seats/40 percent votes) = 0.5, for example—indicates discrimination against the party. For the purposes of the table the ranking of the parties as 1, 2, 3 . . . is based on their percentage of the vote, since to rank them in terms of seats would conceal the very bias it is sought to measure—namely, the bias introduced by the intervening variable of the electoral system that constitutes the mechanism by which votes are translated into seats.

system. Measurements in the absence of normative preferences can neither determine success or failure. In the case of governments some people prefer majorities and other minorities. In Canada the single-member plurality system has produced a reasonable and productive mixture of both.

Tables 1 and 2 show that the winning party almost always (but not always: see 1957 and 1979) gets the most votes. The winner always reaps a higher percentage of seats than its percentage of votes. As for the second, or runner-up party, sometimes (in eight cases) it fares better, sometimes (in twelve cases) it fares worse, and one time (in 1945) its seats and votes were in balance. With the exception of 1968, both major parties benefited in the translation of votes into seats from 1962 through 1980.

Cairns used Tables 2 and 3 to demonstrate that the electoral system also rewarded sectional parties (the Progressives, Social Credit, and the Créditistes). The CCF–NDP, in contrast, has never won seats in proportion to its popular vote. Cairns depicted the electoral system as encouraging the rise of sectional-

TABLE 3 **Minor Parties: Percentages of Seats and Votes**

	Progressives		Reconstruction		CCF–NDP		Soc. Credit		Créditiste	
	Votes	Seats	Votes	Seats	Votes	Seats	Votes	Seats	Votes	Seats
1921	23	28								
1925	9	10								
1926	5	8								
1930	3	5								
1935			9	0.4	9	3	4	7		
1940					9	3	3	4		
1945					16	11	4	5		
1949					13	5	4	4		
1953					11	9	5	6		
1957					11	9	7	7		
1958					10	3	3	—		
1962					14	7	12	11		
1963					13	6	12	9		
1965					18	8	4	2	5	3
1968					17	8	1	—	4	5
1972					18	12	8	6		
1974					15	6	5	4		
1979					18	9	5	2		
1980					20	11	1	—		
1984					19	11				
1988					20	15				

ism, or regionalism, because sectional appeals by small, as well as large, parties proved fruitful in electing more MPs. Meanwhile, a small party (the CCF–NDP) was handicapped for it campaigned on class issues, a cleavage that cuts across all regions. However, from the perspective of the 1990s rather than the 1960s, third-party performance appears differently. The NDP is no longer one of a number of third parties; it is *the* third party. A projection of Cairns's analysis— that sectionally oriented parties would thrive and that a relatively small class-oriented, nationally oriented party like the NDP would weaken and possibly wither—has not materialized. Not since 1968 (with the Créditistes) has a minor party seen its percentage of seats exceed its percentage of votes.

What has happened? Table 3 demonstrates that it has been the CCF–NDP that has exhibited resilience, consistency, and longevity. Along with its predecessor, the Independent Labour Party, this same party has held seats continuously in the House of Commons since 1921, and in 1984 came within ten seats of forming the Official Opposition. Despite the electoral system's tilt against it, the CCF–NDP took root, whereas the "successful" sectional parties—the Progressives, Social Credit, and Créditistes—came and went. Successor sectional parties, like the Confederation of Regions Party and the Reform Party, failed in the 1980s. The bias of the electoral system in translating votes into seats, therefore, neither squelched the NDP nor catapulted more sectional parties into Parliament, as Cairns's analysis implied it would.

The "destructive impact" of the electoral system on the CCF–NDP and its "favourable impact" (to use Cairns's terms) on the fortunes of sectional third parties were not enough to keep a paradoxical result from emerging: a positive outcome for the NDP and annihilation for the "favoured" others. The NDP may not get its "fair share" of the seats, but it has had its "fair share" (and perhaps more) of influence in fashioning the public policy agenda. Moreover, it has sometimes benefited from the vagaries of the electoral system *within* regions. In the seven elections after 1965 it has won more than its "fair share" of seats—three times in Manitoba, four times in Saskatchewan, and three times in British Columbia. On a number of other occasions its share of provincial seats has been reasonably close (within 3 percent) of its share of provincial votes (e.g., 1968 and 1972 in Manitoba; 1984 in Saskatchewan; 1968 and 1979 in British Columbia).

In Table 4 Cairns revealed the distortions produced by the electoral system when comparing a party's total strength in seats and votes in individual provinces. The system made the CCF–NDP appear as a party of protesting Western farmers whereas, in reality, it had more urban supporters, especially in Ontario. In 1945, for example, 18 of the CCF's 28 MPs came from Saskatchewan while none was from Ontario, yet about a third of all CCF voters were in Ontario and only a fifth of them were in Saskatchewan. Since 1965 distortions of this kind have, inevitably, persisted but are rarely so skewed. Sometimes a distorting pattern is broken. In 1974, for example, half the NDP caucus came from Ontario, whereas less than half of all NDP votes did. If there was any doubt about the CCF's mainly urban and class character—a doubt perpetuated by titles such as *Agrarian Socialism*—it was dissolved by the late 1950s. Only once (1980) in the 11 elections since the late 1950s have fewer than 23 percent of the party's MPs been form Ontario. It is also the only time since the fifties that there have been more NDP MPs from Saskatchewan than from Ontario. This demonstrates that distortions in total party strength as reflected in votes and seats by province are fluid rather than fixed. In some cases, however, with Quebec as a good example, the NDP's substantial number of votes have continued to count for naught in terms of seats.

Overall, the post-1957 data show that the NDP is coming closer more consistently to attaining a fairer balance between seats and votes in the various provinces. It has elected MPs from five different provinces in three of the past five elections (1974, 1979, and 1988), whereas it only managed this twice (1949 and 1953) in the preceding twelve elections. Since 1974 the party has also won seats in both Territories and Newfoundland, something it never did before. Of course, individual provincial distortions persist from election to election (such as 44 percent of the NDP's seats in 1988 coming from British Columbia, whereas only 21 percent of its total votes were located there). Nevertheless, the NDP now appears, albeit imperfectly but more consistently than in the past, as a national party. On this score, therefore, the performance of the electoral system has improved marginally. A declining percentage of NDP votes are coming from Manitoba and Saskatchewan, in large measure because a declining percentage of voters live in those provinces. Saskatchewan, the third most populous province from the 1911 through the 1951 census, is now the least populous outside the Atlantic region.

TABLE 4 **Percentages of Total CCF–NDP Strength, in Seats and Votes from Selected Provinces**

	N.S.	QUE.	ONT.	MAN.	SASK.	ALTA.	B.C.
1935 votes	—	2	33	14	19	8	25
seats	—	—	—	29	29	—	43
1940 votes	5	2	16	16	27	9	26
seats	13	—	—	13	63	—	13
1945 votes	6	4	32	13	21	7	15
seats	4	—	—	18	64	—	14
1949 votes	4	2	39	11	20	4	19
seats	8	—	8	23	39	—	23
1953 votes	4	4	33	10	25	4	20
seats	4	—	4	13	48	—	30
1957 votes	2	5	39	12	20	4	19
seats	—	—	12	20	40	—	28
1958 votes	3	7	38	11	16	3	22
seats	—	—	38	—	13	—	50
1962 votes	4	9	44	7	9	4	20
seats	5	—	32	11	—	—	53
1963 votes	3	15	43	6	7	3	22
seats	—	—	35	12	—	—	53
1965 votes	3	18	43	7	8	3	17
seats	—	—	43	14	—	—	43
1968 votes	2	12	44	7	11	4	19
seats	—	—	27	14	27	—	32
1972 seats	3	10	45	7	9	5	19
seats	—	—	35	10	16	—	35
1974 votes	3	11	46	7	9	4	16
seats	6	—	50	13	13	—	13
1979 votes	4	8	43	8	9	4	19
seats	4	—	23	19	15	—	31
1980 votes	4	12	40	7	8	4	20
seats	—	—	16	22	22	—	38
1984 votes	3	13	39	6	9	6	21
seats	—	—	43	13	17	—	27
1988 votes	2	18	35	4	9	8	21
seats	—	—	23	5	23	2	44

Percentages of votes do not total 100 horizontally because the table does not include Newfoundland, Prince Edward Island, New Brunswick, or the territories where the CCF/NDP gained few votes and few seats. The NDP won a seat in the Northwest Territories in 1974, 1979, and 1980. It won a seat in Newfoundland in 1979 and one in the Yukon in 1988.

Table 5 was used by Cairns to show how the electoral system could contribute to divisivness and that it was detrimental to national unity. He observed that Quebec appeared dangerously more Liberal and Ontario more Conservative than either actually were in terms of both parties' national vote totals. This imbalance was reflected in Quebec and Ontario electing lop-sided numbers of Liberals and Conservatives, respectively, between 1921 and 1965. Until 1958 the percentage of all Conservative MPs *always* exceeded the percentage of all Conservative votes located in Ontario. Since 1958, however, the percentage of

TABLE 5 Liberals and Conservatives: Percentages of Total Parliamentary Strength and Total Electoral Support from Quebec and Ontario

| | Conservatives | | | | Liberals | | | |
| | Ontario | | Quebec | | Ontario | | Quebec | |
	Seats	Votes	Seats	Votes	Seats	Votes	Seats	Votes
1921	74	47	—	16	18	27	56	44
1925	59	47	3	18	11	30	60	38
1926	58	45	4	19	20	32	47	33
1930	43	39	18	24	24	34	44	31
1935	63	43	13	25	32	34	32	32
1940	63	49	3	16	32	34	34	31
1945	72	53	3	8	27	35	42	33
1949	61	44	5	23	29	32	35	33
1953	65	44	8	26	30	33	39	34
1957	55	43	8	22	20	31	59	38
1958	32	36	24	26	31	33	51	38
1962	30	37	12	22	44	40	35	29
1963	28	38	8	16	40	39	36	29
1965	26	37	8	17	39	39	43	30
1968	24	37	6	18	41	37	36	32
1972	37	41	2	14	33	37	51	35
1974	26	37	3	15	39	39	43	32
1979	42	42	1	11	28	33	59	43
1980	37	40	1	11	35	35	50	42
1984	32	34	27	28	35	38	43	35
1988	27	32	37	33	52	43	14	25

all Conservative seats has *never* exceeded the percentage of all Conservative votes located in Ontario. In the last four elections they have been fairly balanced, halting the pattern Cairns observed. This is evidence using Cairns's own criteria, of the improved efficiency and performance of the electoral system.

After 1965 and before 1984 Conservative fortunes on this same score were dismal in Quebec, as were Liberal fortunes on the Prairies. Although the ratio of Liberal to Conservative voters in Quebec was 1.9 to 1 between 1921 and 1965, the electoral system puffed this up to 5.6 Quebec Liberal MPs for each Conservative MP. The ratio became more extreme between 1968 and the 1980 elections; the latter had the Liberals receiving 5.4 times as many votes as the Conservatives, but 74 times as many MPs. How could the Conservatives perform an integrative, brokerage function if there was only one Québécois MP in their national caucus? Similarly, Liberal MPs from the Prairies were too few; only two were elected in the 1979 and 1980 elections. Could a Liberal government be expected then to be sensitive and responsive to Western concerns and perceptions? The last two elections, however, have produced an excellent and fair balance for the Conservatives in Quebec. As for the Liberals, they benefited in Quebec seats in every election from 1921 through 1984. In 1988, however, the Quebec "advantage," so long a boost to the Liberals, evaporated, and for the first time they held fewer seats (14 percent) in the province than their total electoral support warranted (25 percent). In Ontario the Liberals have been in a remarkably steady and reasonable balance between total parliamentary strength and total electoral support since 1958. There has also been a shift toward balance for the Conservatives in Ontario. Once again, this is evidence of increased efficiency in and enhanced performance by the electoral system using the same measuring rod offered by Cairns.

CONCLUDING OBSERVATIONS

Cairns's analysis is in need of some revision. If the electoral system fed regional bunching in the parliamentary parties from the 1920s through the 1960s, and if that in turn fed regional tensions in Canadian politics, then the markedly improved performance of the electoral system in the 1980s should have contributed to a lessening of regionalism as a force in national politics. Arguably, it hasn't. In the 1988 election, for example, the Conservatives captured a majority of votes in only two provinces: Quebec and Alberta. Such a development made it more difficult to identify particular parties with particular regions or provinces. Yet, is there more national unity because the governing caucus has a better mix of MPs from the various regions than predecessor Liberal governments? Perhaps Canadian politics were not as driven in the 1960s by sectional cleavages as Cairns suggested them to be; perhaps they are not as integrated now as the party system, moulded by the electoral system (to follow Cairns's logic), suggests them to be. Tensions between East and West, French Canada and English Canada, centre and periphery persist and will likely always persist. The differing values and orientations of Quebecers and Western Canadians might be accommodated in party caucuses as well as in negotiations between and among competing governments with immense resources and social influence. A more regionally balanced parliamentary caucus may contribute to a dialogue on national issues, but institutional forces such as federalism and socioeconomic factors such as the uneven distribution of language groups and natural resources are more significant in understanding the logic and dynamics of regional tensions.

The electoral system in the 1980s produced positive objective conditions for the Conservative and Liberal parties to play more integrative, nationalizing roles. In 1988 the Conservatives won seats in nine provinces, the Liberals in eight, and the NDP in five. There is scant evidence, however, of integration, that the three national parties are now more successful than in the past in containing, mediating, and resolving regional tensions. Too much of the dynamics of regionalism plays itself out outside the national party system. The Constitution Act of 1982 and the failed Meech Lake Accord demonstrate that even when the three national parties agree on such a critical and fundamental issue as the constitution, regional tensions in Canadian politics are not defused but possibly exacerbated. What is the relevance of the Liberals or Conservatives being under- or overrepresented in Quebec or the Prairies if all the MPs in both parties vote the same way on such unquestionably major issues as Canada's constitutional fabric? In the past the electoral system may have been an obstacle to reducing sectionalism. Even as an ally, however, an efficiently operating electoral system is not enough to accomplish a reduction in regional tensions.

Cairns's brilliant study alerted us to the importance of the electoral system and how it could influence the party system and the tone of national politics. "More than anything else, this might be considered the principal achievement of his article; it raised the electoral system to academic consciousness." Cairns recognized that there were limitations in pursuing a single factor analysis. Nevertheless, through his intellectual rigour and critical focus he demonstrated how far one could push, and push powerfully, a single factor analysis. It seemed to help explain so much. The measurably improved output of the system, however, has not yielded the results Cairns implied ought to be forthcoming. The system's outputs in the 1980s somewhat lessened rather than progressively exaggerated sectional tendencies in national party representation. It also produced stable majority governments with effective oppositions. In this sense, therefore, Cairns might have claimed too much for the electoral system's ultimate influence in shaping the tenor of national politics. The distortion of political diversity within regions had been attenuated, yet regional tensions persist as apparently permanent features of Canadian politics. This is logical as they are more firmly rooted in history, socioeconomic cleavages, and institutional structures than in the distorted outputs of the electoral system. The continued absence of successful fourth party candidates in general elections and the more balanced make-up of the larger party caucuses have not led to the evaporation, nor perhaps even the amelioration, of regional tensions, as Cairns's critique implied. For that to happen, something more is needed.

An upshot of Cairns's study was that political scientists went from neglecting the electoral system to suggesting alternatives and modifications. The Parti Québécois proposed proportional representation when it was a victim of the single-member plurality system in the early 1970s. However, elected in 1976 as a beneficiary of the system, the PQ did nothing to change it. The 1979 and 1980 federal elections—the former producing a government without a plurality of the vote and the latter producing Liberal MPs in 74 of 75 Quebec seats but in only 2 of the West's 77 seats—generated new pressures for change. In the aftermath of the last two elections the issue has waned again, as have some of the distortions. From a comparative perspective "the Canadian electoral system does not perform badly, particularly in comparison to other" states with the same system. Canada's experience with its electoral system has been far from ideal. Nevertheless, neither the public nor its politicians have seriously pursued alternatives. That, in itself, testifies to a sense of general satisfaction with the system that exists. The power of tradition, inertia, and the clash of interests that change requires help to perpetuate the system. It may not be perfect, but neither is any other.

[Editor's note: see Chapter 8 for a discussion of proportional representation.]

MIDDLE-OF-THE-ROAD PARTIES ARE THE CANADIAN TRADITION

Paul Fox

Canadian politics and political parties tend to be characterized by the word "moderate." Like Britain and the United States, to which Canadian political parties owe a good deal in formative influences, Canada is a predominantly middle-class nation with middle-class values. This is reflected in the fact that radical parties of either the right or the left are virtually non-existent and that those parties which do exist seek the golden mean in order to get the maximum number of votes.

This tends to diminish the differences between parties and to make them difficult to pinpoint. In some cases it is more a matter of history and traditional loyalty that distinguishes them rather than logic or the planks in their platforms. This is very apparent in comparing the two parties that have dominated Canadian politics since the country became a dominion in 1867, the Conservatives and the Liberals.

CONSERVATIVES

The Conservatives originated in Canada as the colonial equivalent of the British Tory party. In pioneer days they were ardently loyal to the crown and stood for the maintenance of the British connection. Under their first great leader, Sir John A. Macdonald, who was prime minister almost continuously from 1867 until his death in 1891, the party broadened its appeal by incorporating some of the opposing Liberals and by devising a "National Policy" which stressed the development of the country from sea to sea, the construction of transcontinental railways, and the fostering of industry and commerce by the adoption of relatively high tariffs.

These elements left their mark on the party for many years, so much so that it was stigmatized by farmers and French Canadians for decades. The farmers complained that it was the party of "big business," sacrificing the agrarian interests of the three wheat-growing prairie provinces to the financial and commercial demands of the large metropolitan centres (Toronto and Montreal) in the more populous and wealthier provinces of Ontario and Quebec. The French Canadians, Roman Catholic in faith and predominant in Quebec, were alienated by the militant Protestantism and pro-British sentiments of some of the leading Conservatives. When one Conservative government in the nineteenth century executed Louis Riel, a Roman Catholic rebel with French-Canadian blood in his veins, and another Conservative government rigorously implemented universal military conscription during World War I (which French Canadians considered to be a "British" war), the Conservative party

Revised in May, 1990.

went into an eclipse in Quebec from which, after four decades, it recovered in the elections of 1957 and 1958.

In every general election from 1917 to 1957, with one exception, the Conservatives never won more than half a dozen seats in this French-Canadian province which, because of its size, has about one-quarter of the total number of seats in the House of Commons. Conservative weakness in Quebec combined with meagre support in the western agarian provinces explains to a large extent why the Tories went out of power nationally in 1921 and remained out, except for five years, until 1957.

The two elections within ten months in 1957 and 1958 brought about a striking change. In the former the Conservatives under Mr. Diefenbaker secured nine seats out of 75 in Quebec. This provided a bridgehead for future operations. In the succeeding election Mr. Diefenbaker won 50 Conservative seats in Quebec.

At the same time Mr. Diefenbaker, himself a western Canadian who had sat as a western MP for 18 years, was able to revive the cause of Conservatism in that part of the country by the sheer force of his own personality. The result of the election on March 31, 1958, was the most decisive victory in the history of Canadian federal government; the Conservatives were returned with 208 seats out of a total of 265.

Unfortunately for the party, its fortunes varied with its leader's. Mr. Diefenbaker's popularity and command of the situation waned almost as rapidly as they had waxed. The 1962 election returned the Conservatives to the status of a minority government, and the 1963 election found them defeated by the Liberals, who remained in power for the next 16 years. In 1979 the Conservatives regained the government under their new leader, Joe Clark. But his regime was short-lived. After nine months it went down to defeat before the Liberals, who then stayed in office until 1984. In September of that year the Conservatives' new leader, Brian Mulroney, carried his party to a tremendous victory, capturing 211 of the Commons' 282 seats and reducing the Liberals to a mere rump of 40 seats. Fighting an election chiefly on his stand in favour of free trade with the United States, Prime Minister Mulroney retained power in 1988, but with a smaller majority of 169 seats to the Liberals' 83 and the New Democrats' 43 seats.

LIBERALS

Like its British forebear, the Liberal party in Canada commenced as a reform movement. It was a fusion after Confederation of small-scale pioneer farmers of British stock and the more radical and progressive elements in the French-Canadian society known as "Rouges." The colours adopted by the party were red and white in contrast to the Conservatives' blue and white, a distinction that was quite valid. From its birth the Liberal party tended to be more egalitarian, proletarian, and nationalistic. With the advent to leadership of Sir Wilfrid

Laurier, a Roman Catholic French Canadian from Quebec, the party became strongly bi-ethnic and succeeded in gaining power in 1896 and holding it until 1911. World War I and the conscription issue split its two wings apart; most French Canadians and Laurier opposed conscription, while many leading Anglo-Saxons abandoned Laurier and entered a wartime coalition government headed by the Conservatives.

From this crisis the party was rescued by the genius of William Lyon Mackenzie King, who, following his election as leader in 1919, set the Liberals on the path toward a broadly based middle-of-the-road social welfare state. By many artful compromises Mackenzie King kept himself and his party in power almost continuously from 1921 until his retirement in 1948, thereby establishing a personal record as the prime minister in Canada who had held office the longest, 21 years and five months.

He was succeeded by Louis St. Laurent, the second French Canadian (both Liberal) to be prime minister. Though Mr. St. Laurent tried to continue Mr. Mackenzie King's victorious tactic of maintaining the centre-of-the-road policy while moving forward, the process of aging had rendered the Liberal government less flexible and less dynamic, and in 1957, after 22 continuous years of power during which it had won what appeared to be very comfortable electoral pluralities, the party was narrowly defeated by Mr. Diefenbaker's resuscitated Conservatives, who secured 112 seats to the Liberals' 105. Mr. St. Laurent resigned as prime minister and subsequently retired as leader, being replaced by his former secretary of state for external affairs, Mr. Lester B. Pearson. But Mr. Pearson and his Liberals were no match for Prime Minister Diefenbaker's Conservatives who in the 1958 election reduced the number of Liberal seats to 49.

Under Mr. Diefenbaker the Conservatives appeared to take over the mantle of the Liberals as the party of moderate reform and progress appealing to the diverse geographical, economic, religious, and ethnic groups in the country. However, the Liberals regained their ascendancy in 1963, winning a minority government victory that they repeated in 1965, largely by appealing to the middle- and upper-middle class voters in large urban centres.

The new Liberal leader chosen in 1968, Mr. Pierre Elliott Trudeau, was able to enhance this urban, middle-class support, and to win a majority government by combining it with his general personal appeal throughout the country. In 1972 Mr. Trudeau lost his majority and was reduced to leading a minority Liberal government. But in 1974 he regained his majority, winning 141 seats. In 1979 the Liberals lost power to the Conservatives but Mr. Clark's short-lived government lasted only nine months when Mr. Trudeau led the Liberals back to office in 1980 with a majority victory of 147 seats.

Mr. Trudeau retired in 1984 and was replaced by John Turner. Facing ebbing fortunes, the new Liberal leader called an election after being in office only a few months and went down to a severe defeat in September, 1984. The once great Liberal party was reduced to 40 parliamentary seats, the least it had won in any election since 1867. In 1988 the Liberals more than doubled their seats to 83 when John Turner took a strong stand against free trade with the United States, but Mr. Turner was not able to hold out against the pressure for a new leader and in 1990 he was replaced by Jean Chretien.

MINOR PARTIES

Additional proof of the middle-class nature of our politics is that there is no party in Canada on the extreme right wing and the party furthest to the left is virtually extinct. The Communist Party never had much success in Canada. It elected on only one occasion a federal member of Parliament and his career ended ignominiously in prison when he was convicted of conspiracy to turn over government secrets to the Soviet Union in wartime. This assisted in convincing most Canadian voters, if they needed further evidence, that the party was more interested in serving the Kremlin than the Canadian people, and subsequent events such as the Soviet restrictions on Jews and the repression of the Hungarian revolt created serious dissensions within its own ranks. Party membership has fallen to less than a few thousand, and in the federal election of 1988 the Communist party received only 7168 votes out of 13 175 599 cast, or 0.05 percent of the total, which was considerably less than the 275 767 votes won by the farcical Rhinceros party.

Further proof of the need to seek the middle of the road in Canadian politics is presented by the history of minor parties. Canada has had a number of these, but as yet none has been strong enough to form a government at Ottawa. For the most part they have tended to be regional parties representing special interests, in particular western prairie farmers who have been prone to organize their own political movements in protest against the wealthier, more populous "east" (actually central Canada—Ontario and Quebec).

Following the discontents of World War I the farmers created their own Progressive party which, at its zenith in 1921, sent 64 members to the House of Commons , and acquired the balance of power. The party quickly dissolved, however, because of the centrifugal nature of its ultra-democratic organization and its lack of firm leadership. In 1935 the Social Credit party, which espoused unorthodox monetary doctrines and stirred up strong emotional and religious support, elected 17 members to Parliament from Alberta and Saskatchewan, but after reaching a highpoint of 19 in 1957 it was wiped out completely by the Conservative landslide in the following year. It gained great support in Quebec in 1962, electing 26 MPs from that province alone (for a total of 30) but subsequently the Quebec wing split away, electing nine *Ralliement des Créditistes* in 1965 to five for Social Credit. In 1968 the English-speaking Social Credit party was eliminated in Parliament, winning no seats at all, while the *Créditistes* continued with 14 seats. In 1972 Social Credit won 15, in 1974 only 11, in 1979, 6 and in 1980, 1984 and 1988 none at all. Since the Créditistes did not win any seats at all after 1968, it would appear that both wings of the party are dead.

Other small factional parties have developed, however, some speaking for western grievances, such as the Reform party, and others for particular interests, like the Green party, the Confederation of Regions party, the Libertarian party, the Christian Heritage party, the Commonwealth party, and the Rhinoceros party. Altogether, in the 1988 election they polled more than half a million votes, but none elected a member of Parliament, except the Reform party in a subsequent by-election.

NEW DEMOCRATS

A party that attempted to fuse the agrarian interests of the west and the labour forces of the east was born during the depression of the 1930s with the cumbersome title of the Co-operative Commonwealth Federation. Dedicated to the principles of democratic socialism, it has tried to become the Canadian equivalent of the British Labour party but it has not had the success of its model. The number of seats it has won has fluctuated widely, from seven in its first trial in 1935 to 28 in 1945 and back to eight in 1958, though throughout the period its share of the popular vote varied between about 8 and 10 percent. After reorganizing itself as the New Democratic Party in 1961, its fortunes improved electorally. It won 22 seats in 1968, 31 in 1972, 16 in 1974, 26 in 1979, 32 in 1980, 30 in 1984, and 43 in 1988.

The dilemma of the CCF–NDP is that it has been squeezed into an almost impossible position left-of-centre in politics in which it can scarcely find sufficient unique ground on which to make a stand. It fears moving left lest it be accused of being communist, which it abhors, and it cannot move right into the mixed field occupied by Conservatives and Liberals without losing the identity it desires as a working-class party. While it is thus stuck on the horns of a dilemma, the Conservatives and Liberals have appropriated many of its social welfare planks. Its chief obstacle is the hard fact of Canadian middle-class democracy. Like all radical and sectional parties, it can consider broadening its appeal only at the risk of losing its claim to existence.

PROVINCES

In the sphere of the provinces, each government, whatever its political stripe, finds that its most fruitful tactic is to set itself up as the defender of provincial rights against the central administration, particularly in the fields of taxation, finance, and resources. This has become so commonplace that some theorists have suggested that the real opposition to the government of the day at Ottawa comes not in the traditional manner from the benches to the left of the Speaker in the House of Commons but from the provincial regimes, whether or not they are of the same political complexion as the federal government. This may or may not be true, but it is undeniable that any provincial administration tends to make much more of an issue out of its wrangles with Ottawa than out of its own party ideology.

Dogma is either ignored or soft-pedalled, and the provincial governments seek to become all things to all people—or at least to all voters. Like federal governments, the provincial administrations move according to the inexorable fundamental law of Canadian politics toward the centre of the road, or perhaps it would be more precise to say they spread themselves all over the road. Whatever the official label of the party, whatever the planks in its platform before election, it tends to become moderate and eclectic when it obtains power.

This has been true of radical parties like the United Farmers, Social Credit, and the CCF, but also of more orthodox parties like the Conservative and Liberal as well. Thus, in Alberta Social Credit, which drew its strength originally from small towns and farmers, became the darling of urban business men, while the socialist CCF–NDP government in Saskatchewan went all out to attain more private investment in its natural resources. In Quebec the Parti Québécois, which came to power pledged to social democratic reform and sovereignty association, moderated its policies in both these respects in its second term in office. At the same time a Conservative government in Ontario bought a huge private oil company in order to give the public a stake in the marketplace, and it also extended full state financing to all levels of Roman Catholic separate schools. The premier responsible for both these acts summed up the philosophy of moderation superbly when he made the definitive pronouncement, "Bland is best."

Thus, party names and credos do not always establish great differences in Canadian politics where the bland lead the blind down the middle of the road.

ANOTHER EXPLANATION— CLASS DIFFERENCES HAVE BEEN OBSCURED

Janine Brodie and Jane Jenson

INTRODUCTION

. . . In Canada, as in other advanced industrial societies, students of political parties have predicted the arrival of the now-familiar electoral division between the "party of the working class" and the other parties. Since the beginning of

From *Crisis, Challenge and Change: Party and Class in Canada*, Toronto, Methuen, 1980. By permission.

this century, a pattern seemed to develop in most liberal democracies—a pattern which has been described as a "democratic translation of the class struggle." Workers seeking redress form the inequalities of capitalism looked to their own political parties, whether labour, socialist or communist parties, for access to and influence in the political process. This history has led to an equation, in some studies of party politics, of class-based voting and "class politics." Canadian electoral politics, however, seem to provide a case of "non-class politics" because a class cleavage is not observed to a great extent in federal elections. Therefore it is often argued that class differences do not exist or are irrelevant for Canadian federal politics and, instead, parties aggregate preferences on other, often more important, issues.

In at least two fundamental respects, this book [*Crisis, Challenge and Change: Party and Class in Canada*] takes issue with these interpretations of the connection between class and party in Canada. First, a particular conception of political parties is used [here], one which sees parties less as aggregators of individual voters' preferences and more as the actual creators of the pattern of those preferences. Moreover, the patterns created are designed to protect and advance the interests of one social class while suppressing those of others. This conception assigns political parties in liberal democracies a crucial role in the definition of what the substance and form of electoral politics will be. They identify which among a broad range of social differences and tensions will be raised and debated in elections, and they nurture and sustain the criteria by which an electorate will divide against itself in a more or less stable system of partisan alignments. Parties are not alone in this process of issue creation and consideration. Other institutions play important roles, but it is parties, as the organizers of elections, which ultimately have the greatest influence on "the definition of politics."

It is in this process of defining the political, that is selecting the issues and social differences which will be recognized in electoral politics, that specific class interests are either advanced and protected or suppressed and rejected in elections. Class conflict and struggle may take on electoral content or it may not, and whether it does depends upon the actions of political parties, both working class and bourgeois parties, as they organize electoral conflict. The dynamic of the situation is one in which parties of the working class attempt to introduce the language and definition of class politics into elections while the parties of the bourgeoisie use their resources to organize partisan politics around other less threatening social differences. Only if the activity of the working class party succeeds would one expect to see the usual pattern of class voting described above. Indeed, it is precisely the extent to which non-class definitions of politics are the basis for discourse between political parties which hinders the recognition of class politics in elections.

Throughout this study of the history of the Canadian federal party system we show how the two major parties in federal politics have, often with the help of the state which they controlled, advanced the interests of Canadian capital by hindering the organization of the subordinate classes—workers, and to some extent farmers—into their own political parties. They have done this by relying on their considerable resources and prestige, the coercive power of the state and repeated use of two related themes or definitions of Canadian politics. The first theme, bicultural politics, has emphasized that Canadian politics is about the reconciliation of the interests and needs of two separate and self-conscious ethnic groups within a single state. The second theme emphasizes the necessity of consensus amid diversity. The consensual view of Canadian politics stresses the irrelevancy and illogic of class conflict in a country rich in resources and opportunities. Both themes, as we shall see, have been used as substitutes for class-based definitions of Canadian politics. Their use has severely restricted the potential of political parties trying to introduce a class cleavage into the federal system of partisan alignments. Working class parties have confronted formidable obstacles and, as a result, both themes have penetrated deep into the country's political consciousness, reinforced as they are in one election after another.

The second theme underlying [our] analysis of the federal party system is the importance of taking into account the historical context of politics. While the dominant definition of politics may be important in forging any particular pattern of partisan relations (whether cultural or class-based), this system of relations, and its definition, is not given once and for all time. With changes in social forces and with the development of new organizers of these social forces, the definition of politics may change. Bourgeois parties are subject to frequently intense pressure to react to new conditions, just as a renewed opportunity for a party of the Left may come into existence under such circumstances. However, the reactions of new circumstances, while the result of real strategic choice by political parties, also reflect the limits set by previous rounds of electoral competition. Political parties undertake electoral politics in a situation where possibilities for change are shaped and limited by history. The interaction between these limits and possibilities is the story of electoral contests.

The implication of these two perspectives is that electoral politics may not exhibit class-based voting, for reasons of party activity and history. However, the absence of class cleavages in electoral politics should *not* be taken to imply that elections are, as institutions, devoid of class content or importance in class struggle. The electoral organization of class relations occurs if the bourgeois parties, for whatever reasons, can successfully maintain an ideological and organizational dominance which defines politics in non-class terms. It is precisely non-class definitions of politics which disorganize the subordinate classes and place some limits on their demands on private capital.

[*Crisis, Challenge and Change: Party and Class in Canada*] argues that the key to understanding Canada's federal party system is an historical examination of the bourgeois parties' management of the tension between capital and the subordinate classes. Throughout Canadian history, workers and farmers have organized, or attempted to organize, an alternative definition of the political into electoral politics. At certain points, their efforts were a threat to the bourgeoisie and their parties. Yet, up until this point, the challenge of the subordinate classes has not been sustained nor has it resulted in a successful left-wing party in federal electoral politics. In the following chapters we will trace how the bicultural and consensual definitions of Canadian politics were forged and how they have been successfully used to divert demands of subordinate classes into other forms so as to obscure class biases in the political project of Canadian Confederation.

PARTIES AND CLASS IN CANADA: TRADITIONAL VIEWS

Canada provides a somewhat perplexing case study of the partisan organization of class relations in liberal democracies. The country has had an advanced capitalist economy since the turn of the century and high levels of industrialization, particularly since the Second World War. Nevertheless, partisan politics are not organized around the class cleavage between workers and owners which is familiar in countries with similar levels of economic development. There is only minimal evidence of this particular type of partisan organization in the federal party system. In addition, the programs and policies of the Liberal and Conservative parties reveal few real and consistent differences in the class interests that they claim to protect or advance. The New Democratic Party, as its left-wing predecessors, enjoys nowhere near a majority of the support of its claimed constituency—the working class. Instead, study after study has documented that the electorate does not divide its support for political parties according to the occupational structure of capitalist economies or even according to the position voters think they occupy in a status ranking. Rather, in election after election, the bourgeois parties, and particularly the usual government party, the Liberals, gain more votes from workers than Canada's self-styled social democratic party, the NDP.

The apparent absence of a class-based electoral cleavage in Canada's federal party system has evoked several explanations. One explanation is that Canadian politics is not and never has been characterized by conflict between classes because there is no societal basis or need for such conflict. It is argued that geographical and economic conditions have permitted population movement and social mobility which have defused potentially divisive economic cleavages. Instead, Canadian society is considered to be a "middle class" society in which material and social benefits are widely shared. This thesis has led to a depiction of politics as non-conflictual, non-ideological and based only on a concern to share an ever-increasing economic pie. The argument is that, since Canadians seem to have more or less equal access to the benefits and products generated by expansive capitalism and since the distribution of such goods is becoming more and more egalitarian, class politics have never been and are not now necessary. Instead, everyone lives a similar (and middle class) life, and political conflict turns around other questions.

The activities of political parties in such a polity are considered to be those of political brokers in elections, aggregating and accommodating a myriad of differing interests in their electoral coalition. The major parties are depicted as generally neutral political organizations which "do not try to exploit such advantages as they enjoy among particular groups in the population to the exclusion of more general appeals to a larger constituency." Rather, the major parties seek victory by forging a winning electoral coalition, which will shift in response to change in interests and demands.

An underlying assumption of the "brokerage model" is that all interests are equally eligible for accommodation by the political parties. If any criteria for inclusion exist, they depend only on the potential contribution that a group interest can make to the coalition. Some factors, such as the number of voters within each group interest, are relevant in determining whether an interest will be accommodated in the coalition, but it is assumed that the rules of coalition-building do not consistently exclude any interest. If a sufficient number of Canadian workers made demands as workers on the party system, then the major parties, presumably, would accommodate their demands in a broader coalition. Since this is rarely the case, Canadian partisan politics is seen to revolve around other cleavages and issues. It is argued that the political parties, acting as brokers, accommodate the major ethnic, religious, regional and lifestyle cleavages and, thereby, maintain stability and continuity under potentially volatile circumstances.

Both the "middle class" thesis of Canadian society and the "brokerage" theory of political parties predict little explicit organization of the electorate around a class cleavage. Nevertheless, numerous studies of Canadian voting behaviour have attempted to uncover and monitor class voting in federal elections. The principal assumption underlying the search for class voting and specifically working class voting is that there is an inevitable and direct relationship between economic and partisan development. Some marxist and sociological analyses assume that, as a country industrializes, working class parties will emerge and a class cleavage, between workers and owners, will necessarily dominate the electoral system. This view of the ultimate organization of class relations in liberal democracies arises both from deterministic marxism and from political sociologists' observations that labour and socialist parties and class-based voting both emerged and endured in the countries which were earliest to industrialize. Thus, it is predicted that, once nations reach a certain stage of industrial development, the workers will virtually automatically organize and vote according to their class interests.

This formulation of the dynamic of politics in liberal democracies has led to a particular description of electoral politics—notably, that voters' political demands, attitudes and behaviour are determined by their class position. It follows from such a descriptive assumption that politics, organized around this class cleavage, will be concerned primarily with questions of the control over production and the distribution of benefits. A further deduction is that this competition between classes will lead to the general partisan organization of the bourgeoisie, and those supporting the interests of the bourgeoisie, into one party and the workers, and those supporting the interests of workers, into another. Partisan competition is thus assumed to develop between those who have, according to the laws of the economy, control over the production process and its profits and those who have, according to the rules of liberal democracy, some ability to control the production process. In other words, there is an expectation that class relations will be organized by political parties drawing support from the two primary classes characteristic of the capitalist mode of production. It is this particular organization of partisan relations which is missing in Canada, and one can conclude that class-based voting is inconsequential in federal politics in Canada. This conclusion has been taken by some authors as empirical support of the "middle class" and "brokerage" views of Canadian politics.

The apparent absence of working class voting, however, should not be taken to mean, as it sometimes has, that *class politics* does not exist and that elections and partisan politics do not organize class relations in a particular way. The deduction that workers will be organized into one party and the bourgeoisie into another is not the only one possible from the initial assumption about the political importance of classes in capitalist democracy. A class-based electoral cleavage has been observed in many countries, but it is not inevitable. In fact, history has not confirmed the inevitability of a worker-owner partisan cleavage in industrialized liberal democracies. The perspective which emerges from an examination of the last one hundred years of capitalism is the following: While capitalism has proceeded in all countries in similar, although not always exactly the same, directions toward centralization, the growth of monopolistically large corporations and an increase of state intervention in the economy, the partisan expression of classes and class conflict have differed in important ways in the several countries. The politics of capitalism can take and has taken quite different forms. The weakness of the "middle class" thesis, the "brokerage" model and these examinations of class voting is that they regard elections almost as if they occur in a vacuum, lacking an historical legacy. Class structure is treated as an independent datum unaffected by political organization and ideology while elections are studied as if conditions confronting parties, politicians and voters are transient and unstructured.

There is, however, another interpretation of the growth and structure of partisanship in Canada. . . . The Liberal and Conservative parties have, as a result of their strategies for electoral politics over the past century, managed to dominate the field of electoral activity.This strategy has deliberately and successfully retarded, but never eliminated, the growth of class-based parties and voting. The partisan and electoral expression of class conflict has been repeatedly avoided, reinterpreted or simply suppressed. "Third parties" have been plagued by organizational difficulties in the face of this dominance and they have been confined to a minor role in federal elections. Nevertheless, this dominance where the potential for periodic outbreaks of class-based partisan protest, either in the form of new parties or mass migrations between parties, is always present. . . .

THE IDEOLOGICAL TRADITION IN CANADIAN POLITICS

William Christian and Colin Campbell

This essay explores the proposition that political parties are as much a product of differences of political principle as of the lust for power, patronage, and other spoils of office. Political ideologies do exist in Canada, and they suffuse the life of our political parties. In our view there are four principal identifiable political ideologies in Canada today: conservatism, liberalism, socialism, and nationalism, which come to us from our European parent societies. We will not consider nationalism separately but in the context of the major political parties discussed below.

Conservatism is the product of the dominant European political orientation of the sixteenth and seventeenth centuries, rooted in the classical and medieval notions of society as an organic whole arranged in a hierarchy of function and power. Those possessed of high rank enjoyed privileges of wealth and function; the place of those of low rank was to obey their superiors. The corollary of power, however, was duty; the privileged were bound to exercise their power for the general welfare and not out of mere self-interest. In such a properly ordered society the ruled gained from the wisdom and experience of the rulers, and to the rulers was entrusted the welfare of the ruled. There was, therefore, a strong collectivist element, an emphasis on the community as a whole and its welfare, and an assumption that the organized political power of the community was to be used for the common good, if necessary overriding individual goods.

By the eighteenth century this type of conservatism was challenged by the growth of liberalism. Liberalism was, and is, the philosophy *par excellence* of individualism, and its emphasis on the pursuit of individual liberty directly challenged the central collectivist and hierarchical tenets of conservatism.

Prepared in June, 1990 for this edition by the authors, who have incorporated some material that was published originally in their chapter in A. Gagnon and B. Tanguay, (eds.), *Canadian Parties in Transition: Discourse/Organization/Representation*, Toronto, Nelson, 1989, A Division of Thomson Canada Limited. Professor Christian is a member of the Department of Political Studies, University of Guelph, and Mr. Campbell is a Barrister and Solicitor of the Ontario Bar. By permission.

Liberalism consistently opposed restrictions on individual liberty imposed by the pursuit of the collective good, whether in the economic, religious, or strictly political spheres. The liberal fiction of the social contract, of society as a product of the decision of discrete individuals to associate voluntarily, central to John Locke's thought, typified this individualist approach. Tolerance in religious matters, limited government, and free-market economics were its more practical fruits.

Liberalism was also potentially egalitarian. It assumed that all individuals were essentially the same. Liberalism did not produce equality of condition in practice, or of wealth and power, as opposed to equality of status because economic liberty and the free market produced economic inequality.

The social dislocation caused by liberal *laissez-faire* economics—the view that the state should be only minimally involved in the economy—and the Industrial Revolution produced not only resistance from collectivist conservatives but a new challenge in the form of socialism. In the nineteenth century liberalism was challenged on the basis that it not only destroyed established communities and caused social breakdown, but it did not fulfil its inherent promise of equality. Socialists reverted to the conservative idea of collectivism and accepted the conservative premise that the fundamental units of society were groups, not individuals. Socialism defined these groups in terms of their relationship to economic processes, such as industrial workers, rather than to traditional groups or residents of a particular area. Society would use its collective power to promote real equality—equality of condition—and not mere equality of status, or even of opportunity. This use of collective power might restrict the liberty of individuals, but it would promote the real equality of all workers of society and the greater good of society as a whole. Socialism thus combined the collectivism of conservatism and the potential egalitarianism of liberalism.

These different ways of analyzing political and social affairs continued to co-exist in Europe into the twentieth century. In Canada, as Gad Horowitz's seminal work demonstrates, conservative ideas survived in the pre-Enlightenment feudal worldview of French Canadians, the toryism of Loyalist Americans, and Tory assumptions held by many nineteenth century British immigrants. However, because of the attraction of liberalism and the example of the United States, the liberal outlook of many immigrants and the liberal assumptions shared to a degree by virtually all Canadians liberalism became the dominant political ideology, but never the exclusive political ideology. The survival of conservatism also produced the basis for the development of socialism. When Canadians faced the shortcomings of liberal economic policies, in the Great Depression of the 1930s, for example, they had collectivist tools at hand to fashion an alternative view.

Liberalism also developed two different branches. One variant that focuses on the "negative" aspect of removing external restrictions on individual liberty has tended in practice to become identified with the defence of property rights, and we therefore call it business liberalism. On the other hand what we call welfare liberalism places more importance on the "positive" aspect of achieving individual "human" rights and potential more than on the removal of restrictions alone. Consequently, it has been ready to restrict certain economic rights in order to give content and reality to the otherwise empty "freedom" of the poor and disadvantaged. We will examine below the way in which these ideologies have influenced and continue to shape our ideologies.

CANADIAN LIBERALISM

Before Mackenzie King became leader of the Liberals in 1919, the party embodied the "negative," or business liberalism, of classical doctrine. King persuaded the party to commit itself to welfare liberalism. In 1919 the party adopted the goal of eventually achieving a welfare state, including medicare, old age pensions, and unemployment insurance. It saw positive government action in these areas as central to giving real content to individual liberty in the modern industrial world.

King's successors in the Liberal leadership, Louis St. Laurent and Lester Pearson, continued the blend of business and welfare liberalism which King established. As circumstances changed, the policy blend dictated by this ideological orientation necessarily shifted. The experience during the Second World War of massive government intervention in the economy, together with the interventionist economic theories of John Maynard Keynes, convinced the Liberal leadership that welfare liberalism now demanded significantly greater federal government intervention in managing the economy to provide full employment, economic growth, and social welfare policies.

During the 1940s and the 1950s the Liberal party thus became the champion of a strong central government. This fitted well with Pierre Trudeau's subsequent unrelenting opposition to Quebec nationalism and separatism, which in turn reflected his intense commitment to classical liberal individualism. As *Towards a Just Society: The Trudeau Years*, edited by Trudeau and Tom Axworthy and published in 1990, said clearly, "Make no mistake, we were an ideological government—ideological in the sense that we were motivated by an overarching framework of purpose. That framework was grounded in the supreme importance we attached to the dignity and rights of individual human beings."

During his regime Trudeau offered bilingualism policies designed to protect the rights of individual French Canadians to use their language throughout Canada, rather than to protect the collective rights of French Canadians, as advocated by the Parti Québécois and Liberal government of Quebec. The logic of this individualist position also led Trudeau to avoid the reality of other regional identities in Canada, such as those of the West or the Atlantic provinces. The other monument to Trudeau's liberal individualism is the Charter of Rights and Freedoms. Perhaps the most surprising aspect of the Liberal party under Trudeau, however, was its drift toward more interventionist and nationalist economic and cultural policies. Subsequent events in the 1980s challenged, but did not displace, the predominance of welfare liberalism and the party's commitment to strong central government and opposition to Quebec nationalism.

John Turner's victory in the 1984 Liberal leadership campaign at first appeared to signal a resurgence of business liberalism. In the subsequent 1984 election campaign, however, he was forced to downplay this stance and to re-emphasize the old welfare liberal policies in the face of what proved to be a disastrous electoral defeat.

The crushing Liberal defeat in the 1984 election and constant attacks on Turner's leadership effectively countered any inclination he may have had to realign the party's ideological direction. Turner's position as leader was not made easier by the emergence of two overriding issues, both of which spanned the fault lines in the Liberal ideological mixture of business and welfare liberalism: the Meech Lake Accord and the Free Trade Agreement.

MEECH LAKE

The Meech Lake Accord directly challenged the individualist and anti-collectivist assumptions that Trudeau so rigorously applied by suggesting that a particular collectivity, the French-Canadian society within Canada, had certain rights that could override individual rights in some circumstances. Trudeau's own rejection of the Accord was shared by a significant group within the Liberal party—including liberal academics, women's and native groups concerned that the impact of the Charter would be lessened in their cases, and ethnic groups disappointed by the omission of their collective rights. Opponents of the Accord also objected to the limitation on the ability of the federal government to intervene in certain areas of social policy by means of shared-cost programs.

Controversy over Meech Lake arose again with renewed vigour after the 1988 election when the Supreme Court of Canada struck down provisions of Quebec's Charter of the French Language dealing with the use of English in commercial signs. The response of the Bourassa government was to enact new legislation invoking the "notwithstanding" clause in section 33 of the Charter. In turn, this gave Premier Filmon of Manitoba the opportunity to withdraw his support from the Accord, and later provoked many of the smaller Ontario municipalities to adopt "English-only" resolutions.

FREE TRADE

The Free Trade Agreement was similarly troubling for the Liberals. The FTA was clearly responsive to demands of the Canadian business community for market-based economic policies, and it was no surprise that it received overwhelming support from this group. Business opposition, in general, came only from groups such as grape growers and wine producers who were affected adversely by the Agreement, and was not based on broad questions of principle. The FTA reflected the growing strength of business liberalism in the Progressive Conservative party and appealed equally to the business liberals in the Liberal party.

The dominant welfare-liberal wing of the party viewed the FTA very differently. Though they could accept the notion that freer trade would remove external restraints from individual economic liberty and were happy that it connoted internationalism and the rejection of national particularity, Liberals opposed to the FTA, such as John Turner, generally criticized the bilateral nature of the agreement as too favourable to the U.S.A.

They argued that the provisions of the FTA that dealt with energy policy and pricing and with restrictions on United States' investment in Canada directly limited the federal government's ability to act in these areas. Furthermore, in an indirect way closer integration of the Canadian and American economies and more unrestricted competition from American goods and services would create strong pressures to make Canadian social policies, such as medicare, unemployment insurance, welfare and environmental protection, conform to American standards, which were thought to be lower. Such Canadian social policies might be viewed either as forms of subsidies, which would entitle the United States to take countervailing action, or would be attacked by Canadian business as a threat to its ability to compete. By this argument under free trade Canadian and American businesses would be enabled to compete on a "level playing field," but the costs of supporting Canadian business would reduce benefits, thereby threatening Canadian identity.

Turner's view clearly reflected the perception of Canadian welfare liberals (among others) that the United States was a society dominated by business liberalism. In a wider sense the FTA was but one product of the tendency of the Mulroney government to allow market forces a freer reign in Canadian society. This was fully consistent with the dominant business liberalism of the Mulroney government and clearly was ideologically motivated. However, it clashed directly with the growing interventionist tendencies in the Liberal party, which were justified on the basis of the welfare-liberal goal of maximizing the positive liberty of individual Canadians. Fears that the agreement would ultimately force a scaling down of the Canadian social welfare system not only stirred nationalist objections among Liberals, but aroused complaints from those who had long supported the development of such programs. While business and welfare liberals clashed on other fronts in the 1988 election campaign, the free trade issue became the main symbol of ideological conflict.

Many advocates of welfare liberalism also connected the Meech Lake Accord with this assault on welfare-liberal goals. This division, however, was not so clear; the Accord did not place any obstacles in the way of provincial government pursuing such policies. (The Accord was acceptable to welfare liberals in Quebec who were also attracted to French-Canadian nationalism.) Conversely, opposition to the Accord on the basis of a rejection of French-Canadian nationalism was not incompatible with business liberal views.

By relegating business liberalism to a secondary position in the party at the same time as business liberal support was increasing in the Conservative party, the Liberals contributed to a growing polarization in Liberal and Conservative support and reduced the differences between the Liberal party and the New Democrats. Indeed, on many issues, although many leading figures in both parties might disagree with this interpretation, we would argue that the Liberals and the New Democrats have become, personalities aside, indistinguishable. This development is not surprising given the extent to which welfare liberalism predominates in both parties. Paradoxically, the description of Liberals and Conservatives as the Tweedledum and Tweedledee of Canadian politics, so long loved and used by New Democrats, may have become as true of the Liberals and New Democrats as of the Liberals and Conservatives.

The ideological battles in the Liberal party continued into the 1990 leadership contest. Jean Chrétien, the eventual winner, represented the mainline welfare liberalism of the party and called for significant changes to the Meech Lake Accord, reflecting the continuing drift away from the Turner-led initial support of the party for the Accord, and the attack on it led in spirit by Pierre Trudeau. However, as a former finance minister and corporate lawyer, Chrétien also had support from the business community. If he was seen to be on the progressive wing of the Liberal party, he was not dangerously so. It remains to be seen whether he will be able to maintain this balancing act where his predecessor failed. Paul Martin Jr., his major opponent and runner-up, supported Meech Lake and drew on his business experience to appeal for support from the business elements to the party. The failure of the Accord to be ratified, which coincided more or less with the Liberal leadership convention in June of 1990, did not help his bid for the leadership. Martin's defeat also seemed likely to ensure that the ideological polarization between the Liberals and Conservatives, which became so apparent in the 1980s, would continue into the 1990s, though the divisions are unlikely to be as acute as they were during the 1988 election.

CANADIAN CONSERVATISM

Like the Liberals, the other main Canadian political parties have always aimed at attracting a wide ideological coalition. Sir John A. Macdonald expressed this goal when he sought to "enlarge the bounds of our party so as to embrace every person desirous of being counted a progressive Conservative."

The quest to combine the conservative *Bleu* tradition of Quebec, the Tory democracy of Victorian British immigrants, and the pervasive liberalism of Canadian society continued in the Conservative party throughout the late nineteenth and early twentieth centuries by Macdonald's successors, Borden and Meighen.

Toryism by this point was not the elite doctrine of the Family Compact. Under Macdonald and his successors it had been converted into democratic toryism. As the right to vote spread, toryism increasingly accepted the legitimacy of working-class participation in politics and, more importantly, acknowledged the state's responsibility to the victims of urbanization and industrialization.

This aspect of Canadian conservatism went into eclipse for a quarter of a century until it was rescued by John Diefenbaker's selection (on his third attempt) as party leader in 1956. Diefenbaker settled the present character of the Progressive Conservative party. He wrote:

> In discussing our 1957 election platform, I have left until last our program of social justice. This was an essential part of my national vision. To me, government not only had to be of and by the people, but most positively for the people. Unless government concerned itself with the problems of the individual working man and farmer, unless government was cognizant of the problems of the small businessman and not just the corporate giants, unless government acted in the interests of our senior citizens, our veterans, our blind and disabled, unless government sought a basic equality of citizenship, or opportunity, and of well-being for all our people, then government had lost sight of its true purpose.

It was this kind of conservatism that "the Chief" thought would wrest the party out of the hands of the Bay Street and rue St. Jacques crowd. He was only partly successful. Although he acknowledged the influential business liberals who had been dominant in the party under George Drew, and occasionally catered to them, they eventually brought him and the whole government to grief when senior Tory ministers such as Harkness, Hees, and others revolted against Diefenbaker's leadership in 1963. Yet for all his obvious failings Diefenbaker managed to impose his stamp on the party. His commitment to aiding the less fortunate has been shared by all his successors, including Robert Stanfield, a Nova Scotian who was perhaps the most articulate defender of democratic toryism in Canadian politics.

Stanfields' sense of the importance of groups got him into trouble from the beginning. His support for the *deux nations* concept of Canada (i.e., that Canada was composed of two founding peoples) brought Diefenbaker angrily back into the 1967 leadership race. Later, during the 1974 election campaign, Stanfield argued for wage and price controls, a policy that proved to be an electoral liability.

After his party's defeat Stanfield announced his intention to resign before the next election, and as part of his contribution to the party's ideological future, he began a discussion within the caucus on where the party stood. In his view Canadian conservatism favoured individual freedom, tempered by the belief that "a decent, civilized life required a framework of order." This order was not to be taken for granted but was, rather, "quite rare in the world and therefore quite precious." [See Stanfield article, *infra*.]

The need to preserve order "favoured strong and effective government," necessary, among other reasons, "to protect the weak against the excesses of private enterprise and greed." However, as a general rule Stanfield warned about the dangers of state activism. Limited government held a special appeal for three reasons: first, decentralization of power limits the possibility of revolution; second, government is unlikely to accomplish much good because of limitations imposed by the inherent imperfections of human beings; and third, society as a whole is difficult to understand and, therefore, "success in planning the lives of other people or the life of the nation is likely to be limited."

Stanfield's successor, Joe Clark, was a man little known to the general public but was generally thought of as being on the left, or red Tory, wing of the party. Like his predecessor, Clark opposed the party's adoption of a strikingly different set of values. Although Clark led his party to a minority victory in the 1979 election, a series of tactical and other errors defeated his government before he had an opportunity to tackle the major economic and social problems that would have revealed the character of his regime. The decision to privatize Petro-Canada, the most important of his brief span in office, did not receive broad support from his cabinet colleagues and proved a grave liability in the subsequent election.

Although some Conservatives believed Clark should be replaced because he could not win an election against John Turner, others preferred Brian Mulroney because they felt that he represented a clear ideological alternative. Most of the 20 or so MPs who supported Mulroney, such as Sinclair Stevens and Otto Jelinek, were sure that he would take the party in a direction different from Clark's.

In foreign policy Mulroney's supporters hoped to bring Canada closer to the United States. Domestically, they sought to emulate American deregulation of business and at the same time decrease the federal deficit and the size of the civil service. To accomplish these aims, they were also willing (some were eager) to accept a reduction in social welfare programs. If nothing else they were prepared to abandon the principle of universality—only those with proven need would be recipients of governmental transfer payments.

Mulroney's politics turned out to be less clear-cut. Although he had prospered as a business man, his roots were in small-town Quebec, and he thought of himself as the electrician's son who had made good as a negotiator. As a labour lawyer he had made his reputation on the Cliche Commission, which had inquired into the jungle of the Quebec construction industry, and he had acted as a conciliator with the unions when he was president of Iron Ore of Canada.

In the 1984 election campaign he spoke of the "commitment of our party to fundamental fairness and justice" and also of the need for a government "which works with the people to build a society of dignity and compassion, a community where the strong help the weak and the fortunate help the disadvantaged."

Although there was some controversy and confusion in the first year of his government as to where Mulroney stood on these promises, his decision to overrule his finance minister on the de-indexing of Old Age Security payments was completely in harmony with his previous stances. In the important areas of human rights, the role of the social welfare state, and language there is little to distinguish the record of Mulroney from his immediate predecessors in the party.

In economic policy the record of the government has been more distinctive. In attempting to reduce the presence of government in the economy, the Mulroney government has followed, somewhat loosely, the lead of Prime Minister Margaret Thatcher's government in the United Kingdom. It has placed greater emphasis on the role of the private sector in job creation and sought to proceed with deregulation and privatization. It sold government enterprises such as TeleGlobe Canada, floated shares in Air Canada, and announced its intention to privatize Petro-Canada. By introducing income tax reform and a goods and services tax, it has shifted taxes to consumption rather than income.

However, the Conservative government's greatest initiative was the Free Trade Agreement with the United States. As we suggested earlier, the debate in the 1988 election was as clearly ideological as any election in the previous 35 years. From a business-liberal viewpoint, free trade represented a lessening of state involvement in the economy since the government no longer would try to promote and protect certain sectors of the economy through differential tariff rates. The government also forswore the possibility of recreating a national energy policy in the Liberal style.

CANADIAN SOCIALISM

Canadian socialism is Canadian conservatism's younger cousin. We explained earlier that European socialism evolved from toryism, with which it shared a belief in the importance of collectivism, but in contrast to which it placed a high value on social equality.

It would be fair to say that before World War I socialism had met little success in Canada. Even the attempts to form socialist trade unions in the 1880s failed, and the consequences of its lack of success were important for future development of the Canadian ideological system.

For the most part Canadian trade unions followed the lead of the American union leader, Samuel Gompers. A proponent of labourism, Gompers believed that the proper role of a trade union was to seek higher pay, better working conditions, greater security of employment, and other such benefits for its workers. In political action it should support individual candidates who were "friends of labour," no matter what their party, rather than forming its own labour party. In large part because of Gompers' philosophy Canadian workers were sympathetic to Macdonald's Conservatives in the nineteenth century, but they were slowly won over to the Liberals under Laurier and King.

The Bolshevik Revolution of 1917 marked a major watershed for Canadian socialism. When Sir Robert Borden's Unionist government crushed the Winnipeg General Strike of 1919, many Canadian socialists decided that the revolutionary path to a better world was unlikely in a Canadian context, and they turned to the social gospel movement and Christian socialism, which emphasized peaceful persuasion and the gradual achievement of power by parliamentary means. The two MPs who were elected to represent these views in the 1920s were a brilliant parliamentary success, particularly the former Methodist minister, J.S. Woodsworth. In 1932 in Calgary, where the Co-operative Commonwealth Federation (CCF) was founded, and the next year in Regina, where the movement's celebrated Manifesto was adopted, he played a major role in bringing together the farmers' movements and the socialists to form a democratic socialist party which he led and which has now lasted for over half a century.

Under M.J. Coldwell's leadership in the 1940s and 1950s the CCF slowly moved away from its sincere but cautious form of socialism. Many of its founding members, the farmers and trade unionists, were not *bona fide* socialists, but welfare liberals. Both socialists and welfare liberals could agree on the attractiveness of the active, interventionist state, with its assaults on the large corporations, its redistributory effects, and its use of economic and fiscal policy to control the direction of the economy while disagreeing on ends. The socialists wanted the state to move toward equality of condition; the welfare liberals drew back as the state's infringement on individual liberty became excessive.

The modified ideological position did not yield immediate electoral benefits. After the grave electoral setback in the Diefenbaker landslide of 1958, the CCF felt that it was now time to reach out and establish a closer relationship with labour. The Canadian Labour Congress (CLC) had been formed in 1956 by the amalgamation of the two leading trade union groups in Canada. The new body was prepared to abandon the traditional adherence to Gomperism. The outcome was the founding of the New Democratic Party in 1961.

In the three decades of its existence the new party has alternately encouraged and disappointed its partisans. It has held the balance of power in Parliament five times since its foundation, but it has never come close to overtaking either of the major parties, even as Official Opposition. It regularly elects MPs from British Columbia, Saskatchewan, Manitoba, and Ontario, where it has its largest numbers of voters but not seats. Neither it nor its predecessor has had much appeal in the Atlantic region, and it was not until 1990 that it elected its first MP from Quebec.

The NDP's most recent leaders, David Lewis and Ed Broadbent, did not succeed in making the expected breakthrough. After a poor showing in the 1979 election, Broadbent, in concert with Bob Rae, subsequently provincial leader of the Ontario NDP, plotted a strategy designed to neutralize the party's radical image. Broadbent's target was welfare liberals who normally supported the Liberal party. His hope was that they would find a centrist NDP more attractive than a business-oriented Liberal party. Consequently, Broadbent soft-pedalled public references to democratic socialism and sought, instead, to portray New Democrats as the representatives of decent, caring Canadians, committed to the welfare state and the host of established programs that led most Canadians to favour the continuation of welfare state capitalism.

Although the tactic failed in the short run, the enormous pressure Broadbent put on Turner during the 1984 campaign contributed substantially to the final outcome, at which point the Liberals had only ten MPs more than the NDP. The NDP were finally in a position to present themselves as a major party, a serious alternative to the older parties. Reflecting the welfare liberalism dominant in the NDP, Broadbent made it clear that it was equality of opportunity that he supported and not the traditional socialist goal of equality of condition:

> Anyone is naive if he or she argues at some time that there will be a complete equality in incomes. In other circumstances, I would be prepared to offer a moral argument as to why that fact is not even desirable.

The failure of the party to make significant progress in 1988 led to doubts about the strategy. As in 1975 there were those in the NDP who thought that the party was betraying its radical heritage in seeking the centre ground and electoral success.

When the NDP met in Winnipeg in December 1989 to choose a successor to Ed Broadbent, it was paying testimony to its CCF heritage. However, it was not certain in which direction it wanted to go. One choice was former NDP premier of British Columbia, Dave Barrett. He argued that the party would do well to remember its roots in the Western protest movements and its ties with labour, and cease chasing the chimera of immediate national political success. This strategy would necessitate the abandonment of hopes in Quebec in the near future. Against this view economist and federal MP Steven Langdon urged the party to remember its radical origins and to restate in an imaginative way how it would promote great social equality and a more democratic society.

The eventual winner, Audrey McLaughlin, was a relative newcomer to electoral politics. She emerged as a compromise candidate, but it was not clear whether the party chose her because its members could not decide between the rival visions of the other two main contenders. As the first woman to lead a major Canadian national political party, and a single mother, she could be seen to represent part of the so-called Rainbow Coalition of the underprivileged, to whom many in the NDP wanted to open their party. On the other hand she had enough support from labour to satisfy those who saw the maintenance of these ties as essential to the NDP's long-term success. However, it was not clear then or later in what direction she wanted to take the party. Thus, she leaves the party vulnerable to an assault on its welfare liberal support from a renewed Liberal party under the direction of Jean Chrétien.

CONSERVATIVE PRINCIPLES AND PHILOSOPHY

Robert L. Stanfield

PARTIES ARE CONCILIATORS

. . . First, I would like to make a few comments on the role of political parties such as ours in Canada. Not only is it unnecessary for political parties to disagree about everything but some acceptance of common ground among the major parties is essential to an effective and stable democracy. For example, it is important to stability that all major parties agree on such matters as parliamentary responsible government and major aspects of our constitution.

I would like to emphasize too that in the British tradition political parties are not doctrinaire . . . In our parliamentary tradition, which is substantially the British tradition, parties have a unifying role to play. . . . A truly national political party has a continuing role to try to pull things together: achieve a consensus, resolve conflicts, strengthen the fabric of society and work towards a felling of harmony in the country. Success in this role is, I suggest, essential if a party is to maintain a strong position in this country. This role of a national political party, and success in this role, are particularly important in countries as vast and diverse as Canada and the United States.

It is partly because of this that I do not favour the [Senator Ernest] Manning thesis which urges polarization of political viewpoints in this country. In Canada, a party such as ours has a harmonizing role to play, both horizontally in terms of resolving conflicts between regions, and vertically in terms of resolving conflicts between Canadians in different walks of life. It is not a matter of a national party being all things to all people—this would never work. But a national party should appeal to all parts of the country and to Canadians in all walks of life, if it is to serve this essential role, and if it is to remain strong.

CONSERVATIVES STRESS ORDER

Turning now to the consideration of the Conservative Party as such, I would not wish to exaggerate the concern of British Conservatives through the years with principles or theory. After all, they were practising politicians for the most part, pragmatists dealing with problems, and of course, politicians seeking success. There are, however, some threads we can follow through the years. I am, of course, not suggesting that we in Canada should follow British principles or practices slavishly. Nor would I argue that our party in Canada

From a working paper presented to the federal Caucus of the Progressive Conservative Party by the then National Leader, November, 14, 1974. By permission.

has followed a consistent pattern. I believe it has frequently wandered far from the conservative tradition that I believe to be valuable, and conservative principles I accept.

British Conservative thinkers traditionally stressed the importance of order, not merely "law and order," but social order. This does not mean that they were opposed to freedom for the individual; far from it. They believe that a decent civilized life requires a framework of order.

Conservatives did not take that kind of order for granted. It seemed to them quite rare in the world and therefore quite precious. This is still the case. Conservatives attached importance to the economy and to enterprise and to property, but private enterprise was not the central principle of traditional British conservatism. Indeed the supreme importance of private enterprise and the undesirablity of government initiative and interference was Liberal nineteenth century doctrine. It was inherited from Adam Smith and was given its boldest political statement by such Liberals as Cobden and Bright. It was they who preached the doctrine of the unseen hand with practically no reservation.

RESTRICTIONS ON PRIVATE ENTERPRISE AND GOVERNMENT

The Conservative concept of order encouraged Conservative governments to impose restrictions on private enterprise where this was considered desirable. We all studied William Wilberforce and his factory legislation when we were in school. These were logical measures for Conservatives to adopt; to protect the weak against the excesses of private enterprise and greed. That is good traditional conservatism, fully consistent with traditional conservative principles. It is also good Conservatism not to push regulation too far—to undermine self-reliance.

Because of the central importance Conservatives attached to the concept of order they naturally favoured strong and effective government, but on the other hand they saw a limited or restricted role for government for several reasons. Because a highly centralized government is quite susceptible to arbitrary exercise of power and also to attack and revolution, Conservatives instinctively favoured a decentralization of power. National government had to be able to act in the national interest, but there had to be countervailing centres of power and influence. In the past, these might consist of church or the landed gentry or some other institution. Today in Canada, the provinces, trade unions, farm organizations, trade associations and the press would serve as examples. . . .

MAN AND THE WORLD IMPERFECT

Another reason why Conservatives traditionally saw a limited role for government was because Conservatives were far from being Utopians. They adopted basically a Judeo-Christian view of the world. . . . They certainly saw the world as a very imperfect place, capable of only limited improvement; and man as an imperfect being. They saw evil as an ongoing force that would always be present in changing form. It would therefore not have surprised Edmund Burke that economic growth, and government policies associated with it, have created problems almost as severe as those that economic growth and government policies were supposed to overcome.

A third reason for Conservatives taking a limited view of the role of government was that men such as Edmund Burke regarded man's intelligence as quite limited. Burke was very much impressed by how little man understood what was going on around him. . . .

Burke questioned whether any one generation really had the intelligence to understand fully the reasons for existing institutions or to pass judgement on those institutions which were the product of the ages. Burke pushed this idea much too far, but Conservatives have traditionally recognized how limited human intelligence really is, and consequently have recognized that success in planning the lives of other people or the life of the nation is likely to be limited. Neither government nor its bureaucracy is as wise as it is apt to be believed. Humility is a valuable strain in Conservatism, provided it does not become an excuse for resisting change, accepting injustice or supporting vested interests. . . .

THE NATIONAL VIEW

There is another important strain to traditional Conservatism. Conservatism is national in scope and purpose. This implies a strong feeling for the country, its institutions and its symbols; but also a feeling for all the country and for all the people in the country. The Conservative Party serves the whole country and all the people, not simply part of the country and certain categories of people. . . .

I suggest that it is in the Conservative tradition to expand the concept of order and give it a fully contemporary meaning. The concept of order always included some concept of security for the unfortunate, although the actual program may have been quite inadequate by our present-day standards.

The concept of order certainly includes the preservation of our environment. And the concept of order, linked to Conservative concern for the country as a whole, certainly includes concern about poverty.

SOCIAL GOALS

For a Conservative in the Conservative tradition which I have described, there is much more to national life than simply increasing the size of the gross national product. A Conservative naturally regards a healthy economy as of great importance, but increasing the size of the gross national product is not in itself a sufficient goal for a civilized nation, according to a Conservative. A healthy economy is obviously important, but a Conservative will be concerned about the effects of economic growth—what this does to our environment, what kind of living conditions it creates, what is its effect on the countryside, what is its effect on our cities; whether all parts of the nation benefit or only some parts of the nation, and whether a greater feeling of justice and fairness and self-fulfilment result from this growth, thereby strengthening the social order and improving the quality of national life.

. . . Any particular economic dogma is not a principle of our party, fond as most Conservatives may be of that particular dogma at any particular time.

At any given time our party is likely to contain those whose natural bent is reform and those whose natural bent is to stand pat or even to try to turn the clock back a bit. I think it is fair to say that Conservative statesmen we respect most were innovators. They did not change Conservative principles, but within those principles they faced and met the challenges of their time.

Traditional Liberalism started with the individual, emphasizing liberty of the individual and calling for a minimum of government interference with the individual. Conservatives, on the other hand, emphasized the nation, society, stability and order.

In this century, Liberals have resorted to the use of government more and more. Today big government and Liberalism are synonymous in Canada. . . .

Some Conservatives want to move to the old individualistic position of nineteenth century Liberalism—enshrining private enterprise as the most fundamental principle of our party, and condemning all government interference. The Conservative tradition has been to interfere only where necessary, but to interfere where necessary to achieve social and national objectives. Conservatives favour incentives, where appropriate, rather than the big stick.

Of course, it has always been and remains important to Conservatives to encourage individual self-reliance; and certainly red tape and regulation have today gone too far, especially in the case of small business. Self-reliance and enterprise should be encouraged, but Conservatism does not place private enterprise in a central position around which everything else revolves.

Conservatism recognized the responsibility of government to restrain or influence individual action where this was in the interests of society. Whether a government should or should not intervene was always a question of judgement, of course, but the Conservative tradition recognized the role of government as the regulator of individual conduct in the interests of society. . . .

REFORM AND JUSTICE

. . . I would not suggest that Conservatives have tried or would try to build a radically different society from that which they have known. But to reform and adapt existing institutions to meet changing conditions, and to work towards a more just and therefore a truly more stable society—this I suggest is in the best Conservative tradition. . . .

This is a period when true Conservative principles of order and stability should be most appealing. Principles of conservation and preservation are also high in the minds of many Canadians today, and a Conservative can very legitimately—and on sound historical ground—associate with these. Again I emphasize that these kinds of bedrock principles are national in scope and reflect an overriding concern for society at large. . . .

Enterprise and initiative are obviously important; but will emphasis upon individual rights solve the great problems of the day: I mean the maintenance of acceptable stability—which includes price stability, acceptable employment, and an acceptable distribution of income? Would we achieve these goals today by a simple reliance on the free market, if we could achieve a free market?

It would certainly be appropriate for a Conservative to suggest that we must achieve some kind of order if we are to avoid chaos; an order which is stable, but not static; an order therefore which is reasonably acceptable and which among other things provides a framework in which enterprise can flourish. That would be in the Conservative tradition. . . .

A DEFINITION OF LIBERALISM

Robert F. Nixon

● ● ● The root of the liberal philosophy remains today as it has always been—a passionate dedication to the freedom of the individual. But the liberal does much more than espouse this freedom: he strives continually to expand the amount of individual freedom in society. In other words, he works to liberate as many individuals from the confining influences of poverty, ignorance, background, geography and nature. The liberal, therefore, is a *liberator* (the very word comes from the Latin verb to liberate); he is not the liberated person. Hence the ever-present concern with reform, human betterment and progress in the hearts of liberals everywhere. Almost instinctively the liberal approaches issues and problems with the questions, What are the weak points of this or that program? How can we improve the present situation? What is the best machinery to utilize? The conservative, as I understand, instinctively reacts by defending the status quo, demanding clear proof of the need for

From Robert F. Nixon, ed., *The Guelph Papers*, Toronto, Peter Martin Associates, 1970. By permission. The Hon. Robert F. Nixon was formerly the Leader of the Ontario Liberal Party, Treasurer of Ontario, 1985–1990, and Interim Leader, 1990.

change and then reforming to the smallest degree necessary to remedy the problem.

This, then, is the essence of liberalism—the perpetual pressing forward to a freer society where individuals can develop to their full potential, a continual removing of barriers blocking the avenues of individual progress. The reason for this passion is the realization that the best society can be achieved only through the individual efforts of all our people. The task of the liberal is to fight for this elusive goal—a society where every individual will have an equal opportunity to learn, to work, to strive, to grow, to achieve, and to succeed. This does not mean, of course, that every individual will be equal or will secure an equal share of the fruits of society. People have always been, and will continue to be, unequal in ability and diligence. Their rewards will therefore differ and should differ—but until each person has an equal opportunity to succeed, our society will have need of liberals.

From what I gather, conservatism prizes freedom of the individual as well as does liberalism. My impression, however, is that conservatives are more concerned with *potential freedom* than with the *real freedom* which liberals strive towards. One cannot have real freedom unless the conditions within society permit each individual actually to exercise his freedom. The difference is between *freedom in theory* and *freedom in fact*. It is the latter which liberals wish to create. For example, a man has the freedom to choose a doctor if he is ill and to select a lawyer if he is in trouble. But this is only a theoretical freedom if he has no money to pay the doctor or lawyer. Potentially anyone can become the prime minister of Canada, or the president of the CBC, the CNR, GM or GE, but liberals know that this is not a real freedom unless a person has been properly educated and has the right family background. Liberals want to change this potential freedom into real freedom and to do this they wish to liberate people from their ignorance by providing equal educational opportunity.

To provide this atmosphere of freedom, liberals are prepared to utilize government actively. They view government as an instrument to be used for human betterment. It is not the enemy of the people but their servant, and they should use it willingly. Conservatives tend to avoid governmental action, preferring solutions to problems by non-governmental intervention. Conservatives seem to prefer reluctant government, whereas liberals advocate more involved government.

Liberals are more prepared to sacrifice economic freedoms to provide wider personal freedom. Property rights, while they are respected by liberals, are revered by conservatives. . . . Liberals believe that often those who cry out for economic freedom are really only disguising their lack of devotion to individual freedom. To liberals, where the two conflict the choice is easy. Economic freedom yields to the superior claim of individual freedom. ● ● ●

CANADIAN SOCIALISM: "THE SOCIETY OF FRIENDS"

Desmond Morton

Currently more than one Canadian voter in five supports Canada's New Democratic Party (NDP). In 1990 New Democrats formed the government in Ontario and the Yukon and the official opposition in the four western provinces and claimed a small legislative outpost in Nova Scotia. Even in Quebec the NDP had finally won a seat, if only in a by-election. That might be a long way from the national victory New Democrats had promised themselves at their founding convention 25 years before, but it is also a reminder that the NDP's moderate brand of democratic socialism has remained politically viable even in seemingly conservative times. At a moment in history when worldwide capitalism seemed triumphant, Canada's version of democratic socialism appeared to be holding its own.

Few of the NDP's supporters identify "socialism" as their bond to the party. Polls indicate that voters welcome the NDP's record of "standing up for working people," its defence of social programs and public funding for the arts, or its support for civil liberties. Like its predecessor, the Co-operative Commonwealth Federation (CCF), the NDP and its policies are seen as a bulwark against the "Americanization" of Canada. The alternative to economic continentalism, embodied in the 1988 Free Trade Agreement, is the kind of planned, interventionist economic system which only New Democrats have consistently advocated.

If socialism is rarely mentioned by the NDP's supporters and if Canadian socialists differ passionately about its significance, the word itself provides a core ideology for the democratic left in Canada. Significantly, too, socialism is not the kind of mind-blinding political curseword in Canada that it often seems to be in the United States. One reason is that socialism in Canada "owes more to Methodism than to Marx," even more than in Britain where the phrase originated. There were socialists in Canada who were as dry, didactic, and sectarian as any in the world. The first avowed socialists elected anywhere in the British Empire won mining constituencies in British Columbia in 1902. Their Socialist Party of Canada denounced unions and strikes as mere reformism and, for a time, compelled would-be members to pass an examination in Marxist ideology. Yet socialism only spread in Canada when it became reformist and when it became the ideological fuel for a host of causes and movements, from the Protestant social gospel of Salem Bland to the feminist causes of Flora Denison or Thérèse Casgrain. American populism, spread by the slogan of "a co-operative commonwealth" and the pages of *Appeal to Reason*, was as powerful a component of Canadian socialism as the passionate rhetoric of British or eastern European radicals.

Revised in September, 1990, by the author, who is a member of the Department of History, University of Toronto, and Principal, Erindale College. By permission.

From the outset, socialism in Canada has drawn on a faith, inherent in a pioneering people, that the "Great Society" remains to be built. James Shaver Woodsworth, the frail, bearded founder of Canada's CCF–NDP tradition offered the House of Commons a definition of his political faith that reflected the intensely moral roots of Canadian radical reform. "Socialism," he explained, "comes from the good old Latin word *socius*, or friend." It was a vision, Woodsworth insisted, of what society could be if men and women were free to treat each other as friends.

Such a vision was no more universally acceptable to Woodsworth's listeners in 1926 than it may be 70 years later. There were those then as now who considered society a Hobbesian struggle of all against all, with the added Darwinian gloss that the fittest would triumph. There were those too of an undemocratic socialist persuasion, who insisted that human society would work together only under external coercion. Fear or hunger, not love or curiosity, were the true human motivators. In its struggle with idealism, realism wins most of the battles; must it win the war? Socialism remains an idealist's choice, but the realistic alternatives are ugly. Can humanity outlive nuclear weapons, racial hatred, shrinking resources, and increasingly visible extremes of wealth and poverty unless it becomes Woodsworth's "society of friends?"

Democratic socialism in Canada found its first effective form when the representatives of tiny western labour, farmer, and socialist parties met in Calgary in 1932 to proclaim a Co-operative Commonwealth Federation and elect Woodsworth as their president. At Regina a year later the new CCF adopted a manifesto chiefly drafted by a University of Toronto professor. Despite its slightly old-fashioned prose, Frank Underhill's preamble still summarizes the dominant vision of Canadian socialism:

> We aim to replace the present capitalist system, with its inherent injustice and inhumanity, by a social order from which the domination and exploitation of one class by another will be eliminated, in which economic planning will supersede unregulated private enterprise and competition, and in which democratic self-government, based upon economic equality, will be possible.

Tucked into this statement are three concepts earlier immortalized as the motto of the French Revolution: Liberty, Equality and Fraternity. With discreet modifications for a more gender-conscious age, socialism in the CCF–NDP tradition involves a combination of three goals: freedom, equality, and community. Their interdependence is crucial. By itself, as the NDP's Tommy Douglas used to say, freedom is the liberty of elephants to dance among the chickens. Equality without freedom is the status of the galley slave. A community without freedom or equality is a fair definition of feudalism. Innumerable regimes that masquerade as socialist, from the Soviet Union to Cuba, have met and failed a tough test. Collectivism, whether in the service of state or of IBM, is not freedom. Materialism, currently celebrated as "neo-liberalism," leaves equality and community unfulfilled and real liberty reserved for very few.

As our ancestors recognized when they restricted the right to vote to wealthy men, freedom has an economic dimension. Effective democracy is impossible amidst the cruel disparities of wealth and poverty that characterize the Third World; it is painfully difficult in Canadian communities where a quarter or a third of the working population is unemployed. It is meaningless for women if they are held as family chattels. Ed Broadbent, a political philosopher long before he became NDP federal leader from 1975 to 1989, once wrote of the bold expectations democratic socialists placed on freedom:

A fully democratic society for us is one in which the opportunity for self-realization is equally available to all. And self-realization for us means the free development of our moral, intellectual, aesthetic, and sensual capacities. . . . The second characteristic of a fully developed democracy is that the average citizen should possess direct or indirect control over all those decisions affecting his day-to-day life— in particular in the economic institution in which he is likely to spend most of his living time.

Freedom and equality are possible only within a community, whether in a workplace or a neighbourhood, a city, province or country, or, most fundamentally, membership in that endangered species called humanity. Outside a community, freedom and equality become meaningless and, ultimately, impossible. Community is vital if our civilization is to survive in the face of human and ecological threats.

A British socialist, Graham Wallas, added the concept of "political image" to our understanding. In Canada the image of democratic socialism over the past half-century has usually taken the shape of the CCF–NDP and is a succession of leaders from J.S. Woodsworth to Audrey McLaughlin. More than anyone Woodsworth insisted that socialism in Canada must be based on elected legislatures, public education, and what his British Fabian mentors called "the inevitability of gradualness." For the passionate radicals of the Canadian Left patience has been a bitter constraint. At almost every CCF–NDP convention a remarkably consistent third of the delegates have identified with a "more socialist" and extra-parliamentary alternative. The majority (and the grumbling minority) struggle on to the minor victories and frequent frustrations of electoral politics and community education. Canadian reform is largely based on policies pirated from the NDP: there is no patent on a good idea.

In the "Great Consensus" of postwar Canada, the Left's frustrations were many. Free enterprise and welfarism had apparently combined to reform a century's worth of injustice and inequality. Canadians hardly needed alternative political ideas. As of the 1990s that age is over. Today, the two postwar generations seem almost an accidental interlude in our history. The moulders of conventional wisdom now promise us an age of harsh sacrifices and "new realities" in which the future will be worse than the past. The comfortable incomes, social security, and prospects for the young that most Canadians learned to take for granted are a fading memory. The affluent, secure middle class is shrinking; the extremes of wealth and poverty are growing in Canada, as they already have in the United States. A polluted globe poses challenges that selfish greed cannot adequately overcome.

In such a setting democratic socialism emerges as a persuasive political vision. Canadians are not yet Americans, and most of the real distinctions between the two neighbours, from the CBC to Medicare, to legal safeguards for equality as well as freedom, are linked to a quiet, persistent socialist tradition. Put to the test, most Canadians shudder at the Conservative alternative of merciless struggle and stark disparities.

In the 1990s Canada's socialist tradition is relevant, powerful, and necessary. Both as Canadians in North America and as human beings in this menacing world, only a "society of friends" can save us.

BIBLIOGRAPHY

Federal Parties and Politics

(See also Bibliography in Chapter 8.)

Archer, K. "The Failure of the New Democratic Party: Unions, Unionists, and Politics in Canada." *C.J.P.S.*, 18, 2, June, 1985.

Archer, K., and Whitehorn, A. "Opinion Structure Among New Democratic Party Activists: A Comparison with Liberals and Conservatives." *C.J.P.S.*, 23, 1, March, 1990.

Aucoin, P., (ed.). *Party Government and Regional Representation in Canada*. Toronto: U.T.P., 1985.

Bashevkin, S. *Toeing the Line: Women and Party Politics in English Canada*. Toronto: U.T.P., 1985.

Baum, G. *Catholics and Canadian Socialism:Political Thought in the Thirties and Forties*. Toronto: Lorimer, 1980.

Bercuson, D., Granatstein, J.L., and Young, W.R. *Sacred Trust? Brian Mulroney and the Conservative Party in Power*. Toronto: Doubleday, 1986.

Bouchard, P. "Feminisme et marxisme: un dilemme pour la Ligue communiste canadienne." *C.J.P.S.*, 20, 1, March, 1987.

Bradley, M. *Crisis of Clarity: The New Democratic Party and the Quest for the Holy Grail*. Toronto: Summerhill Press, 1985.

Brennan, J.W., (ed.). *Building the Co-operative Commonwealth: Essays on the Democratic Socialist Tradition in Canada*. Regina: Canadian Plains Research Centre, 1985.

Brodie, J. *Women and Politics in Canada*. Toronto: McG.-H.R., 1985.

Brodie, J., and Jenson, J. *Crisis Challenge and Change: Party and Class in Canada Revisited*. Ottawa: C.U.P., 1988.

Caplan, G., Kirby, M., and Segal, H. *Election [1988]: The Issues, the Strategies, the Aftermath*. Scarborough: P.-H., 1989.

Carty, K. "Is There Life After Losing the Race?" *J.C.S.*, 24, 2, Summer, 1989.

Christian, W., and Campbell, C. *Political Parties and Ideologies in Canada*. Toronto: McG-H.-R, 3rd ed., 1990.

Courtney, J. C. *The Selection of National Party Leaders in Canada*. Toronto: Macmillan, 1973.

Coyle, J., *et al. Sinc: The Incredible Story of the Sinclair Stevens Investigation*. Toronto: F. and W., 1987.

Erickson, L. "CCF–NDP Popularity and the Economy." *C.J.P.S.*, 21, 1, March, 1988.

Forbes, D. "Hartz-Horowitz at Twenty: Nationalism, Toryism and Socialism in Canada and the United States." *C.J.P.S.*, 20, 2, June, 1987. "Comment" by Wiseman, N., and "Rejoinder" by Forbes, D., *ibid.*, 21, 4, December, 1988.

Fraser, G. *Playing for Keeps: The Making of the Prime Minister, 1988*. Toronto: M. & S., 1989. [1988 Election]

Frizzell, A., and Westell, A. *The Canadian General Election of 1984: Politicians, Parties, Press and Polls*. Ottawa: C.U.P., 1985.

Gagnon, A. "Third Parties: A Theoretical Framework." *A.R.C.S.*, 11, 1, Spring, 1981.

Gagnon, A., and Tanguay, B., (eds.). *Canadian Parties in Transition: Discourse, Organization, Representation*. Toronto: Nelson, 1989.

Goldfarb, M., and Axworthy, T. *Marching to a Different Drummer: An Essay on the Liberals and Conservatives in Convention*. Toronto: Stoddard, 1988.

Gollner, A., and Salée, D., (eds.). *Canada Under Mulroney: An End of Term Report*. Montreal: Vehicule Press, 1989.

Graham, R. *One-Eyed Kings: Promise and Illusion in Canadian Politics*. Toronto: Collins, 1986.

Grant, G. *Lament for a Nation*. Toronto: M. & S., 1965.

Gratton, M. *"So What Are the Boys Saying?" An Inside Look at Brian Mulroney in Power*. Toronto: McG-H.R., 1987.

Heggie, G.F. *Canadian Political Parties, 1867–1968: A Historical Bibliography*. Toronto: Macmillan, 1977.

Hiemstra, J.L. *Trudeau's Political Philosophy: Its Implications for Liberty and Progress*. Toronto: I.S.C., 1983.

Horn, M. *The League for Social Reconstruction: Intellectual Origins of the Democratic Left in Canada 1930–1942*. Toronto: U.T.P., 1980.

Horowitz, G. "Conservatism, Liberalism, and Socialism in Canada: An Interpretation." *C.J.E.P.S*, 32, 2, June, 1966.

Hoy, C. *Friends in High Places: Politics and Patronage in the Mulroney Government*. Toronto: Key Porter, 1987.

Irvine, W. *The Farmers in Politics*. Toronto: Macmillan, 1978.

Johnston, R., and Percy, M.B. "Reciprocity, Imperial Sentiment, and Party Politics in the 1911 Election." *C.J.P.S.*, 13, 4, December, 1980.

Kerr, D.C., (ed.) *Western Canadian Politics: The Radical Tradition*. Toronto: U.T.P., 1981.

Kornberg, A., Smith, J., and Clarke, H.D. *Citizen Politicians—Canada: Party Officials in a Democratic Society*. Durham, North Carolina: Carolina Academic Press, 1979.

Lee, R.M. *One Hundred Monkeys: The Triumph of Popular Wisdom in Canadian Politics*. [1988 Election]. Ottawa: Macfarlane, Walter and Ross, 1989.

Lévesque, T.J. "On the Outcome of the 1983 Conservative Leadership Convention: How They Shot Themselves in the Other Foot." *C.J.P.S.*, 16, 4, December, 1983. (See also comments by Woolstencroft and Perlin, *ibid*.)

Loomis, D.G. *Not Much Glory: How Trudeau's Army Killed the F.L.Q.*. Toronto: Deneau, 1985.

Lyon, V. "The Future of Parties—Inevitable . . . Obsolete?" *J.C.S.* , 18,4, Winter, 1983–84.

MacLaren, R. *Consensus: A Liberal Looks at His Party*. Oakville, Ontario: Mosaic Press, 1984.

McCall-Newman, C. *Grits: An Intimate Portrait of the Liberal Party*. Toronto: Macmillan, 1982.

Meisel, J. *Working Papers on Canadian Politics*. Montreal: McG.- Q.U.P., 2nd enlarged edition, 1975.

Melnyk, O. *No Bankers in Heaven: Remembering the CCF*. Toronto: M.H.-R., 1989.

Morton, D. *The New Democrats, 1961–1986: The Politics of Change*. Toronto: Copp Clark, 1987.

Morton, W.L. *The Progressive Party in Canada*. Toronto: U.T.P., 1950.

Noel, S.J.R. "Dividing the Spoils: The Old and New Rules of Patronage in Canadian Politics." *J.C.S.*, 22, 2, Summer, 1987.

Penner, N. *The Canadian Left: A Critical Analysis*. Toronto: P.- H., 1977.

Penner, N. *Canadian Communism: The Stalin Years and Beyond*. Toronto: Methuen, 1988.

Penniman, H., (ed.). *Canada at the Polls, 1979 and 1980*. Washington: American Enterprise Institute, 1981.

Penniman, H., (ed.). *Canada at the Polls, 1984.* Washington: American Enterprise Institute, 1988.

Perlin, G.C. *The Tory Syndrome: Leadership Politics in the Progressive Conservative Party.* Montreal: Mc.G.-Q.U.P., 1980.

Perlin, G., (ed.). *Party Democracy in Canada: The Politics of National Party Conventions.* Scarborough: P.-H., 1988.

Petry, F. "The Policy Impact of Canadian Party Programs: Public Expenditure Growth and Contagion from the Left." *C.P.P.* 14, December, 1988.

Pickersgill, J.W. *The Road Back: By a Liberal in Opposition.* Toronto: U.T.P., 1986.

Pinard, M. *The Rise of a Third Party: A Study in Crisis Politics.* Montreal: Mc.G.-Q.U.P., 1975.

Preece, R. "The Myth of the Red Tory." *Canadian Journal of Political and Social Theory,* 1, 1, 1977. (Comments by G. Horowitz, *ibid.* 1.3; W. Christian, 2,2; Reply, 2,2.)

Preece, R. "The Anglo-Saxon Conservative Tradition." *C.J.P.S.,* 13, 1, March, 1980.

Quinn, H.F. *The Union Nationale: A Study in Quebec Nationalism.* Toronto: U.T.P., 2nd ed., 1979.

Richards, J., and Kerr, D., (eds.). *Canada, What's Left?: A New Social Contract Pro and Con.* Edmonton: NeWest Press, 1986.

Roberts, J. *Agenda for Canada: A Vision of Liberalism.* Toronto: L.& O.D., 1985.

Salutin, R. *Waiting for Democracy: A Citizen's Journey* [1988 Election]. Toronto: Viking, 1989.

Schwartz, M.A. *Politics and Territory: The Sociology of Regional Persistence in Canada.* Montreal: McG.-Q.U.P., 1974.

Simpson, J. *Discipline of Power: The Conservative Interlude and the Liberal Restoration.* Toronto: Macmillan, 1984.

Simpson, J. "Political Patronage." *Q.Q.,* 95, 2, Summer, 1988.

Simpson, J. *Spoils of Power: The Politics of Patronage.* Toronto: Collins, 1988.

Smith, D. *The Regional Decline of a National Party: Liberals on the Prairies.* Toronto: U.T.P., 1981.

Snider, N. *The Changing of the Guard: How the Liberals Fell From Grace and the Tories Rose to Power.* Toronto: L. & O.D., 1985.

Stanfield, R.L. *National Political Parties and Regional Diversity.* Kingston: Queens University, I.I.R., 1985.

Thorburn, H.G., (ed.). *Party Politics in Canada.* Scarborough: Ontario, P.-H., 5th ed., 1985.

Underhill, F.H. *In Search of Canadian Liberalism.* Toronto: Macmillan, 1960.

Wearing, J. *The L-Shaped Party: The Liberal Party of Canada, 1958–1980.* Toronto: McG.-H.R., 1980.

Wearing, J. "Political Bucks and Government Billings: A Preliminary Enquiry into the Question of Linkage Between Party Donations by Business and Government Contracts." *J.C.S.,* 22, 2, Summer, 1987.

Wearing, J. *Strained Relations: Canada's Parties and Voters.* Toronto: M.& S., 1988.

Weinrich, P.H. *Social Protest from the Left in Canada, 1870- 1970.* Toronto: U.T.P., 1982.

Whitaker, R. *The Government Party: Organizing and Financing the Liberal Party of Canada, 1930–58.* Toronto: U.T.P., 1977.

Whitaker, R. "Between Patronage and Bureaucracy: Democratic Politics in Transition." *J.C.S.,* 22, 2, Summer, 1987.

Young, W.D. *The Anatomy of a Party: The National C.C.F. 1932- 61.* Toronto: U.T.P., 1969.

Provincial Politics

(See also Bibliography, Chapter 4, Provinces and Territories, and Chapter 8. For Quebec, see Chapter 5.)

Barthomeuf, J. *Governing Nova Scotia*. Halifax: Himbus, 1985.

Blake, D.E., Carty, K., and Erickson, L. "Federalism, Conservatism and the Social Credit Party in British Columbia." *B.C. Studies*, 81, Spring, 1989.

Blake, D., Carty, K., and Erickson, L. "Ratification or Repudiation: Social Credit Leadership Selection in British Columbia." *C.J.P.S.*, 21, 3, September, 1988.

Boyle, T.P. *Elections: British Columbia: The Unique Guide for Provincial Election Participants and Spectators*. Vancouver: Lion's Gate Press, 1982.

Bullen, J. "The Ontario Waffle and the Struggle for an Independent Socialist Canada: Conflict Within the NDP." *C.H.R.*, 64, 2, 1983.

Chorney, H., and Hansen, P. "Neo-Conservatism, Social Democracy and 'Province-building': The Experience of Manitoba." *C.R.S.A*, 22, 1, February, 1985.

Conway, J.F. *The West: The History of a Region in Confederation*. Toronto: Lorimer, 1983.

Doyle, A. *The Premiers of New Brunswick*. Fredericton: Brunswick Press, 1983.

Dyck, R. *Provincial Politics in Canada*. Scarborough: P.-H., 1986.

Eager, E. *Saskatchewan Government: Politics and Pragmatism*. Saskatoon: Western Producer, 1980.

Elkins, D.J., and Simeon, R. *Small Worlds: Parties and Provinces in Canadian Political Life*. Toronto: Methuen, 1980.

Finkel, A. *The Social Credit Phenomenon*. Toronto: U.T.P., 1989.

Garr, A. *Tough Guy: Bill Bennett and the Taking of British Columbia*. Toronto: Key Porter, 1985.

Gauvin, M., and Jalbert, L. "The Rise and Fall of the Parti Acadien." *C.P.R.*, 10, Autumn, 1987.

Irving, J.A. *The Social Credit Movement in Alberta*. Toronto: U.T.P., 1959.

Kavic, L.J. *The 1200 Days, A Shattered Dream: Dave Barrett and the N.D.P. in B.C., 1972–75*. Coquitlam, B.C.: Kaen Publishers, 1979.

Kornberg, A., Mishler, W., and Clarke, H.D. *Representative Democracy in the Canadian Provinces*. Scarborough: P.-H., 1982.

Laycock, D. *Populism and Democratic Thought in the Canadian Prairies, 1910–1945*. Toronto: U.T.P., 1989.

Lipset, S.M. *Agrarian Socialism: The Co-operative Commonwealth Federation in Saskatchewan*. New York: Anchor Books, Doubleday, 1968.

Macpherson, C.B. *Democracy in Alberta: The Theory and Practice of A Quasi-Party System*. Toronto: U.T.P., 1953.

Magnusson, W., (ed.) *After Bennett: A New Politics for British Columbia*. Vancouver: New Star, 1986.

Mason, G. *Fantasyland: Inside the Reign of Bill Vander Zalm*. Toronto: M.H.-R., 1989.

McAllister, J.A. *The Government of Edward Schreyer: Democratic Socialism in Manitoba*. Montreal: McG.-Q.U.P., 1985.

McCormick, P. "Is the Liberal Party Declining? Liberals, Conservatives and Provincial Politics, 1867–1980." *J.C.S.*, 18, 4, Winter, 1983–84.

Michelmann, H.J., and Steeves, J.S. "The 1982 Transition in Power in Saskatchewan: The Progressive Conservatives and the Public Service." *C.P.A.*, 28, 1, Spring, 1985.

Morley, J.T. *et al. The Reins of Power: Governing British Columbia*. Vancouver: Douglas and McIntyre, 1983.

Morley, J.T. *Secular Socialists: The CCF–NDP in Ontario, a Biography*, Montreal: McG.-Q.U.P., 1984.

Murray, P. *From Amor to Zalm*. Vancouver: Orca, 1989.

Paine, R., (with Lamson, C.). *Ayatolahs and Turkey Trots: Political Rhetoric in the New Foundland*. St. John's: Breakwater Books, 1981.

Palmer, B.D. *Solidarity: The Rise and Fall of an Opposition in British Columbia*. Vancouver: New Star, 1987.

Persky, S. *Bennett II: The Decline and Stumbling of Social Credit Government in B.C., 1979–83*. Vancouver: New Star, 1983.

Persky, S. *Fantasy Government: Bill Vander Zalm and the Future of Social Credit*. Vancouver: New Star, 1989.

Pottle, H. *Newfoundland, Dawn Without Light: Politics, Power and People in the Smallwood Era*. St. John's: Breakwater, 1980.

Pratt, L., (ed.). *Socialism and Democracy in Alberta: Essays in Honour of Grant Notley*. Edmonton: NuWest, 1986.

Robin, M., (ed.). *Canadian Provincial Politics: The Party Systems of the Ten Provinces*. Scarborough: P.-H., 2nd ed., 1978.

Rowe, F. W. *The Smallwood Era*. Toronto: McG.-H.R., 1985.

Smith, D.E. *Prairie Liberalism, The Liberal Party in Saskatchewan 1905–1971*. Toronto: U.T.P., 1975.

Smitheram, V., Milne, D., and Dasgupta, S., (eds.). *The Garden Transformed: Prince Edward Island, 1945–80*. Charlottetown: Ragweed Press, 1982.

Spafford, D. "Highway Employment and Provincial Elections." *C.J.P.S.*, XIV, 1, March, 1981.

Speirs, R. *Out of the Blue: The Fall of the Tory Dynasty in Ontario*. Toronto: Macmillan, 1986.

Stein, M.B. *The Dynamics of Right-Wing Protest: Social Credit in Quebec*. Toronto: U.T.P., 1973.

Stewart, D. "Delegate Support Patterns at Nova Scotian Leadership Conventions." *Dalhousie Review*, 69, 1, Spring, 1989. 95–126.

Thatcher, C. *Backrooms: A Story of Politics*. Saskatoon: Western Producer, 1985.

White, G., (ed.). *The Government and Politics of Ontario*. Toronto: Nelson, 4th ed., 1990.

Wilson, B. *Politics of Defeat: The Decline of the Liberal Party in Saskatchewan*. Saskatoon: Western Producer Prairie Books, 1981.

Wilson, J. "The Canadian Political Cultures: Towards a Redefinition of the Nature of the Canadian Political System." *C.J.P.S.*, VII, 3, September, 1974.

Wiseman, N. *Social Democracy in Manitoba: A History of the CCF/NDP*. Winnipeg: University of Manitoba Press, 1983.

City Politics

(See also Bibliography, Chapter 4, Municipalities, and Chapters 5 and 8.)

Colton, T.J., *Big Daddy: Frederick G., Gardiner and the Building of Metropoliltan Toronto*. Toronto: U.T.P., 1980.

Freeman, B., and Hewitt, M., (eds.). *Their Town, the Mafia, the Media and the Party Machine*. [Hamilton, Ontario], Toronto: Lorimer, 1979.

Frisken, F. *City Policy-making in Theory and Practice: The Case of Toronto's Downtown Plan*. London: University of Western Ontario, 1988.

Harris, R. *Democracy in Kingston: Social Movement in Urban Politics, 1965–1970*. Montreal: McG.-Q.U.P., 1988.

Higgins, D.J.H. *The Politics and Government of Canada's Cities: Urban Canada.* Toronto: Gage, rev. ed., 1986.
Kaplan, H. *Reform, Planning, and City Politics: Montreal: Winnipeg, Toronto.* Toronto: U.T.P., 1982.
Leonard, J.-F., and Leveillee, J. *Montreal After Drapeau.* Montreal: Black Rose, 1987.
Lorimer, J., and MacGregor, C., (eds.). *After the Developers.* Toronto: Lorimer, 1981.
Lyon, D.M., and Fenton, R. *The Development of Downtown Winnipeg: Planning Plans and Policy, 1874–1984.* Winnipeg: University of Winnipeg, 1984.
Magnusson, W., and Sancton, A., (eds.). *City Politics in Canada.* Toronto: U.T.P., 1983.
Masson, J. *Alberta's Local Governments and Their Politics.* Edmonton: U.A.P., 1985.
McKenna, B., and Purcell, K.S. *Drapeau.* [Montreal], Toronto: Clarke Irwin, 1980.
Williams, D. *Mayor Gerry: The Remarkable Gerald Grattan McGeer.* Vancouver: Douglas & McIntyre, 1986.

Political Biographies

Aiken, G. *The Backbencher: Trials and Tribulations of a Member of Parliament.* Toronto: M. & S., 1974.
Anderson, D. *To Change the World: A Biography of Pauline Jewett.* Toronto: Irwin, 1987.
Archer, J. H., and Munro, J.A., (eds.). *One Canada: Memoirs of the Rt. Hon. John G. Diefenbaker: The Crusading Years, 1895–1956.* Toronto: Macmillan, 1975.
Beck, M. *Joseph Howe: Vol. II, The Briton Becomes Canadian 1848- 1873.* Montreal: McG.-Q.U.P., 1983.
Bélanger, R. *Wilfrid Laurier: Quand la politique devient passion.* Montréal: P.U.M., 1986.
Bissell, C. *The Imperial Canadian: Vincent Massey in Office.* Toronto: U.T.P., 1986.
Black, C. *Duplessis.* Toronto: M. & S., 1977.
Bothwell, R. *Pearson, His Life and World.* Toronto: McG.-H.R., 1978.
Bothwell, R., and Kilbourn, W. *C.D. Howe: A Biography.* Toronto: M. & S., 1979.
Brown, R. *Being Brown: A Very Public Life.* Toronto: U.T.P., 1989.
Brown, R.C. *Robert Laird Borden: A Biography,* Vol. I. *1854- 1914.* Toronto: Macmillan, 1975; Vol. II, *1914–1937:* 1980
Cahill, J. *John Turner.* Toronto: M. & S., 1984.
Chrétien, J. *Straight from the Heart.* Toronto: Key Porter, 1985.
Conrad, M. *George Nowlan: Maritime Conservative in National Politics.* Toronto: U.T.P., 1986.
Copps, S. *Nobody's Baby: A Survival Guide to Politics.* Toronto: Deneau, 1986.
Davey, K. *The Rainmaker: A Passion for Politics.* Toronto: Stoddard, 1986.
Dawson, R.M. *William Lyon Mackenzie King: A Political Biography 1874–1923.* Vol. I, Toronto: U.T.P., 1958. (See *infra,* Neatby for Vols. II and III.)
Deering, L. *W.A.C. Bennett.* Toronto: F. and W., 1983.
Desbarats, P. *René: A Canadian in Search of a Country.* Toronto: M. & S., 1976.
Donaldson, G. *Eighteen Men: Canada's Prime Ministers from Macdonald to Trudeau.* Toronto: Doubleday, 1985.
Durant, V. *War Horse of Cumberland, The Life and Time of Sir Charles Tupper.* Hantsport, N.S.: Lancelot, 1985.
Elliott, D., and Miller, I. *Bible Bill: A Biography of William Aberhart.* Edmonton: Reidmore Books, 1987.

English, J. *Shadow of Heaven: The Life of Lester Pearson*, Vol. 1, 1897–1948. Toronto: U.T.P., 1989.

English, J. *Borden: His Life and World*. Toronto: McG.-H.R., 1977.

English, J., and Stubbs, J.O., (eds.). *Mackenzie King: Widening the Debate* Toronto: Macmillan, 1978.

Esberey, J. E. *Knight of the Holy Spirit: A Study of William Lyon Mackenzie King*. Toronto: U.T.P., 1980.

Ferns, H. *Reading from Left to Right: One Man's Political History*. Toronto: U.T.P., 1986.

Fleming, D.M. *So Very Near: The Political Memoirs of the Honourable Donald M. Fleming*. Toronto: M. & S., 1985, 2 vols.

Gibson, G. *Bull of the Woods: The Gordon Gibson Story*. Vancouver: Douglas and McIntyre, 1980.

Goodman, E. *The Life of the Party: The Memoirs of Eddie Goodman*. Toronto: Key Porter, 1988.

Gordon, W. *A Political Memoir*. Toronto: M. & S., 1977.

Granatstein, J.L. *Man of Influence: Norman A. Robertson and Statecraft, 1929–68*. Toronto: Deneau, 1981.

Gwynn, R. *The Northern Magus: Pierre Trudeau and Canadians, 1968- 80*. Toronto: M. & S., 1980.

Harrop, G. *Advocate of Compassion: Stanley Knowles in the Political Process*. Hantsport, Nova Scotia: Lancelot, 1984.

Haycock, R. *Sam Hughes: The Public Career of a Controversial Canadian, 1855–1916*. Waterloo: W.L.U.P., 1986.

Hellyer, P. *Damn the Torpedoes: My Fight to Unify Canada's Armed Forces*. Toronto: M. & S. 1990.

Horner, J. *My Own Brand*. Edmonton: Hurtig, 1980.

Horwood, H. *Joey: The Life and Political Times of Joey Smallwood*. Toronto: Stoddart, 1989.

Hoy, C. *Bill Davis: A Biography*. Toronto: Methuen, 1985.

Jerome, J. *Mr. Speaker: The Man in the Middle*. Toronto: M. & S., 1985.

Johnston, C.M. *E.C. Drury: Agrarian Idealist*. Toronto: U.T.P., 1985.

Johnston, D. *Up the Hill*. Montreal: Optimum, 1986.

Johnston, D., (ed.). *With a Bang, Not a Whimper: Pierre Trudeau Speaks Out*. Toronto: Stoddart, 1988.

Leclerc, A. *Claude Ryan: A Biography*. Toronto: NC Press, 1980.

Lévesque, R. *Attendez que je me rappelle*. Montreal: Editions Québec/Amérique, 1988.

Lévesque, R. *Memoirs*. Toronto: M. & S., 1986.

Lewis, D. *The Good Fight: Political Memoirs, 1909–1958*. Toronto: Macmillan, 1981.

Lynch, C. *A Funny Way to Run a Country: Further Memoirs of a Political Voyeur*. Edmonton: Hurtig, 1986.

MacDonald, Donald C. *The Happy Warrior: Political Memoirs*. Toronto: F. and W., 1988.

MacDonald, L. I. *Mulroney: The Making of the Prime Minister*. Toronto: M. & S., 1984.

MacLaren, R. *Honourable Mentions: The Uncommon Diary of an M.P.*. Toronto: Deneau, 1986.

Mann-Trofimenkof, S. *Stanley Knowles: The Man from Winnipeg North Centre*. Saskatoon: Western Producer, 1982.

Mardiros, A. *William Irvine: The Life of a Prairie Radical*. Toronto: Lorimer, 1979.

Martin, P. *A Very Public Life*, Vol. I, *Far From Home*. Ottawa: Deneau, 1983; Vol. II, *So Many Worlds*: 1985.

McDougall, A.K. *John P. Robarts: His Life and Government.* Toronto: U.T.P., 1985.

McIlroy, T. *Diefenbaker: Remembering the Chief.* Toronto: Doubleday, 1984.

McIlroy, T. *A Rose is a Rose: A Tribute to Pierre Elliott Trudeau.* Toronto: Doubleday, 1984.

McKenna, B., and Purcell, S. *Drapeau,.* Toronto: Clarke Irwin, 1980.

McLeod, T., and McLeod, I. *Tommy Douglas: The Road to Jerusalem.* Edmonton: Hurtig, 1988.

Mitchell, D. *W.A.C. Bennett and the Rise of British Columbia.* Vancouver: Douglas and McIntyre, 1983.

Mulroney, B. *Where I Stand.* Toronto: M. & S., 1983.

Munro, J. A., and Inglis, A. I., (eds.). *Mike: The Memoirs of the Right Honourable L. B. Pearson,* Vol. II, *1948–1957,* Toronto: U.T.P., 1973; Vol. III, *1957–1968.* 1975. [See *infra,* Pearson for Vol. I.]

Murphy, R., Chodos, R., and Auf der Maur, N. *Brian Mulroney: The Boy from Baie-Comeau.* Halifax: Goodread Biographies, 1985.

Neatby, H. B. *William Lyon MacKenzie King, 1924–1932: The Lonely Heights,* Vol. II, Toronto: U.T.P., 1963; Vol. III, *1932–39: Prism of Unity,* 1976. (See *supra.* Dawson for Vol. I.)

Nielsen, E. *The House Is Not A Home.* Toronto: Macmillan, 1989.

Oliver, P. *Unlikely Tory: The Life and Politics of Allan Grossman.* Toronto: L. & O. D., 1985.

Ondaatje, C. *The Prime Ministers of Canada: Macdonald to Mulroney 1867–1985.* Toronto: Pagurian, 1985.

O'Sullivan, S., with McQueen, R. *Both My Houses: From Politics to Priesthood.* Toronto: Key Porter, 1986.

Pearson, L. B. *Mike, The Memoirs of the Right Honourable L.B. Pearson,* Vol. 1 *1897–1948.* Toronto: U.T.P., 1972. (See *supra,* Munro and Inglis for Vols. II and III.)

Pelletier, G. *Years of Choice, 1960–1968.* Toronto: Methuen, 1987.

Petrie, A.R. *Henri Bourassa.* Markham, Ontario: F. and W., 1980.

Radwanski, G. *Trudeau.* Toronto: Macmillan, 1978.

Robinson, B. *Diefenbaker's World: A Populist in Foreign Affairs.* Toronto: U.T.P., 1989.

Rooke, P.T., and Schnell, R.L. *No Bleeding Heart: Charlotte Whitton: A Feminist on the Right.* Vancouver: U.B.C.P., 1987.

Salutin, R. *Kent Rowley, A Canadian Hero.* Toronto: Lorimer, 1980.

Scott, F. *A New Endeavour: Selected Political Essays, Letters, and Addresses,* edited by Horn, M. Toronto: U.T.P., 1986.

Shackleton, D. *Tommy Douglas.* Halifax: N.S., Goodread Biographies, 1983.

Smith, C. *Unfinished Journey: The Lewis Family.* Toronto: Summerhill Press 1989. [Stephen and David Lewis]

Smith, D. *Gentle Patriot—A Political Biography of Walter Gordon.* Edmonton: Hurtig, 1973.

Stacey, C.P. *A Very Double Life: The Private World of Mackenzie King.* Halifax: Goodread Biographies, 1985.

Starr, R. *Richard Hatfield: The Seventeen Year Saga.* Halifax: Formac Publishing, 1987.

Steed, J. *Broadbent: The Search for Integrity.* Markham, Ontario: Viking, 1988.

Stursberg, P., (ed.). *Diefenbaker: Leadership Gained, 1956– 62,* Vol. I. Toronto: U.T.P., 1975; Vol. II, *Diefenbaker: Leadership Lost, 1962–67.* 1976.

Stursberg, P., (ed.). *Lester Pearson and the Dream of Unity.* Vol. I. Toronto: Doubleday, 1978; Vol. II, *Lester Pearson and the American Dilemma,* 1980.

Swift, J. *Odd Man Out: The Life and Times of Eric Kierans.* Vancouver: Douglas & McIntyre, 1988.

Thomas, L.H., (ed.). *The Making of a Socialist: The Recollections of T.C. Douglas*. Edmonton: U.A.P., 1984.

Waite, P.B. *Macdonald: His Life and World*. Toronto: McG.-H.R., 1975.

Waite, P.B. *The Man from Halifax: Sir John Thompson, Prime Minister*. Toronto: U.T.P., 1985.

Ward, N., and Smith, D. *Jimmy Gardiner: Relentless Liberal*. Toronto: U.T.P., 1990.

Whelan, E. *Whelan: The Man in the Green Hat*. Toronto: Irwin, 1986.

Wilson, K. *John A. Macdonald and Confederation*. Toronto: Irwin, 1982.

Wood, D. *The Lougheed Legacy*. Toronto: Key Porter, 1985.

Young, W., (ed.). *Paul Martin: The London Diaries, 1975–1979*. Ottawa: U.O.P., 1988.

Zolf, L. *Just Watch Me: Remembering Pierre Trudeau*. Toronto: Lorimer, 1984.

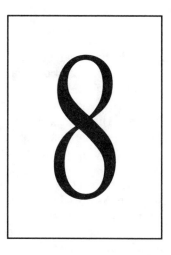

ELECTIONS AND
VOTING BEHAVIOUR

TELEVISION AND THE 1988 CAMPAIGN:
DID IT MAKE A DIFFERENCE?

Frederick J. Fletcher and Robert Everett

Since 1968, the most vivid memories of Canadian federal election campaigns come from television visuals. From clips of Pierre Trudeau dropping in on a political rally by helicopter in 1968 to the free trade "sound bite" in 1988, television pictures have had a profound influence on our perceptions of political leaders.

Not surprisingly, therefore, political strategists have increasingly focussed their resources on television, especially newscasts and political spots. Yet academics studying campaigns have remained skeptical, arguing that the primary effect of campaign coverage has been to reinforce voters' preconceptions and that media effects are limited by other influences, such as family and friendship networks.

During the 1988 campaign, three veteran political observers—Craig Oliver, Jack Webster and Mike Duffy—agreed on an October 12 broadcast that the 1984 debates had been the turning point in that campaign. Yet one of Canada's leading voting behaviour specialists, Lawrence LeDuc of the University of Toronto, concluded after a careful analysis of survey data that "even in . . .

From *SCAN*, Vol. 2, No. 3, January/February, 1989, a magazine for CBC television producers and directors. By permission of the authors.

1984, where the campaign produced apparent wide shifts in public opinion and the debates produced sharp distinctions between the performances of the leaders, little real effect on voting is found."

At another level, of course, there is widespread agreement on the impact of television on campaign practices. The very existence of television has altered political campaigns, reducing the importance of traditional loyalties and increasing voter volatility. In 1988, all three parties ran their national campaigns primarily for television news.

For example, the Conservative campaign prior to the leaders' debates was a classic front-runners' campaign. Its objective was to control the news. The key element was a visit by the prime minister to a factory or school each morning to provide photo opportunities related to a policy text that he would deliver to a convenient group at noon. Each text contained a brief passage intended to provide the "sound bite" for the evening newscasts. The partisan rallies were less central but were deemed necessary to rally the troops. All three major party leaders followed a similar basic script.

In Mr. Mulroney's case, he usually offered a suitable "sound bite" in both official languages regardless of where he was speaking. Indeed, the party carried on quite different campaigns in French and English, and strategists were unhappy when The National began reporting what he said in French to its English-speaking audience.

The concern of the strategists with the "sound bites" and their frequent complaints about the coverage are testimony to the importance they attach to television news coverage.

In the final analysis, however, it is difficult to find evidence—or design research—to demonstrate unequivocally the independent influence of television on actual election outcomes. There are too many variables to disentangle, and the campaign is shaped not only by the parties and the media organizations, all struggling to influence the agenda, but also by the public through polls.

Nevertheless, there is considerable circumstantial evidence to suggest that the choices that television newsworkers made in the 1988 campaign were an important factor in its development.

It seems clear that Liberal leader John Turner entered the campaign with a very low personal standing in the polls, not only because of his own failings and the problems in the Liberal organization, but also because television news had selected—consciously or unconsciously—these two elements as the narrative line around which they would organize their coverage of his campaign. Coverage focussed on slips and splits, even when there were other angles available. Every backgrounder on the 1984 election that we saw in this campaign used the patronage sound bite from the debates.

The Conservatives had suffered in the polls as a result of similar personal and organizational factors. Once again, however, it is arguable that these problems were reinforced in the public mind by the tendency of television news to focus on scandals and gaffes at the expense of more abstract matters, such as economic growth.

The rhetoric of the leaders was also clearly shaped by the needs of television. For example, Turner could not adopt a more nuanced position on the free trade agreement than his rip-it-up stance in large part because it would not play on television.

Certainly the campaign, with its unprecedented number of national polls, was marked by a great deal of voter volatility. According to Decima's post-election survey, more than 60 per cent of voters interviewed made up their minds after the election call on October 1, significantly higher than usual, and 27 per cent reported changing their minds at least once during the 52 days of the campaign.

In the same survey, reported in *Maclean's* (December 8), 51 per cent reported finding the media coverage helpful in their vote decisions. In addition, 45 per cent said the debates were helpful and 26 per cent even found the party television spots useful. How influential these sources of information were remains uncertain, however, at least until more sophisticated statistical analysis can be done.

It seems clear that media polls played an unprecedented role in 1988. There were more than two dozen national polls during the 52-day campaign, more than twice as many as in 1984, when 20 per cent of all television news items on the campaign mentioned poll results. The number must have been significantly higher in 1988, and it seems likely that this continual taking of the electoral pulse contributed to the volatility of voter preferences. As will be seen, the immediate post-debate polls appear to have had a notable influence on both the media and the voters.

Together the two leaders' debates were the "main event" of the campaign. The stakes were high, given the volatility of the electorate, and each leader had to cope with pre-existing expectations. John Turner was the consensus winner of both sets of debates, the relatively sedate French version and the more confrontational English set-to. After each debate, Liberal pollster Martin Goldfarb asked respondents if each leader had done better or worse than expected and found that Turner had a net score of +27 for the French debate and +44 for the English, scores that put him far ahead of his rivals.

Although Turner was not declared the winner in the instant analysis that followed the English debates, which was more equivocal than in 1984, a consensus emerged within 48 hours that pictured Turner as the victor and NDP leader Ed Broadbent as the loser (despite the fact that many pundits had declared him the winner on points immediately after Encounter '88).

On the basis of American studies and the 1979 case, where the consensus took 72 hours to form, many observers have suggested that news coverage of the debates, and especially the declaration of winners and losers, has greater influence on public perceptions than the debates themselves. In 1988, however, the initial effect appears to have been direct, as it was in 1984, but it seems likely that the swing was exaggerated by the subsequent coverage. Michael Adams of Environics found that there was little difference in perceptions of leader performance between respondents who had actually seen the debates and those who had formed their opinions solely on the basis of news coverage (one-quarter of the sample).

In both 1984 and 1988, it seems likely that the selection of the main "sound bite" was crucial. While the network newscasts carried a number of clips, including dramatic disputes over NATO (Broadbent pressed by Turner) and child care (Mulroney on the defensive in an exchange with Broadbent), the "sharpest confrontation," in the words of Peter Mansbridge, became the clip that was featured in subsequent coverage. That confrontation, in which Turner told Mulroney he had "sold us out" in signing the free trade agreement and the latter defended his patriotism, became the symbol of the debates, as the patronage exchange had become in 1984.

It is interesting to note that the child care exchange, in which Mulroney disparaged the judgement of advocacy groups, got lost in the shuffle, though some observers saw it as a major gaffe (for example, *Le Devoir* columnist Michel Vastel, commenting on CBC radio). It is interesting to speculate about what difference it would have made had that clip been the focus of the coverage.

In the event, the result was the one Tory strategists had most tried to avoid: a single issue campaign in which they were on the defensive. In addition, John Turner had risen from the ashes of his campaign organization. Having been damaged by television's intolerance for those who appear to lack confidence in 1984, Turner was able to use television to communicate confidence, conviction and sincerity in 1988, and to escape, to some extent at least, the image established over the previous four years.

Within 48 hours of the debates, party polls showed a significant shift to the Liberals, and within a week they were ahead in every province but Alberta and appeared at one time to be headed for a majority government.

The 1988 results suggest that the public response, as reported by the polls, influenced the subsequent television news coverage as much as the coverage influenced public perceptions. The causal sequence seems to have been as follows: (1) Turner performed well in the first three weeks of the campaign but could not alter the preconceptions of the media and, therefore, could not reach most of the public; (2) the debates allowed him to gain public attention and to dispel the image that he was a "stumblebum"; (3) voters who disliked or distrusted Mulroney and were concerned about the free trade agreement now saw Turner as a credible alternative; (4) this shift showed up quickly in post-election polls and influenced media coverage, which in turn reinforced the public perception.

All the polls showed Turner as the winner. His personal competence rating in the polls jumped from 9 per cent at the beginning of the campaign—when party strategists feared that they would win only 28 seats—to 30 per cent, just behind the prime minister. Turner's media strategists, who had taught him to use television effectively, could take some of the credit.

The story of the erosion of what proved to be a temporary Liberal lead also revolves around television and its impact. While part of of the loss of Liberal momentum may be attributed to natural erosion as the memory of a dramatic event fades, the Tory counterattack and the failure of the Liberals to attract media attention to the rest of their agenda also played a part.

The Conservatives adopted a three-pronged strategy based on their polling, which showed that Turner had gained new supporters by exceeding expectations on performance and communicating sincerity on the free trade issue, which tapped the concerns of many voters regarding the agreement. However, the Decima polling also showed that 40 per cent of voters doubted that Turner was sincere in opposing the deal. As Tory pollster Allan Gregg put it: "We saw that the bridge that joined the growing fear of free trade and the growing support for the Liberal party was John Turner's credibility. So we had to get all the planes in the air and smash the bridge. . . ."

The counterattack began with the prime minister hitting back at Turner and a hit squad of senior cabinet ministers challenging his credibility. Within a week, the Conservatives had produced two hard-hitting television commercials and purchased a great deal of air time to reach as many voters as possible. The spots had the appearance of interviews with ordinary voters (actually Tory workers) who questioned Turner's competence and the strength of his team. The primary purpose of the ads, according to Decima President Ian McKinnon, was to undermine Turner's credibility, in particular to undermine the sincerity of his opposition to free trade by questioning his motivation. The tactic was to portray him as just another politician who was exaggerating the risks associated with free trade to save his political career.

The Decima numbers showed that the tactic, which was reinforced by reassurances from business and credible non-partisan figures regarding the deal, was stunningly successful. The spots first aired November 4, when the proportion of voters who believed Turner was sincere on free trade was over 50 per cent; by November 12, the figure was 25 per cent. Turner's image as a crusader had been successfully undermined for a good many voters.

Liberal polling showed that Turner needed another issue to maintain momentum in the weeks after the debates and, in addition, to communicate a positive program. As with the pre-election attempts to draw attention to the themes of social and economic justice in the party's 40-point platform, Turner's efforts to make the proposed national sales tax an issue and to get the national media to pay some attention to the party platform essentially failed. The networks were still trying to respond to the public hunger for more information on free trade and had little willingness to adjust to a new narrative line.

The Decima polls showed that the Tory slide stopped early in November and that by November 12 the Conservatives had a 5-point lead, a lead that grew over the next few days, until they were able to project a majority six days before the vote. The prime minister had, in fact, moved ahead of Turner on honesty and trust, providing further evidence of the effectiveness of the Tory counterattack.

The first report of the National Election Study—conducted by the Institute for Social Research at York University, under the supervision of political scientists from the University of British Columbia, Laval University, and the University of Chicago—suggests a similar pattern. Focussing on the relationship between support for free trade and for Prime Minister Mulroney, Richard Johnston and André Blais (*The Globe and Mail*, December 19) found that Mulroney reduced support for the deal by about 5 per cent before the debate and by 14 per cent in the week following. Late in the campaign, however, his image no longer hurt support for the deal and by the last week may have helped it.

If we assume that the rehabilitation of Mulroney's popularity is a function of a decline in the popularity of the other two leaders, since voters most likely make their judgements in a comparative context, then this finding can be traced to the drop in Broadbent's popularity as a result of responses to the debates and the effectiveness of the Conservative ads in reminding voters of Turner's long-standing image problems.

In general terms, then, we can say that the television news coverage, especially in the context of the media polls, the narrative lines established by the media for covering the leaders, the debates, and the party advertisements all had some effect on the nature of the campaign and its outcome. Disentangling the specific effects is, as noted above, extremely difficult, but the increasingly sophisticated media and academic polling may allow scholars to uncover some of the mysteries before the next election.

In the meantime, it seems clear that the choices made by newsworkers and the media strategies of the parties do make a difference. It also seems clear that the superior financial resources of the Conservatives and the additional air time available to them under the electoral regulations were a factor in the outcome, as were the "third party" advertisements, though probably to a lesser extent.

Certainly the coverage did draw attention to the free trade issues, perhaps at the expense of other issues. News organizations, like the opposition parties, had to scramble to deal with the changed situation after the debates. However, by voting day, according to the National Election Study, 80 per cent of those polled had an opinion on the deal and 90 per cent of those voted consistent with their opinions.

Scholars, newsworkers and party strategist will be discussing this election for a long time to come.

SINGLE ISSUE POLITICS: IS ABORTION A TEST CASE?

Jeffrey Simpson

OTTAWA

... As a political issue, abortion is no big deal. Despite the conventional wisdom, abortion doesn't elect or defeat politicians, except in their imagination. Put another way, there are few, if any, issues where the impression of political consequences is more evidently mismatched with the political reality.

This gap between perception and reality is due, in large part, to the interest groups for and against abortion. They scream, yell, demonstrate, petition, threaten, wave placards, swear undying fidelity to their cause and promise to make life miserable for all who disagree with them, especially politicians. Because they are so vocal and active, the media (print and electronic) flock to their demonstrations, press conferences and other public manifestations of putative strength.

It's all a facade. As Professors Barry Kay and Steve Brown of Wilfrid Laurier University and Professors Ronald Lambert and James Curtis of Waterloo University note in their study of abortion in the 1988 campaign, the political consequences of abortion are wildly exaggerated. (By the way, their findings closely mirror findings by the Tories' own pollsters, Decima Research.)

The four professors looked at the electoral fate of the 125 candidates supported by *Vitality*, a magazine of the Coalition for the Protection of Human Life. By comparing the votes these candidates received with the party swing from the 1984 to 1988 elections, they found 67 did better, 56 did worse and two performed the same.

They tried the same analysis for the candidates supported by the pro-abortion groups, and got nearly the same result. The conclusion: there was not a "significant influence of either pro-life or pro-choice advocates upon the electoral process."

Just to be sure, the professors then zeroed in on the ridings of Kitchener and Waterloo. In Kitchener, the Conservative MP, John Reimer, was a well-known and high-profile abortion opponent. They looked at the feelings of voters pro- and anti-abortion, then blended those findings with voting intentions. They discovered, although they stated this finding tentatively, that "most voters who claimed that abortion was important either were unaware or unmoved by where the candidates stood on the issue."

These findings mirror other national surveys that concluded that the majority of Canadians do not have strong feelings about abortion. How a question is put definitely influences the outcome, but most surveys, including the professors', discovered that most Canadians feel abortion should be available with some restrictions. About one-quarter of Canadians favor unrestricted access to abortion; about 15 per cent resolutely oppose abortion.

From *The Globe and Mail*, September 22, 1989. By permission.

. . . [The authors conclude that] "the evidence . . . suggests that MPs should cast their votes free from much concern about the electoral fallout."

[⬛]

REGULATING FEDERAL ELECTION SPENDING

Joseph Wearing

The current federal law governing election spending dates from 1974. Earlier legislation was of two sorts. First, there were laws against so-called "corrupt practices"—chiefly, bribery and treating—which predated Confederation. Then in 1874, following the Pacific Scandal, a new law required every parliamentary candidate to have an agent with sole responsibility for campaign funds (the so-called "doctrine of agency") and to issue a statement of campaign expenditures. The corrupt practices legislation regularly produced a flood of charges and invalidated elections. Between 1875 and 1878 almost a quarter of the MPs lost their seats! But the law requiring disclosure was frequently ignored and, with a single exception, went unenforced.

Public revulsion over the Watergate affair in the United States forced legislators in many countries, including Canada, to produce much tougher laws regulating party finance. The federal law of 1974 was one of the most comprehensive. Its chief features are that it extends the doctrine of agency to political parties as well as candidates; it requires parties and candidates to disclose both income and expenditures; it imposes limits on what parties and candidates can spend during the campaign period; it provides for the reimbursement from public funds of a portion of those expenditures; and it gives tax credits to those who make political contributions. (The size of contributions is not limited.)

Overall, the legislation has been much more effective than anything that existed previously; election financing is now more open and equitable than it was before. However, with the passage of time the limits of the legislation have been put to the test. Imperfections have come to light, and in 1985 a government White paper proposed a complete overhaul of the legislation. However, these changes were not passed into law before the 1988 election, and in 1990 the Mulroney government set up a royal commission in the hope of finding a consensus on amending the current law.

Responsibility for enforcing the Act lies with a commissioner of Canada Elections who is appointed by the chief electoral officer. Since the new legislation came into effect, compliance has generally been impressive. After the 1972

Prepared in 1990 by the author for this edition, based on an earlier, unpublished version which was written for the Royal Commission on Electoral Reform and Party Financing, Ottawa. The author is a member of the Department of Political Studies at Trent University. By permission.

election, for example, only 75 percent of the candidates filed expenditure statements as they were required by law to do. Now almost all candidates submit their statements of contributions and expenditures and the delinquents are fined. Following the 1984 election there were just 14 convictions for violations related to election expenses. (The largest number of charges—73— were for the Victorian vice of selling alcoholic beverages on election day.)

DISCLOSURE

Although there has been a very high degree of compliance with the disclosure requirements, the requirements themselves overlook some important aspects of election finance. Only national parties are required to disclose what they have spent outside the campaign period. Riding organizations are also exempt from this requirement, as are nominated candidates. Furthermore, those seeking to be candidates do not have to say how much they spent in their nomination campaigns nor where the money came from. Similarly, leadership campaigns are not covered by any disclosure requirements.

The annual expenditure statement required from national parties is not particularly informative, since there are just ten lines required in the statement. In some years miscellaneous expenses have comprised about one-third of the total operating expenses of both the Liberal and New Democratic parties, while printing and stationery appears to be a similar sort of omnibus item for the PC party. Some Liberal party members were shocked that a good chunk of their contributions had been used to cover expenses and salaries in the opposition leader's office and in his official residence, but none of that information could have been gleaned from the party's annual statement to the chief electoral officer.

The amount of information that needs to be provided about contributions is also somewhat limited. Only the contributor's name and the amount are given (when it is over $100). Not even the contributor's province is given. For corporate donations it is a relatively easy matter to get this information from other sources, but an individual with a common surname might just as well be making an anonymous contribution.

Another area where disclosure is not required—but might have been— concerns the trust funds that have traditionally been set up to supplement the income of the PC and Liberal leaders and other trust funds that are usually under the control of a regional party bagman. A close friend of Mackenzie King created a fund that was discreetly placed with a trust company in Boston. King apparently knew how much each of his benefactors had contributed, and in the late 1920s the fund amounted to almost a quarter of a million dollars—a very large sum in those days. Half a century later there was flurry of interest in a fund that paid for building a swimming pool for Pierre Trudeau at the prime minister's official residence, but no further details were ever revealed.

EXPENDITURE LIMITATIONS

One of the principal goals of the 1974 legislation was to put a brake on soaring campaign expenditures. The consensus initially was that the legislation was tough. Indeed, for the first election under the new law, that of 1979, campaign spending by the PC and Liberal parties on their national campaigns fell by 23 percent. On the other hand the NDP's national campaign spending jumped from a very low level so that it approached the level of the other two parties. At the riding level total reported spending by candidates of all three parties went up, although part of this increase was simply due to the fact that only three-quarters of the candidates had reported their expenditures under the old law. In many ridings the new limits were a real constraint on expenditures, and certainly budgetary controls had to be much tighter than they had ever been in the past.

At first the expenditure limits were not indexed to the cost-of-living index, but indexation was introduced before the 1988 election. Consequently, a party with candidates in every constituency across the country saw its expense limit of $4.5 million for its 1979 national campaign rise to just over $8 million in 1988. The limits for the party's candidates likewise increased from $7.6 million to $13.8 million over the same period.

By 1988 it was clear that there were more problems arising from the expenditure limits than from any other aspect of the legislation. One problem arises from an unforeseen loophole in the 1974 legislation—the distinction between election expenses and campaign expenses. The difference between the two can appear to be arcane, but it has important implications, since the spending limitations apply only to election expenses, not to campaign expenses. Election expenses include all the costs of directly promoting a candidate or party during an election period. Campaign expenses are anything else and can include such items as volunteers' expenses and polling research. The distinction became very controversial following the 1984 election when PC cabinet minister, Marcel Masse, declared election expenses of $32,941—his limit was $35,500—and campaign expenses of another $16,876.

The chief electoral officer has complained that the term "election expenses" is so vaguely defined in the current legislation as to make it extremely difficult to apply. The parties cannot agree on closing the loophole, since the cash-rich Conservatives want to transfer as much as possible into the campaign expense category, while the cash-poor Liberals and New Democrats want more items included in the election expense category, which earns them a 50 percent rebate.

At the national level a similar problem arises from the vague boundary line separating the parties' election expenses from the cost of their ongoing, annual expenditures, most of which are the operating expenses of the national office and some operations at the provincial level. Obviously, a good portion of a party's expenses during the campaign period can be considered part of its ongoing operation, and these do not come under the legislated limits for election expenses. Since the legislation does *not* limit annual expenses, a party with high election expenditures will be sorely tempted to report some of these as annual expenditures. Admittedly, the line between the two is very difficult to draw.

To deal with this and other problems arising from implementing a complex piece of legislation, an *"ad hoc* committee" of party representatives was set up to work out the detailed application of the spending rules. But in practice this has meant that the parties have been given complete discretion over how each of them wants to allocate ongoing national office expenses to the election period. In order to maximize their reimbursement and also stay within the limits set for the election period, the parties in effect use national office expenses as an "adjustable" item. In 1984, according to Paltiel, it was in the NDP's interest to put as much national office spending as possible into the election period, because otherwise it would fall short of the election spending limit and qualify for a smaller reimbursement. The PC party, on the other hand, risked going over the limit, so it allocated only a small proportion of national office expenses to the election period. In other words the so-called limit on election expenses has become a balancing item that allows the three major parties to maximize their reimbursement and stay within the law by shifting any excess spending into their annual expenditures, which have no limit.

This is clearly seen in the accompanying figures. Figure 1 (PC Income and Expenditure) shows that PC national office expenditures increased sharply in 1984 and 1988—years of federal elections. Figure 2 (Liberal Income and Expenditure) reveals a similar situation with respect to the Liberal party in 1984, but in 1988 annual spending was below that of the previous election year, no doubt because of the party's accumulated debt. Because the NDP chooses to report its annual spending as a combined total for both federal and provincial activities, it is not possible to chart the party's national expenditures during election and nonelection years. Generally, the party's annual expenditures appear not to rise dramatically in election years because, as noted previously, the party wants to maximize its election expenditure and does not have to worry about going over the limit. What is very striking in the case of all three parties is that income and expenditure are very closely related; income appears to be a far more effective check on party expenditure—both annually and during election campaigns—than any statutory limitations.

At the riding level the expenditure limitations are similarly incomplete since they do not include spending done before the election is called. The most notorious recent case was that of Broadview-Greenwood in the 1988 election. The Liberal candidate, Dennis Mills, admitted spending $130,000 before the election was called—an expenditure he justified by pointing to the publicly financed resources available to his opponent, Lynn McDonald, over the four years of her incumbency.

In one sense Mills has a point in arguing that limitations in the prewrit period

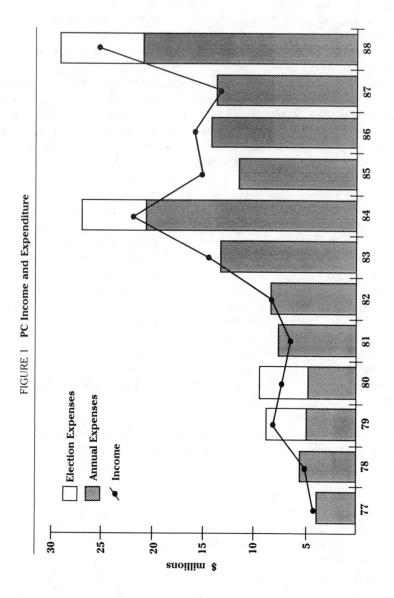

FIGURE 1 **PC Income and Expenditure**

FIGURE 2   **Liberal Income and Expenditure**

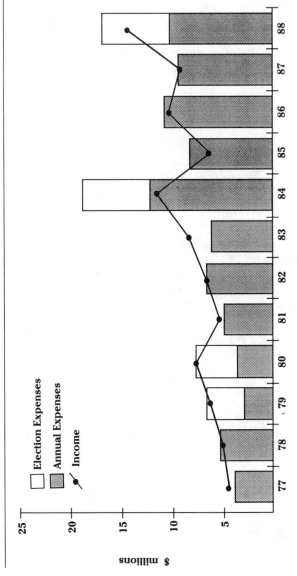

would be unfair to challengers. An incumbent usually has four years in office when he or she can work at maintaining a high visibility in the riding. The resources available to an MP include free mailing privileges, a riding office, and a free trip back to the riding once a week when Parliament is in session. Palda estimated these communications resources to be worth about $100,000 a year, whereas the average campaign spending limit for candidates in 1988 was $46,887. Accordingly, he argues that spending limits are not only unfair but even undemocratic, because studies in Canada and the United States have shown that turnout is directly related to election spending. He concludes that spending limits are a "barrier erected by incumbents to lower competition in the electoral arena." If spending limits were abolished completely, victory would not necessarily go to the highest spenders, he argues, because of the diminishing returns from each extra increment of campaign spending. A U.S. study of Congressional elections found that incremental returns reached zero at about $175,000, and this figure probably would be lower in Canada because of our less heavily populated constituencies.

This line of analysis might well lead one to conclude that expenditure limits should be put on all stages of the electoral cycle from one election to the next—at the same time trying to make some adjustment for advantage accruing to sitting MPs through the publicly financed advertising which they get. Or one might argue that there should be no limits at all. In any case the present law is illogical and simply encourages wealthy parties and candidates to do their spending outside the campaign period.

THIRD-PARTY ADVERTISING

Recently, the attempt to legislate expenditure limits has been called into question by so-called third-party advertising. This is advertising originating not with a candidate or party but with a private individual or interest group. Obviously, parties and candidates cannot monopolize the debate on election issues. It would be undemocratic to ban all election-related expenditures by those who are neither parties nor candidates. On the other hand, should private individuals and groups be permitted to spend whatever they want in promoting or attacking parties and candidates? It makes no sense to legislate limits on what parties and candidates can spend but to have no limits on what these so-called third parties can spend.

Moreover, Canadian politicians have been alarmed by the political clout exercised by such groups in the United States. Since the 1960s these political action committees (PACs) have grown remarkably, both in numbers and in wealth. In 1986 there were over four thousand that spent $156 million in election campaigns. Most PAC money goes to parties and candidates and these amounts are limited by law. However, it is the spending done by PACs independently of candidates that undoubtedly make Canadian politicians particularly anxious. In 1982 in the United States, for example, the conservative association, NCPAC, spent over $3 million attempting to defeat certain Democratic senators, without much success. For the most part PACs tend to support incumbents in order to get access to members of Congress for their lobbying activities.

One of the principles behind the Canadian 1974 election expenses legislation was to require every registered party and candidate to have an official agent, who would be completely accountable for all spending on behalf of that party or candidate. There would be no point in legislating spending limits if other groups could spend money on the party's or the candidate's behalf. Indeed, there would be nothing to prevent a party or candidate from channelling money through separate organizations to get round these limits. The 1974 legislation did allow third-party expenditures if these were made "in good faith . . . for the purpose of gaining support for views held . . . on an issue of public policy, or for the purpose of advancing the aims of any organization or association other than a political party or an organization or association of a partisan political character. . . . " However, MPs and the chief electoral officer were increasingly concerned about the activities of various single-issue groups and feared an assault by American-style PACs.

In 1983 Parliament passed various amendments to the election expenses legislation (Bill C-169) that, among other things, removed the "good faith" clause. The National Citizens Coalition (NCC) challenged the legislation on the ground that it conflicted with the Charter's guarantees of free speech, and the Alberta Court of Queen's Bench decided in favour of the NCC. Although binding only on Alberta, the decision effectively curtailed any prohibition of third-party activity that supports or opposes parties and candidates.

As a result of this ruling a number of groups were particularly active in the 1988 election, including the NCC. It was especially anxious to combat the rise in popularity of the NDP and Broadbent before the 1988 election, so it launched a $500,000 advertising campaign on radio, television, and in newspapers, calling Broadbent "very, very scary," "a socialist who means what he says." Because these advertisements were run before the campaign, they would not have been prohibited by the 1983 legislation. Nevertheless, they are a dramatic illustration of how third-party groups can intervene in a most partisan way. Even more striking was the campaign supporting free trade during the last few weeks of the 1988 election. Estimates of what was spent by these third-party groups range from $2 million to $10 million. Ironically, this advertising could continue right up to the day before the election, while the parties themselves were subject to the traditional 24-hour advertising blackout.

A complete *prohibition* on third-party activity would likely violate the Charter's protection of freedom of speech. However, one would assume that Parliament would be within the Charter's reasonable limits of a free and democratic society if it sought to regulate third-party spending in the way that it now regulates spending by political parties. That is, third-party groups might be required to disclose their income and expenditures and to limit their overtly partisan spending. To leave third-party groups completely free of regulation would ultimately defeat the purpose of the legislation now in place. (This still leaves open the question of whether newspaper editorials and government advertising are also loopholes to the present law.)

SUBSIDIZATION OF ELECTION SPENDING

The 1974 Act, for the first time in Canada, provided for parties and candidates to have a portion of their election expenses subsidized out of public funds. The formulas that determine the level of subsidies are generous—especially to the three major parties—though not always logical. The reimbursement for a political party is 22.5 percent of its actual election expenses, provided it spends at least 10 percent of what it is allowed to spend. In 1984 the three major parties were reimbursed $3.9 million; none of the other parties received anything. In 1988 the big three got $4.9 million, while one smaller party, the Christian Heritage Party, was entitled to $48,906.

At the riding level all candidates receive a small reimbursement for auditing expenses, otherwise they must get at least 15 percent of the vote in their ridings in order to qualify for the very substantial reimbursement that amounts to half of their election expenses. In 1984 candidates of the three major parties got $11.1 million, while all the other candidates received just $55,210. In 1988 PC, Liberal, and NDP candidates qualified for reimbursements of $13.6 million, but only 11 Reform candidates and one Independent were eligible for reimbursements totalling $184,192. Candidates for the smaller parties got 5 percent of the votes but just 1.3 percent of all the reimbursement.

Smaller parties experience similar discrimination in their access to free-time broadcasting. In 1984 the Liberals got 173 minutes out of the six-and-a-half hours available; the PC party had 129 minutes, the NDP 69, the Rhinos 8 minutes, and each other party had 5.5 minutes. In 1988 the PC party had half the available time.

Other countries that provide public support for political parties are more concerned to provide equal opportunities for all. For example, in France during the 1978 National Assembly elections, the parties shared seven-and-a-half hours of free time on primetime television. The majority and the opposition parties each got two hours, while parties not in the Assembly (but with candidates in at least 75 districts) got 19 minutes each.

There is no particular logic or any consistency to the various thresholds that parties and candidates now have to cross in order to qualify for subsidization. The formula that requires a party to spend at least 10 percent of its permitted limit in order to qualify for reimbursement actually encourages spending, particularly by smaller parties, and so it appears to conflict with one of the intentions of the act—that of limiting expenditures. In 1988 the only small party to qualify for reimbursement (the Christian Heritage Party) received only 0.78 percent of the vote. The NDP got 32 percent of the reimbursement, but only 20 percent of the vote. By way of comparison subsidization in the Federal

Republic of Germany is fairer, as well as being more generous. Any party that gets 0.5 percent of the votes receives a reimbursement of 5 DM (about $3.50) per voter to compensate them for the costs of conducting election campaigns.

The discrimination against smaller Canadian parties appears to ignore the contribution made by such parties through much of our political history. Independent Labour parties, the Progressives, Social Credit, the CCF, the Reconstruction party, the Bloc populaire, and others would have been at a severe disadvantage if they had entered the electoral scene under the present law.

Another more general observation needs to be made about the way in which political parties are subsidized. That is, we subsidize election campaigns, we subsidize the parties in Parliament through grants for research offices of the various party caucuses, but we provide nothing for the year-to-year operations of the national party offices. This further accentuates an imbalance that has existed within Canadian political parties for a long time—the extra-parliamentary party that represents the rank-and-file is completely overshadowed by the parliamentary and electoral wings of the party, and has become little more than a fund-raising operation with virtually no policy capability. Once again, by contrast, West German parties are encouraged to do policy research and political education by means of grants that are given to the research foundations of the parties represented in Parliament. In 1983 these amounted to 83.3 million DM.

TAX CREDITS FOR POLITICAL CONTRIBUTIONS

One of the main achievements of the 1974 Act was to encourage modest political contributions by individuals. Previous efforts by the parties to broaden their fund-raising bases had not been particularly successful. A Conservative popular fund-raising campaign in the 1940s failed completely. The Liberals had more success with fund-raising dinners in the 1960s, but the two older parties were heavily dependent on contributions from a relatively small number of wealthy individuals and corporations. The CCF-NDP had a broader fund-raising base, as befitted a social democratic party, but the party was always very short of funds. The election expenses legislation suddenly made contributing to a political party both respectable and attractive to those of modest means. Whereas previously a political contribution provided no tax benefit, contributors now get a generous tax credit of 75 percent for the first $100. Above that amount the percentage decreases up to a maximum credit of $500. (Political contributions now produce a more attractive tax break than charitable donations. For example, an Ontario taxpayer who gave $100 each to a charity and a political party would get tax credits of about $26 for the charitable donation and $75 for the political contribution.)

As a consequence of the new legislation the parties substantially increased their contributions from individuals so that, by the late 1970s, that source accounted for about half their income. Figures 3, 4, and 5 show contributions

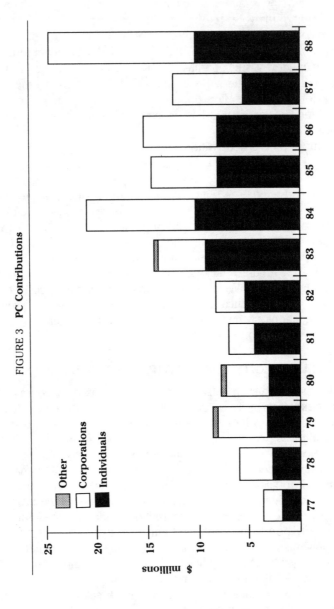

FIGURE 3   PC Contributions

FIGURE 4 Liberal Contributions

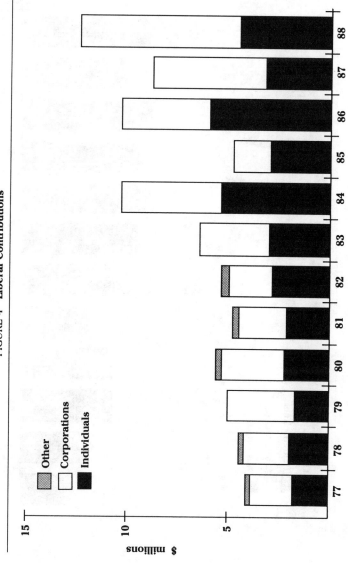

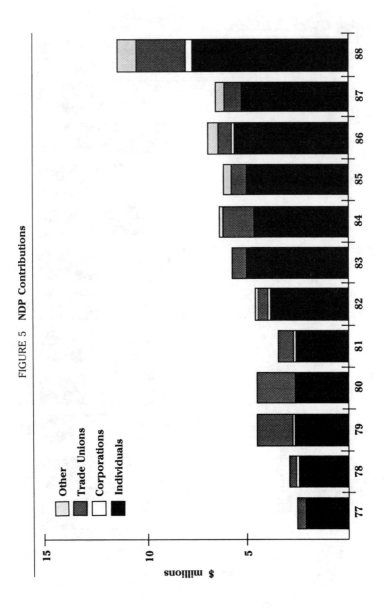

FIGURE 5   NDP Contributions

FIGURE 6   **Individual Contributors**

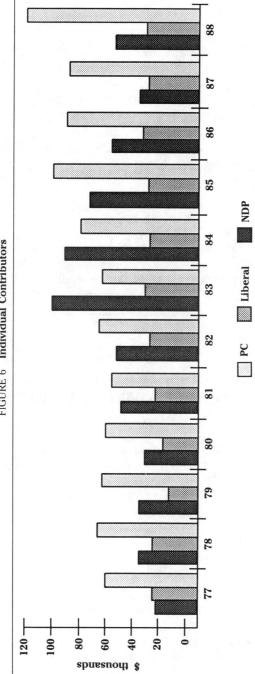

to the three major parties by size and by source over a 12-year period. (Contributions to provincial sections of the NDP have been excluded so as to allow for a direct comparison with the other two parties.) Figure 6 shows the actual number of individual contributors. Several things should be noted. First, the PC party gets more from individual contributors than either of the other two. (The party got even more from corporations during the last two election years.) Second, the number of individuals contributing to the PC party reached a maximum in 1983 and has been on a downward trend since then, though average contributions have increased. Third, individuals contributing to the NDP have substantially increased in number, although dollar amounts reached a plateau in the years leading up to the 1988 election. Fourth, individual contributors to the Liberal party have stagnated at around 30 000, and in three of the last five years the party has raised less from individuals than the NDP and less from individuals than from corporations.

CONCLUSION

Fifteen years of Canada's first comprehensive election expenses legislation have shown that, on the whole, it is an effective law. But time has also shown that further amendments and refinements are needed. Whether the parties can agree on the next stage of reform remains to be seen.

RECENT CANADIAN PROVINCIAL ELECTION RESULTS

Paul Fox

The tables that follow present basic data from the results of the two most recent general elections in each province. The second table is a continuation of the first and should be read as though it were a horizontal extension to the right.

All of the results shown are derived from the reports of the provincial chief electoral officers.

Similar details of provincial election results for the period from 1905 to 1982 are provided in the fifth edition of *Politics: Canada*, pages 655–693, and for 1982 to 1986 in the sixth edition, pages 413–415.

Some of the information in the tables needs to be explained. In British Columbia, which has some two-member ridings where voters may vote for each of two candidates, party percentages have been determined by dividing in half the party vote in each of those two-member constituencies. However, the unadjusted, valid votes by party are given in all cases. The totals of votes given in Prince Edward Island are the totals for both assemblymen and councillors, since all voters in P.E.I. may cast a vote for a candidate for each of the two positions in the legislature. For all provinces except British Columbia and P.E.I. the number of rejected ballots can be calculated by subtracting the total vote from the number of eligible voters who voted.

Because the tables have been constructed to reflect the results for the parties that are customary in elections in most of the provinces, the categories do not fit too well the situation in British Columbia and in Quebec. In the latter province, which tends to have its own slate of parties, the Parti Québécois is listed as the fourth party when, in fact, in the past two elections it has been the second party. Note also that in the 1989 election in Quebec the Equality party elected 4 members out of 19 candidates, obtaining 125 726 votes, or 3.7 percent of the total votes cast, though these results are obscured in the tables by the fact that the Equality party's results are included within the general category of Others (O.)

Recent Canadian Provincial Election Results

Province / Date of Election	Seats	Candidates						Elected					Popular Vote			
		L	C	NDP	4th	O	Total	L	C	NDP	4th	O	Liberal	%	Conservative	%
Prince Edward Island																
April 21, 1986	32	32	32	16	—	1	81	21	11	—	—	—	75 187	50.3	68 062	45.5
May 29, 1989	32	32	32	17	—	—	81	30	2	—	—	—	85 982	59.6	50 731	35.2
Newfoundland																
April 2, 1985	52	52	52	49	—	5	158	15	36	1	—	—	102 016	36.7	134 893	48.6
April 20, 1989	52	52	52	36	—	6	146	31	21	—	—	—	137 271	47.2	138 609	47.6
Nova Scotia																
Nov. 6, 1984	52	52	52	52	14	4	174	6	42	3	1	—	129 310	31.3	209 298	50.6
Sept. 6, 1988	52	52	52	52	7	—	163	21	28	2	1	—	186 007	39.6	204 150	43.4
New Brunswick																
Oct. 12, 1982	58	58	58	54	10	6	186	18	39	1	—	—	158 840	41.0	182 467	47.1
Oct. 13, 1987	58	58	58	58	10	—	184	58	—	—	—	—	246 702	60.0	116 798	28.4
Quebec																
Dec. 12, 1985	122	122	39	90	122	293	666	99	—	—	23	—	1 910 307	56.0	35 210	1.0
Sept. 25, 1989	125	125	—	—	125	307	557	92	—	—	29	4	1 702 808	49.9	—	—
Ontario																
Sept. 10, 1987	130	130	130	130	36	69	495	95	16	19	—	—	1 788 214	47.3	931 473	24.7
Sept. 6, 1990	130	130	130	130	68	157	615	36	20	74	—	—	1 301 948	32.4	944 723	23.5
Manitoba																
April 26, 1988	57	57	57	57	14	44	229	20	25	12	—	—	190 913	35.4	206 180	38.3
Sept. 11, 1990	57	57	57	57	6	22	199	7	30	20	—	—	138 146	28.1	206 032	41.9
Saskatchewan																
May 18, 1982	64	64	64	64	40	18	250	—	55	9	—	—	24 134	4.5	289 311	54.1
Oct. 20, 1986	64	64	64	64	9	10	211	1	38	25	—	—	54 739	10.0	244 382	44.6
Alberta																
May 8, 1986	83	63	83	83	46	58	333	4	61	16	2	—	87 239	12.2	366 783	51.4
Mar. 20, 1989	83	83	83	83	6	12	267	8	59	16	—	—	237 787	28.7	367 244	44.3
British Columbia																
May 5, 1983	57	52	12	57	57	46	224	—	—	22	35	—	44 074	2.5	19 143	1.4
Oct. 22, 1986	69	55	12	69	69	32	237	—	—	22	47	—	130 505	6.7	14 074	0.7

Recent Canadian Provincial Election Results

| Province | Popular Vote (continued) | | | | | | | | Voter Turnout | | |
	NDP	%	4th Party	%	Party	Others	%	Total	Registered Electorate	Voters Who Voted	%
P.E.I.											
1986	5 965	4.0	—	—	—	280	0.2	149 494	86 813	76 101	87.7
1989	4 902	3.4	—	—	—	—	—	141 615	89 230	72 132	80.9
Newfoundland											
1985	39 954	14.4	—	—	—	778	0.3	277 641	359 087	278 502	77.6
1989	12 924	4.4	—	—	—	2 138	0.7	290 947	361 913	291 785	80.6
Nova Scotia											
1984	65 876	15.9	8 322	2.0	Labour Party	630	0.2	413 436	614 899	415 160	67.5
1988	74 038	15.8	5 638	1.0	Independent	—	—	469 833	623 586	472 437	75.8
New Brunswick											
1982	39 211	10.1	3 331	0.9	Parti Acadien	708	0.2	384 557	471 798	387 251	82.6
1987	43 083	10.4	1 933	0.5	Independents	—	—	408 516	501 646	411 136	82.0
Quebec											
1985	82 588	2.4	1 320 008	38.7	Parti Québécois	63 494	1.9	3 411 607	4 576 600	3 464 232	75.7
1989	—	—	1 369 067	40.2	Parti Québécois	337 034	9.9	3 408 909	4 670 690	3 501 068	74.9
Ontario											
1990	1 509 440	37.6	110 952	28.3	Family Coalition	151 157	3.8	4 018 220	6 311 180	4 069 433	64.5
1987	970 813	25.7	48 110	1.3	Family Coalition	38 701	1.0	3 777 311	6 067 378	3 803 969	62.7
Manitoba											
1988	126 954	23.6	7 100	1.3	Confederation of Regions	6 263	1.2	537 410	728 319	538 738	74.0
1990	141 328	28.72	1 564	0.3	Confederation of Regions	3 630	0.7	490 700	712 747	492 161	69.1
Saskatchewan											
1982	201 390	37.6	17 487	3.3	Western Can. Concept	2 763	0.5	535 085	640 216	537 165	83.9
1986	247 683	45.2	458	0.1	Western Can. Concept	668	0.1	547 930	669 716	549 995	82.1
Alberta											
1986	208 561	29.2	36 656	5.1	Representative Party	14 415	2.0	713 654	1 514 182	715 376	47.2
1989	217 972	26.3	3 939	0.5	Social Credit	2 247	0.3	829 189	1 550 867	831 240	53.6
British Columbia											
1983	741 680	44.2	821 284	50.6	Social Credit	22 970	1.3	1 649 151	1 768 063	1 366 877	77.3
1986	824 544	42.6	954 516	49.3	Social Credit	11 814	0.6	1 935 453	1 770 000	1 366 193	77.2

Canadian General Elections, 1867–1988
Party Standings in House of Commons

Date of Election	Cons.	Lib.	Prog.	CCF-NDP	SC	SCR	Other	Total Seats
August 7–September 20, 1867	101	80						181
July 20–September 3, 1872	103	97						200
January 22, 1874	73	133						206
September 17, 1878	142	64						206
June 20, 1882	139	71					1	211
February 22, 1887	126	89						215
March 5, 1891	121	94						215
June 23, 1896	88	118					7	213
November 7, 1900	80	133						213
November 3, 1904	75	138					1	214
October 26, 1908	85	135					1	221
September 21, 1911	134	87						221
December 17, 1917	153*	82						235
December 6, 1921	50	116	64				5	235
October 29, 1925	116	99	24				6	245
September 14, 1926	91	128	20				6	245
July 28, 1930	137	91	12				5	245
October 14, 1935	40	173		7	17		8	245
March 26, 1940	40	181		8	10		6	245
June 11, 1945	67	125		28	13		12	245
June 27, 1949	41	193		13	10		5	262
August 10, 1953	51	171		23	15		5	265
June 10, 1957	112	105		25	19		4	265
March 31, 1958	208	49		8				265
June 18, 1962**	116	100		19	30			265
April 8, 1963	95	129		17	24			265
November 8, 1965	97	131		21	5	9	2	265
June 25, 1968	72	155		22		14	1	264
October 30, 1972	107	109		31	15		2	264
July 8, 1974	95	141		16	11		1	264
May 22, 1979	136	114		26	6			282
February 18, 1980	103	147		32				282
September 4, 1984	211	40		30			1	282
November 21, 1988	169	83		43				295

*Unionist.

**Figures include results of service vote and deferred election in Stormont held July 16, 1962. CCF became NDP July 31, 1961.

Results of Federal General Elections in 1988 and 1984
Seats Won by Parties by Provinces in 1988 (1984 results in brackets)

Province	PC		Lib.		NDP		Ind.		Totals	
Newfoundland	2	(4)	5	(3)					7	(7)
Prince Edward Island		(3)	4	(1)					4	(4)
Nova Scotia	5	(9)	6	(2)					11	(11)
New Brunswick	5	(9)	5	(1)					10	(10)
Quebec	63	(58)	12	(17)					75	(75)
Ontario	46	(67)	43	(14)	10	(13)		(1)	99	(95)
Manitoba	7	(9)	5	(1)	2	(4)			14	(14)
Saskatchewan	4	(9)			10	(5)			14	(14)
Alberta	25	(21)			1				26	(21)
British Columbia	12	(19)	1	(1)	19	(8)			32	(28)
Yukon		(1)			1				1	(1)
Northwest Territories		(2)	2						2	(2)
Totals	169	(211)	83	(40)	43	(30)			295	(282)

From *Report of the Chief Electoral Officer, Thirty-Fourth General Election, Appendices (Revised), 1988*, p. 21. For results prior to 1984 see previous editions of *Politics: Canada.*

[   ]

SHOULD CANADA ADOPT PROPORTIONAL REPRESENTATION?

Paul Fox

Democracy can be defined as rule by the majority, although Canadian governments are not often elected that way. At both federal and provincial levels it is common for governments to be elected by less than half the voters who go to the polls (and they, of course, are considerably fewer than the total number of citizens eligible to vote).

Governments gain power frequently by winning a plurality of parliamentary seats and popular votes rather than by a majority, that is, by getting more seats in the Commons and more votes in the country than any other party, but not more than 50 percent of the places and votes. In fact, under our curious system of voting it is even possible for a party to become the government although it has received fewer seats and votes than another party. While this does not happen often, it is certainly true that most federal and provincial governments that have been elected recently have come to power with more people voting against them than for them.

That has happened in 18 out of the past 21 federal elections—and in many provincial contests as well. Only twice since 1921 has the winning party in a national election received more than 50 percent of the total popular vote. The Liberals got 51.5 percent in 1940, while the Conservatives received 53.6 percent in 1958, and exactly 50 percent in 1984.

Revised in May, 1990.

MINORITY WINS

How do minority wins occur? They arise when the victorious party carries a large number of constituencies by pluralities rather than by majorities. For instance, in the 1988 federal election the Tory candidate in a south-western Ontario riding got 22 400 votes while the Liberal received 19 344, the New Democrat 11 571, and others 325. Thus, although the Tory candidate had fewer people voting for him than against him—22 400 to 31 240—he won.

When this sort of result is repeated in constituency after constituency, a party can easily win an election by obtaining more seats than any other party or all the other parties combined and still not have had even half the voters supporting it.

The appearance of important smaller parties, like the NDP, has had much to do with this sort of outcome. But the minor parties are not the real cause of the weakness. The actual defect is in the electoral machinery. It works in such a way that the winning party ordinarily gets far more seats in the House of Commons than its share of the vote entitles it to.

At the same time the opposition parties usually receive far fewer. In every federal election since 1896 the incoming government has ridden into power with more seats than its portion of the national vote gave it. Sometimes the discrepancies have been truly shocking, as the figures for 1984 show in the table accompanying this article entitled "Discrepancies Between Percentages of Seats Gained and Percentages of Valid Votes Won by Parties Nationally in 1988 and 1984."

In 1984 Brian Mulroney's Conservatives captured the government by winning exactly 50 percent of the popular vote. But that even split gave them 74.8 percent of the seats in the House of Commons, or nearly half as many seats again as the actual vote warranted. Of course, the opposition parties paid the price by receiving far fewer places in Parliament than their share of the vote justified. The Liberals got 28 percent of the vote but only 14 percent of the seats, while the NDP received about 19 percent of the vote and 11 percent of the seats.

Discrepancies Between Percentages of Seats Won and Percentages of Valid Votes Won by Parties Nationally in 1988 (1984 results in brackets)

	PC	Lib.	NDP
Seats[1]	57.3 (74.8)	28.1 (14.1)	14.6 (10.7)
Valid Votes[2]	43.0 (50.0)	31.9 (28.0)	20.4 (18.8)

[1] Calculated from data given in the Chief Electoral Officer's *Report, Appendices (Revised)*, 1988, p. 21, and *Report, 1984*, p. 34.
[2] From *Report, Appendices (Revised), 1988*, p. 20, and *Report, 1984*.
From *Report of the Chief Electoral Officer, Thirty-Fourth General Election, 1988, Appendices (Revised)*, and *Report of the Chief Electoral Officer, Thirty-Third General Election, 1984*. For discrepancies for earlier elections see previous editions of *Politics: Canada*.

The distortions were not as egregious in 1988, but even though the Conservatives had lost a good deal of their popular support, they still profited from the lop-sided system. The Tories got 43 percent of the vote but more than 57 percent of the seats. Again, the opposition parties made up the difference, the Liberals receiving about 32 percent of the votes and 28 percent of the seats, and the NDP 20.4 percent of the votes and 14.6 percent of the seats.

Provincial election results are sometimes even more startling. The 1976 Quebec election brought the separatists to power, and the Parti Québécois, which had been grossly underrepresented in the Assembly, suddenly became overrepresented by jumping from 6 seats to 71, although its share of the popular vote had risen from 30 to only 41 percent. In other words a 30 percent increase in votes produced a 1000 percent increase in seats.

In the provincial election in New Brunswick in 1987 the Liberals won 60 percent of the votes cast, which was a remarkably sweeping victory in popular votes for any party anywhere, but the results in terms of seats were even more remarkable. In fact, it was the ultimate, since the Liberals won 100 percent of the seats in the legislature. The opposition parties, with 40 percent of the vote, got zilch.

Absurd results like these bring our present system of voting into question and raise the issue, what can be done to remedy the defects? The answer is "not much" as long as we retain our existing plurality system (or "first past the post") which permits a candidate to win not by getting a majority but only more votes than the next runner-up.

Should we scrap our present system then and try something different? Few Canadians realize that we came close to doing this in the 1920s.

ALTERNATIVE VOTING

In 1924, and again in 1925, the federal government introduced a bill to abolish our present method of election and to replace it by alternative voting. These bills were never passed. But about the same time Manitoba and Alberta switched over to the new system, followed by British Columbia in 1952, though they all dropped it later.

The big difference between alternative or preferential voting and our present federal method is that the voter gets as many choices as there are candidates and marks his or her ballot in order of preference: 1, 2, 3, 4, 5, and so on. When the polls close, the first choices for each candidate are counted, and if no one has a clear majority the contestant with the fewest votes is dropped and the second choice on his ballots are distributed. If there's still no majority, the next lowest candidate is put out and the second choices on the ballots are distributed. And so it goes until someone finally gets a majority.

The great advantage to this method (which is used in Australia for the House of Representatives) is, of course, that it ensures that the winner finally gets a majority and that nobody gets in by a plurality. But that's about all it does. It doesn't solve the problem of the wasted votes for the losing parties and it doesn't give the minorities any representation. It can also encourage a little skullduggery because it enables two parties to co-operate at an election to knock out a third. (Party A and Party B pass the word along to their supporters to vote their own party first and the other party second, but under no circumstances to cast a ballot for Party C). This is what happened in British Columbia in 1952 when Liberal and Conservative voters helped Social Credit capture the government by winning more seats than the CCF, which was the most popular party.

The truth is that no system of voting will guarantee equal weight to all votes and fair representation to minority groups so long as we stick to our present method of electing only one member of Parliament from each constituency.

The big weakness of single-member districts is that only one person and one party can be chosen to represent all the voters living in that area.

This is unrealistic if there are many different points of view in the riding. The only sure way of giving them representation is to enlarge the constituency so that it has a number of seats and to fill these seats in proportion to the way the electorate votes.

PROPORTIONAL REPRESENTATION

This, in a nutshell, is the system of voting known as proportional representation. It had quite a vogue in Canada about 40 years ago when cities like Winnipeg, Calgary, Edmonton, and Vancouver adopted it. It is still popular in some countries like Denmark, Ireland, and Israel. Australia uses it for senate elections.

There are about as many different systems of proportional representation as there are ideas about government. Somebody once counted three hundred varieties, but they all work much the same way. Under the Hare System, which is probably the best known in Canada, electors go to the polls and vote for all candidates in order of preference. There will likely be a large number of candidates, at least as many as there are persons to be elected multiplied by the number of political parties, for each party will want to nominate a full slate. A minimum of five candidates is essential to make proportional representation work well.

The quota necessary for election is figured out by dividing the number voting by the number of seats to be filled plus one, the one being added to reduce the quota a bit to allow for such contingencies as spoiled ballots.

The next step is to count the first choices for each candidate. Anyone who has secured the quota is declared elected. If he or she has more than the quota, the surplus is transferred to the second choices. If none of the hopefuls has a quota, or if too few have it, then the person with the least first choices is eliminated and the second preferences on his or her ballots are distributed as marked. If this is not enough, the next lowest candidate is put out and second choices are allocated. This goes on until the required number of candidates reaches the quota.

The supporters of proportional representation say it has been tried in Canada in cities like Winnipeg and that is has worked well. They argue that its greatest asset is that it eliminates the startling discrepancy between the popular vote for parties and the number of seats they win in the legislature.

Representation in Parliament of political parties becomes identical to the proportion of votes they get at the polls: no more plurality wins, no more narrow-majority wins for one party in a lot of constituencies and a huge "wasted" vote for the other parties; no more overrepresentation of one party and underrepresentation of the others with a small knot of voters swinging an election one way or the other and converting a small shift in votes into a landslide in seats.

Instead, there would be an exact mathematical similarity between proportion of popular vote and proportion of seats and completely unbiased treatment for both minor and major parties. There would also be a seat for any minority that could muster a quota, and as many seats for the larger groups as would be proportional to their voting strength.

If proportional representation is such a cure-all, why not adopt it in Canada?

DISADVANTAGES

Oddly enough, the best argument for it is also the best argument against it. The fact is that proportional representation produces *too* accurate a resemblance between public opinion and representation in Parliament.

If we used it across the country, it would be rare for a party to get a majority in the House of Commons, at least judging by the voting since 1921. This would change completely the basis of our system of cabinet government, which depends on the party in power having enough strength to get its legislative program through Parliament. A party without a majority would be forced to battle every proposal through the Commons, or to enter into a coalition with some other party or parties.

There are other arguments against proportional representation. A favourite is that it multiplies the number of parties because it gives them a better chance of securing representation in the legislature. This is not as true as most people think. In France and Belgium, for example, there are no more parties now than there were before proportional representation was introduced.

But there is a danger in a country like Canada, which has strong regional feelings and interests, that proportional representation might foster a large number of regional parties in the federal House. Even under the existing system, the tendency in that direction is strong. Another difficulty is that proportional representation increases the size of constituencies in thinly populated areas to almost unreasonable dimensions. If proportional representation were put into effect in Canada and no riding were to have less than five members, it might well be, for example, that the whole of Manitoba outside of Winnipeg and its suburbs would become one or two gigantic electoral districts. Candidates would have a tremendous and expensive task trying to campaign over such a huge area and the voters might never get a glimpse of their MP.

Actually none of the disadvantages of proportional representation is as significant as the one overwhelming argument that if it were introduced all across Canada it would jeopardize our system of parliamentary government. And that limitation is so serious that it makes it impossible to recommend the wholesale adoption of proportional representation in this country.

Is there no solution, then?

The remedy seems to be to mix the two systems together judiciously to get the good effects of each. This could be done quite easily. One way would be to retain our present system for large rural areas while substituting proportional representation for it in large, densely populated urban centres. This was first suggested and debated in Parliament 60 years ago. Vancouver, Toronto, and Montreal would be obvious places to start.

If that kind of combination is not acceptable, there is another possibility which has been receiving a good deal of attention lately.

RECENT PROPOSALS

In the past decade there has been renewed concern about the damaging effects that our present voting system has on the representativeness of our political parties. Because they are limited or squeezed out of getting members elected in certain regions even though they have reasonable popular votes there, our parties tend to be less representative of the whole country. For years, for instance, the Conservatives had almost no members elected from Quebec, the Liberals few MPs from west of Winnipeg, and the NDP far less representation in southern Ontario and Montreal than its popular support warranted.

Lacking MPs from certain areas, the parties appear to be less than national— and they are, to the extent that these regions have little or no voice in the party caucus.

In the 1988 election, for instance, though the maldistribution was not as bad as it has been many times in the past, the Liberals won only one seat from the three provinces of Saskatchewan, Alberta, and British Columbia. Yet if seats in the Commons had been assigned to parties in proportion to their vote by province, the Liberals would have received 12 or 13 seats in this western part of Canada. Similarly, the NDP would have won ten in Quebec instead of none, and the party might also have picked up one or two in Atlantic Canada where it received none. Even the Conservatives would have profited by winning one or two in Prince Edward Island instead of being blanked out.

In 1979 the Pepin-Robarts Task Force on Canadian unity was so disturbed by this weakness in our present system that it said, "The regional polarization

**Composition of the House of Commons following the Federal Election
of February 18, 1980, if Pepin-Robarts' Proposal Had Been Applied**

Province	Lib.	Cons.	NDP	Créd.	Rhino	Total
Newfoundland	5	2				7
Prince Edward Island	2	2				4
Nova Scotia	5	6	1			12
New Brunswick	7	3				10
Quebec	74	12	3	1	1	91
Ontario	59	46	12			117
Manitoba	4	5	7			16
Saskatchewan	3	7	7			17
Alberta	6	21	1			28
British Columbia	9	16	12			37
North		2	1			3
Totals	174	122	44	1	1	342

of federal political parties corrodes federal unity." To overcome the danger
and to give the parties better regional representation, the Task Force recommended a mixed electoral system. While the present plurality, single-member
system would be continued for the existing seats in the Commons (which
then numbered 282), an additional 60 seats would be allocated in proportion
to the popular vote for parties, either by province or nationally using the
d'Hondt formula.

The accompanying table shows what the results would have been if the
Pepin-Robarts' proposal had been applied in the 1980 election.

Comparing this distribution of seats to the actual outcome, it is clear that
all three main parties would have benefited by obtaining greater regional
representation.

The essence of the Pepin-Robarts' plan caught on, particularly in light of the
misshapen results of the 1980 election. Soon after the election the leader of
the federal NDP, Ed Broadbent, proposed that 50 new members be added to
the House of Commons, ten for each of five regions, in proportion to the
parties' shares of the votes in each region. The Canada West proposal was
very similar. Saskatchewan Premier Allan Blakeney suggested a House with
182 members elected directly in single-member constituencies and another
100 selected by proportional representation. The Quebec Liberal party, following their leader, Claude Ryan, proposed a completely proportional system.

In a book which is the most definitive Canadian study of the problem,
Professor William Irvine of Queen's University devised a mixed system which,
like Mr. Broadbent's, is somewhat similar to the one used in West Germany
since 1949. There would be 188 constituency seats and 166 "provincial seats"
based on proportional representation. If a party did not secure a percentage
of constituency seats equal to its proportion of the popular vote in the province,
its deficiency would be made up by giving it the required number of provincial
members from a ranked list of candidates submitted in advance by the party
itself. (This is similar to the List system of proportional representation used in
Israel and elsewhere.)

In well-reasoned articles noted in the bibliography, Professor John Courtney has commented critically on these various proposals and the assumptions on which they are based. In *The Parliament of Canada* (pages 62–66) Professor C.E.S. Franks also has criticized the proposals trenchantly on seven different counts. The then federal Conservative Leader Joe Clark and Premier Peter Lougheed of Alberta declined to accept the new systems, no doubt because that very acceptance would make it even more difficult for the Conservatives to dislodge the Liberals from power.

Having already expressed support for proportional representation during the 1980 campaign, Prime Minister Trudeau said he was interested in Mr. Broadbent's proposal, and his government promised in the subsequent throne speech to set up a parliamentary committee to study alternatives to the present system of voting.

However, this promise was muted in January, 1982 when the government announced postponement of the committee's establishment to a later session of Parliament. There appeared to be opposition to the idea of a new electoral system from within the Liberal caucus as well as from within the NDP itself. MPs and others expressed dissatisfaction with having two different kinds of members in the House. Liberals were reported to be worried also by the prospect of their members from Quebec being diminished, particularly if the Parti Québécois fulfilled its threat to run candidates federally and got them elected by means of the new system.

Since Mr. Mulroney has come to power, there have been no further developments.

VOTING FOR FREE TRADE?: THE CANADIAN VOTER AND THE 1988 FEDERAL ELECTION

Lawrence LeDuc

On November 21, 1988, Canadians voted in a general election which was widely considered to have been one of the most important and dramatic in our history. Centring around the Canada–U.S. Free Trade Agreement (hereafter called the FTA), the election yielded a solid majority of seats for the incumbent Progressive Conservative government which had negotiated the agreement. With this outcome, the Canadian electorate seemed to signal its approval of the FTA in a decisive election which many considered to have been a kind of "referendum" on the agreement. At the same time Canadian voters re-

An original article prepared for this edition by the author, who is a Professor of Political Science at the University of Toronto. By permission.

warded Brian Mulroney with a majority government, the first prime minister to achieve two consecutive parliamentary majorities since Louis St. Laurent did so in 1953.

Yet there is much left unexplained in these seemingly simple interpretations of the 1988 election. In this paper I will argue that Canadian voters in 1988 did not deliver a positive "mandate" on free trade, did not reward the governing party for a "job well done," and for the most part did not view their participation in the events of 1988 in positive terms. Rather than the "referendum" on free trade that it was widely thought to be, the 1988 election was, for all of its moments of high political drama, a quite typical contest for political power in which the critical issues of the day were carefully manipulated for short-term political advantage. While seemingly yielding a decisive outcome, the major policy question of that campaign was left largely unresolved insofar as the public was concerned, and the party that emerged as the victor generated little public enthusiasm and support.

This chronic failure of our political institutions to more fully involve the public in major new policy directions and to present coherent choices in elections has contributed much to the growing levels of public cynicism and discontent that have been evident in national politics in recent years. Frustration with other recent political questions of major importance such as the Meech Lake Accord and the Goods and Services Tax seems certain to drive public distrust to even higher levels.

VOLATILITY AND DISCONTENT

Like Americans and Europeans, we have come to expect more from government and at the same time are demanding a greater voice in the public decisions that affect our lives. Yet the political processes that should make this possible are increasingly seen as unresponsive and untrustworthy. Canadians in alarming numbers have come to believe that their representatives in Parliament are "out of touch" with the people, and that the federal government "doesn't care much" about the public's wishes. As Figure 1 shows, in 1988 both of these standard indicators of what political scientists call political efficacy stood at or near the peak of an increasingly negative trend over the last 25 years, rising even above levels that were already fairly high. Canadians have come to feel a growing sense of disillusionment with their politics and politicians.

National surveys of the public, conducted regularly with each federal election beginning in 1965, have consistently portrayed an electorate which holds little long-term loyalty to political parties and is easily susceptible to sudden and often dramatic swings in voting choice. Elections in Canada generally have not been orderly, predictable affairs. In the dozen federal elections that have taken place since Louis St. Laurent achieved his second majority in 1953, half have produced majority governments and half have resulted in minorities. Exactly

FIGURE 1   **Indicators of External Political Efficacy in Canada: 1965–88**

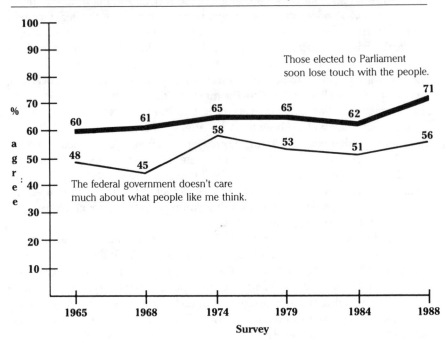

half of these elections have been won by the Progressive Conservatives (1957, 1958, 1962, 1979, 1984 and 1988) and half by the Liberals (1963, 1965, 1968, 1972, 1974, and 1980). In every one of these elections except 1958, "third" parties have polled at least 20 percent of the total vote, often gaining enough parliamentary seats to deny a majority to the winner.

In these 12 elections that form the modern Canadian political era, five federal governments have gone down to electoral defeat (St. Laurent in 1957, Diefenbaker in 1963, Trudeau in 1979, Clark in 1980, and Turner in 1984), and one came precariously close (Trudeau in 1972). Even some victories have been pyrrhic, such as the failure of Diefenbaker and Pearson to obtain majorities in 1962 and 1965, respectively. Although the Liberals were the governing party for nearly two-thirds of the period since 1957 (20 of 33 years), their hold on power was only rarely more secure than that of their opponents. Even those governments that have enjoyed considerable political success have often found their standing with the Canadian public to be at risk. The most popular federal political leaders of the modern era—Diefenbaker and Trudeau—both faded quickly in public esteem during their early years in office, turning majority governments into minorities within four years of an overwhelming election victory. Virtually every federal government in the past two decades has found itself behind in the public opinion polls after less than two years in office.

In spite of his record majority achieved in the 1984 election, Brian Mulroney has fared even more poorly in the affections of the public than most of his predecessors. At the beginning of 1988 the Conservatives stood third in the Gallup poll, preferred by only 28 percent of a national sample. Only 25 percent of that sample felt that Brian Mulroney was the best choice for prime minister. The Liberals, led by the same John Turner who had brought his party to such a crushing defeat in the 1984 election, enjoyed a comfortable lead in the polls during much of Mulroney's first term in office, even though only 11 percent felt that Turner would be a better prime minister. Within but a few months of his 1988 election victory Mulroney's Conservatives again found themselves trailing their adversaries in most polls. Within two years they had begun to register new record lows in public support.

The reasons for continued volatility in Canadian elections over the past 30 years may be found in Canadians' attitudes toward government and in the nature of the Canadian party system. In earlier studies of the attitudes of the public toward government and politics in Canada, we found an overwhelmingly negative view of the political world, and widespread discontent with government, parties, and politicians. Rising inflation and unemployment in those years had produced a pessimistic public outlook toward the economy, and nurtured doubts that governments were capable of finding solutions to protracted economic difficulties. There has been a clear tendency to place much of the blame on the shoulders of those in power. Canadians, of course, are not unique among citizens of Western democracies in expressing discontent with government. But, while in some instances such discontent has precipitated a withdrawal from the political process or the formation of protest movements, in Canada it has more often been manifested in a willingness to "throw the rascals out" when the opportunity arose.

PARTIES, LEADERS, AND ISSUES

The Canadian party system to a considerable degree magnifies and encourages this tendency toward volatility in elections. While most Canadians express some degree of allegiance toward a political party, relatively few are strongly partisan. In the 1984 national election study only 23 percent were found to be "very strong" supporters of any political party. Many also hold different party attachments at the federal and provincial levels of government, a uniquely Canadian pattern that explains part of the volatility in federal partisanship and voting behaviour. A substantial number of Canadians change their party identification, often over fairly short periods of time. Between 1974 and 1980, for example, a national panel study found that 41 percent of the sample had either changed or abandoned their party identification. While some may later return to support their former party, this degree of movement nevertheless demonstrates the precariousness of the base of public support on which the parties depend.

FIGURE 2 **Party Identification in the Canadian Electorate, 1974, 1984**

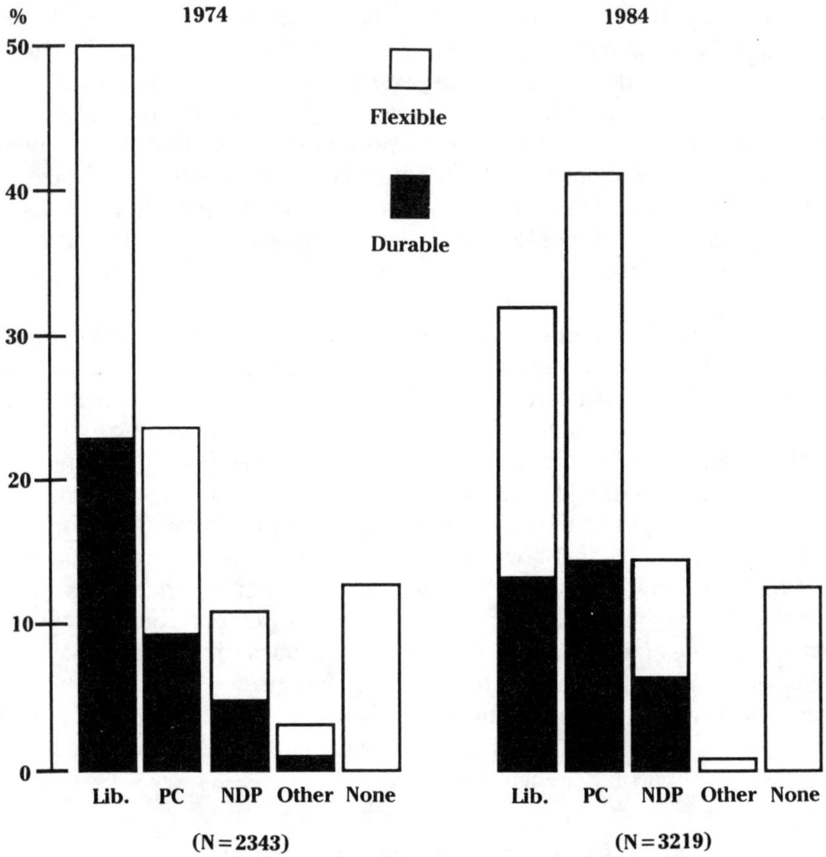

Using a classification scheme developed in *Political Choice in Canada* (McGraw-Hill Ryerson, 1979, 1980), we estimated in 1974 that slightly over a third of the electorate could be thought of as "durable" partisans—reasonably dependable, fairly strong supporters of a particular party—while about two-thirds were "flexible" partisans, whose actual voting decisions would often be determined by the personalities, issues, and events of a particular election campaign. The proportions of flexible partisans found in the electorate sampled in 1984 or 1988 were slightly higher, even though the balance between the parties had shifted in favour of the Conservatives (Figure 2). The flexible Conservative supporters of Brian Mulroney in 1988 are potentially no more reliable in the future than were the flexible Liberals who abandoned Pierre Trudeau in 1972 or 1979, but the two larger parties are now fairly evenly matched in terms of "durable" partisans. Each, however, has only a very small

FIGURE 3   **The Structure of Political Party Images in Canada, 1974, 1984**

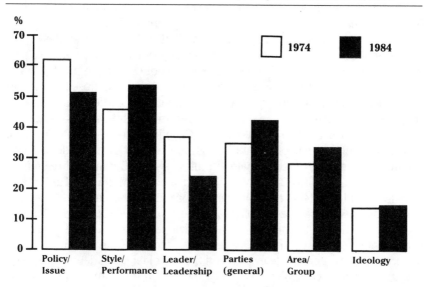

cohort of strong adherents on whose support they can safely rely over the course of several elections.

Unlike some European democracies it has not been possible to explain the dynamics of Canadian party politics by examining long-term forces such as social class, religion, or group alignments. Ideology has been notably weak as a factor in Canadian partisanship, and the Canadian party system has long defied a simple, left-right characterization. Religion, once a factor in the political alignments of an earlier era, is also no longer very useful in understanding Canadian party politics. Linguistic and regional patterns are sometimes strong, and are often highly visible in national politics. But such factors, even when added to other demographic characteristics, can explain only on average about one-tenth of the variation in support for any given party in any election. Rather than calling upon legions of loyal supporters whose attitudes are reinforced by strong group or ideological alignments, Canadian parties must act as "brokers" between competing interests, and attempt to harness the increasingly negative attitudes and impulses of a de-aligned electorate to serve their own short-term goals.

The way in which Canadians tend to view political parties has not changed fundamentally over the period for which national level survey data on this topic are available. In 1984, as in previous years, the largest components of the images that people held of the various parties were those having to do with issues and public policy, followed closely by those characterized as "style" or "performance" (Figure 3). The parties are most commonly viewed in terms of the dominant policies or issues of the day, and/or in terms of their performance, particularly when in government. Parties are much less likely to be viewed in ideological terms, and references to groups, regions, etc., are also distinctly lower than the two predominant categories. For the most part the images of parties that recur with the greatest frequency are those that tend to be most responsive to change over time. Images of parties that might be shaped by long-term social or political forces are much less in evidence.

Party leaders also figure prominently in Canadians' perceptions of political parties. Through much of the 1970s various references to Trudeau (both positive and negative) predominated in this category. But in 1984 references to party leaders declined somewhat, in part because Mulroney, Turner, and Broadbent did not tend to ignite strong passions in quite the same way that Trudeau was capable of doing, and they were therefore somewhat less dominant in shaping the public images of their parties than he had been. This is not to suggest, however, that leaders have declined in importance. If anything, the pervasiveness of television and the use of televised debates between leaders in election campaigns has made them even more important. What is noteworthy is that images of political parties are shaped by current political trends and can be subject to quite rapid change. Strong political leaders have often been able to reshape their parties around their own image. One of the quickest and surest ways for a Canadian political party to give itself a new image is to choose a new leader. But leaders can also drag their parties down. In 1988 the esteem in which the public held all of the party leaders had declined sharply (Figure 4), and these negative perceptions of their leaders reflected on the parties as well.

While issue and policy references are consistently the largest single element in Canadians' perceptions of political parties, issues themselves have demonstrated a high degree of volatility in federal politics. Each of the last four federal elections has seen an abrupt and dramatic shift in the particular issues that attracted the attention of the public and provided the main focus of the campaign. Not infrequently, parties have been able to manipulate issues for strategic purposes, or to invent new issues that promote their own interests. Sometimes, however, certain issues force themselves onto the agenda whether or not the parties wish to emphasize them. But knowing the issues which had been important in the thinking of parties and public alike in one election campaign would be of little help to us in predicting the issues which are likely to arise in the next one. Parties seize upon the issues of the day, and shape their own political strategies around them.

THE CHANGING CANADIAN VOTER

The picture of the Canadian electorate portrayed here is of relatively weak, long-term attachments to parties, low ideological commitment, and high

FIGURE 4   **Mean Thermometer Scores for Party Leaders, 1968–88**

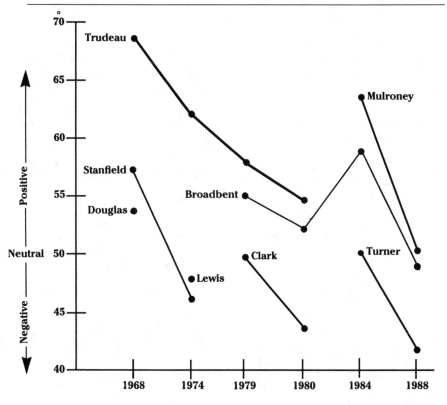

responsiveness to short-term factors such as leaders, issues, or political events. The public tends to react to events as they unfold rather than to ideological or other longer term stimuli. Only a quarter to a third of Canadian voters may be said to have their minds made up with respect to voting choice well in advance of an election. As many as half of all voters may make their voting decisions during the approximately eight weeks of an election campaign, and at least one in five generally reports that their voting decision was made in the final week. Both the 1984 and 1988 elections saw considerable movement in the polls in the immediate period leading up to the election call. And while the sharp movements in the polls which took place during the 1988 campaign were more extreme than normal, they are entirely consistent with the behaviour and characteristics of the Canadian electorate described in previous studies of elections.

Some evidence of typical patterns of voting change in Canadian elections

FIGURE 5   **Stability and Change in Four Federal Elections, 1974–1988**

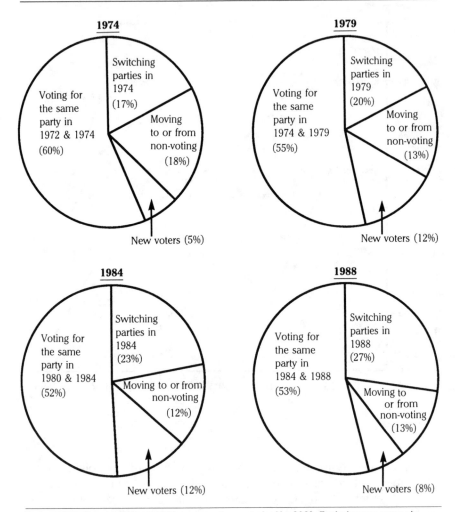

Notes: 1974. Calculated from 1974 cross-section sample. N = 2060. Excludes non-voters in both 1972 and 1974, and new voters not voting in the 1974 election.

1979. Calculated from 1974–79 panel and 1979 cross-section samples. N = 2276. Excludes non-voters in both 1974 and 1979, and new voters not voting in the 1979 election.

1984. Calculated from 1984 cross-section sample. N = 2693. Excludes non-voters in both 1980 and 1984, and new voters not voting in 1984.

1988. Calculated from 1984–88 panel study. N = 1057. Excludes non-voters in both 1984 and 1988. New voters are estimated from census data.

The 1980 election is not included because of some difficulties in comparison.

are found in Figure 5, which compares data from four federal elections over the past two decades. In each of the four cases, what might be considered "stable" patterns of individual voting account for slightly more than half of the total electorate. The similarity of the patterns is especially striking when it is considered that these four elections produced quite different results. The percentage of voters switching is fairly high in each of them, and has increased with each successive election. But one of these elections (1988) produced a comfortable majority for the Conservatives, another (1984) a landslide victory, the third (1979) a precarious minority government, and the other (1974) a Liberal majority.

The source of change in elections is not of course limited to the switching of votes from one election to the next, because the electorate itself is a continually (but gradually) changing entity. Some voters are "replaced" in each election both in the short term as a result of abstentions and in the longer term due to the enfranchisement of new voters. New voters enter the electorate in every election, varying only slightly in total numbers depending upon the interval between elections and long-term population trends. Voting turnout has fluctuated only modestly in Canada from one election to another, and has not thus far exhibited the long-term downward trend found in some other countries, notably the United States. On the other hand the approximate average of 75 percent of eligible Canadians who vote in federal elections should not be taken to imply that it always the same 75 percent. There is a considerable degree of recirculation of nonvoters in federal elections over time, and the proportion of Canadians who are found not to have voted in at least one of several elections over a period of time is quite low. There are therefore in each election a number of previous nonvoters who return to the electorate, and a number of previous voters who leave it, as well as voters becoming eligible to participate for the first time.

The percentage of new voters entering the electorate in 1984 was about the same as in 1979, and turnout rates in these two elections were similar, the proportion of former voters re-entering or leaving the electorate offsetting each other. Population growth is also a potentially important catalyst of change, even though younger voters have thus far not shown characteristics of partisanship or behaviour that would distinguish them sharply from older age cohorts. The lowering of the voting age to 18 in 1970, coupled with higher postwar birth rates, has added about two million new voters to the electorate at each four- or five-year interval since 1968. Immigration has been a smaller, although also important, source of population change. At the time of the 1984 election, one-third of the eligible electorate was under the age of 30. Lower birth rates have now begun to slow down the growth of the electorate, but nearly 1.5 million new voters were nevertheless added to the enumeration lists in 1988. Approximately 17.5 million Canadians were eligible to participate in the 1988 election, reflecting the demographic trends of recent years.

AN ELECTION NOT A REFERENDUM

The events of the 1988 election can be used to illustrate many of the characteristics of voting and elections in Canada described in earlier studies. Following their massive victory in the 1984 election, the Conservatives quickly slipped in the public opinion polls, falling behind the Liberals for the first time as early as mid-1986. Like other federal governments of recent years, the Mulroney government provoked large, negative public sentiment, an improving economy notwithstanding. Yet the prospects for its electoral recovery were always present, as the volatility of the polls in the pre-election period showed. But the improvement in Conservative standing in the public opinion polls during the summer of 1988 leading up to the election call was due at least as much to the problems of the Liberals under John Turner as to better public perception of the Tories or of Brian Mulroney. In studies of the past several federal elections, reasons given by voters for switching from one party to another have often tended to be more negative than positive—an expression of discontent or disillusionment with a party previously supported rather than attraction to a new party or leader.

Although some support existed among both advocates and opponents of the FTA for the idea of a referendum on the free trade issue, there is little indication that this option was ever taken very seriously by either the government or the opposition parties. Rather, each of the three political parties saw the issue as closely linked to its own prospects in the next federal election, which by law had to occur by September 1989 at the latest. As the centrepiece of Conservative economic policy, the FTA represented a tangible policy accomplishment of Mulroney's first term in office. For the Liberals and NDP, it attracted support from economic nationalists and also provided a convenient rallying point for opposition to government economic policies.

But each of the three parties also had serious strategic problems with free trade. After the conclusion of negotiations in October 1987, and the publication of the draft agreement, the Conservatives saw public opinion, which had generally been favourable to the concept of free trade, become much more narrowly divided. As attention shifted from the abstract issues of the Canadian/American relationship to the details of the FTA, the grounds for opposition became more clearly focused. Two months after the text of the agreement became public, a Globe/Environics poll found 40 percent in favour, 40 percent against, and 20 percent undecided, a decline of 15 percent in support for free trade from the levels registered in a poll by the same organization only six months earlier.

The Liberals also had problems with their position on free trade. John Turner came out strongly against the FTA as soon as it was published, vowing to "tear it up" if the Liberals were returned to office. But there were many Liberals who supported the principles of free trade, if not necessarily every detail of the proposed agreement. Free trade was to some degree a Liberal policy, having been proposed by the Macdonald Commission, as well as being associated with the objectives of past Liberal governments. Turner's strong opposition, while helping to revive his sagging leadership credentials in the short term, ran the risk of dividing his party.

For the NDP the issue was made even more complex by Turner's strategy. Accustomed to setting itself up as the only real alternative to "the two old parties," the NDP found itself potentially marginalized by a Liberal–Tory fight over the FTA. Further, even though the party itself was more united against the pact than were the Liberals, the NDP's traditional strength in the West and its hopes of making a breakthrough in Quebec, both areas where free trade was more popular, presented some electoral difficulties. The Conservatives had hoped to have the FTA in place well before an election, thereby avoiding the need to fight a campaign specifically on the free trade issue. But the protracted nature of the negotiations and parliamentary ratification process pushed the conclusion of the agreement ever further into their planned election timetable. As the debate continued in Parliament, Turner announced that he had instructed the Liberal majority in the Senate to block the FTA until a federal election had been held.

Caught in this impasse, the Conservatives delayed their election plans until the last possible moment consistent with a fall election date and the January implementation of the agreement. In spite of the low esteem in which much of the public held John Turner (11 percent of a Gallup sample felt that Turner was the best choice for prime minister), the Tories had been running behind in public opinion polls for some time. A Gallup poll published in August 1988 (just before the Liberals' strategy for blocking the FTA was announced) placed the governing party at 34 percent, the Liberals at 35 percent, and the NDP at 30 percent. As the Conservative government fought to regain control of the political agenda, however, it found its private polls more encouraging. By the time of the election call on October 1, Conservative support as measured by Gallup had risen to 43 percent and the NDP had fallen back to 22 percent.

Surprisingly, as the election finally got under way all three parties seemed determined to circumvent the free trade issue. With public opinion sharply divided, it represented an area of high political risk for all parties. Instead of calling for a popular mandate on their free trade policy, the Conservatives began to stress environmental protection and housing policy (issues scoring high in their private polls), and adopted the vague concept of "managing change" as their campaign theme. The Liberals, having forced free trade onto the election agenda with their parliamentary strategy and Turner's vow to tear up the FTA, feared that a campaign fought solely around one issue would not be credible. Instead, they opened the campaign with the release of position papers on 40 different policy areas, and commenced a strategy of having the leader discuss one of these policy areas in each daily speech. This format was designed to take the emphasis off free trade and also to make the Liberals appear as a party of depth, well prepared to return to government.

The New Democrats' campaign strategy likewise was designed to de-emphasize free trade. With a leader more popular than either Mulroney or Turner, the party sought to downplay ideology and to highlight Broadbent's leadership qualities, adopting as its campaign themes the issue of "fairness" and the needs of the "average family." Seeking to hold its strength among organized labour (where the FTA was not popular), as well as in the West (where it was), party strategists quickly realized that free trade was not the best focus for the NDP campaign. Further, the necessity of sharing opposition to the FTA with the Liberals meant that the party was vulnerable to sounding like a weak echo to Turner's sometimes fiery rhetoric on this issue. Thus, the election which was supposed to "let the people decide" the fate of the FTA began with a campaign in which the agreement received little attention and in which each of the three parties sought to hedge its bets. Three weeks into the campaign Gallup placed Conservative support at 40 percent, the Liberals at 28 percent and the NDP at 29 percent.

It is rare that a single event such as a debate can by itself produce a sudden and dramatic change in a party's political fortunes. In this instance, however, Turner's performance in the two debates temporarily turned the campaign around. The most dramatic segment of the English debate, later used in Liberal campaign spots, occurred when Turner lectured Mulroney on the FTA:

"I happen to believe that you've sold us out. . . . With one stroke of a pen . . . you have thrown us into the North-South influence of the United States . . . And when the economic levers go, political independence is sure to follow."

Turner's success in the debates had several immediate effects. It eclipsed the possibility that the NDP might supplant the Liberals as the principal opposition party, and effectively restored the campaign to a Liberal–Conservative contest. It threw the smooth-running Conservative campaign off stride, and created a new atmosphere of political uncertainty. But, most importantly, it turned the remaining four weeks of the campaign into a debate on free trade, the very issue which all three parties, each for its own reasons, had been treating with such caution.

Public opinion polls quickly confirmed what many of those who saw the debates sensed almost immediately. The Gallup poll taken in the week following the debates (November 6) gave the Liberals 43 percent, Conservatives 31 percent, and NDP 22 percent (Table 1). An 11-point gain in the Liberal percentage from the poll published a week earlier, it was the largest single shift ever recorded by the Gallup organization in Canada. At the same time public support for the trade agreement itself declined sharply. A Globe/Environics poll taken after the debates found only 31 percent in favour of the FTA and 51 percent opposed. Similar results were obtained in the post-debate wave of the 1988 National Election Study (R. Johnston, A. Blais, and J. Crête), in which 33 percent were found to be supportive of the agreement and 47 percent

TABLE 1   **Vote Intention as Measured by Gallup and Other Polls, and by 1988 National Election Study, Weekly Reports, Oct. 1–Nov. 21, 1988**

Week of:	Gallup			Other poll*				NES**		
	PC	**Lib.**	**NDP**	**PC**	**Lib.**	**NDP**		**PC**	**Lib.**	**NDP**
Oct. 2	43	33	22	45	26	27	(R)	—	—	—
Oct. 9	41	32	26	42	25	29	(E)	46	25	24
Oct. 16	39	29	28	42	25	29	(CBC)	48	26	22
Oct. 23	40	28	29	43	25	30	(CTV)	—	—	—
Oct. 30	38	32	27	31	37	26	(E)	37	36	22
Nov. 6	31	43	22	35	37	24	(E)	39	36	22
Nov. 13	35	35	26	39	39	20	(CTV)			
								47	35	16
Final poll	40	35	22	43	32	20	(CTV)			

*Date of publication nearest to that of Gallup report. Angus Reid (R), Environics (E), CBC, or CTV.
**From R. Johnston, A. Blais, H. Brady and J. Crête, "Free Trade and the Dynamics of the 1988 Canadian Election," paper presented to the annual meeting of the American Political Science Association, Atlanta, 1989. Interviews for Oct. 4–8 and 26–30 are combined with those of the following week. Last entry is aggregate for final week (Nov. 14–20).

opposed, a net shift of 7 percent from the wave of interviews conducted only one week earlier.

Had the election taken place in the week following the debates, the Liberals might conceivably have won. But the Conservatives' recovery began swiftly. The party's official campaign organization turned its fire directly on John Turner, emphasizing issues of "trust" and "competence," borrowing selectively from the negative tactics seen in the U.S. election campaign only a few weeks earlier. At the same time outside groups, financed heavily by the business community, mounted an enormous advertising campaign to save the FTA. While not mentioning party affiliation, and therefore falling largely outside the campaign finance laws, it was clear that free trade could be "saved" only by the election of a Conservative majority government. By election day Gallup was forecasting a Conservative majority, and other polls likewise showed the Conservatives regaining much of the lost ground. Few, however, were willing to venture firm predictions in a setting that had proven so volatile. Most observers expected a close election, and a minority government seemed a real possibility until the very end.

The Conservative election victory in 1988 was achieved as much in spite of the free trade issue as because of it. While a large segment of the press in Canada and elsewhere insisted on calling the election a "referendum" on the FTA, I have argued here that such an interpretation is highly questionable. Although Conservative support recovered steadily in the final three weeks of the campaign, in part because of the effectiveness of the campaign against Turner, public attitudes toward the FTA never fully recovered. The final Gallup poll which forecast a Conservative majority government continued to show a plurality of 41 percent opposed to the agreement, with only 34 percent in favour. One-fourth of the respondents in this poll remained undecided, and uncertainty about the FTA continued to be voiced by many voters. The final wave of the National Election Study sample, in the last week, found 45 percent opposed to the agreement, 38 percent in favour, and 17 percent undecided. An exit poll conducted by the Carleton School of Journalism Survey Centre found 44 percent opposed, 42 percent in favour, and 14 percent undecided. There is thus a great deal of consistency in the survey evidence. While the Conservatives won the election decisively, they lost the battle for the hearts and minds of the Canadian electorate on free trade.

Utilizing data available from several of the studies conducted of the 1988 electorate, including one that contains a large panel component of 1984 voters, it is possible to show that attitudes toward the FTA did have a strong impact on the behaviour of voters, particularly in comparison with the effects of issues in past elections. Both the direction of opinion and its intensity were factors in the voting decision. Among those who held strong opinions on the issue, voting patterns were relatively predictable. Eighty-nine percent of those respondents in the 1988 Carleton Panel Study who were strongly favourable to the FTA voted for the Conservatives. Conversely, the Tories received few votes among those respondents who strongly opposed the agreement. But the slippage between attitudes and vote is greater among some of the other groups. Twenty percent of those whose opinions were favourable to the FTA but not strongly held voted Liberal. Among those who remained undecided about free trade, the Conservatives did fairly well, gaining 42 percent of the vote compared to 31 percent for the Liberals and 21 percent for the NDP.

What is most evident in these data, however, is the effectiveness of the split in votes between Liberal and NDP candidates in contributing to the re-election of the Conservative government. While opposition to the FTA helped the Liberals generally in the campaign, the necessity of sharing this opposition with the NDP all but assured the success of the Conservatives' campaign strategy so long as free trade remained the main focus of the campaign. Although there were small numbers of active opponents of the agreement in various parts of the country who advocated tactical voting strategies in an attempt to defeat Conservative candidates, such efforts were clearly ineffectual. Few members of the public at large are potential tactical voters. In the Canadian electoral system, where only a single vote is available with which to express one's preferences for party, leader, and local candidate, there was not much room left for the voter to express an opinion on the FTA.

A categorization of the entire electorate, as sampled on election day in the Carleton Exit Poll, illustrates the difficulty inherent in attempting to infer broad public support for free trade in the 1988 voting patterns. Just under 38 percent of the electorate supported the FTA and voted Conservative. Even when combined with Liberal and NDP supporters of the agreement, this does not come remotely close to a majority of the electorate. Under a European-style system of proportional representation, the election outcome would have been either a Conservative minority government or a Liberal–NDP coalition, in either case

TABLE 2 **An Election Day Map of the Canadian Electorate: Attitude Toward Free Trade Agreement and Vote (Carleton Exit Poll)**

	(Diagonal percentages)*			
	Lib.	**PC**	**NDP**	**Other**
Favour	2.5	37.7	1.5	1.6
Opposed	24.2	1.9	17.0	1.2
DK, Undecided	2.7	5.3	3.8	0.7
				/ 100%
				(N = 1832)

*Percentages sum to 100 percent.

effectively killing the FTA. Had it been a California-style ballot proposition, the agreement probably would have been defeated.

The intensity of the final weeks of the campaign placed unusually great pressure on Canadian voters. The unprecedented advertising blitz waged by nonparty groups on behalf of the FTA seemed to imply that the election was truly a one-issue affair. At the same time, however, the official Conservative campaign was de-emphasizing free trade in its advertising and focusing its attention on the leadership qualities of John Turner. It may have been an easy choice for the voter who was persuaded by both of these arguments. But it was a difficult one for those who sought to register their views on a major policy question while at the same time being asked to pass judgment on individual leaders and candidates. Implicitly, a contest between three or more political parties for parliamentary seats can never really be a referendum on any single issue, even one as important as the Canada–U.S. Free Trade Agreement.

It is perhaps surprising to discover that fewer than half of those sampled in the 1988 panel study reported that their vote was affected by free trade "a great deal" (48 percent). Nearly one voter in five responded to this item by indicating that free trade had little to do with his or her voting choice. There are only small differences between voters for the three main parties on this item, although a slightly larger proportion of Conservative voters took a middle position, indicating that attitudes toward free trade had "something" to do with their vote. This might be expected, given that a Conservative vote was, for many Canadians, an implied positive judgment on Mulroney's first term in office and on the government's policies more generally, only one of which was the FTA.

Perhaps one of the most unexpected findings in the various surveys was that over two-thirds of those sampled in the panel study felt that they did not have sufficient information about the FTA. It would have seemed that nearly a year of public discussion of the agreement, culminating in an intensive election campaign where the trade issue was the central focus, would have produced a quite different response. But the strategic interests of the parties did not point in the direction of sending clear signals to the voters or of presenting clear choices. Rather, the normal operation of the electoral system made the choice extremely difficult for many voters, even had they not been subjected to campaign strategies designed as much to confuse and obscure as to clarify. Repeatedly told that the election was the "most important in their history," many Canadians found frustration rather than satisfaction in their vote. On the surface the 1988 election seemed a classic exercise in democracy, seeking the approval of the voting public for a major new policy direction. But the reality was far different. In retrospect it is difficult to see the outcome as anything more than one in which the views of a well-organized and heavily financed minority ultimately prevailed, and in which the electoral system again failed to deliver a clear mandate.

On free trade as on other political questions in Canada, few voters approached the issue from an ideological or strongly partisan perspective. The events of the 1988 election were perhaps unusual in their intensity and dramatic impact, but they were in many ways typical of the type of volatility that has been a feature of Canadian politics for the past three decades. The perceptions of the party leaders, the state of the economy, and the ongoing debate on the FTA, all accounted to some degree for the shifts in party popularity documented by the polls in the pre-election period. But as the campaign took hold, the activities of the leaders and the respective strategies of the parties began to affect the attitudes of the public. In particular the televised leader debates and the rise of the free trade issue to a dominant position in the campaign were the types of events capable of producing sharp swings among large numbers of voters. There were two different types of volatility at work in this process— the shift of the attention of the electorate to a new issue, and the revision of opinions on the issue itself. As a result the 1988 election outcome was in some doubt almost until the very end.

It is likely that the Canadian political world of the 1990s will continue to exhibit many of these same characteristics. While it will reflect the partisan trends of the recent past, it will also be subject to influences from new problems, policies, or leaders. The proportion of flexible partisans in the electorate continues to be high, and it is high in virtually every age cohort, every region of the country, and every significant voting group. Responsiveness to short-term factors such as issues, party performance and style, the personalities of leaders, or the intrusion of new political or economic problems will be greater than responsiveness to ideology, group loyalty, or other longer term forces. But it will also be a world in which discontent with politics and politicians is pervasive, and in which there are new firmly anchored partisan alignments. In such an environment, the re-election of a governing party with a clear parliamentary majority could well become an increasingly rare event.

BIBLIOGRAPHY

The Electoral Process

(See also the Bibliography in Chapter 7)

Adamson, A. "We Were Here Before—The Referendum in Canadian Experience." *P.O.*, I, 1, March, 1980.

Aucoin, P. *Party Government and Regional Representation in Canada.* Toronto: U.T.P., 1985.

Boyer, J.P. *Election Law in Canada: The Law and Procedure of Federal, Provincial and Territorial Elections.* Toronto: Butterworths, 1982.

Boyer, J.P. *Lawmaking by the People: Referendums and Plebiscites in Canada.* Toronto: Butterworths, 1982.

Boyer, J.P. *Political Rights: The Legal Framework of Elections in Canada.* Toronto: Butterworths, 1982.

Boyer, J.P. *Money and Message: The Law Governing Election Financing, Advertising, Broadcasting and Campaigning in Canada.* Toronto: Butterworths, 1983.

Boyer, J.P. *Local Elections in Canada: The Law Governing Elections of Municipal Councils, School Boards and Other Local Authorities.* Toronto: Butterworths, 1983.

Canada, [Hnatyshyn, R.]. *White Paper on Election Law Reform.* Ottawa: S. and S., June, 1986.

Canada, Task Force on Canadian Unity, [Pepin-Robarts Report], *A Future Together: Observations and Recommendations.* Ottawa: S. and S., 1979.

Carty, R.K. "The Electoral Boundary Revolution in Canada." *A.R.C.S.,* 15, 2, Autumn, 1985.

Coulson, M. "Reforming Electoral Distribution." *P.O.,* 4, 1, January–February, 1983.

Courtney, J.C. "Recognition of Canadian Political Parties in Parliament and in Law." *C.J.P.S.,* 11, 1, March, 1978.

Courtney, J.C. "Reflections on Reforming the Canadian Electoral System." *C.P.A.,* 23, 3, Fall, 1980.

Courtney, J.C. "The Defeat of the Clark Government: The Dissolution of Parliament, Leadership Conventions, and the Calling of Elections in Canada." *J.C.S.,* 17, 2, Summer, 1982.

Courtney, J. "Parliament and Representation: The Unfinished Agenda of Electoral Redistributions." *C.J.P.S.,* XXI, 4, December, 1988.

Dobell, W.M. "A Limited Corrective to Plurality Voting." *C.P.P.,* VII, 1, Winter, 1981.

Doucet, P. and Finn, J.-G. "Eléments de réforme du système électoral du Nouveau-Brunswick." *J.C.S.,* 18,4, Winter, 1983–84.

Elton, D., and Gibbins, R. *Electoral Reform: The Time Is Pressing, The Need Is Now.* Calgary: Canada West Foundation, 1980.

Fillmore, N. "The Big Oink: How Business Swallowed Politics." *This Magazine,* 22, March-April, 1989. [Campaign finance].

Forest, P.-G. "Les techniciens de la représentation: contribution à l'histoire des études électorales." *C.J.P.S,* 19, 4, December, 1986.

Hiebert, J. "Fair Elections and Freedom of Expression Under the Charter." *J.C.S.,* 24, 4, Winter, 1989–90.

Hyson, S. "The Horrible Example." *P.O.,* 9, 8, October, 1988. [The electoral system]

Irvine, W.P. *Does Canada Need a New Electoral System?* Kingston: Queen's University, I.I.R., 1979.

Irvine, W.P. "Power Requires Representation." *P.O.*, 1, 4, December-January, 1980–1981.

Johnston, J.P., and Pasis, H.E., (eds.). *Representation and Electoral Systems: Canadian Perspectives.* Toronto: P.-H., 1990.

Lovink, J.A.A. "On Analysing the Impact of the Electoral System on the Party System in Canada." *C.J.P.S.*, 3, 4, December, 1970. (Reply by A.C. Cairns, *ibid.*)

Lovink, J.A.A. "Is Canadian Politics Too Competitive?" *C.J.P.S.*, 6, 3, September, 1973.

Mintz, E. "Election Campaign Tours in Canada." *Political Geography Quarterly*, 4, 1, January, 1985.

Ontario Commission on Election Contributions and Expenses. *A Comparative Survey of Election Finance Legislation.* 1983.

Stanbury, W.T. "The Mother's Milk of Politics: Political Contributions to Federal Parties in Canada, 1974–1984." *C.J.P.S.*, 19, 4, December, 1986.

Stevenson, A.B. *Canadian Election Reform: Dialogue on Issues and Effects.* Toronto: Ontario Commission on Election Contributions and Expenses, 1982.

Wearing, J., and Wearing, P. "Mother's Milk Revisited: The Effect of Foreign Ownership on Political Contributions." *C.J.P.S.*. 23, 1, March, 1990.

Voting Behaviour, Political Culture, Socialization, Participation

(See also Bibliographies in Chapters 4, 5, 6, 7.)

Apostle, R., Kasdan, R.L., and Hanson, A. "Political Efficacy and Political Activity in Southwest Nova Scotia: A Research Note." *J.C.S.*, 19, 1, Spring, 1984.

Archer, K. "A Simultaneous Equation Model of Canadian Voting Behaviour." *C.J.P.S.*, 20, 3, September, 1987.

Archer, K., and Johnson, M. "Inflation, Unemployment and Canadian Federal Voting Behaviour." *C.J.P.S.*, 21, 3, September, 1988.

Archer, K., and Kornberg, A. "Issue Perceptions and Electoral Behavior in an Age of Restraint, 1974–1980." *A.R.C.S.*, 15, 1, Spring, 1985.

Baer, D.E., and Curtis, J.E. "French Canadian-English Canadian Differences in Values: National Survey Findings." *C.J.S.*, 9, 4, Fall, 1984.

Bashevkin, S., (ed.). *Canadian Political Behaviour: Introductory Readings.* Toronto: Methuen, 1985.

Beck, J.M. *Pendulum of Power: Canada's Federal Elections.* Toronto: P.-H., 1968.

Berkowitz, S.D. *Models and Myths in Canadian Society.* Toronto: Butterworths, 1981.

Black, J.H. "Revisiting the Effects of Canvassing on Voting Behaviour." *C.J.P.S.*, 17, 2, June, 1984.

Black, J.H. "The Practice of Politics in Two Settings: Political Transferability among Recent Immigrants to Canada." *C.J.P.S.*, 20, 4, December, 1987.

Blake, D.E. "1896 and All That: Critical Elections in Canada." *C.J.P.S.*, 12, 2, June, 1979.

Blake, D.E. "The Consistency of Inconsistency: Party Identification in Federal and Provincial Politics." *C.J.P.S.*, 15, 4, December, 1982.

Blake, D.E. *Two Political Worlds: Parties and Voting in British Columbia.* Vancouver: U.B.C.P., 1985.

Brown, S. *et al.* "In the Eye of the Beholder: Leader Images in Canada." *C.J.P.S.*, 21, 4, December, 1988.

Brym, R. *et al.* "Class power, class mobilization, and class voting: the Canadian Case." *C.J.S.*, 14, 1, Winter, 1989.

Canada, *Report of the Chief Electoral Officer, Thirty-Fourth General Election, 1988.* Ottawa: S. and S., 1989. (Previous *Reports* for each election.)

Clarke, H.D. *et al.. Political Choice in Canada.* Toronto: McG.-H.R., 1979. (Abridged ed., 1980.)

Clarke, H.D. *et al.* "Voting Behaviour and the Outcome of the 1979 Federal Election: The Impact of Leaders and Issues." *C.J.P.S.*, 15, 3, September, 1982.

Clarke, H.D. *et al. Absent Mandate: The Politics of Discontent in Canada.* Toronto: Gage, 1984.

Clarke, H.D., Kornberg, A., and Stewart, M. "Parliament and Political Support in Canada." *American Political Science Review*, 78, 2, June, 1984.

Cooper, A.F., (ed.). *Canadian Culture: International Dimensions.* Toronto: C.I.I.A., 1985.

Dahlie, J., and Fernando, T. *Ethnicity, Power and Politics in Canada.* Toronto: Methuen, 1981.

Elkins, D.J., and Simeon, R. *Small Worlds: Parties and Provinces in Canadian Political Life.* Toronto: Methuen, 1980.

Feigert, F. *Canada Votes: 1935–1988.* Durham, North Carolina: Duke University Press, 1989.

Frizzell, A., Pammett, J., and Westell, A., (eds.). *The Canadian General Election of 1988.* Ottawa: C.U.P., 1989.

Frohlich, N., and Boschmann, I. "Partisan Preference and Income Redistribution: Cross-National and Cross-Sexual Results." *C.J.P.S.*, 19, 1, March, 1986.

Gerber, L.M. "The Federal Election of 1968: Social Class Composition and Party Support in the Electoral Districts of Ontario." *C.R.S.A.*, 23, 1, February, 1986.

Gibbins, R., and Nevitte, N. "Canadian Political Ideology: A Comparative Analysis." *C.J.P.S.*, 18, 3, September, 1985.

Gidengil, E. "Class and Region in Canadian Voting: A Dependency Interpretation." *C.J.P.S.*, 22, 3, September, 1989.

Hamilton, R., and Pinard, M. "The Parti Québecois Comes to Power: An Analysis of the 1976 Quebec Election." *C.J.P.S.*, 11, 4, December, 1978.

Happy, J. "Economic Performance and Retrospective Voting in Canadian Federal Elections." *C.J.P.S.*, 22, 2, June, 1989.

Hunter, A.A., and Denton, M. "Do Female Candidates 'Lose Votes'?: The Experience of Female Candidates in the 1979 and 1980 Canadian General Elections." *C.R.S.A.*, 21, 4, November, 1984.

Johnston, R. "The Reproduction of the Religious Cleavage in Canadian Elections." *C.J.P.S.*, 18, 1, March, 1985. (Comment by W.P. Irvine, *ibid.*)

Kay, B.J. "By-Elections as Indicators of Canadian Voting." *C.J.P.S.*, 14, 1, March, 1981.

Kornberg, A., Mishler, W. and Clarke, M. *Representative Democracy in the Canadian Provinces.* Toronto: P.-H., 1982.

Kornberg, A., and Clarke, H.D., (eds.). *Political Support in Canada: The Crisis Years.* Durham, North Carolina: Duke University Press, 1983.

Kornberg, A., and Clarke, H.D. "Governmental Performance, Political Socialization and Parliamentary Support: The Case of Canada." *A.R.C.S.*, 16, 2, Summer, 1986.

Krashinsky, M., and Milne, W.J. "Some Evidence on the Effect of Incumbency in Ontario Provincial Elections." *C.J.P.S.*, 16, 3, September, 1983.

Krashinsky, M., and Milne, W.J. "Additional Evidence on the Effect of Incumbency in Canadian Elections." *C.J.P.S.*, 18, 1, March, 1985.

Lambert, R.D. "Question Design, Response Set and the Measurement of Left/Right Thinking in Survey Research." *C.J.P.S.*, 16, 1, March, 1983.

Lambert, R.D. *et al.* "Effects of Identification with Governing Parties on Feelings of Political Efficacy and Trust." *C.J.P.S.*, 19, 4, December, 1986.

Lambert, R. *et al.* "The left/right factor in party identification." *C.J.S.*, 13, 4, Fall, 1988.

Lambert, R. *et al.* "The Social Sources of Political Knowledge." *C.J.P.S.*, 21, 2, June, 1988.

LaPonce, J.A. *Left and Right: The Topography of Political Perceptions.* Toronto: U.T.P., 1981.

LaPonce, J.A. "Left or Centre? The Canadian Jewish Electorate, 1953–1983." *C.J.P.S.*, 21, 4, December, 1988.

LeDuc, L. "Canada: The Politics of Stable Dealignment." In Dalton, R.J., *et al.*, (eds.) *Electoral Change in Advanced Industrial Democracies.* Princeton: P.U.P., 1984.

LeDuc, L. "Canada." In Crewe, I., Denver, D., (eds.). *Electoral Changes in Western Democracies.* New York: St. Martin's Press, 1985.

LeDuc, L. *et al.* "Partisan Instability in Canada: Evidence from a New Panel Study." *American Political Science Review*, 78, 2, June, 1984.

MacDermid, R. "The Recall of Past Partisanship: Feeble Memories or Frail Concepts?" *C.J.P.S.*, 22, 2, June, 1989.

Martinez, M.D. "Intergenerational Transfer of Canadian Partisanships." *C.J.P.S.*, 17, 1, March, 1984.

McCormick, P. "Voting Behaviour in Alberta: The Quasi-Party System Revisited." *J.C.S.*, 15, 3, Fall, 1980.

Meisel, J. *Working Papers on Canadian Politics.* Montreal: McG.-Q.U.P., 2nd enlarged ed., 1975.

Mishler, W. *Political Participation in Canada: Prospects for Democratic Citizenship.* Toronto: Macmillan, 1979.

Nevitte, N., Bakvis, H., and Gibbins, R. "The Ideological Contours of 'New Politics' in Canada: Policy, Mobilization, and Partisan Support." *C.J.P.S.*, 22, 3, September, 1989.

Nevitte, N., and Gibbins, R. "Neoconservatism: Canadian Variations on an Ideological Theme." *C.P.P.*, 10, 4, December, 1984.

Ornstein, M.D., and Stevenson, H.M. "Ideology and Public Policy in Canada." *British Journal of Political Science*, 14, 3, 1984.

Ornstein, M.D., Stevenson, H.M., and Williams, A.P. "Region, Class and Political Culture in Canada." *C.J.P.S.*, 13, 2, June, 1980.

Penniman, H.R., (ed.). *Canada at the Polls, 1979 and 1980.* Washington: American Enterprise Institute for Public Policy Research, 1981.

Penniman, H.R., (ed.). *Canada at the Polls, 1984.* Washington: American Enterprise Institute for Public Policy Research, 1988.

Simeon, R., and Elkins, D. "Regional Political Cultures in Canada." *C.J.P.S.*, 7, 3, September, 1974.

Stevenson, M. "Ideology and Unstable Party Identification in Canada: Limited Rationality in a Brokerage Party System." *C.J.P.S.*, 20, 4, December, 1987.

Ullman, S. "The Political Attitudes of New Brunswick's Acadians and Anglophones: Old Wine in Old Bottles." *A.R.C.S.*, 16, 2, Summer, 1986.

Wilson, J. "The Canadian Political Cultures: Towards a Redefinition of the Canadian Political System." *C.J.P.S.*, 7, 3, September, 1974.

Wilson, R.J. "Geography, Politics and Culture: Electoral Insularity in British Columbia." *C.J.P.S.*, 13, 4, December, 1980.

Wiseman, N. "The Use, Misuse and Abuse of the National Election Studies." *J.C.S.*, 21, 1, Spring, 1986. (See also: Archer, K., "The Meaning and Demeaning of the National Election Studies," *ibid.*, 24, 4, Winter, 1989–90; Wiseman, N., "The National Election Studies Revisited." *ibid.*)

PUBLIC POLICY
MAKING

THE EXECUTIVE:
CROWN, PRIME MINISTER, CABINET

THE VALUE OF THE MONARCHY

Frank MacKinnon

A constitutional monarchy protects democracy from some peculiarities of political power. It has been retained in our system because it works. Other reasons, such as nostalgic recollections of the past and sentimental ties with Britain, are secondary—to some, irrelevant—and should not obscure basic facts of government. One of these facts is a tendency of man, whether deep-sea diver or astronaut on the one hand or politician on the other, to suffer from the "bends" during rapid rises from one level of pressure and atmosphere to another.

History clearly indicates how common and serious are the "bends" in government. Even small rises from private citizen to mayor may bring on giddiness while major ascents from backbencher to minister or from minister to head of government can cause acute distress of the equilibrium. Constitutions have prescribed various remedies. Complicated procedures select those who are to make the political climb; ascent by stages is sometimes provided—perhaps by planned pauses in the back benches or the opposition; control of those on high is arranged through established contacts with those below; and,

From *The Dalhousie Review*, Vol. 49, No. 2, Summer, 1969, by permission of the author and publisher.

most difficult of all, some arrangement must be made to end the stay in political orbit of those who have been there long enough and can not or will not come back by themselves. A sure cure has not yet been devised, however, and the "bends" remain a major occupational hazard of rulers, which some overcome for varying periods and to which others fall quick and tragic victims.

To relieve this difficulty at the heights of political power is the main purpose of the constitutional monarchy. Some human being must be at the summit of government, and much depends on his stability. Unfortunately great talent, public acclaim and hero worship, and even assumptions of "divine right" have not been reliable stabilizers when the head of state wields power. We therefore place two persons at the top: one is at the very summit and he stays there permanently and is accustomed to living at that level; the other is temporary and he is made to understand that his status is sponsored and may be ended at any time.

The monarch holds power in the state on behalf of the people, and he or she is the personal symbol of authority which man finds necessary in every system. Heredity makes his tenure unquestioned and ensures a rigid training for the job. Pomp and ceremony attract respect and provide the show which people always expect from heads of state. But the monarch is not allowed to wield the power of head of state by himself; the pomp and ceremony are all that he can manage safely at his level and he must wield the power only on the advice of others.

These others are the sovereign's ministers, especially the prime minister, who is the head of government. A prime minister is almost at the summit but not quite, and that difference is crucial to democracy. He is given no power whatever; he advised the Crown on the exercise of the Crown's power; and that difference is also crucial to democracy. He has no pomp of his own, so that he knows that he is not an indispensable symbol. He is a trustee into whose hands is placed the exercise of power but not power itself.

This separation of pomp and power at the top took centuries to develop and was the result of the mistakes of many sovereigns and ministers. Other arrangements for such separation in other systems did not go so far as the British who make the monarch so colourful and the prime minister so powerful and responsible an adviser that each, regardless of the personalities concerned, knows his place. . . .

The monarchy therefore serves democracy. It keeps the ministers in second place as servants of the state—electable, responsible, accountable, criticizable, and defeatable—a position necessary to the operation of parliamentary government. The people and their parliament can control the head of government because he cannot identify himself with the state or confuse loyalty to himself with allegiance to the state and criticism with treason. He is discouraged from the common tendency of officials, whether elected or not, to regard and make themselves indispensable, to entrench themselves in expanding power structures, to resent accountability and criticism, and to scoff at the effects of prolonged tenure of office or advancing years. Moreover, such control avoids the charges of treason, executions, assassinations, revolutions, and miscellaneous other expensive upheavals which so often accompany attempts to control and change governments that take themselves too seriously.

The democratic sensibilities of some people are disturbed by the idea of an élite, a symbol, an official who is neither elected nor chosen by someone who is elected. They err if they think the withdrawal of monarchy will remove such elements from government. These elements are characteristic of government itself, whatever its form, and are simply transferred to other institutions when a monarchy disappears. Whatever their system, men will have élites and symbols. Heads of government, elected or not, will take to themselves if they can the prestige and power of monarchs, disguised perhaps, but with the same basic elements; they find them a natural and necessary feature of government authority. The existence of a monarch protects the prime minister from such temptations . . .

Monarchical phenomena are common in other activities of society. The cult of the celebrity is as dominant in our day as it ever was in history. How often is "I touched him!" heard in a screaming crowd. The élite in athletics have always been admired and well paid. Universities feature academic ceremonial. There are many resemblances between churches and royal courts—the raiment, titles, powers of clergy, even the throne, tiara, and crown. And in the smallest communities the dignities and regalia of fraternal and religious lodges are reminiscent of the potentates and knights of old. These are such natural and acceptable phenomena that it is not difficult to understand government officials taking advantage of them. Man has found, however, that in government it is hard to criticize and advise a tremendous swell in robes or uniform who also has power, a retinue, and a palace. Our system discourages these things as much as possible for working politicians, but, since they are inevitable anyway, they are placed with the Crown, partly to provide a good show, mainly to strengthen the democratic state.

All systems, including democracy, contain the means for their own destruction. It is in time of crisis, when some serious and unexpected dislocation takes place for which there is no normal remedy, that systems break down for good. . . . Parliamentary government presupposes change as required; but such change means orderly alterations of power, not conditions of general panic and destruction. When an electoral system is stalemated, when a parliament breaks down, when a prime minister dies in office and there is no obvious successor, when a leader becomes very ill or insane and everyone knows it but himself and the public—these are among the times when political paralysis is brought on by shock and uncertainty. In such circumstances a constitutional monarch provides a symbol of continuity, order, and authority. He cannot, of course, step in and take over; he can only encourage others and sponsor the search for an orderly solution of the difficulties. He is above suspicion and can command confidence because of his prestige, because he is above politics and ambition for personal aggrandizement, and because he does not exercise power on his own initiative. Even in such modest periods of upheaval as elections, he represents the state as a whole while the parties involved, including the government, can oppose each other to even the most vituperative extremes—a process which should never be taken for granted. No political leader can be a symbol of the whole state either in crisis or in elections, nor should he be in a parliamentary democracy. That is the job of a monarch.

There are other purposes of the monarchy: the encouragement of dignity and respect for government, the example of a royal family, the colour of pageantry, the sponsorship of good works and the inevitable social activities of government; the source of honours and awards; a continuing focus of loyalty and emotion; a unifying force among a people; and, in our monarchy, a headship for a family of nations, the Commonwealth. Each of these functions has its own merits and weaknesses. Whether or not we approve of any or all of them, we must remember that none is irrelevant or disposable: each one crops up in some form in every system of government. When a monarchy disappears, other institutions soon take them on. Then trouble begins because of the transfer of such functions to the power structure. Officials and political parties from right to left have found many ways of using them to protect themselves and their powers and prestige from the legitimate operation of democracy. They are in safer hands, and are more effective, with the Crown.

An elected non-political president is often used as an alternative to a monarch. His main problem, aside from the temporary and relatively uninteresting and colourless character of his office, is the ease with which he can be overshadowed by the prime minister and, worse, the ease with which he can compete with the prime minister. Everyone concerned knows exactly where the monarch and his advisers stand in relation to one another and to the people. This arrangement, as already noted, is not so clear in a republic because two elected heads can get in each other's way and trespass on each other's powers.

An elected political president wielding power directly is a completely different institution at the head of a different system of government. He could not function in the parliamentary system as we know it. As every American president has testified, this kind of official also finds burdensome the combination of head of government and head of state. . . .

Canadians have retained the Crown as represented by the Sovereign, the Governor-General, and the Lieutenant-Governors. All the reasons for the Crown have applied in both federal and provincial governments, and, on the whole, the relations between the Crown and the ministers have worked extremely well. The twelve incumbents together cost a little more than two cents per citizen per year. By no stretch of the imagination can the Governors-General or the Lieutenant-Governors be considered to have played any significant role in actual government in our time, or to have obstructed or overshadowed their

Premiers. Their job has been to occupy the top levels in their respective jurisdictions and to handle the decorative and emergency functions, while leaving the Prime Ministers and Premiers to handle the powers of government without actually possessing them, and to be electable, responsible, accountable, criticizable, and removable. The Governors-General and the Lieutenant-Governors are something more than constitutional presidents; they have Sovereign's auspices to signify authority, to enhance their prestige, and to clearly mark the line between pomp and power. . . .

Those who worry about the monarchy sometimes doubt the relevance in Canada of the Sovereign herself because she is Queen of several countries. Such a situation is common in Canada; many citizens owe allegiance to outside heads of their business, churches, unions, international political parties, and other groups. Nevertheless, a shared head of state is controversial. We need to remember that under our constitution the Sovereign is a part of Parliament and is the formal, ultimate source of political power, and the law sets out the facts of power with clarity for all to see and recognize as authentic. Governments in Canada may have quarrelled over which may do what, but power to govern has itself been unassailable and unquestioned from colonial times to the present. This stability of law is by no means universal around the world in an age when constitutions have been unusually short-lived and unreliable and when human rights have enjoyed only modest protection. Governments and their supporters come and go, but the Canadian people know that their rights and the powers of their state enjoy a solid, recognized base and the validations of centuries of usage. The sovereign is the legal expression and permanent non-partisan symbol of that fact. . . .

THE PRIME MINISTER
Marc Lalonde

HISTORY OF THE OFFICE

In analysing the role and function of the prime minister, one must be suspicious of a text book approach. A purely constitutional description of his office would reveal that it has changed little during the past century in Canada. A constitutional analysis, however, would be subject to severe limitations. It

Adapted by the editor from an article by Marc Lalonde, former Principal Secretary to the Prime Minister, which appeared under the title "The Changing Role of the Prime Minister's Office" in *Canadian Public Administration*, 14, 4, Winter, 1971, published by the Institute of Public Administration of Canada. By permission.

would inevitably ignore the "pith and substance" of his office which can only be revealed by considering the daily discharge of his responsibilities. . . . What has happened is that greater demands for his accountability and participation made by ministers, members of Parliament, public administrators, the press, pressure groups and the public in general have required the Canadian prime minister fully to assume the powers that he has always had under the constitution.

For some time, many concerned Canadians have been wondering whether the Canadian Parliamentary system is evolving into a presidential system. When asked about this, it is only half jokingly that I usually answer by asking the question, "Why should the Canadian prime minister, who occupies one of the most powerful elected offices in the world, seek to implement a congressional style of government and accept in so doing a reduction of his powers?"

Within the political framework of the British North America Act of 1867 and following British practice, the prime minister is recognized as the chief minister of a committee known as "the cabinet." The cabinet in turn is part of the Privy Council established under section 11 of the British North America Act. Considering the extensive power exercised by the prime minister and the cabinet, it is rather remarkable that the BNA Act nowhere mentions the office of prime minister nor specifically the institution of cabinet. Though power is not explicitly vested in the prime minister and cabinet by the law, they exercise it formally through some other body in accordance with the custom of the constitution. The vital aspects of prime ministerial and cabinet power rest, therefore, on constitutional conventions.

Some idea of the basis for the pre-eminent position of the prime minister can be gleaned from an official statement of his functions. . . .

The most recent minute of Council on this subject is P.C. 3374 of October 25, 1935, which reads as follows:

1. A meeting of a Committee of the Privy Council is at the call of the Prime Minister and, in his absence, of that of the senior Privy Councillor, if the President of the Council be absent;

2. A quorum of the Council being four, no submission, for approval to the Governor General, can be made with a less number than the quorum;

3. A Minister cannot make recommendations to Council affecting the discipline of the Department of another Minister;

4. The following recommendations are the special prerogative of the Prime Minister:

Dissolution and Convocation of Parliament

Appointment of

Privy Councillors;

Cabinet Ministers;

Lieutenant-Governors; (including leave of absence to same);

Provincial Administrators;

Speaker of the Senate;
Chief Justices of all Courts;
Senators;
Sub-Committees of Council;
Treasury Board;
Committee of Internal Economy, House of Commons;
Deputy Heads of Departments;
Librarians of Parliament;
Crown Appointments in both Houses of Parliament;
Governor General's Secretary's Staff;
Recommendations in any Department. . . .

While this official statement is useful, it is far from complete. To gain a fuller understanding of the extent of the prime minister's power, it is necessary to examine the fundamental political reality upon which his position rests. He is chosen by a popular convention of a major party; he ordinarily commands substantial and deeply rooted support amongst the electorate; he is the directing force in both cabinet and Parliament; he has a key role in the Commons, answers many questions there, and takes the lead in explaining and defending his government's policies and activities; he must be consulted on important decisions by all cabinet ministers; to a large extent he prescribes the functions of his colleagues and he can, if necessary, advise the Governor General to dismiss a minister; he recommends most important appointments to the cabinet; he has a special responsibility for external affairs; and he has the important prerogative of advising the Governor General when Parliament should be dissolved.

The powers of the prime minister are, therefore, potentially enormous. How they are wielded, however, depends in large measure on his personality and on his interpretation of his leadership role. In the words of Lord Oxford and Asquith, "The office is what its holder chooses and is able to make of it."

PRIME MINISTER AND PARLIAMENT

. . . The traditional duties of the prime minister in the House of Commons have changed very little in the past century. When in the House of Commons, he is inevitably the chief spokesman for the Chamber. He is the dominant figure, and his position and responsibilities are recognized by the House as a whole. . . .

Among those traditional duties is participation in Question Period, undoubtedly one of the institutions most cherished by the members of the House. . . . Whereas cabinet ministers are frequently called upon to answer questions that touch their respective departments, the prime minister, on the other hand, is expected to answer questions which involve general issues or the interrelationships of the various departments. . . .

A vitally important aspect of the prime minister's parliamentary responsibilities concerns his relationship with the government caucus. Every Wednesday morning, unless he is out of Ottawa, he meets with the members of the caucus to hear their questions and opinions and to offer answers and guidance in reply. This weekly meeting with caucus is by no means the only contact between the prime minister and party members. On the occasion of his daily presence in the House, they have another opportunity to raise various questions with him. . . .

Finally, the prime minister, like all other members, represents a particular electoral riding and, as such, he has a direct responsibility to his constituents. . . .

PRIME MINISTER AND CABINET

. . . For a time it was popular to refer to the prime minister as *primus inter pares* or as *inter stellas luna minores*. [Neither interpretation does] justice to his office. He cannot be first among equals because in a political sense no individual is his equal. It would be wrong, however, to assume that the prime minister stands in a position of unquestionable supremacy over his colleagues in the cabinet. Unlike the president of the United States, the prime minister is not in a position of strength superior to that of the total cabinet. Members of the Canadian cabinet are responsible to the House of Commons; and while they acknowledge the leadership of the prime minister, and will in fact bow to his decisions, they have important political and administrative responsibilities which they must discharge independently of the prime minister. It must also be remembered that ministers who are dissatisfied with their leader retain the weapon of resignation—they can resign of their own free will, and if enough ministers were to resign, a prime minister would face serious difficulties.

One of the most important factors distinguishing the prime minister from his cabinet colleagues is the manner in which he obtains and relinquishes his office. He is requested by the Governor General to form a government, while he himself issues the invitation to all other members. Whenever the prime minister vacates his office, the act normally carries with it the resignation of all those who compose the government; but whenever any other member leaves, the tenure of the remainder is undisturbed.

The powers of the prime minister in cabinet derive from his position as chairman. He controls the agenda and is the principal guiding force in helping the cabinet arrive at decisions. He is both co-ordinator and arbitrator of the executive decision-making process; he is concerned with the total activity of the government and is principally responsible for its policies, style and thrust; he oversees the operation of his colleagues' departments and ensures that harmonious relations exist between his ministers. Supported by the doctrine of cabinet solidarity, his task is to crystallize the collective point of view and to infuse into cabinet decision-making a sense of direction, coherence, efficacy and unity.

The relationship of the prime minister of the various committees of cabinet is most important. He is responsible for appointing members to the standing committees. He also chairs . . . Priorities and Planning. . . . Functioning at the level of Federal-Provincial Conferences, a growing number of which involve him directly, he acts as convenor and chairman, negotiator and arbitrator. The constitutional review process in particular has demanded considerable amounts of the prime minister's time and energy. As chairman of the Priorities and Planning Committee, he concerns himself with the setting of government priorities, planning for the orderly development of integrated policy, and evaluating ongoing programs.

Any discussion of the prime minister's executive duties should include some mention of his control over the power of appointment. . . . The great majority of public servants are now appointed by the Public Service Commission. Nonetheless, with the growth in the number of governmental departments and agencies, a large number of senior appointments are still made by Order-in-Council. Approximately four hundred appointments are made every year by cabinet. While the initiative for recommendations to cabinet for a large number of them lies with individual ministers, the prime minister must ensure that such recommendations carry the assent of his colleagues and have been the subject of adequate investigation. In addition, many appointments [250] are presented to cabinet upon the initiative of the prime minister himself. . . .

Some appointments are a mere formality, others require the prime minister's involvement in numerous hours of consultations and discussions. For instance, a cabinet shuffle is likely to involve individual discussions with most members of the cabinet, or appointments of deputy ministers might require consultations with ministers concerned as well as with senior officials. . . .

PRIME MINISTER AND THE PARTY

The prime minister is the leader of his party and is ultimately responsible for its direction. To remain in office he must be master of his party and enjoy its confidence and support. In this respect, the relationship of prime minister and his party has changed little in the last century. What has changed, however, is the role of the party itself as a political instrument and as a vehicle of citizen involvement. Parties are being subjected to a technocratic and professional transformation. More important citizens are seeking greater involvement in influencing party decisions. . . .

The democratization of the Liberal party has affected the position of the prime minister in some additional ways. The constitution of the party now requires the leader formally to "account" to the membership of the party at its biennial National Policy Convention and to submit to a "leadership convention ballot" at the first national meeting of the party following a general election. . . .

PRIME MINISTER AND THE PUBLIC

. . . Changes in the nature of the body politic have had a profound effect upon relations between the public and the executive, and in particular between the public and the prime minister. . . .

This new style of politics has required heads of government to make themselves more available to more and more people. Direct communication between the public and the prime minister has required him to devote an increasing amount of time to the media and to travel outside of Ottawa. . . .

But a voice on radio, a TV image or a press report, however faithful, do not sufficiently satisfy the public's desire for communication. Canadian voters also wish face-to-face contact with their political leaders, and more particularly with the prime minister. . . .

CONCLUSIONS

My conclusions . . . stem from my observation of the evolution and possible future development of the office of prime minister.

(i) The prime minister will continue to maintain his pre-eminent position in the government apparatus because of the continuing and pressing need for centralized planning, co-ordination and control. His pre-eminence should not compromise the authority of Parliament. So long as the prime minister remains responsible to the House of Commons, the advent of a *de facto* presidency is impossible.

(ii) The pre-eminent position of the prime minister as a national leader is likely to continue as well. Politics in democratic countries has tended to become more personalized and this phenomenon has unquestionably taken root in Canada.

(iii) The prime minister's contacts with the public will continue to expand because of the changing nature of public needs, expectations and demands. As a consequence, his symbolic, motivational and pedagogic roles will inevitably increase in importance.

(iv) The prime minister's power and influence is unlikely to emasculate the role of the cabinet or Parliament. The growing demands of the body politic have brought to all these bodies an increase in work, responsibility, power and influence.

(v) If future prime ministers are to meet their expanded responsibilities, they will have to maintain in their service a personal staff of adequate proportions. The alternatives are quite unpalatable—assumption of these functions by the administration or by the extra-parliamentary party.

THE CABINET AND MINISTERS

Timothy Plumptre

CABINET

As the senior decision-making body next to Parliament, Cabinet exercises an extraordinary influence on all the workings of government. It is a powerful vortex drawing towards it the policy proposals of the public service. As an executive body its "outstanding duty . . . is to provide the country and Parliament with a national policy and to devise means for coping with present emergencies and future needs," constantly gauging, as it does so, where it stands in relation to public opinion. As a legislative entity, it generally controls the House of Commons; it dominates legislation in Parliament; and it enacts "subordinate legislation" in the form of orders-in-council or minutes dealing with a huge range of matters, not least of which are the numerous appointments to top positions of departments, agencies, government corporations and boards of directors.

In Britain, a distinction is drawn between the "ministry" and the Cabinet. There may be several dozen ministers at any time, but not all are in the Cabinet, which is restricted to about 20 of the most senior ministers. In Canada, however, all ministers are, by convention, in the Cabinet, the result of which is an unwieldy, inefficient body for decision-making. The issue of the size of Cabinet has been an ongoing object of debate. When Canada's first Cabinet was formed in 1867, the Opposition argued that 13 ministers were too many and suggested that seven or eight would suffice. However, when the Government changed, the former Opposition found it necessary to create a Cabinet of 14 members. Ever since, efforts to diminish the size of Cabinet have foundered on the need for representation of a broad cross-section of interest groups, of French and English interests, and of the many geographic regions of a sprawling country.

Since the selection of Cabinet members is based as much upon representational considerations as upon experience or ability, a Canadian Cabinet usually comprises a mixed bag. Particularly in a newly elected Government, Cabinet members may have had only superficial exposure to the many complex issues of public policy before assuming their posts. In administration, many Cabinet members (and members of Parliament as well) often have very limited background. In the 40-member Cabinet of Prime Minister Brian Mulroney in 1987, for example, more than half the members come from backgrounds in the professions or small business; only half a dozen or so have had senior managerial experience (such as holding the position of a president or vice-president

From *Beyond the Bottom Line: Management in Government*, Halifax, The Institute for Research on Public Policy, 1988. By permission.

of a large institution). A Canadian deputy minister who had worked with ten different ministers over the years observed, "Most ministers are not as bright as the officials they are leading . . . in my experience, a minister in Canada is typically a former small businessman or a walk-up lawyer or a farmer; he or she has little or no executive experience and little by way of shared values with a department."

Because Cabinet is so large, much of its work is transacted in committees. In the last two decades or so, Canada has had between nine and 12 Cabinet committees, dealing with such issues as priorities and planning (the most influential committee, sometimes referred to as the "inner Cabinet"), government expenditure and management (Treasury Board), legislation and the planning of House of Commons business, foreign policy and defence, communications, security and intelligence, economic policy and social policy. . . .

Most of the work of Cabinet and its committees involves proposals contained in memoranda to Cabinet, or Cabinet documents, formally sponsored and signed by ministers, but nearly all prepared by public servants. Once a document has been considered by committee, and subsequently approved by Cabinet, a record of decision conveying ministerial intent is prepared by central agency officials and forwarded to the responsible department(s). Knowledge of these procedures constitutes the stock-in-trade of any moderately senior government official.

As governments grow, so do the number of Cabinet documents and the complexity of the issues they address. In the decade from 1957 to 1967, the number of Cabinet documents considered in Canada rose from around 400 to 800 a year. More recent statistics indicate that by the early 1980s, about 900 documents a year were being processed, resulting in about 750 records of decision. . . .

In any large government, the volume and length of Cabinet documents present a dilemma. Almost two decades ago, a former Secretary to the federal Cabinet in Canada was lamenting "the relentless daily servitude our ministers now face when Parliament is in session," pointing out the "enormous difficulties" associated with the volume of legislation and Cabinet material. Departmental officials, in attempting to do justice to complicated policy questions, produce long and detailed memoranda. Seeking to reduce ministers' workload to human proportions, central agencies call for shorter documents and executive summaries. Departmental officials protest that such summaries are superficial and inadequate as a basis for decision-making. It is a problem with no obvious solution. A modern Cabinet is severely stretched, if not seriously overloaded. Cabinet members just do not have the time to do justice to the host of complex issues brought before them.

Most ministers read the documents on a highly selective basis, depending on their officials to notify them of difficult or topical issues. Increasingly, for less contentious issues, the Cabinet document system is primarily an instrument to ensure effective interdepartmental consultation before the confirmation of a decision by Cabinet. Ministers, of course, retain the power to intervene, and they do on important issues; but on less significant questions, the Cabinet document serves as a record of agreements struck and compromises evolved through channels subordinate to the Cabinet itself. Cabinet simply provides the final seal of approval—often with a rubber stamp.

It seems unlikely that ministers have ever been able to afford much time for abstract strategic policy issues or for conceiving grand schemes. Running one portfolio is more than sufficient challenge for most. Efforts to engage the Canadian Cabinet in a form of corporate planning during the 1970s, under Prime Minister Pierre Trudeau, were judged by many observers to have been unsuccessful. . . .

Cabinet is ill-constituted to provide an overall strategic plan for governmental activity or even a framework of assumptions that could be used by departments as a basis for their own planning. There are important areas of public policy where Cabinet cannot easily afford to communicate its assumptions, even with the bureaucracy. For example, planning in some areas of the public service is significantly affected by future movements of the exchange rate, by the pay which government is prepared to offer its employees, by interest rates and by the rate of inflation. It could be useful to some departments if Cabinet were to tell them its assumptions on such topics. However, there is too great a risk that the market could learn Cabinet's expectations, and take action that might undermine government efforts to attain critical policy objectives.

In any event, Cabinets tend to operate on an issue-by-issue basis in planning and formulating policy. In many areas of policy, departments have to make their own assumptions, groping as best they can for indications of intent in the Government's actions and announcements, hoping that their own plans and policies will result in some sort of co-ordinated thrust and some consistency of direction.

Participation in Cabinet and its committees is hard work for ministers. Issues brought before Cabinet are often complicated, involving difficult technical points derived from scientific disciplines; complex financial or economic assessments related to major government investments, monetary policy or international negotiations; subtle legal points embodied in agreements with other levels of government or foreign powers; or critical political calculations that could affect the balance of power in the next election. Many documents are the result of years of preparation and countless hours of staff work within the public service. Yet Cabinet must dispose of them within the course of one or two meetings.

MINISTERS' RELATIONSHIPS

Cabinet is only one dimension of a minister's job. As well, ministers maintain a bewildering array of relationships outside Cabinet: with the prime minister and his or her office, with colleagues, with constituents, with party officials, with regional interest groups, with other interest groups of Parliament including opposition parties, with their departments, and with Crown corporations and other advisory bodies for which they may be responsible (including the members of the boards of those bodies).

Maintaining these relationships and acting as a spokesman for the Government demand a great many public appearances at which the minister must be able to articulate and defend not only the policies for which he or she is directly responsible, but also the general thrust of the Government's stand on other issues. The principle of Cabinet solidarity requires a minister to stand fast with the key directions of government policy, even on issues of a moral or ethical nature with which they might not personally agree. From time to time, Cabinet ministers are publicly reminded of their responsibilities in this regard, as happened in March 1985 when the Premier of Nova Scotia instructed his Cabinet on its response to the abortion issue:

> ... Premier John Buchanan has defended his threat to expel any Cabinet minister who publicly disagrees with the government's stand against Dr. Henry Morgentaler's plan to open a Halifax abortion clinic ....
>
> "They have a right to free speech but not in a matter which is a government decision," Buchanan said. ... "That is Cabinet solidarity. ... "

Constant pressure from the media can make a ministerial job extremely stressful. One minister from the Cabinet of former Prime Minister Pearson, Maurice Lamontagne, stated that

> the mass media have ... a great deal of influence on the politician. ... If a minister enjoys a good press, he will be envied and respected or feared by his colleagues. If he has no press, he has no future. And, if he has a bad press, he is in serious trouble, because he will be viewed even by his own associates as a political liability, in spite of the qualities he may have.

Lamontagne suggested that the increasing complexity of Cabinet business, the growing role of the state, and the unending demands for personal appearances are gradually rendering ministers ineffectual, turning them into figureheads for the Government. He argued that ministers succumb to maintaining a positive image, responding to the media's superficial stress on sensation and on "surface" rather than on "performance." Competent ministers are sometimes destroyed simply because they show themselves to be human; conversely, ineffectual ministers may continue to have good ratings.

With respect to their constituents, ministers must exercise caution. With the exception of the rare minister appointed to Cabinet from the upper house, ministers can never forget that they are members of Parliament first, and members of Cabinet second. Although travel to and from a riding can be time-consuming and physically exhausting, ministers must appear in their constituencies frequently. Those who do not, often fail to secure re-election.

It is a rash minister who will tell electors that constituency concerns take second place to regional or national issues. Some relatively inconsequential local issue may be the determining factor on how an important group of voters will mark their ballots at the next election. . . .

Ministers must also maintain good relationships with members of their own party, especially if they have long-term political ambitions (such as party leadership) which will make it necessary to seek the support of party members at some future date. The bigger the Government majority in the House of Commons, the more party members there are to consider.

Ministers who pay attention to their relationship with the House of Commons as a whole and who maintain good relations with the opposition parties can find their role greatly simplified; an arrogant or uncaring minister may often encounter heavy weather. "[F]rom the viewpoint of almost all parliamentarians, question time in the Commons is central to the principle of parliamentary government. . . . " This is when the opposition tries to score debating points against the Government, and perhaps tries to force it to reveal damaging information, or to embarrass a minister who is ill-prepared. Question period is the focal point of House of Commons activity, and in general tends to attract much more attention than other debates. Ministers go to considerable lengths to avoid embarrassment by preparing to cope with even the most trivial question (and many of them *are* trivial) related to their portfolios.

The need for ministers to be able to deal personally with queries raised by voters, either from their own constituencies or from elsewhere, through questions raised in question period or perhaps in caucus, has very important implications for the operation of the public service. In business, chief executives can afford to delegate less important matters to subordinates; such matters, once delegated, are usually off their desks for good. Not so a minister of the Crown . . . much of the trivia comes back to the minister's office.

By comparison with the private sector, the problem of "two-ended program delivery" creates a much greater need for staff support positions, such as assistants-to, at top levels of departments. It clogs up the priorities of organizational units, such as planning offices or policy shops, with relatively unimportant paper. It consumes more of the time of ministers and senior officials than they would like. It gets in the way of line managers trying to run their programs on a systematic basis. It is a classic example of the urgent driving out the important. But it is a fact of life in government . . . a minister typically has only "a few hours a week to spend on his department," according to a Canadian study.

MINISTERS AND THEIR DEPARTMENTS

New ministers—who have often never run anything larger than a law office, a political campaign or a small business—suddenly find themselves at the head of an organization which may have many decades of history, engrained traditions, several thousand employees, and operations that extend across the country. Many ministers are quite unprepared for their departmental responsibilities. They have no experience in directing a big institution, and have difficulty understanding that ocean liners do not change course as easily as dinghies.

Sometimes ministers are appointed to portfolios for which they are well prepared, as when, for example, an MP who was the party's critic of industrial policy while in opposition is named to an economic development post. However, often ministers are selected to lead a department without much warning. Since the prime minister must consider many factors besides the personal interest or suitability of the potential incumbent, often an MP is assigned to a portfolio in which he or she has little background or even interest. With little time to prepare, new ministers may arrive at their post with scant knowledge of departmental policy concerns and with no clear agenda of what they wish to accomplish. One former deputy minister of finance commented on his minister's views on policy: "My experience as often as not was that the minister had no view . . . and I don't say that critically."

As a result, new ministers, especially those of a newly elected Government, can be somewhat unpredictable, and may treat their departments with a mixture of intense suspicion and distrust. One Canadian deputy minister characterized this aspect of government as a sort of "institutionalized unfriendly takeover" in the private sector. If ministers do not grow to trust their departments, relations with the public service can be tense, tiring and frustrating for both sides throughout the tenure of the minister. Fortunately, in most cases, departments and their ministers reach an accommodation that is mutually acceptable if not entirely satisfactory; and sometimes, a highly successful partnership emerges.

Some ministers make the mistake of thinking that it is their job to run their department—to direct the day-to-day work, hire staff, structure the organization. Such ministers have to be gently educated by their officials and by central agencies in such mysteries as the merit principle, the responsibilities of the collectivity and the role of central agencies. Most ministers are not managers in any event, either by temperament or experience. While managerial questions occupy rather more ministerial time than they used to . . . most ministers would probably agree with former Saskatchewan Premier Allan Blakeney: "If there is one thing a minister should not be, it is the administrative head of his department."

Blakeney has proposed two roles for a minister in relation to a department: to explain departmental policies to the public, and to interpret to officials public reaction to the department's policies. In his view, the first role is well understood by officials whereas the second is less so. Blakeney believes that the essence of the minister's job is to ensure that policies in place are those which "are in the range of public acceptability," not necessarily those which are technically ideal.

The key aspect of the minister's relationship to his or her department has to do with the development of policy. If ministers and departments share common views about this aspect of their work, the relationship is generally happy. If they do not, it is more difficult. Sometimes there is some doubt as to who is running things. . . . [see articles by MacDonald and Sharp, *infra*.]

Ministers are clearly in charge of the development of new policy: they are obviously in a position to enforce their will over the public service but within certain constraints. Most important, they must be able to carry their Cabinet colleagues with them.

Except for those exceptionally gifted, it is difficult for ministers to provide leadership in policy fields with which they are unfamiliar. Public servants with years of experience in a particular area of policy usually have quite strong ideas about what works and what does not. Ministers who come to that field with no background and few preconceptions of their own, inevitably have a lot of catching up to do. . . .

Ministers clearly can prevail when they want to; but wise ministers pick their issues. Those who seize a few strategic objectives, and who are not overwhelmed by day-to-day pressures, can undoubtedly have a major impact on policy.

From time to time, politics attracts individuals who make a mark because of their vision and their strength of character. Leaders tend to be characterized by focus and by persistence. Ministers who come to office equipped principally with the generalities of their party's election platform and some rather vague ideas of their own will have to take cues from officials, perhaps more often than they would like. But that, after all, is hardly a reasonable basis upon which to criticize public servants, nor does it suggest that there is (as is sometimes suggested) a public service "plot" to stifle the elected Government. The fact is, some ministers are more able than others. The able ministers lead; the less able ones are carried with the tide. This does not necessarily result in poor government, but it obviously places a very important responsibility on the public service to ensure that the policy proposals they advance are soundly analyzed and sensitive to public opinion. . . .

Former Premier Blakeney argues that the minister's function is to be attuned to public views; he must circulate, consult and listen. In addition, Blakeney recommends that "the minister must hold himself aloof from the decision-making process until that process is in its final stages." Not all ministers would agree with this; some believe it is critical to affect the shape of policy at an early stage, before it goes through the interdepartmental mill. However, Blakeney's belief is that if ministers get involved too early they do not have time to perform what he calls their political function—that is, they lose the capacity to criticize proposals from a public perspective. "This has the effect in many cases of making the minister a captive of his department," (and therefore less effective in his other roles as a member of Cabinet, as a depart-ment leader or as a representative of his constituents).

It must be said that elected Governments do not make it easy for ministers to be effective departmental leaders. The great impediment is the Cabinet shuffle—the practice of shifting ministers from one portfolio to another every year or two. Shuffling ministers is a technique used by prime ministers to "launder" a Cabinet sullied by crises and misjudgment. It helps to create a fresh face with which the Government can confront the public. It may also be thought to give the public an illusion of action and to keep the Government's name in the headlines. In addition, shuffles may be initiated because prime ministers want to prevent ministers from becoming too committed to the interest groups associated with their existing portfolio. Ministers too long in one portfolio may be thought to be in danger of becoming the "prisoners" of their department.

Cabinet shuffles occur several times during the normal four- or five-year term of many Governments. Most people need a year or so in a new job before they can start to be fully effective. Thus, ministers are often just starting to hit their stride—and officials are just getting used to working with them—when they are hustled off to a new portfolio. This diminishes ministerial effectiveness while leaving public servants in a state of recurring uncertainty as to what the appropriate policy emphasis should be for their department. Ministers are seldom in place long enough to complete the initiatives they start. Even though, following a shuffle, a new minister will come from the same party as the previous one, he or she is likely to have different views about priorities and about how the department should operate. The prevailing practice of "musical chairs" may entail short-run political gains for a Government, but it impedes ministers' ability to achieve anything of substance in their portfolios, and it is extraordinarily disruptive for public servants trying to administer programs consistently and efficiently.

To summarize, ministers are, in principle, able to prevail powerfully over their departments. However, their ability to provide substantive, rather than cosmetic, leadership on major issues is often constrained by too many other responsibilities and by Cabinet shuffles. They are forced to rely heavily upon the public service in the development of new policies. There are times when ministers must feel like the pilot of a large aircraft, ultimately in charge, but inadequately prepared for the job and overburdened with other tasks, therefore having to accept advice and guidance from the ground simply in order to stay in the air.

THE CABINET DECISION-MAKING SYSTEM: A PROCESS WITHOUT A NAME

Evert A. Lindquist

On January 30, 1989, Prime Minister Brian Mulroney announced a cabinet shuffle and a reorganization of the cabinet decision-making system. The new

An original article prepared for this edition in June, 1990 by the author, who is a member of the Department of Political Science, University of Toronto. By permission.

system, which has not yet received a formal title, operates under a different logic than its predecessor, the Policy and Expenditure Management System (PEMS), which had been in place since the late 1970s. One reason for the change was to introduce a strong bias within the process against increasing expenditures and the deficit. Therefore, our discussion below will touch upon aspects of the expenditure budget process. However, cabinet decision making embraces the full range of policy concerns and instruments and is not simply geared to making expenditure decisions.

Before delving into the particulars of the new system, it is worth reflecting on the range of considerations, from individual personalities to external challenges, that feed into the design of any cabinet decision-making system. First, the design will reflect the style and preferences of the prime minister who, relying on the advice of political advisors, cabinet colleagues, and the Clerk of the Privy Council and Secretary to Cabinet, is the primary architect of the system. Second, whether the system is new or old, its design must reflect the capabilities of the ministers appointed to cabinet; no matter how impeccable its logic, a system will lose its integrity if the limitations of ministers are not taken into account. Third, the processes and structures of cabinet must reflect the strategic priorities (fiscal and political) of the prime minister and the government. Fourth, the system must be designed not only to come to grips with the complexity of managing the civil service (the federal government is Canada's *largest* employer), but also the broad range of policy problems and challenges which emerge from inside and outside Canada.

Although Prime Minister Mulroney has reshaped the cabinet decision-making system, it has yet to be dignified with a label comparable to that of PEMS or PPBS. The reluctance to name the new system may be rooted in a feeling that it should not be touted as a solution to current problems, therefore lowering expectations about what can be achieved. None of the succession of much-vaunted budgetary systems were viewed as successes; to coin a name might serve to "jinx" the system. Another possible reason is that the prime minister and his officials refuse to label a design that will inevitably change— why try to name or describe a moving target until is has coalesced, if ever? Although very elegant and logical on paper, PEMS never worked according to plan and was always in a state of flux. Indeed, given the many factors which impinge on the design of cabinet decision processes, perhaps it is more appropriate to downplay the notion of a system, with all of its logical and mechanical connotations, and suggest instead the metaphor of a balancing act, which emphasizes both craft and politics.

THE NEW SYSTEM

Under the current system the key policy-making body is the Priorities and Planning Committee, chaired by the prime minister and consisting of his most senior and trusted ministers. It determines government priorities and approves major policy initiatives and expenditures. (Expenditure decisions deemed not deserving of the detailed attention of the Priorities and Planning Committee are referred to the Treasury Board.) Even more importantly, the committee is responsible for managing the policy reserve, the only source of funds for new projects or initiatives of any significance. Most other work is delegated to other cabinet committees, since Priorities and Planning cannot handle all cabinet business, but it does have its own specific responsibilities such as oversight of the equalization program. However, assisted by the Privy Council staff, the Priorities and Planning Committee monitors and ratifies the decisions and recommendations of the other committees. There is nothing radical about the committee; it has been a fixture of modern cabinet systems in Canada. But with an eye cast firmly toward expenditure restraint and the political bottom line, Prime Minister Mulroney has introduced key innovations to increase the control P&P has over the policy agenda and the decision-making process.

These innovations include the creation of two new cabinet committees, the Operations Committee and the Expenditure Review Committee, to assist the Priorities and Planning Committee. The Operations Committee, chaired by the deputy prime minister, co-ordinates and manages the short-term activities of cabinet on a week-to-week basis. It, in effect, manages the agenda of the Priorities and Planning Committee, and serves as a preliminary screening mechanism for a new policy proposals. The Expenditure Review Committee reviews existing programs to determine the potential for cutbacks within existing programs. This activity is cyclical as it tends to take place during the months preceding the annual budget. Given their proximity and responsibilities toward the Priorities and Planning Committee, these two Committees have become powerful entities in their own right.

What about the rest of the cabinet committee system? First, the responsibilities of other co-ordinating committees—the Treasury Board and the Federal–Provincial Relations, Legislation and House Planning, and Communications committees—remain intact. However, it is worth noting that the position of the Treasury Board and the Treasury Board secretariat appears to have been strengthened under the new system. The Treasury Board, of course, has status as the "manager" of the civil service, a role that embraces a wide range of responsibilities. In addition, it administers the only other two "reserves" in town, the Program Reserve and the Operations Reserve. The latter exists to compensate departments for unexpected increases in workload, and the former is a pool of funds for policy initiatives that are not sufficiently large, controversial, or politically sensitive to demand review by the Priorities and Planning Committee. In addition to assisting the Treasury Board in fielding funding requests and preparing the Main Estimates, the secretariat provides data to the Expenditure Review Committee.

The new system revamps the organization, responsibilities, and relationship of the policy committees to the Priorities and Planning Committee. Under PEMS there were two policy committees of cabinet (Economic Policy and Social Policy), consisting of the ministers with departments and programs in those broad sectors. Each committee had broad authority for the allocation of funds within its respective sector and administered its own policy reserve. They were assisted by their own staff complement, the Ministry of State for Economic Development and the Ministry of State for Social Development. The Priorities and Planning Committee, using the advice of officials from the Department of Finance, set the parameters for the activities of these committees by determining the fiscal framework and the broad allocation of funds across sectors (these were called envelopes). Under the new system there are far more policy committees with smaller membership—Human Resources, Income Support and Health; Cultural Affairs and National Identity; Environment; Economic Policy; Foreign and Defence Policy; Trade Executive; and the Special Committee of Council, responsible largely for processing orders in council, privatization, and regulatory affairs. These committees no longer have the authority to allocate or authorize funds—instead they review and generate policy proposals for the Priorities and Planning Committee.

This shift of power back to Priorities and Planning has been done in the name of expenditure restraint, reducing paperwork, and strengthening the control of the prime minister over the policy process. But it easy to lose sight of the fact that cabinet systems can never be just "top-down" planning systems—they are "bottom-up" systems which must respond to the surfeit of ideas and proposals emanating from departments. Consider the path that any new initiative follows. Departmental officials prepare a proposal, a memorandum to cabinet, which must be approved by their deputy minister and minister before moving toward cabinet. If the proposal is consistent with the current policy priorities set out by the Priorities and Planning Committee, it is routed by Privy Council officials (who ensure that the proposal has received preliminary screening from other key players such as Treasury Board, the Department of Finance, and pertinent line departments) to the appropriate policy committees for review and recommendations. If the proposal is endorsed by the committees, it returns to the Priorities and Planning Committee for final approval. If significant new funds are requested, the Operations Committee screens the proposal before sending it to policy committees and then reviews their recommendations before putting the proposal on the Priorities and Planning agenda. The Operations Committee can veto or derail the proposal at either point. This policy development process is not only layered on top of the annual expenditure budget cycle, which produces the Main Estimates and operational plans for each department, but also moves in tandem with the ongoing assessments of the Expenditure Review Committee.

When the new committee system was introduced, it was billed as a wholesale change from PEMS. The reality is that new system reflects an accumulation of changes that occurred over a fairly long period of time. The lynchpins of PEMS, the ministries of State for Economic and Social Development, were disbanded by John Turner during his brief spell as prime minister in 1984. During his first mandate Prime Minister Mulroney encouraged a more informal approach to cabinet business, reflecting his "brokerage style" of politics. The Operations Committee was established before the 1989 reorganization. This is not to say that the new system has not changed significantly; there has been a definite shift in power within cabinet, particularly with regard to the allocation of reserves and the approval of new small to medium expenditures.

SOME ISSUES TO CONSIDER

1. There is much merit in centralizing power within cabinet to facilitate expenditure restraint and to maintain control of the policy agenda. For this strategy to work, those who wield power must stay on top of all business moving onto the committee agenda—their staff must keep them well informed. However, many of the changes in the decision-making process are designed to reduce the flow of paper in the system and to buffer cabinet members from having to make too many small decisions. Thus, an interesting tension emerges between protecting the Priorities and Planning Committee from information overload and ensuring that its members have enough information to make good decisions. Does the new system strike an adequate balance, thereby permitting the government to achieve its key policy objectives?

2. The new system uses the Operations and Expenditure Review committees to assist the Priorities and Planning Committee to achieve the overarching objectives of the government. One of the more interesting features is the overlapping membership on the three committees. An implicit premise behind the design of the system is that ministers find it difficult to retain their commitment to expenditure reduction and other key policy priorities. The solution is to have them wear different hats by sitting on different committees. This not only serves to expand the constituency for expenditure reduction within cabinet, but also permits the magic of "groupthink" to sustain the resolve of key ministers sitting on those committees. This raises the following question: are the new committees a substitute for exercising political will or are they necessary for nurturing this will?

3. Under PEMS ministers and their departmental officials had incentive to search for efficiency gains and to propose cutbacks because they would have some claim to the savings when they were re-allocated by the sectoral committees as reserves. Under the new system savings revert to the policy reserves managed by the Priorities and Planning Committee. As a result some departments might want to "hide" the savings they find or may not see the merits in searching for improvements. One response is for the prime minister to search for ways to better "police" recalcitrant departments: strengthening central agencies like the Treasury Board and, at the level of cabinet, creating the Expenditure Review Committee. But there is a potentially more positive approach that involves instilling a different set of values in ministers and officials. Rather than base promotions of ministers and senior officials on the size of their staff and budgets, much greater weight could be given to their record on efficiency gains and meeting program objectives over the medium term. In this connection two key initiatives must be noted: the Increased Managerial Authority and Accountability (IMAA) program managed by the Treasury Board, and the Public Service 2000 task force currently in progress. Each seeks to lessen the restrictions on deputy ministers and other senior officials in obtaining and arranging inputs, as well as focusing more attention on improving efficiency and performance. Only time will tell whether these initiatives are more effective than a policing approach.

4. Recognizing that the full cabinet no longer sets policy priorities for a government, Katherine Graham has referred to it as the "inner caucus." This characterization understates the importance of cabinet in the policy process in several regards. First, under the new system policy committees vet and refine proposals and, until there is evidence to the contrary, we must assume that these committees do have a significant role in the policy process. Second, cabinet is an important link when developing and selling major policy initiatives: following a decision of the Priorities and Planning Committee, the prime minister must take the proposal to cabinet and seek approval before submitting it to the scrutiny of caucus, the House of Commons, and the public. If serious reservations are expressed in cabinet, chances are that the proposal will have to be reworked—the politics of getting the proposal through cabinet provide a good glimpse of possible public reactions. And third, while cabinet no longer acts as a *collective* decision-making body on most issues, it is a *collection* of decision makers, albeit each with different responsibilities and varying degrees of authority.

WHO IS ON TOP? THE MINISTER OR THE MANDARINS?

Flora MacDonald

As a new Secretary of State for External Affairs, it seemed to me that I ought to establish a foreign policy with the twin objectives that Canada should receive maximum advantage from its foreign relations and that it should play a fully responsible role in the international scene. I was convinced that this required both broad public support for foreign and aid policies and an ability, on my part, to weigh independently the advice I received from public servants.

It is natural that advice from public servants would be based on a continuation of existing policy—policy which, in large part, had had its genesis within the Department. And while it was not necessarily wrong, neither was it neces-

From an address by the Hon. Flora MacDonald to the Annual Meeting of the Canadian Political Science Association in Montreal, June 3, 1980. Printed in *Policy Options*, 1, 3, September–October, 1980, published by The Institute for Research on Public Policy. By permission.

sarily right. A new Minister must be able to assess, for himself or herself, where we have been and where we ought to be going.

This did not mean a wholesale rejection of everything that had gone on before or was currently in process; but, given my desire to develop a foreign policy attuned to the turbulent 1980s, I was determined that advice as to how we could achieve that goal should come from more than one quarter. It was, and is, natural that senior bureaucrats would have their own methods of gaining approval for the decisions they both needed and especially wanted. A new Minister, just trying to find his or her way through the labyrinth of bureaucracy, is indeed vulnerable to such practices. A new Minister in a new government who had not paced the corridors of power for some sixteen years is not only vulnerable but, indeed, almost without protection.

To reduce this dependency on bureaucratic advice and to provide a mechanism that would ensure political input into the decision-making process, a cabinet committee system was devised by the Prime Minister which aimed to establish a better equilibrium between Ministers and mandarins. While this mechanism was being set up at the cabinet level, I personally moved on two fronts to ensure that I was the recipient of independent advice I considered would be critical to my own survival as an effective Minister.

First, I determined that my personal staff would play a critical role in the evaluation of all sensitive policy issues. Although few in number, their independent and sometimes irreverent analysis of these issues was invaluable.

Secondly, with the co-operation of some interested persons from outside government circles—experts, primarily but not exclusively from the ranks of academe—I had taken the initial steps in developing what I hoped would be a mildly formalized structure to offer ongoing advice.

Without some such protective mechanisms, the Minister is indeed at the mercy of bureaucratic domination, not because of some devious manipulative plot, but simply because that is the way the system had been allowed to develop. To emphasize the point, and the concerns that flow down from it, and because others have documented it so much better than I, I will refer to the memoirs and speeches of several cabinet members who faced a similar situation.

Anthony Wedgewood Benn began a recent lecture, entitled "Manifestos and Mandarins," with the statement:

> ... It would be a mistake to suppose that the senior ranks of the civil service are active Conservatives (or in Canada, Liberals) posing as impartial administrators. The issue is not their personal political views, nor their preferences for any particular government. The problem arises from the fact that the civil service sees itself as being above the party battle, with a political position of its own to defend.
>
> Civil service policy—and there is no other way to describe it—is an amalgam of views that have been developed over a long period of time. It draws some of its force from a deep commitment to the benefits of continuity, and a fear that adversary politics may lead to sharp reversals by incoming governments of

policies devised by their predecessors, which the civil service played a great part in developing.

In a country like Canada with a long history of one-party dominance, this tendency is even more entrenched. Benn goes on to list the techniques employed by the doyens of Whitehall when ministerial views differ from their own.

By briefing Ministers—the document prepared by officials for presentation to incoming ministers after a general election comes in two versions, one for each major party.

It is a very important document that has attracted no public interest, and is presented to a Minister at the busiest moment of his life—when he enters his department and is at once bombarded by decisions to be made, the significance of which he cannot at that moment appreciate.

The brief may thus be rapidly scanned and put aside for a proper reading when the pressure eases, which it rarely does.

Thus Ministers are continually guided to reach their decisions within that framework. Those Ministers who seek to open up options beyond that framework are usually unable to get their proposals seriously considered.

By the control of information—the flow of necessary information to a Minister on a certain subject can be made selective, in other ways restricted, delayed until it is too late, or stopped altogether.

By the mobilisation of Whitehall—it is also easy for the Civil Service to stop a Minister by mobilising a whole range of internal forces against his policy.

The normal method is for officials to telephone their colleagues in other departments to report what a Minister is proposing to do; thus stimulating a flow of letters from other Ministers (drafted for them by their officials) asking to be consulted, calling for inter-departmental committees to be set up, all in the hope that an unwelcome initiative can be nipped in the bud.

Tony Benn's lecture dealt with the interface between cabinet ministers generally and their senior mandarins. Henry Kissinger in his recent book *The White House Years* deals with the particular problems which confront a Secretary of State:

Cabinet members are soon overwhelmed by the insistent demands of running their departments. On the whole, a period in high office consumes intellectual capital; it does not create it. Most high officials leave office with the perceptions and insights with which they entered; they learn how to make decisions but not what decisions to make. And the less they know at the outset, the more dependent they are on the only source of available knowledge: the permanent officials. Unsure of their own judgement, unaware of alternatives, they have little choice except to follow the advice of the experts.

This is a particular problem for a Secretary of State. He is at the head of an organization staffed by probably the ablest and most professional group of men and women in the public service. They are intelligent, competent, loyal, and hardworking. But the reverse side of their dedication is the conviction that a lifetime of service and study has given them insights that transcend the untrained and shallow-rooted views of political appointees.

When there is strong leadership, their professionalism makes the foreign service an invaluable and indispensable tool of policymaking. In such circumstances the foreign service becomes a disciplined and finely honed instrument, their occasional acts of self-will generate an important, sometimes an exciting dialogue. But when there is not a strong hand at the helm, clannishness tends to overcome discipline. Desk officers become advocates for the countries they deal with and not spokesmen of national policy; assistant secretaries push almost exclusively the concerns of their areas. Officers will fight for parochial interests with tenacity and a bureaucratic skill sharpened by decades of struggling for survival. They will carry out clear-cut instructions with great loyalty, but the typical foreign service officer is not easily persuaded that an instruction with which he disagrees is really clear-cut.

Finally Richard Crossman, in his very revealing diaries, has this to say:

> Now for my impressions of the ministry and of the civil service. The main conviction I had when I got there was that the civil service would be profoundly resistant to outside pressure. Was that true? I think it was. I found throughout an intense dislike of bringing people in, whether they are politicians or experts.
>
> I should say that in general I have found profound resistance in the civil service to a Minister who brings in outside advisers and experts, and profound resistance to interference by anybody with direct access to the Minister. What they like is sole ministerial responsibility because they are convinced that under this system the amount of outside influence exerted is minimal.

Am I exaggerating when I use these British and American examples of resistance to ministerial attentiveness to outside advice and apply them here in Canada? I do not think so. But I think that this resistance resides almost entirely among those who really have their hands on the levers of power—the senior mandarins. And I sometimes felt they reacted as negatively to the creativity and imaginative proposals of those in the less senior ranks of the foreign service as they did to outside advice. One of my constant frustrations was to find ways in which to penetrate senior management levels so as to tap this well-spring of fresh ideas, creativity and provocative questioning which I know from some experience exists.

I found myself as vulnerable as any new minister in any new government to the techniques Tony Benn attributes to the mandarins in Whitehall. He refers to them as techniques; I often thought of them as entrapment devices. Let me give you some examples:

(a) The unnecessarily numerous crisis corridor decisions I was confronted with—here is the situation; (breathless pause), let us have your instructions.
(b) The unnecessarily long and numerous memos; one of my great triumphs was that, in the wake of an abject plea for mercy, the senior re-write personnel agreed to reduce their verbiage by half.
(c) The late delivery to me of my submissions to cabinet, sometimes just a couple of hours (or less) before the meeting took place, thus denying me the opportunity for a full and realistic appraisal of the presentation I was supposed to be making to my cabinet colleagues. On a number of occasions my aides

resorted to obtaining bootleg copies of such documents on their way through the overly complex bureaucratic approval system.

(d) The one-dimensional opinions put forward in memos. I was expected to accept the unanimous recommendations of the Department, though of course there was always the possibility that I might reject it. Seldom, if ever, was I given the luxury of multiple-choice options on matters of major import.

I mentioned earlier that in order to ensure political input into the decision-making process, the cabinet committee system grouped together ministers whose responsibilities were interrelated. Thus, all those ministers whose duties took them into the international field were members of the cabinet committee on foreign and defence policy, the one body where the initiatives could be co-ordinated. I was mandated by the Prime Minister to be chairman of that committee.

As such, I had to be rigorously scrupulous not to allow my departmental interests to prejudice my impartiality as chairman of the committee. The system was designed to provide an independent source of information to ministers, and particularly to cabinet committee chairmen, through the cabinet secretariat of the Privy Council Office. Memos for the chairmen, drafted by secretariat officials, analysed the issues on the committee's agenda and pointed out the strengths and weaknesses of the various departmental positions. Deputy ministers or other officials participated in such cabinet committee meetings only if the agenda item required their attendance.

There was no comparable committee at the deputy minister level. In my view that would have undermined the decision-making role of ministers.

Not that such a committee of deputy ministers wasn't suggested. It was urged on me in a succession of proposals which I consistently rejected. Such a committee headed by a deputy whose mandate was solely that of chief officer in the department of External Affairs would, I felt, hardly be acceptable to National Defence, Industry, Trade and Commerce, Immigration, etc., as the person to co-ordinate their policies at the bureaucratic level. In addition, such a committee of deputy ministers would usurp or at least conflict with the function of the cabinet secretariat in the PCO. One senior mandarin used these words to describe it when he first heard of the proposal: "A mechanism to facilitate conflict."

I thought it was a dead duck; now I hear it has been activated and given the impressive title of Mirror Committee of Deputies. One wonders how many such mirror committees of deputies a cabinet minister can cope with before he or she ends up surrounded by a wall of mirrors each one reflecting the wisdom of the other into infinity. Even Alice in Wonderland might have difficulty in finding her way through what is likely to become a looking glass jungle, presenting the illusion of ministerial control.

Not only did I discover, after the takeover of the current administration, that senior mandarins had been successful in establishing this committee whose very operation must conflict with that of the cabinet secretariat, but I have also been led to believe that during my tenure copies of the private and confidential analysis done for me as a cabinet committee chairman by the PCO cabinet secretariat found their way to my deputy's desk, without my knowledge or indeed without the knowledge of those who drafted the memoranda.

This would have permitted one senior official to be in a position to have access to privileged information not available to other deputy ministers, not indeed to cabinet ministers other than the committee chairman. One need hardly speculate on the important role control of information plays in the bureaucratic game.

On a more philosophical level, I am concerned that the proliferation of senior management co-ordinating committees—co-ordinating advice not only to senior ministers but now to groups of ministers—will seriously impair the decision-making role of ministers. Such a system effectively filters out the policy options that an entire committee might otherwise consider. Too many bureaucrats, I fear, have the mistaken impression that vigorous debate of policy options by cabinet ministers is an indication that they—the bureaucrats— have somehow failed to properly channel and co-ordinate views before the cabinet meeting takes place.

Regrettably too few Canadian ministers have followed the example of Richard Crossman, Tony Benn, Harold MacMillan, Henry Kissinger or Dean Acheson in providing a first-hand account of the relationship between the minister and the bureaucracy. Regrettably as well, academics in this country have not paid as much attention as they should to the interface between ministers and the senior echelons of their departments.

The effective management of the relationship is what distinguishes parliamentary government from bureaucratic management. As Anthony Wedgewood Benn concluded: "In considering these issues, we do not want to find new scapegoats or pile blame upon ministers or civil servants who have let the system grow into what it is. What matters now is that we should examine what has happened to our system of government with fresh eyes and resolve to reintroduce constitutional democracy to Britain" and, I might add, to Canada.

A REPLY FROM A FORMER MINISTER AND MANDARIN

Mitchell Sharp

In a recent article in *Policy Options* Flora MacDonald says "Regrettably too few Canadian ministers have provided a first-hand account of the relationship

From *Policy Options*, Vol. 2, No. 2, May–June 1981, published by The Institute for Research on Public Policy. By permission.

between the minister and the bureaucracy." I am among the few who have done so and I do so again because my account differs substantially from that given by Miss MacDonald.

I have been on both sides of the relationship. For 16 years—between 1942 and 1958—I was a senior civil servant. Towards the end of that period the media called me a mandarin. For 13 years—between 1963 and 1976—I was a minister. In between I was, for five years, a businessman.

My previous experience as a civil servant helped me enormously when I became a minister. I understood the functions of my departmental advisers. I consulted them daily, every morning that I was in town, following the pattern of strong independent ministers under whom I had served like Ilsley, Abbott and Howe. I asked questions and listened to their answers. Sometimes I agreed; sometimes I didn't. In the end I made my decisions and they carried them out. Once they knew my views, they prepared drafts of policy speeches and announcements for my consideration.

Top public servants are powerful persons in the machinery of government at the federal level in Canada. They wield great influence. They do so because they are, in the main, professionals who have been selected for proven administrative ability and who devote their full time to government. In many cases, they have a greater influence upon the course of events than have ministers, particularly the weaker and less competent ministers.

This may seem somehow to be anti-democratic but it needn't be and in my experience it isn't. Government is, in fact, a specialized affair which cannot be run successfully by amateurs without professional advice and professional execution. With rare exceptions, in a parliamentary system politicians are amateurs in any field of government administration, at least at the beginning of their political careers.

Few of them will be experts in fiscal and monetary policy, or in nuclear policy, or in foreign affairs, for example, when they offer themselves as candidates in a local constituency. Yet they may find themselves having to make decisions in any or all those complex fields once in office. Prime ministers are limited in their selection of ministers to those of their party who have been elected. Sometimes, given the necessity in a federal state for geographical distribution in cabinet, the choice may be extremely limited.

At a political meeting . . . I was asked by a young man in the audience what qualifications I had to be foreign minister of Canada. I replied that my essential qualification was that I had been elected to Parliament.

Politicians, particularly ministers, require the best impartial advice that they can get if they are to make wise decisions. Sycophants who echo their boss's views are of little value; indeed they can be positively dangerous as advisers if they are not prepared from time to time to tell their bosses the painful truth that a pet idea is unworkable. That is one of the reasons why I am not in favour of the principle, which is sometimes advanced, that the top positions—the heads of departments—should be filled by those who are in sympathy with the views of the party in power, who should depart with their ministers when the government is replaced.

After some 35 years observing the process of government at close range, I am also more convinced than I was at the beginning that there is virtue in continuity in the senior administrative jobs, and in promoting career public servants to them. Competent people are not going to be prepared to enter the public service and make a career of it if they are to be denied access to the top jobs where they can bring their talents fully to bear.

The contrary argument that senior civil servants would resist change in the event that a government with radically different views from its predecessor took office has never been very convincing to me. In the first place, knowing my own country and its political parties, I doubt that any change would be in fact very radical. In the second place, it is precisely under those circumstances, were they to come about, that an experienced senior civil service would be most valuable, one that could guide a new government in the implementation of its innovative policies and enable it to avoid the administrative pitfalls of which it might otherwise not be aware.

I can testify from my own experience and my own observation that changes of government such as occurred in 1957 and 1979 were considered in the civil service as providing a challenge, an opportunity to prove that the service is non-partisan, notwithstanding the long years of Liberal administration. It is useful in this connection to observe that nearly all the deputy ministers at the time of both changes were drawn from the ranks of public servants who had originally qualified for entry to the public service by the independent Public Service Commission. As nearly as I can determine, something like 80 per cent of the present heads of departments are drawn from the ranks of non-political civil servants.

That there were some transitional difficulties in 1957 and 1979 is not surprising. Even when there is no change of government—only change of minister—there are bound to be some awkward adjustments in relations between the incoming minister and the incumbent deputy minister, which sometimes necessitate a switch in responsibilities. However, I neither saw nor heard evidence that the transition was difficult because the senior public service was committed to the policies of the previous government and was determined to resist change.

What a new minister finds—I had the experience four times in my political career—when he or she takes over a department is that the problems are more complicated than they looked to be from the outside and that he or she needs plenty of advice to avoid making mistakes.

There is need, of course, for ministers to have in their offices men and women to help them perform as members of Parliament and political leaders. Such temporary appointees, however valuable they may be, are no substitute for permanent non-partisan senior civil servants.

From time to time, too, governments may wish to be able to call on the services for qualified Canadians from the business or professional world who have special expertise of one kind or another. This they should be able to do and are able to do. I myself inherited a deputy minister appointed by the Diefenbaker administration who had not been drawn from the ranks of the permanent public service. I advised Mr. Pearson to retain him, which he did. The test of such appointments should be the competence of the appointee and not his or her personal politics.

Admittedly the system does give rise to serious questions. Do senior civil servants exert too much influence upon the government? Are ministers puppets being manipulated by the mandarins, as is sometimes asserted or implied? These are difficult questions to answer satisfactorily because so much depends upon the way individual ministers react to advice. I don't think anyone who knew him though that C.D. Howe was manipulated by his civil service advisers, yet he had excellent working relationships with them. The key to that good working relationship was that Mr. Howe gave them his confidence and they responded with loyalty and respect.

When I was a civil servant, I think it is fair to say that individual ministers and the cabinet as a whole depended more upon the advice of senior civil servants than they do today and they did so deliberately. When a difficult problem arose, the customary response was to refer it for study and report to a committee of senior public servants. There was also a period during the war and in the immediate post-war years when influential public servants like Clifford Clark, Norman Robertson, Graham Towers and Donald Gordon were active promoters of new ideas and approaches that they persuaded their ministers and the cabinet to adopt.

The federal mandarins then, however, were a tightly knit group of personal friends drawn from various walks of life who had been invited to Ottawa to join the public service during both Conservative and Liberal regimes. They were not lifetime civil servants recruited at time of graduation who had risen through the ranks, as is now the pattern.

Today when difficult problems arise, they are more often referred to ministerial committees than to committees of civil servants. Innovative ideas still emerge from the civil service, but the process of decision-making at the cabinet level is so complex nowadays that individual contributions are quickly submerged in a deluge of documentation. The present ministers, I suspect, long for a return of the general rule, under which I operated as a civil servant, which was that memoranda for ministers should not exceed two pages, otherwise they might not be read.

I sympathise with those ministers who like myself had to wade through pages and pages of memoranda, some of which became available barely in time to be read before decisions had to be taken. However, it was our own fault for letting the system get out of hand.

I sometimes thought that as ministers we were much too zealous and that, particularly under Mr. Trudeau, we worked far too hard and spent far too much time in cabinet and cabinet committees reading and discussing each other's proposals. Decisions might have taken less time, we might have had a better perspective on events and more time for politics, had we delegated more to our civil service advisers and left more time for reflection.

A first-class non-partisan public service dedicated to the public interest is one of the bulwarks of parliamentary government. It enables the elected amateurs, gifted or otherwise, to make the political decisions and govern the country.

BIBLIOGRAPHY

(See also Bibliographies in Chapter 7 and 12.)

The Crown

Benoît P. "Remembering the Monarch." *C.J.P.S.*, 15, 3, September, 1982.
Courtney, J.C. "The Defeat of the Clark Government: The Dissolution of Parliament, Leadership Conventions, and the Calling of Elections in Canada." *J.C.S.*, 17, 2, Summer, 1982.
Forsey, E.A. *The Royal Power of Dissolution of Parliament in the British Commonwealth*. Toronto: O.U.P., 1968.
Hendry, J.McL. *Memorandum of the Office of Lieutenant-Governor of a Province: Its Constitutional Character and Functions*. Ottawa: Department of Justice, 1955.
La Forest, G.V. *Disallowance and Reservation of Provincial Legislation*. Ottawa: Department of Justice, 1965.
Monet, J. *The Canadian Crown*. Toronto: Clarke Irwin, 1979.
MacKinnon, F. *The Crown in Canada*. Calgary: Glenbow-Alberta Institute, McClelland and Stewart West, 1976.
Saywell, J.T. *The Office of Lieutenant-Governor*. Toronto: U.T.P., rev. ed., 1985.
Woods, S.E. *Her Excellency, Jeanne Sauvé*. Toronto: Macmillan, 1986.

Cabinet, Prime Minister

Aucoin, P. "Organizational Change in the Machinery of Canadian Government: From Rational Management to Brokerage Politics." [Trudeau and Mulroney.] *C.I.P.S.*, 29, 1, March, 1986.
Axworthy, T. "Of Secretaries to Princes." *C.P.A.*, 31, 2, Summer, 1988.
Bakvis, H. "Regional Ministers, National Policies and the Administrative State in Canada: The Regional Dimension in Cabinet Decision-making, 1980–1984." *C.J.P.S.*, 21, 3, September, 1988.
Bakvis, H. "Regional Politics and Policy in the Mulroney Cabinet, 1984– 88: Towards a Theory of the Regional Minister System in Canada." *C.P.P.*, 15, June, 1989.
Barker, P. "The Canada Health Act and the Cabinet Decision-making System of Pierre Elliott Trudeau." *C.P.A.*, 32, 1, Spring, 1989.
Campbell, C. *Governments Under Stress: Political Executives and Key Bureaucrats in Washington, London, and Ottawa*. Toronto: U.T.P., 1983.
Campbell, C. "Federal Cabinets in Canada." In Mackie, T., Hogwood, B., (eds.). *Unlocking the Cabinet: Cabinet Structures in Comparative Perspective*. Beverly Hills: Sage, 1985.
Chenier, J.A. "Ministers of State to Assist: Weighing the Costs and the Benefits." *C.P.A.*, 28, 3, Fall, 1985.
Clark, I. "Recent Changes in the Cabinet Decision-Making System in Ottawa." *C.P.A.*, 28, 2, Summer, 1985.
Clark, J. "A Prime Minister's View of the Office." In Fox, P. (ed.). *Politics: Canada*. Toronto: McGraw-Hill Ryerson, 6th ed., 1987.
Courtney, J.C. "Prime Ministerial Character: An Examination of Mackenzie King's Political Leadership." *C.J.P.S.*, 9, 1, March, 1976. (Also, Esberey, J.E., "An Alternative View," *ibid.*)

Donaldson, G. *Eighteen Men: Canada's Prime Ministers.* Toronto: Doubleday, 1985.

Edwards, J.L.J. *The Attorney General, Politics and the Public Interest.* Toronto: Methuen, 1984.

Gossage, P. *Close to Charisma: My Years Between the Press and Pierre Elliott Trudeau.* Toronto: M.& S., 1986.

Hay, M. "Understanding the PCO-The Ultimate Facilitator." *O.*, 13–1, 1981.

Hockin, T., (ed.). *Apex of Power: The Prime Minister and Political Leadership in Canada.* Scarborough: P.-H., 2nd ed., 1977.

Lammers, W.W., and Nyomarkay, J.L. "The Canadian Cabinet in Comparative Perspective." *C.J.P.S.*, 15, 1, March, 1982.

Leger, P. C. "The Cabinet Committee System of Policy-Making and Resource Allocation in the Government of New Brunswick." *C.P.A.*, 26, 1, Spring, 1983.

Maslove, A.M., (ed.). *Budgeting in the Provinces: Leadership and the Premiers.* Toronto: IPAC, 1989.

Matheson, W.A. *The Prime Minister and the Cabinet.* Toronto: Methuen, 1976.

Pal, L.A., and Taras, D., (eds.). *Prime Ministers and Premiers: Political Leadership and Public Policy in Canada.* Scarborough: P.-H., 1988.

Pitfield, M. "The Shape of Government in the 1980s." *C.P.A.*, 19, 1, Spring, 1976.

Punnett, R.M. *The Prime Minister in Canadian Government and Politics.* Toronto: Macmillan, 1977.

Savoie, D.J. "The Minister's Staff: The Need for Reform." *C.P.A.*, 26, 4, Winter, 1983.

Schultz, R., *et al. The Cabinet as a Regulatory Body: The Case of the Foreign Investment Review Act.* Ottawa: E.C.C., 1980.

Seymour-Ure, C. "Prime Ministers, Political News and Political Places." *C.P.A.*, 32, 2, Summer, 1989.

Sharp, M. "Decision-making in the Federal Cabinet." *C.P.A.*, 19, 1, Spring, 1976.

Stewart, E.E. *Cabinet Government in Ontario: A View from Inside.* Halifax: I.R.P.P., 1989.

Stewart, I. "Of Custom and Coalitions: The Formation of Canadian Parliamentary Alliances." *C.J.P.S.*, 13, 3, September, 1980.

Van Loon, R. "Stop the Music: The Current Policy and Expenditure Management System in Ottawa." *C.P.A.*, 24, 2, Summer, 1981.

Van Loon, R. "The Policy and Expenditure Management System in the Federal Government: The First Three Years." *C.P.A.*, 26, 2, Summer, 1983.

Weller, P. "Inner Cabinets and Outer Ministers: Some Lessons from Australia and Britain." *C.P.A.*, 23, 4, Winter, 1980.

Weller, P. *First Among Equals: Prime Ministers in Westminster Systems.* Sydney, Australia: George Allen & Unwin, 1985.

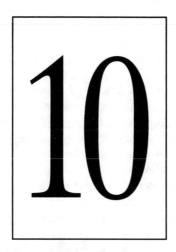

THE HOUSE OF COMMONS

FUNCTIONS OF THE HOUSE OF COMMONS

Graham White

The Canadian House of Commons is a fundamentally important political institution. Its importance, however, is often misunderstood. The House of Commons does not govern nor, with few exceptions, does it make policy or render decisions on important issues. Instead, its significance lies in representing various interests and viewpoints, in holding the government accountable for its actions, in legitimizing policy, and in setting out before the voters the political parties' positions on important issues.

This essay explores some of the functions of the House of Commons. Before doing so it discusses two elements crucial to an understanding of Parliament: party discipline and the position of an MP. The paper concludes with a look at recent reforms in the House.

PARTY DISCIPLINE

Many of the constitutional principles underlying Parliament predate the rise of disciplined political parties in Britain and Canada in the latter part of the nineteenth century. Nevertheless, the parliamentary system as Canadians have

An original article prepared in 1990 by the author, who is Assistant Professor of Political Science at Erindale College, University of Toronto. By permission.

come to know it is absolutely incomprehensible except in terms of disciplined political parties.

Party discipline often is confused with cabinet solidarity, since both involve strict adherence to a position once it has been adopted. The two are, however, quite different. Cabinet solidarity is a constitutional and political principle, breech of which may have serious constitutional implications, whereas party discipline is solely a matter of politics. A breakdown in party discipline may have serious political consequences (for example, in 1988 a single wayward NDP backbencher brought down the Pawley government in Manitoba), but it involves no violation of Constitutional principles. Moreover, cabinet solidarity—which, of course, applies only to the cabinet—comes into play once the cabinet has itself taken a decision, but party discipline does not imply that the MPs who are subject to it have any say whatsoever in the decision they are expected to support.

In the Canadian House of Commons party discipline is very strong—stronger, for example, than in Britain. Among the important implications of this strong party discipline is that the key number in the House is not 295 but three: not 295 individual members of Parliament, but three political parties acting as cohesive, disciplined units. It is rare for MPs to publicly voice disagreement with their parties and rarer still for them to vote against their parties. As a consequence the power of MPs who are not in cabinet is severely limited. Opposition MPs lack power because they are simply outnumbered by a solid phalanx of government members. Government MPs might seem to be in a strong position to influence policy, but because of the dominant position enjoyed by cabinet, reinforced by party discipline, this tends not to be the case. Backbench members on the government side have better informal lines of communication with ministers, but usually have substantially less clout in determining party policy than MPs in opposition.

Why do members of Parliament tolerate such strong party discipline, which leads to accusations that they are no better than "trained seals?" To some extent discipline is effective because of the rewards and sanctions involved. The rewards are far more enticing on the government side: cabinet posts, parliamentary secretaryships, plum committee assignments, future prospects for prized patronage jobs, and the like. For the opposition the immediate rewards are not nearly so impressive, but MPs belonging to the party forming the Official Opposition toe the line in anticipation of similar rewards should they form the government. Sanctions are much less in evidence, though MPs are aware that they may be enforced, as occurred in early 1990 when two Alberta MPs were expelled from the Conservative caucus for publicly disagreeing with the government's proposed goods and services tax.

Members of Parliament are not immune in their belief in some of the "fairy tales" about parliamentary government set out by Forsey and Eglington in the following article in this book. In particular, the myth that any government defeat in the House entails either the government's resignation or an election is very much alive on Parliament Hill. Party leaders, whips, and House leaders regularly propagate this myth because it makes it easier to manage their MPs.

For all this, however, the most important basis for party discipline is that the MPs believe in it. They prefer to be team players because of the social support they receive from their colleagues and because they see this as the most effective route to power.

The cohesion of the parties stands as both cause and effect of the relentlessly adversarial nature of Parliament. The very layout of the chamber, with the parties arrayed along long rows of benches facing one another, contributes to the "us against them" mentality that pervades the House. The dynamic of the House is premised on a fundamental division between government and opposition, who rarely compromise on fundamentals. The adversarial proceedings in the House resemble the adversarial character of our judicial system, with the entire electorate serving as the jury.

THE LOT OF THE MEMBER OF PARLIAMENT

Members of Parliament are subject to frequent criticism, but the lot of the MP is not an easy one. (As with other groups such as doctors, people tend to be supportive of their own MP but critical of MPs as a group.) MPs are fairly well paid: approximately $83,000 a year as of 1990, plus a generous pension plan. For those who give up positions in the private sector, however, this may well represent a significant cut in income. Moreover, their job security lasts no further than the next election, and some have trouble attempting to return to their former professions after losing their seats.

The real hardships, though, are not financial but personal. MPs have to live away from home for more than half the year; for many this means being separated from their families for extended periods. Even if their ridings are thousands of kilometres from Ottawa, their constituents expect them to come home on a regular basis. Accordingly, MPs often leave Ottawa on Friday after a full week, endure many hours travelling to spend a good part of the weekend meeting constituents and attending various events in their ridings, and return to Ottawa for Monday. MPs suffer invasions of their privacy that many citizens would not tolerate. In addition, they face enormous job frustration; they are often unable to realize their policy goals or even to contribute meaningfully to the policy process.

Three or four decades ago members of Parliament were in an even weaker position because they lacked resources in the form of the most elemental facilities and staff support. Among the resources available to a present-day MP are several personal staff, publicly funded offices in his or her riding, and access to professional research assistance supplied by the Library of Parliament, by the party caucuses, and by the parliamentary committees on which he or she serves. Some of these resources are directed toward fulfilling the MPs' legislative role, that is, developing and promoting policy ideas (which on the opposition side may include acting as the party's "critic," or spokesperson, for a particular government department). MPs also devote a good deal of their resources to constituency concerns.

The typical MP does not stay in Parliament for long. Relatively few are in the House for even a decade; data compiled by C.E.S. Franks in *The Parliament of Canada* indicate that roughly 80 percent of MPs have served less than seven years at the beginning of each Parliament. Some quit because they no longer wish to put up with the frustrations and the personal sacrifices. Most, however, simply lose their seats at election time. Whatever the cause, the result is a tendency to one- and two-term members of Parliament. The advantage of bringing new blood into the House is outweighed by the inexperience and insecurity felt by MPs. Moreover, as Franks has put it, "a high proportion of Canadian MPs are learning their job, and an equally large proportion are planning to leave, expecting to leave, going to leave, or all three."

THE FUNCTIONS OF PARLIAMENT

It is not at all necessary that the MPs or the parties intend that the House perform various functions for those functions to be fulfilled. Few MPs, for example, approach Question Period with the noble goal of keeping the government accountable, and yet as a result of the partisan hurly-burly, accountability is achieved. Similarly, MPs do not defend or attack government policies with a view to maintaining the legitimacy of the overall political system, though this is certainly one by-product of the parliamentary process.

Among the functions performed by Parliament are:

Representation—parliament is a representative institution in several senses. Individual MPs and their staffs spend considerable time and energy serving as representatives of their constituents in their dealings with government: advising in immigration matters, intervening in denials for unemployment insurance benefits, and any number of similar problems. In addition to this "ombudsman function," MPs contribute to representation by bringing forward, both in debate and behind the scenes, regional and ideological viewpoints, as well as the perspectives of various social groups.

This last point raises the question of how socially representative MPs are, and if it matters whether, as a group, they reflect the make-up of Canadian society. In region, language (at least French and English), and religion, MPs fairly mirror the Canadian population. In other respects, however, they are not at all a representative group. MPs are overwhelmingly male and tend to come from middle-class professions, especially business and law; they are better educated and wealthier than their constituents. Not only are women, the poor, and those of working-class background dramatically underrepresented, but so too are Canadians from the so-called visible minorities (including, until recently, Natives), the disabled, and the young.

Does it matter that the House of Commons is unrepresentative in these and other ways? On the one hand members do strive to understand and to promote the concerns of their constituents. Aside from believing that it is their duty to do so, MPs recognize that it is in their electoral interest. On the other hand it is hard to argue that the interests of single mothers, the disabled, and unemployed youth would not be taken more seriously by government were there more MPs from these and similar groups. As well, the legitimacy of Parliament as an institution is undermined when substantial numbers of citizens perceive that the central democratic institution in Canada has few, if any, members like them.

Policy-making—Parliament is not so much a law-making body as a law-passing body. Virtually all principal decisions of government policy are made by the cabinet and the bureaucracy. Many, but by no means all, major decisions must be brought forward for parliamentary approval either in the form of spending estimates or in bills. For the most part, though, such approval is not in doubt, and only amendments acceptable to the government succeed. Because of the overloaded parliamentary agenda government bills may fail to pass for lack of time; but for high priority bills the uncertainty about their passage is a matter of when rather than if.

Nevertheless, the tremendous concentration of power in the cabinet and the constraints of party discipline do not mean that MPs, individually or as a collectivity, are denied influence on policy. Through the adversarial approach the opposition may be able to get the government to change its mind or to alter its policy by embarrassing it, by mobilizing and channeling public opinion against it, or by delaying key items in its program. Success in influencing policy in this way—on those infrequent occasions when it occurs—is a matter of being critical, obstreperous, and confrontational. When Parliament operates in a consensual fashion, that is, with members working together in disregard of party lines, the emphasis is on compromise, force of argument, and evidence rather than on power politics. MPs can often influence the details of policy, if not the principles, in this fashion. In addition, in developing new policy ideas, especially on issues in which the parties (or the government) have not taken firm positions, considerable leeway exists for MPs to influence the process.

Debates in the House and procedures such as private members' bills can play a role in the policy formulation process, but the principal means by which MPs participate in policy formulation is through the committee system. Parliamentary committees engage in a number of tasks, such as scrutinizing the government's spending estimates, approving (and amending) bills on a clause-by-clause basis, and reviewing the effectiveness of programme administration. On occasion committees conduct special enquiries designed to produce new policy proposals. The cabinet is under no obligation to accept and implement the recommendations that emerge from these studies, but if the committee has done a thorough job and produced a report supported by MPs from all parties, the committee's views will be seriously considered and may well result in policy changes. This is not to suggest that parliamentary committees or the MPs who serve on them are typically key players in the policy process, for as a rule they are not. The scope does exist, however, for MPs to influence policy in some circumstances.

Fostering Accountability—Parliament plays a crucial role in holding the government accountable for its policies and for the administration of those policies. During the daily Question Period ministers, including the prime minister, must answer the criticisms of their principal political opponents in the most public forum imaginable. Committees such as the Public Accounts Committee conduct more low key, but more detailed, public investigation of the government's performance.

The exchanges in Question Period are often superficial or thinly veiled partisan attacks, and only a small proportion of government activities can be subjected to the more intense scrutiny of parliamentary committees. It would, however, be incorrect to conclude that Parliament is ineffective in promoting accountability. The threat of what might happen or what might be said is often more important than what actually takes place. Ministers and senior bureaucrats know that the likelihood of serious embarrassment or political damage arising from errors, questionable policies, and ineffective administrative practices is fairly low. Yet such unwelcome consequences are a real possibility; one can never take Parliament for granted. Accordingly, by forcing government to act in anticipation of possibly embarrassing criticism, Parliament and its committees foster accountability and shape government policy choices.

Debating the Issues—John Stuart Mill argued in the last century that Parliament must be "an arena in which not only the general opinion of the nation, but that of every section of it, can produce itself in full light and challenge discussion." In other words Parliament can provide a forum for debate of the great issues of the day. The adversarial nature of the process encourages the parties to confront and to criticize one another's policies (and thereby to refine and clarify their own policies), to mobilize the proponents of specific policy causes, and to educate the public on important issues of public policy. To be sure, parliamentary treatment of many issues is superficial and inadequate, but in recent years Parliament has served as a focus for discussion and a spur to public debate about such issues as free trade with the United States, the goods and services tax, immigration policy, unemployment insurance, and fisheries policy.

Maintaining Legitimacy—All political systems require legitimacy, the recognition by the citizens that the state has legitimate authority over them, coupled with a willingness on the citizens' part to accept policies that they do not personally favour. To say that a political system is legitimate is not equivalent to saying that the government of the day is popular; indeed, the real significance of legitimacy becomes clear when a government makes unpopular decisions.

Major government policies are debated and approved in the House of Commons by the elected representatives of the people; thus it contributes significantly to legitimacy. Moreover, legitimacy is enhanced when those affected by decisions participate in making them, or at least believe that they are participating (or can participate). It may well be that the public hearings held by parliamentary committees on proposed policy changes and on pending legislation, as well as the letters and calls received by MPs on various topics, have little discernible impact on policy outcomes. Nevertheless, the very existence of a public process through which interest groups and citizens can make their voices heard to members of Parliament serves to maintain the legitimacy of the political system.

THE REFORM OF PARLIAMENT

In the early and mid-1980s Parliament underwent extensive scrutiny by its own members and by outside observers in an effort to counteract the manifold problems it faced. A series of significant reforms emerged from this process, principally through the work of two parliamentary committees, the Lefebvre committee (1982–83) and the McGrath committee (1984–85).

The catalyst for serious reform was the infamous "bells incident" early in 1982. As a means of pressuring the government over its controversial energy legislation, the Conservative opposition refused to take part in a vote; Parliament was paralyzed for 15 days as the division bells rang. The bells crisis pointed up sharply the futility of Parliament and the desperate need for reform. Shortly thereafter the government agreed to establish a Commons Special Committee on Procedure.

The special committee, chaired by veteran Liberal backbencher Tom Lefebvre, issued ten reports between July 1982 and September 1983. Several of the committee's key recommendations were accepted by the government and came into effect early in 1984; others had to await the election of the Conservative government for implementation. The most significant of these reforms relate to the parliamentary calendar, the hours of sitting, the role of parliamentary committees, and the length of members' speeches.

Until 1984 on most days the House began its business at 2:00 p.m. and continued (with a two-hour supper break) until 10:30 p.m. or later. Not only were MPs asked to work impossibly long hours—most spent their mornings at committee meetings or working in their offices—but they were unable to plan their schedules with any certainty. The House was in session for roughly seven or eight months a year, but no one knew in advance which seven or eight months. Since MPs are expected by their constituents and by their party leaders to be in Parliament when it is sitting, this made it difficult for MPs to plan the work they have to do in their ridings, as well as their personal schedules with their families.

Almost all night sittings have now been eliminated, though some committees meet in the evening. The House sits from 11:00 a.m. until 6:00 p.m. In addition, although the government retains the power to convene special emergency sessions, a "parliamentary calendar" dictates which weeks and months of the year the House will be in session so that MPs know well in advance when they will have to be in Ottawa. It speaks volumes about the need for reform that such a sensible, business-like approach to the timing of House sittings was agreed to only recently.

On most occasions MPs must now limit their speeches to 20 minutes, rather than the previous limit of 40 minutes. This represents a significant saving of time and makes for more concise, pointed speeches. Another innovation is that after a member speaks, there is now a ten-minute period in which other members can ask questions or take issue with the member. This reform has not raised the tone of debate as much as had been hoped. Still, it has gone some way toward turning the dry recitation of set-piece speeches, in which MPs talked past one another, into something more closely resembling what the public thinks of as "debate."

Parliamentary committees have been substantially strengthened as a result of the Lefebvre committee's proposals. They were reduced in size from about 20 MPs to between 10 and 15, and their membership was made more stable to improve their effectiveness. More significantly, they were given the ability to examine just about any aspect of government policy without first seeking approval of the government. Although under a majority government the government MPs on a committee can still vote to prevent or to limit discussion of a particular subject, this is a very important extension of the power of committees and of the private members who sit on them.

Shortly after assuming office in 1984, Prime Minister Mulroney expressed strong support for the process of reform and appointed another special committee to continue the work. This committee was chaired by Jim McGrath, one of the most senior and respected members of the House. Significantly, whereas the Lefebvre committee had been instructed to limit its recommendations to the formal rules and procedures of the House, the McGrath committee was given free rein to examine all aspects of parliamentary reform. It reaffirmed almost all of the Lefebvre recommendations that had yet to be acted upon and moved on to cover new ground. In June of 1985 the committee released its final report, which its chairman rightly termed "the most ambitious attempt to pursue major and comprehensive reform" in the history of Canada's Parliament.

The *Report of the Special Committee on Reform of the House of Commons* set out recommendations aimed at improving various aspects of the workings of Parliament and the services available to it and to its members. Many were relatively minor or dealt with important but arcane administrative matters, but all were proposed, in the committee's words, "to restore the private members an effective legislative function, to give them a meaningful role in the formation of public policy, and, in so doing, to restore the House of Commons to its rightful place in the Canadian political process." The government was not comfortable with all of the committee's ideas, but after intense behind-the-scenes activity it accepted, with relatively few modifications, most of the important recommendations which came into force in February 1986.

One of the most notable reforms arising from the McGrath report has been the election of the Speaker by secret ballot. Prior to 1986, although nominally elected by the House, Speakers were, in effect, chosen by the prime minister. A strong, independent Speaker, who enjoys the trust and support of all MPs, is essential to an effective, smoothly running Parliament. But it was difficult for Speakers to achieve independence and members' respect because they were seen not as Parliament's choice but as the prime minister's. Not only is a Speaker elected by secret ballot a more independent Speaker, he or she enjoys far better relations with the MPs since they were responsible for the choice. John Fraser, the first Speaker elected under the new rules, has been widely perceived as a successful, well-respected Speaker; to an important extent this reflects the process by which he became Speaker.

As proposed by McGrath, the size of committees was further reduced to between 7 and 15 members. The early tendency had been to appoint the minimum rather than the maximum. A new species of *ad hoc* legislative committee has been created. These committees deal with specific bills as they pass through the House and are disbanded once the bills are sent back to the House. The idea was to rationalize the workload of committees, which might previously have been asked to deal with several items of business at once. However, complications of scheduling so many committees and other additional problems have rendered this change a mixed success.

Committees' ability to hire expert staff to help with their work has been enhanced, and a new rule requires that the government must, if requested, publish comprehensive formal responses to committee reports. This does not guarantee that governments will act on the recommendations, but it does not mean that they cannot ignore the recommendations.

Another important and controversial power given committees is the power to review "order-in-council appointments." Deputy ministers, heads of crown corporations, ambassadors, and others appointed by the cabinet to high government positions (excluding judgeships) may now be called before parliamentary committees empowered to consider the advisability of their appointments. The committees are not permitted to veto such appointments (as the McGrath report had proposed for certain cases), but the very fact that committees composed of MPs from all parties can meet in public to examine the suitability of government appointments may well cause the government to reconsider possible appointments (and possible appointees to reconsider their acceptance).

The rules governing private members' business have also been overhauled in the hope of giving some meaning to backbench MPs' ability to propose laws and ideas to the House. Until these new rules came into force, even the most innocuous private members' bills rarely passed. Instead, they were debated for an hour and then dropped to the bottom of a long list, from which they never returned. Now 20 items of private members' business are selected in a random ballot and are referred to a committee of the House. This committee considers the merits of each item and picks those to be debated for as much as five hours, after which they must come to a vote.

It is still quite unusual for a private member's bill to become law, though NDP MP Lynn MacDonald was successful in having a far-reaching smokers' rights bill enacted. Nevertheless, the prospects for backbench MPs influencing public policy have improved significantly as a result of the new rules. The impact of private members' bills often depends less on the likelihood that they will be passed than on their success in mobilizing public opinion and generating enthusiasm and credibility for the proposed policy so that the government will agree to adopt it as its own measure.

Among the other rule changes adopted in 1986 were measures to enhance the Speaker's power to discipline unruly MPs and to limit the time that the opposition could delay proceedings by ringing the bells. In most circumstances the bells will ring for only 30 minutes. Either the government whip or the Official Opposition whip may request that the vote be deferred for as much as a day, but during this time the House continues with normal business.

These reforms have generally been well received and have unquestionably given private members and parliamentary committees a more effective role in advising and scrutinizing the government. Yet even the most optimistic reformer recognizes that changes to formal rules and procedures can go only so far in enhancing Parliament's significance in the governing process. The McGrath committee rightly focused on the need for fundamental attitudinal changes on the part of MPs and of government. So long as MPs rarely speak out against their parties' positions, let alone vote against them in the House, the prospects for a truly effective Parliament in which independent-minded members contribute to policy making are dim.

The McGrath report argued for a looser approach to the key issue of confidence votes, which many regard as the heart of party discipline. It recommended that all parties adopt an approach similar to that prevalent in Britain, where MPs frequently vote against their parties without fear of retribution or of causing an election. In Canada the Mulroney government signified acceptance in principle of the need for a less restrictive interpretation of the confidence convention, but none of the parties has taken any significant steps toward relaxing party discipline.

It may be unfair to describe the reforms of the 1980s as merely tinkering, but certainly the fundamental power relationships within Parliament have not altered. The cabinet retains enormous power, while backbench MPs on both government and opposition sides of the House are essentially powerless. Fundamental change to the House of Commons depends rather less on reforms to the rules, although these can certainly help, than it does on the attitude held by the parties (especially the party in power) toward giving MPs a share of the power now exercised almost exclusively by the government.

[   ]

TWENTY-FIVE FAIRY TALES ABOUT PARLIAMENTARY GOVERNMENT

Eugene Forsey and Graham Eglington

Even after acknowledging the many and serious limitations on the exercise of deliberative judgment by members of the Commons, there can be room for independence of thought and action so long as members, ministers, prime ministerial assistants and advisers, Opposition strategists, civil servants and media commentators, reporters and columnists are not blinded or led astray by the fairy tales about responsible government that have grown up, gained wide currency and been embellished in the retelling. Ironically, one of the most vocal groups of story-tellers are Opposition Leaders and spokesmen as they try to wring political advantage from temporary government difficulties in the House, or cause the government to appear to lose face because of some set-back there.

What are these widespread misconceptions?

1. The pattern of parliamentary government implies that the government must win every vote.

No. The government must maintain its majority in the sense of retaining the House's confidence, or give way to another. These two principles are *not* the same. It is a curious belief, unsupported by history or practice, whether in Canada, Britain or elsewhere in the Commonwealth, that "responsible government" means that every vote in the House of Commons must be won by the government, and that any defeat is a resigning or dissolving matter. This belief appears to have achieved the status of a religious doctrine in some quarters. It can, therefore, be described as a heresy used by unscrupulous persons and journalists to support the more immediately visible sanctions against tendencies to rebellion in members of the House of Commons.

2. The temporary possession of a majority in the House of Commons constitutes the possessors of it for the time being absolute autocrats, able to insist that the House endorse every measure, every clause of every bill, and every line in the Estimates, and turn back every critical report or resolution.

From *The Question of Confidence in Responsible Government*, a study prepared for the Special Committee on the Reform of the House of Commons, Ottawa, 1984. By permission.

No again. This view is wholly at variance with theory, practice and precedent.

3.   The administrative convenience of the executive is a basic principle of the Constitution for the sustaining of which the government's majority must be employed to carry skeletal bills, to confer vast delegated powers and enormous discretions on the executive and to turn back all criticism of delegated legislation or administrative action.

Again, this is an entirely fallacious doctrine, though no doubt one holding great attraction for ministers and their advisers, and especially for civil servants.

4.   The government is responsible only to the electorate. It may do as it pleases, and insist that its parliamentary followers allow it to do as it pleases, in between elections. In between elections the House may not *control* the executive or amend its measures by direct action but only by acting as a sounding board for outside opinion leading the government to amend its draft legislation.

No, yet again. Limitation of the House in this way is wholly unsupported by convention, theory or history.

5.   The general confidence accorded by the electorate is an endorsement before the event of every measure a government may bring forward and of all means it may choose to implement its policies.

If this were so Parliament would serve practically no purpose at all and the job of criticism and exposure could be handed over to the media.

6.   Every debatable or votable matter in the House of Commons is a matter of principle and hence of confidence on which the government must be sustained. Machinery clauses in bills, hostile or even slightly critical committee reports, the rare opportunities accorded to affirm or disallow regulations and other delegated legislation, all are matters on which a government cannot give way and matters on which a private member may at best be absent.

This is merely a variant or summary of the preceding five myths.

7.   Members of Parliament are powerless in the present circumstances.

They are not powerless. They *choose* not to exercise their power, especially in clause by clause consideration of bills or in the scrutiny of delegated legislation. Their choice may be dictated by reason, principally fear of a government black mark and the arrest of their careers, party loyalty and distaste for the other side, but the choice is theirs to make.

8.   A government which is defeated in the House must resign or secure a dissolution.

No. This is a fiction, the only purpose of which can be to intimidate members and mislead the electorate.

9.   Amendments made to a bill in committee must be reversed at the report stage and any defeat by the government at that stage must result in resignation or an election.

Yet another fiction.

10.   A government defeated in the House is *entitled* to a dissolution.

This is a persistent and dangerous falsehood which, if ever finally accepted as a constitutional convention, would destroy democratic government.

11.   If a minority government is defeated in the House there *must* be an election.

This is a popularised version of No. 10, often seen in newspapers. It is wholly without foundation. Defeat of a minority government in the House may result in:

a)   that government continuing, accepting the consequences, whatever they are, of the vote lost in the House;
b)   resignation of the government and formation of a new government by one or other, or by more than one of the other parties in the House;
c)   a request for a dissolution which is refused, leading to resignation and formation of a new government; or
d)   a request for a dissolution which is granted, and hence an election.

12.   Any money measure—a taxation proposal or an Estimate—is a matter of confidence so that any government defeated on one must resign or secure a dissolution.

Wrong. There have been many such defeats, in Canada and throughout the Commonwealth, which have been accepted by the government of the day which has carried on and neither resigned nor sought an election.

13.   A defeat in the House on a measure and especially a financial matter "terminates the government."

On the contrary, it remains in office until the prime minister resigns or is dismissed. If he asks for and is granted a dissolution the government remains in office throughout the election and beyond until resignation or dismissal.

14.   A defeat of the government in the House on any matter, and especially a financial matter, robs the House of its right to sit.

This is incorrect. The House may adjourn while the government considers its position, but the House continues in existence until it is dissolved and continues in session until prorogued. Even the practice of adjournment after defeat has fallen into abeyance in Britain.

15.   The defeat of any proposal in the budget entails resignation of the government or dissolution.

Defeat of the government on the general budget motion—"That this House approves in *general* the budgetary policy of the government"—or the carrying of an amendment to it clearly expressing the House's censure of that policy entails resignation or dissolution, as in December 1979 [when the Clark government was defeated]. Once the general motion is approved, the way is wide open for amendments to budget proposals. Particular provisions may be amended by making changes which the government can take or not take as matters of confidence, as it considers wise. This is a most important safeguard for the rights of private members.

The House's freedom is limited only by the basic rule of responsible government that it cannot increase a tax proposed by the government, or substitute another tax for that proposed. When dealing with Estimates, the House can reduce or eliminate them or any of them. But it cannot increase any Estimate.

16.   A government condemned or censured in the House, or defeated on a major measure central to its programme, or being at the end of a string of defeats which have destroyed its credibility and honour, can say to the House "you really didn't mean it" and ask for a vote of confidence.

To allow such a principle is to make a mockery of the doctrine of confidence and to place an intolerable burden on private members who may be forced to vote against their party and colleagues time and time again until they break.

17.   The House may question and debate the policies and measures of the government but may not reject them or any part of them: it may only criticize and scrutinize.

This is merely a generalization extracted from what is thought usually to have happened in the House in this century. It is more a criticism than an accurate summary. It is not borne out by practice and precedent in Britain, or even in Canada.

18.   The function of a member is confined to assisting his constituents in their conflicts with bureaucracy, securing grants and public works for his constituency, obtaining grants and contracts for his constituents and their employers, and making appeals to ministers to alter policies or measures which offend public opinion or sectional interests.

Important as all these activities are, they are not, or should not be, the whole extent of a member's functions. He is to consider the content and text of legislation and budget proposals, express himself in those areas of policy in which he has interest and knowledge, and, it is to be hoped, take some part in monitoring and controlling public administration and delegated legislation.

19.   The government must control House business at all times. Any loss of control is a matter of confidence leading to resignation or dissolution.

This is not supported by precedent. Even serious reversals on House business leading to effective loss of legislation have been accepted by governments which have simply carried on.

20.   Adverse committee reports must be treated as matters of confidence and rejected by the House.

This is without foundation. It is of course, conceivable that an adverse committee report could raise some issue which a government could, or even should in the political circumstances, treat as a resigning matter. But it will be rare that a committee report falls into that category. Governments are foolish to try to insist on bromide reports.

The Canadian House of Commons unanimously concurred in a report critical of the way increases in postal charges were effected. The government did not fall; neither were the increased charges abandoned, although they were later validated retroactively by legislation introduced by the succeeding government.

21.   Provision for disallowance of regulations and other delegated legislation cannot be allowed because such legislation, being made or approved by the governor-in-council or by ministers, must be treated as a matter of confidence, and any vote for disallowance must be regarded as one of want of confidence.

This is a peculiarly Canadian nostrum. It is contrary to experience, practice, and precedent in those jurisdictions where disallowance in the House as a control mechanism is possible. No one in Britain or in Australia seems even to have suggested that disallowance of delegated legislation involves automatically either collective responsibility or confidence.

22.   Censure of an individual minister must be treated as censure of the entire ministry, and, as such, a matter of confidence.

Censure of individual ministers is now rare. Past practice and precedent show that a government need not treat a motion of censure of a particular minister as a question of confidence in the whole ministry. Governments may be tempted to do so, and certainly can be expected to call upon all their supporters to vote in defence of the minister under attack.

23.   The Constitution, its conventions and practices must be entirely consistent with some all-pervading theory.

We have always had a mixed Constitution which has been made to work by practical adjustments to the power of its several elements. The objects are reasonable, stable and effective government, and freedom. These will not be secured by a system of governance set out in accordance with some theory dreamed up to suit the circumstances of the moment, but by the maintenance of a healthy tension between executive and Parliament, and between lower and upper Houses, and by the preservation and use, when necessary, of the reserve powers of the crown.

24.   The sovereign or governor general must always act in accordance with the advice of ministers.

This may be true in connection with those matters on which advice is taken. But it is not true of the reserve powers of the crown: appointment and dismissal of prime ministers and dissolution of Parliament.

25.   Defeats in the House cannot be conceded by the government for fear of losing face and being ridiculed by the media as weak.

This need only be so if defeats are inflicted on a government which has set its face against any concessions in or to the House. If a government were to concede that it need not win every vote and carry every clause in order to stay in office, what face would there be to lose? Media education and management seems to be common enough in other areas of government. Let it be employed in the matter of confidence too.

QUESTION PERIOD AND DEBATE IN THE HOUSE
C.E.S. Franks

The main modes of discussion in a parliamentary system are debate and question period. In theory, a debate is an argument between two sides in which one side wins because its arguments are the more persuasive—such, for example, are the famous arguments in Thucydides, or Burke's speeches in the great age of parliamentarism. In theory, also, the purpose of a question is to ask something in the expectation of obtaining an answer. But in the Canadian House of Commons practice belies the theory. Debates rarely persuade and questions are not asked so that the interrogator will learn from an informative answer. As George Hees has noted, "the unwritten rule is never to ask a question unless you know the answer." John Reid has argued that "the

From *The Canadian House of Commons: Essays in Honour of Norman Ward*, pages 1, 2, 3 & 4, 1985, by permission of The University of Calgary Press.

purpose of most debates in the House of Commons is not to enlighten but to beat one's opponents to death by dullness." In effect, the questions are not real questions, and the debates, with the conclusion foregone, are not real debates.

Debate and question period are problems. They occupy most of the time of the Canadian House of Commons, the most important political forum in the country. But they do not perform the functions that their names imply. They must be of value or even the slow processes of changing parliamentary procedure would have modified them. But their values are not the obvious ones. . . .

The setting for both debate and question period in the Canadian House of Commons is adversarial. The chamber is rectangular. On the Speaker's right sit the government members, with the prime minister and cabinet ministers (the heads of the executive branch) occupying the front rows. To the Speaker's left sit the opposition. Each of the 282 [now 295] members, including the Speaker, has a desk on the floor of the House. In former times this was all the office a member had, but nowadays each member has a suite of offices in Ottawa as well as an office in his constituency, paid for by Parliament. This is far better accommodation than that of his British counterpart. Members, while the House is in session, often sit at their desks reading correspondence, or writing, or performing other chores. The physical setting of the Canadian House of Commons is quite different from the British, which is much smaller. The British House of Commons has benches instead of desks, and there is not enough room for the 640 MPs to sit at one time. Although the British setting was originally an accident of history, it was perpetuated by choice to ensure an intimate, informal style.

The adversarial structure of the House, and its division into government and opposition, is a great simplifier. There are only two sides to every issue. A member is either for a motion or against. All different shades of opinion are forced into these two aggregations. There is no room for single-issue politics in the parliamentary system. The parties and the members win or lose on the basis of their total choices, policies, and decisions; the individual member is protected by party discipline from single-issue pressure groups. But he must also pay the price of conforming to that discipline. The physical setting of the House reflects that discipline and simplifying aggregation. "We shape our buildings," Churchill said in discussing the rebuilding of the British House of Commons after it was destroyed by bombing during the Second World War, "and afterwards our buildings shape us."

This is not to say, of course, that there are only two shades of opinion expressed in Parliament. With at least three and occasionally four or five parties represented in the House, at least that variety of opinions will be expressed. There are also many shades of opinion within each party. The Liberal caucus under Pierre Trudeau, despite its monolithic unanimity in public, had vigorous debates in private. The Progressive Conservative party has often been better known for its disagreements than for its party unity. Members of the NDP frequently vote against party positions on matters of conscience. But when it comes to a vote in the House, the choice is aye or nay; and a member's record is never far from the aggregation of ayes and nays expressed by his party.

The Canadian House lacks the intimate atmosphere of its British counterpart. While it is crowded for question period, for most of the time it is nearly deserted with only twenty or thirty members present. A member speaks from his desk, while before him stretches a vast wasteland of empty desks with inattentive colleagues reading, letter signing, or conducting other business. This physical setting, with its lack of closeness, audience, contact, or excitement, is enough to make speaking in the House a difficult matter. Since 1977 the House has been televised. The picture that the television audience sees, however, is quite different from that of a spectator in the gallery. Members on the side of the MP who is speaking often crowd into the desks around him so the narrow frame of the television camera gives the illusion that the House itself is crowded. In reality only the few seats close to the member speaking are occupied, and most of the House is deserted. Except on grand or urgent occasions the chamber is an intimidating and depressing place in which to speak, and this contributes to the dullness of debate.

Question period occurs five times a week while Parliament is sitting. From Monday to Thursday it occupies 45 minutes between 2:15 and 3:00 P.M.; on Friday it is in the morning. Unlike debates, question period is a time of excitement. Most members are at their places, the press gallery is full and so is the visitors' gallery. The Canadian question period is unique. For 45 minutes opposition members attack the government. Most questions are of the "have you stopped beating your wife yet" variety. They are, in effect, miniature speeches in which the questioner claims that some problem or desperate situation exists and asks the government what it is going to do, or stop doing, about it. The opposition parties have in recent years organized themselves as they make a systematic choice of which ministers, policy, and problem to attack. They also decide who shall be questioners. The Speaker, for the bulk of question period, follows lists of questions given to him by the opposition parties. Each question is normally followed by supplementaries, in which the initial questioner or a colleague tries to elicit further confessions from the minister who, in turn, tries to give as good as he gets.

Questions are in order as long as they are, in fact, questions (though this rule is often bent, if not broken), are asked about something for which the minister is responsible and answerable, and are in parliamentary language. Answers by the minister are acceptable as long as they are relevant, in order, and in parliamentary language. A minister can choose not to reply, but rather to sit and ignore the question.

Question period is a free-wheeling affair with tremendous spontaneity and vitality. The main topics are often those on the front pages of the major newspapers, or ones raised on national television news the previous evening. No notice is usually given for questions. However, the ministers' staff are at least as diligent in spotting possible questions and briefing their ministers with answers as opposition members and their research staff are in preparing questions and supplementaries. The Speaker's role in question period is to ensure that the rules of order and procedure are respected. He is not responsible for ensuring that topics are adequately covered, or that ministers give useful answers, and his role in ensuring that all opposition members have the opportunity to participate has been severely curtailed since the parties themselves began to choose their own batting order.

The bulk of the television and newspaper coverage of Parliament comes from question period. After it is over there is a remarkable exodus; where there were 280 members there are now twenty-five; where the press gallery was packed, only two or three remain; the public galleries are empty.

In Britain, questions are written and there is notice of at least a week during which ministers and their staff can prepare answers. Though supplementaries introduce an element of spontaneity, much of the British question period is a ponderous dance in which the ministers give carefully phrased replies to questions that are at least a week old. Question period in Britain is sophisticated and frequently clever but it is rarely as spontaneous or dynamic as [in Canada].

Question period is a contest between two cohesive and disciplined teams, the government and the opposition. Neither the prime minister nor any other government official has any control over whether question period will occur, or what will be asked. It is a gruelling, regular occasion, on over 150 days of the year, during which the rulers of the country are forced to listen and respond to the complaints and grievances of the nation as expressed by the opposition, in the spotlight of intensive coverage by the media. In the United States, neither presidential press conferences, where questions are limited, pre-selected and orchestrated, nor presidential State of the Union addresses to Congress, where there are no questions, compare with the Canadian question period.

The bulk of the rest of the House of Commons' time is occupied with debate. In a given year, fifteen or sixteen days will be taken up with opening the session, the throne speech and budget debates. After deducting the twenty-five opposition supply days, there will be about 110 days left for government business, or about 400 hours. This, the bulk of the House of Commons' time, is spent primarily on bills. But a few times each year the normal routine will be interrupted by debate on a motion under Standing Order 26, to discuss a matter of urgent public importance.

We have already noted that debate is protracted and dull. A recent study found that even though the House spends far more time debating bills than on question period, newspaper coverage of question period exceeds coverage of debate on government bills by a ratio of thirty-five to one. The normal speech is wordy, unnecessarily long and repetitious and, in the British House, would be drowned out and terminated by catcalls and the shuffling of feet. Only because nobody is listening does this not happen in Canada. Similarly, debates themselves are overly long and repetitious. Virtually every interesting point to be made in a debate can be found in the first three and the last three speeches—those of the leading party spokesmen. The dozens of speeches and hours in between are chaff, best lost in the winds of time. Recently, on the recommendation of a Special Committee on Procedure, the length of most speeches was reduced to twenty minutes from forty. At the same time provision was made for a brief give and take question and answer session after each speech. This, it was hoped, would give some spontaneity and life to debate. So far it appears to have had moderate success but the problem of length and dullness of debate still remains.

[   ]

A PRIVATE MEMBER SPEAKS HER MIND
Lise Bourgault

The role of yesterday's MP is not that of today's. That of tomorrow's MP will be different still. In the past, parliamentarians took the initiative in legislative measures; their current role is limited to mere approval. In the future they will be called upon to check legislation before they approve it. The political evolution of the people, largely due to the introduction of electronic media, is the reason for the change in attitude over time. Our party-based democratic system must be redesigned so that the real capabilities of Parliament and the MPs correspond to what the electors expect of them, or think them capable of doing. . . .

Parliamentary reform has been a topic of discussion in every country with a parliamentary government as long as democratic elections have been held. In 1774 the British parliamentarian Edmund Burke said that a member is not a member for a riding, ". . . he is a Member of Parliament." Earlier in the same speech, he refers to the member's first loyalty as ". . . not local purpose, not local prejudices . . . but the general good, resulting from the general reason of the whole." . . .

The question today is whether or not voters would appreciate an MP who did not fight for their aspirations in the House, even if those aspirations were opposed to those of the majority. The MP's role is shaped by constituent expectations and party realities. How would the party leader react if an MP on the government side of the House voted against a government motion, even if it were directly opposed to the aspirations of the MP's constituents?

The role of an MP in 1985 is very complex. Party directives, government legislation, constituent expectations, position in parliament, all affect the MP's behaviour. In my opinion, existing Canadian parliamentary institutions must be

From *Canadian Parliamentary Review*, 8, 3, Autumn, 1985. By permission. The author is a member of Parliament.

rethought from the bottom up. Do they still correspond to their responsibilities? Parliament is the very foundation of the democratic system. It must be reformed before any other changes can be made. We must all change our attitudes. Everything I have read or heard on the subject points in the same directions: MPs must change their attitudes toward themselves and an information campaign on the proper role of the MP would help Canadians understand the dilemmas the MP faces every single day.

THE MP AND THE PRESS

The press plays a major role in an MP's life. If the newspapers do not talk about us enough, people wonder what we are doing. The press is looking for spectacular information. I have great respect for freedom of the press. It is still difficult for an MP to read that he is never in the riding, because one reporter was at some function or other and the MP was not. Directives from the party and the government warn MPs not to divulge secrets to the press on the way out of caucus. I agree up to a point. The government is after all responsible for its policies; it is perfectly logical that the government should announce major decisions. I do not solicit press interviews. Neither do I refuse to answer questions.

I have also learned that even in committee you cannot express yourself freely, or the next day you may see your name on the front page, especially if you criticize a government measure. Of course the press always interprets any criticism as dissidence.

This leads to the question of televising committee meetings. I have some doubts as to whether it is a good idea unless someone can convince me that I will be able to express myself quite freely and be reported fairly. The president of the Press Gallery told the reform committee there is room for a change in the attitude of the press, and asked only for the co-operation of MPs.

Attitudes will change when parliamentarians stop thinking that only complimentary, even flattering articles are important, and/or the press ceases to consider it a duty to engineer the re-election or defeat of members. . . . I recently had a poll taken in my riding; it revealed that only 40 per cent of what the newspapers say about me interests the constituents; they would rather make up their own minds. And 85 per cent of them prefer the electronic to the written media.

THE MP AND THE PARTY

I consider myself a moderate in that I follow the general ideology of my party without, however, approving a policy that is contrary to my own opinion and/ or that of my constituents. To never oppose a measure supported by the party for fear of being ignored when appointments are handed out is a disservice to the MP, the government, the party and, especially, the constituents.

During the election campaign, some of my constituents were afraid I would become a "yes woman." I soon learned that the majority of constituents have no idea of the party discipline an MP is subjected to. They elected a party leader and a program although they become uncompromising when the same government prepares to pass legislation contrary to their interests.

. . . it seems to me that our system should allow freedom of expression within the framework of party affiliation. Let us suppose that in committee and at meetings of commissions, an MP, as a party member, could speak freely on matters of conscience and general interest. Such an attitude would promote in-depth study of government administration and of the parties, and contribute to reinforcing the image Canadians have of our system. It is not because of occasional disagreements that an MP should be labelled a dissident or a rebel.

True parliamentary reform will not be possible until the political parties carry out internal reforms, change their attitudes to caucus members, and stop believing that their political future depends solely on a rigid discipline that puts all personal initiative on hold.

Comparatively speaking we are still a young Parliament. Many other countries have become aware that the evolution of society has necessitated changes in their political institutions. Do we need a new electoral system? The answer is yes, unless we introduce measures that will promote the MP's initiative and independence, leaving to individual conscience the reconciliation of personal opinion and party affiliation.

MEMBERS AND MINISTERS

The accountability of ministers and the government must be exercised through House of Commons committees. This is one of the conclusions of the report of the Special Committee, and of numerous reports on the question published by public, para-public and private organizations. Why is this not the case at present? In my opinion it is largely because of the size and pervasiveness of the public service. Because ministers have too much responsibility, they give senior civil servants too much latitude not only in departmental administration but in advising on policy.

The best place for consultations is the House of Commons itself! An MP knows his riding and the people who live there. Yet ministers feel the need to take exhausting trips to consult the population of Canada. The practice does not give them the true pulse of the nation; they simply do not have time to meet everyone concerned about a particular question. Think of all the time and energy wasted when the MP usually has the information the minister requires. Recommendations in our report are aimed at correcting this situation and also drastically reducing the number of royal commissions and other commissions of inquiry. Outside inquiry is all too often simply an expensive exercise in futility. The MPs have the knowledge to advise the government on national issues.

One of the anomalies of the existing system is that a newly appointed minister must do an about face and begin defending the same civil servants he criticized in opposition. There appears to be too great a difference in the powers of ministers and MPs. This is not meant as a criticism of ministers. I have far too much respect for their enormous responsibilities and the difficult decisions they have to make. But ministers are all too often restricted by cabinet solidarity. When you meet with a minister, you learn that his or her mind is already made up about proposed legislation. A minister in a majority government presumes that the House will approve the legislation; that is the party line.

The attitudes of MPs and ministers must change. This change of attitude is the aim of the new committee structure proposed in the McGrath report. Ministers would be directly accountable to committees. Because legislation would go to committee after first reading, MPs would have a means of expressing their opinions, amending a bill and/or reaching a better understanding of it. It will take a good year to test the new procedure and determine whether or not it meets the requirements of the House and cabinet.

THE MP AND CONSTITUENTS

Naturally, one of the things I like best about being an MP is meeting my constituents. At home, in my own riding, the electors do not expect us to perform miracles. It is enough for them to know that we have taken the trouble to do something for them.

I feel it is extremely important that an MP hire reliable staff and give them more autonomy of action in the office. I place great importance on my riding staff and, as a result, the constituents get to know and trust them all. This practice allows me to delegate responsibility and free myself for other things. Our constituents are demanding in part because our salaries come out of their taxes. They see us as their employees and they require us to be visible. They do not understand that we cannot accept all the invitations we receive.

It seems to me that many MPs currently devote too much time to their ridings and too little to the House. This is why legislation is adopted without the MPs being familiar with it. I used to think it was my duty to accept everything that came along. It was not long before I realized I could not keep up that pace. I decided to spend four days in Ottawa, two days in the riding, one day at home. Every two weeks I change the schedule to four days in Ottawa, one day in the riding and two days at home. My constituents understand, and say so. The reaction of constituents to an MP who seems to be everywhere is just as bad as their reaction to one who is nowhere to be seen. All it takes is a little common sense. The current system allows an MP no individuality, no personal opinion. Today's MP is elected to go and tell the government what his constituents want him to say.

CONCLUSION

... Every MP in Canada has to sell parliamentary reform. Canada's House of Commons is often used as a model for provincial legislative assemblies, and vice versa. The role of the member of a provincial legislature is closely linked to the reform we are proposing. In Quebec, a committee chaired by Denis Vaugeois concluded: "Parliamentary reform has often been taken to mean re-evaluation of the role of the member. Using this approach it has even been suggested that, since members had too little to do, work must be found for their idle hands. What is needed is not more work for members, but the opportunity for members to make a different sort of contribution, one compatible with their mandate from the voters and Parliament as an institution. In other words, the members must be given more power."

I believe this is an important statement because, in fact, few constituents have a true idea of the work done by an MP every day. We must insist on a public information campaign, so that MPs can stop having to justify their use of time.

Can we "sell" parliamentary reform, now and in the future? I sincerely hope so, in our own interest, that of our constituents, our party, our government and, primarily, that of democracy itself.

BIBLIOGRAPHY

Parliamentary Procedure

Bourinot, J.G. *Parliamentary Procedure and Practice in the Dominion of Canada.* Toronto: Canada Law Book Co., 3rd ed., 1903.

Canada, Parliament, House of Commons. *Standing Orders of the House of Commons, 1990.* Ottawa: S. and S., 1990.

House of Commons, Table Research Branch. *Precis of Procedure.* Ottawa: 2nd ed., 1987.

Fraser, A., Dawson, W., and Holtby, J. *Beauchesne's Rules and Forms of the House of Commons of Canada.* Toronto: Carswell, 1989.

Stanford, G. *Bourinot's Rules of Order.* Toronto: M. & S., 3rd rev. ed., 1980.

Stewart, J.B. *The Canadian House of Commons: Procedure and Reform.* Montreal: McG.-Q.U.P., 1977.

Functioning of Legislatures

Archer, K., Ellis, F., and Nestoruk, P. "Legislators and Their World: A Study of Alberta MLAs." *C.P.R.*, Summer, 1989.

Atkinson, M.M., and Mancuso, M. "Do We Need a Code of Conduct For Politicians? The Search For an Elite Political Culture of Corruption in Canada." *C.J.P.S.*, 18, 3, September, 1985.

Atkinson, M.M., and Nossal, K.R. "Executive Power and Committee Autonomy in the Canadian House of Commons: Leadership Selection, 1968–1979." *C.J.P.S.*, 13, 2, June, 1980.

Aucoin, P., (ed.). *Institutional Reforms for Representative Government.* Toronto: U.T.P., 1985.

Barrie, D., and Gibbins, R. "Parliamentary Careers in the Canadian Federal State." *C.J.P.S.*, 22, 1, March, 1989.

Canada, Parliament, House of Commons. *Report of the Special Committee on Standing Orders and Procedure.* [Lefebrve report]. Ottawa: November 5, 1982.

Canadian Bar Association. *Report of the Canadian Bar Association Committee on the Reform of Parliament (Parliament as Lawmaker).* Ottawa: 1982.

Canadian Government Publishing Centre. *The Federal Legislative Process in Canada.* Ottawa: S. and S., 1986.

Clarke, H.D. *et al.* (eds.). *Parliament, Policy and Representation.* Toronto: Methuen, 1980.

Clarke, H.D., and Price, R.G. "Freshman MPs' Job Images: The Effects of Incumbency, Ambition and Position." *C.J.P.S.*, 13, 3, September, 1980.

Clyne, J.V. "Reforming Parliament." *P.O.*, 4, 6, November, 1983.

Colwell, R., and Thomas, P. "Parliament and the Patronage Issue." *J.C.S.*, 22, 2, Summer, 1987.

Corry, J.A. "Sovereign People or Sovereign Governments." *P.O.*, 1, 1, March, 1980.

Courtney, J.C., (ed.). *The Canadian House of Commons: Essays in Honour of Norman Ward.* Calgary: University of Calgary Press, 1985.

D'Aquino, T. Doern, G.B., and Blair, C. *Parliamentary Democracy in Canada: Issues for Reform.* Toronto: Methuen, 1983.

Danis, M. "The Speakership and Independence: A Tradition in the Making." *C.P.R.*, 10, Summer, 1987.

Dobell, R. "Policy-Planning MPs." *P.O.*, 3, 4, July-August, 1984.

Dunn, C. "The Budget Process in Western Canadian Legislative Assemblies." *C.P.R.*, 10, Winter 1987–88.

Dunn, C. "Executive Dominance in Provincial Legislatures." *C.P.R.*, 13, 1, Spring, 1990.

Fleming, R.J., (ed.). *Canadian Legislatures 1987–1988*. Ottawa: Ampersand Communications Services, 1988. (Annual from 1979.)

Franks, C.E.S. "Borrowing from the United States: Is the Canadian Parliamentary System Moving Toward the Congressional Model?" *A.R.C.S.*, 13, 3, Autumn, 1983.

Franks, C.E.S. "Debates and Question Period in the Canadian House of Commons: What Purpose Do They Serve?" *A.R.C.S.*, 15, 1, Spring, 1985.

Franks, C.E.S. *The Parliament of Canada*. Toronto: U.T.P., 1987.

Gillies, J., and Pigott, J. "Participation in the Legislative Process." *C.P.A.*, 25, 2, Summer, 1982.

Happy, J., and Kyba, P. "The 'Myth' of Business Over-representation in the Canadian House of Commons." *Journal of Commonwealth and Comparative Politics*, 24, 3, November, 1986.

Henderson, J. "Groupthink Must Go." *P.O.*, 9, 5, June, 1988 [Party discipline]

Holland, D., and McGowan, J. *Delegated Legislation in Canada*. Toronto: Carswell, 1989.

Huntington, R. and Lachance, C.-A. "Accountability: Closing the Loop." *C.P.R.*, 5, 4, Winter, 1982–83.

Jackson, R.J., and Atkinson, M.M. *The Canadian Legislative System*. Toronto: Macmillan, 2nd rev. ed., 1980.

Jerome, J. *Mr. Speaker*. Toronto: M. & S., 1986.

Kent, T. "Making Representative Government Work." *P.O.*, 1,1, March, 1980.

Kilgour, D. and Kirsner. "Call off the Party." *P.O.*, 10, 3, March, 1989. [Party discipline]

Kohn, W.S.G. "Women in the Canadian House of Commons." *A.R.C.S.*, 14, 3, Fall, 1984.

Kornberg, A., and Mishler, W. *Influence in Parliament: Canada*. Durham, North Carolina: Duke University Press, 1976.

Landry, R. "Parliamentary Control of Science Policy in the Quebec National Assembly." *C.P.R.*, 3, 4, Winter, 1980.

Laundy, P. *The Office of Speaker in the Parliaments of the Commonwealth*. London: Quiller Press, 1984. [Chap. 4, The Speakership in Canada.]

L'école Nationale d'Administration Publique. *Le Contrôle de l'Administration et la Réforme Parlementaire*. Québec: 1984.

Lemco, J., and Regenstreif, P. "Less Disciplined MPs." *P.O.*, 6, 1, January, 1985.

Lever, N.S. "Private Members' Business: Whats Happened Under the New Rules?" *C.P.R.*, 11, Autumn, 1988.

Levy, G. "A Night to Remember: The First Election of a Speaker by Secret Ballot." *C.P.R.*, 9, 4, Winter, 1986/87.

Levy, G., and White, G., (eds.). *Provincial and Territorial Legislatures in Canada*. Toronto: U.T.P., 1989.

Maine, F.W. "Parliamentary Scrutiny of Science Policy." *C.P.R.*, 3, 4, Winter, 1980.

Normandin, P.G., (ed.). *Canadian Parliamentary Guide, 1989*. Toronto: INFOGLOBE, 1989. (Annual)

Parliamentary Government. Special issue on "Parliamentary Secretaries," 4, 3, 1983.

Parliamentary Government. Special issue on "Caucus," 4, 1, 1983.

Parliamentary Government. Special issue on "Question Period," 5, 4, 1985.

Parliamentary Government. Special issue on "Question Period," Summer, 1989.

Pross, P. "Parliamentary Influence and the Diffusion of Power." *C.J.P.S.*, 18, 2, June, 1985.

Rae, Bob "Changing the Confidence Convention in Ontario." *C.P.R.*, 8, 4, Winter, 1985–86.

"Responsible Government Reconsidered." A collection of articles on Parliament, *J.C.S.*, 14, 2, Summer, 1979.

Reynolds, B. "Twelve Days With the sub-committee On Women and the Indian Act." *C.P.R.*, 5, 4, Winter, 1982–83.

Smith, D.P. "Parliament Innovates: A New Style of Committee." *P.O.*, 2, 2, May–June, 1981.

Stanfield, R.L. "The State of the Legislative Process in Canada." *P.O.*, 1, 2, June–July, 1980.

Taras, D., (ed.). *Parliament and Canadian Foreign Policy.* C.I.I.A., 1985.

Thomas, P. "The Role of House Leaders in the Canadian House of Commons." *C.J.P.S.*, 15, 1, March, 1982.

Thomas, P. "Practicable Reforms for Parliament." *P.O.*, 4, 1, January–February, 1983.

Vanderhoff-Silburt, M. "The Role of Parliamentary Secretaries." *C.P.R.*, 6, 4, Winter, 1983–84.

White, G. *The Ontario Legislature: A Political Analysis.* Toronto: U.T.P., 1989.

Williams, R.J. "The Role of Legislatures in Policy Formulation." In Landry, R. (dir.) *Introduction à l'Analyse des Politiques.* Québec: P.U.L., 1980.

Wilson, J. "In Defence of Parliamentary Opposition." *C.P.R.*, 11, Summer, 1988.

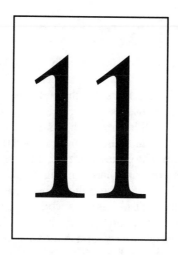

THE SENATE

CANADA NEEDS A TRIPLE E SENATE

Peter McCormick

[*Editor's note: For an account of events and other proposals for Senate reform leading to the suggestion of a Triple E Senate, see the section on Senate Reform in Garth Stevenson's article, "Co-operative, Executive, and Intrastate Federalism" in Chapter 3, supra.*]

The three basic elements of the Triple E Senate are straight-forward: . . . the first "E" stands for "elected," the second for "equal" and the third "E" for "effective."

The argument in favour of electing Senators is obvious, even more so in the light of recent developments in Ottawa. The present Senate has over the last few years finally started doing what any self-respecting Senate should have been doing right through the past century: it has been taking a firm stand on controversial issues, and speaking out when it thinks that the Commons has got something wrong. But in the process, it has only managed to reveal publicly and dramatically precisely what is wrong with the Senate as it now stands. As soon as Senators start doing what they should have been doing every day, every month, every year, we wonder out loud what claim they have to hold

From *The Canadian Senate: What Is To Be Done?*, Edmonton, The Centre for Constitutional Studies at the University of Alberta, 1989.

up national legislation, and who they are really speaking for, and what is really on their agenda. . . .

It is rather sad that the Senate is caught in such a double bind: if it does nothing, it is condemned as useless; and if it does something it is condemned for its lack of credibility. But this only highlights again how limited our Senate's capacity really is, and what a sad missed opportunity it represents. The problem is not that the individual Senators are incompetent or lazy, because they aren't. Many are very conscientious and hardworking, which makes it all the more wasteful to put them in the Senate, where they labor under such massive disadvantages. Senators don't represent anybody except the Prime Minister who appointed them; and they can't effectively speak for anybody because an appointed chamber lacks legitimacy for a democratic age; and every time they arouse furor by speaking up and delaying the legislative process, they simply remind us how much could be accomplished legitimately and credibly by Senators who clearly represented the people who had elected them.

The second E is Equality: the principle that every province would enjoy equal representation regardless of population. This is the E that . . . causes a lot of people to swallow hard as the wild idea of Newfoundland or Prince Edward Island having the same number of Senators as mighty Ontario. But is it precisely because the large provinces are so large, and the small provinces so small, that we need equal representation. Suppose that the people of Canada had been obliging enough to spread themselves equally across all the provinces . . . then we would already enjoy the equal representation of the provinces, and maybe we wouldn't have to talk about this kind of Senate reform. No province would have to worry about being outvoted so massively and so often that the interests of its citizens faded to political marginality. But Canada's population distribution is far from equal, and it is precisely because Ontario is so massive a presence in Canadian politics, because the two central provinces can automatically dominate the Commons whenever their interests coincide, that we *need* equal representation in the Senate. The more difficult it is for a radical democrat to accept provincial equality, the more desperately necessary it is for a federalist to push for it.

I don't feel any need to apologize for the second of the E's. Denying the equality of the provinces is pernicious in its consequences: critics seize upon the comparison between Ontario and Prince Edward Island to ridicule the idea, but what they really mean in practice is that Alberta cannot enjoy the same powers as Ontario, and British Columbia must enjoy a perpetual Senate back seat to Québec. But it is also objectionable at its very core, because for constitutional purposes a province is a province. This is a principle that Americans take for granted; it is a principle that Australians take for granted, and it baffles me that it is somehow a principle that Canadians cannot even consider without being accused of defying democracy or logic or common sense.

The third E is "effective." I'm sure everyone is aware that the only reason we use the word "effective" in this context is because it starts with the letter "E"; the word we really wanted was "powerful," but it destroys the symmetry, and "Triple E" has such a nice ring to it. So for the present purposes let's forget about the word "effective" and go right behind it to the real word, "powerful." You don't want to go to all the bother of reforming the Senate to find you've created a modern counterpart to the Russian Duma which can meet and talk all it wants to but can never actually do anything. If we were foolish enough to settle for that, then the substance of Canadian politics would go on the way it has been for the last hundred years, and this is precisely what Senate reformers want to get away from. If you reform the Senate at the cost of denying its power, you haven't accomplished anything.

Now, strangely enough, the third "E" is the one respect in which the existing Canadian Senate is just fine. Our Senate now has all the formal legal power that the most fiery-eyed Triple E maniac could ever dream of, including a total veto on any and all government legislation. The problem of the present Senate is not a lack of power, but the lack of the credibility and legitimacy that would allow it to use that power on a regular basis. An elected Senate would have that legitimacy. So of the three, the third "E" is the least problematic; just leave things as they are, and everything would be fine. Some Senate reformers want to add new powers to the Senate, such as ratifying treaties or approving judicial appointments, but I don't see any need to be that greedy.

Now, if we created a Triple E Senate by waving a magic wand or something, obviously everything else would not carry on just as it does not. Reforming a national institution is not like buying a new bumper sticker—just slap it on the outside and that's all there is to it. It's more like putting one person into a crowded room—everybody else has to shift a bit to make room for a new arrival. A Triple E Senate would affect all the other components of our political process, and I don't want to give the impression that Senate reformers are unaware of this impact, or have failed to work out its implications. Indeed, the effect that a Triple E Senate would have on other national institutions is argu-ably one of the strongest arguments in its favor.

First, Senate reform would affect the national government. A Triple E Senate could be thought of as a new set of bumpers in the great pinball machine of Canadian politics, that would cause the ball to travel differently and the final score to change, possibly dramatically. Since many Western Canadians are not too pleased with the way the ball has been bouncing the last decade or so, and since much of the agitation for Senate reform grows out of this dissatisfac-tion, such an outcome is not only to be accepted but actively desired. The standard reply, of course, is that Canada is an enormously difficult country to govern, and the additional set of complications represented by such a Senate would be the final straw that could shut things down altogether. I don't attach much significance to this complaint, the more so as it tends to come from government members or government officials who can be presumed not to be entirely impartial about the matter. Politics is the art of the possible; for any government at any time, what you do is some prioritized selection from the range of things that you are able to do. If a Canadian government confronted by a reformed Senate were obliged to work a little harder, to build a few more compromises into their policies, to fine-tune things a little more rigorously—then fine, so be it. I don't believe that this country is so close to total paralysis that it is beyond the imagination of federal politicians to find their way around one more set of obstacles, although I can believe it is in that interest to persuade us that it is.

Second, Senate reform would affect provincial governments, most specifically the role that provincial premiers have come to assume in recent decades. You can describe that assumption in various ways—either as provincial premiers meddling in matters that have nothing to do with their mandate, or as provincial premiers generously sliding into an institutional vacuum to provide regional input on national policies—but the substance is much the same whichever wording you use. The point is that the wholesale mixing of national issues and provincial issues is a rather disturbing development. The problem can cut either way—you can worry about a premier elected on the basis of public school funding and reform of the provincial public service swanning off to rewrite Canada's international trade commitments; or about having a provincial election decided on the issue of how a premier would respond to some proposed national program—but both types of scenario are disturbing enough that I don't see why it is necessary to choose. Even if we concede that the separation between regional and national issues can never be perfect or airtight, there are real benefits in keeping them as separate as possible, and in creating a new national institution to deal with regional input and regional sensitivities on national policy.

Thirdly, a reformed Senate would have an impact on the House of Commons. I share the general concern with the way contemporary legislatures at all levels are very much in the shadow or the executive. The House of Commons already feels (and rightly so) that it is beleaguered and unappreciated, and we must be cautious about doing something that might block even more of their sunlight, that might squeeze their role and significance even harder than it is being squeezed right now. That's why I think it is important to stress that the Triple E model envisages an absolute ban on drawing cabinet members from the Senate, so that the House of Commons would remain the only access point to cabinet membership and the only place where cabinet members are directly and routinely responsible. A Triple E Senate is not trying to crowd its way into the House of Commons game, but rather to play its own distinctively different game off to one side. Confidence and responsibility and ambitious people aiming at national office—that should be the absolute monopoly of the Commons. Regional representation by elected members on national policy—that should be the pre-emptive raison d'être of the Senate. The two roles are distinct, and it is important to keep them distinct.

Fourth, a reformed Senate would have an impact on the party system, although this is harder to specify in any detail because of the variety of options that remain even after one has specified that the new Senate would be elected. For example, suppose Senatorial elections coincided with provincial general elections. The present extent of organization separation between national and provincial political parties would become a luxury that could not always be afforded. Suppose, for example, that Senate approval of a controversial piece of federal legislation hinged on the defeat of a Senator whose re-election campaign had been triggered by a premier calling a provincial election; how could any national party not be directly involved? A degree of mutual understanding, an ongoing modus vivendi, between provincial and federal parties (and not always or necessarily those sharing the same party label) would become necessary. For another example, suppose Senators were elected by single transferable vote in province-wide constituencies, an option I very much favor. Under such a system, voters choose not just the party they wish to support, but the precise segment of opinion within that party. Would a Conservative voter want Kindy or Clark, Mazankowski or Kilgour? Why not give them a chance to say—and in the process give the candidates some incentive to spell out how they differ from their party colleagues, why a voter should support one of their party's candidates rather than another. To the extent that our present electoral system narrows our choice to a single set of candidates within a single riding, the province-wide STV option would expand the voter's opportunity to cast an informed and nuanced vote. Even if many citizens did not do much with their opportunity, such a democratic experiment seems well worth trying.

Finally, a reformed Senate might have an impact on the very conception of a political role in national politics. For example: in the United States, there are many Senators for whom that position is the perfectly satisfactory culmination of a political career, that allows them to have an impact on policy, a high profile, and an important national role without ever seeking an executive position. In the United Kingdom, the size of the House of Commons and the large number of safe seats creates members who are "House of Commons man" [sic], who find real satisfaction in serving and representing their constituents as an end in itself, and for whom a lengthy career in Parliament is an attractive option even if it never culminates in a cabinet appointment. By contrast, I think that Canadian national politics has a very unhealthy focus on government and cabinet that drives backbench MPs into obscurity, frustration and early retirement. It turns every political career into a successful or a failed shot at cabinet rank, and contributes to the docility of backbenchers who are afraid of getting their name on the wrong list by rocking the boat. Maybe an elected Senate, a national institution constitutionally cut off from cabinet appointments, would contribute to a less government-centred notion of politics.

Although the Triple E Senate concept is a fairly recent arrival—ten years ago it was virtually unheard of—it has come to be very much in the centre of the Senate Reform stage. Whether it moves further, whether it makes the difficult transition from talk to action, will depend on a number of factors, one of which is a wider understanding of its details and implications. . . .

NO—MORE THAN A TRIPLE E SENATE IS NEEDED

Eugene Forsey

Nearly everyone agrees that our present Senate is unsatisfactory. The New Democratic Party wants to abolish it. Most people in the other parties want to reform it. Most of the reformers want to elect it, though they differ about how it should be elected, its size and its powers.

ABOLITION OF THE SENATE?

Abolition is not really on the cards. For one thing, it would require the consent of every provincial Legislature, which is unlikely. The smaller provinces have always been afraid that Ontario and Quebec, with their huge majority in the House of Commons, might ride rough-shod over the Atlantic provinces and the West; and Quebec has wanted extra protection against the English-speaking majority. So the Maritimes, Quebec, and in due course the West, insisted on equal representation by region in the Senate: twenty-four seats for Ontario, twenty-four for Quebec, twenty-four for the Maritimes, twenty-four for the West. Six Senators for Newfoundland and two for the Territories throw this equality a little out of whack. But the fact remains that the two central provinces, with nearly two-thirds of the population, have slightly fewer than half the Senators. As long as the Senate has the legal power to throw out—and keep on throwing out—any Bill passed by the House of Commons, the other provinces can, theoretically, protect themselves against central Canadian domi-nation. As the Senate is appointed, not elected, it has very little political clout: it has not thrown out a Bill from the Commons for almost fifty years. So the protection, in fact, does not amount to much. But, such as it is, the smaller provinces are not likely to give it up. They want more protection, not less; and if just *one* refuses to consent to abolition, the proposal is dead.

Reform, giving the smaller provinces more seats, and the Senate more real power, is another matter. But any change in the number of Senators from any province, or in the method of selecting Senators (for example, to election, or to appointment by provincial Governments), or in the powers of the Senate (up or down), now requires the consent of the Legislatures of at least seven provinces with at least half the population of the ten. This means that it must have the consent of *either* Ontario *or* Quebec and of at least six other provinces. Under the Meech Lake Accord, it would have to have the consent of all ten. Any single Legislature could kill it.

DILEMMA OVER THE NUMBER OF SEATS

Most of the reform proposals would give the West more seats, and nearly everyone agrees that this is necessary. But how many more? Neither Quebec

From a chapter by the author in Robert J. Fleming, General Editor, *Canadian Legislatures, 1987–1988*, Ottawa, Ampersand Communications Services Inc., 1988. By permission.

nor the Atlantic provinces will consent to any significant reduction in their proportion of the total number of seats.

For example, the Alberta "Triple E" proposal would give every province six seats. The four Western provinces and Newfoundland have six now. No objection there. Prince Edward Island would go up from four to six. Delight there. But Nova Scotia and New Brunswick would each go down from ten to six; Quebec and Ontario each from twenty-four to six. All four of those provinces would balk. Four from ten leaves six. To pass the amendment needs seven.

Changing the number from six each to ten might win the consent of Nova Scotia and New Brunswick (though their proportion of the total would still go down). But to carry the amendment still requires either Ontario or Quebec. Their number of seats would go down by more than half, and their proportion of the total by almost two-thirds. To consent to this would call for heroic self-abnegation.

Changing the number to twenty-four each would produce a gargantuan Senate, in which Ontario and Quebec together would have only about one-fifth of the total, and Quebec only about one-tenth. Neither province would accept that.

The Meech Lake Accord would compound the problem. For one thing, any single province could block any change. For another, the Accord gives the nomination of Senators from every province to the provincial Governments. No provincial Government, having once got its hands on this delicious piece of fail-safe patronage, will be eager to give it up; and if just *one* refuses, the thing is dead.

The reformers will insist on some change in numbers. But most of them will insist even more strongly that the Senate must be elected.

ELECTED HOW?

By single-member constituencies, with the first-past-the-post system, like the House of Commons? But that would give us simply a facsimile of the House of Commons. Many of the reformers would object that this would mean the same under-representation of minorities (for example, the Liberals in the West, the Conservatives formerly in Quebec, and the New Democrats all round) as in the Commons. For many reformers, getting rid of this under-representation has been one of the main objectives. The answer would be proportional representation. But neither the Liberals nor the Conservatives have ever shown any enthusiasm for that. With the present system, they can, and usually do, win only a minority of the popular vote, but this may, and usually does, win them a majority of the seats. Under proportional representation, neither the Liberals nor the Conservatives might ever get a majority of the seats. The nearer the New Democrats get to power, the less they are likely to be ready to forfeit the chance that they too, with a minority of the popular vote, might win a majority of the seats (which is precisely what happened in British Columbia the only time they ever won an election there).

A QUESTION OF POWER

Even if enough provincial Legislatures were (miraculously) to agree on the numbers, on election rather than provincial appointment, and on the method of election, there would remain the crucial question of the *powers* of an elected Senate.

All the reformers want the Senate to have more real power. But how much?

The Meech Lake Accord's "transitional" Senate, nominated by the provincial governments, would have all the present Senate's legal powers, notably the absolute veto on every Bill. It could stop Supply. It could throw out the Budget.

It would, of course, take some time to produce a Senate all of whose members had been nominated by the provincial Governments. But eventually, as the present Senators died, or reached the age limit, or resigned, or became aliens or bankrupts, or were convicted of some felony or infamous crime, or lost their residence qualification, or took jobs which made them ineligible for the Senate; that is what we would have. And that Senate would be no paper tiger. It would have substantial political clout, and no hesitation about using it. Its members would not be beholden to any national political party, but only to the respective provincial governments. They would not have to face elections. If they objected to a Bill passed by the House of Commons, but disliked by the provincial Governments, they would have no qualms about throwing it out. They would argue, with truth, that the Senate was originally set up partly to protect provincial interests; that the provincial Governments, or several, or most, of them, objected to this Bill. Very well, let the Senate do the job it was set up to do, and if the federal Government, or the Leader of the Opposition or the whole House of Commons didn't like it, let them eat cake.

One prominent reformer has said publicly, on television, that he wants an elected Senate with "teeth, muscle, claws", and that this meant an absolute veto on all legislation. An elected Senate with that power would most certainly use it. If the House of Commons remonstrated that it represented the people, the elected Senators would reply, "So do we". If they had been elected more recently, or by proportional representation, they might add, "and better than you do. No noise from the cheap seats"!

The House of Commons, whose consent is necessary for any constitutional amendment, will "brook, like the Turk, no brother near the throne". Nor will any federal Government. Neither will accept an elected Senate with an absolute veto on all legislation, or on Supply, or the Budget, or anything more than a short-term suspensive veto on Supply or the Budget and a rather longer one on other legislation.

Probably a formula could be hammered out that would be strong enough to give the smaller provinces, notably the West, a reasonable degree of satisfaction, and weak enough to pass the House of Commons, provided the numbers and the method of selection could also be agreed on. But getting "the time, the place and the loved one all together" would be far from easy.

The acute problem is Western alienation. To allay or mitigate that would require an elected Senate with enough Western members and enough power to stop, or at least seriously delay, legislation the West considered oppressive or injurious. Even the present seven-province formula for constitutional amendment is a formidable obstacle. The Meech Lake unanimity formula might prove insuperable. The Accord guarantees an annual discussion of Senate reform by the First Ministers' Conference. But that is all it guarantees.

This is discouraging. But it need not be as discouraging as it looks. There is a tendency in some quarters to think that Senate reform would solve all our problems, especially Western problems. It would not. For example, some Manitobans seemed to think a reformed Senate could have prevented the CF-18 contract from going to Montreal instead of Winnipeg. It could not have. A reformed Senate could have done nothing whatever about the CF-18 contract, except denounce it (and any private citizen can do that, and with precisely the same effect: none), unless a constitutional amendment had explicitly conferred that power; and no Government will ever accept that. Furthermore, no Senate, reformed or unreformed, will ever be empowered to throw out a Government with a majority in the House of Commons. The most a reformed Senate could do would be to force a Government to a fresh election by vetoing or delaying a Bill the Government considered essential or urgent. The notion that if anything happens in the body politic which the West, or any other region, dislikes, a reformed Senate could kiss the place and make it well is nonsense.

CHANGES THE SENATE COULD MAKE

Does all this mean that we are stuck with what we have?

No. Much can be done to improve the Senate without any constitutional amendments at all, and the Senate's Lamontagne Committee of 1980 set it down in black and white. Some of it would require only ordinary legislation. Some of it the Senate could do itself.

One of the problems with the present Senate is dead wood: members who do not turn up regularly, let alone work. This is often exaggerated. My own experience is that at least two-thirds of the members do attend pretty regularly, and at least half do work hard and conscientiously when the Senate is sitting and in committees, which often sit when the Senate itself is in recess. Many are also active in their home communities, involved in various public activities, often doing constituency work which would ordinarily be done by a member of the House of Commons. But some dead wood there undoubtedly is.

The Lamontagne *Report* proposed three measures to get rid of it, all of them requiring only a simple Act of Parliament. First, a fixed term of ten years, renewable for further terms of five years on the recommendation, by secret ballot, of a bi-partisan Senate Committee.

Second, provision to enable Senators who had reached the age of sixty-five, with fifteen years' service (or seventy, with ten years'), to retire, like judges, on full pension.

Third, provision to vacate the seat of any Senator who failed, for two consecutive years, to attend at least one-third of the sittings in each year. The Constitution already stipulates that any Senator who fails to turn up at least once in two consecutive sessions loses his seat; and a fair number have lost their seats accordingly. But others have been literally wheeled in once in two sessions and so retained their seats. Moreover, a single session may now last for years (a recent one lasted for three), so that a resolute valetudinarian or scrimshanker could retain his or her seat by a single appearance in seven or eight years—"A lovely apparition sent to be a moment's ornament".

NEW STANDING COMMITTEES

The *Report* also proposed four things the Senate itself could do.

First, establish a Standing Committee on Regional Affairs; second, a Standing Committee on Official Languages, with half the members French-speaking, half English-speaking; third, a Standing Committee on Human Rights; fourth, regional all-party caucuses.

The Fathers of Confederation intended the Senate not only to revise Bills sent to it by the House of Commons (a job the present Senate does thoroughly on the often wretchedly drafted legislation the Lower House hands it), but also to protect the interests of the provinces in matters under federal jurisdiction, and to protect minorities. It has not done much to protect the provinces; partly because the courts have so much narrowed federal jurisdiction; partly because the task has been performed by the provinces' representatives in the Cabinet. It has not done much to protect minorities, partly because in some cases (the Manitoba school question, for example) the House of Commons has taken over the job. But it could, and should, do more in both fields.

The *Report* recommended the new Standing Committees because the Senate does most of its work in committees. The new Standing Committee on Human Rights might be of special importance if the House of Commons passed a Bill curtailing those rights, by virtue of section 33 of the Charter of Rights and Freedoms (the "notwithstanding" section), which enables Parliament to override, for a renewable period of five years, section 2 and 7 to 15 of the Charter.

One question the Lamontagne Committee ought to have dealt with, and did not, is that of vacant seats. No Senate seat should be left vacant for more than a specified short period, perhaps six months. There have been cases of seats left unfilled for years (in one instance, eight years). This should be forbidden by law, if need be by a constitutional amendment, which, for once, should not be hard to carry.

The Lamontagne *Report* proposed also that half the Senators should be appointed by the federal Government from lists submitted by the provincial Governments. The Meech Lake Accord provides that *all* Senators should be so appointed.

There is something to be said for either proposal. Both could give parties unrepresented in the House of Commons representation in Parliament, and parties under-represented in the Commons fuller representation in Parliament. Both could mean a more varied membership in the Senate, politically, economically and socially, and less danger of huge, long-lasting one-party majorities. The federal Government's power to refuse a provincial nominee would enable it to weed out dead-beats, has-beens and dedicated enemies of effective national government.

The present method of appointment has obvious defects. It gives us too few women in the Senate, too few Native people, too few from ethnic groups, too few from Labour, and too many party faithful (some of whom, however, turn out to be first-rate Senators: hardworking, independent, productive). Provincial nomination and federal appointment might help to redress the balance; but they might not.

It is sometimes suggested that the Government should appoint more "eminent persons"—scholars, poets, scientists, philosophers. Perhaps it might, but pretty certainly it will not; and not without reason. The Senate is primarily a legislative body. It is not a supernumerary Royal Society of Canada or Authors' Association, or a permanent Conference of Learned Societies (though it does, in fact, include Fellows of the Royal Society, authors, learned men, and at least one poet). A few more scholars, poets, scientists, philosophers, might help to leaven the legislative lump, and bring valuable expert knowledge to Parliament. But the bulk of the Senators should be, as in fact most of them are now, people capable of helping to make good laws.

NOT QUITE HARMLESS GAMES

Most Senate reformers will say that the Lamontagne *Report* is totally inadequate. They want much more. But what they want and what they have any reasonable chance of getting are very different things. If this were 1864, or if we were drafting a Constitution with a blank sheet, what they want might have some chance. But it is not 1864, and we have not a blank sheet. It is 1988, and we have the Constitution Act, 1982, which has given us a very rigid Constitution, very hard to amend, notably in regard to the Senate. We have the Meech Lake Accord, which, if it is approved by all the provincial Legislatures, will give us an even more rigid Constitution, even harder to amend and, again, notably in regard to the Senate. That being so, it is hardly too much to say that those who draw up or promote Senate reform proposals that would require constitutional amendments are merely playing games; and not quite harmless games either, since they distract attention from changes that would be easy to make and that would make the Senate more representative and more effective. They set people chasing wandering fires, will-o'-the-wisps, rainbows; blowing bubbles. To change the metaphor: I am sorry to be the boy who points out that the Emperor has no clothes on. But it has to be done.

Editor's Note   When asked what internal changes, in his view, could take place in the Senate, regardless of constitutional considerations or the Meech Lake Accord, Dr. Forsey provided the following check list.

1. Abolition of the property qualifications for Senators.
2. Fixed term of office: ten years, renewable for a further term of five years, on recommendation, by secret ballot, of a bi-partisan Senate Committee.
3. Loss of seat for failure to attend at least one-third of the sittings of the Senate in each of two consecutive years.
4. Full pension at sixty-five after fifteen years' service (or at seventy, with ten years).
5. Establishment of Standing Committees on Regional Affairs, on Official Languages (with half the members French-speaking) and on Human Rights.
6. Establishment of regional all-party caucuses.

DOING ITS THING—PROVIDING "SOBER SECOND THOUGHT": THE CANADIAN SENATE, 1984–1990
Lorna R. Marsden

INTRODUCTION

The Canadian Senate is one of the checks and balances in the complexity of Canada's democracy. Not only is it intended to play that role, but it plays it in a subtle way, although it is not well understood by Canadians.

The Senate is always under consideration for reform. Since the late nineteenth century Canadians have objected to various aspects of the Senate, including the method of appointment, the distribution of Senate representation among the provinces and regions, the powers of the Senate, the lack of power of the Senate, the work of the Senate that is seen to reflect the interests of certain sectors, and the lack of work of the Senate that is seen to reflect the patronage nature of appointments. There have been numerous studies of

An original article prepared for this edition in May, 1990 by the author, who is a member of the Senate of Canada and of the Department of Sociology, University of Toronto. By permission.

Senate reform on the part of the federal government, both directly (for example, *Report*, Special Joint Committee on Senate Reform, 1984) and indirectly (for example, Macdonald Royal Commission, Vol. 3, 1985), as well as proposals from many individual scholars and groups. In June 1988 the reference section of the Library of Parliament published a bibliography on the Senate of 71 pages of references, of which 37 pages were devoted exclusively to published works on Senate reform. The most recent proposals for reform are on the Meech Lake agenda entrenched in the Accord. The next items for consideration are Senate reform and fish.

In the period of 1984 to 1990, when the majority Conservative government in the House of Commons clashed several times with the Liberal majority in the Senate, the public's perception of these disputes was that they were partisan conflicts, fuelling speculation about the role of a triple-E Senate or other reforms. However, from inside the Senate each of the major disputes of the past six years—the Borrowing Authority in 1984–85, the Pharmaceutical Bill in 1987, the amendments to the constitution in the Meech Lake Accord (1987–88), the Unemployment Insurance Bill amendments in 1989–90, the "clawback" tax amendments (An Act to Amend the Income Tax Act . . .) in 1990, and the Goods and Services Tax amendments in 1990—has represented a different point of parliamentary principle or public interest.

In reviewing these clashes one can see the way in which the Senate and its committees work and the role the Senate plays as a chamber of "sober second thought." But it should be noted that of the 269 bills sent to the Senate since 1984, 251 have passed without amendment, 18 with amendment, and none has been rejected.

The role of the Senate is not now, nor ever has been and cannot be, a popular one. The Senate acts as a check on the power of the House of Commons by reviewing, amending, and delaying legislation passed by the House. Delay normally results in public debate, and it is public pressure that has an impact on the government of the day. Because of this the Senate is intrinsically unpalatable to any prime minister and most members of Parliament. Throughout the years of Liberal government, with a Senate Liberal majority, the number of checks put on that government were significant, but the bargaining and negotiating occurred among "friends" and was less publicly contentious.*

---

*For a summary of the bills amended by the Senate see various reviews published by the Library of Parliament. Through the period 1968 to 1979, an unpublished study by the Library indicates that the Senate made 436 amendments or changes to legislation emanating from the Commons. This was in the era of pre-study when the Senate changes were accepted by ministers before legislation passed the House. See *Amendments to Legislation Initiated by the Senate, 1968–1979*; *Senate Amendments to House of Commons Bills 1961–1974—Preliminary Report*; and *Amendments to Legislation Initiated by the Senate, 1980–1987*. All are reports prepared by the Research Branch of the Library of Parliament on request of members.

It should be noted that Mr. Trudeau's government was forced to withdraw several bills stalled in the Senate when the amendments proposed by the Senate (or its committees) were highly contentious. See reports cited above.

The cases that follow illustrate the variety of checks and balances used in that six-year period. The lessons to be derived have to do with the division of powers between the two houses that create checks and balances, a crucial matter in considering reform.

1. THE CASE OF BORROWING AUTHORITY, 1984

In the period 1984 to 1990 the government assumed at the outset that its large popular mandate would allow it to override Senate decisions. This notion was defeated very early on. Late in 1984 the government introduced a Borrowing Authority Bill into the House of Commons, which extended the government's borrowing into a fiscal year for which the Main Estimates (how government intends to spend) had not yet been tabled in the House of Commons. Although this bill passed the House of Commons without much attention, when it appeared in the Senate the knowledge of senators came into play: there was no precedent to be found in our Parliament or in Britain's Parliament for giving a government authority to borrow very large sums of money without indicating through the Main Estimates how that borrowed money was to be spent. On these historical grounds the Senate delayed the Borrowing Authority Bill until the Main Estimates were tabled. Alternatively, the Senate proposed that the government could split the Bill in two, one part covering the borrowing for the previous estimates and a second part to be brought in with the new estimates.

The majority government interpreted this as a political clash instead of a procedural one. Had the government been of the same party as the Senate, that clash would have occurred as well, but with "back corridor" negotiations before the matter became public. If private discussions with the responsible minister had not had the desired effect, other means would have been available. The weekly national caucuses of the parties include both senators and MPs, and some Liberal senator would have pointed out to the Liberal government that this bill was in an unacceptable and unprecedented format and would have stopped it.

In the 1984 case, however, the Conservative government misjudged the situation and took on the Senate in a highly public and partisan way. Mr. John Crosbie, then minister of justice, put a motion in the House to curtail the powers of the Senate. But such a change would require the assent of the provinces, which were reluctant to go along with such a hasty venture. In the end, after much blustering, the government tabled the Estimates and the Senate passed the bill. Public pressure came from Canadian constitutional experts who made it clear to government that the Senate was perfectly correct. The majority of Canadians did not see the point of the dispute and regarded it as partisanship on the part of the Liberal majority.

This case indicates one of the major roles of the Canadian Senate, which is to examine and pass on parliamentary safeguards for the public. As Sir John A. Macdonald said in the debates over Confederation:

> There would be no use of an Upper House if it did not exercise, when it thought proper, the right of opposing or amending or postponing the legislation of the Lower House. It would be of no value whatever were it a mere chamber for registering the decrees of the Lower House. It must be an independent House, having a free action of its own, for it is only valuable as being a regulating body, calmly considering the legislation initiated by the popular branch, and preventing any hasty or ill-considered legislation which may come from that body, but it will never set itself in opposition against the deliberate and understood wishes of the people.

2. THE CASE OF THE PHARMACEUTICAL BILL

A second and entirely different clash arose in 1987 in the case of the pharmaceutical bill. The object of this legislation was to remove some of the patent protection of generic drugs, putting them into the brandname market more quickly. The government's purposes were to increase competition and research and development and, at the same time, to contain prices through regulation. The public feared that the price of generic drugs would rise rapidly, creating a hardship for people with disabilities, the population on fixed incomes—who were mainly retired Canadians—and the poor. This case indicates a quite different role of the Senate, which is to take up the public's desire for review of legislation when a majority in the House has overridden the legitimate concerns of the opposition.

The Senate established a committee to hold public hearings on this bill and over several months heard briefs from the consumers, producers, regulators, and others. Ten amendments to the bill were proposed, the Commons agreed to one, amended two, and turned down seven. The Senate then sent the bill back to the Special Committee which reported eight amendments to the Commons in October, 1987. The Commons accepted some amendments, but having heard the public protests and put them on record, having improved the bill, and having tried to persuade the government of public concerns, the Senate did not insist on its amendments and the bill passed and received royal assent.

3. THE CASE OF THE MEECH LAKE CONSTITUTIONAL ACCORD

On April 30, 1987, the prime minister and ten provincial premiers met at Meech Lake and proposed a series of amendments to the Constitution of Canada known as the Meech Lake Accord. Thirty-four days later, they met again at the Langevin Building in Ottawa from where, after a night of negotiation, they emerged with a slightly modified agreement. This was to be ratified by Parliament and the legislature of each province before June 23, 1990.

The details of the Accord and its fate are well known, but the work of the Senate on this momentous document is far less well known. Parliament struck a special joint committee of the Senate and the House of Commons to examine the Constitutional Accord on August 6, 1987. The committee heard about one hundred briefs and reported without amendment to Parliament in the fall of 1987. In the House, opposition members moved amendments, but they were all defeated. Many of the proposed amendments had to do with the rights of aboriginal people, the territories, women and other minorities, federal spending powers, executive federalism, and the distinct society concept. In the vote that followed 242 MPs voted in favour of the unamended Accord, 16 opposed, and 4 abstained. Thirty-three members were absent.

The Accord was tabled in both Houses simultaneously and the Senate was asked to concur. Under the revised constitution of 1982 the Senate has only a suspensive veto of 180 days on constitutional amendments, although it retains the absolute veto on all other legislation. So the Senate had 180 days, until April 23, 1988, in which to study the legislation and persuade the government to make changes. Since the prime minister had announced, supported by the premiers, that only "egregious errors" would persuade him to change even a comma, the prospects for change were slim. The minister responsible for federal-provincial relations was the Leader of the government in the Senate, Lowell Murray, and, as chief salesman of the Accord, he wanted the Senate to pass it quickly. But the Senate never did pass the Accord. Rather, the 180 days lapsed and the government proclaimed the Accord as having passed through Parliament.

From the time of the Langevin Agreement, however, the Senate took up the issues in the Accord. Forming into the Committee of the Whole on the Meech Lake Constitutional Accord on 22 June, 1987, it held hearings in the Senate chamber itself on Wednesday afternoons from June, 1987, to April, 1988. That testimony is to be found in the Debates of the Senate, Wednesday editions. Heard from were many constitutional authorities, including the Honourable Eugene Forsey who appeared three times, historians, lawyers, political scientists, groups such as those representing aboriginal peoples, women, visible minorities, and those affected by changes to the federal spending powers clause. In addition, former Prime Minister Pierre Trudeau appeared in a televised session on March 30, 1988, and spoke for six hours, arguing the case point by point. These hearings developed a loyal following of interested Canadians both in the galleries during the hearings and by distribution of the testimony. The Senate record provides more well-informed and thoughtful opinion on the Meech Lake Accord than most of the published works.

Second, that Committee of the Whole, chaired by Senator Gil Molgat of Manitoba, responded to the frustration of northern Canadians who had not been part of the first ministers' group and whose future was affected by the requirement of unanimity to create new provinces. On August 13, 1987, the Committee created a Task Force on the Meech Lake Constitutional Accord and on the Yukon and the Northwest Territories. Eight senators travelled to the Yukon and Northwest Territories and heard testimony on the question of the creation of new provinces and other matters from 59 witnesses. Based on these hearings and many written submissions, the Senate published a report in February, 1988 which made seven recommendations for amendment.

Having completed a task which neither the Special Joint Committee nor the government of Canada allowed, that is, to let the people speak, the Senate issued a final report proposing amendments in many areas. But because of the suspensive veto no change was made to the Accord. This shows how the Senate, through its own powers to set up investigative committees and task forces, can respond to the expressed needs of people abandoned by the majority in the House of Commons. It shows, as well, how the suspensive veto, long on the table for Senate reform, renders the upper chamber powerless.

4. THE CASE OF UNEMPLOYMENT INSURANCE

Other non-constitutional cases have arisen in the past six years when popular sentiment has been clearly against the government's legislation. This has been the case with bills changing the unemployment insurance scheme and imposing the goods and services tax. In both cases regional and demographic protest was universal. In both cases only a very narrow band of support, largely from the largest employers, favoured the legislation, while the protests came from a whole range of people across the country of different ages, sexes, ethnicities, language groups, and social classes. In both cases the bills were "money bills," legislation that can be initiated only in the Commons on the recommendation of the crown.

The course of events on the unemployment insurance legislation was the following. The bill passed the House of Commons against the combined opposition votes. It received first and second reading in the Senate and was sent to committee. A special legislative committee was struck, chaired by Senator Jacques Hebert, which held public hearings for all those interested parties that had been denied a hearing by the Commons. The committee reported the bill back to the Senate with several amendments. The legislation proposed to change the fundamental nature of unemployment insurance by removing the contribution to the fund from the general revenues, or the government. In other words, in future only workers and employers would pay into this fund. The key amendment was one that kept the government's contribution to the fund at a reduced rate of about 1.75 billion dollars. The amendments passed the Senate and were sent back to the House of Commons. The Commons accepted several of the amendments, but not the key amendment, and sent the bill back to the Senate. The Senate studied the government's proposals, but insisted upon the key amendment, and sent the bill back to the Commons.

Throughout parliamentary history, at this stage a government has three choices. Either it can accept the amendments, withdraw the legislation and reintroduce it another time, or it can call a conference between the two Houses for the purposes of negotiation. The government chose none of those courses of action, thus precipitating a constitutional challenge which at the time of writing has yet to be resolved.

Another interesting aspect of this case is that when the Senate first returned the bill with amendments, the minister challenged the constitutionality of the Senate's key amendment on the grounds of the royal recommendation noted above and asked for a ruling from the Speaker of the House of Commons.

After studying the powers of the Senate with respect to money bills, the Speaker concluded the Senate was within its powers. (See the report of the Standing Senate Committee on National Finance entitled *The Form and Use of Royal Recommendations*, February, 1990.)

This is probably the best example of "sober second thought" at work—the precise examination of parliamentary process and countermanding an attempt to change the social contract of Canadians.

At the time of writing the GST Bill is under study through public hearings by the Banking, Trade, and Commerce Committee, but it, too, will be affected by the outcome of the constitutional challenge to the amendments on the unemployment insurance bill. These two clashes are entirely different from that on the pharmaceutical legislation in that they affect spending and governmental financial planning. Should a majority government have the right to make such changes, unmodified by the very institutions (Opposition, Senate, and popular will) set up to check the power of the majority? These questions are fundamental to proposals for the reform of the Senate.

These examples of clashes between the legislative will of the House and that of the Senate have illustrated one of the major contributions senators make to the checks and balances of democracy: to allow citizens to make presentations when they have been denied that right in the House of Commons and to reflect their concerns in proposed amendments (the pharmaceutical bill, for example); to maintain parliamentary logic and precedent (the Borrowing Bill of 1984); to provide new information to the interested public (the Meech Lake Constitutional Accord hearings); and to maintain the social contract (the unemployment insurance amendments) through the use of constitutional powers. But there are other ways in which the Senate also contributes to checks and balances.

SPECIAL STUDIES

The Senate is best known for its special studies, such as the study of poverty by Senator David Croll, of soil erosion by Senate Herb Sparrow, of media concentration by Senator Keith Davey, of science and technology by Senator Maurice Lamontagne, and many others. These are subject matters referred to the Senate's standing or special committees to carry out research and look in depth at major problems facing the nation. These studies, which are often less expensive versions of royal commissions, may shape future legislation, reveal new problems or new evidence about problems, and influence public opinion. The research is carried out by the staff of the library of Parliament's research branch, or by contract with other agencies and individuals. These reports reflect not only the priority of problems but also the interests and special knowledge of senators involved. They offer an opportunity for expert in-depth knowledge to be made available to Canadians on a subject chosen not by government but by independent Senate committees.

INDEPENDENT ACTION

Non-financial bills can be, and often are, introduced in the Senate, although the government from 1984–1990 has not done so. But various housekeeping bills, such as changes to the incorporation of churches and professional associations, emerge in the Senate. In addition, a senator can introduce a Private Member's bill.

For example, in 1989 I introduced a Private Member's bill to amend the Copyright Act. The 1924 Copyright Act is well out of date, but amendments by the government in 1988 left teachers, researchers, and scholars in a precarious positions with increased penalties for violation of the Act. Since the government had promised, but not produced, educational exemptions, both creators and producers have been left on tenterhooks. Bill S-8 provides a narrow exemption for not-for-profit educational users should licences not be available for copyrighted materials under reasonable terms and conditions. The bill passed the first two stages and was sent to the Senate Standing Committee on Banking, Trade and Commerce which heard a great many witnesses representing both creators and users who had an interest in copyright. The bill was passed in the Banking, Trade and Commerce Committee in May of 1990 and reported to the Senate without amendment. Such a bill serves as a strong signal to the government that citizens are unhappy about, not their legislation, but their *lack* of legislation. This is another type of balance in the access of citizens to government.

CONCLUSION

Reform of the Senate requires reform of the powers of that chamber and of the House of Commons and other players in the checks and balances of power. The illustrations of the variety of ways in which legislation, special studies, and independent action can occur in the Senate—and have occurred in the past six years—have shown that this is not a simple question. The division of powers cannot be created *de novo*. Not only are there factors like long parliamentary tradition and precedent to be taken into account, since they can be called upon in future actions, but there are many players in the game, including the provinces, the courts, and the people. If Senate reform is to be realized, the current checks and balances must be understood and assessed carefully. If the Senate does not perform this role, who will? But above all both reformers and senators require some better grasp of the will of the people, as reflected in the revised constitution, with respect to a reformed Senate.

<hr />

THE SENATE AS AN INSTRUMENT OF BUSINESS AND PARTY

John McMenemy

INTRODUCTION

The Canadian Senate has usually been dismissed as a "comparatively unimportant and ineffective body" not far removed from "obscurity and obsolescence" (R. MacGregor Dawson), and "a senior but minor partner in the process of parliamentary government" (J.R. Mallory). However, since the Conservative party formed the federal government in 1984, the Senate has been a focus of public attention on several counts. First, the Liberal-dominated upper chamber has held up major government legislation, including the free trade agreement, drug patent legislation, deregulation of the transportation industry, copyright measures, a supply bill, amendments to income tax legislation and unemployment insurance, and legislation implementing the goods and services tax.

At the same time Senate reform has become an important item in constitutional negotiations and debate. The Constitutional Amendment, 1987 (the Meech Lake Accord) proposed provincial government involvement in the appointment process and included Senate reform on the "entrenched" agenda of the to-be-entrenched constitutional conference. However, it also proposed that Senate reform require the unanimous approval of Parliament and the provincial legislatures rather than of Parliament and two-thirds of the legislatures that together represent 50 percent of the population of all provinces, as the Constitution Act, 1982 required.

Finally, public attention has focused on the Senate in recent years as a result of RCMP investigations of two senators. In 1990 seven charges involving

Revised May, 1990 from an original article prepared for the previous edition and published here with the permission of the author, who is a member of the Department of Political Science, Wilfrid Laurier University. For comparable information re the Senate in the 1960s and 1970s, see previous editions.

criminal fraud, theft, and breach of trust with respect to Senate funds had been laid against Liberal Senator Hazen Argue. In November 1989 the RCMP began an investigation of allegations that Conservative Senator Michel Cogger had received payment from a private company for helping to secure a federal grant after his appointment to the Senate in 1986, and also received legal fees from a federal crown corporation. Also, a civil suit in Quebec Superior Court disclosed that the Senator had received payment from a company for lobbying activities on its behalf. The Parliament of Canada Act prohibits parliamentarians from receiving compensation for influencing government business or from a government contract. Also, the Lobbyists Registration Act, which among other things requires lobbyists to be publicly registered, came into effect in September 1989.

For his part, Senator Cogger, a lawyer, said that the fees paid arose out of other work he had done for a law firm, and that while he had arranged meetings he had not lobbied federal officials on behalf of private interests. Senator Cogger's case in particular attracted public interest because of his close connections with the prime minister. He had organized Brian Mulroney's campaign for the party leadership in 1983 and was co-chairman of the party's campaign committee in 1988.

Reformed or not, the Canadian Senate and its members in recent years have given lie to the conventional view of the upper house as an obscure, obsolete legislative body. The "unreformed" Senate has actively performed the function of legislative review in a partisan context as noted above. But it has also engaged in general policy reviews, for example, on tax reform and the future of Canadian financial institutions. Given the nature of representation in the appointed Senate, does that body perform its legislative role in a pluralist fashion, or is there reason to conclude that the Senate's legislative role supports the view that unequal class representation in state structures facilitates public policy in the interest of a dominant class?

The conventional critical view of the Senate as a legislative and political irrelevancy inhabited by superannuated politicians ignores the activities of particular senators who have an impact on the formal and informal aspects of the policy process and the electoral fortunes of particular parties. While many senators have no doubt been appointed in recognition of past service to a party, if not country, prime ministers make some senatorial appointments precisely to facilitate present and future party service, and many senators are still active in or useful to private corporations—including such key sectors of the business community as finance, manufacturing, energy, communication, and transportation—which have a direct and continuing interest in federal legislation and administrative regulations and decisions. Indeed, it can be argued that the conventional burlesque image of senators provides a useful screen behind which some senators can more easily conduct private business with respect to government policy. There has only been one scholarly assessment of the Senate that has taken major account of this corporate connection.

In 1978 Colin Campbell published an analysis of senators' standing among the country's economic elite, the entrenchment of sympathetic reviews of business policy, and senatorial role choices which have led to the creation of a dominant "lobby from within" the parliamentary system.

In 1990 senators' perquisites included an indexed parliamentary "indemnity" of $62,100 and a non-taxable expense allowance of $9,800, a free office on Parliament Hill, secretarial service, answering service, franking privileges, and free long-distance telephone. Senators appointed before 1965 who are still sitting hold life-long tenure, while those appointed since then retire at 75 years of age. This article discusses the active connections of senators with private corporations and the electoral organizations of political parties in the context of the debate on Senate reform.

THE CORPORATE CONNECTION

A federal government Green Paper on conflict of interest which dealt with the conduct of senators and MPs and which included a suggested Independence of Parliament Bill was tabled by the Liberals in 1973. The Liberals left office 11 years and one brief Conservative inter-regnum later with no such statute to their credit. Following a plague of scandals involving ministers and backbenchers, the Mulroney government introduced conflict of interest legislation late in its first term. It died on the order paper in 1988, but was re-introduced in November 1989 after the announcement of the police investigation of allegations concerning Senator Cogger. Under the proposed legislation, parliamentarians and their spouses would be required to declare their assets and sources of income to an ethics commission, which would have investigatory powers and could order an MP or senator to make changes if there could be a conflict of interest. Since September 1989 the Lobbyists Registration Act has required paid lobbyists to register publicly and describe their business in some detail.

At present, then, there is no federal law requiring parliamentarians to disclose, let alone restrict, directorships, property and financial holdings; nor, despite the Parliament of Canada and the Lobbyists Registration acts, does there seem to be effective control of legal affiliations and related activities that might be construed as lobbying. Senators who are appointed to the cabinet are required to follow existing prime ministerial guidelines for ministers. Most senators, however, are bound only by a rule under which they are not allowed to vote on any question in which they have "a pecuniary interest not available to the general public." Senators may define pecuniary interests in a very narrow way; but, in any case, voting in the Senate or in a committee is not the most effective way to influence a legislative issue.

The focus of the corporate connection is the Senate's standing committee on banking, trade and commerce. An examination of that committee's activity suggests that during the protracted but desultory public discussions since 1973 of parliamentary conflict of interest, senators on the whole may have become more sensitive to public appearances. Still, as we shall see, in the 1980s senators were essentially left with their own consciences to decide upon conflicts of interest.

In a review of budget legislation in 1981, committee witnesses included spokesmen for oil companies, the Institute of Chartered Accountants, the Independent Petroleum Association, the Canadian Daily Newspaper Publishers' Association, and the Brewers' Association of Canada. The brewing industry, for example, was concerned about the automatic and quarterly indexing of the excise tax on alcoholic beverages. As their representative was about to be heard, Senator Hartland Molson declared that, because of his private interests, he would not take "an active part" in the meeting.

Following the collapse of two chartered banks in 1985, the federal government tabled a Green paper on the regulation of financial institutions and introduced legislation to compensate the uninsured (that is, large) depositors. At the committee's first meeting to examine the Conservative government's parliamentary response to this crisis in the financial community, the committee members discussed conflicts of interest.

Two senators, including the committee's new deputy chairman, declared conflicts, as each was an "active participant" in the industry. "Some people might consider that my position [on the committee] would be in some way compromised because of my associations," Ian Sinclair told his colleagues. "I unfortunately have to recognize that some people think that way [although] I certainly do not feel that my associations would affect my judgment." Other committee members declared shareholding interests and indirect directorship interests (some without specifying them). After one senator read Senate rules on conflict of interest, Senator John M. MacDonald remarked: "Have we embarked on a truth and tell session? If we have come down to a matter of shareholdings in financial institutions, I think we just lost a committee." Committee chairman, Senator Lowell Murray, declared that at present there was no legal opinion that shareholding required withdrawal from the committee. Senator John Godfrey added that when the committee received a legal opinion on conflict of interest from the legal office of Senate, he would "not feel in any way bound by that opinion."

Senate rules facilitate changes in committee membership, even from day to day. It is also common for a Senate committee to allow non-members to attend and participate. On one occasion during consideration of the Green paper, the nine members of the banking committee in attendance were outnumbered by ten attendant non-member senators.

Industry witnesses who appeared before both the House of Commons committee on finance and the Senate committee strongly opposed key aspects of the Green paper, especially with regard to increased federal government regulation. However, the Senate committee's response to the Green paper and implicitly to the earlier published report of the House committee was clearly more sympathetic to the industry. In its report in 1986 the Senate committee rejected both the Green paper's and the House committee's recommendation for increased federal regulation. The Senate committee would require increased public disclosure and more responsibility for directors and auditors in the industry; at the same time it would permit increased commercial lending and leasing by financial institutions within conglomerates through holding companies, which would have to allow 35 percent of their shares to be publicly traded.

Earlier in 1985 the committee had conducted a pre-study of government legislation tabled in the House, but not yet in the Senate, to replace the Foreign Investment Review Agency with the less restrictive Investment Canada. The committee met three times, heard two supportive private representations— including the Canadian Manufacturer's Association whose brief the committee published in its *Proceedings*—before submitting its report to Senate.

While the bank failures were certainly a matter of importance to the national business community, so too had been the previous Liberal government's foreign investment review policy. On the earlier issue senators had protested that their judgment would not be affected by their corporate connections. On this last issue, which apparently posed no direct conflict, there was little doubt that their informed judgment as senators was that the Conservative "new broom" legislation, also of interest to the business community, should receive only nominal, but supportive attention. The committee would not sponsor an extended parliamentary debate over the question of controls on foreign investment.

In 1989 the Senate authorized the committee to study "the future of Canadian financial institutions in a globally competitive and evolving environment and, in particular, the ownership of such institutions." In 1989 and 1990 the committee heard from senior officials of chartered banks, trust companies, and companies whose holdings included financial institutions. The committee also entertained the views of associations of trust companies, insurance brokers, credit unions, life and health insurance companies, and bankers.

The committee chairman, Senator Sidney Buckwold, established the general policy-making atmosphere in which the committee held its study:

> ... the government seems not to be moving as quickly as was earlier anticipated in bringing down legislation involving financial institutions. I think that means the work of this committee becomes even more important than it was and that the kind of in-depth study we are doing ... may be very useful to the government in determining the direction in which they will move.

The atmosphere in which the executives of the finance industry were heard was extremely congenial. The chairman introduced the chairman and CEO of BCE Inc., which owns a trust company, as "a distinguished representative of his industry. ... I express the admiration of all members of this committee for the great contribution that you have personally made to the business and economic life of this country. We are looking forward with a great deal of interest to what you have to say. . . ."

At this time many of the committee members, including the chairman, Senator Buckwold, and the deputy chairman, Senator Jean-Marie Poitras, were on the boards of directors of various financial institutions. According to the *Financial Post Directory of Directors* (1990), the *Canadian Parliamentary Handbook* (1989), and the *Canadian Parliamentary Guide* (1989), the following members of the Senate committee on banking, trade and commerce in early 1990 held these business positions [for comparative purposes, see the 1975 list in 4th edition, pages 458–59, the 1982 list in 5th edition, pages 454–46, and the 1987 list in the 6th edition, pages 538–50]:

Margaret Jean Anderson (businessperson): president, W.S. Anderson and Co. Ltd.

Jack Austin (lawyer): chairman, Elite Insurance Management Ltd., First Toronto Mining Corp., Giant Pacific Petroleum, Inc.; director, Ark-La-Tex Industries Ltd., Morgan Financial Corp., Westmount Resources Ltd.

Sidney Buckwold (businessperson): pres., Buckwolds Ltd., dir., Mutual Life Assurance Co. of Canada, Mutual of Canada Financial Corp. (U.S.).

Michel Cogger (corporate and securities lawyer): corporate director (*CPH*, 1989); no directorships listed (*FPDD*, 1990).

Philippe Deane Gigantes (journalist): none.

"Jerry" Grafstein (lawyer): dir., Consolidated HCI Holdings Corp., Toronto Life Magazine.

William Kelly (executive, corporate director, civil engineer): pres., Kelco Management Inc.; chairman, Rothmans Inc.; dir., Contrans Corp., First City Financial Corp. Ltd., First City Trust Co., First City Trustco Inc., Lavalin Industries, Inc., Rothmans, Benson and Hedges.

Michael Kirby (academic; former prime ministerial aide and senior civil servant): vice-president, Goldfarb Consultants; dir., Crownx Inc., The Goldfarb Corp., The Quaker Oats Co. of Canada Ltd.

Leo Kolber (lawyer, corporate executive): vice-chairman and dir., CEMP Investments Ltd., chairman and dir., Cadillac Fairview Corp. Ltd., dir., I D B Bankholding Corp. Ltd., Canada-Israel Dev. Ltd., Standard Broadcasting Corp. Ltd. (*CPG*, 1989): chairman, Claridge Inc.; dir., E.I. DuPont de Nemours and Co., The Seagram Co. Ltd., The Toronto-Dominion Bank (*FPDD*, 1990).

Fernande-E. Leblanc (chartered accountant): none.

Philip Derek Lewis (lawyer): dir., CT Financial Services Inc., The Canada Trust Co., Canada Trustco Mortgage Co., Canada Trust Realtor.

"Bud" Olson (farmer and businessperson): pres., Farmer Stockman Supply Ltd.

Gerald Ottenheimer (former Newfoundland cabinet minister): none.

Ray Perrault (advertising and public relations counsel): dir. Citizens Trust, Northwest Sports Enterprises Ltd. (NHL franchise).

Jean-Marie Poitras (businessperson): dir., The Laurentian Mutual Insurance, The Imperial Life Assurance Co. of Canada, Alcan Aluminum Ltd., Bomem Inc., The Laurentian Group Corp., The Laurentian Life Insurance Co. Inc., Sodarcan Inc.

Duff Roblin (former premier of Manitoba and former president of Canadian Pacific Investments Ltd.): none.

Jean-Marie Simard (chartered accountant, former New Brunswick cabinet minister): none.

While the foregoing has dealt with senators in their deliberative, parliamentary role, it is not solely in that capacity that senators are able to assist private interests. Senators may use their publicly financed resources to establish a favourable environment for particular business interests elsewhere in the legislative process, notably among ministers and senior administrators, although the Parliament of Canada Act prohibits parliamentarians from receiving compensation for lobbying activities and the Lobbyists Registration Act requires public registration of lobbyists.

The matter of senators acting as lobbyists is relevant as approximately one-half of the members of the Senate committee on banking, trade and commerce in 1990 had legal and accounting backgrounds. Lawyers, in particular, are reluctant to disclose privileged information even as to who their clients might be; for example, denying the assertion that senators were lobbyists, then-senators David Walker and John Connolly distinguished lawyers acting on behalf of clients from lobbyists. The press had noted Senator Connolly's representations on behalf of corporations. Speaking of Connolly, Senator Walker, a colleague in law and on the Senate committee, said:

> Now in the practice of his [law] profession in Ottawa, as may be expected, he has been consulted by corporate and other clients who have problems to be solved within various departments of the federal government. These include tax problems, custom matters, contract settlements, and other matters requiring the service of lawyers. . . . I am sure that no official in . . . government . . . would ever feel that, because the honourable gentleman happens to be a senator when he appears before them as a lawyer with a client, he is doing any more than his professional duty requires him to do for a client.

Senator Connolly observed: "When professional people from outside come [to Ottawa] to interview [government lawyers, accountants, engineers], they do not come to seek favours, they come to try to find solutions for the problems of their clients. . . ."

However, this distinction between the activities of lawyers and lobbyists may be less than clear for non-lawyers, who are especially concerned when the lawyer in question is a senator and a member of the committee on banking, trade and commerce.

According to journalist Terrence Belford in *The Globe and Mail*, November 10, 1973, Senator Connolly's clients included Gulf Canada Ltd. and

IBM Canada Ltd. Senator Connolly asserted that his relationship with both companies was that of lawyer to client. But Belford quoted Gulf President Jerry McAfee as saying that the senator "occasionally opens doors for us and provides the proper atmosphere" for discussion with government officials. "With his knowledge of the people and scene there . . . he keeps us up to date on who are there, who is who, and what is what."

This question arose in 1989 in connection with allegations against Senator Cogger with respect to his activities as a lawyer while also a senator. "It is my understanding that several senators act in a similar capacity," he told the Senate. A Liberal lawyer-senator later responded: "If the insinuation is that other senators are receiving public monies, my response is: I do not." "All I meant was that several senators work for law firms. End of similarity," Senator Cogger told a journalist.

THE ACTIVE PARTY CONNECTION

Undeniably, the Senate includes former party activists and leaders. Indeed, Dalton Camp, one-time president of the national Progressive Conservative party and more recently advisor to Prime Minister Brian Mulroney, describes this as "the true value of the Senate." According to Camp, "It permits a prime minister to reform his government, to retire ministerial colleagues who are inept or weary, to open seats for newcomers to the cabinet, and to give sanctuary to those who have soldiered in his cause."

Despite indications of reformist intentions in the early years of his ministry, most of Prime Minister Pierre Trudeau's appointments reflected the principle of partisan reward and manipulation. Even on eve of his retirement in 1984 Trudeau's whirlwind of patronage appointments—some implemented by his successor, John Turner—included ten senatorial appointments, three of whom were cabinet ministers and three backbenchers. Turner's government was defeated in the election shortly thereafter, due in part to public reaction against these political rewards.

The Senate is not well recognized, however, as a publicly financed and prestigious repository for active organizers and fund-raisers. In recent years active Liberal party organizers and fund-raisers in the Senate have included M. Lorne Bonnell, Jean-Pierre Côté, John Godfrey, Alasdair Graham, Paul C. Lafond, Gildas Molgat, Ray Perrault, Maurice Riel (these appointed to the Senate by Trudeau), and Keith Davey, Earl Hastings, Harry Hays, and Richard Stanbury (these appointed to the Senate by Prime Minister Lester Pearson). Fund-raising aside, recent federal Liberal campaign organizations have included these senators: Keith Davey (co-chairman, responsible for all areas with the exception of Quebec, 1979 and 1980); Jack Austin (chairman, campaign committee for Yukon and Northwest Territories, 1979 and 1980); Derek Lewis (Newfoundland campaign committee chairman, 1979 and 1980); Royce Frith (Ontario campaign committee chairman, 1979); and David Steuart (Saskatchewan campaign committee chairman, 1979). Other campaign chairmen in the provinces included some prominent Liberals from the Commons. The fewer number of senators leading the organization in the 1980 campaign may have reflected the party's defeat in 1979 rather than a trend to remove senators from this role in general. In the 1984 campaign Turner attempted to discard the "Trudeau machine," but campaign problems, occasioned in part by inexperienced staff, resulted in the return of veteran organizer Senator Davey as campaign director. Senator Grafstein, a Trudeau appointment, headed Red Leaf Communications, an organization that handled Liberal campaign advertising. In the 1988 election Senator Alasdair Graham was co-chairman of the Liberal campaign committee and Senator Michael Kirby headed the national strategy committee.

The Conservative party has exploited Senate appointments similarly, although more infrequently, since the Tories have been in office for less time. In 1986 Prime Minister Mulroney appointed Norman Atkins and Michel Cogger to the Senate. Cogger had organized Mulroney's campaign for the party leadership. Atkins, formerly the successful head of the Ontario Conservative party's "Big Blue Machine," had been chairman of the federal Conservative campaign in 1984. Senators Atkins and Cogger were co-chairmen of the national Conservative campaign committee in 1988. Though in office for only nine months in 1979–1980, Prime Minister Joe Clark found time to place in the Senate Lowell Murray, who was his 1979 campaign chairman. In 1986 Mulroney appointed Murray to his cabinet as government leader in the Senate and minister of state for federal-provincial relations, responsible for constitutional negotiations. Though not occupying a visible position in the formal campaign structure in 1988, Senator Murray's role in the successful campaign has been described as "pivotal." After the election Senator Murray continued as government leader in the upper house and minister responsible for constitutional negotiations, including Senate reform. Senator Finlay McDonald has also been cited as an informal source of sound counsel in the 1988 Conservative campaign.

Mulroney's and Clark's actions were similar to those of their Conservative predecessor in office, John Diefenbaker, who appointed his key campaign advisor, Allister Grosart, to the Senate in 1962. Also, former Senator Gunnar Thorvaldson, appointed by Diefenbaker, was a fund-raiser for the federal and provincial Conservative parties in Manitoba. According to newspaper columnists Douglas Fisher and Harry Crowe, Senator Thorvaldson's role was to seek "contributions from those who got contracts in Manitoba through the federal [Conservative] government and from those out-of-province firms that got contracts from the provincial [Conservative] government." Senator William Kelly, an Ontario Conservative fund-raiser, was appointed by Trudeau on the recommendation of Premier William Davis in 1982 to fill a seat previously held by a Conservative.

CONCLUSION

Recent political and scholarly analyses of the Senate focus on the need for equitable and effective regional representation. Otherwise, the widely held perception of the Senate as an inactive or weak deliberative body neglects or minimizes the intensive and influential activities of many senators. The focus here has been on those activities that relate to the scrutiny of proposed legislation or current policy affecting private corporations, their organization and activities, and political party organization and fund-raising.

In the latter case, the question arises as to whether the public is well served by its subsidy of high party officialdom appointed by the government party-of-the-day. In the former case the public may wonder if it is well served by senators, particularly those on the committee on banking, trade and commerce, who have extensive corporate interests and whose intellectual values are those of large-scale business. There has been considerable discussion of conflict of interest legislation for parliamentarians since the publication of the Green paper in 1973, although no legislation has been enacted. In contrast the recently increased activity of professional lobbyists has resulted in the Lobbyists Registration Act. Even if senators have become sensitized to the question of personal conflicts of interest, there remains the question of the representativeness of senators and the exploitation of Parliament by an internal, publicly funded "business" lobby. The lack of conflict of interest legislation underscores this evidence of unequal class representation in Canada's federal state structures and the policy process.

BIBLIOGRAPHY

Alberta, Legislative Assembly. *Strengthening Canada: Reform of Canada's Senate, Report of the Alberta Select Special Committee on Senate Reform*. Edmonton: 1985.

Alberta. *A Provincially Appointed Senate: A New Federalism for Canada*. Edmonton: 1982.

Aucoin, P. *Institutional Reforms for Representative Government*. Toronto: U.T.P., 1985.

Bosa, P. "A Reformed But Not Elected Senate." *C.P.R.*. 5, 3, Autumn, 1982.

Campbell, C. *The Canadian Senate: A Lobby from Within*. Toronto: Macmillan, 1978.

Canada, Parliament, Senate. *Report of the Special Joint Committee on Senate Reform*. Ottawa: S. and S. 1984.

Canada, Parliament, Senate. *Rules of the Senate of Canada*. Ottawa: S. and S. 1976.

Canadian Parliamentary Review. Special issue on Senate reform, 7, 1, Spring, 1984.

Dobell, P.C. "The New Senate." *P.O.*, 10, 4, April, 1989.

Elton, D., Engelman, F.C., and McCormick, P. *Alternatives: Towards the Development of an Effective Federal System for Canada*. Amended Report. Calgary: Canada West Foundation, 1981.

Engelmann, F.C. "A Prologue to Structural Reform of the Government of Canada." *C.J.P.S.*, 19, 4, December, 1986.

Franks, C.E.S. "The Canadian Senate in an Age of Reform." *Q.Q.*, 95, 3, Autumn, 1988.

Franks, C.E.S. "The Senate and its Reform." *Q.L.J.*, 12, 3, 1988.

Frith, R. "Senators by Election." *P.O.*, 4, 3, May, 1983.

Galligan, B. "An Elected Senate for Canada? The Australian Model." *J.C.S.*, 20, 4, Winter, 1985–86.

Gibbins, R. *Senate Reform: Moving Towards the Slippery Slope*. Kingston: I.I.R., Queen's University, 1983.

Kunz, F.A. *The Modern Senate of Canada, 1925–1963, A Re-appraisal*. Toronto: U.T.P., 1965.

Lemco, J. "The Futility of Senate Reform in Canada." *Australian Journal of Politics and History*, 32, 3, 1986.

Lemco, J., and Regenstreif, P. "Let the Senate Be." *P.O.*, 6, 4, May, 1985.

MacKay, R.A. *The Unreformed Senate of Canada*. Toronto: M. & S., revised edition, 1963.

McConnell, H. "The Case for a 'Triple E' Senate." *Q.Q.*, 95, 3, Autumn, 1988.

Parliamentary Government. Special issue on Senate Reform, 5, 1 and 2, 1984.

Roblin, D. "The Case for an Elected Senate." *Canadian Parliamentary Review*, 5, 3, Autumn, 1982.

Smiley, D. *An Elected Senate for Canada? Clues from the Australian Experience*. Kingston: Queen's University, I.I.R., 1985.

University of Alberta Centre for Constitutional Studies. *The Canadian Senate: What Is to Be Done?* Edmonton: 1989.

Watts, R.L. "Second Chambers in Federal Political Systems." *Ontario Advisory Committee on Confederation: Background Papers & Reports*, Vol. 2, Toronto: Queen's Printer, 1970.

White, R. *Voice of Region: The Long Journey to Senate Reform in Canada*. Toronto: Dundurn Press, 1990.

Wudel, D. "A Job Description for Senators." *P.O.*, 7, 3, April, 1986.

Yurko, W. "A Third Way for Senate Reform." *P.O.*, 3, 5, September–October, 1982.

THE ADMINISTRATION

THE ADMINISTRATIVE MACHINE IN CANADA

Paul Thomas

BUREAUCRACY

Describing the public service as the administrative machinery of government refers to its bureaucratic nature. In popular usage the term bureaucracy has acquired the pejorative connotations of arbitrariness and red tape, but social scientists use it to describe any large organization, whether public or private, in which specialized experts play a dominant role.

Employment and promotion within bureaucratic organizations are based on technical qualifications and seniority. In structuring the organization a division of labour is followed so that specialized knowledge is involved in the performance of specified tasks. In addition to a division of labour there is emphasis on hierarchy, status, and a clear chain of command, with each member of the organization accountable to a superior for his or her decisions. Formal rules for decision making are to be applied uniformly and consistently to ensure that personalities do not interfere with the efficient and objective discharge of responsibilities. All of these principles are intended to ensure that the bureaucratic organization is both predictable and reliable. In a democracy,

An original article prepared for this edition in May, 1990, by the author, who is a member of the Department of Political Studies, University of Manitoba. By permission.

if we are to avoid arbitrary rule by experts in large public bureaucracies, we must ensure that the public service can take both political direction and is subject to ultimate democratic control through our elected representatives in cabinets and legislatures.

In all political systems reliance upon and the influence of the bureaucracy in formulating and implementing policy have grown during this century. Since Confederation the federal public service has multiplied several thousand-fold in response to the broadening scope and the complexity of government activity. Similar growth has also taken place at the provincial level; in fact, during recent decades provincial bureaucracies grew more rapidly than the federal public service. In addition to possessing a virtual monopoly on the expert knowledge necessary for modern policy making, contemporary public services have been granted, or have acquired, extensive discretionary powers over many aspects of our daily lives.

There is today, therefore, a vast, submerged level of policy making taking place through the development and application of rules to particular cases, a process largely controlled by the bureaucracy. A recent federal report identified no less than 14 885 types of discretionary powers that were exercised by ministers (usually acting on bureaucratic advice), departments, commissions, boards and tribunals. In quantitative terms, at least, the real lawmakers are found today not in the legislatures, but in the departments and non-departmental bodies that compose modern government. If at Confederation there might have been one elected representative for every one hundred public servants, today the proportion is probably one legislator for every several thousand public servants. Growth of the public bureaucracy in Canada has slowed in recent years, and there may be actual decline in some instances, but no one seriously disputes that the bureaucracy continues to play a crucial role in modern government.

While the image of the bureaucracy as a machine fits with the ideal of efficient rationality, in other respects the metaphor is misleading. It implies that someone, perhaps the prime minister, can climb into the driver's seat and steer the administrative apparatus of government in the direction he wants it to go. This may be true up to a point, but in practice no one, not even the prime minister, can arrange to be present, or even to influence, significant levels across the wide expanse of government. Much of what happens in government, though seldom completely random, nonetheless occurs in an unplanned and unco-ordinated manner. Serendipity, or chance, plays a role in how governments work (or fail to work) and Murphy (of Murphy's law fame) lurks everywhere. Bureaucratic influence has some limits, but so does the capacity of the bureaucracy to act in a rational, objective manner.

In recent years "bureaucrat bashing" has become one of Canada's more popular indoor sports. Brian Mulroney's Conservatives attacked the bureaucracy as being ineffective, wasteful, self-serving, arrogant, and perhaps uncontrollable. This negative stereotype apparently struck a responsive chord with the public. Controls over bureaucratic expansion were tightened, and efforts were made to actually reduce the size of the federal public service.

Bureaucracies are said usually to cherish stability and to resist change. However, it has been the capacity of the federal public service to adapt to economic, technological, social, and political change that has increased its influence, while other parts of the political system, like cabinets and legislatures, have been slower to adapt their structures and methods of operation to meet new demands. Bureaucratic change has been slow during some periods and rapid during others; growth, for example, has not been smooth; it has come in spurts. Even during periods of relative organizational stability there are often internal reorganizations and shifts in program responsibilities taking place among and within departments in a manner that escapes public notice.

ORGANIZATION

Contrary to the popular image the federal bureaucracy is not a homogeneous monolithic entity. Rather, it is a diverse agglomeration of organizations performing widely varying types of functions. There are three basic forms of organization: departments which constitute the main body of the public service, crown agencies which enjoy some measure of freedom from direct political control and are widely varied in their structures, and advisory bodies which also take on several different organizational formats. There are also the so-called "central agencies" which have achieved greater prominence over the last two decades. These categories overlap to some degree.

Statistics on government employment are recorded broadly along the lines of these three types of organization. Depending upon which statistical source is consulted, different conclusions can be drawn about the magnitude of the expansion or the reduction in the total size of the federal public sector. There are three sources for statistics on such employment. First, the *Public Service Commission's Annual Reports* record the number of people employed under the terms of the Public Service Employment Act (PSEA). These jobs constitute the main body of the public service represented by the regular departments of government. They are also the most regulated, protected, and visible type of government employment. A second, overlapping population is covered by reports from the Treasury Board, which is the legal representative of the government as an employer. Employees hired both within and outside the PSEA are included in the Treasury Board count so that total employment is larger than the PSC count. In other words the Treasury Board's statistics add to the PSC count those individuals who work for the various crown agencies, as well as Governor-in-Council (GIC) appointments made by the federal cabinet to various senior positions throughout the bureaucracy. Finally, Statistics Canada counts everyone who is on the payroll of a publicly funded organization. This is the most inclusive and therefore the largest inventory of public sector employment.

SIZE

The diagram presents the relative size of these three overlapping universes of public sector employment. The diagram shows that as of December, 1988 there were 211 993 employees in the PSC universe, 227 427 employees in the TB universe, and 565 398 employees in the Statistics Canada universe. Understanding these three reporting categories is necessary to enable comparisons over time to be made accurately. For example, one study reported that the public service population (that is, employment in regular departments) grew by 54 percent from 130 000 to almost 200 000 employees from 1960 to 1968. While the figures might suggest uncontrolled expansion, this would be misleading since much of this growth consisted of the extension of the provisions of the PSEA to a larger number of government workers.

In addition to this reporting change, note that federal employment since 1960 actually lost ground slowly in comparison to provincial employment, which belies the popular image promoted by provincial politicians that Ottawa is overrun with bureaucrats. Even during the 1960s when jobs in the public sector multiplied, the rate of growth in the labour force in general was higher. Total public employment in Canada has been almost stable in relation to the labour force since 1971, and now stands at about 20 percent. In summary, the image of an increasing percentage of Canadians making their daily living on the public payroll is inaccurate.

However, there is no disputing that the decades of the 1960s and 1970s were turbulent for the federal public service. Compared to the stability and tranquillity of the 1950s, the changes were rapid. Eight new departments were added between 1966 and 1971, and existing ones were expanded. Departmental reorganizations were common. Outside of the regular departments new crown corporations were created, with more established during the Trudeau decade from 1968 to 1979 than during any similar period in the past. New regulatory agencies were also established. As new areas of responsibility emerged, promotions for public servants became the order of the day.

To keep track of this spreading bureaucratic empire, the Trudeau government strengthened existing central control agencies and added new ones. Organizations like the Prime Minister's Office, the Privy Council Office, and the Federal-Provincial Relations Office gained power as co-ordinating bodies and as alternative sources of policy advice to that which flowed from the regular departments. Beginning in 1971 ministries of state for urban affairs and for science and technology emerged as policy planning units, and their successors after 1979, the ministries of state for social development and for economic development, were used to integrate policy formulation with budgetary allocation. In alphabet soup fashion new budgetary and management systems (PPBS, MBO, PEMS, and IMMA) were tried in official Ottawa. In 1967 the Treasury Board Secretariat was separated from the Department of Finance to become the financial watchdog over departmental spending. After 1978 it was joined

NUMBER OF FEDERAL GOVERNMENT EMPLOYEES

Viewed by Statistics Canada, the Treasury Board, and the Public Service Commission,
December, 1988

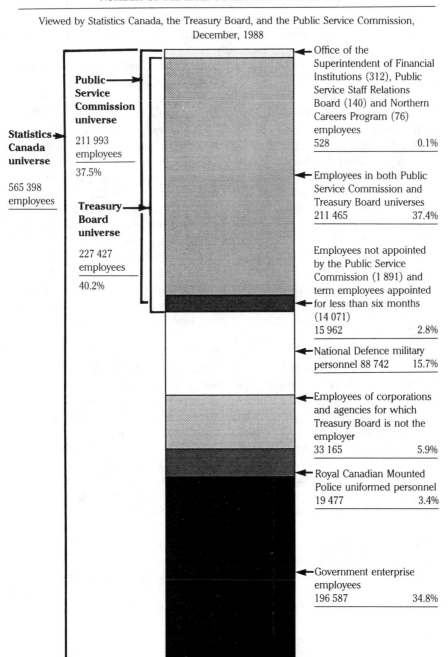

Public Service Commission universe

Statistics Canada universe

211 993 employees
37.5%

565 398 employees

Treasury Board universe

227 427 employees
40.2%

◄— Office of the Superintendent of Financial Institutions (312), Public Service Staff Relations Board (140) and Northern Careers Program (76) employees
528   0.1%

◄— Employees in both Public Service Commission and Treasury Board universes
211 465   37.4%

Employees not appointed by the Public Service Commission (1 891) and term employees appointed
◄— for less than six months (14 071)
15 962   2.8%

◄— National Defence military personnel 88 742   15.7%

◄— Employees of corporations and agencies for which Treasury Board is not the employer
33 165   5.9%

◄— Royal Canadian Mounted Police uniformed personnel
19 477   3.4%

◄— Government enterprise employees
196 587   34.8%

Source: Public Service Commission of Canada, *Annual Report, 1988*. By permission.

by the Office of the Comptroller General, whose mandate was to ensure that all departments practised sound financial management and possessed the capability to evaluate programs to ensure that value for money was being obtained.

The increased size of the bureaucracy brought increased concern that it was insufficiently accountable. A kind of "counter bureaucracy" began to appear in the 1970s in the form of various surveillance and review agencies which reported directly to Parliament. An Official Languages Commissioner (1969), a Human Rights Commission (1977), a strengthened Auditor General (1977), a Freedom-of-Information Commissioner (1983), a Privacy Commissioner (1983), and other auxiliary agencies appeared. Most of these newer bodies were part of a trend that saw the traditional bureaucracy itself become the target of public policy, rather than just the means through which policies were implemented. Official bilingualism, collective bargaining for public servants, affirmative action, pay equity, privacy protection, and freedom of information were adopted within the bureaucracy, and the new surveillance agencies reported to Parliament on the progress being obtained in these fields. By following the philosophy of "setting a bureaucrat to catch a bureaucrat," the government may have added unintentionally to the public perception that "big government" was growing uncontrollably. Growth in the "political establishment," that is, individuals working in ministerial offices, added to the public perception of bureaucratic expansion.

In the late 1970s in response to mounting deficits the Trudeau government began to restrain the growth of the public service, without much ideological fanfare. In 1984 the Mulroney government took office with an ideological commitment to less public sector employment as an end in itself, irrespective of other programmatic goals. A five-year Workforce Adjustment Program announced in the May 1985 budget set a target for the net reduction in the public service by 15 000 person years by the end of the fiscal year 1990–1991. The population covered by the Public Service Commission dropped from 224 026 in 1984 to 211 993 in 1988, which suggests that the Mulroney government would achieve its target for reducing the public service. By 1988 the regular public service had returned to the size it was in 1974. Restraint has also been applied to the other two universes of government employment. However, according to a detailed analysis prepared by Sharon Sutherland, actual layoffs have been minor compared to reductions achieved through attrition. Limited or no growth has led to problems of an aging workforce, limited mobility, the plateauing of careers, and a growing malaise within the public service, caused in part also by mounting, outside criticism of its role.

STRUCTURE

The Main Estimates for 1989–1990 listed 26 departments, the principal units by which the federal government delivers its programs and services. A department has been defined as "an administrative unit comprising one or more organizational components over which a minister has direct management and control." With the exception of the Privy Council Office, departments are created through statutes passed by Parliament, but the cabinet has discretionary authority to alter the duties of a department as well as its internal organization.

Departments vary considerably in function, size, and administrative structure. Some departments have enormous policy and political significance (for example, National Health and Welfare, and Environment), whereas others are mainly administrative in their functions (for example, Public Works, and Supply and Services) and are less politically visible. No consistent pattern, or principle, appears to have been followed in the creation and reorganization of departments; rather, each instance has represented a response to such factors as new functions of government, to perceived imbalances in responsibilities among departments, and as a way to recognize political demands.

The three largest departments in 1989–1990 were National Defence (33 191 person years), Employment and Immigration (24 817 person years), and Transport Canada (20 961). As large operational units involved in direct delivery of services and programs, these departments are more decentralized than others. Bureaucratic clout cannot be measured by size alone. National Health and Welfare had only 8833 employees in 1989–1990, but it spent approximately 40 percent of the total federal budget, mainly in the form of transfer payments to individuals and to other governments. And no one disputes the power of the relatively small Department of Finance which has only 845 employees, but is still the pre-eminent economic department within government.

Relatively new features on the political and bureaucratic landscape are two types of ministers of state. "Ministers of state to assist" can be described as junior cabinet ministers, whose role is to assist senior department ministers. In the Mulroney cabinet of 40 members there were at the start of 1990 no fewer than 11 such ministers to assist. Their numbers had increased since the early 1970s, partly to help ensure that political goals were translated into bureaucratic action, to provide job training for prospective senior ministers, and to give symbolic recognition to the demands of various outside groups.

The second category, "ministers of state for designated purposes," also appeared in the early 1970s as a way to co-ordinate the government's policy response to policy problems that slipped between the bureaucratic cracks of existing departments. Unlike the first category of ministers of state, ministers in this second group were the political heads of organizations called ministries of state. Since 1971 there have been four instances of this type of ministry of state, the only surviving one being the Ministry of State for Science and Technology. As small organizations with little direct program responsibility, the ministries of state were supposed to wield influence on the basis of their policy expertise, but most ended up taking a "back seat" in policy terms to the regular departments.

Under the doctrine of ministerial responsibility, cabinet ministers are placed in charge of their departments and must answer to Parliament for their activities. The pure theory of ministerial responsibility suggests that every act of a public servant will be regarded as an act of the minister, and in the event of a grave error by the department the minister must resign. In practice ministers have increasingly refused to accept liability for the actions of officials of which they had no prior knowledge and do not approve. Also, in practice the minister does not manage the department on a daily basis. This is the responsibility of the deputy minister, who is the most senior public servant in the department.

Deputy ministers are appointed by order in council (that is, by the cabinet) upon the recommendation of the prime minister, and they serve "at the pleasure of the crown," which means in practice as long as the prime minister wishes. During earlier decades civil servants who became deputies spent most of their careers in one department, eventually rising to the top. Beginning with Trudeau, prime ministers have shuffled deputies among departments every couple of years. When governments change, most deputies remain with the public service. For example, when Brian Mulroney took office in 1984 he brought in only a few outsiders to the senior public service, despite his election rhetoric that there would be wholesale changes. Continuity at the upper levels of the Canadian bureaucracy has distinguished it from its American counterpart in Washington.

The role of the deputy minister has both an administrative and a policy component, though in practice the two activities intermingle. As "general managers" of their departments, deputies are expected to plan for the department, staff it, delegate responsibility, appraise performance, supervise budgeting, and represent the department in various forms. As the chief administrator of the department, the deputy minister must adhere to the procedures and standards for staffing decisions and financial transactions which are laid down by such central administrative bodies as the Public Service Commission, the Treasury Board Secretariat, and the Office of the Comptroller General.

As policy advisers deputy ministers are expected to anticipate trends and to perceive emerging problems. Particularly during times when governments or individual ministers change, the deputy becomes important in assuring continuity in policy making. It is a deputy's legitimate function to initiate policy ideas as well as to react to the ideas of others. Deputies must warn, criticize, and object if a minister's plans are seen to be unwise or impractical, but such resistance must obviously stop short of obstruction or sabotage. There is a growing recognition that deputy ministers play a key role in policy formulation and its implementation, and this has led to suggestions that deputies should be held directly and separately accountable to Parliament for the administrative aspects of the department's performance, which are seen as beyond the practical control of cabinet ministers.

Most ministers are answerable not only for their departments, but also for various agencies, boards, commissions, and advisory bodies (collectively referred to as crown agencies). Depending upon the exact definition used, there are between four and five hundred crown agencies at the federal level, ranging from the giant Canadian National Railway to the tiny Canadian Institute for International Peace and Security. As their number grew during this century, so too did the concern that they were not sufficiently accountable. As so-called "arms-length" agencies, these non-departmental bodies enjoy some measure of independence from continuous ministerial direction and control, which supposedly characterizes regular departments. The autonomy enjoyed by crown agencies varies. They usually have a different management structure, with other than a deputy minister at the top, are not subject to the regular estimates-approval-process for budgeting, and do not follow the procedures of the Public Service Commission for the recruitment of personnel. Since the extent of ministerial involvement with their activities varies, so too does the willingness of ministers to accept political responsibility for their performance.

Crown corporations have played a significant role in Canada's economic and social development since Confederation, but it was during and after the Second World War that their expansion gained momentum. The majority of crown corporations now in existence have been created since the war, many during the prosperous decade from the late 1960s to the late 1970s. Economically, crown corporations have been used as a form of "defensive expansionism," to foster growth in situations where the market was not working or to withstand the natural north-south flow of economic activity. In addition to promoting national and provincial development, crown corporations have been used to cushion the impact of negative economic changes, for example, to salvage failing private sector operations when jobs were at stake. A desire to protect certain sensitive functions from partisan abuse (for example, broadcasting through the CBC or the award of grants through the Canada Council) is why crown corporations have been preferred over regular departments in some instances. At times this latter reason really amounts to distancing the government from criticism as, for example, when the post office was changed in 1981 from a department to a crown corporation, in part to deflect away from ministers criticisms about higher rates and poor services.

During the postwar period the crown corporation sector became almost a second public service, and the existing accountability arrangements proved inadequate. In 1984 the Financial Administration Act (FAA), the statute governing crown corporations, was extensively amended. New requirements were set for the creation of crown corporations and subsidiaries, for the approval of corporate plans and long-range budgets, for the role of boards of directors, and for annual reports and external audits. According to Parliament's financial watchdog, the auditor general, the new accountability framework for crown corporations is working quite well. When the FAA was amended in 1984, it applied to 66 crown corporations which were wholly owned by the government of Canada. Since then the Mulroney government has sold some of its crown holdings.

Privatization, or the selling of crown corporations to private sector owners, is now an internationally accepted approach to economic renewal, and Canada has shared in this trend. Discarding crown corporations that no longer serve a public policy purpose, coping with the deficit, eliminating barriers to private sector expansion, and an ideological preference for market solutions have been the reasons behind the privatization drive. From 1984 to the end of 1989 the Mulroney government fully privatized 13 crown corporations, including Air Canada, and sold its investments in another five companies. Compared to the accumulated public debt of $350 billion, the yield of $3.2 billion from the sale of crown corporations seemed paltry, but the auctioning off of money-losing crown corporations also sent a powerful symbolic message to beleaguered taxpayers.

Independent or semi-independent regulatory agencies have also come under increased scrutiny over the last two decades at both the federal and provincial levels of government. Such agencies formulate and apply economic and social regulations with respect to agriculture, communications, consumer protection, energy, the environment, financial institutions, health and safety, human rights, labour, and transportation. More visible agencies like the Canadian Radio-Television and Telecommunications Commission and the National Transportation Agency regulate entire sectors of the economy, whereas more obscure regulatory agencies like the Canadian Dairy Commission have a narrower scope. All agencies receive their objectives and powers from enabling legislation, which typically is quite vague and grants the members of a board or commission considerable latitude in policy making. Members are appointed by the cabinet, often for fixed terms. Other protections are provided also to ensure freedom from political interference. While the direct costs to government for regulatory agencies are relatively small, the indirect costs to the private sector in order to comply with regulatory provisions are held to be significant.

Recently, concern has been expressed that government regulation contributes to economic inefficiency and that regulatory agencies are insufficiently accountable. Provision for the cabinet to issue binding policy directives, extension of the right to appeal regulatory decisions before cabinet, parliamentary review of order in council appointments to such bodies and of their annual reports, intervenor funding for citizen groups appearing in their hearings, the prepublication of proposed regulations to allow for public commentary, and the deregulation of certain types of economic and social behaviour are among the changes introduced or contemplated under the general label of regulatory reform.

The final type of non-departmental body is of an advisory nature. There are various kinds, for example, advisory councils, royal commissions, and task forces. They all are set up on a permanent or *ad hoc* basis to supply governments with policy advice. Several advisory councils, such as the Economic Council of Canada and the Science Council of Canada, are also crown corporations. All such councils must walk the fine line between maintaining their independent policy stance without alienating the government and/or the regular bureaucracy. Royal commissions and task forces are created to investigate an area of public concern and to make recommendations for government action. In contrast to task forces, royal commissions tend to conduct inquiries which typically take longer to complete, have larger budgets and staffs, and sponsor more research. To the cynics both types of studies are seen as a way for a government to handle "political hot potatoes," since they allow for delay and the government is not obliged to act on the eventual recommendations.

During earlier decades there was greater consensus about the role that governments should play in economic and social development. Recent debates over various aspects of bureaucratic performance reflect the wider context of ideological disagreement over the role of government in general. So long as there is the current level of dissensus about government, the bureaucracy will remain at the centre of a swirl of controversy.

[⬚]

THE BUDGETARY PROCESS
Evert A. Lindquist

CANADIAN REVENUE BUDGET PROCESS

The Canadian revenue budget process has four distinct stages:

- ongoing analysis, consultation and planning;
- active budget development;
- budget presentation until first reading of the budget bills; and
- parliamentary review and approval.

FIRST STAGE: ONGOING ANALYSIS, CONSULTATION AND PLANNING

The budget process does not begin with the announcement that a budget is to be presented. The decision by the Minister of Finance and the Prime Minister is the product of a continual process of analysis, consultation and planning.

An important element of formulating any budget is the adoption of a "budget stance"—the general direction of policy in the budget. Hartle emphasizes that the Department of Finance, which bears the responsibility for preparing the budget document, always has a stance upon which it bases its activities in the area of monetary policy, fiscal policy, and international trade policy. The

From *Consultation and Budget Secrecy: Reforming the Process of Creating Revenue Budgets in the Canadian Federal Government*, Ottawa, The Conference Board of Canada, 1985, pp. 7–14, supplemented by additions by the author in 1990. By permission.

prevailing stance not only shapes the decision about whether to have a budget but also influences the stance taken in the budget. The Cabinet Committee on Priorities and Planning develops an overall economic strategy each fall which is modified throughout the year. This strategy also contributes to the decision to have a budget and to its general policy direction.

The perception of a need for a budget grows out of the normal activities of the Department of Finance and the government. Such activities and related sources of information include:

- the ongoing analysis and monitoring of the economy by the Department of Finance and other groups inside and outside the government;
- Cabinet and caucus discussions;
- regular consultations with groups and journalists; and
- federal-provincial government meetings.

In these inter-budget periods, the Department of Finance does not usually reveal which alternatives it is considering seriously or what the anticipated budget date is. So, although consultation does take place with the Department of Finance, it tends to take the form of information gathering and listening by the department rather than a two-way exchange of ideas. The extent of these tendencies at this stage is, of course, conditioned by the style of the Minister of Finance.

SECOND STAGE: ACTIVE BUDGET DEVELOPMENT

Decision to Have a Budget

There are two aspects of budget timing: the date of the budget and the amount of time the Department of Finance will be given to produce the budget. Typically, the Minister of Finance and the Deputy Minister of Finance determine the need for a budget and agree upon a tentative date. This recommendation is discussed with the Prime Minister to obtain his support and to ensure that the budget does not interfere with other government plans. Once the approval is given, the Deputy Minister focuses the work of the department on the budget.

Budget Analysis and Formulation

Given the suggestions generated in the first stage of the process and the "general budget stance," it becomes the task of the less senior officials to convert the collected ideas into specific proposals. The Assistant Deputy Minister for Tax Policy will assume a central role in most budgets because of expertise among the officials in that division.

To co-ordinate work on the various parts of the budget a budget committee is formed within the Department of Finance. The committee is composed of the most senior officials in the department, the Deputy Minister, the Associate

Deputy Ministers and the Assistant Deputy Ministers. However, membership on the committee can vary depending on the thrust of the budget. Some officials at the level of Director may be included. Even though the budget is formulated under the direction of the Minister of Finance, the budget committee is responsible for developing alternative budget proposals and for drafting the budget speech.

In consultation with the Minister of Finance, the budget committee considers various alternatives, especially in the area of tax policy, which have been generated from within Finance or outside the department. Some additional proposals are generated during this period of active budget development. The budget committee sets a "tone" for the speech itself and this of course partially determines the type of economic and tax policy that will be included in the budget.

Budget Approval

When the budget committee has produced a draft of the budget speech, the Minister of Finance reviews the document, revising it to add a more personal flavour. At this stage there should be nothing in the budget speech that surprises the minister.

A week before the budget is to be presented, the Minister of Finance goes over the draft speech with the Prime Minister. Usually, there will have been general discussion about the contents of the budget before this. There should be no real surprises for the Prime Minister, even though he will not have been involved in the formulation of the details. The main role of the Prime Minister is one of legitimation and support for the Minister of Finance in Cabinet and in public.

The involvement of the Cabinet in the formulation of the budget is extremely limited and mainly passive. Outlines of the budget are often circulated to the Cabinet Committee on Priorities and Planning or its equivalent but the full Cabinet does not learn of the budget plans until a week before budget night, after the Prime Minister has given his approval. Cabinet learns of the details of the budget only a day or two before it is presented to the House of Commons and the public. However, if the budget committee alters the general stance of the budget in a significant fashion at any time after the beginning of the second stage (active budget development) by convention members of Cabinet are informed of this.

THIRD STAGE: BUDGET NIGHT UNTIL FIRST READING

It is a popular misconception that when the Minister of Finance rises to present the budget in the House of Commons he is presenting the actual legislation that will be voted upon by the Members of Parliament. In fact, the period that follows can be used for serious revision and refinement of the measures that are proposed in the budget speech. Only when the budget bills have been submitted for first reading in the House of Commons is the government committed.

When the Minister of Finance rises in the House of Commons his opening statement consists of a motion to approve the general economic policy of the government. The debate and vote that follow during the next few days are concerned with the general thrust of the budget and not necessarily the specific measures it contains.

The speech that the Minister of Finance presents follows a fairly standard format;

- a review of economic conditions and problems based on information from a white paper tabled a few days earlier;
- a statement of government revenues and expenditures over the past year and a comparison with the previous budget's projections;
- an estimate of government expenditures and revenues for the upcoming year and the surplus or deficit; and
- notices of any ways and means motions—that is, motions to introduce bills to amend various tax acts.

Ways and means motions involve a series of steps leading to the normal procedure for considering legislation in the House of Commons. The normal procedure includes a vote on the introduction of the legislation (first reading); a debate on the principle of the legislation followed by a vote (second reading); consideration of the legislation's details in a committee of Members of Parliament, who report their recommendations to the legislature (report stage); and a final vote on the legislation (third reading). Budget legislation is introduced as a result of a resolution (passage of a motion). Although it served different and important purposes in the past, today this extended procedure enables the government to put forward legislative ideas without irrevocably committing itself. Upon completion of the speech, the House of Commons debates the budget speech for no more than six days.

The introduction of ways and means motions is important because it allows the government much room to manoeuvre and provides a role for consultation on specific measures. What is presented in the budget speech is a notice of the ways and means motions that the government intends to submit to Parliament. The notice of ways and means motions includes information about intended tax changes and the dates on which the measures are to take effect, but not the specific technical details.

Each ways and means motion that is later introduced must be consistent with the notice that preceded it. If the government decides it wants to alter a proposal it has made, a new notice is tabled.

The government can allow certain policy initiatives to "die" simply as notices of ways and means without ever being translated into legislation. In other words, the government does not have to be committed to the whole of the Minister of Finance's budget, although it risks embarrassment in this. Of course, if a budget contains too many measures that have to be withdrawn or changed, tremendous pressure is placed on the Minister of Finance to resign or for the entire budget and general economic policy of the government to be rethought.

A development of the ways and means motions involves tabling draft legislation along with the notice on budget night or shortly thereafter. This is known as a "comprehensive" ways and means motion. It allows for technical review of the proposed legislation by tax professionals. After changes have been incorporated, the comprehensive ways and means motions eventually have to be reintroduced with a new notice.

Once individual ways and means motions are finalized by the government they are presented to the House of Commons and are voted upon individually. There is no debate in anticipation of these votes.

Much of the delay that has been observed in transforming budget measures into law occurs at this stage. The delays have two causes. First, the Department of Finance may introduce notices of ways and means without having considered and prepared the legislation that must follow them. What may be politically feasible can present severe difficulties when an attempt is made to translate it into tractable legislation. If the legislation is not in a fairly advanced draft form then it may take much time to complete. Second, if the proposals have been submitted in the form of comprehensive ways and means motions and the measures under consideration are complex, groups outside the Department of Finance must be allowed an adequate amount of time to review and comment upon the draft legislation. This can also result in substantial delay.

Once the ways and means motions have been approved, the actual legislation is introduced to the House of Commons for first reading. At this point, the normal legislative process begins. The Department of Justice plays a key role in drafting the final legislation.

FOURTH STAGE: PARLIAMENTARY REVIEW AND APPROVAL

The final stage of the budget process is concerned with the way legislation is examined by Members of Parliament once it has been formally introduced as a bill. This stage is important because many of the proposed reforms suggest modifying this part of the process. Indeed, the entire parliamentary process has been the subject of much concern and the focus of many proposals for reform.

After being voted upon and passed at first reading, the bills are presented to the House of Commons for second reading. At this point the principle of the bill is debated. Following passage of the bill at second reading, budget bills are not sent to a House of Commons Standing Committee for review. Instead, the bills are sent to the Committee of the Whole; that is, the entire House of Commons sitting as a committee. The Committee of the Whole reviews the legislation clause by clause. Unlike standing committees, the Committee of the Whole cannot call witnesses to be questioned on aspects of the bills.

Amendments can be made to the legislation but, as is normally the case, they cannot be contrary to the original purpose of the bill.

Following the detailed consideration of the financial legislation, the Committee of the Whole reports the legislation back to the House of Commons as an entire bill. This is called the "report stage." The bill is then given "third reading" and upon passage is sent to the Senate for approval. Following Senate approval, after three readings, the bill is given Royal Assent and becomes law upon proclamation.

It would be misleading to leave the impression that members of the Senate are limited to a cursory approval of the financial legislation. Once the final bills are introduced in the House of Commons, the Senate Committee on Banking, Trade and Commerce reviews the legislation, holds hearings and writes a report, which is submitted to the Committee of the Whole before it begins its clause-by-clause analysis.

> The Senate Committee engages outside consultants to assist in its deliberations, and it hears witnesses, including representatives of the Departments of Finance and National Revenue. The review by this Committee is comprehensive and not only deals with important matters of substance but also gives detailed consideration to technical aspects of the legislation. This contributes substantially to the extensive analysis received by tax bills before their enactment.

Finally, the budget process does not end when the budget bills have become law. It is rare that any sort of legislation is drafted unambiguously and without unwanted side effects. The Department of Finance and the Department of National Revenue will often be involved in extensive consultations on how to implement and interpret the law. Out of the experience gained from having the law in effect, officials or other affected parties may seek to have portions of the law amended. This can be done inside or outside the budget process. With this type of consultation, the budget process has gone the full circle and essentially has returned to the stage of "ongoing consultation."

RECENT DEVELOPMENTS IN THE
CANADIAN REVENUE BUDGET PROCESS

Perhaps more than any other process associated with key policy instruments (taxation, expenditure, regulation, public enterprise), the revenue budget or tax policy process has changed the least during the past decade. Indeed, the previous paragraphs should provide a reasonably accurate account of how the process worked during the 1970s and the 1980s. It would be very difficult to make the same claim for the many renderings of the expenditure process over the same time period! Nevertheless, some changes have taken place in the revenue budget process, and though they are not radical departures from previous practice, any account would be incomplete without making note of them.

INCREASED COMMITMENT TO CONSULTATION

There has always been some degree of consultation prior to budgets, particularly with major business and labour groups. But the budget produced by Finance Minister Allan MacEachean in November 1981 caused a storm of controversy because it introduced a package of significant tax reform without any warning or public consultation. It soon became apparent that not only was the department surprised by the virulent reaction to the budget, but it had no obvious plan in place to "sell" the budget. There was a concerted effort on the part of affected interests to roll back key provisions in the budget which, in the end, was largely successful.

This episode was a traumatic experience for politicians and officials alike. Questions were raised about the competence of the department, and a decline in morale among staff soon followed. More importantly, no government in Canada can long afford the appearance of disarray in its central policy-making portfolio—it is a fundamental tenet of Canadian politics that it is necessary for the business community and the public to have confidence in both the Minister and Department of Finance if a government is to survive.

Under the leadership of Prime Minister Trudeau, the Liberal government took several steps to ameliorate the situation and restore confidence in the Department of Finance, initiatives that were sustained under subsequent Mulroney governments. First, Trudeau appointed Marc Lalonde, his strongest and most competent minister, to the Finance portfolio (Mulroney did the same by appointing Michael Wilson.) Second, a new branch was established within the department to increase its capacity for strategic planning, co-ordination, and consultation for both revenue budgets and major policy initiatives. Third, there has been extensive use of discussion papers, consultations, and parliamentary committees to vet new tax-related reform proposals. Finally, as will be discussed below in more detail, the Mulroney government has regularized the budget process.

INSTITUTIONALIZATION OF AN ANNUAL REVENUE BUDGET

Prior to 1985, one of the distinctive features of the Canadian revenue budget process was its *ad hoc* nature. Together, the Prime Minister and the Minister of Finance could, at any time, announce that a budget was in the offing. This stood in great contrast to the rigid timetable associated with the expenditure side of the process (producing the Main Estimates) as well as the revenue budget processes found in other parliamentary democracies such as Australia, the United Kingdom, and the United States, which were part of an annual budget cycle tied to the expenditure processes. One problem was that "snap budgets" often caught outside interests and other government departments off-guard, lessening their opportunity to provide input into the formation of policy. At a different level, the rush to produce a budget meant that the draft legislation necessary to implement the announced policy could not be produced with the budget, and taxes then would be collected without the enabling legislation.

In 1985, the Mulroney government made a commitment to regularize its revenue budget process. One reason was to counter increasing concern in the business community about the uncertainty surrounding economic policy. Another reason was to encourage more constructive consultations leading up to the budget process; adopting an annual budget meant that outside groups and departments as well as the Department of Finance could plan to direct sufficient resources to this end. Since 1985, revenue budgets have been held sometimes during the spring, usually during February and March. The most recent budget, for example, was released on February 20, 1990. However, it seems that the first budget of each mandate (May 1985 and April 1989) was delayed until late spring. Presumably, this occurred because these are key budgets which are intended to set the tone and economic framework for the rest of the mandate. It is also worth mentioning that major budget-related measures such as free trade and tax reform, which have involved extensive consultations, have been handled largely outside the annual budget process.

However, shifting to an annual budget cycle has not been without difficulty. Time is a scarce resource, and the major policy initiatives undertaken by the Mulroney government have, at times, put considerable pressure on sticking to a regular budget timetable. Indeed, the Mulroney government recently decided not to hold pre-budget consultations in advance of the February 1990 budget. Much time and effort had been expended on the marketing of, and the consultations for, the proposed Goods and Services Tax in 1989. This meant that if standard pre-budget consultations were to be initiated in early 1990, the budget would have not been produced for several months. In the end, the government revealed its determination to continue with a predictable budget cycle.

RECENT CONTROVERSY OVER BUDGET SECRECY

There have been many controversies associated with the revenue budget process, all related in some way to the convention of budget secrecy. They include the resignation of Walter Gordon following the 1963 federal budget, advance rumours of a national sales tax in a forthcoming budget of Jean Chretien in 1978, the "good guess" of pundits about some of the contents of John Crosbie's 1979 budget, and the inadvertent revelation of some budget figures by Marc Lalonde during a photo session the day before the 1983 budget. Although questions were raised about whether the leaking of information had created the potential for financial gain in these latter three incidents, and allegations were made about holding these Ministers to the British precedent of resignation for breaching the convention of budget secrecy, this was largely treated as posturing by Opposition parties and the media, and there was not sufficient pressure to force the resignations of the implicated Ministers of Finance.

But the leak associated with the April 26, 1989, budget was different. Not only was the entire budget leaked to reporter Doug Small, but this happened while financial markets were still open. This incident raised a host of important questions concerning accountability and responsibility. There were very legitimate concerns about whether or not financial gain had occurred and whether or not the Department of Finance had taken adequate steps to maintain security in printing and distributing budget papers before they were made public. On the other hand, the Minister of Finance maintained that the event was not a breach of budget secrecy because an employee had committed a criminal act by releasing the information. Even the act of laying charges soon became controversial because critics held that the policy investigation was politically motivated to shift responsibility from the government. At the time of writing, the case has yet to be resolved in court, but it remains that in anticipation of the February 1990 budget the Minister of Finance announced that fewer copies of the budget would be available for release immediately following the Budget speech and that there would be new lock-up procedures for the press corps and other observers.

[   ]

FREEDOM OF INFORMATION IN CANADA

John Eichmanis

The notion that government-held information should be accessible to the public as a right is of relatively recent origin in Canada. Following in the British political tradition, Canadian governments at the federal and provincial levels have held, and some still do, that secrecy is synonymous with good government. In the context of British parliamentary conventions of ministerial responsibility and cabinet solidarity, it has been argued that access to information legislation invites the debasement of these conventions or, at the very least, the creation of a "fish-bowl effect" that would adversely affect the deliberative processes of government. Freedom of information, in other words, would inhibit frank and open discussion of policy matters by ministers and their civil servants. Opponents of access also pointed to the negative impact that such legislation would have on law enforcement, international relations, and the like. The debate on these issues was largely resolved when all sides of the

An original article prepared for this edition in 1990 by the author, who is the Manager, Strategic Planning and Policy Development in the Office of Information and Privacy Commissioner/Ontario. The views expressed are not necessarily those of the Office of Information and Privacy Commissioner/Ontario. By permission.

argument acknowledged that certain information could be legitimately withheld from public disclosure.

The origins of what could be called the "freedom of information movement" lie in the 1970s, when much soul-searching was done by politicians, political commentators, and academics over the state of liberal democratic political institutions. There was a growing perception, best illustrated by the Watergate scandal in the United States, that democratic institutions were under siege and were failing to deal with rising public expectations. Much of the debate turned on the need for greater accountability of those engaged in the public's business and for increased public participation in various decision-making processes of government.

One way advanced for strengthening the legitimacy of liberal democratic institutions was freedom of information, which posits as its first principle the right of everyone to have access to government-held information. Such a right had never been defined in law. True, Sweden had as early as the eighteenth century passed its famous freedom of the press law which guaranteed a certain degree of access to government information; but for most governments in the twentieth century, public access to government information had been determined by various official secrets laws placed on the statute books in reaction to wartime conditions when concern for national security was paramount.

Moreover, in countries that followed British practices, government information was the property of the crown, safeguarded by Her Majesty's ministers. Ministers both individually and collectively were responsible for determining what information should be publicly disclosed in the public interest. However, it became apparent to many that whatever the merits of keeping secret matters pertaining to international relations, national security, and defence, the notion that the crown should in some abstract, and even in a real, sense be the keeper of all government information seemed an anachronism. Particularly when we recognize that in the second half of the twentieth century governments have become the largest repositories of socially useful information on a wide range of topics and issues. With the rise of the "interventionist state," governments in fulfilling their regulatory roles collect large amounts of information on individuals, companies, and organizations. Similarly, their policy roles in economic and social planning require the collection of vast amounts of statistical and related information. There were those who argued that such information should be publicly available to private individuals and organizations for their decision-making purposes.

In Canada in the 1970s "Jed" Baldwin, Conservative MP, began a campaign to introduce freedom of information at the federal level. By the late 1970s he had succeeded in converting his own party to the need for such legislation, and pressed the Liberals to follow suit when they returned to power in 1980. In 1982 the Liberals passed the Access to Information Act.

In some provinces there was also noticeable interest in such legislation. In the maritimes Nova Scotia passed an access law (which is now being revised), followed by New Brunswick and Newfoundland. In Ontario the Conservative minority government of 1977 was pressured by the Liberals and NDP to set up the Williams Commission to study not only this issue but also protection of privacy. While its report was issued in 1980, not until the Liberals formed a minority government in 1985 was the Freedom of Information and Protection of Privacy Act passed. A few years earlier Quebec had passed its law, modelled to large extent on the recommendations of the Williams report. Manitoba passed its law in 1985, but not until 1989 did it receive royal assent. And, as of writing, Saskatchewan has introduced its access legislation in the legislature.

Ontario and Quebec are unique in having integrated freedom of information and protection of privacy principles within one piece of legislation; the federal Parliament passed two parallel acts, one dealing with access and the other with privacy, both using the same legislative design.

As modern technology finds new ways to keep close watch over all of us, the issue of privacy will receive increasing public attention over the next few years. Where privacy commissioners are in place, one of their roles has been to monitor government programs and legislation for their impact on privacy. The wide use of the SIN, or Social Insurance Number, has been a particular concern to the federal privacy commissioner, who sees this use as opening the door to potential privacy abuses.

As for freedom of information legislation, it usually begins with a clause providing everyone with a general right of access to government-held information. This is the reverse of what prevailed in the past. If information contained in a record is now to be denied this denial must be based on specific exemptions. These exemptions detail the legitimate interests that should be protected and have now become generally standard in all freedom of information legislation; they include cabinet records, records that reveal the advice given to government by civil servants and others, law enforcement records, certain commercial and related information provided to governments by the private sector, records that deal with national security and defence, and records that touch on intergovernmental relations. Additional exemptions deal with records that involve solicitor-client priviledge, personal privacy, and the health and safety of individuals. These exemptions are usually required to be interpreted narrowly to ensure that as much information as possible is disclosed, without damaging the interest that the exemption seeks to protect.

There is, as could be expected, a continuing debate over whether the exemptions are too broad in favouring governments' interest in keeping secret as much information as possible.

Armed with the right to ask for any record (information, as such, cannot be requested), the individual makes application for the record(s) to the government entity that most likely possesses that record. The government entity has a specified period of time in which it must reply to the individual. If the request is turned down, the entity must provide a written reason, citing the exemption(s) it has relied on to make its decision.

At this point access legislation provides for some sort of independent appeal or review mechanism. That the appeal or review mechanism must be independent of government is a firmly established principle in access legislation. Certainly, the requester, but also the government, must have confidence that the appeal body will decide the dispute fairly and objectively. The body that resolves the appeal varies to some extent from jurisdiction to jurisdiction. At the federal level there is an information commissioner, who acts much like a classical ombudsman in that he or she makes a recommendation to the government entity proposing a resolution of the dispute. The government of Canada, or, more specifically, the particular department, is not obliged to accept the information commissioner's recommendation. If the individual is not satisfied with the government's response, he or she can take the matter further by appealing to the Federal Court, whose decision is then final.

This "ombudsman" approach is the preferred method of resolving appeals in Canada, though there are individual variations in different provinces. The most interesting, perhaps, is Ontario. Its legislation provides for a commissioner, but instead of only having the power to make recommendations, the Ontario commissioner has the power to make a binding order, much like a court does. This power to make a binding order represents a major innovation in freedom of information legislation in the context of British parliamentary government. Ordinarily, only the courts have the power to determine issues that involve the release of government information. This order cannot be challenged except on matters affecting the interpretation of the law. The Quebec Access Commission has similar powers, though its orders can be challenged in the provincial court.

By and large, freedom of information legislation in Canada has been relatively successful. The legislation is in place and people are beginning to use it. At the federal level, and in Ontario and Quebec, the number of requesters has risen over the years, though more could be done to inform the public of the existence of such legislation. In other jurisdictions the situation is somewhat mixed; the initial legislation has been perceived to have been inadequate in the case of Nova Scotia, and in other jurisdictions the public has failed to use the legislation as intended. As for the appeal and review bodies, they are attempting in most cases to clearly define the scope of the various exemptions, while holding the various government entities to their commitment to abide by the spirit of the legislation.

Freedom of information legislation in Canada has been in place a relatively short time. Whether the long-standing traditions of secrecy and confidentiality have been altered or attitudes changed by these laws, it is too early to tell. In the long run changing the attitudes of governments and their civil servants is critical if these access laws are to work in the way they were intended.

THE ESSENTIALS OF STRATEGIC POLICY MAKING

Thomas S. Axworthy

● ● ● The recent spate of stories on backroom advisers and their supposed shadowy intrigues raises once again questions about leadership and democratic accountability. Do those in power—whether kings, presidents or prime ministers—always require a loyal retinue? If so, what is the proper role of a leader's personal office? And what sort of qualities should he or she seek in a personal staff? Perhaps the most critical question of all is whether even a superbly advised leader can impose a pattern upon events. Have our problems become too large, our systems too complex, our society too lacking in consensus for our politicians? They can preside but can any one lead?

To help answer these questions, I will argue a three-part thesis:

- It is indeed possible to keep to a political agenda, and to prevent the urgent from overwhelming the important. But to do so, it is necessary to adopt a strategic approach to government. *Strategy necessitates choice.*
- To run a strategic prime ministership it is critical to recruit a highly competent personal staff. Nostalgia for the simpler days of Laurier or King is an inadequate response to the modern demands of government. A prime minister must make decisions on a host of matters about which he or she is not expert. *Choice necessitates advice.*
- In recruiting a personal staff a leader must distinguish between the demands of partisanship and the virtues of a professional civil service. Partisans bring creativity; public servants provide perspective. The political arm makes things move; bureaucratic routines prevent errors. Both kinds of counsel are necessary, but in Canada we are now in danger of doing permanent damage to the concept of a neutral civil service. Paradoxically, a strongly partisan personal office is the best way to defend an apolitical public service. *Good advice necessitates different kinds of expertise.* ● ● ●

THE LAW OF ACCELERATION

Even the greatest of political leaders have often wearily agreed with Emerson that "things are in the saddle, and ride mankind." Lincoln confessed that "I claim not to have controlled events, but confess plainly that events have controlled me." Bismarck, no shrinking violet when it came to self-confidence, believed that "man cannot create the current of events. He can only float with it and steer."

The pessimism of such great statesmen about their ability to master the

An abridgement by the editor of an article by the author entitled "Of Secretaries to Princes," which appeared in *Canadian Public Administration*, Vol. 31, No. 2, Summer, 1988, published by the Institute of Public Administration of Canada. By permission.

forces transforming the nineteenth century is all the more striking because today the pace of change is accelerating at an exponential rate. Technology strides ahead. The number of actors on the global scene shoots upwards. Interactions increase. Interdependence expands. No state, not even the most powerful, is any longer in complete control of its own destiny. Historian Arthur Schlesinger Jr., for example, has calculated that the last two lifetimes have seen more change than the planet's first 798 put together.

The cumulative impact of such revolutions leaves man breathless. One part of us rejoices at the affluence and leisure that new technology brings. Another side of our soul hungers for stability. Politicians are caught in the middle, not knowing whether to welcome the new world or to defend the old ways. But as Henry Adams warned, "a law of acceleration, definite and constant as any law of mechanics, cannot be supposed to relax its energy to suit the convenience of man."

Canada has not been immune from Adams's law of acceleration. Statistics tell the story. In 1867, in the era when Lincoln and Bismarck found it so difficult to cope with society's complexities, the new government of Canada spent less than $14 million. In 1987 Finance Minister Wilson plans to spend more than $116 billion. In 1867 Canada's public service could comfortably be fitted within the East Block; even in 1909 the newly created Department of External Affairs was housed entirely above a barber shop on Ottawa's Bank Street, and the total federal public service only numbered about twenty thousand souls. In 1987, the federal Main Estimates authorized over 236,000 person years, exclusive of the military, while External Affairs now resides in solitary splendour on Sussex Drive in a brown, squat imitation of an Egyptian pyramid.

The demands placed on the time, energy and physical resources of our leaders by this complex machinery are enormous. . . . Pressures on ministers were intense: in 1982–83, for example, there were three hundred meetings held of full cabinet or cabinet committees, nine hundred cabinet memoranda circulated (how many read?), seven hundred and fifty policy decisions taken, seventy-five bills drafted, four thousand order-in-council appointments made, and six thousand Treasury Board spending decisions taken. As an additional example, a case study showed that the Department of Regional and Industrial Economic Expansion alone made a further forty-seven hundred spending decisions, all of them theoretically under the purview of the minister. No human being could long keep up even with the press of this government business, let alone the equally heavy demands of constituents, party militants, media and interest groups. To survive, one must choose. And to choose well one needs a strategic conception of the job.

A STRATEGIC PRIME MINISTERSHIP

In a healthy democracy politics should mean more than a single-minded pursuit of office. Tyrants need seek only power. But leaders in a self-governing democracy must build a reciprocal relationship of trust and support with their fellow citizens. Democratic politics, therefore, is fundamentally a debate about conviction, while democratic leadership is the ability to educate, arouse and energize citizens to work for goals that represent mutual values.

Put simply, a strategic approach to politics is the intelligent application of priorities to the complicated world of clashing values and interests. There is no magic to it: one decides on objectives, assesses the difficulties in achieving them, and calculates the resources available to throw into the contest. Yet, while easy to outline, strategic politics is excruciatingly difficult to implement. A leader must choose from among a vast array of problems of which three or four issues will receive his or her individual attention. Once the choice is made, events, or the competing priorities of colleagues, can too easily edge aside the top items of the agenda. With a plethora of ministries and a multiplicity of decision makers, even politicians with the best of intentions may not be able to coordinate action or concentrate sufficient resources to make headway.

In this endless battle to rescue an element of choice from the pressure of events, you may fail even with a strategic approach. But you are certain to fail without it. . . . To achieve this, four different components should interconnect:

Policy: where do you want to go?
Politics: how do you get there?
Structure: how do you distribute authority?
Process: how do you run the system?

POLICY

Politicians are expected to have a five-point platform on every problem facing government. Yet, while it is easy to design such a program, if a leader has not made a real intellectual and emotional commitment to the ideas, they remain only fodder for campaign speeches. If a leader has not identified those few policy themes most fundamental to his or her conception of the job before arriving in office, he or she will have difficulty putting an imprint on affairs while in office.

In a four-year term a prime minister has the time to concentrate extensively on four or five issues at most. This is not to suggest that a prime minister can or should ignore the routine of government. Mistakes avoided are just as important as bills passed. It simply means that a leader can expend a significant amount of personal energy only on relatively few subjects. Since the most valuable resource in Ottawa is the time of the prime minister, to work intensively on four or five problems requires saying no to hundreds of other requests.

In a strategic prime ministership it is the task of the PMO to deal with the disgruntled. In the 1980–84 government, for example, the four priorities of constitutional reform, the national energy program, anti-inflation policy and the peace initiative took up much of the time of the prime minister. . . .

If prime ministers can at best immerse themselves in four of five policy areas, the cabinet can devote substantial effort to only a further twenty-five or thirty problems. . . . It is a sobering thought that the reputation and impact of a government rests on only the twenty-five issues that receive the top priority out of the one thousand plus cabinet memoranda that will be produced by the bureaucracy in a four-year term. . . . The success of a strategic prime ministership rests on which twenty-five issues are chosen.

POLITICS

Timing, organization and communication are the very stuff of politics. Knowing when to proceed and when to delay, sensing when to be bold and when to be prudent, calculating the forces pro and con—these are the intuitive arts possessed by all great politicians. Timing makes or breaks a government. . . .

Organizational politics is coalition building, pure and simple. Who can you bring onside and with what degree of intensity? Every government needs allies, especially those with media credibility. Over time, for example, the Trudeau government lost the support of business. . . .

The traditional cry of losing governments is that "our policies weren't wrong, they were simply not understood." More often than not, citizens understand their governments very well and that is exactly why the party in power loses, but the centrality of good communications can hardly be in doubt. Every great leader is a master of the communication medium of the age: Lincoln the outdoor rally, Roosevelt the radio, and Trudeau the television set. It is no good decrying the age of the thirty-second clip: one must simply master it, or disappear.

Policies that ignore politics quickly come to grief. Ukases that come down from on high with neither public support nor a plan to garner any are more commonly a failure of government than an administration with few ideas. Politicians who become so convinced of the righteousness of their cause that they expect the public meekly to follow reflexively their banner forget that leadership in a democracy is reciprocal: the leader must first identify with the needs, aspirations and values of the public before he can begin to educate. Moral leadership emerges from and always returns to the fundamental values of society. And party politics is the main venue for this debate over values.

A prime minister must lead a party before he leads a government. Parties represent a particular constellation of values, interests, blocs and localities. Politics is a never-ending process of satisfying your supporters, disengaging the supporters of your opponents and attracting the uninterested. The ideas which drive policy must somehow connect with the public. Thus, communicating the values inherent in a policy directive is just as important as writing a bill. Building a coalition to organize around an idea is just as important as passing a law. Ministering to a party, knowing the needs of the militants and maintaining the sinews of organizational strength are crucial to a successful prime ministership. The party base should never be forgotten.

Policy and politics should intersect most dramatically at election time, but in Canada the conduct of modern campaigns is invariably a record of opportunities lost. The duty of the party is to define problems and find answers. In Great Britain political parties issue detailed manifestos outlining their vision of the future. In Canada personal image rather than policy substance drives the race. Policy announcements are too often viewed as tactical devices to be dropped whenever media attention is flagging. The press, which must be fed, is daily doled out a policy Gainsburger. . . .

A strategic prime ministership, therefore, should begin to put down its roots in the campaign headquarters. The kind of campaign waged has a direct bearing on the nature of the government to follow. In the heat of an election it is difficult to have such discipline: one more promise to one more group may win one more seat. But by a curious process, the seeds of the next defeat are often sown in the moment of a seeming triumph.

STRUCTURE

The structure of decision-making can determine whether a strategic prime ministership will work or not. While the pattern of authority must give the chief executive enough time to work on the central agenda, it must also allow the government as a whole to get on with its business. A prime minister may define a set of priorities, but his or her cabinet colleagues will have their own concerns and the routine of government involves hundreds of daily decisions. A prime minister who has a well-developed policy sense but who continually finds his government blown off course by a series of minor crisis is perilously neglecting structure. . . .

PROCESS

Pierre Trudeau ran a collegial government and no apologies need be made for that style. He seldom reserved decisions for himself and loved instead to have his cabinet and caucus debate issues at length. The Trudeau style was undoubtedly time-consuming and even frustrating to the ministers involved but, as Bismarck once remarked, people with weak stomachs should not observe the manufacture either of sausages or new laws. . . .

. . . ministers see themselves as being the spokesperson of their departmental interest to the prime minister and cabinet. Thirty ministers in a room usually leads to thirty definitions of the public interest. A prime minister must bring order out of this babel and find the common thread that unites.

Discussion invites participation. Participation increases involvement. Involvement may lead to commitment. Such a progression is central to the concept of a strategic prime ministership. Ordering ministers or caucus members to toe a line is far less effective than winning their support through engagement. To persuade the thirty members of cabinet or the one hundred and forty members of caucus to put aside their parochial concerns to take up a central quest is the essence of parliamentary leadership. . . .

THE GUARDIANS

Access to power, Plato advised, should be confined to men who are not in love with it. Yet, as with many of Plato's ideals, human nature keeps getting in the way . . . we should at least revisit Plato's critical question: what virtues should the city demand of its guardians?

. . . Advisers should be recruited to fill the gaps in a leader's experience. The first rule of the office, therefore, is to recruit complementary skills. . . . Balance should be sought not only between the leader and the staff but also within the office staff. Enthusiasm must be tempered with experience. . . . A sagacious leader will insist on a staff that has already learned from mistakes made elsewhere.

Loyalty is perhaps the virtue most praised and least practised among politicians. Leaders hunger for loyalty because it is so rare. "Power is poison," wrote Henry Adams. He meant by that not only the corrosive effect authority has on the character of a leader, but also the predatory environment in which he or she must live. Everyone wants something. Supplicants want to use a leader's power for their ends, the leader wants to persuade them that his objectives should be their objectives. In this heated atmosphere, having the support of people who genuinely want to promote your interest, as opposed to their own, is a valued commodity. . . .

But loyalty is not the same as sycophancy. As Cardinal Richelieu warned, "there is no plague more capable of ruining a state than the host of flatterers." The best single test of loyalty is to tell the truth. Often the greatest service rendered to a leader is to force him to face unpalatable realities. To be able to do so requires a relationship of trust and respect. . . .

A PARTISAN OFFICE

In 1873 the new Liberal prime minister, Alexander Mackenzie, with not even a secretary to handle his mail, answered all letters himself, complaining "as letters come in bushels I have to answer them as fast as I can drive the pen." In 1983 Mr. Trudeau received nine thousand pieces of mail a week, a volume that not even the industrious Mr. Mackenzie could have kept up with. Unsurprisingly, as the scope of government has expanded in Canada, so too has the size of the prime minister's personal office.

In 1968 Mr. Trudeau initiated one of the most significant structural changes in the history of Canadian government. Before Mr. Trudeau, prime ministers' personal staffs were almost all seconded from the civil service. Sometimes the adviser was personally recruited by the prime minister to enter his service, as was Arnold Heeney in 1938 or Tom Kent in 1963. . . . Mr. Trudeau changed all that, by making it clear that his personal staff would be openly partisan. Thus a new category of official was created—the political adviser. The role of such individuals differed from that of the public service; they would advise on the interaction of policy and politics and not be subject to the formal rules of the public service. They could enter government without examination and they would leave government without the protection of the Public Service Act. . . .

In his last year as prime minister, in 1983–84, Mr. Trudeau's personal office employed eighty-seven people and had an estimated budget of $4.2 million. The prime minister's civil service secretariat—the Privy Council Office and Federal Provincial Relations division—had two hundred and seventy-five positions. . . . The PMO has grown, further, under Prime Minister Mulroney: in 1985/86 it expanded to one hundred and seventeen with a budget of $6.6 million.

As is often pointed out in the literature, the Trudeau PMO was double the size of Mr. Pearson's. But these numbers can be deceiving, since three-quarters of the staff slots were taken up by secretarial or correspondence positions. Most people in the PMO simply answered the mail or the telephones. Only twenty or so persons were senior advisers. While twenty is not a large number for such an office, my preference would be for an even smaller number. In 1979 after the election defeat, as leader of the opposition, Mr. Trudeau's staff was reduced by 60 per cent to only thirty with twelve senior people. Even though there were obvious differences, that small staff functioned more cohesively with as much impact as the larger PMOs which preceded and followed it. A prime minister requires a few assistants, not another layer of bureaucracy. . . .

The personal office of the leader should make contributions to the four dimensions of the strategic prime ministership outlined above:

Policy: knowing the trends.
Politics: promoting the party perspective.
Structure: knitting things together.
Process: keeping a grip during a crisis.

POLICY INTELLIGENCE

Information is power. This may be a cliché but it is still a powerful insight. The PMO must connect daily with other assistants on the Hill, with the caucus, the party and the media to keep abreast of events. My foremost objective—not often reached—was to avoid surprises. . . .

Party activists help create the climate of values to which decision makers respond. Individual members of cabinet and caucus bring regional perspectives to bear. The great departments of state have their own interests and are a vast reservoir of expertise. The Prime Minister's Office must balance the competing priorities by assessing them against a standard of public acceptability. The PMO is more often a policy synthesizer than a policy initiator.

PARTISANSHIP

The PMO, along with party headquarters, is a central partisan agency. Just as Finance brings economic expertise to a discussion, and External Affairs advances foreign policy considerations, the role of the PMO is to promote a partisan perspective. While the partisan perspective does not always carry the day, it is essential that ministers understand the political implications of policy discussions. To that end PMO advisers in Mr. Trudeau's office spent their time on major theme documents like the speech from the throne or the annual planning agenda meetings of the cabinet. Operational responsibilities were few, coordinating and goal-setting responsibilities were uppermost.... The feeling grew that the PMO was not transmitting party views so much as manipulating them. Such tensions, while perhaps inevitable, are ultimately self-defeating. Since the partisan perspective must compete with real power-holders like Finance, a divided political wing simply means that bureaucratic priorities rather than political necessities will prevail.

COORDINATION

James Coutts, my predecessor as principal secretary, described the PMO as "a switchboard" and that metaphor is apt. As a central political agency it connects the party with the bureaucracy. More time of the PMO is spent on coordination than any other activity....

With thirty government departments, twelve provincial party associations, and nearly three hundred ridings, the job of meshing the various components of this huge machine is enormous. Even a simple task like organizing the speaking engagements of ministers, so that Canada's outlying regions receive some attention, takes hundreds of phone calls. A strategic prime ministership must choose relatively few central themes, not only because of the time demands on the prime minister, but also because it takes a herculean effort to coordinate the government machine.

CRISIS MANAGEMENT

Only crises came to the PMO: the easier problems got solved elsewhere. The critical clearing house of the PMO from 1981–84 was a daily 8:30 a.m. meeting chaired by the principal secretary and including all senior staff. Here information was exchanged and tactics discussed. The operations, policy and communications divisions of the office also attempted to have weekly planning meetings to anticipate future crises rather than reacting to daily concerns. Despite this heroic goal, such meetings often dissolved into tactical fire-fighting sessions. The only compensation in all this was knowing that the ability to defuse a crisis, promote calm and instill confidence is among the most important characteristics of a central political staff. The only infallible rule is that crises are a true test of whether an office has the creativity and good humour to master events.

PRESERVING THE PUBLIC SERVICE

I believe in a strong partisan Prime Minister's Office. If politics is a debate about values, there is a need for a contingent of value-driven people to influence the direction of the state. Commitment fosters creativity. It is the political dynamic of our system which brings about reform. But good government needs other virtues besides creativity. Impartiality, experience and caution are equally important components to policy-making. These virtues the public service provides. The Canadian system of government with its amalgam of partisan advisers and neutral public servants combines equal doses of commitment and consistency.

A close partnership between the principal secretary and the clerk of the Privy Council is crucial to the workings of a strategic prime ministership. Since both officers have equal access to the prime minister, it is essential that they establish between them an atmosphere of trust. . . .

I fear that we are about to damage seriously our system of government by confusing the function of the partisan and the public servant. I favour stronger partisan advisers, not a more partisan public service. . . .

AN EVALUATION

. . . The crucial question in a strategic approach, then, is which big items?

The big items chosen by Mr. Trudeau between 1980 and 1984 provide lessons, both about the concept of a strategic prime ministership and the role of the PMO. The National Energy Program (NEP) was the most purely political priority. . . . But the attempt to use energy as a building block for a more independent economy and a strengthened federal treasury did not survive the Liberal defeat in 1984. Only Petro-Canada and the national sentiment in favour of a Canadian-owned oil industry remain as a legacy of the Trudeau energy policy. Public support for the NEP, while substantial, was not intensely felt. Bureaucratic support was always tepid. These two factors allowed the Conservatives to make sweeping changes. . . .

In the battle to patriate the constitution and entrench the Charter of Rights and Freedoms all four components of the strategic approach were synchronized. The policy was far-reaching. The decision to have a parliamentary committee hold public hearings helped create a vast constituency in favour of the Charter of Rights and by this device policy reform and organizational politics meshed as one. Structurally, the prime minister used cabinet and the Planning and Priorities Committee to discuss fully the general items, while Justice Minister Jean Chrétien employed his considerable skills in the day-to-day negotiations with the provinces. The Liberal party made constitutional reform central to its political appeal. Both caucus and the cabinet believed that they had moved Mr. Trudeau to take even bolder steps than he had originally contemplated. The circle of commitment, therefore, was large and deep. And it had to be for, even with all this in place, provincial opposition to the Charter was so intense that the battle for constitutional reform was, in the words of Wellington at Waterloo, "the nearest run thing you ever saw in your life."

By contrast, tax reform in 1981 was a major failure. . . .

The sad history of the 1981 budget also suggests that whatever the four or five overall priorities of a government, the economy must always be one of them. Politically the economy may be a no-win issue, but neglect will turn it into a clear loss. Living standards are nearly always the principal object of public concern and no government can afford to ignore this reality. Expectations will always exceed results but the resulting dissatisfaction is simply a fact of twentieth century political life. . . .

CONCLUSIONS

Government can make a difference only if there is true appreciation of how difficult and crucial it is to retain an element of choice from the welter of changing events. The urgent is always crowding out the important. A strategic approach and a strong partisan office, however, can help a leader master events. In summary, my recommendations are as follows:

- to have an agenda before you go in;
- to use the election campaign to seek a policy mandate;
- to concentrate on only a few themes, to know the trade offs, and never to ignore the economy;
- to combine policy and politics, structure and process into a coherent plan;
- to keep the personal staff small and to give them thematic, not operational, responsibilities;
- never to forget that a political party is made up of volunteers; and
- never to blur partisan and public service roles. Each has a different contribution to make.

Finally, despite the current attention focused on advisers and the backroom, we should never forget that it is the elected politicians who make our system of self-government run. As Machiavelli recognized, "it is an infallible rule that a prince who is not wise himself cannot be well advised."

BIBLIOGRAPHY

(See also Bibliographies in Chapters 1, 4, 5, 6, and 7)

General

Adie, R., and Thomas, P. *Canadian Public Administration: Problematic Perspectives*. Toronto: P.-H., 2nd ed., 1988.

Aucoin, P., (ed.). *The Politics and Management of Restraint in Government*. Montreal: I.R.P.P., 1981.

Aucoin, P., (ed.). *Regional Responsiveness and the National Administrative State*. Toronto: U.T.P., 1985.

Bolduc, R. "Les questions d'éthique dans les années 1980." *C.P.A.*, 24, 2, Summer, 1981.

Canada, [Treasury Board]. *Organization of the Government of Canada, 1980*. Ottawa: S. and S., 13th ed., 1980.

Chandler, M., and Chandler, W. "Public Administration in Canada's Provinces." *C.P.A.*, 25, 4, Winter, 1982.

Doerr, A.D. *Machinery of Government in Canada*. Toronto: Methuen, 1981.

Dussault, R. "Le rôle du juriste fonctionnaire dans l'aménagement des relations entre l'administration et les citoyens." *C.P.A.*, 24, 1, Spring, 1981.

Dussault, R., and Borgeat, L. *Administrative Law: A Treatise*. Toronto: Carswell, 3 vols, 1986, 1988, 1989.

Dwivedi, O.P., (ed.). *The Administrative State in Canada*. Toronto: U.T.P., 1982.

Dwivedi, O.P., and Woodrow, R.B., (eds.) *Public Policy and Administrative Studies*, Vol. 2. Guelph: Department of Political Studies, University of Guelph, 1985.

Fox, D. *Public Participation in the Administrative Process*. Ottawa Law Reform Commission, 1980.

Gow, J. *et al. Introduction à l'administration publique: une approche politique*. Montréal: Gâetan Morin, 1987.

Grasham, W.E., and Julien, G. *Canadian Public Administration Bibliography*. Toronto: I.P.A.C., 1972. *Supplement I*, 1971–72, 1974; *Supplement II*, 1973–75, 1977; *Supplement III*, 1976–78, 1980; *Supplement IV*, 1979–82, *Supplement V* 1983–85, 1988.

Hicks, M. "Evaluating Evaluation in Today's Government." *C.P.A.*, 24, 3, Fall, 1981.

Kernaghan, K. "Representative Bureaucracy: The Canadian Perspective." *C.P.A.*, 21, 4, Winter, 1978.

Kernaghan, K., (ed.). *Canadian Public Administration: Discipline and Profession*. Toronto: Butterworths, 1983.

Kernaghan, K., (ed.). *Public Administration in Canada: Selected Readings*. Toronto: Methuen, 5th ed., 1985.

Kernaghan, K., and Kuper, O. *Coordination in Canadian Governments—A Case Study of Aging Policy*. Toronto: Toronto Monograph Series, I.P.A.C., 1983.

Kernaghan, K., and Siegel, D. *Public Administration in Canada: A Text*. Toronto: Methuen, 1987.

Laframboise, H.L. "Causes of Organizational Disarray in the Federal Public Service." *O.*, 16, 1, 1985.

McCready, D.J. *The Canadian Public Sector*. Toronto: Butterworths, 1983.

Morgan, N. *Implosion: An Analysis of the Growth of the Federal Public Service in Canada (1945–1985)*. Montreal: I.R.P.P., 1985.

Morton, F.L., and Pal, L.A. "The Impact of the Charter of Rights on Public Administration." *C.P.A.*, 28, 2, Summer, 1985.
Palumbo, D.J., and Harder, M.A. *Implementing Public Policy.* Toronto: Heath, 1981.
Paquet, G. "An Agenda for Change in the Federal Public Service." *C.P.A.* 28, 3, Fall, 1985.
Rowat, D.C., (ed.). *Global Comparisons in Public Administration.* Ottawa: Carleton University, 1981.
Sage, G.A. *The Completely Civil Servant: The Bible of Survival and the Key to Prospering in the Civil Service.* Montreal: Eden, 1985.
Savoie, D.J. "The General Development Agreement Approach and the Bureaucratization of Provincial Governments in the Atlantic Provinces." *C.P.A.*, 24, 1, Spring, 1981.
Sutherland, S.L., and Doern, G.B. *Bureaucracy in Canada: Control and Reform.* Toronto: U.T.P., 1985.
Task Force on Conflict of Interest. *Ethical Conduct in the Public Sector.* Ottawa: S. & S., May, 1984.
Wilson, V.S. *Canadian Public Policy and Administration: Theory and Environment.* Toronto: McG.-H.R., 1981.

Bilingualism and Biculturalism

(See also Bibliography in Chapter 2.)

Borins, S.F. *The Language of the Skies: The Bilingual Air Traffic Control Conflict in Canada.* Montreal: McG-Q.U.P., 1983.
Borins, S.F. "Language Use in the Federal Public Services: Some Recent Survey Results." *C.P.A.*, 27, 2, Summer, 1984.
Cloutier, S. "Senior Public Service Officials in a Bicultural Society." *C.P.A.*, 11, 4, Winter, 1978.
Kanungo, R.N. *Biculturalism and Management.* Toronto: Butterworths, 1980.
Wilson, V.S., and Mullins, W.A. "Representative Bureaucracy: Linguistic/Ethnic Aspects in Canadian Public Policy." *C.P.A.*, 21, 4, Winter, 1978.

Bureaucrats and Politicians

(See also Bibliography in Chapter 9)

Atkinson, M.M., and Coleman, W. "Bureaucrats and Politicians in Canada: An Examination of the Political Administrative Model." *Comparative Political Studies*, 18,1, 1985.
Axworthy, L. "Control of Policy." *P.O.*, 6, 3, April, 1985.
Blakeney, A. "Goal-setting: Politicians' Expectations of Public Administrators." *C.P.A.*, 24, 1, Spring, 1981.
Bourgault, J., and Dion, S. "Brian Mulroney, a-t-il politisé les sous- ministres?" *C.P.A.*, 32, 1, Spring, 1989.
Bourgault, J., and Dion, S. "Governments Come and Go, but What of Senior Civil Servants? Canadian Deputy Ministers and Transitions in Power." *Governance*, 2, 2, 1989.
Campbell, C. *Governments Under Stress: Political Executives and Key Bureaucrats in Washington, London, and Ottawa.* Toronto: U.T.P., 1983.
Cullen, J. "The Disinterested Public Service: Growth and Change." *O.*, 19, 1, 1988–89.

D'Aquino, T. "The Public Service of Canada: The Case for Political Neutrality." *C.P.A.*, 27, 1, Spring, 1984.

Dion S. "La politisation des administrations publiques: éléments d'analyse stratégique." *C.P.A.*, 29, 1, Spring, 1986.

Granatstein, J.L. *The Ottawa Men: The Civil Service Mandarins 1935–1957.* Toronto: O.U.P., 1982.

Hodgetts, J.E. "The Deputies' Dilemma." *P.O.*, 4,3, May, 1983.

Johnson, A.F., and Daigneault, J. "Liberal 'Chefs de Cabinets ministeriels' in Quebec: Keeping Politics in Policy-making." *C.P.A.*, 31, 4, Winter, 1988.

Kernaghan, K. "Power, Parliament and Public Servants in Canada: Ministerial Responsibility Re-examined." *C.P.P.*, V, 3, Summer, 1979.

Kernaghan, K., and Langford, J. *The Responsible Public Servant.* Toronto: I.P.A.C., 1989.

Manion, J. "New Challenges in Public Administration." *C.P.A.*, 31, 2, Summer, 1988.

Osbaldeston, G. "The Public Servant and Politics." *P.O.*, 8, 1, January, 1987.

Osbaldeston, G. "Job Description for Deputy Ministers." *P.O.*, 9, 1, 1988.

Parliamentary Government. Special issue on "Conflict of Interest," 5, 3, 1985.

Plasse, M. "Les chefs de cabinets ministeriels au Québec: la transition du gouvernement libéral au gouvernement péquiste (1976–1977)." *C.J.P.S.*, XIV, 2, June, 1981.

Plumptre, T. "New Perspectives on the Role of the Deputy Minister." *C.P.A.*, 30, 3, Fall, 1987.

Plumptre, T. "Renewing the Public Service." *P.O.*, 10, 10, December, 1989.

Political Rights. Comments by Kernaghan, K., *et al. C.P.A.*, 29, 4, Winter, 1986.

"Responsibility and the Senior Public Service." Nine papers given at the Seventeenth National Seminar, I.P.A.C., *C.P.A.*, 27, 4, Winter, 1984.

Robertson, G. "The Deputies' Anonymous Duty." *P.O.*, 4, 4, July, 1983.

Savoie, D.J. "Putting Deputies Through the Hoops." *P.O.*, 7, 1, January, 1986.

Business-Government Relations

(See also Chapter 1, "Business and Society".)

Atkinson, M., and Coleman, W. *The State, Business, and Industrial Change in Canada.* Toronto: U.T.P., 1989.

Baetz, M., and Thain, D. *Canadian Cases in Business-Government Relations.* Toronto: Nelson, 1989.

Bartha, P. "Organizational Competence in Business-Government Relations: A Managerial Perspective." *C.P.A.*, 28, 2, Summer, 1985.

Bon, D.L., and Hart, K.D. *Linking Canada's New Solitudes: The Executive Interchange Program and Business Government Relations.* Ottawa: The Conference Board of Canada, 1983.

Brander, J.A. *Government Policy Toward Business.* Toronto: Butterworths, 1988.

Brooks, S. *Who's in Charge?: The Mixed Ownership Corporation in Canada.* Halifax: I.R.P.P., 1987.

Coleman, W. *Business and Politics: A Study of Collective Action.* Montreal: McG.-Q.U.P., 1988.

Fleck, J.D., and Litvak, I.A., (eds.). *Business Can Succeed: Understanding the Political Environment.* Toronto: Gage, 1984.

Gillies, J. *Where Business Fails: Business-Government Relations at the Federal Level in Canada.* Montreal: I.R.P.P., 1981.

Gillies, J. *Facing Reality.* Montreal: I.R.P.P., 1986.

Grant, W. *Government and Industry: A Comparative Analysis of the US, Canada and the UK.* Brookfield, Vermont: Gower, 1989.

Islam, N., and Sadrudin, A.A. "Business Influence on Government: A Comparison of Public and Private Sector Perceptions." *C.P.A.*, 27, 1, Spring, 1984.

Lermer, G., (ed.). *Government and the Market Economy.* Vancouver: The Fraser Institute, 1983.

Murray, V.V., (ed.). *Theories of Business-Government Relations.* Toronto: Trans-Canada Press, 1985.

Murray, V.V., and McMillan, C.J. "Business-Government Relations in Canada: A Conceptual Map." *C.P.A.*, 26, 4, Winter, 1983.

Rea, K., and Wiseman, N., (eds), *Government and Enterprise in Canada.* Toronto: Methuen, 1985.

Collective Bargaining and Political Activity

Christensen, S. *Unions and the Public Interest: Collective Bargaining in the Government Sector.* Vancouver: Fraser Institute, 1980.

Daubney, D. "Freedom to Think." [political rights of civil servants], *P.O.*, 7, 5, June, 1984.

Finkleman, J., and Goldenberg, S. *Collective Bargaining in the Public Service.* Montreal: I.R.P.P., 1983, 2 vols.

Gallant, E. "Service Above Party." [political rights of civil servants]. *P.O.*, 7, 2, March, 1986.

Gunderson, M., (ed.). *Collective Bargaining in the Essential and Public Service Sectors.* Toronto: U.T.P., 1975.

Kernaghan, K., and Kuruvilla, P.K. "Merit and Motivation: Public Personnel Management in Canada." *C.P.A.*, 25, 4, Winter, 1982.

Ontario Law Reform Commission. *Report on Political Activity, Public Comment and Disclosure by Crown Employees.* 1986.

Swimmer, G., and Thompson, M. *Conflict and Compromise: The Future of Public Sector Industrial Relations.* Montreal: I.R.P.P. 1984.

Crown Corporations and ABCs

Bernier, I., and Lajoie, A., (eds.). *Regulations, Crown Corporations and Administrative Tribunals.* Toronto: U.T.P., 1985.

Borins, S.F., and Brown, L. *Investments in Failure: Five Government Corporations that Cost the Canadian Taxpayer Billions.* Toronto: Methuen, 1986.

Brooks, S. "The State as Financier: A Comparison of the Caisse de dépôt et placement du Québec and the Alberta Heritage Savings Trust Fund." *C.P.P.*, 13, 3, September, 1987.

Gordon, M. *Government in Business.* Montreal: C.D. Howe Institute, 1981.

Green, C. "Agricultural Marketing Boards in Canada: An Economic and Legal Analysis." *U.T.L.J.*, 33, 4, Fall, 1983.

Hardin, H. *The Privatization Putsch.* Halifax: I.R.P.P., 1989.

Hull, W.H.N. "Captive or Victim: The Board of Broadcast Governors and Bernstein's Law, 1958–68." *C.P.A.*, 26, 4, Winter, 1983.

Kirsch, E. *Crown Corporations as Instruments of Public Policy: A Legal and Institutional Perspective.* Ottawa: E.C.C., 1986.

Langford, J.W. "The Identification and Classification of Federal Public Corporations: A Preface to Regime Building." *C.P.A.*, 23, 1, Spring, 1980.

Langford, J.W. "The Question of Quangos: Quasi-public Service Agencies in British Columbia." *C.P.A.*, 26, 4, Winter, 1983.

Laux, J., and Molot, M. *State Capitalism: Public Enterprise in Canada*. Ithaca, New York: Cornell University Press, 1988.

Law Reform Commission, *Independent Administrative Agencies*. Ottawa: S. and S., 1980.

Lucas, A.R. "Judicial Review of Crown Corporations." *A.L.R.*, 25, 3,1987.

McKay, P. *Electric Empire*. [Ontario Hydro]. Toronto: Between the Lines, 1983.

Peers, F.W. *The Politics of Canadian Broadcasting, 1920–51*, Vol. I. Toronto: U.T.P., 1969; *The Public Eye: Television and the Politics of Canadian Broadcasting, 1952–68*, Vol. II. Toronto: U.T.P., 1979.

Privy Council Office, *Crown Corporations: Direction, Control, Accountability*. Ottawa: S. and S., 1977.

Stewart, W. *Uneasy Lies the Head: The Truth About Canada's Crown Corporations*. Toronto: Collins, 1987.

Thomas, P. "Uneasy Crowns." *P.O.*, 8, 1, January, 1987.

Tupper, A., and Doern, B., (eds.). *Public Corporations and Public Policy in Canada*. Montreal: I.R.P.P., 1981.

Tupper, A., and Doern, B., (eds.). *Privatization, Public Policy and Public Corporations in Canada*. Halifax: I.R.P.P., 1989.

Walker, M., (ed.). *Privatization: Tactics and Techniques*. Vancouver: Fraser Institute, 1988.

Financial Management and Accountability

Baker, W.A. "Accountability, Responsiveness and Public Sector Productivity." *C.P.A.*, 23, 4, Winter, 1980.

Balls, H.R. "The Watchdog of Parliament: The Centenary of the Legislative Audit." *C.P.A.*, 21, 4, Winter, 1978.

Brown, M.P. "Responsiveness versus Accountability in Collaborative Federalism: The Canadian Experience." *C.P.A.*, 26, 4, Winter, 1983.

Canada. *Final Report, Royal Commission on Financial Management and Accountability*. [Lambert Report]. Ottawa: S. & S., 1979. (For an extensive review of the Report, see the Seminar Publication, *Financial Management and Accountability*. I.P.A.C., Toronto: 1980, and McLeod, T.H., "The Special National Seminar on Financial Management and Accountability: An Appraisal." *C.P.A.*, 23, 1, 1980.)

Cassidy, R.G., and Neave, E.H. "Accountability and Control in the Federal Government." *Q.Q.*, 87, 1, Spring, 1980.

Chapman, I.D., and Farina, C.. "Accountability and the Science Research Councils." *J.C.S.*, 17, 4 Winter, 1983.

Cutt, J. "Zero-Base Budgeting in the Government of British Columbia." *C.T.J.*, 32, Jan.–Feb., 1984.

Cutt, J. "Accountability, Efficiency and the 'Bottom Line' in Non-profit Organizations." *C.P.A.*, 25, 3, Fall, 1982.

Cutt, J., and Ritter, R. *Public Non-Profit Budgeting: The Evolution and Application of Zero-Base Budgeting*. Toronto: I.P.A.C., 1984.

Doern, B., Maslove, A., and Prince, M. *Public Budgeting in Canada: Politics, Economics, Management*. Ottawa: C.U.P., 1988.

Dwivedi, O.P. "Accountability of Public Servants: Recent Developments in Canada." *International Journal of Public Administration*, 26, 3, July–September, 1980.

Hartle, D.G. "The Report of the Royal Commission on Financial Management and Accountability: A Review." [The Lambert Report]. *C.P.P.*, 5, 3, Summer, 1979.

Hodgetts, J. E. "Government Responsiveness to the Public Interest: Has Progress Been Made?" *C.P.A.*, 24, 2, Summer, 1981.

Jones, L.R. "Financial Restraint Management and Budget Control in Canadian Provincial Governments." *C.P.A.*, 29, 2, Summer, 1986.

Kent, T. "Advancing Accountability." *P.O.*, 4, 1, January–February, 1983.

Kirkwood, D. "Accountability and the Deputy Minister." *O.*, 13, 2, 1982.

Laframboise, H.L. "Conscience and Conformity: The Uncomfortable Bedfellows of Accountability." *C.P.A.*, 26, 3, Fall, 1983.

Marson, B. "The Transformation of a Public Agency: British Columbia's Office of the Comptroller General." *C.P.A.*, 31, 4, Winter, 1988.

Maslove, A., (ed.). *Budgeting in the Provinces: Leadership and the Premiers.* Toronto: I.P.A.C., 1989.

McCaffery, J. "Canada's Envelope Budgeting System." *A.R.C.S.*, 14, 1, Spring, 1984.

Osbaldeston, G. "How Deputies Are Accountable." *P.O.*, 8, 7, September, 1987.

Osbaldeston, G. *Keeping Deputy Ministers Accountable.* Toronto: M-H. R., 1988.

Parliamentary Government. Special issue on "Scrutiny and Accountability." 3, 2, Spring, 1982.

Pitfield, M. "The Office of Auditor General as a Way to Parliamentary Reform." *O.*, 15, 1, (1984).

Report of the Independent Review Committee on the Office of the Auditor General of Canada. Ottawa: Information Canada, 1975.

Sinclair, S. *Cordial But Not Cosy: A History of the Office of Auditor General.* Toronto: M. & S., 1979.

Strick, J.C. *Canadian Public Finance.* Toronto: H.R.W., 3rd ed., 1985.

Sutherland, S.L. "On the Audit Trail of the Auditor General: Parliament's Servant, 1973–80." *C.P.A.*, 23, 4, Winter, 1980.

Sutherland, S.L. "The Politics of Audit: The Federal Office of the Auditor General in Comparative Perspective." *C.P.A.*, 29, 1, Spring, 1986.

Thomas, P. "Public Administration and Expenditure Management." *C.P.A.*, 25, 4, Winter, 1982.

Van Loon, R. "The Policy and Expenditure Management System in the Federal Government: The First Three Years." *C.P.A.*, 26, 2, Summer, 1983.

Veilleux, G., and Savoie, D. "Kafka's Castle: The Treasury Board of Canada Revisited." *C.P.A.*, 31, 4, Winter, 1988.

Wildavsky, A. "From Class Comes Opportunity: The Movement Toward Spending Limits in American and Canadian Budgeting." *C.P.A.*, 26, 2, Summer, 1983.

Freedom of Information, Secrecy, Security

Law Reform Commission. Access to Information: Independent Administrative Agencies. Ottawa: 1979.

Canada, Commisssion of Inquiry Concerning Certain Activities of the Royal Canadian Mounted Police [McDonald Commission]. *First Report: Security and Information.* Ottawa: S. and S., 1980; *Second Report: Freedom and Security Under the Law.* Vols. 1 and 2, August, 1981; *Third Report: Certain RCMP Activities and the Question of Government Knowledge.* August, 1981. (Ancillary studies: Edwards, J.L. *Ministerial Responsibility for National Security*, 1980; Franks, C.E.S. *Parliament and Security Matters*, 1980; Friedland, M.L. *National Security: The Legal Dimensions*, 1980.

Cordell, A.J. *The Uneasy Eighties: The Transition to an Information Society and Summary of Background.* Ottawa: Science Council of Canada, 1985.

Franks, C.E.S. *Dissent and the State.* Toronto: O.U.P., 1989.

MacDonald, B.A. "Information Management in the Public Service, Summary of Discussions," (with papers from the Eighteenth National Seminar of I.P.A.C.). *C.P.A.,* 29, 1, Spring, 1986.

McCamus, J.D., (ed.). *Freedom of Information: Canadian Perspectives.* Toronto: Butterworths, 1981.

Ontario. *Public Government for Private People, The Report of the Commission on Freedom of Information and Individual Privacy.* Toronto: Queen's Printer, 1980, 3 Volumes. (See also the Research Publications, Numbers 1 to 17.)

Pal, L. "Simpler Access." *P.O.,* 6, 3, April, 1985. [Access to Information]

Public Access to Information. Comments by Sharp, M., *et al. C.P.A.,* 29, 4, Winter, 1986.

Rankin, M. "National Security: Information, Accountability and the Canadian Security Intelligence Service." *U T.L.J.,* 36, 3, Summer, 1986.

Rowat, D.C., (ed.). *The Right to Know: Essays on Governmental Publicity and Public Access to Information.* Ottawa: Department of Political Science, Carleton University, 3rd ed., 1981.

Rowat, D.C., (ed.). *The Making of the Federal Access Act: A Case Study of Policy Making in Canada.* Ottawa: Dept. of Political Science, Carleton University, 1985.

Weller, G. "The Canadian Security Intelligence Service under Stress." *C.P.A.,* 31, 2, Summer, 1988.

Management

Aucoin, P., and Bakvis, H. *The Centralization-Decentralization Conundrum: Organization and Management in the Canadian Government.* Halifax: I.R.P.P., 1988.

Bellavance, M. "Le ministère de l'Education du Québec et la gestion de l'enseignement supérieur." *C.P.A.,* 24, 1, Spring, 1981.

Best Practices in the Management of Complex Operational Departments. Nineteenth National Seminar, *C.P.A.,* 30, 2, Summer, 1987.

Brown-John, L., LeBlond, A., and Marson, B. *Public Financial Management: A Canadian Text.* Toronto: Nelson, 1988.

Campbell, C., and Szablowski, G.J. *The Superbureaucrats: Structure and Behaviour in Central Agencies.* Toronto: Macmillan, 1979.

Chénier, J. "Sunsetting Programs." *P.O.,* 7, 3, April, 1986.

Coulombe, P.E. "Evolution de la gestion des ressources humaines dans la fonction publique québécoise." *C.P.A.,* 27, 3, Fall, 1984.

Langford, J., (ed.). *Fear and Ferment: Public Sector Management Today.* Toronto: I.P.A.C., 1986.

McLaren, R. "Organizing Government Departments: Experience from Saskatchewan." *C.P.A.,* 32, 3, Fall, 1989.

McQueen, J. "Integrating Human Resource Planning with Strategic Planning." *C.P.A.,* 27, 1, Spring, 1984.

Plumptre, T. *Beyond the Bottom Line: Management in Government.* Halifax: I.R.P.P., 1989.

Simeon, J. "The Neilsen Task Force on Program Review and the Reorganization of the Federal Government." *O.* 20, 1, 1989.

Savoie, D.J. "Government Decentralization: A Review of Some Management Considerations." *C.P.A.,* 28, 3, Fall, 1985.

Treasury Board of Canada. *Principles for the Management of the Public Service of Canada.* Ottawa: S. and S., 1983.
Treasury Board of Canada, Secretariat. *Roles and Responsibilities of the Treasury Board of Canada and the Public Service Commission of Canada in Personal Management.* Ottawa: Vol. 1, 1982.
Zussman, D., and Jabes, J. *The Vertical Solitude: Managing in the Public Sector.* Halifax: I.R.P.P., 1989.

Ombudsman

Canada. *Report of the Committee on the Concept of the Ombudsman.* Ottawa: Government of Canada, 1977.
Friedmann, K.A. "The Public and the Ombudsman: Perceptions and Attitudes in Britain and in Alberta." *C.J.P.S.*, X, 3, September, 1977.
Friedmann, K.A. "The Ombudsman in Nova Scotia and Newfoundland." *Dalhousie Law Journal*, 5, 2, 1979.
Friedmann, K.A., and Milne, A.G. "The Federal Ombudsman Legislation: A Critique of Bill C–43." *C.P.P.*, VI, 1, Winter, 1980.
Lavoie, J. *Le protecteur de citoyen du Québec.* Paris: Presses Universitaires, 1977.
Lundvik, U. *The Ombudsmen in the Provinces of Canada.* Edmonton: International Ombudsman Institute, 1981.
Rowat, D.C. "We Need a Federal Ombudsman Commission." *P.O.*, 3, 2, March–April, 1982.
Rowat, D. C. *The Spread of the Ombudsman Plan in Western Europe.* Edmonton: International Ombudsman Institute, Occasional Paper No. 21, 1983.
Rowat, D.C. *The Ombudsman Plan: The Worldwide Spread of an Idea*, Lanham, Maryland: University Press of America, 2nd ed. rev., 1986
Runciman, R. "Ombudsmen and Legislatures: Allies or Adversaries?" *C.P.R.*, 7, 3, Autumn, 1984.
Stacey, F. *Ombudsmen Compared.* Toronto: O.U.P., 1978.

Public Policy and Decision-Making

(See also Bibliography in Chapter 1.)

Atkinson, M.A., and Chandler, M.A., (eds.). *The Politics of Canadian Public Policy.* Toronto: U.T.P., 1983.
Baker, W. *Organization Under Stress: The Reorganization of Canada's Department of Public Works, 1970–73.* Ottawa: Centre for Policy and Management Studies, 1980.
Bella, L. "The Provincial Role in the Canadian Welfare State: The Influence of Provincial Social Policy Initiatives on the Design of the Canadian Assistance Plan." *C.P.A.*, 22, 3, Fall, 1979.
Bellavance, M. *Les politiques gouvernementales: élaboration, qestion, évalation.* Montréal: Agence d'Arc, 1985.
Blais, A., (ed.). *Industrial Policy.* Toronto: U.T.P., 1985.
Blais, A. *The Political Sociology of Industrial Policy.* Toronto: U.T.P., 1985.
Bonin, B., (ed.). *Immigration: Policy-Making Process and Results.* Toronto: U.T.P., 1985.
Brooks, S. *Public Policy in Canada: An Introduction.* Toronto: M.& S., 1989.
Bryden, K. *Old Age Pensions and Policy-Making in Canada.* Montreal: McG.-Q.U.P., 1974.

Bryden, K. "Public Input into Policy-Making and Administration." *C.P.A.*, 25, 1, Spring, 1982.

Campbell, R. *Grand Illusions: The Politics of the Keynesian Experience in Canada 1945–75*. Peterborough, Ontario: Broadview, 1987.

Chandler, M., and Chandler, W. *Public Policy and Provincial Politics*. Toronto: McG-H.R., 1977.

Campbell, R., and Pal, L. *The Real World of Canadian Politics: Cases in Process and Policy*. Peterborough, Ontario: Broadview Press, 1989.

Coleman, W.D., and Skogstad, G., (eds.). *Policy Communities and Public Policy in Canada: A Structural Approach*. Toronto: C.C., 1990.

Denton, T., and Burns, J. "A Better Way to Make the Budget." *P.O.*, 4, 3, May, 1983.

Dobell, A.R., and Mansbridge, S.H. *The Social Policy Process in Canada*. Montreal: I.R.P.P., 1986.

Doern, G.B., (ed.). *The Politics of Economic Policy*. Toronto: U.T.P., 1985.

Doern, G.B., and Morrison, R.W., (eds.). *Canadian Nuclear Policies*. Montreal: I.R.P.P., 1980.

Doern, G.B., and Phidd, R. *Canadian Public Policy: Ideas, Structure, Process*. Toronto: Methuen, 1983.

Doerr, A. "The Role of Coloured Papers." *C.P.A.*, 25, 3, Fall, 1982.

Dupre, J.S. *et al. Federalism and Policy Development: The Case of Adult Occupational Training in Ontario*. Toronto: U.T.P., 1973.

Dwivedi, O.P., (ed.). *Resources and the Environment: Policy Perspectives for Canada*. Toronto: M. & S., 1980.

French, R.D. *How Ottawa Decides: Planning and Industrial Policy- Making, 1968–1981*. Toronto: Lorimer, 2nd ed., 1984.

Good, D.A. *The Politics of Anticipation: Making Canadian Federal Tax Policy*. Ottawa: School of Public Administration, Carleton University, Lorimer, 1980.

Graham, K., (ed.). *How Ottawa Spends 1990–91: Tracking the Second Agenda*. Toronto: C.U.P., 1990. (Annual; previous editions edited by G.B. Doern, A. Maslove and M. Prince.)

Jenkin, M. *The Challenge of Diversity: Industrial Policy in the Canadian Federation*. Ottawa: Science Council of Canada, S. and S., 1983.

Johnston, R. *Public Opinion and Public Policy in Canada*. Toronto: U.T.P., 1985.

Jones, L.R., and McCaffery, J.L. *Government Response to Financial Constraints: Budgetary Control in Canada*. New York: Greenwood, 1989.

Kent, T. *A Public Purpose: An Experience of Liberal Opposition and Canadian Government*. Montreal: McG-Q.U.P., 1988.

Lutz, J. "Emulation and Policy Adoptions in the Canadian Provinces." *C.J.P.S.*, XXII, 1, March, 1989.

Macintosh, D. *et al. Sports and Politics in Canada: Federal Government Involvement since 1961*. Toronto: McG.-Q.U.P., 1987.

Malcolmson, P. "Zero-base Budgeting: Panacea or Gimmick?" *O.*, 14, 2, 1983.

Maslove, A.M., Prince, M.J., and Doern, G.B. *Federal and Provincial Budgeting*. Toronto: U.T.P., 1985.

McAllister, J.A. "The Fiscal Analysis of Policy Outputs." *C.P.A.*, 23, 2, Fall, 1980.

Ohashi, T.M. *et al. Privatization; Theory and Practice: Distributing Shares in Private and Public Enterprises*. Vancouver: Fraser Institute, 1980.

Paehlke, R., and Torgerson, D., (eds.). *Managing Leviathan: Environmental Politics and the Administrative State*. Peterborough, Ontario: Broadview, 1990.

Pal, L. "The Finance View: The Case of Unemployment Insurance, 1970–1978." *C.T.J.*, 33, 4, July-August, 1985.

Pal, L. *State, Class, and Bureaucracy: Canadian Unemployment Insurance and Public Policy*. Montreal: McG.-Q.U.P., 1988.

Pal, L. *Public Policy Analysis: An Introduction*. Toronto: Methuen, 1987.

Paquin, M. "La répartition du pouvoir de décision dans l'administration publique: l'apport de la théorie de l'organisation." *C.P.A.*, 23, 4, Winter, 1980.

Phidd, R.W., and Doern, G.B. *The Politics and Management of Canadian Economic Policy*. Toronto: Macmillan, 1978.

Prince, M.J., and Chenier, J.A. "The Rise and Fall of Policy Planning and Research Units: An Organizational Perspective." *C.P.A.*, 23, 4, Winter, 1980.

Pross, P., and McCorquodale, S. *Economic Resurgence and the Constitutional Agenda: The Case of the East Coast Fisheries*. Kingston: Queen's University, 1987.

Rowat, D. *Cases on Canadian Policy-making*. Ottawa: C.U.P., 1988.

Savoie, D. "La bureaucratie représentative: une perspective régionale." *C.J.P.S.*, XX, 4, December, 1987.

Savoie, D. *The Politics of Public Spending in Canada*. Toronto: U.T.P., 1989.

Schultz, R.J. *Federalism, Bureaucracy, and Public Policy: The Politics of Highway Transport*. Montreal: McG.-Q.U.P., 1980.

Simeon, R. "Studying Public Policy." *C.J.P.S.*, IX, 4, December, 1976.

Skogstad, G. *The Politics of Argricultural Policy-Making in Canada*. Toronto: U.T.P., 1987.

Solomon, P.H. "Government Officials and the Study of Policy-Making." *C.P.A.*, 26, 3, Fall, 1983.

Stevenson, G. *The Politics of Canada's Airlines: From Diefenbaker to Mulroney*. Toronto: U.T.P., 1987.

Taylor, M.G. *Health Insurance and Canadian Public Policy: The Seven Decisions that Created the Canadian Health Insurance System*, rev. ed. Montreal: McG.-Q.U.P., 1988.

Trebilcock, M.J. *et al. The Choice of Governing Instrument*. Ottawa: E.C.C., 1982.

Woodside, K. "Policy Instruments and the Study of Public Policy." *C.J.P.S.*, XIX, 4, December, 1986.

Regulation

Baldwin, J.R. *The Regulatory Agency and the Public Corporation: The Canadian Air Transportation Industry*. Cambridge: Massachusetts: Ballinger, 1975.

Brown-John, C.L. *Comprehensive Regulatory Agencies: An Introduction*. Toronto: Butterworths, 1981.

Buchan, R.J. *et al. Telecommunications Regulation and the Constitution*. Montreal: I.R.P.P., 1982.

Doern, G.B., (ed.). *The Regulatory Process in Canada*. Toronto: Macmillan, 1978.

Economic Council of Canada. *Reforming Regulation*. Ottawa: 1981.

Globerman, S. *Cultural Regulation in Canada*. Montreal: I.R.P.P., 1983.

Janisch, H.N., *et al. The Regulatory Process of the Canadian Transport Commission*. Ottawa: Law Reform Commission, 1978.

Kane, T. *Consumers and the Regulators: Intervention in the Federal Regulatory Process*. Montreal: I.R.P.P., 1980.

Regulating the Regulators: Science, Values and Decisions. Ottawa: Science Council of Canada, 1982.

Schultz, R.J. *Federalism and the Regulatory Process*. Toronto: Butterworths, 1979.

Stanbury, W.T., (ed.). *Studies on Regulation in Canada*. Toronto: Butterworths, 1979.

Stanbury, W.T., (ed.). *Government Regulation: Scope, Growth, Process*. Ottawa: E.C.C., 1980.

Stanbury, W.T., and Lermer, G. "Regulation and the Redistribution of Income and Wealth." *C.P.A.*, 26, Fall, 1983.
Stanbury, W.T., and Thompson, F. *Regulatory Reform in Canada*. I.R.P.P., 1982.
Woodrow, B., and Woodside, K. *The Introduction of Pay-TV in Canada*. Montreal: I.R.P.P., 1983.

Royal Commissions

Aucoin, P. "Royal Commissions and Task Forces as Mechanisms of Program Review." *Canadian Journal of Program Evaluation*. 2, 2, Oct–Nov, 1987.
Bashevkin, S. "Does Public Opinion Matter? The Adoption of Federal Royal Commission and Task Force Recommendations on the National Question." *C.P.A.*, 31, 1, Fall, 1988.
Canada, Library of Parliament, Information and Reference Branch. *Commissions of Inquiry Under the Inquiries Act, Part I, 1867 to Date*. Ottawa: August, 1983. (Photocopied typescript)
Canada. *Report of the Royal Commission on the Economic Union and Development Prospects for Canada*, [Macdonald Commission]. Ottawa: S. and S., 1985, 3 volumes and 72 research studies.
Canadian Public Policy. Special issue on "The Macdonald Report," 12, 1, February, 1986.
Drache, D., and Cameron, D., (eds.). *The Other Macdonald Report*. Toronto: Lorimer, 1985.
Fox, P. "Royal Commissions." In *The Canadian Encyclopedia*, Vol. III, Edmonton: Hurtig, 1985.
Gorecki, P.K., and Stanbury, W.T., (eds.). *Perspectives on the Royal Commission on Corporate Concentration*. Toronto: Butterworths, 1979.
Henderson, G.F. *Federal Royal Commissions in Canada, 1867–1966: A Checklist*. Toronto: U.T.P., 1967.
Provincial Royal Commissions of Inquiry, 1867–1982: A Selective Bibliography. Ottawa: National Library of Canada, 1986.
Resnick, P. "State and Civil Society: The Limits of a Royal Commission." *C.J.P.S.*, 20, 2, June, 1987.

THE JUDICIARY

THE STRUCTURE AND PERSONNEL OF THE CANADIAN JUDICIARY

Carl Baar

STRUCTURE OF THE CANADIAN COURT SYSTEM

The Canadian court system was conceived as a unitary system, in explicit contrast to the dual system of courts in the United States. Thus, while the United States has both a federal court system (for federal law and a diversity of citizenship matters) and 50 state court systems, Canada's constitution envisaged a national court of last resort, limited specialized federal courts, and fully developed provincial court systems. What makes the Canadian system unitary is the provision in section 96 of the original British North America Act that judges of the provincial superior, county, and district courts would be appointed by the federal government. Section 96 thus contemplated a system of provincially organized and administered courts staffed by federally appointed judges.

This constitutional scheme is still the basis of contemporary Canadian court structure. The Supreme Court of Canada sits atop the national judicial pyramid.

From an article in K. Holland and J. Waltman, *The Political Role of Law Courts in Modern Democracies*, London and Basingstoke, Macmillan, 1988, revised and updated by the authors in May 1990. By permission. U.S. rights courtesy of St. Martin's Press.

Directly below are the provincial Courts of Appeal. Below the courts of appeal are the superior courts of each province. Names vary: Court of Queen's Bench (Alberta, Saskatchewan, Manitoba, and New Brunswick), Supreme Court (British Columbia, P.E.I., Nova Scotia, and Newfoundland), cour supérieure (Quebec), and the Ontario Court of Justice (General Division). The ten superior courts function as central trial courts for their provinces, following the English model of the High Court of Justice, whose members sit centrally and travel on circuit to various county towns and trial centres. However, as populations and caseloads have increased, superior court judges now reside in an increased number of major cities within each province. The days when B.C. Supreme Court justices resided only in Vancouver and Victoria, or—in the most extreme case—when some 50 Ontario High Court justices resided in Toronto and travelled to over 40 other trial centres, are now history.

At the next level in the traditional trial court hierarchy were the county or district courts, originally conceptualized on the English scheme as a set of local courts which would "bring justice to every man's [sic] door." Throughout Canada's first hundred years every province except Quebec had a system of county or district courts. However, since 1973 the county or district courts of eight provinces have been legislated out of existence, merged with their respective superior courts. After British Columbia and Ontario phase out their county and district courts in the summer of 1990, only Nova Scotia's county courts will remain, and a provincial study commission is likely to recommend some form of merger for that province as well.

The merger of county courts with superior courts has not altered the basic constitutional scheme of provincially organized courts staffed by federally appointed judges. However, other developments over the past 20 years have multiplied the exceptions to the original design. At the federal level, a Federal Court of Canada, with trial and appeal divisions, was created in 1971. It took over the specialized financial jurisdiction of the century-old Exchequer Court, and added jurisdiction over appeals from federal administrative agencies, long a responsibility of provincial superior courts. In 1983 a Tax Court was created by upgrading the status of the pre-existing Tax Review Board.

More fundamental evolutionary changes have occurred in the provinces, where courts have grown up staffed by provincially appointed judges. In the late nineteenth and early twentieth centuries these were the minor courts staffed by lay magistrates and justices of the peace, with authority to hear minor civil matters, violations of local by-laws, and preliminary matters in criminal cases (authorizing warrants, setting bail, hearing first appearances). By the mid-twentieth century a number of provinces had devolved jurisdiction over family and juvenile matters to provincial appointees, and expanded their responsibility for criminal cases. Lawyers began being appointed to replace lay magistrates. By the 1960s first Quebec, then Ontario renamed the magistrates judges, and magistrates' courts provincial courts. Throughout the 1970s other provinces followed suit. By the 1980s only Newfoundland still appointed lay judges to its Provincial Court, and it then sends the appointee to law school after a period of three years on the bench.

The evolution of provincial courts has added a substantial layer to the court systems of every province, to the point where the reorganization of provincial courts has moved into a new consolidation phase in the country's two largest provinces. By the mid-1980s Quebec had developed an elaborate set of courts staffed by provincially appointed judges: the Cour de sessions de la paix (the Sessions Court) with jurisdiction over all criminal cases not tried by a jury; the Tribunal de la jeunesse (Youth Court) for young offenders and social welfare matters; and a Provincial Court with civil jurisdiction in matters involving up to $15,000, well beyond the traditional small claims limit. At the close of the decade these separate courts were merged into a single Cour du Québec organized into eight regions. Within each region separate divisions were retained for criminal, civil, and youth matters, but the existence of a single court would allow the shifting of provincially appointed judicial personnel across divisions as work required. In Ontario three provincial court divisions— criminal, family and civil—were operating by the late 1980s, but the same legislation that merged the two section 96 trial courts into a single General Division consolidated the Criminal Division and Family Division of the Provincial Court into a single Provincial Division (with the civil division abolished and its judges and jurisdiction transferred to the new General Division).

By 1990 every province vests all juvenile and substantial criminal jurisdiction in its Provincial Court; seven provincial courts have extensive family law jurisdiction, and four have civil jurisdiction, usually from one to three thousand dollars. Quebec also has a unique layer of municipal courts—four with full-time judges and 140 with part-time judges—separate from the Cour du Québec; these courts handle minor criminal offences, provincial offences, and by-law violations.

The growth and development of courts staffed by provincially appointed judges represents the major change in Canadian court structure since Confederation, and can be accounted for by a number of factors:

1. Pressure to upgrade the status and professionalism of lower court judges.

2. Willingness of federally appointed judges to give up jurisdiction over "minor" matters.

3. Willingness of the federal Parliament to enlarge the jurisdiction of provincial courts in criminal matters.

4. Federal-provincial conflict over appointments. It is not unusual for different parties to be in power at different levels of government, encouraging a province to appoint "its judges" rather than having the courts staffed by members of that province's bar chosen by the party in power in Ottawa. Some provinces have magnified the issue still further; thus, one reason for Quebec having expanded the jurisdiction of its provincially appointed judges to the

greatest extent has been the desire of nationalist governments to minimize the impact of Ottawa on institutions within the province.

5. A traditionally liberal interpretation of the BNA Act by the Supreme Court of Canada and the Judicial Committee to allow the devolution of jurisdiction, particularly in family matters. This factor has been minimized in recent years, as the Supreme Court has restricted the devolution of jurisdiction in a number of cases involving criminal, family, and administrative law matters.

A court structure paralleling that of the ten provinces has also been established in the Yukon and the Northwest Territories. Each has a Supreme Court staffed by federally appointed judges (one for the Yukon, two for the NWT). Each has a Territorial Court analogous to the provincial courts south of the fifty-fourth parallel, with judges appointed by the territorial government. There is also a Yukon Court of Appeal, along with a Northwest Territories Court of Appeal, but these are "foreign" courts: the British Columbia Court of Appeal serves that function for the Yukon, the Alberta Court of Appeal for the NWT.

The growth of provincial courts staffed by provincially appointed judges has also altered the purely hierarchical nature of the court systems of the provinces. Traditionally, a serious criminal case would begin in a magistrates' court and then move to a county court or a superior court for trial. Now, while that path would still be followed in a jury trial, the overwhelming majority of serious criminal cases are dealt with in the Provincial Court. In practice, in criminal as well as family matters, the provincial courts have become identified as subject-matter specialists rather than merely the lowest layer in a hierarchical system.

While trial courts have evolved a division of labour based on subject matter, appeals courts continue to hear a full range of issues. More important for comparative purposes, constitutional matters are not segregated from other legal issues. Any of the courts described in this section can rule on a constitutional question arising in litigation validly before it. At the same time constitutional issues were rare prior to enactment of the Charter of Rights in 1982. While the Supreme Court of Canada might hear a half-dozen constitutional matters per term in the 1970s, it averaged two or three annually for most of its history.

An overview of trial court structural change must also note an even more fundamental proposal, now pending in Ontario and under consideration in other provinces, to create a single trial court by combining the section 96 superior court and the Provincial Court. The Ontario proposal, labelled "Phase Two" because it was made at the same time as "Phase One" proposals to merge the province's supreme and district courts and consolidate its provincial court divisions, would unify the remaining trial courts. Unification has already been widely proposed for family matters; Ontario would expand that concept to criminal matters. At the same time, however, full unification would alter the traditional supervisory role of the superior courts, substantially change procedure in criminal cases, and shift all appointments (at least in form) to the federal government—controversial issues that have generated opposition from lawyers and judges. The debate over unification could dominate court structural issues, at least in English Canada, for several years.

JUDICIAL PERSONNEL

Canadian judgeships are appointed positions. No Canadian judge is elected, nor do Canadian judges (even in Quebec's civil law system) follow the career model of continental Europe. Judges are appointed by the cabinet (either federal or provincial), with the major role played by the minister of justice/ attorney general. Federally appointed judges must be members of the bar of the province for which they are appointed (under sections 97 and 98 of the Constitution Act, 1867), and in addition "a barrister or advocate of at least ten years standing at the bar of any province" (under section 3 of the Judges Act, a federal law that establishes the number of and salaries for federally appointed judges). Provincially appointed judges have similar minimum qualifications, as lay judges have been phased out of all provinces save Newfoundland over the past decade.

Since the late 1960s a variety of efforts have been made to constrain the discretion of cabinets over judicial appointments, on the grounds that partisan political considerations have reduced the overall quality of persons appointed to the bench. . . . [See the following article.]

Despite these trends, the importance, even if not dominance, of partisan considerations in judicial appointments has been a fact of Canadian political life. It is reflected in the oft-repeated maxim that "to become a judge in the United States, you must be elected; to become a judge in Canada, you must be defeated." Efforts to improve the quality of judicial appointments have had some effect, but have rarely led to the appointment of a Conservative by a Liberal government, a Liberal by a Conservative government, or a New Democratic party member by either one. The issue of patronage in judicial appointments reached a new level of public concern in the summer of 1984 when the federal Liberal government on the eve of an election call appointed a number of party faithful (including the minister of justice himself) to judgeships, and other long-term appointments. The appointments became an election issue and the opposition Conservatives swept to power, giving added visibility to the work of the Canadian Bar Association study committee on judicial appointments created during the same period. The CBA recommendations went in the direction of the nominating council model used for provincially appointed judges in British Columbia, but the federal government's eventual scheme stopped short of constraining the minister of justice to the extent demanded by critics of patronage. The new system of federal appointments does shift the focus of applications and screening away from Ottawa to committees in each province, but experience is not yet sufficient to pass judgment on the impact of the new system.

The most formalized and best-known constraints on judicial appointments affect the Supreme Court of Canada. By law and convention the nine members of the court must represent the various regions of the country. The fundamental difference between Quebec and the nine common law provinces is reflected in the requirement that three of the nine justices must come from the bar of "the civil law province." This one-third representation was incorporated in the original Supreme Court Act of 1875, and is now included in the patriated 1982 Constitution. The other six justices are by convention distributed geographically by region. The four Atlantic provinces are entitled to one justice. Thus when the justice from Nova Scotia retired in the fall of 1984, no one contemplated appointing a replacement from outside the region. The four western provinces have normally had two justices, and Ontario has had three. The two western justices normally rotate among the four provinces, so it has been unlikely that a justice from one western province will be succeeded by a justice from the same province. Deviations are minimal. For example, in the early 1980s an Ontario vacancy was filled by an appointee from British Columbia, in anticipation of the retirement the following year of an Alberta appointee, who was in turn replaced by a person from Ontario.

Regional representation is the most clearly established pattern in appointments to the Supreme Court of Canada. It also serves partially as a proxy for other forms of representation. Thus, linguistic differences have been traditionally reflected by the 6–3 division between common law provinces and Quebec, producing three French-Canadian justices. At certain points in the court's history, one of the three civil law appointees has been an anglophone, but the current pattern of all three Quebec justices being francophones is likely to hold. No francophone appointments from outside Quebec had ever been made until 1984, when an Ontario appointment went to Quebec-born Gerald LeDain; a year later, the Atlantic province appointment went to Gérard LaForest of New Brunswick, the first Acadian to sit on the Supreme Court of Canada. Only two justices have ever been appointed from outside the British Isles or French ethnic communities. The first was Bora Laskin, of Russian-Jewish heritage, appointed in 1970, and currently sitting is John Sopinka, of Ukrainian background. While the first woman was not appointed to the Supreme Court of Canada until 1982, the court now includes three women, the largest proportion of women on a court of last resort anywhere in the common law world.

The other major constraint on Supreme Court appointments beyond regional representation is the convention that appointees have been superior court judges, and normally judges of the courts of appeal of the provinces. Eight of the nine current justices had been appeal judges prior to their appointments. Justices have occasionally been appointed directly from the senior ranks of the bar (Sopinka is the current example), but only once in the last 80 years has a cabinet minister or member of Parliament been named directly to the Supreme Court. Canadian practice thus diverges sharply from American practice, where justices of the Supreme Court of the United States have been more commonly drawn from legal and political rather than judicial careers.

While this Canadian practice may remove the Supreme Court of Canada further from the centre of political debate, it may also have reinforced the more legalistic and restrained approach to constitutional issues that has contrasted the Canadian and the American Supreme Court.

Recruitment and representational patterns are more varied among judges appointed to provincial courts by the federal government. Court of appeal judges are commonly appointed from the superior trial courts, but often directly from the senior ranks of the legal profession, and sometimes from among legal academics or high-ranking officials in provincial or federal ministries of justice. Representation of particular areas or communities within a province may figure in an appointment, but the most important explicit factor may be the need for an individual with a particular subject matter competence (for example, criminal or family law).

Section 96 (that is, federally appointed) trial judges are sometimes drawn from the provincially appointed judiciary, but this pattern is not common. The most common internal judicial "promotion" is currently from a superior trial court to a court of appeal. Members of the bar chosen for section 96 judgeships are typically drawn from the litigation bar, and range from 45 to 60 years of age. Women and ethnic minorities are more frequently appointed than in the past (no woman held a superior court judgeship until 1969). At the provincial court level judges are typically appointed before reaching age 45, and are often drawn from specialized criminal or family law practices.

All federally appointed and all full-time provincially appointed judges serve during good behaviour, that is, they hold continuing appointments and are removable only for cause or upon reaching a mandatory retirement age. Every judicial appointment now made in Canada is subject to mandatory retirement: age 75 for the Supreme Court of Canada and all section 96 courts, and age 65 for most provincially appointed judges. Some provinces also provide for continued service after age 65 at the discretion of a chief judge or judicial council. Federally appointed judges can opt for supernumerary (semi-retired) status, with reduced salary and reduced workload, but may not continue after age 75.

Tenure during good behaviour begs the question of how misbehaviour is defined. There is no written code of ethics for judges; even unofficial attempts to develop such a code have been discouraged. At the same time the norms of judicial conduct that have developed have been relatively rigid, in keeping with the caution and conservatism of Canadian judges. Judges may, but rarely do, write books, give public speeches, or testify before public bodies on judicial needs. Federally appointed judges are prohibited by the federal Elections Act from even voting, lest their impartiality be questioned in litigation over a contested election. Thus, controversial judicial conduct could be deemed misbehaviour in Canada even when it may be acceptable within other legal cultures.

Discussions of removal of judges focus primarily on the methods for removal. Thus superior court judges and justices of the Supreme Court and Federal Court of Canada may be removed only by joint address—a procedure in which the governor general, acting on behalf of the cabinet, presents a bill of particulars to the Senate and House of Commons, which is then subject to debate and vote. No Canadian judge has ever been removed by joint address, although three attempts at removal were made in the nineteenth century, and one in 1967. County and district court judges may be removed by order in council, that is, a cabinet directive made without reference to Parliament, and that procedure was used on two occasions in the 1930s.

In the early 1970s the Canadian Judicial Council, consisting entirely of federally appointed judges, was created and given authority to investigate complaints against section 96 judges, and make recommendations to the cabinet. Legally, a Council recommendation is not required for the pre-existing removal procedures to be invoked, but it is likely that such a recommendation will be required as a matter of practice. No judge has been removed under the new provisions; however, judges have resigned pending or following a Council investigation. Early in 1990 two judges retired from the Nova Scotia Court of Appeal shortly before the most controversial inquiry in Council history: an examination of the conduct of the five judges who ruled in 1982 on Donald Marshall Jr.'s conviction for a murder he did not commit.

Provincial removal mechanisms are more diverse. Councils exist to consider removal or censure in a majority of provinces, but responsibility generally has remained in the hands of provincial cabinets, sometimes operating under vague or broad mandates. A number of provincially appointed judges have been removed in recent years, while for most of Canadian history provincially appointed judges have held office at pleasure. Thus, security of tenure is a relatively new concept at this level of the court system.

One set of judicial officials still hold office at pleasure, or for carefully circumscribed terms: the justices of the peace appointed by the various provinces. Justices of the peace generally carry out quasi-judicial administrative functions (for example, signing arrest warrants), but they have increasingly taken on the minor functions associated with the provincial police magistrates of the early twentieth century. Justices of the peace in many provinces do bail hearings and handle parking tickets; in Ontario they deal with a wide range of provincial offences such as liquor violations, highway traffic matters, and even environmental offences. Justices of the peace have generally not been viewed or studied as judicial officers, but as provincial court judges have grown in status, the JPs have come to take on an increasing volume and variety of routine judicial tasks, and their uncertain status has become the object of public debate and well-publicized court battles.

No formal training is required of any judicial appointee; however, an increasing range of in-service training programs have been developed across the country. Most important has been the recent creation of the Canadian Judicial Centre, which co-ordinates existing annual seminars on procedural and substantive law and orientation programs for newly appointed section 96 judges, and has designed programs of its own on subjects as diverse as computers, caseflow management, and gender bias. Training programs for provincially appointed judges vary considerably from national workshops and conferences to provincial and regional seminars on new legislation.

The wide range of Canadian courts suggests that Canadian judges range equally widely across the status hierarchy. Thus provincially appointed judges may be drawn from practitioners in small towns and in criminal and family practices—hardly the legal elite of Canada or most other countries. On the other hand superior court judges at both trial and appeal level are commonly drawn from among high-prestige members of the bar of various provinces. Prominent counsel have rejected judicial appointments—usually because of the difficulty of moving to another community, taking a cut in salary, or enduring the travel associated with the circuit systems in some superior courts. However, despite the narrowness sometimes bred by considerations of political patronage, the judiciary has been drawn from members of the legal profession active in their own communities and equal in status to other professionals and community leaders. ● ● ●

MULRONEY'S JUDICIAL APPOINTMENTS AND THE NEW JUDICIAL ADVISORY COMMITTEES

Peter H. Russell and Jacob S. Ziegel

I

The extent of the federal government's judicial appointing power in Canada is not widely recognized. Most Canadians are surprised to learn that each year the federal government appoints 50 to 60 judges. Appointments to the Supreme Court of Canada receive considerable public attention. But even when turnover on the Supreme Court is brisk—and it has never been brisker than in recent years—there will be only one or two appointments a year. There is very little public awareness that under section 96 of the Constitution the federal government appoints the judges of the higher courts of all the provinces (and territories). Nor has the increase in the federal government's judicial appointing power through the growth of the lower federal courts—the Federal Court and the Tax Court—been generally recognized.

An abridged version of an article which was completed by the authors in May, 1990 and which will be published in a forthcoming issue of the *University of Toronto Law Journal*. Professor Russell is a member of the Department of Political Science at the University of Toronto and Professor Ziegel is a member of the Faculty of Law at the same institution. The abridgement, which has been prepared by the editor, is published with the permission of the authors and University of Toronto Press.

The significance of the federal appointing power stems not only from the number of judges who are federally appointed each year, but from the positions they hold in the Canadian judicial hierarchy. While provincially and territorially appointed judges outnumber the federally appointed judiciary (approximately 1250 to 750), section 96 of the Constitution bars them from performing any of the essential functions of a superior court. Thus, most important civil and criminal trials as well as virtually all appellate jurisdiction in provincial as well as federal matters are the responsibility of federally appointed judges. Clearly, the selection of these judges will have an enormous impact on the quality of justice throughout the country.

Who is responsible for selecting these judges? Formally, the appointing power is vested in the governor general or the governor general in council. In practice, the power of selecting these judges has been concentrated in the hands of the minister of justice and the prime minister. The minister of justice plays the lead role in bringing forward to cabinet the names of persons to fill most of the judgeships at the disposal of the federal government. Other members of the cabinet, particularly strong regional ministers, may have a considerable influence on the selection process. The prime minister is directly involved in the appointment of Supreme Court justices, the chief justice of the Supreme Court, and chief justices of the provincial superior courts, the Federal Court of Canada, and the Tax Court of Canada. Since the mid-1970s each minister of justice has appointed a "special advisor" to his staff to collect the names of judicial candidates. From 1967 to 1988 a committee of the Canadian Bar Association advised the minister of justice on whether or not persons being considered by the government for appointment were qualified to act as judges.

In theory the minister of justice's and the prime minister's answerability to Parliament renders them accountable for these federal judicial appointments. That has always been the justification for keeping the power of appointment in ministerial hands. In practice this theory has had little, if any, reality. One looks in vain through the pages of *Hansard* for any review of the quality of judicial appointments. There is, on the contrary, a well-established tradition that specific appointments should not be questioned in Parliament. The new procedure for parliamentary review of order-in-council appointments has not been extended to the judiciary. The information given to the public through the press release announcing each appointment is very sparse, confined to setting out the bare bones of the appointee's *professional* career.

That a more systematic review of the quality of federal judicial appointments may be needed is evident from the criticism the federal appointing process has received in professional circles over the years. . . . In the 1980s the Canadian Bar Association (CBA) and the Canadian Association of Law Teachers (CALT) conducted studies of the judicial appointing process in Canada. Both found serious fault with the federal process and recommended the adoption of broadly based nominating committees.

The direct target of most of this criticism has been the excessive role of patronage, or "political favouritism," in the selection of federally appointed judges. There is abundant evidence that a good connection with an influential member of the governing party in Ottawa has unduly influenced the selection of judges. The point of this criticism is not that an involvement in partisan politics should disqualify a person for appointment to the bench, but that partisan connections should be irrelevant in identifying the most talented candidates for judicial office.

. . . The nominating committees proposed by the CBA and the CALT in 1985 aimed at bringing to bear on the selection process a much broader and stronger base of local intelligence. Although the final decision on whom to appoint would remain with responsible ministers, nominating committees in each province and territory representing both levels of government, the bench, the bar, and the general public would play the primary role both in seeking out and in evaluating candidates. The reports also envisaged—and this was a key issue—that the nominating committees would compile a short list of candidates who, in their view, were best qualified to fill a given vacancy.

The Mulroney government rejected this proposal. Instead, Raymon Hnatyshyn, the then minister of justice, unveiled a plan in the spring of 1988 which, in effect, amounts to replacing the screening committee of the CBA with new provincial and territorial screening committees. These committees bear a superficial resemblance to the committees proposed by the CBA and CALT in that their (much smaller) membership includes the same elements as were to constitute the nominating committees. But the key point is that the Hnatyshyn committees were not to be nominating committees. Their function, like that of the CBA's National Committee on the Judiciary, is not to seek out and develop a short list of the best candidates, but simply to report on whether or not persons whose names are sent to them from Ottawa are "qualified." . . .

II

The data we have collected on the Mulroney administration's first term judicial appointments [1984–1988] are presented in this section. . . .

First, we should note the distribution of the 228 judicial appointments. . . . By far the bulk of these appointments, over 90 percent, are to the section 96 courts, that is, the provincial and territorial courts presided over by federally appointed judges. . . .

Sixty-seven of the 228 appointments were promotions within the judicial system. . . .

There is a real promotional ladder from the highest provincial trial court (the General Jurisdiction Trial Court) to the Court of Appeal, and then to the Supreme Court of Canada. Indeed, over half of the appointments to the provincial courts of appeal were "elevations" from the superior trial court. It is pleasantly surprising to find that as many as 13 judges were promoted from the lower provincial courts and that these were spread across the country. In the past such promotions have been very rare. Perhaps their increased frequency reflects the improvements many of the provinces have made in their method of selecting judges....

Women comprised 17.5 percent of the appointees, and these appointments were spread proportionately among the various positions and levels. Certainly this is a clear improvement over the situation at the beginning of the decade when Pauline Jewett reported to the House of Commons that only 3 percent of the federally appointed judiciary were women ... this suggests a conscious effort at affirmative action to redress the gender imbalance on the bench.

It would appear that this move in the direction of appointing more women judges has not been at the expense of merit. All but one of the 13 appointees whose professional reputation were in the lower of categories—"fair" or "weak"—were men. It is indeed an "old boys network" that enables less qualified lawyers to obtain appointments.

... There is certainly no evidence of a youth movement in these recent appointments. Indeed, 24 percent of the lawyers appointed had over 30 years of professional experience and must have been in their late fifties or older at the time of their appointment.

... the great majority of appointees have come from private practice. There were complaints during the Trudeau years that the federal government was appointing too many of its own government lawyers to the bench. Our data show very few such appointments during the Mulroney first term and more appointments from the provincial attorney general ministries than from the federal Department of Justice....

... Because of the broad jurisdiction of our higher courts, criminal law will figure prominently in the judicial work of all the appointees except the 11 appointed to the Federal Court and to the Tax Court. Yet, only one in ten of the appointees specialized in criminal law. We understand that this is a long-established trend....

[There was] a distinct tendency for appointees to come from smaller law firms. Indeed, 58 percent of those on whom we have this item of information came from firms with ten lawyers or less. Only four came from what might be considered large firms— that is, firms with one hundred or more lawyers. It would appear that whatever influence the large big city law firms have in lobbying government, they do not use it to obtain judicial appointments for their members. The underrepresentation of large firms may also have something to do with the fact that the incomes earned by partners in these firms will nearly always considerably exceed judicial salaries....

... Bar politics rivalled, and at times even surpassed, partisan politics as the main avenue of judicial recruitment.... Just over one-half of the appointees (and here we include information on promoted judges as well as new appointees) have held at least one leadership position in their provincial law society, the local branch of the Canadian Bar Association, or some similar organization.... Nearly one in three at some time took a leading role in the activities of the Canadian Bar Association, for example, by serving on some committee or in an executive office. . . .

. . . It seems safe to conclude that scholarly or academic experience is not regarded by the federal government as an important credential for judicial appointment.

We turn now to information about the political background of the appointees. We organized this information by placing each appointee in one of five categories: those who had a major involvement with the Conservative party, those who had a lesser involvement or association with that party, those with *no known* political association, those who have had a relatively low level of involvement with an opposition party, and those who have been involved in a major way with an opposition party. A major involvement with a party includes running for elected office under the party's banner, serving as a party official or "bagman," and active involvement in election or leadership campaigns. Lesser partisan associations include minor constituency work, financial contributions, as well as close personal and professional associations with party leaders. . . .

The appointment of a lawyer associated with an opposition party may well be politically motivated. There are well-known incidents in Canadian history where a political opponent received an appointment in order to make it easier to elect a government member in the appointee's constituency. . . .

What our "political background" data do show is that patronage, or "political favouritism," to use the CBA's phrase, continued to have a major influence on judicial appointments during the first Mulroney government. One hundred and eight of the appointees, just under half of the total number (48 percent), had known political associations with the Conservative party. For just under a quarter—24 percent—this was a strong involvement with the party. Mr. Mulroney's government, it would appear, so far as judicial appointments are concerned, did not exercise its options much differently from those of the Trudeau/Turner Liberal administration. . . .

In five provinces—Manitoba, New Brunswick, Nova Scotia, Prince Edward Island, and Saskatchewan—the percentage of appointees with a known connection to the Conservative party ranges from P.E.I.'s 71.5 percent to Manitoba's 87.5 percent. This finding closely resembles the Canadian Bar Association Committee's findings on judicial appointments from 1978 to 1985. It reported that in New Brunswick, Nova Scotia, Prince Edward Island, and Saskatchewan "political favouritism has been a dominant, though not the sole, consideration; most appointees have been active supporters of the party in power." . . .

Political favouritism has not been concentrated on appointments to the lowest level. On the contrary, the percentage of appointees with ties to the Conservative party was greater—over 50 percent—among those appointed to the provincial courts of appeal and superior courts than to the county or district courts, where it was 40 percent. In this respect our results differ from those of the Bar Committee, which found that under the Trudeau and Clark administrations the influence of political favouritism was generally greater at the county and district court level.

While the influence of political favouritism is less marked [in regard to promotion], it is still strong: 29 of the 66 judges and one court administrator who were promoted by the Mulroney administration were known to have had an involvement or association with the Conservative party, while 11 had opposition party affiliations. . . .

This observation is disturbing. Judicial promotions have always been a delicate issue. In the common law world some observers have expressed concern that the desire for promotion may colour an appointee's conduct on the bench so that he or she will be well thought of by the appointing authority. . . . Our data show, however, that promotions are frequent and not necessarily based on merit, and that some may well have a political flavour. In the next section we note that promotions have been excluded from the reformed judicial appointing process. . . .

On the whole the persons appointed by the Mulroney government in its first term appear to be well regarded within the profession. Nearly a quarter of them are considered outstanding, and 86 percent are considered at least to be good. It is significant that appointees with a high political profile, at either end of the spectrum, were not rated as highly as those with weak political connections: for example, only 19.2 percent of appointees with strong Conservative party connections were rated as outstanding, compared with 30.85 percent with weak Conservative party linkages, and 41.7 percent for appointees with slight opposition party linkages. However, these differentials become much less significant when the percentages for outstanding and outstanding/ good reputations are combined in each of the categories. Only 13 appointees, 6.1 percent of those appraised, were considered by both assessors to be weak or only fair.

On the basis of this part of our research, some might question the need to reform the traditional appointing system. . . . But we think there are at least three reasons for dissatisfaction. . . .

First, it should be noted that among the most poorly regarded appointees— those considered fair or weak—there is a disproportionately large number with political connections to the government—10 out of 13, or nearly 77 percent. . . .

Second, we believe Canadians should strive for a system that is designed so far as possible to appoint not simply persons who will make acceptable judges but those who are best qualified for judicial service. . . .

Third, there is also the danger of producing a judiciary which is ideologically imbalanced. Canadians have reason to be especially sensitive to this danger now that their judges are playing such a significant policy-making role in interpreting the Charter of Rights and Freedoms. We should be looking for a reasonable balance in the political and philosophical perspectives represented on the bench. . . .

Finally, but not least, . . . there is a highly subjective component in assessing the merits of appointees, a difficulty which argues strongly in favour of using committees to assess candidates for judicial office. With the benefit of hindsight we now also recognize that our categories were too broad and that there is a large gap between an "outstanding" appointee and a "good" one. . . .

III

Let us now turn to the federal government's new judicial appointment process—the process that will govern federal judicial appointments in the Mulroney government's second term.

. . . The new process breaks the appointing system into three basic components: recruitment, screening, and selecting. The changes in the process concern the first two of these components, recruitment and screening, not the crucial matter of selection.

For the recruitment stage of the process the commissioner of Federal Judicial Affairs replaces the minister of justice and the minister's staff. The commissioner's office was created in 1977 to provide an independent administration of the salaries and benefits of federally appointed judges. Under the new system a secretariat working under the Commissioner, currently Pierre Garceau, will "solicit and maintain records of all those interested in appointment to a federal judicial position." . . . The Commissioner then refers the names of all who meet the statutory requirement to the appropriate provincial or territorial assessment committee.

These committees are said to "constitute the heart of the new appointment system." There is to be a five-person committee for each province or territory made up as follows:

- a nominee of the provincial or territorial law society
- a nominee of the local branch of the Canadian Bar Association
- a federally appointed judge nominated by the chief justice of the province or territory
- a nominee of the provincial attorney general or territorial minister of justice
- a nominee of the federal minister of justice.

At least as initially conceived, these committees are confined to performing strictly a vetting, or screening, function. For each of the names submitted to them they are "empowered to make either of two assessments: 'qualified' or 'not qualified.' " . . .

Even the committees' limited screening function does not apply to all candidates. Candidates for "elevation" (that is, for promotion) are not to be screened by the committees. In the government's view "it would be inappropriate for the provincial committee, because of the nature of its composition, to attempt to rate the performance of a judge in office." So the minister of justice through consultation with "the chief justice and attorney general concerned" will decide who is "qualified" for promotion to a higher court. Also, Supreme Court of Canada appointments are entirely exempt from the new procedure, as the federal government is relying on the adoption of the Meech Lake Constitutional Accord and the arrangements it contains for appointing supreme court justices to regulate their future mode of selection.

Thus, the new provincial and territorial assessment committees—the "heart" of the new system—are supposed to play only a negative role in the selection process. They may remove from consideration those who are deemed to be not qualified. . . . And even in performing this negative function, the committees' decisions are not authoritative, for the minister of justice retains "the ultimate right to recommend an appointment regardless of a negative assessment by a committee."

The new assessment committees were appointed in the fall of 1988 and began to function early in 1989. There has been no public account of how these committees are functioning. . . .

IV

Based on the analysis of the data and other developments described in this report, our conclusions are that there were only marginal improvements in the system of selection of judges by the Mulroney government during its first term of office. Political patronage in judicial appointments was still pervasive. . . .

The federal government's much delayed response to the CALT and CBA recommendations was deeply disappointing and does little to address the basic flaws in the appointing system. . . . The fact remains that the new committees are essentially toothless. They are not authorized to rank candidates, they have no staff to assist them to do well the limited task assigned to them, and they are not even required and, for the most part, do not have the resources to interview candidates before determining whether or not they are qualified for judicial office. . . .

The committees face the further invidious task of being asked to give reasons for not deeming a candidate suitably qualified and of having their assessments reversed on appeal by the minister of justice, a politician who does not strike us as well qualified to serve in an appellate capacity. Most disturbing of all, the new screening process will not prevent the federal government from continuing to promote candidates on political and personal grounds or to appoint even highly qualified candidates for the wrong reasons. There is an almost irresistible inference that the wish to cling to the important political patronage power, if not for the sake of the patronage then for the power itself, is the federal government's primary reason for refusing to allow the advisory committees the right to rank candidates. ● ● ●

BIBLIOGRAPHY

(See also the Bibliography in Chapter 2.)

Abella, R. "Equality, the Public and the Legal System." *Q.Q.*, 95, 4, Winter, 1988.

Barnes, J. "The Law Reform Commission of Canada." *Dalhousie Law Journal*, 2, 1, February, 1975.

Batten, J. *Lawyers*. Toronto: Macmillan, 1980.

Batten, J. *In Court*. Toronto: Macmillan, 1982.

Batten, J. *Judges*. Toronto: Macmillan, 1986.

Bernier, I., and Lajoie, A., (eds.). *The Supreme Court of Canada as an Instrument of Political Change*. Toronto: U.T.P., 1985.

Canadian Bar Association. *Report on the Appointment of Judges in Canada*. Ottawa: 1985.

Griffiths, C.T., Klein, J. J., and Verdun-Jones, S.N. *Criminal Justice in Canada*. Toronto: Butterworths, 1980.

Law Reform Commission. *Judical Review and the Federal Court*. Ottawa: S. and S., 1980.

Millar, P.S., and Baar, C. *Judical Administration in Canada*. Montreal: McG.-Q.U.P., 1981.

Morton, F.L. *Law, Politics and the Judicial System in Canada*. Calgary: University of Calgary Press, 1984.

Mullan, D.J. *"The Federal Court Act: A Study of the Court's Administrative Law Jurisdiction*. Ottawa: Law Reform Commission, 1978.

Ratner, R.S., and McMullan, J.L., (eds.). *State Control: Criminal Justice Politics in Canada*. Vancouver: U.B.C.P., 1988.

Russell, P.H. *Bilingualism and Biculturalism in the Supreme Court of Canada*, Document of the Royal Commission on Bilingualism and Biculturalism, Ottawa: Queen's Printer, 1970.

Russell, P.H. "The Political Role of the Supreme Court in Its First Century." *C.B.R.*, 53, 3, September, 1975.

Russell, P.H. "History and Development of the Court in National Society: The Canadian Supreme Court." *Canada-United States Law Journal*, 3, Summer, 1980.

Russell, P.H. "Constitutional Reform of the Judicial Branch, Symbolic Versus Operational Consideration." *C.J.P.S.*, 17, 2, June, 1984.

Russell, P.H. "The Supreme Court and Federal-Provincial Relations: The Political Use of Legal Resources." *C.P.P.*, 11, 2, June, 1985.

Russell, P.H. *The Judiciary in Canada: The Third Branch of Government*. Toronto: McG.-H.R., 1987.

Snell, J.G., and Vaughan, F. *The Supreme Court of Canada: History of an Institution*. Toronto: U.T.P., 1985.

Snell, J.G. "The Deputy Head in the Canadian Bureaucracy: A Case Study of the Registrar of the Supreme Court of Canada." *C.P.A.*, 24, 2, Summer, 1981.

Wilson, B. "Decision-making in the Supreme Court." *U.T.L.J.*, 36, 3, Summer, 1986.

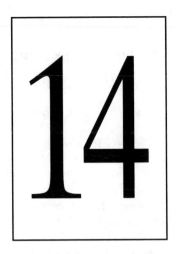

GOVERNMENT PUBLICATIONS

A DESCRIPTION AND GUIDE TO THE USE OF CANADIAN GOVERNMENT PUBLICATIONS

Brian Land

A government publication has been defined as "any publication originating in, or issued with the imprint of, or at the expense and by the authority of, any office of a legally organized government or international organization."* Government publications range in scope from the formal papers, journals and debates of our legislatures, and from the annual reports of the various departments, agencies, boards and commissions, to the more popular periodicals and pamphlets for tourists, and to how-to-do-it booklets for the handyman or housewife.

The following paragraphs describe some of the more important publications of the federal government such as the journals, debates, committee reports, statutes, regulations, gazettes, and reports of commissions of inquiry, and review some of the more important guides, catalogues, indexes, and checklists for identifying publications issued by the federal, provincial, and territorial governments.

---

*The ALA Glossary of Library and Information Science, edited by Heartsill Young, Chicago, American Library Association, 1983, p. 106.

Revised June 1990 for this book by the author, who is Executive Director, Ontario Legislative Library and Professor, Faculty of Library and Information Science, University of Toronto.

PART 1. PARLIAMENTARY PUBLICATIONS

1. DAILY AGENDA

House of Commons

Projected Order of Business/Ordre projeté des travaux is a brief, unofficial outline of the anticipated order of business of the House for each sitting day. In addition to listing the order of business and the text of motions to be debated, it notes the length of time Members may speak and any special order attached to an item of business. The *Projected Order of Business*, which is subject to change without notice, is not subsequently cumulated or republished.

The *Order Paper and Notice Paper/Feuilleton et Feuilleton des Avis*, a bilingual pamphlet, is issued daily by the House of Commons when it is in session. The **Order Paper** is the official agenda for the House and lists all of the items of business that may be brought forward during the day's sitting including the order of business, orders of the day and government orders, private members' business and questions. It also contains a "Weekly Review of Business", providing information on items introduced or considered during the week, which is subsequently published in the weekly *Status of Bills and Motions*. The *Notice Paper* contains notice of all items Members wish to introduce in the House including questions, notices of motion for the production of papers, private Members notices, and notices relating to the report stage of bills. The *Order Paper and Notice Paper* is not subsequently cumulated or republished.

The *Monthly Supplement to the Order Paper: Questions/Supplément mensuel au Feuilleton: Questions* commenced publication January 17, 1983. Written questions appear on the *Notice Paper* once when notice is given and are then transferred to the "Questions" section in the daily *Order Paper* for the remainder of the month. At the beginning of each succeeding month, all outstanding questions are printed in the *Monthly Supplement to the Order Paper: Questions*. When a question has been answered, made an Order for Return or withdrawn, this fact is noted in Part II of the *Monthly Supplement*.

Senate

A section, "Order of Business/Ordre des travaux," appears in the *Minutes of the Proceedings of the Senate/Procès-verbaux du Sénat*, a bilingual pamphlet which is issued daily when Senate is in session. This section constitutes the official agenda for each day's business and includes information about the presentation of petitions, reading of petitions, reports of committees, notices of inquiries, notices of motions, question period, orders of the day, inquiries and motions. It is not subsequently cumulated or republished.

2. DAILY PROCEEDINGS

House of Commons

Votes and Proceedings/Procès-verbaux is published daily in pamphlet form in a bilingual format when the House is in session and constitutes its official record of decisions and other transactions. The *Votes and Proceedings* include the daily transactions of the House, the Speech from the Throne, the Address in Reply to the Speech from the Throne, proclamations regarding the summoning and dissolution of Parliament, titles of bills read and assent to bills, recorded votes in the House, Speaker's rulings, lists of returns and reports deposited with the Clerk, a list of Orders in Council passed each month, rosters of committees and reports of committees dealing with bills and estimates. The *Votes and Proceedings* are bound at the end of each session to form the *Journals* of the House of Commons.

Senate

The *Minutes of the Proceedings of the Senate/Procès-verbaux du Senat*, published daily in pamphlet form in a bilingual format when the Senate is in session, constitutes its official record. It corresponds to the *Votes and Proceedings* of the House of Commons and contains similar information. At the end of each session, the *Minutes of the Proceedings* and such appendices as it is decided to include are published with an index in the bound *Journals of the Senate*.

3. JOURNALS

House of Commons

The bound *Journals/Journaux*, published in a bilingual format since 1976, constitute the permanent official record of the proceedings of the House. They consist of the edited and corrected version of the daily *Votes and Proceedings* to which are added lists of the Ministry and parliamentary secretaries; standing, special, joint committees and subcommittees; legislative committees, members of the House of Commons; constituencies represented in the House; principal officers and officials of the House; Acts passed during the session; and minutes of proceedings and evidence of standing, special, joint and legislative committees and subcommittees not tabled in the House. An index to *Journals* is included in the final volume for each session. Reports of Commons committees are included in the index under the names of the respective committees, e.g., Agriculture Standing Committee.

Senate

The bound *Journals of the Senate of Canada/Journaux du Sènat du Canada*, published in a bilingual format, constitute the permanent official record of the proceedings of the Senate. The *Journals* incorporate the edited and corrected version of the daily *Minutes of the Proceedings* to which are added special lists similar to those published in the *Journals* of the House of Commons. The *Journals* contain an index which includes reports of standing and special committees gathered together under "Committees." Other reports are indexed under "Reports, Orders in Council and other Documents laid on the Table."

4. DEBATES (HANSARD)

The most familiar of the parliamentary publications are the debates, which give an almost complete verbatim account of what is said in Parliament. The several volumes each session record the daily debates of the House, messages of the Governor General and varying information such as lists of members of the House and of the ministry. Like those of the British Parliament, debates of the Canadian Parliament are referred to as "Hansard" in honour of the Hansard family, which reported and published the British debates in the nineteenth century.

The only example of printed debates as we know them today which were published before Confederation are the *Parliamentary Debates on the Subject of the Confederation of the British North American Provinces*, published in 1865 and republished in 1951. An *Index to Parliamentary Debates on the Subject of the Confederation of the British North American Provinces*, compiled by M.A. Lapin and edited and revised by J.S. Patrick, was published by the Public Archives of Canada in 1951.

The debates of the early Canadian Parliaments, as in most countries, were not officially reported, and the only records are, with a few exceptions, the so-called *Scrapbook Debates*, which are in the Library of Parliament. These debates consist of clippings from contemporary newspapers, which have been mounted in scrapbooks and for which handwritten indexes have been prepared. The *Scrapbook Debates* cover the period from Confederation to 1874, and are available on microfilm, having been published by the Canadian Library Association, Ottawa, in 1954. From 1870 to 1872 three volumes of debates of both Houses were published but were unofficial in origin. These are referred to as the *Cotton Debates* after the *Ottawa Times* reporter, John Cotton, who covered the sessions. Not until 1875 did the House of Commons itself begin reporting its debates. From 1875 to 1879 the contract for reporting these debates was awarded to private reporters, but in 1880 an official staff of reporters was appointed to secure continuity and uniformity.

House of Commons

The *Debates* of the House of Commons covering the first three sessions of the first Parliament, November 6, 1867 to May 12, 1870, were collated and edited from contemporary newspaper accounts by Professor Peter B. Waite of Dalhousie University under the auspices of the Library of Parliament as part of the

1967 Centennial project of the Parliament of Canada. These reconstituted debates were subsequently published by the Queen's Printer.

The daily edition of the *House of Commons Debates: Official Report (Hansard)* is issued in pamphlet form during each session of Parliament on the morning following each day's sitting and contains the speeches in English as delivered and the English translation of speeches delivered in French. There is a corresponding French-language edition entitled *Débats de la Chambre des communes: Compte rendu officiel (Hansard)* which contains the speeches in French as delivered and the French translation of speeches delivered in English. Prior to publication of the daily edition, preliminary proofs of their speeches or remarks are sent to members for suggested changes, which must be confined to the correction of errors and essential minor alterations. At the end of each session revised bound volumes are published as *House of Commons Debates: Official Report.*

The *Debates* for each Wednesday contain several useful appendices: officers of the House; an alphabetical list of members of the House of Commons with their constituencies, addresses, and political affiliations; a list of standing and standing joint committees, special committees, and legislative committees, with the membership of each; members of the ministry (i.e., cabinet) according to precedence; and a list of parliamentary secretaries. In recent years an index to the daily House of Commons *Debates* has been issued in pamphlet form at intervals during the session; at present, the index is issued four times a year. The complete revised index for each session is subsequently published in bound form.

Senate

The *Debates of the Senate* are also referred to as "Hansard" from their prototype, the parliamentary debates of Great Britain. For the years from 1870 to 1872 inclusive unofficial nonverbatim versions of the Senate debates appear in the *Cotton Debates* referred to above. As part of the 1967 Centennial project cited to above, *Debates of the Senate* covering the first three sessions of the first Parliament, November 6, 1867 to May 12, 1870, were edited by Professor Waite and subsequently published by the Queen's Printer. In 1871 the Senate began publishing its own *Debates.* From 1871 to 1916 the contract for reporting was awarded to various persons, but in 1917 an official staff was appointed by the Senate to provide this service.

The *Debates of the Senate: Official Report (Hansard)*, like those of the House of Commons, are recorded and published in pamphlet form daily when the Senate is in session. The corresponding French-language edition is titled *Débats du Sénat.* As in the House of Commons, the same opportunity is afforded members of the Senate to amend or correct errors and omissions in the daily *Debates,* so that the bound edition at the end of the session may be complete and correct. The amount and extent of corrections in *Hansard* are subject to discussion and agreement in each House, respectively.

The *Debates of the Senate* for the first Thursday of each month contain several lists: officers of the Senate; the ministry (i.e., the cabinet); a list of senators according to seniority, alphabetically and by provinces and territories; and a list of standing, special, and joint committees with their membership. Each Thursday issue of the *Debates of the Senate* includes an appendix, "Progress of Legislation," which indicates the status of government bills as well as members' and senators' public bills. Occasionally, an index to the *Debates of the Senate* is issued in pamphlet form at intervals during the session, and a complete revised index is published in bound form at the end of each session.

5. SESSIONAL PAPERS AND ANNUAL DEPARTMENTAL REPORTS

During the course of each session of Parliament, certain reports and papers are received which, when deposited with the Clerk and tabled in the House or Senate, are designated as sessional papers.

House of Commons

In the House of Commons each sessional paper, whether printed or unprinted, is assigned a distinctive number and listed in the daily *Votes and Proceedings* along with the name of the minister or parliamentary secretary who deposited the paper with the clerk. Published sessional papers are listed in the various checklists and catalogues issued by the Canadian Government Publishing Centre; photocopies of current unpublished sessional papers are available for a fee from the Journals Directorate of the House of Commons.

Senate

Some sessional papers are deposited with the Clerk of the Senate and tabled in the Senate as well as in the House of Commons. In addition, the leader of the government in the Senate may table other reports and papers for the information of Senators. As in the case of the House of Commons, some sessional papers are printed and listed in the checklists and catalogues of publications issued by the Canadian Government Publishing Centre. Photocopies of current unpublished sessional papers may be obtained for a fee from the Journals Branch of the Senate.

Sessional Papers Series

From 1867–68 to 1925, sessional papers were published in a collected series. This series included most of the reports that came before Parliament and were ordered printed with the exception of the reports of committees which were printed as appendices to the *Journals* of each House. There were several volumes of sessional papers for each session, and each volume includes both an alphabetical and numerical list of the papers for that session. The series is not paged continuously, and indexes refer to the number of each document rather than to pages. Much of the material published in the *Sessional Papers* series was also published elsewhere, e.g., a branch report might appear in the *Sessional Papers*, be published separately, and published as part of a departmental report, as well as being issued in both English and French. The government ceased publication of the *Sessional Papers* series in 1925 after having published some 923 volumes since Confederation, but the departmental reports formerly included were continued in the series of *Annual Departmental Reports* described below.

General Indexes to the Journals of the House and to Sessional Papers

In order to facilitate their use, a consolidated *General Index to the Journals of the House of Commons of Canada, and of the Sessional Papers of Parliament* was published on five occasions covering the following periods: 1867–1876; 1877–1890; 1981–1903; 1904–1915; and 1916–1930.

Annual Departmental Report Series

From 1924-25 to 1929-30 *Annual Departmental Reports* were issued in a series. This series included reports of some commissions as well as continuing the departmental reports issued in *Sessional Papers* up to 1924. Since this series also duplicated material issued in other forms, it was dropped in 1930 as an economy measure. Annual departmental reports are now published separately by the respective departments, agencies, boards, and commissions.

6. PARLIAMENTARY COMMITTEES AND THEIR PUBLICATIONS

House of Commons

Unlike the royal commission or commission of inquiry, which are creatures of the executive, the parliamentary committee is a vital part of the legislative arm of the government—the House of Commons and the Senate. Parliamentary committees in the House are of four kinds: the Committee of the Whole House, standing committees, special committees, and legislative committees.

The main function of the Committee of the Whole House, which consists of all members of the House sitting as a committee, is deliberation rather than inquiry, and clause-by-clause consideration of money bills or, on occasion, other bills to expedite their passage. Discussion is facilitated by relaxation of the formal rules of debate and party discipline. The proceedings of the Committee of the Whole House are reported without a break in the *Debates* and in the *Journals*, and there is no special problem in locating them.

Standing committees are provided for in the *Standing Orders of the House of Commons*. Standing committees are appointed for the life of a Parliament to examine matters relating to specified government departments, or to consider subject matters referred to them by the House, and to report their findings and recommendations to the House for its consideration. The *Standing Orders* give each standing committee an ongoing mandate or order of reference, and also provide for certain automatic referrals such as annual reports and Order in Council appointments and nominations. Standing committees may on their own initiative or by order of the House appoint some of their members to constitute a subcommittee to consider a matter that has been referred to the main committee. Subsequently, the subcommittee reports its findings and recommendations to its parent committee, which in turn may report to the House.

The standing committees, which are listed in the *Standing Orders*, are: aboriginal affairs; agriculture; communications and culture; consumer and corporate affairs and government operations; privileges and elections; energy, mines, and resources; environment; external affairs and international trade; finance; forestry and fisheries; health and welfare, social affairs, seniors, and the status of women; human rights and the status of disabled persons; industry, science, and technology, regional and northern development; justice and solicitor general; labour, employment and immigration; management and members' services; multiculturalism and citizenship; national defence and veterans affairs; public accounts; and transport.

The *Standing Orders* also make provision for standing joint committees, which are made up of a proportionate number of members of both the House of Commons and the Senate. At present, these include official languages and scrutiny of regulations.

Special committees are appointed by the House on an *ad hoc* basis to inquire into or deal with specific matters. The purpose of each special committee, its powers, the number of members, and the date on which it is to report to the House are set out in its order of reference, and the committee ceases to exist when it makes its final report to the House, when its deadline expires, or at the end of the session.

Legislative committees, the newest type of House committee, are appointed on an *ad hoc* basis to examine and inquire into bills on a clause by clause basis. Unless the House orders otherwise, all bills except those based on a supply motion are referred to a legislative committee after second reading. Once a legislative committee has reported the bill to the House, with or without amendment, it ceases to exist.

The deliberations of House Committees—standing, special, and legislative—are published in pamphlet form in bilingual format as *Minutes of Proceedings and Evidence/Procès-verbaux et témoignages* as their meetings occur. Separate indexes to the respective *Minutes of Proceedings and Evidence* of standing committees are published at the end of the session; in the case of special committees and legislative committees, an index to the *Minutes of Evidence and Proceedings* is published after the final report has been made to the House. At present, *Proceedings* less than 100 pages in length are not indexed.

From the late 1960s to 1981 the complete text of all House of Commons committee reports was published in its *Votes and Proceedings*. In addition, each report was published in an issue of the committee's *Minutes of Proceedings and Evidence*. Substantive committee reports were also published separately as special issues. On December 11, 1981, the Speaker informed the House that committee reports on bills and estimates tabled in the House would continue to be published both in its *Votes and Proceedings* and in the committee *Minutes of Proceedings and Evidence*. But since that time committee reports on subject matter other than bills and estimates have been published in the regular issues of the committee's *Minutes of Proceedings and Evidence* only and not in the *Votes and Proceedings* or as special issues. A list of reports of committees of the House is included in its *Journals* under "Appendices to *Journals*." In addition, committee reports are indexed in the *Journals* under the names of the respective committees.

Senate

Standing committees set up under the Rules of the Senate include: aboriginal peoples, agriculture and forestry; banking, trade and commerce; energy and natural resources; fisheries; foreign affairs; legal and constitutional affairs; national finance; social affairs, science and technology; standing rules and orders; and transport and communications. The Senate may also establish special committees to consider and report on particular subjects.

The deliberation of committees of the Senate, as well as joint committees of the Senate and the House, are published in pamphlet form in a bilingual format as their meetings occur under the title of *Proceedings/Délibérations*. Reports of Senate committees may be published in the respective committee *Proceedings*, in the *Minutes of the Proceedings of the Senate*, and in the *Debates of the Senate*. Occasionally, Senate committee reports, especially those dealing with the study of a special subject, have not been printed in these publications but have been published separately. A list of Senate committee reports appears in the index to its *Journals* under "Committees."

7. BILLS, ACTS, AND STATUTES

Bills

After first reading all bills originating in the House of Commons or Senate are printed in pamphlet form in a bilingual format with English and French text in parallel columns. Bills originating in the House of Commons are distinguished by the letter "C" and numbered chronologically as introduced. The numbers from C-1 to C-200 have been reserved for government bills; numbers from C-201 to C-1000 have been allocated to private members' public bills; and C-1001 upwards to private members' private bills. The progress of bills through the three readings and committee stage is recorded in the *Order Paper and Notice Paper* previously cited. At the end of each session a list of Acts passed is included in the *Journals* of the House; in addition, a list of bills introduced during the session is included in the index to the *Journals* under "Bills, House of Commons."

Bills originating in the Senate are distinguished by the letter "S" and numbered chronologically as introduced. They also are printed in pamphlet form in a bilingual format. The progress of bills through the three readings and committee stage is recorded in the *Minutes of the Proceedings of the Senate* previously cited. At the end of each session a list of bills may be found in the index of the *Journals* of the Senate under "Bills, General data respecting."

After third reading, bills of the House of Commons and Senate are printed as passed. Parliament issues no bound volume of bills that have failed to pass, and few libraries other than the Library of Parliament and provincial legislative libraries keep such bills beyond the session during which they were proposed.

Status of Bills

Cumulative information on the respective stages of public or private bills before the House of Commons may be found in *Status of Bills and Motions*. This publication, begun in October 1986, is issued weekly by the House when it is in session and is intended as a guide to each stage of bills and motions before it. Coverage includes all government bills, private members' public bills and private bills. The Senate publishes similar information about the status of bills. Its "Progress of Legislation" appears each Thursday as an appendix to the *Debates of the Senate*.

Acts

When a bill has successfully passed through three readings of both the House of Commons and Senate and received royal assent from the Governor General, it becomes an Act. Each Act is then assigned a chapter number, coupled with the name of the reigning sovereign and the regnal year(s) of the session, e.g., 36-37 Elizabeth II, c. 65, Canada-United States Free Trade Agreement Implementation Act, 1988. Since February 1990, bills that have received Royal Assent have been published as a series of Individual Chapters. New Acts are also published in *Part III* of the *Canada Gazette* in order to expedite their distribution to the public. New Acts may also be published by the Queen's Printer in pamphlet form known as Separate Chapters. In addition, Acts may be published from time to time in unofficial pamphlet form as Office Consolidations, with or without the related regulations, for the convenience of court officials, lawyers, and the public generally.

Statutes of Canada

The Acts passed each year are gathered together in one or more volumes entitled *Acts of the Parliament of Canada/Lois du Parlement du Canada*. In bound form the Acts are more commonly known as the *Statutes of Canada/ Statuts du Canada*. Part 1 of the *Statutes* consists of Public General Acts; Part II of Local and Private Acts. Currently, each annual volume of *Statutes* has a table of contents listing Acts by their short title, a separate English and French Index to Public General Acts, a list of Proclamations of Canada, and a Table of Public Statutes from 1907 to date.

In 1983 a *Table of Local and Private Acts: Statutes of Canada, 1867 to 1979/ Tableau des Lois d'Intérêt local ou privé: Statuts du Canada, 1867 à 1979* was published in bilingual format under the authority of the Statute Revision Act. This table lists all local and private Acts, other than those dealing with divorce, enacted since 1867, including any amendments thereto or the repeal thereof, and published in the *Statutes of Canada*. The first supplement covering the period from March 27, 1979, to November 4, 1984, was published in 1985.

Revised Statutes of Canada

The *Revised Statutes of Canada*, which bring legislation amended since its original passage up to date, have been issued six times since Confederation: 1886, 1906, 1927, 1952, 1970 and 1985. The *Revised Statutes of Canada, 1985, (R.S.C., 1985)*, proclaimed in force December 12, 1988, are the first to be available in both a bound and a loose-leaf edition, although only the bound volumes have evidentiary value. The eight basic volumes of the *R.S.C., 1985* include laws enacted on or before December 31, 1984. However, as a general rule amendments enacted but not yet in force at the end of 1984 are excluded from the text.

The complete set of the *R.S.C., 1985* consists of 16 volumes made up of eight volumes of statutes, five supplemental volumes covering Acts passed or amended between December 31, 1984, and December 12, 1988; one volume of appendices; one volume containing the Table of Concordance; and a one-volume index. The *English Index* was prepared by the Canadian Law Information Council and the *Index francais* was prepared by the Societe québécoise d'information juridique. The contents of the index to both the bound and loose-leaf editions will be updated and replaced periodically.

8. THE CANADA GAZETTE, ORDERS IN COUNCIL AND REGULATIONS

Canada Gazette

The *Canada Gazette*, published under the authority of the Statutory Instruments Act, is issued in three parts in a bilingual format and is the official gazette of Canada. All matters under the control of Parliament and requiring publication are published in the *Canada Gazette* unless some other mode of publication is required by law.

The *Canada Gazette, Part I,* is published every Saturday and contains notices of a general character, certain Orders in Council required to be published by the enabling Act but not by the Statutory Instruments Act, proposed regulations, notices of hearings and decisions, proposed government purchases, and various other classes of statutory notice placed by both the government and private sector. Orders in Council are designated by the letters PC (for Privy Council), followed by the year and a chronological number. Extras and supplements of *Part I* are published as required. Each issue is indexed, and there are also non-cumulative quarterly indexes but no annual index.

The *Canada Gazette, Part II*, is published every second Wednesday with special editions as required. It contains proclamations into force of Acts passed into law, all regulations as defined in the Statutory Instruments Act, and certain other classes of statutory instruments and documents required to be published therein. Each item in *Part II* is listed by its registration number assigned in the Privy Council Office as either statutory orders and regulations (SOR) or Statutory Instruments other than regulations (SI) and the numbers are consecutive within each series and year. All regulations and other statutory instruments (other than regulations), and other documents that have been made under statutory or other authority and that were in force at any time since January 1 of the current calendar year, are indexed in the *Consolidated Index of Statutory Instruments*, a quarterly publication. For instruments in force in other than the current calendar year, reference should be made to the *Consolidated Index* of December 31st of the year in question.

The *Canada Gazette, Part III*, contains the public Acts of Canada and their enactment proclamations as soon as is reasonably practicable after they have received Royal Assent in order to expedite their distribution to the general public. *Part III* contains certain other ancillary information, including a list of proclamations of Canada from the date of the previous number to the date of the most recent number, showing when Acts have been proclaimed in force. From time to time, a Table of Public Statutes from 1907 to date, and a Table of Acts and the Ministers responsible for their administration are published. *Part III* is published whenever there are sufficient Acts to warrant publication.

The three parts of the *Canada Gazette* include the separate publication of Supplements, Extra Editions to meet specific requirements, Extracts and Indexes. These publications are published at various intervals during the year.

Orders in Council and Regulations

Orders in Council were first published in the *Statutes of Canada* for 1872. From 1874 to 1939, certain statutory orders and regulations having the force of law were published in the preliminary section of the *Statutes of Canada*. On two occasions during this period, consolidations were published by the federal government: *Orders in Council, Proclamations, Departmental Regulations, etc., Having the Force of Law in the Dominion of Canada* (1875), and *Consolidated Orders in Council of Canada* (1889).

Since 1939 there has been a steady increase in the number of statutes that confer power to make orders and regulations on the minister. The systematic publication of statutory orders "of general or widespread interest or concern" is a fairly recent development. It began in 1940 with the publication of *Proclamations and Orders in Council (relating to the War)*. Eight volumes of this series were published covering the period from August 26, 1939 to September 30, 1942. During the period from 1940 to 1942 the federal government also published three volumes of the consolidated *Defence of Canada Regulations*. In October 1942 a new publication, *Canadian War Orders and Regulations*, began publication. Its title changed to *Statutory Orders and Regulations* in October 1945, and it ceased publication in January 1947.

Since January 1, 1947 provision has been made for publication of statutory orders and regulations in the *Canada Gazette, Part II*. In 1950 a *Statutory Orders and Regulations Consolidation* was published, bringing together all statutes that conferred the power to make orders or regulations, and all orders and regulations having a general effect. A later consolidation was published in 1955.

A "Summary of Orders in Council Passed During the Month," which lists Orders in Council, is tabled in the House of Commons and is included in its *Votes and Proceedings*. For the period 1867–1971 the Privy Council Office has prepared an annual index of orders in council which is available on microfilm from the National Archives of Canada. Unpublished Orders in Council for the current Parliament may by acquired at cost from the Privy Council Office; older unpublished Orders in Council may be purchased at cost from the National Archives of Canada.

Consolidated Regulations of Canada

In 1978 the *Consolidated Regulations of Canada* were published in 19 volumes. Briefly stated, the consolidation includes: statutory orders and regulations published in the 1955 consolidation of *Statutory Orders and Regulations*; regulations, statutory instruments, and other documents published in the *Canada Gazette, Part II*, since the 1955 consolidation; and regulations that, prior to the date of the coming into force of the Statutory Instruments Act, were not published in the *Canada Gazette* but were registered after that date with the Clerk of the Privy Council and were in force on December 31, 1977 and are of general application. It contains as well certain regulations not included in the 1955 consolidation and certain unpublished statutory orders that are still in force and of general application.

To assist users in updating the *Consolidated Regulations of Canada, 1978*, a special two-volume issue of the *Canada Gazette, Part II*, was published. The material contained in the special issue is essentially a re-publication of regulations and other instruments published in 1978 that amend or revoke regulations found in the 1978 consolidation. It does not include regulations published as new regulations during that period.

Each amending regulation and other instrument appearing in the first 16 issues of *Part II* of the *Canada Gazette* in 1979 was footnoted by title and section number or subdivision thereof to indicate its relation to the 1978 *Consolidated Regulations* where applicable. Commencing with the 17th issue, any material published in *Part II* of the *Canada Gazette* and affecting the 1978 consolidation refers in the body to the text to a chapter number and, if re-numbering has taken place, to new section numbers. In addition, each amendment or revocation of a regulation or other instrument is footnoted to cite previous relevant amendments of each section or subdivision thereof that is being amended or revoked.

For information about regulations and other instruments in force since January 1, 1978, reference should be made to the *Consolidated Index of Statutory Instruments* for the most recent year. This is a quarterly index that cumulates annually from the date of the consolidation.

PART 2.   PUBLICATIONS OF COMMISSIONS OF INQUIRY AND TASK FORCES

REPORTS OF ROYAL COMMISSIONS AND COMMISSIONS OF INQUIRY

Royal commissions, or commissions of inquiry as they are now generally called, are appointed under the terms of the Inquiries Act or other empowering statutes by the executive arm of government, i.e., the cabinet, to carry out full and impartial investigations of specific problems and to report their findings so that decisions may be reached and appropriate action taken. When the cabinet has approved of the setting up of a royal commission, or commission of inquiry, it issues an order in council which is published in *The Canada Gazette, Part 1*, giving the terms of reference, powers, and names of the commissioners. The commission is usually empowered to call witnesses and to hold public hearings. When the commission has completed its investigation and made its report to the prime minister, the report is subsequently published. There has been a recent trend toward the commissioning of research studies that are prepared as supplements to the main report; for example, 72 research studies were published as background papers for the *Report of the Royal Commission on the Economic Union and Development Prospects for Canada*. Usually commissions are popularly referred to by the names of their chairmen; hence, the so-called "Deschenes report" is the 1986 *Report of the Commission of Inquiry on War Criminals*, chaired by Mr. Justice Jules Deschenes.

A useful reference work for locating royal commission and commission of inquiry reports is *Federal Royal Commissions in Canada, 1867–1966; A Checklist*, by George F. Henderson, published by the University of Toronto Press in 1967. It has been updated by *Commissions of Inquiry under the Inquiries Act, Part 1, 1967 to Date*, compiled by Denise Ledoux and published in 1986 by the Information and Reference Branch of the Library of Parliament, Ottawa. In addition, *The Canada Year Book* contains a list of newly appointed royal commissions and commissions of inquiry, both federal and provincial, indicating the name of the chief commissioner or chairman and the date of appointment.

REPORTS OF TASK FORCES

The term "task force" became a common expression during World War II when it was used to describe a military force, frequently involving different services, assembled to undertake a specific task. In the jargon of government the term is used to describe a group of experts gathered together to tackle a particular problem of public concern. In Canada the use of task forces to help formulate government policy on such topics as labour relations, the government's role in sport, and housing became fashionable in the late 1960s. In its composition and operation the task force stands somewhere between a royal commission and a parliamentary committee. Usually, the task force is made up of academics and other experts from outside government who work closely with senior civil servants. The task force may commission special studies, invite briefs, and hold public hearings. A recent example is the Task Force on Program Review, chaired by Erik Nielsen, whose report was published in 1985-86.

PART 3. PUBLICATIONS OF THE FEDERAL COURTS

The principal publications of the judicial arm of the federal government consist of the reports of cases tried before the two federal courts, the Federal Court of Canada (formerly known as the Exchequer Court of Canada) and the Supreme Court of Canada. From 1876 to 1922 there was a series of *Reports of the Exchequer Court of Canada*; from 1923 to 1969 the series was known as *Canada Law Reports: Exchequer Court of Canada*; in 1970 the title was changed to *Canada Exchequer Court Reports*, and when the Federal Court replaced the Exchequer Court in 1971, its judgments were contained in a new series called *Canada Federal Court Reports*. From 1876 to 1922 there was also a series known the *Reports of the Supreme Court of Canada*; from 1923 to 1969 the series was called *Canada Law Reports: Supreme Court of Canada*; and since 1970 the series has been known as *Canada Supreme Court Reports*.

PART 4. BIBLIOGRAPHIES AND CATALOGUES
OF GOVERNMENT PUBLICATIONS

1. FEDERAL GOVERNMENT PUBLICATIONS

Bibliographies

There are several useful bibliographies and catalogues that can help identify government publications. One such guide is *Canadian Federal Government Publications; A Bibliography of Bibliographies*, by Mohan Bhatia, published in 1971 by the University of Saskatchewan and divided into three parts; general bibliographies, bibliographies of parliamentary publications, and bibliographies of departmental publications.

Although out of date, the manual on *Canadian Government Publications*, compiled by Marion V. Higgins and published in 1935 by the American Library Association, remains the outstanding historical and descriptive bibliography in its field. It includes federal publications beginning with the united Province of

Canada, 1841–1867. Publications are arranged according to the issuing office, and brief histories of the various governmental agencies are supplied along with a list of their publications. These publications are divided into two large groups; serial publications and special publications. For serials, inclusive dates of publication are shown with a note as to whether or not the reports appeared in the *Sessional Papers* series and *Annual Departmental Reports* series. The section on special publications includes all of these publications issued by each governmental agency that were not published in the *Journals* or *Sessional Papers*. There is a general subject index.

Government Publications Catalogues Issued Before 1953

For federal government publications issued prior to 1953, the indexes and catalogues available were incomplete, spasmodic, and originated from many difference sources. From 1892 to 1938 the *Annual Report* of the Department of Public Printing and Stationery contained a list of government pamphlets and miscellaneous monographs issued during the fiscal year and arranged according to the issuing agency. No bibliographical details were given except paging. From 1894 to 1927 this department also issued a *Price List of Government Publications* which was superseded by the *Catalogue of Official Publications of the Parliament and Government of Canada*. This latter publication was issued irregularly from 1928 to 1948 in different forms, later being known as the *Government Publications Annual Catalogue*. It was simply a list of titles and prices of all official publications procurable from the King's Printer, and no bibliographical details were supplied. It had supplements at intervals up to 1952, when it was replaced by a new series of daily, monthly and annual catalogues.

Government Publications Catalogues Issued Since 1953

In 1953 the Queen's Printer published the *Canadian Government Publications Consolidated Annual Catalogue*, a basic work which superseded the old *Annual Catalogue* of 1948 and its supplements to 1952. The *Consolidated Annual Catalogue* attempted to include all federal government publications in print as of September 1953. The *Canadian Government Publications Annual Catalogue*, 1954, supplemented the *Consolidated Annual Catalogue*, 1953, and listed federal government publications issued between October 1953 and December 1954. Both the 1953 and 1954 editions were also published separately in French.

From 1955 to 1977 a bilingual annual *Catalogue* was published. This annual *Catalogue* superseded issues of the bilingual *Canadian Government Publications Monthly Catalogue* which, in turn, cumulated issues of the bilingual *Daily Checklist of Canadian Government Publications*. The purpose of these catalogues was to provide a comprehensive listing of all official publications, public documents and papers not of a confidential nature printed or processed at government expense by authority of Parliament or of a government agency, or bought at public expense for distribution to members of Parliament, public servants, or the public. These publications made it possible to check the bibliographic details, price, and distribution policy of any current federal government publication. The *Monthly Catalogue* and the annual *Catalogue* were indexed by personal author, title, and subject. From 1963 to 1978, the *Monthly Catalogue* also indexed articles in about two dozen Canadian government periodicals by personal author, title, and subject. From 1963 to 1977 this index was cumulated in the annual *Catalogue*.

Since 1978 the federal government has introduced a number of changes for economic reasons in the content and frequency of its major checklists and catalogues. In November 1978 a *Weekly Checklist of Canadian Government Publications/Liste hebdomadaire des publications du gouvernement du Canada* superseded the *Daily Checklist*. In 1979 the *Government of Canada Publications Quarterly Catalogue/Publications du gouvernement du Canada catalogue trimestrial* replaced the *Monthly Catalogue* and the indexing of government periodicals was dropped. The final cumulated edition of the annual *Catalogue* covered the year 1977. Since 1978 a *Government of Canada Publications Quarterly Catalogue Index/Publications du gouvernement du Canada catalogue trimestrial index* has been issued annually but, because this publication does not cumulate the contents of the *Quarterly Catalogue*, it is necessary to refer from the annual *Index* to the *Quarterly Catalogue* for full information about publications.

The Canadian Government Publishing Centre of the Department of Supply and Services periodically issues a *Special List of Canadian Government Publications/Liste spéciale des publications du gouvernement du Canada*, a bilingual pamphlet highlighting selected publications available free from the issuing department, as well as a selection of publications for sale by the Publishing Centre.

In 1976 the Publishing Centre began to issue *Selected Titles*, the purpose of which is to acquaint booksellers, librarians, and the general public with a selection of the wide variety of priced publications issued by the federal government. *Selected Titles*, which suspended publication from 1979 to 1985, is now published twice yearly. The French-language edition is *Titres choisis*.

In 1977, the Publishing Centre began issuing a series of *Subject Lists* to inform bookstores, libraries, and the general public about the availability of priced government publications. *Subjects Lists* are published on an irregular basis and group related topics under nine broad categories. The corresponding French-language series is entitled *Vedette-matière*.

Sectional and Departmental Catalogues

From 1963 to 1970 the federal government published seven sectional catalogues which were especially useful for providing a detailed subject approach to the many hundreds of publications issued by selected departments and agencies. The sectional catalogues were: 10, *Labour* (1963); 11, *Northern*

Affairs and National Resources (1963); 12, *Mines Branch* (1967); 13, *Forestry* (1963); 14, *Dominion Bureau of Statistics* (1964); 15, *Canada Treaty Series* (1967); and 16, *National Museums of Canada* (1970). This series was discontinued in 1970.

Certain federal government departments and agencies, such as the Department of Agriculture, the Geological Survey, the National Research Council of Canada, and Statistics Canada, periodically issue excellent guides or indexes to their respective publications giving greater detail than is possible in the general catalogues issued by the Canadian Government Publications Centre.

Canadiana

In 1951 the National Library of Canada (then known as the Canadian Bibliographic Centre) began issuing *Canadiana*, a national monthly bibliography listing books about Canada, published in Canada, or written by Canadians. Since 1952, *Canadian* has included federal government publications and all listings are in full bibliographic form giving author, title, edition, publisher, date and place of publication, paging, series notes, and other pertinent information. Coverage of federal government publications in *Canadian* is not as comprehensive as in the *Quarterly Catalogue*. Nevertheless, the bibliographical description for each item listed is considerably more complete, often supplying details about previous publications in the same series. Since 1953 *Canadiana* has also listed current publications of provincial governments. *Canadiana* is cumulated annually.

Commercial Indexes

In January 1977 Micromedia Limited of Toronto began publication of *Publicat Index*, a bibliographic reference tool covering Canadian federal government publications of general reference value. Designed to supplement the *Daily Checklist* and *Special List* issued by the Publishing Centre, the *Publicat Index* provided comprehensive coverage of current publications and serials not appearing in the government's own checklists and catalogues. In addition, the *Publicat Index* included selected monographs of reference value which might also have appeared on the government checklists. The *Publicat Index*, which was published monthly and cumulated annually, was superseded in 1979 by the *Microlog Index*, which includes not only Canadian federal publications but also selected provincial and municipal government publications. Retitled *Microlog: Canadian Research Index* in 1988, this bilingual *Index* is issued monthly and cumulated annually by Micromedia Limited, and can be accessed by subject, by personal author or corporate body, and by title or series. Abstracts are provided for each title.

2. PROVINCIAL AND TERRITORIAL GOVERNMENT PUBLICATIONS

In general, publications of the provincial governments parallel the types issued by the federal government. Most provinces publish debates, votes and proceedings, journals, sessional papers, annual departmental reports, and gazettes. Because of a dearth of published indexes or catalogues, provincial publications have in the past been much more difficult to locate than those of the federal government. The situation has improved considerably in recent years but some provinces still do not publish catalogues of their publications on a regular basis. A useful reference work is *Canadian Provincial Government Publications; Bibliography of Bibliographies*, compiled by Mohan Bhatia and published by the Library of the University of Saskatchewan in 1971.

Another valuable reference work for provincial government publications was *Profile Index*, which was issued monthly from 1973 to 1978 and cumulated annually. Published by Micromedia Limited of Toronto, *Profile Index* was superseded in 1979 by *Microlog Index* (now *Microlog: Canada Research Index*) described above, which includes a selection of provincial government publications.

A Guide to the Identification and Acquisition of Canadian Provincial Government Publications: Provinces and Territories, prepared by Catherine Pross, and published in a second edition in 1983 by the Dalhousie University Libraries and the School of Library Service, Halifax, is an extremely useful for those seeking information about publications issued by provincial governments.

3. PROVINCIAL AND TERRITORIAL GOVERNMENT PUBLICATIONS

Retrospective bibliographies and current checklists and catalogues of provincial and territorial government publications are listed below.

Alberta

Retrospective

MacDonald, Christine. *Publications of the Government of the North-West Territories, 1876–1905, and of the Province of Saskatchewan, 1905–1952.* Regina: Legislative Library, 1952. Includes early material relating to the area which is now Alberta.

Forsyth, Joseph. *Government Publications Relating to Alberta: A Bibliography of Publications of the Government of Alberta from 1905 to 1968, and of Publications of the Government of Canada Relating to the Province of Alberta from 1867 to 1968.* 8 vol. Ann Arbor, MI: University Microfilms International, 1979. (F.L.A. thesis).

Current

In 1974, the Alberta Public Affairs Bureau issued a *Publications Catalogue* covering the year 1973. From 1974 to 1987 the *Publications Catalogue* was issued quarterly and cumulated annually. In 1988, it was renamed *Alberta Government Publications* and began semi-annual publication.

British Columbia

Retrospective
Strathern, Gloria M. *Navigations, Traffiques and Discoveries, 1774–1848; A Guide to Publications Relating to the Area Now British Columbia.* Victoria: University of Victoria, 1970. Includes government publications.

British Columbia. Provincial Archives. *Dictionary Catalogue of the Provincial Archives of British Columbia.* 8 vol. Boston: G.K. Hall, 1971. Includes government publications.

Lowther, Barbara. *A Bibliography of British Columbia: Laying the Foundations, 1849–1899.* Victoria: University of Victoria, 1968. Includes government publications.

Holmes, Marjorie C. *Publications of the Government of British Columbia, 1871–1947.* Victoria: Provincial Library, 1952.

Edwards, Margaret H. and Lort, John C.R. *A Bibliography of British Columbia; Years of Growth, 1900–1950.* Victoria: University of Victoria, 1975. Includes government publications.

Current
British Columbia Government Publications Monthly Checklist, compiled and issued by the Legislative Library of British Columbia, Victoria, began in January 1970. From 1982 to 1984 it was cumulated annually into *British Columbia Government Publications*; in 1989 *Checklist* became a bimonthly publication.

Manitoba

Retrospective
Morley, Marjorie. *A Bibliography of Manitoba from Holdings in the Legislative Library of Manitoba.* Winnipeg: Legislative Library of Manitoba, 1970.

Looking for Manitoba Government Publications; An Annotated Bibliography of Books and Pamphlets. Edited by John Tooth. Winnipeg: Public Library Services Branch, Dept. of Tourism, Recreation and Cultural Affairs, 1979.

Current
Manitoba Government Publications Received in the Legislative Library of Manitoba was issued three times a year and cumulated annually from 1970 to 1974. In 1975 it was superseded by the *Manitoba Government Publications Monthly Checklist*, which is compiled and edited by the Manitoba Legislative Library and published by Manitoba Culture, Heritage and Recreation. From 1975 to 1983 the *Checklist* was cumulated into an annual catalogue; from 1984 to 1988 it was published on a monthly basis only; and in 1989 it once again was cumulated into an annual catalogue.

New Brunswick

Retrospective
Bishop, Olga B. *Publications of the Governments of Nova Scotia, Prince Edward Island, New Brunswick, 1758–1952.* Ottawa: National Library, 1957.

Guilbeault, Claude. *Guide des publications officielles de la province de Nouveau-Brunswick/Guide to Official Publications of the Province of New Brunswick, 1952–1970.* Ottawa: University of Ottawa Library School, 1974. (M.L.S. thesis).

Atlantic Provinces Checklist. Halifax: Maritime Library Association in cooperation with the Atlantic Provinces Economic Council, v. 1–9, 1957–1965. Annual. Includes government publications.

Current
New Brunswick Government Documents; A Checklist of New Brunswick Government Documents received at the Legislative Library, Fredericton, NB, during the Calendar Year/Publications gouvernementales du Nouveau-Brunswick établié à la Bibliothéque de l'Assemblée législative au cours de l'annee has been published annually since 1956 by the Queen's Printer. Since January, 1986 it has been supplemented by the *Quarterly Checklist.*

Newfoundland

Retrospective
Bibliography of Newfoundland, compiled by Agnes C. O'Dea and edited by Anne Alexander. 2 vol. Toronto: University of Toronto Press, 1986. Includes government publications.

Current
List of Publications of the Government of Newfoundland and Labrador was issued by the Newfoundland Information Service on an irregular basis from 1974 to 1979 when it suspended publication.

Nova Scotia

Retrospective
Bishop, Olga B. *Publications of the Governments of Nova Scotia, Prince Edward Island, New Brunswick, 1758–1952. Ottawa: National Library, 1957.*

Atlantic Provinces Checklist. Halifax: Maritime Library Association in co-operation with the Atlantic Provinces Economic Council, v. 1–9, 1957–1965. Annual. Includes government publications.

Current
Publications of the Province of Nova Scotia is an annual checklist of provincial publications compiled by the Legislative Library. The first issue covered the year 1967. In June 1980 *Publications of the Province of Nova Scotia: Quarterly Checklist*, a list of publications received at the Legislative Library during the

quarter, began publication; in June 1987, this publication became the *Monthly Checklist.*

Publications Catalogue: Nova Scotia Government Bookstore, has been published on an irregular basis since the late 1970s.

Ontario

Retrospective
Bishop, Olga B. *Publications of the Government of the Province of Upper Canada and of Great Britain Relating to Upper Canada, 1791–1840.* Toronto: Ministry of Citizenship and Culture, 1984.

Bishop, Olga B. *Publications of the Government of the Province of Canada, 1841–1867.* Ottawa: National Library of Canada, 1963. The Province of Canada consisted of Canada West (Ontario) and Canada East (Quebec.)

Bishop, Olga B. *Publications of the Government of Ontario, 1867–1900.* Toronto: Ministry of Government Services, 1976.

MacTaggart, Hazel I. *Publications of the Government of Ontario, 1901–1955: A Checklist Compiled for the Ontario Library Association.* Toronto: University of Toronto Press for the Queen's Printer, 1964.

MacTaggart, Hazel I., and Sundquist, Kenneth E. *Publications of the Government of Ontario, 1956–1971: A Checklist.* Toronto: Ministry of Government Services, 1975.

Current
Ontario Government Publications Monthly Checklist/Publications du gouvernement de l'Ontario Liste mensuelle, compiled and edited by the Legislative Library, has been published by the Ministry of Government Services since May 1971. Since 1972, it has cumulated into the *Ontario Government Publications Annual Catalogue/Publications du gouvernement de l'Ontario Catalogue annuel.*

Prince Edward Island

Retrospective
Bishop, Olga B. *Publications of the Governments of Nova Scotia, Prince Edward Island, New Brunswick, 1758–1952.* Ottawa: National Library, 1957.

Atlantic Provinces Checklist. Halifax: Maritime Library Association in co-operation with the Atlantic Provinces Economic Council, v. 1-9, 1957-1965. Annual. Includes government publications.

Current
Prince Edward Island Provincial Government Publications Checklist, compiled and edited since 1976 by the Island Information Service, Charlottetown, is published monthly.

Quebec

Retrospective
Vlach, Milada et Yolande Buono. *Catalogue collectif des impressions Québécoises, 1764–1820.* Montréal: Bibliothéque nationale du Québec, 1984. Includes government publications.

Hare, John E. and Jean-Pierre Wallot, *Les imprimés dans le Bas-Canada, 1801–1941.* Montréal: Presses de l'Université de Montréal, 1967. First of a series; includes government publications.

Bishop, Olga B. *Publications of the Government of the Province of Canada 1841–1867.* Ottawa: National Library of Canada, 1963. The Province of Canada consisted of Canada West (Ontario) and Canada East (Quebec).

Beaulieu, André; Jean-Charles Bonenfant; and Jean Hamelin. *Répertoire des publications gouvernementales du Québec, 1867–1964.* Québec: Imprimeur de la Reine, 1968.

Beaulieu, André, Jean Hamelin, and Gaston Bernier. *Répertoire des publications gouvernementales du Québec: Supplément, 1965–1968.* Québec: Editeur officiel du Québec, 1970.

Current
Bibliographie du Québec: Liste mensuelle des publications québécoises ou relatives au Québec établie par la Bibliothéque nationale du Québec, published in Montreal since 1968, contains a section on current government publications of the province.

Liste bimestrielle des publications du gouvernement du Québec, issued by Direction générale des publications gouvernementales du Ministère des Communications, began publication in April 1981. From 1981 to 1987 it was published monthly; since 1988 it has been published bi-monthly. It is supplemented by an annual *Index des titres de l'année and Liste annuelle des périodiques du gouvernement du Québec*.

Les publications du Québec: Catalogue, published twice a year since 1985 by Direction générale des publications gouvernementales du Ministère des Communications, highlights about 250 priced publications in each issue.

Saskatchewan

Retrospective
MacDonald, Christine. *Publications of the Governments of the North-West Territories, 1876–1905, and of the Province of Saskatchewan, 1905–1952.* Regina: Legislative Library, 1952.

Current
Checklist of Saskatchewan Government Publications has been compiled since 1977 by the Legislative Library of Saskatchewan. From 1977 to 1982 it was published annually; from July 1982 to December 1984 it was published

monthly with an annual cumulation; and since January 1985 it has been published monthly only.

Northwest Territories

Retrospective

MacDonald, Christine. *Publications of the Governments of the North-West Territories, 1876–1905, and of the Province of Saskatchewan, 1905–1952.* Regina: Legislative Library, 1952

Current

Publications Catalogue, published annually from 1977 to 1986 by the Department of Information, is now published by the Department of Culture and Communications.

Yukon Territory

Retrospective

Yukon Bibliography (1897–1963). Ottawa: Department of Northern Affairs and National Resources, 1964. Update 1963–1970; 1971–1973; 1974–1975; 1976–1977; 1978–1979; 1980–1981. Edmonton: Boreal Institute of Northern Studies. Published periodically since 1982, this bibliography includes some government publications.

BIBLIOGRAPHY

Part 5. Selective Bibliography

Banks, Margaret, A. *Using a Law Library: A Guide for Students and Lawyers in the Common Law Provinces of Canada*, 4th ed., Toronto: Carswell, 1985.

Bishop, Olga B. *Canadian Official Publications*. Oxford, Pergamon Press: 1981. (*Guides to Official Publications*, Vol. 9).

Canada, Parliament, House of Commons, Committee Directorate. *Committee of the House of Commons of Canada; Practical Guide*, 2nd ed. Ottawa: 1989.

Canada, Parliament, House of Commons, Table Research Branch. *Précis of Procedure*, 2nd ed. Ottawa: Clerk of the House of Commons, 1987.

Canada, Treasury Board, Administrative Policy Branch. *Administrative Policy Manual, Chapter 335, Publishing, December 1978*. Ottawa: 1979.

Canada, Treasury Board Secretariat. *Administrative Policy Manual: Chapter 480, Government Communications Policy, July, 1988*. Ottawa: 1988.

MacEllven, Douglass T. *Legal Research Handbook*. Toronto: Butterworths, 1986.

Maillet, Lise. *Provincial Royal Commissions and Commissions of Inquiry, 1867–1982*. Ottawa: National Library of Canada, 1986.

Sinclair, Mary Jane T. *Updating Statutes and Regulations for All Canadian Jurisdictions*, 3rd ed. Ottawa: Canadian Law Information Council, 1989.

APPENDIX

CONSTITUTION ACT, 1982*

PART I

CANADIAN CHARTER OF RIGHTS AND FREEDOMS

Whereas Canada is founded upon principles that recognize the supremacy of God and the rule of law:

Guarantee of Rights and Freedoms

1. The *Canadian Charter of Rights and Freedoms* guarantees the rights and freedoms set out in it subject only to such reasonable limits prescribed by law as can be demonstrably justified in a free and democratic society.

Fundamental Freedoms

2. Everyone has the following fundamental freedoms:
   (a) freedom of conscience and religion;
   (b) freedom of thought, belief, opinion and expression, including freedom of the press and other media of communication;
   (c) freedom of peaceful assembly; and
   (d) freedom of association.

Democratic Rights

3. Every citizen of Canada has the right to vote in an election of members of the House of Commons or of a legislative assembly and to be qualified for membership therein.

4. (1) No House of Commons and no legislative assembly shall continue for longer than five years from the date fixed for the return of the writs at a general election of its members.
   (2) In time of real or apprehended war, invasion or insurrection, a House of Commons may be continued by Parliament and a legislative assembly may be continued by the legislature beyond five years if such continuation is not opposed by the votes of more than one-third of the members of the House of Commons or the legislative assembly, as the case may be.

5. There shall be a sitting of Parliament and of each legislature at least once every twelve months.

Mobility Rights

6. (1) Every citizen of Canada has the right to enter, remain in and leave Canada.

---

*Enacted as Schedule B to the *Canada Act 1982* (U.K.) 1982, c. 11, which came into force on April 17, 1982. Reproduced with permission of the Minister of Supply and Services Canada

(2) Every citizen of Canada and every person who has the status of a permanent resident of Canada has the right

(*a*) to move to and take up residence in any province; and

(*b*) to pursue the gaining of a livelihood in any province.

(3) The rights specified in subsection (2) are subject to

(*a*) any laws or practices of general application in force in a province other than those that discriminate among persons primarily on the basis of province of present or previous residence; and

(*b*) any laws providing for reasonable residency requirements as a qualification for the receipt of publicly provided social services.

(4) Subsections (2) and (3) do not preclude any law, program or activity that has as its object the amelioration in a province of conditions of individuals in that province who are socially or economically disadvantaged if the rate of employment in that province is below the rate of employment in Canada.

Legal Rights

7. Everyone has the right to life, liberty and security of the person and the right not to be deprived thereof except in accordance with the principles of fundamental justice.

8. Everyone has the right to be secure against unreasonable search or seizure.

9. Everyone has the right not to be arbitrarily detained or imprisoned.

10. Everyone has the right on arrest or detention

(*a*) to be informed promptly of the reasons therefor;

(*b*) to retain and instruct counsel without delay and to be informed of that right; and

(*c*) to have the validity of the detention determined by way of *habeas corpus* and to be released if the detention is not lawful.

11. Any person charged with an offence has the right

(*a*) to be informed without unreasonable delay of the specific offence;

(*b*) to be tried within a reasonable time;

(*c*) not to be compelled to be a witness in proceedings against that person in respect of the offence;

(*d*) to be presumed innocent until proven guilty according to law in a fair and public hearing by an independent and impartial tribunal;

(*e*) not to be denied reasonable bail without just cause;

(*f*) except in the case of an offence under military law tried before a military tribunal, to the benefit of trial by jury where the maximum punishment for the offence is imprisonment for five years or a more severe punishment;

(*g*) not to be found guilty on account of any act or omission unless, at the time of the act or omission, it constituted an offence under Canadian or international law or was criminal according to the general principles of law recognized by the community of nations;

(*h*) if finally acquitted of the offence, not to be tried for it again and, if finally found guilty and punished for the offence, not to be tried or punished for it again; and

(*i*) if found guilty of the offence and if the punishment for the offence has been varied between the time of commission and the time of sentencing, to the benefit of the lesser punishment.

12. Everyone has the right not to be subjected to any cruel and unusual treatment or punishment.

13. A witness who testifies in any proceedings has the right not to have any incriminating evidence so given used to incriminate that witness in any other proceedings, except in a prosecution for perjury or for the giving of contradictory evidence.

14. A party or witness in any proceedings who does not understand or speak the language in which the proceedings are conducted or who is deaf has the right to the assistance of an interpreter.

Equality Rights

15. (1) Every individual is equal before and under the law and has the right to the equal protection and equal benefit of the law without discrimination and, in particular, without discrimination based on race, national or ethnic origin, colour, religion, sex, age or mental or physical disability.

(2) Subsection (1) does not preclude any law, program or activity that has as its object the amelioration of conditions of disadvantaged individuals or groups including those that are disadvantaged because of race, national or ethnic origin, colour, religion, sex, age or mental or physical disability.

Official Languages of Canada

16. (1) English and French are the official languages of Canada and have equality of status and equal rights and privileges as to their use in all institutions of the Parliament and government of Canada.

(2) English and French are the official languages of New Brunswick and have equality of status and equal rights and privileges as to their use in all institutions of the legislature and government of New Brunswick.

(3) Nothing in this Charter limits the authority of Parliament or a legislature to advance the equality of status or use of English and French.

17. (1) Everyone has the right to use English or French in any debates and other proceedings of Parliament.

(2) Everyone has the right to use English or French in any debates and other proceedings of the legislature of New Brunswick.

18. (1) The statutes, records and journals of Parliament shall be printed and published in English and French and both language versions are equally authoritative.

(2) The statutes, records and journals of the legislature of New Brunswick shall be printed and published in English and French and both language versions are equally authoritative.

19. (1) Either English or French may be used by any person in, or in any pleading in or process issuing from, any court established by Parliament.

(2) Either English or French may be used by any person in, or in any pleading in or process issuing from, any court of New Brunswick.

20. (1) Any member of the public in Canada has the right to communicate with, and to receive available services from, any head or central office of an institution of the Parliament or government of Canada in English or French, and has the same right with respect to any other office of any such institution where

(a) there is a significant demand for communications with and services from that office in such language; or

(b) due to the nature of the office, it is reasonable that communications with and services from that office be available in both English and French.

(2) Any member of the public in New Brunswick has the right to communicate with, and to receive available services from, any office of an institution of the legislature or government of New Brunswick in English or French.

21. Nothing in sections 16 to 20 abrogates or derogates from any right, privilege or obligation with respect to the English and French languages, or either of them, that exists or is continued by virtue of any other provision of the Constitution of Canada.

22. Nothing in sections 16 to 20 abrogates or derogates from any legal or customary right or privilege acquired or enjoyed either before or after the coming into force of this Charter with respect to any language that is not English or French.

Minority Language Educational Rights

23. (1) Citizens of Canada

(a) whose first language learned and still understood is that of the English or French linguistic minority population of the province in which they reside, or

(b) who have received their primary school instruction in Canada in English or French and reside in a province where the language in which they received that instruction is the language of the English or French linguistic minority population of the province,

have the right to have their children receive primary and secondary school instruction in that language in that province.

(2) Citizens of Canada of whom any child has received or is receiving primary or secondary school instruction in English or French in Canada, have the right to have all their children receive primary and secondary school instruction in the same language.

(3) The right of citizens of Canada under subsections (1) and (2) to have their children receive primary and secondary school instruction in the language of the English or French linguistic minority population of a province

(a) applies wherever in the province the number of children of citizens who have such a right is sufficient to warrant the provision to them out of public funds of minority language instruction; and

(b) includes, where the number of children so warrants, the right to have them receive that instruction in minority language educational facilities provided out of public funds.

Enforcement

24. (1) Anyone whose rights or freedoms, as guaranteed by this Charter, have been infringed or denied may apply to a court of competent jurisdiction to obtain such remedy as the court considers appropriate and just in the circumstances.

(2) Where, in proceedings under subsection (1), a court concludes that evidence was obtained in a manner that infringed or denied any rights or freedoms guaranteed by this Charter, the evidence shall be excluded if it is established that, having regard to all the circumstances, the admission of it in the proceedings would bring the administration of justice into disrepute.

General

25. The guarantee in this Charter of certain rights and freedoms shall not be construed so as to abrogate or derogate from any aboriginal, treaty or other rights or freedoms that pertain to the aboriginal peoples of Canada including
(a) any rights or freedoms that have been recognized by the Royal Proclamation of October 7, 1763; and
(b) any rights or freedoms that now exist by way of land claims agreements or may be so acquired.*

26. The guarantee in this Charter of certain rights and freedoms shall not be construed as denying the existence of any other rights or freedoms that exist in Canada.

27. This Charter shall be interpreted in a manner consistent with the preservation and enhancement of the multicultural heritage of Canadians.

28. Notwithstanding anything in this Charter, the rights and freedoms referred to in it are guaranteed equally to male and female persons.

29. Nothing in this Charter abrogates or derogates from any rights or privileges guaranteed by or under the Constitution of Canada in respect of denominational, separate or dissentient schools.

30. A reference in this Charter to a province or to the legislative assembly or legislature of a province shall be deemed to include a reference to the Yukon Territory and the Northwest Territories, or to the appropriate legislative authority thereof, as the case may be.

31. Nothing in this Charter extends the legislative powers of any body or authority.

Application of Charter

32. (1) This Charter applies
(a) to the Parliament and government of Canada in respect of all matters within the authority of Parliament including all matters relating to the Yukon Territory and Northwest Territories; and
(b) to the legislature and government of each province in respect of all matters within the authority of the legislature of each province.
(2) Notwithstanding subsection (1), section 15 shall not have effect until three years after this section comes into force.

33. (1) Parliament or the legislature of a province may expressly declare in an Act of Parliament or of the legislature, as the case may be, that the Act or a

*As amended June 21, 1984.

provision thereof shall operate notwithstanding a provision included in section 2 or sections 7 to 15 of this Charter.

(2) An Act or provision of an Act in respect of which a declaration made under this section is in effect shall have such operation as it would have but for the provision of this Charter referred to in the declaration.

(3) A declaration made under subsection (1) shall cease to have effect five years after it comes into force or on such earlier date as may be specified in the declaration.

(4) Parliament or a legislature of a province may re-enact a declaration made under subsection (1).

(5) Subsection (3) applies in respect of a re-enactment made under subsection (4).

Citation

34. This Part may be cited as the *Canadian Charter of Rights and Freedoms*.

PART II

RIGHTS OF THE ABORIGINAL PEOPLES OF CANADA

35. (1) The existing aboriginal and treaty rights of the aboriginal peoples of Canada are hereby recognized and affirmed.

(2) In this Act, "aboriginal peoples of Canada" includes the Indian, Inuit and Métis peoples of Canada.

(3) For greater certainty, in subsection (1) "treaty rights" includes rights that now exist by way of land claims agreements or may be so acquired.*

(4) Notwithstanding any other provision of this Act, the aboriginal and treaty rights referred to in subsection (1) are guaranteed equally to male and female persons.*

35.1 The government of Canada and the provincial governments are committed to the principle that, before any amendment is made to Class 24 of section 91 of the *Constitution Act, 1867*, to section 25 of this Act or to this Part,

(a) a constitutional conference that includes in its agenda an item relating to the proposed amendment, composed of the Prime Minister of Canada and the first ministers of the provinces, will be convened by the Prime Minister of Canada; and

(b) the Prime Minister of Canada will invite representatives of the aboriginal peoples of Canada to participate in the discussions on that item.*

PART III

EQUALIZATION AND REGIONAL DISPARITIES

36. (1) Without altering the legislative authority of Parliament or of the provincial legislatures, or the rights of any of them with respect to the exercise of

---

*Subsections 35(3) and 35(4) and section 35.1 were added to the original *Constitution Act, 1982* by amendments proclaimed on June 21, 1984.

their legislative authority, Parliament and the legislatures, together with the government of Canada and the provincial governments, are committed to
(a) promoting equal opportunities for the well-being of Canadians;
(b) furthering economic development to reduce disparity in opportunities; and
(c) providing essential public services of reasonable quality to all Canadians.

(2) Parliament and the government of Canada are committed to the principle of making equalization payments to ensure that provincial governments have sufficient revenues to provide reasonably comparable levels of public services at reasonably comparable levels of taxation.

PART IV.1*

CONSTITUTIONAL CONFERENCES

37.1 (1) In addition to the conference convened in March 1983, at least two constitutional conferences composed of the Prime Minister of Canada and the first ministers of the provinces shall be convened by the Prime Minister of Canada, the first within three years after April 17, 1982 and the second within five years after that date.

(2) Each conference convened under subsection (1) shall have included in its agenda constitutional matters that directly affect the aboriginal peoples of Canada, and the Prime Minister of Canada shall invite representatives of those peoples to participate in the discussions on those matters.

(3) The Prime Minister of Canada shall invite elected representatives of the governments of the Yukon Territory and the Northwest Territories to participate in the discussions on any item on the agenda of a conference convened under subsection (1) that, in the opinion of the Prime Minister, directly affects the Yukon Territory and the Northwest Territories.

(4) Nothing in this section shall be construed so as to derogate from subsection 35(1).

PART V

PROCEDURE FOR AMENDING CONSTITUTION OF CANADA

38. (1) An amendment to the Constitution of Canada may be made by proclamation issued by the Governor General under the Great Seal of Canada where so authorized by
(a) resolutions of the Senate and House of Commons; and
(b) resolutions of the legislative assemblies of at least two-thirds of the provinces that have, in the aggregate, according to the then latest general census, at least fifty per cent of the population of all the provinces.

(2) An amendment made under subsection (1) that derogates from the legislative powers, the proprietary rights or any other rights or privileges of the

---

*Part IV.1 was added by amendment on June 21, 1984. The former Part IV, which provided for the 1983 constitutional conference, was automatically repealed on April 17, 1983.

legislature or government of a province shall require a resolution supported by a majority of the members of each of the Senate, the House of Commons and the legislative assemblies required under subsection (1).

(3) An amendment referred to in subsection (2) shall not have effect in a province the legislative assembly of which has expressed its dissent thereto by resolution supported by a majority of its members prior to the issue of the proclamation to which the amendment relates unless that legislative assembly, subsequently, by resolution supported by a majority of its members, revokes its dissent and authorizes the amendment.

(4) A resolution of dissent made for the purposes of subsection (3) may be revoked at any time before or after the issue of the proclamation to which it relates.

39. (1) A proclamation shall not be issued under subsection 38(1) before the expiration of one year from the adoption of the resolution initiating the amendment procedure thereunder, unless the legislative assembly of each province has previously adopted a resolution of assent or dissent.

(2) A proclamation shall not be issued under subsection 38(1) after the expiration of three years from the adoption of the resolution initiating the amendment procedure thereunder.

40. Where an amendment is made under subsection 38(1) that transfers provincial legislative powers relating to education or other cultural matters from provincial legislatures to Parliament, Canada shall provide reasonable compensation to any province to which the amendment does not apply.

41. An amendment to the Constitution of Canada in relation to the following matters may be made by proclamation issued by the Governor General under the Great Seal of Canada only where authorized by resolutions of the Senate and House of Commons and of the legislative assembly of each province:

(a) the office of the Queen, the Governor General and the Lieutenant Governor of a province;

(b) the right of a province to a number of members in the House of Commons not less than the number of Senators by which the province is entitled to be represented at the time this Part comes into force;

(c) subject to section 43, the use of the English or the French language;

(d) the composition of the Supreme Court of Canada;

(e) an amendment to this Part.

42. (1) An amendment to the Constitution of Canada in relation to the following matters may be made only in accordance with subsection 38(1):

(a) the principle of proportionate representation of the provinces in the House of Commons prescribed by the Constitution of Canada;

(b) the powers of the Senate and the method of selecting Senators;

(c) the number of members by which a province is entitled to be represented in the Senate and the residence qualifications of Senators;

(d) subject to paragraph 41(d), the Supreme Court of Canada;

(e) the extension of existing provinces into the territories; and

(f) notwithstanding any other law or practice, the establishment of new provinces.

(2) Subsections 38(2) to (4) do not apply in respect of amendments in relation to matters referred to in subsection (1).

43. An amendment to the Constitution of Canada in relation to any provision that applies to one or more, but not all, provinces, including
(a) any alteration to boundaries between provinces, and
(b) any amendment to any provision that relates to the use of the English or the French language within a province,
may be made by proclamation issued by the Governor General under the Great Seal of Canada only where so authorized by resolutions of the Senate and House of Commons and of the legislative assembly of each province to which the amendment applies.

44. Subject to sections 41 and 42, Parliament may exclusively make laws amending the Constitution of Canada in relation to the executive government of Canada or the Senate and House of Commons.

45. Subject to section 41, the legislature of each province may exclusively make laws amending the constitution of the province.

46. (1) The procedures for amendment under sections 38, 41, 42 and 43 may be initiated either by the Senate or House of Commons or by the legislative assembly of a province.
(2) A resolution of assent made for the purposes of this Part may be revoked at any time before the issue of a proclamation authorized by it.

47. (1) An amendment to the Constitution of Canada made by proclamation under section 38, 41, 42 or 43 may be made without a resolution of the Senate authorizing the issue of the proclamation if, within one hundred and eighty days after the adoption by the House of Commons of a resolution authorizing its issue, the Senate has not adopted such a resolution and if, at any time after the expiration of that period, the House of Commons again adopts the resolution.
(2) Any period when Parliament is prorogued or dissolved shall not be counted in computing the one hundred and eighty day period referred to in subsection (1).

48. The Queen's Privy Council for Canada shall advise the Governor General to issue a proclamation under this Part forthwith on the adoption of the resolutions required for an amendment made by proclamation under this Part.

49. A constitutional conference composed of the Prime Minister of Canada and the first ministers of the provinces shall be convened by the Prime Minister of Canada within fifteen years after this Part comes into force to review the provisions of this Part.

PART VI

AMENDMENT TO THE CONSTITUTION ACT, 1867

50. The *Constitution Act, 1867* (formerly named the *British North America Act, 1867*) is amended by adding thereto, immediately after section 92 thereof, the following heading and section:

"Non-Renewable Natural Resources, Forestry Resources and Electrical Energy

92A. (1) In each province, the legislature may exclusively make laws in relation to
(a) exploration for non-renewable natural resources in the province;
(b) development, conservation and management of non-renewable natural resources and forestry resources in the province, including laws in relation to the rate of primary production therefrom; and
(c) development, conservation and management of sites and facilities in the province for the generation and production of electrical energy.

(2) In each province, the legislature may make laws in relation to the export from the province to another part of Canada of the primary production from non-renewable natural resources and forestry resources in the province and the production from facilities in the province for the generation of electrical energy, but such laws may not authorize or provide for discrimination in prices or in supplies exported to another part of Canada.

(3) Nothing in subsection (2) derogates from the authority of Parliament to enact laws in relation to the matters referred to in that subsection and, where such a law of Parliament and a law of a province conflict, the law of Parliament prevails to the extent of the conflict.

(4) In each province, the legislature may make laws in relation to the raising of money by any mode or system of taxation in respect of
(a) non-renewable natural resources and forestry resources in the province and the primary production therefrom, and
(b) sites and facilities in the province for the generation of electrical energy and the production therefrom,
whether or not such production is exported in whole or in part from the province, but such laws may not authorize or provide for taxation that differentiates between production exported to another part of Canada and production not exported from the province.

(5) The expression "primary production" has the meaning assigned by the Sixth Schedule.

(6) Nothing in subsections (1) to (5) derogates from any powers or rights that a legislature or government of a province had immediately before the coming into force of this section."

51. The said Act is further amended by adding thereto the following Schedule:

"THE SIXTH SCHEDULE

Primary Production from Non-Renewable Natural Resources and Forestry Resources

1. For the purposes of section 92A of this Act,
(a) production from a non-renewable resource is a primary production therefrom if
(i) it is in the form in which it exists upon its recovery or severance from its natural state, or
(ii) it is a product resulting from processing or refining the resource, and is not a manufactured product or a product resulting from refining crude oil, refining upgraded heavy crude oil, refining gases or liquids derived from coal or refining a synthetic equivalent of crude oil; and

(b) production from a forestry resource is primary production therefrom if it consists of sawlogs, poles, lumber, wood chips, sawdust or any other primary wood product, or wood pulp, and is not a product manufactured from wood."

PART VII

GENERAL

52. (1) The Constitution of Canada is the supreme law of Canada, and any law that is inconsistent with the provisions of the Constitution is, to the extent of the inconsistency, of no force or effect.

(2) The Constitution of Canada includes
(a) the *Canada Act*, including this Act;
(b) the Acts and orders referred to in Schedule I; and
(c) any amendment to any Act or order referred to in paragraph (a) or (b).

(3) Amendments to the Constitution of Canada shall be made only in accordance with the authority contained in the Constitution of Canada.

53. (1) The enactments referred to in Column I of Schedule I are hereby repealed or amended to the extent indicated in Column II thereof and, unless repealed, shall continue as law in Canada under the names set out in Column III thereof.

(2) Every enactment, except the *Canada Act*, that refers to an enactment referred to in Schedule I by the name in Column I thereof is hereby amended by substituting for that name the corresponding name in Column III thereof, and any British North America Act not referred to in Schedule I may be cited as the *Constitution Act* followed by the year and number, if any, of its enactment.

54. Part IV is repealed on the day that is one year after this Part comes into force and this section may be repealed and this Act renumbered, consequential upon the repeal of Part IV and this section, by proclamation issued by the Governor General under the Great Seal of Canada.

54.1 Part IV.1 and this section are repealed on April 18, 1987.*

55. A French version of the portions of the Constitution of Canada referred to in Schedule I shall be prepared by the Minister of Justice of Canada as expeditiously as possible and, when any portion thereof sufficient to warrant action being taken has been so prepared, it shall be put forward for enactment by proclamation issued by the Governor General under the Great Seal of Canada pursuant to the procedure then applicable to an amendment of the same provisions of the Constitution of Canada.

56. Where any portion of the Constitution of Canada has been or is enacted in English and French or where a French version of any portion of the Constitution is enacted pursuant to section 55, the English and French versions of that portion of the Constitution are equally authoritative.

---

*Section 54.1 was added by amendment on June 21, 1984.

57. The English and French versions of this Act are equally authoritative.

58. Subject to section 59, this Act shall come into force on a day to be fixed by proclamation issued by the Queen or the Governor General under the Great Seal of Canada.

59. (1) Paragraph 23(1)(a) shall come into force in respect of Quebec on a day to be fixed by proclamation issued by the Queen or the Governor General under the Great Seal of Canada.

(2) A proclamation under subsection (1) shall be issued only where authorized by the legislative assembly or government of Quebec.

(3) This section may be repealed on the day paragraph 23(1)(a) comes into force in respect of Quebec and this Act amended and renumbered, consequential upon the repeal of this section, by proclamation issued by the Queen or the Governor General under the Great Seal of Canada.

60. This Act may be cited as the *Constitution Act, 1981*, and the Constitution Acts 1867 to 1975 (No. 2) and this Act may be cited together as the *Constitution Acts, 1867 to 1981*.

61. A reference to the *Constitution Acts, 1867 to 1982* shall be deemed to include a reference to the *Constitution Amendment Proclamation, 1983.**

---

*Section 61 was added by amendment on June 21, 1984.

SCHEDULE 1

to the

CONSTITUTION ACT, 1981

MODERNIZATION OF THE CONSTITUTION

Item	Column I Act Affected	Column II Amendment	Column III New Name
1.	British North America Act, 1867, 30-31 Vict., c. 3 (U.K.)	(1) Section 1 is repealed and the following substituted therefore: "1. This Act may be cited as the *Constitution Act, 1867.*" (2) Section 20 is repealed. (3) Class 1 of section 91 is repealed. (4) Class 1 of section 92 is repealed.	Constitution Act, 1867
2.	An Act to amend and continue the Act 32-33 Victoria chapter 3; and to establish and provide for the Government of the Province of Manitoba, 1870, 33 Vict., c. 3 (Can.)	(1) The long title is repealed and the following substituted therefor: "*Manitoba Act, 1870.*" (2) Section 20 is repealed.	Manitoba Act, 1870
3.	Order of Her Majesty in Council admitting Rupert's Land and the North-Western Territory into the Union, dated the 23rd day of June, 1870		Rupert's Land and North-Western Territory Order
4.	Order of Her Majesty in Council admitting British Columbia into the Union, dated the 16th day of May, 1871		British Columbia Terms of Union
5.	British North America Act 1871, 34-35 Vict., c. 28 (U.K.)	Section 1 is repealed and the following substituted therefor: "1. This Act may be cited as the *Constitution Act, 1871.*"	
6.	Order of Her Majesty in Council admitting Prince Edward Island into the Union, dated the 26th day of June, 1873		Prince Edward Island Terms of Union
7.	Parliament of Canada Act, 1875, 38-39 Vict., c. 38 (U.K.)		Parliament of Canada Act, 1875

8. Order of Her Majesty in Council admitting all British possessions and Territories in North America and islands adjacent thereto into the Union, dated the 31st day of July, 1880		Adjacent Territories Order
9. British North America Act, 1886, 49-50 Vict., c. 35 (U.K.)	Section 3 is repealed and the following substituted therefor: "3. This Act may be cited as the *Constitution Act, 1886*."	Constitution Act, 1886
10. Canada (Ontario Boundary) Act, 1889, 52-53 Vict., c. 28 (U.K.)		Canada (Ontario Boundary) Act, 1889
11. Canadian Speaker (Appointment of Deputy) Act, 1895, 2nd Sess., 59 Vict., c. 3 (U.K.)	The Act is repealed.	
12. The Alberta Act, 1905, 4-5 Edw. VII, c. 3 (Can.)		Alberta Act
13. The Saskatchewan Act, 1905, 4-5 Edw. VII, c. 42 (Can.)		Saskatchewan Act
14. British North America Act, 1907, 7 Edw. VII, c. 11 (U.K.)	Section 2 is repealed and the following substituted therefor: "2. This Act may be cited as the *Constitution Act, 1907*."	Constitution Act, 1907
15. British North America Act, 1915, 5-6 Geo. V, c. 45 (U.K.)	Section 3 is repealed and the following substituted therefor: "3. This Act may be cited as the *Constitution Act, 1915*."	Constitution Act, 1915
16. British North America Act, 1930, 20-21 Geo. V, c. 26 (U.K.)	Section 3 is repealed and the following substituted therefor: 3. This Act may be cited as the *Constitution Act, 1930*."	Constitution Act, 1930
17. Statute of Westminster, 1931, 22 Geo. V, c. 4 (U.K.)	In so far as they apply to Canada, (*a*) section 4 is repealed; and (*b*) subsection 7(1) is repealed.	Statute of Westminster, 1931
18. British North America Act, 1940, 3-4 Geo. VI, c. 36 (U.K.)	Section 2 is repealed and the following substituted therefor: "2. This Act may be cited as the *Constitution Act, 1940*."	Constitution Act, 1940
19. British North America Act, 1943, 6-7 Geo. VI, c. 30 (U.K.)	The Act is repealed.	

20.	British North America Act, 1946, 9-10 Geo. VI, c. 63 (U.K.)	The Act is repealed.	
21.	British North America Act, 1949, 12-13 Geo. VI, c. 22 (U.K.)	Section 3 is repealed and the following substituted therefor: "3. This Act may be cited as the *Newfoundland Act*."	Newfoundland Act
22.	British North America (No. 2) Act, 1949, 13 Geo. VI, c. 81 (U.K.)	The Act is repealed.	
23.	British North America Act, 1951, 14-15 Geo. VI, c. 32 (U.K.)	The Act is repealed.	
24.	British North America Act, 1952, 1 Eliz. II, c. 15 (Can.)	The Act is repealed.	
25.	British North America Act, 1960, 9 Eliz. II, c. 2 (U.K.)	Section 2 is repealed and the following substituted therefor: "2. This Act may be cited as the *Constitution Act, 1960*."	Constitution Act, 1960
26.	British North America Act, 1964, 12-13 Eliz. II, c. 73 (U.K.)	Section 2 is repealed and the following substituted therefor: "2. This Act may be cited as the *Constitution Act, 1964*."	Constitution Act, 1964
27.	British North America Act, 1965, 14 Eliz. II, c. 4, Part I (Can.)	Section 2 is repealed and the following substituted therefor: "2. This Part may be cited as the *Constitution Act, 1965*."	Constitution Act, 1965
28.	British North America Act, 1974, 23 Eliz. II, c. 13, Part I (Can.)	Section 3, as amended by 25-26 Eliz. II, c. 28, s. 38(1) (Can.), is repealed and the following substituted therefor: "3. This Part may be cited as the *Constitution Act, 1974*."	Constitution Act, 1974
29.	British North America Act, 1975, 23-24 Eliz. II, c. 28, Part I (Can.)	Section 3, as amended by 25-26 Eliz. II, c. 28, s. 31 (Can.), is repealed and the following substituted therefor: "3. This Part may be cited as the *Constitution Act (No. 1), 1975*."	Constitution Act (No. 1), 1975
30.	British North America Act, (No. 2), 1975, 23-24 Eliz. II, c. 53 (Can.)	Section 3 is repealed and the following substituted therefor: "3. This Act may be cited as the *Constitution Act (No. 2), 1975*."	Constitution Act (No. 2), 1975

CONSTITUTION ACT, 1867*

[THE BRITISH NORTH AMERICA ACT, 1867]

30 & 31 Victoria, c. 3.

(Consolidated with amendments)

An Act for the Union of Canada, Nova Scotia, and New Brunswick, and the Government thereof; and for Purposes connected therewith.

(29th March, 1867.)
WHEREAS the Provinces of Canada, Nova Scotia and New Brunswick have expressed their Desire to be federally united into One Dominion under the Crown of the United Kingdom of Great Britain and Ireland, with a Constitution similar in Principle to that of the United Kingdom:

And whereas such a Union would conduce to the Welfare of the Provinces and promote the Interests of the British Empire:

And whereas on the Establishment of the Union by Authority of Parliament it is expedient, not only that the Constitution of the Legislative Authority in the Dominion be provided for, but also that the Nature of the Executive Government therein be declared:

And whereas it is expedient that Provision be made for the eventual Admission into the Union of other Parts of British North America:

I.—PRELIMINARY.

1. This Act may be cited as the *Constitution Act, 1867.*

• • •

VI.—DISTRIBUTION OF LEGISLATIVE POWERS.

Powers of the Parliament.

91. It shall be lawful for the Queen, by and with the Advice and Consent of the Senate and House of Commons, to make Laws for the Peace, Order, and good Government of Canada, in relation to all matters not coming within the Classes of Subjects by this Act assigned exclusively to the Legislatures of the Provinces; and for greater Certainty, but not so as to restrict the Generality of the foregoing Terms of this Section, it is hereby declared that (notwithstanding anything in this Act) the exclusive Legislative Authority of the Parliament of Canada extends to all Matters coming within the Classes of Subjects next hereinafter enumerated; that is to say,—

1. Repealed.
1A. The Public Debt and Property.
2. The Regulation of Trade and Commerce.
2A. Unemployment insurance

---

* As amended by the *Constitution Act, 1982*. Reproduced with permission of the Minister of Supply and Services Canada.

3. The raising of Money by any Mode or System of Taxation.
4. The borrowing of Money on the Public Credit.
5. Postal Service.
6. The Census and Statistics.
7. Militia, Military and Naval Service, and Defence.
8. The fixing of and providing for the Salaries and Allowances of Civil and other Officers of the Government of Canada.
9. Beacons, Buoys, Lighthouses, and Sable Island.
10. Navigation and Shipping.
11. Quarantine and the Establishment and Maintenance of Marine Hospitals.
12. Sea Coast and Inland Fisheries.
13. Ferries between a Province and any British or Foreign Country or between Two Provinces.
14. Currency and Coinage.
15. Banking, Incorporation of Banks, and the Issue of Paper Money.
16. Savings Banks.
17. Weights and Measures.
18. Bills of Exchange and Promissory Notes.
19. Interest.
20. Legal Tender.
21. Bankruptcy and Insolvency.
22. Patents of Invention and Discovery.
23. Copyrights.
24. Indians, and Lands reserved for the Indians.
25. Naturalization and Aliens.
26. Marriage and Divorce.
27. The Criminal Law, except the Constitution of Courts of Criminal Jurisdiction, but including the Procedure in Criminal Matters.
28. The Establishment, Maintenance, and Management of Penitentiaries.
29. Such Classes of Subjects as are expressly excepted in the Enumeration of the Classes of Subjects by this Act assigned exclusively to the Legislatures of the Provinces.

And any Matter within any of the Classes of Subjects enumerated in this Section shall not be deemed to come within the Class of Matters of a local or private Nature comprised in the Enumeration of the Classes of Subjects by this Act assigned exclusively to the Legislatures of the Provinces.

Exclusive Powers of Provincial Legislatures

92. In each Province the Legislature may exclusively make Laws in relation to Matters coming within the Classes of Subject next hereinafter enumerated; that is to say,—
1. Repealed.
2. Direct Taxation within the Province in order to the raising of a Revenue for Provincial Purposes.
3. The borrowing of Money on the sole Credit of the Province.
4. The Establishment and Tenure of Provincial Offices and the Appointment and Payment of Provincial Officers.
5. The Management and Sale of the Public Lands belonging to the Province and of the Timber and Wood thereon.

6. The Establishment, Maintenance, and Management of Public and Reformatory Prisons in and for the Province.
7. The Establishment, Maintenance, and Management of Hospitals, Asylums, Charities, and Eleemosynary Institutions in and for the Province, other than Marine Hospitals.
8. Municipal Institutions in the Province.
9. Shop, Saloon, Tavern, Auctioneer, and other Licences in order to the raising of a Revenue for Provincial, Local, or Municipal Purposes.
10. Local Works and Undertakings other than such as are of the following Classes:—
    (*a*) Lines of Steam or Other Ships, Railways, Canals, Telegraphs, and other Works and Undertakings connecting the Province with any other or others of the Provinces, or extending beyond the Limits of the Province;
    (*b*) Lines of Steam Ships between the Province and any British or Foreign Country;
    (*c*) Such Works as, although wholly situate within the Province, are before or after their Execution declared by the Parliament of Canada to be for the general Advantage of Canada or for the Advantage of Two or more of the Provinces.
11. The Incorporation of Companies with Provincial Objects.
12. The Solemnization of Marriage in the Province.
13. Property and Civil Rights in the Province.
14. The Administration of Justice in the Province, including the Constitution, Maintenance, and Organization of Provincial Courts, both of Civil and of Criminal Jurisdiction, and including Procedure in Civil Matters in those Courts.
15. The Imposition of Punishment by Fine, Penalty, or Imprisonment for enforcing any Law of the Province made in relation to any Matter coming within any of the Classes of Subjects enumerated within this Section.
16. Generally all Matters of a merely local or private Nature in the Province.

Non-Renewable Natural Resources, Forestry Resources and Electrical Energy.

92A. (1) In each province, the legislature may exclusively make laws in relation to
(*a*) exploration for non-renewable natural resources in the province;
(*b*) development, conservation and management of non-renewable natural resources and forestry resources in the province, including laws in relation to the rate of primary production therefrom; and
(*c*) development, conservation and management of sites and facilities in the province for the generation and production of electrical energy.
(2) In each province, the legislature may make laws in relation to the export from the province to another part of Canada of the primary production from non-renewable natural resources and forestry resources in the province and the production from facilities in the province for the generation of electrical energy, but such laws may not authorize or provide for discrimination in prices or in supplies exported to another part of Canada.
(3) Nothing in subsection (2) derogates from the authority of Parliament to enact laws in relation to the matters referred to in that subsection and, where such a law of Parliament and a law of a province conflict, the law of Parliament prevails to the extent of the conflict.

(4) In each province, the legislature may make laws in relation to the raising of money by any mode or system of taxation in respect of
(a) non-renewable natural resources and forestry resources in the province and the primary production therefrom, and
(b) sites and facilities in the province for the generation of electrical energy and the production therefrom,
whether or not such production is exported in whole or in part from the province, but such laws may not authorize or provide for taxation that differentiates between production exported to another part of Canada and production not exported from the province.

(5) The expression "primary production" has the meaning assigned by the Sixth Schedule.

(6) Nothing in subsections (1) to (5) derogates from any powers or rights that a legislature or government of a province had immediately before the coming into force of this section.

Education

93. In and for each Province the Legislature may exclusively make laws in relation to Education, subject and according to the following Provisions:—

(1) Nothing in any such Law shall prejudicially affect any Right or Privilege with respect to Denominational Schools which any Class of Persons have by Law in the Province at the Union:

(2) All the Powers, Privileges, and Duties at the Union by Law conferred and imposed in Upper Canada on the Separate Schools and School Trustees of the Queen's Roman Catholic Subjects shall be and the same are hereby extended to the Dissentient Schools of the Queen's Protestant and Roman Catholic Subjects in Quebec:

(3) Where in any Province a System of Separate or Dissentient Schools exist by Law at the Union or is thereafter established by the Legislature of the Province, an Appeal shall lie to the Governor General in Council from any Act or Decision of any Provincial Authority affecting any Right or Privilege of the Protestant or Roman Catholic Minority of the Queen's Subjects in relation to Education:

(4) In case any such Provincial Law as from Time to Time seems to the Governor General in Council requisite for the due Execution of the Provisions of this Section is not made, or in case any Decision of the Governor General in Council on any Appeal under this Section is not duly executed by the proper Provincial Authority in that Behalf, then and in every such Case, and as far only as the Circumstances of each Case require, the Parliament of Canada may make remedial Laws for the due Execution of the Provisions of this Section and of any Decision of the Governor General in Council under this Section.

STUDENT REPLY CARD

In order to improve future editions, we are seeking your comments on *Politics: Canada, seventh edition,* by Fox/White

    After you have read this text, please answer the following questions and return this form via Business Reply Mail. *Thanks in advance for your feedback!*

1. Name of your college or university: _____

2. Major program of study: _____

3. Your instructor for this course: _____

4. Are there any sections of this text which were not assigned as course reading? _____
   If so, please specify those chapters or portions:

5. How would you rate the overall accessibility of the content? Please feel free to comment on reading level, writing style, terminology, layout and design features, and such learning aids as chapter objectives, summaries, and appendices.

— — — — — — — — — — — FOLD HERE — — — — — — — — — — — —

6. What did you like *best* about this book?

7. What did you like *least?*

If you would like to say more, we'd love to hear from you. Please write to us at the address shown on the reverse of this card.

CUT HERE

- - - - - - - - - - - - - - - *CUT HERE* - - - - - - - - - - - - -

- - - - - - - - - - - - - *FOLD HERE* - - - - - - - - - - - - -

**BUSINESS
REPLY MAIL**

**No Postage Stamp
Necessary If Mailed
in Canada**

Postage will be paid by

Attn: Sponsoring Editor, Social Sciences
The College Division
McGraw-Hill Ryerson Limited
300 Water Street
Whitby, Ontario
L1N 9Z9

TAPE SHUT

CUT HERE